The Little, Brown Handbook *Brief Version*

LB *Brief*

SECOND EDITION

JANE E. AARON

New York Boston San Francisco
London Toronto Sydney Tokyo Singapore Madrid
Mexico City Munich Paris Cape Town Hong Kong Montreal

Senior Vice President and Publisher:	Joseph Opiela
Senior Acquisitions Editor:	Lynn M. Huddon
Development Manager:	Janet Lanphier
Development Editor:	Carol Hollar-Zwick
Senior Supplements Editor:	Donna Campion
Media Supplements Editor:	Nancy Garcia
Executive Marketing Manager:	Megan Galvin-Fak
Production Manager:	Donna DeBenedictis
Project Coordination, Text Design, and Electronic Page Makeup:	Nesbitt Graphics, Inc.
Cover Design Manager:	Wendy Ann Fredericks
Cover Designer:	Kay Petronio
Senior Manufacturing Buyer:	Alfred C. Dorsey
Printer and Binder:	Webcrafters, Inc.
Cover Printer:	The Lehigh Press, Inc.

Library of Congress Cataloging-in-Publication Data

Aaron, Jane E.

LB brief : the Little Brown handbook, brief version / Jane E. Aaron.— 2nd ed.

p. cm.

Includes bibliographical references and index.

ISBN 0-321-20781-5

1. English language—Grammar—Handbooks, manuals, etc. 2. English language—Rhetoric—Handbooks, manuals, etc. I. Title.

PE1112.A22 2005

808'.042—dc22

2004007997

Please visit us at *http://www.ablongman.com/littlebrown.*

ISBN 0-321-20781-5

3 4 5 6 7 8 9 10—WC—07 06 05 04

Grateful acknowledgment is made to the following sources for the use of their material in this book:

"At what point do national security and common sense collide? Join the conversation." Ad in *Time*, October 7, 2002. Reprinted by permission of the photographer, Steve Liss.

Big Audio Dynamite. "Rush" by Mick Jones from *The Globe*. Recorded by Big Audio Dynamite for Columbia Records. © 1991 The Voice of London Inc. (BMI). All rights reserved. Reprinted with permission of the author.

Brooks, Gwendolyn. "The Bean Eaters" from *Blacks* by Gwendolyn Brooks. Reprinted by consent of Brooks Permissions.

Dickinson, Emily. Lines from "A narrow Fellow in the Grass." Reprinted by permission of the publishers and the Trustees of Amherst College from *The Poems of Emily Dickinson*, Thomas H. Johnson, ed., Cambridge, MA: The Belknap Press of Harvard University Press, Copyright © 1951, 1955, 1979 by the President and Fellows of Harvard College.

(*continued on p. 556*)

Preface for Students

LB Brief contains the basic information you'll need for writing in and out of school. Here you can find out how to get ideas, use commas, search the Internet, cite sources, craft an argument, and write a résumé—all in a convenient, accessible package.

This book is mainly a reference for you to dip into as needs arise. You probably won't read the book all the way through, nor will you use everything it contains: you already know much of the content anyway, whether consciously or not. The trick is to figure out what you *don't* know—taking cues from your own writing experiences and the comments of others—and then to find the answers to your questions in these pages.

The next two pages detail the many ways you can find information in the handbook. Note four features especially:

- The beginning of every chapter poses and briefly answers a frequently asked question (FAQ) about the topic of that chapter. All the FAQs are gathered inside the front cover of the book.
- The mouse icon shown here signals tips for using computers productively for all kinds of writing activity, from discovering ideas through citing sources.
- Also using the mouse icon, green boxes at chapter openings direct you to the handbook's companion Web site at *http://www.ablongman.com/littlebrown*. On the site you will find video tutorials, downloadable exercises and checklists from the handbook, additional interactive exercises, and links to other helpful sites.
- The symbol CULTURE LANGUAGE flags material for students who are using standard American English as a second language or a second dialect. A guide to all this material appears on the third-to-last page of the book.

Before you begin using this book, you may need to clear your mind of a very common misconception: that writing is only, or even mainly, a matter of correctness. True, any written message will find a more receptive audience if it is correct in word choice, grammar, punctuation, and similar matters. But these concerns should come late in the writing process, after you've allowed yourself to discover what you have to say, freeing yourself to make mistakes along the way. As one writer put it, you need to get the clay on the potter's wheel before you can shape it into a bowl, and you need to shape it into a bowl before you can perfect it. So get your clay on the wheel and work with it until it looks like a bowl. Then worry about correctness.

Finding What You Need

Use a directory.

- **Frequently Asked Questions,** printed inside the front cover and repeated at the start of each chapter, provide questions in everyday language that are commonly asked about the book's main topics.
- The **Contents,** inside the back cover, provides a detailed guide to the entire book.

Use the index.

On the last pages of the book, the **Index** is an alphabetical list of every topic, term, and problem word or expression mentioned in the book.

Use the glossary.

The **Glossary of Usage** (pp. 543–55) clarifies more than 250 words that are often confused or misused, such as *affect/effect* or *emigrate/immigrate.*

Use the elements of the page.

❶ Chapter number and title.
❷ Frequently asked question about the chapter topic.
❸ A boldfaced term being introduced and defined for the first time.
❹ Examples, always indented. Color underlining highlights sentence elements and revisions.
❺ Mouse icon: a tip for using computers effectively.
❻ Page tab, containing the code of the nearest chapter or section heading (**31**) and the symbol or abbreviation for the topic being discussed (**pn agr**).
❼ Culture-language pointer for students using standard American English as a second language or a second dialect.
❽ Box defining secondary terms used on the page. Refer to these white boxes whenever a term is unclear. Otherwise, ignore them.
❾ Web box linking to the handbook's Web site and specifically to its coverage of the topic being discussed: here, a video tutorial, interactive Web exercises, a downloadable exercise from the handbook, and links to other Web sites.
❿ Section heading, a main convention or topic labeled with the section code **31d**: the chapter number (**31**) and the section letter (**d**).
⓫ Exercise providing practice with a key topic. Many exercises are downloadable from the handbook's Web site, and answers to selected exercises appear at the back of the book.

1 31 Agreement of Pronoun and Antecedent

2 Is this the right pronoun?

3

The right pronoun is the one that matches its **antecedent**—the word to which it refers—in person, number, and gender. This chapter focuses on agreement in number: singular and plural antecedents and the pronouns that replace them.

4

Homeowners fret over their tax bills.
antecedent pronoun

Its constant increases make the tax bill a dreaded document.
pronoun antecedent

5 **Note** Grammar and style checkers cannot help with agreement between pronoun and antecedent because they cannot recognize the intended relation between the two. You'll need to check for errors on your own.

6 pn agr 31

7 CULTURE LANGUAGE The gender of a pronoun should match its antecedent, not a noun that the pronoun may modify: *Sara Young invited her* [not *his*] *son to join the company's staff.* Also, nouns in Eng-

8 Key terms

	Number	
Person	**Singular**	**Plural**
First	*I*	*we*
Second	*you*	*you*
Third	*he, she, it,* indefinite pronouns, singular nouns	*they,* plural nouns
Gender		
Masculine	*he,* nouns naming males	
Feminine	*she,* nouns naming females	
Neuter	*it,* all other nouns	

9 *http://www.ablongman.com/littlebrown*
➤ Sentences and words
➤ Video tutorials ➤ Recognizing pronoun-antecedent problems
➤ Web exercises ➤ Exers. 41–43
➤ Downloads ➤ Chapter 31 exercise in electronic format
➤ Web links ➤ Pronoun-antecedent agreement

10 **31d Collective nouns such as *team* take singular or plural pronouns depending on meaning.**

Use a singular pronoun with a collective noun when referring to the group as a unit:

The committee voted to disband itself.

When referring to the individual members of the group, use a plural pronoun:

The old group have gone their separate ways.

11 **EXERCISE 31.1**
Revising: Pronoun-antecedent agreement

Revise the following sentences so that pronouns and their antecedents agree in person and number. Some items have more than one possible answer. Try to avoid the generic *he* (see opposite). If you change the subject of a sentence, be sure to change the verb as necessary for agreement. If a sentence is already correct as given, circle the number preceding it. Answers to starred items appear at the end of the book.

Preface for Instructors

LB Brief provides writers with a reliable, accessible, and affordable reference. Merging the authority of its parent, *The Little, Brown Handbook,* and a concise format, this handbook answers frequently asked questions about the writing process, critical thinking, computers in writing, grammar and style, research writing, and more. With its cross-curricular outlook, easy-to-use format, and assumption of little or no experience with writing or handbooks, *LB Brief* helps students of varying interests and skills.

This second edition improves on the handbook's strengths while keeping pace with the rapid changes in writing and its teaching. In the context of the handbook's many functions, the following pages highlight as **New** the significant additions and changes.

A guide to writing in and out of school

New Part II collects chapters that students can draw on for their college courses and beyond. In addition to critical reading and writing, argument, writing about literature, writing online, and writing for business, the part includes two new chapters:

- **New** "Academic Writing" discusses subject, purpose, and audience, establishing a context for college writing.
- **New** "Making Oral Presentations" offers a concise guide to planning and delivering a speech.

A guide to writing with computers

LB Brief integrates computers into all stages of writing, explaining how they can help and also when they cannot.

- More than ninety computer tips are signaled by the mouse icon shown here.
- Specific, problem-centered advice helps students use spelling and grammar/style checkers effectively.
- Up-to-date coverage of computers in research writing assists students with searching electronically and evaluating and documenting online sources.
- **New** A Web box for every chapter points to specific content on the handbook's Web site, described below.

An integrated text and Web site

New Throughout the text, newly designed Web boxes point to specific pages on the handbook's, vastly expanded Web site, a powerful online resource for students and teachers.

- More than thirty video tutorials provide explanations, examples, tips, and student interviews to help students understand concepts and techniques. Topics include narrowing a subject online, finding an argument topic, using e-mail, recognizing comma splices, conducting online keyword searches, and designing a *PowerPoint* presentation.
- Nearly a thousand interactive exercises provide immediate feedback for every answer and are cross-referenced to the text.
- More than a hundred exercises and checklists from the handbook can be downloaded for practice, invention, and revision.
- Hundreds of Web links direct students to helpful sites on the writing process, critical thinking, argument, grammar, research, writing in the disciplines, and more.
- The online "Glossary of Usage" allows students to test their knowledge and practice usage.
- A database includes seven student papers from across the disciplines.

An introduction to critical thinking and argument

Chapters 9 and 10 provide helpful, specific discussions of forming a critical response and constructing an effective argument:

- The step-by-step approach to critical reading and writing includes a sample annotated reading, an extended example of analyzing a Web site, and a sample student critique.
- **New** A section on critically viewing images offers a method of analysis and a case study of an ad for *Time* magazine.
- The distinctive treatment of argument covers claims, assumptions, evidence, appeals to readers, organization, and fallacies.
- **New** An annotated sample argument asserts the virtues of television.

A guide to research writing

The handbook gives close attention to research writing, mindful of the dramatic changes in the methods and challenges of research.

- The discussion emphasizes managing information, evaluating and synthesizing sources, integrating sources, and avoiding plagiarism.
- **New** A focus on the library as Web gateway includes using the library's Web site (with a case study on navigating a subscription service) and distinguishing between library and other online sources.
- **New** A detailed case study illustrates evaluating a Web site.
- **New** A section covers integrating quotations in the humanities, the social sciences, and the natural sciences.

- **New** A separate chapter on avoiding plagiarism includes a section on Internet term-paper sites and detection software, more examples of plagiarism and its correction, and special advice on using sources in Web compositions.

A guide to documenting sources

Cited for its meticulous attention to source documentation, *LB Brief* includes extensive chapters on MLA and APA styles.

- **New** Updated MLA style reflects the sixth edition of the *MLA Handbook* (2003) and includes thorough explanations and annotated examples for electronic sources.
- APA style reflects the fifth edition of the APA *Publication Manual* (2001), including detailed coverage of electronic sources.

A guide for culturally and linguistically diverse students

The handbook provides extensive rhetorical and grammatical help for writers whose first language or dialect is not standard American English.

- **New** Notes labeled CULTURE LANGUAGE supplant former ESL notes and now cover dialect as well as language differences.
- Fully integrated coverage, instead of a separate section, means that students can find what they need without having to know which problems they do and don't share with native SAE speakers.
- "Guide to CULTURE LANGUAGE Topics," just before the back endpapers, pulls all the integrated coverage together in one place.

A uniquely accessible reference

LB Brief opens itself to students, featuring not only a convenient spiral binding but also numerous features designed to help students find what they need and then use what they find:

- "Frequently Asked Questions," both on the front endpapers and at the beginning of every chapter, provide a common-language portal for reaching the handbook's contents.
- An unusually direct organization arranges topics in ways that students can easily grasp.
- Rules and other headings use minimal terminology, with examples replacing or supplementing terms.
- "Key terms" boxes define secondary terms used on each page and minimize cross-references.
- Nearly fifty checklist and summary boxes highlight key reference information, such as questions about audience, uses of the comma, and indexes to documentation formats.

A source for examples and exercises

Bringing concepts to earth, *LB Brief* provides examples for students to emulate and exercises for them to practice on:

- Hundreds of illustrations use color underlining to show clearly both the look of errors and the means of correcting them.
- Nine complete student papers model a wide range of writing assignments, from personal narrative to critique of a reading to fully documented research paper.
- More than 120 exercise sets offer hands-on work with words, sentences, paragraphs, and whole essays—all drawing on content from across the disciplines, all in connected discourse, and about half of each set answered in the back of the book.

Supplements

In addition to its Web site (pp. viii–ix), *LB Brief* is accompanied by a large array of supplements.

For instructors and students

- *MyCompLab* provides many multimedia resources on one easy-to-use site: guided assistance through each step of the writing process; *Exchange*, Longman's online peer-review program; the tutorial "Avoiding Plagiarism"; diagnostic grammar tests and more than 2,500 exercises; and *Research Navigator*™, a database with thousands of magazines and academic journals, the subject-search archive of the *New York Times*, "Link Library," and more. Tour the site at *www.mycomplab.com*.
- *CourseCompass* is an online course-management system powered by *BlackBoard*. Easy to use, the program enables instructors to tailor content and features to their own needs. For more information and a demo, visit *www.coursecompass.com*.

For instructors

- Separate answer keys are available for the exercises in *LB Brief* and for the *Developmental Exercises to Accompany LB Brief*.
- An extensive assessment package includes Competency Profile tests, sample CLAST and TASP exams, and *Diagnostic and Editing Tests and Exercises*. (All testing supplements are available in both print and electronic formats.)

For students

- *Developmental Exercises to Accompany LB Brief*, by Kathryn Riley, provides practical activities for developing writers.
- *The Longman English Tutor Center* offers registered students feedback on their drafts from experienced writing teachers.
- *Research Navigator Guide for English*, by H. Eric Branscomb and Linda R. Barr, offers students advice on the research process

and shows how to conduct high-quality online research and document sources properly. This guide also includes an access code to *Research Navigator*™ (previous page).

- *Take Note! 2.0* is a cross-platform CD-ROM that provides an information-management tool for students as they take notes from sources, outline, and prepare a bibliography.
- *ESL Worksheets*, by Jocelyn Steer and Dawn Schmid, provides nonnative speakers with practice in troublesome areas.

Other supplements for students include *The Longman Writer's Journal, The Longman Researcher's Journal,* the Literacy Library Series (*Public Literacy, Workplace Literacy,* and *Academic Literacy*), *Analyzing Literature: A Guide for Students,* and *A Guide for Peer Response.* In addition, *LB Brief* may be packaged with other books at a discount: *Merriam-Webster's Collegiate Dictionary*, a hardcover desk dictionary; *The New American Webster Handy College Dictionary*, a briefer paperback; and, in conjunction with Penguin Putnam, a variety of Penguin titles, such as Arthur Miller's *Death of a Salesman* and Julia Alvarez's *How the Garcia Girls Lost Their Accents*.

Acknowledgments

This edition of *LB Brief* owes much to the instructors who offered thoughtful and insightful suggestions for improvement. I am grateful to Crystal W. Brantley, Vance-Granville Community College; Jean Ferguson Carr, University of Pittsburgh; John Dudley, Southern Arkansas University; Richard F. Gaspar, Hillsborough Community College; Margaret Graham, Iowa State University; Shari Horner, Shippensburg University; Mahbub Jamal, Prince George's Community College; Gary M. Levine, Ashland University; Michelle Paulsen, University of Missouri, Rolla; Milton Moreland, Huntingdon College; David Morse, Long Beach City College; Capper Nichols, University of Minnesota; Judith Wrase Nygard, Mercer County Community College; and Sherry R. Truffin, McHenry County College.

Many others contributed to *LB Brief* as well. Daniel Anderson, University of North Carolina, provided the foundation for the book's coverage of technology. Sylvan Barnet, Tufts University, lent his expertise in the chapter "Reading and Writing About Literature," which is adapted from his *A Short Guide to Writing About Literature* (with William E. Cain) and *An Introduction to Literature* (with William Burto and William E. Cain). At Longman, Lynn Huddon, assisted by Esther Hollander, captained the project thoughtfully and supportively. During development Carol Hollar-Zwick once again proved a superb idea source, sounding board, and hand holder. And during production Susan McIntyre worked miracles of scheduling without ever dropping her high standards. My thanks to all these colleagues.

I

The Writing Process

1 The Writing Situation

How should I tackle a writing assignment?

Many writers find it helpful to break writing tasks into manageable steps. Such steps are part of the **writing process**—the term for all activities, mental and physical, that go into creating what eventually becomes a finished piece of work.

There is no one writing process: no two writers proceed in the same way, and even an individual writer adapts his or her process to the task at hand. Still, most experienced writers pass through certain stages that overlap and circle back on each other:

- *Analyzing the writing situation,* especially considering subject, audience, and purpose (this chapter).
- *Invention and planning:* generating ideas, gathering information, focusing on a central theme, and organizing material (Chapters 2–3).
- *Drafting:* expressing and connecting ideas (Chapter 4).
- *Revising and editing:* rethinking and improving structure, content, style, and presentation (Chapter 5).

As you complete varied assignments and try the many techniques included in this book, you will develop your own writing process.

1a Analyze the writing situation.

Any writing you do for others occurs in a **writing situation** that both limits and clarifies your choices. You are communicating within a particular context, about a particular subject, to a particular audience of readers, for a specific reason. You may need to conduct research. You probably face a length requirement and a deadline. And you may be expected to present your work in a certain format.

Analyzing the elements of the writing situation at the very start of a project can tell you much about how to proceed. (For more in-

http://www.ablongman.com/littlebrown
➤ The writing process
  ➤ Video tutorials ➤ Narrowing a subject online
  ➤ Web exercises ➤ Exers. 1 and 2
  ➤ Downloads ➤ Questions about audience
  ➤ Web links ➤ The writing situation

formation about any of the following elements, refer to the page numbers given.)

Context (pp. 88–160)

- Are you writing for a course in school, for work, or in some other context? What do you know of the requirements for writing in this context?
- How much leeway do you have for this writing? Is there a stated or implied assignment?

Subject (pp. 4–6)

- What does your writing assignment instruct you to write about? If you don't have a specific assignment, what do you want to write about?
- What interests you about the subject? What do you already have ideas about or want to know more about?
- What does the assignment require you to do with the subject?

Audience (pp. 6–8)

- Who will read your writing? What do your readers already know and think about your subject?
- Do your readers have any characteristics—such as educational background, experience in your field, or political views—that could influence their reception of your writing?
- What is your relationship to your readers? How formal or informal should your writing be?
- What do you want readers to do or think after they read your writing?

Purpose (pp. 9–10)

- What aim does your assignment specify? For instance, does it ask you to explain something or argue a point?
- Why are you writing? What effect do you intend your writing to have on readers? What do you want to accomplish?
- How can you best achieve your purpose?

Research (pp. 406–71)

- What kinds of evidence—such as facts, examples, and the opinions of experts—best suit your subject, audience, and purpose?
- Does your assignment require you to consult sources of information or conduct other research, such as interviews, surveys, or experiments?
- Besides the requirements of the assignment, what additional information do you need to develop your subject? How will you obtain it?

- What style should you use to cite your sources? (See pp. 466–68 on documenting sources in the academic disciplines.)

Deadline and length

- When is the assignment due? How will you complete the work you have to do in the available time?
- How long should your writing be? If no length is assigned, what seems appropriate for your topic, audience, and purpose?

Document design

- What organization and format does the assignment require? (See p. 74 on formats in academic disciplines and pp. 146–52 on formats in business.)
- Even if a particular format is not required, how might you use margins, headings, illustrations, and other elements to achieve your purpose? (See pp. 75–85.)

EXERCISE 1.1
Analyzing a writing situation

The following assignment was made in a survey course in psychology. What does the assignment specify and imply about the elements of the writing situation? Given this assignment, how would you answer the questions on page 3 and above?

When is psychotherapy most likely to work? That is, what combinations of client, therapist, and theory tend to achieve good results? In your paper, cite studies supporting your conclusions. Length: 1500 to 1800 words. Post your paper online to me and your discussion group by March 30.

1b Find an appropriate subject.

A subject for writing has several basic requirements:

- It should be suitable for the assignment.
- It should be neither too general nor too limited for the length of paper and deadline assigned.
- It should be something you care about.

When you receive an assignment, study its wording and its implications about your writing situation to guide your choice of subject:

- *What's wanted from you?* Many writing assignments contain words such as *discuss, describe, analyze, report, interpret, explain, define, argue,* or *evaluate.* These words specify the way you are to approach your subject, what kind of thinking is expected of you, and what your general purpose is. (See pp. 9–10.)

- *For whom are you writing?* Some assignments will specify your readers, but usually you will have to figure out for yourself who your audience is and what it expects of you. (For more on analyzing your audience, see pp. 6–8.)
- *What kind of research is required?* Sometimes an assignment specifies the kinds of sources you are expected to consult, and you can use such information to choose your subject. (If you are unsure whether research is required, check with your instructor.)
- *Does the subject need to be narrowed?* To do the subject justice in the length and time required, you'll often need to limit it. (See below.)

Answering these questions about your assignment will help set some boundaries for your choice of subject. Then you can explore your own interests and experiences to narrow the subject so that you can cover it adequately within the space and time assigned. Federal aid to college students could be the subject of a book; the kinds of aid available or why the government should increase aid would be a more appropriate subject for a four-page paper due in a week.

One helpful technique for narrowing a subject is to ask focused questions about it, seeking one that seems appropriate for your assignment and that promises to sustain your interest through the writing process. The following examples illustrate how questioning can scale down broad subjects to specific subjects that are limited and manageable:

Broad subjects	Specific subjects
Communication on the Internet	What are the advantages of online communication? How, if at all, should the government regulate Internet content? How might the Internet contribute to social and economic equality?
Mrs. Mallard in Kate Chopin's "The Story of an Hour"	What changes does Mrs. Mallard undergo? Why does Mrs. Mallard respond as she does to news of her husband's death? What does the story's irony contribute to the character of Mrs. Mallard?
Lincoln's weaknesses as President	What was Lincoln's most significant error as commander-in-chief of the Union army? Why did Lincoln delay emancipating the slaves? Why did Lincoln have difficulties controlling his cabinet?

Here are guidelines for narrowing broad subjects:

- *Ask as many questions about your broad subject as you can think of.* Make a list.
- *For each question that interests you and fits the assignment, roughly sketch out the main ideas.* Consider how many paragraphs or pages of specific facts, examples, and other details you would need to pin those ideas down. This thinking should give you at least a vague idea of how much work you'd have to do and how long the resulting paper might be.
- *Break a too-broad question down further,* repeating the previous steps.

EXERCISE 1.2
Narrowing subjects

Choose three of the following broad subjects and, using the techniques above, narrow each one to at least one specific question that can be answered in a three- to four-page paper.

1. Bilingual education
2. Training of teachers
3. Distribution of music by conventional versus electronic means
4. Dance in America
5. The history of women's suffrage
6. Food additives
7. Immigrants in the United States
8. Space exploration
9. The effect of television on professional sports
10. Child abuse
11. African Americans and civil rights
12. Successes in cancer research
13. Television evangelism
14. Treatment and prevention of AIDS
15. Women writers
16. Campaign finance reform
17. Genetic engineering
18. Trends in popular music
19. Immigration in your community
20. The World Wide Web and popular culture

1c Consider your audience.

The readers likely to see your work—your **audience**—may influence your choice of subject and your definition of purpose. Your audience certainly will influence what you say about your subject and how you say it—for instance, how much background information you give and whether you adopt a serious or a friendly tone. Consider, for instance, these two memos written by a student who worked part-time at a small company and wanted to persuade the company to recycle paper:

Addressed to coworkers

Ever notice how much paper collects in your trash basket every day? Well, most of it can be recycled with little effort, I promise. Basically, all you need to do is set a bag or box near your desk and deposit wastepaper in it. I know, space is cramped in these little cubicles. But what's a little more crowding when the earth's at stake? . . .

Information: how employees could handle recycling; no mention of costs

Role: cheerful, equally harried colleague

Tone: informal, personal (*Ever notice; you; what's; Well; I know, space is cramped*)

Addressed to management

In my four months here, I have observed that all of us throw out baskets of potentially recyclable paper every day. Considering the drain on our forest resources and the pressure on landfills that paper causes, we could make a valuable contribution to the environmental movement by helping to recycle the paper we use. At the company where I worked before, the employees separate clean wastepaper from other trash at their desks. The maintenance staff collects trash in two receptacles, and the trash hauler (the same one we use here) makes separate pickups. I do not know what the hauler charges for handling recyclable material. . . .

Information: specific reasons; view of company as a whole; reference to another company; problem of cost

Role: serious, thoughtful, responsible employee

Tone: formal, serious (*Considering the drain; forest resources; valuable contribution;* no *you* or contractions)

For much academic and business writing, readers have definite needs and expectations. Thus Chapter 8 discusses academic writing, and Chapter 13 discusses business writing. Even in these areas, you must make many choices based on audience. In other areas where the conventions of structure and presentation are vaguer, the choices are even more numerous. The box on the next page contains questions that can help you define and make these choices. You can download these questions from this book's Web site: see the box on page 2. Duplicate the list for each writing project, write appropriate answers, and print a copy for reference as you compose.

CULTURE LANGUAGE If English is not your native language, you may not be accustomed to appealing to your readers when you write. In some cultures, for instance, readers may not expect such an appeal or may accept a writer's statements with little or no questioning. When writing in English, try to reach out to readers by being accurate, fair, interesting, and clear.

Questions about audience

Identity and expectations

- Who *are* my readers?
- Why are readers going to read my writing? What will they expect?
- What do I want readers to know or do after reading my work, and how should I make that clear to them?
- What is my relationship to my readers? How formal or informal will they expect me to be? What role and tone should I assume? What role do I want readers to play?

Characteristics, knowledge, and attitudes

- How will readers' characteristics, such as those below, influence their attitudes toward my topic?

  Age and sex
  Occupation: students, professional colleagues, etc.
  Social or economic role: adult children, car buyers, potential employers, etc.
  Economic or educational background
  Ethnic background
  Political, religious, or moral beliefs and values
  Hobbies or activities

- What do readers already know and *not* know about my topic? How much do I have to tell them?
- If my topic involves specialized language, how much should I use and define?
- What ideas, arguments, or information might surprise readers? excite them? offend them? How should I handle these points?
- What misconceptions might readers have of my topic and/or my approach to the topic? How can I dispel these misconceptions?

Uses and format

- What will readers do with my writing? Should I expect them to read every word from the top, to scan for information, or to look for conclusions? Can I help with a summary, headings, illustrations, or other aids? (See pp. 74–86 on document design.)

EXERCISE 1.3
Analyzing audience

Choosing one of the topics you worked with in Exercise 1.2, use the questions above to determine as much as you can about the probable readers of an essay based on that topic. What does your analysis reveal about the specific information your readers would need? What role would you want to assume, and what tone would best convey your attitude toward your topic?

1d Define your purpose.

Your **purpose** in writing is your chief reason for communicating something about your subject to a particular audience of readers. Most writing you do will have one of four main purposes. Occasionally, you will *entertain* readers or *express yourself*—your feelings or ideas—to readers. More often you will *explain* something to readers or *persuade* readers to respect and accept, and sometimes even act on, your well-supported opinion. These purposes often overlap in a single essay, but usually one predominates. And the dominant purpose will influence your particular slant on your subject, the details you choose, and even the words you use.

Many writing assignments narrow the purpose by using a signal word, such as the following:

- *Report:* survey, organize, and objectively present the available evidence on the subject.
- *Summarize:* concisely state the main points in a text, argument, theory, or other work.
- *Discuss:* examine the main points, competing views, or implications of the subject.
- *Compare and contrast:* explain the similarities and differences between two subjects. (See also p. 65.)
- *Define:* specify the meaning of a term or a concept—distinctive characteristics, boundaries, and so on. (See also p. 63.)
- *Analyze:* identify the elements of the subject and discuss how they work together. (See also pp. 63–64 and 98.)
- *Interpret:* infer the subject's meaning or implications.
- *Evaluate:* judge the quality or significance of the subject, considering pros and cons. (See also p. 101.)
- *Argue:* take a position on the subject and support your position with evidence. (See also pp. 109–24.)

You can conceive of your purpose more specifically, too, in a way that incorporates your particular topic and the outcome you intend:

> To explain how Annie Dillard's "Total Eclipse" builds to its climax so that readers appreciate the author's skill.
>
> To explain the steps in a new office procedure so that staffers will be able to follow it without difficulty.
>
> To persuade readers to support the college administration's plan for more required courses.
>
> To argue against additional regulation of health-maintenance organizations so that readers will perceive the disadvantages for themselves.

EXERCISE 1.4
Finding purpose in assignments

For each of your narrowed topics in Exercise 1.2 (p. 6), suggest a likely purpose (entertainment, self-expression, explanation, persuasion) and try to define a specific purpose as well. Make audience part of your suggestions: what would you want readers to do or think in each case?

2 Invention

How do writers get ideas?

Writers use a host of techniques to discover ideas for their writing projects, from keeping a journal to making lists to reading magazines and books. There are many such **invention** techniques, but they don't all work for every writer. As you read through this chapter, try a few of the invention strategies that appeal to you. If they don't work, try others.

Whichever of the techniques you use, do your work in writing, not just in your head. That way, your ideas will be retrievable, and the very act of writing will lead you to fresh insights.

CULTURE LANGUAGE The discovery process encouraged here rewards rapid writing without a lot of thinking beforehand about what you will write or how. If your first language is not standard American English, you may find it helpful initially to do this exploratory writing in your native language or dialect and then to translate the worthwhile material for use in your drafts. This process can be productive, but it is extra work. You may want to try it at first and gradually move to composing in standard American English.

2a Keep a journal.

A **journal** is a diary of ideas kept on paper or on a computer. It gives you a place to record your thoughts and can provide ideas for writing. Because you write for yourself, you can work out your ideas without the pressure of an audience "out there" who will evaluate

http://www.ablongman.com/littlebrown
➤ The writing process ➤ Web links ➤ Invention

logic or organization or correctness. If you write every day, even just for a few minutes, the routine will loosen your writing muscles and improve your confidence.

You can use a journal for varied purposes: perhaps to confide your feelings, explore your responses to movies and other media, practice certain kinds of writing (such as poems or news stories), think critically about what you read (see p. 91), or pursue ideas from your courses. In both examples following, the students planted the seeds for essays they later wrote. Megan Polanyis pondered something she learned from her biology textbook:

> *Ecology* and *economics* have the same root—the Greek word for "house." Economy = management of the house. Ecology = study of the house. In ecology the house is all of nature, ourselves, other animals, plants, earth, air, the whole environment. Ecology has a lot to do with economy: study the house in order to manage it.

Sara Ling responded to an experience:

> Had an exchange today on the snowboarding forum with a woman who joined the forum a while ago. She says she signed on at first with a screen name that didn't give away her gender, and she didn't tell anyone she was a woman. She was afraid the guys on the forum might shout her down. She waited until she'd established herself as an experienced snowboarder. Then she revealed her gender, and no one reacted badly. She asked me about my experiences, since my screen name says Sara. Had to admit I'd had problems of the what-does-a-girl-know sort. Wish I'd taken her approach.

(Further examples of Ling's writing appear on p. 13 and in the next three chapters.)

CULTURE LANGUAGE A journal can be especially helpful if your first language is not standard American English. You can practice writing to improve your fluency, try out sentence patterns, and experiment with vocabulary words. Equally important, you can experiment with applying what you know from experience to what you read and observe.

2b Observe your surroundings.

Sometimes you can find a good subject—or gather information about a subject—by looking around you, not in the half-conscious way most of us move from place to place in our daily lives but deliberately, all senses alert. On a bus, for instance, are there certain types of passengers? What seems to be on the driver's mind? To get the most from observation, you should have a tablet and pen or pencil handy for notes and sketches. Back at your desk, study your notes and sketches for oddities or patterns that you'd like to explore further.

2c Freewrite.

Writing into a subject

Many writers find subjects or discover ideas by **freewriting:** writing without stopping for a certain amount of time (say, ten minutes) or to a certain length (say, one page). The goal of freewriting is to generate ideas and information from *within* yourself by going around the part of your mind that doesn't want to write or can't think of anything to write. You let words themselves suggest other words. *What* you write is not important; that you *keep* writing is. Don't stop, even if that means repeating the same words until new words come. Don't go back to reread, don't censor ideas that seem dumb or repetitious, and above all don't stop to edit: grammar, punctuation, spelling, and the like are irrelevant at this stage.

The physical act of freewriting may give you access to ideas you were unaware of. For example, the following freewriting by a student, Robert Benday, gave him the subject of writing as a disguise:

> Write to write. Seems pretty obvious, also weird. What to gain by writing? never anything before. Writing seems always—always—Getting corrected for trying too hard to please the teacher, getting corrected for not trying hard enuf. Frustration, nail biting, sometimes getting carried away making sentences to tell stories, not even true stories, *esp.* not true stories, *that* feels like creating something. Writing just pulls the story out of me. The story lets me be someone else, gives me a disguise.

(A later phase of Benday's writing appears on p. 15.)

If you write on a computer, you can ensure that your freewriting keeps moving forward by turning off your computer's monitor or turning its brightness control all the way down so that the screen is dark. The computer will record what you type but keep it from you and thus prevent you from tinkering with your prose. This **invisible writing** may feel uncomfortable at first, but it can free the mind for very creative results. When you've finished freewriting, simply turn the monitor on or turn up the brightness control to read what you've written, and then save or revise it as appropriate. Later, you may be able to transfer some of your freewriting into your draft.

CULTURE LANGUAGE Invisible writing can be especially helpful if you are uneasy about writing in standard American English and you tend to worry about errors while writing: the blank computer screen leaves you no choice but to explore ideas without regard for their expression. If you choose to write with the monitor on, concentrate on *what* you want to say, not *how* you're saying it.

Focused freewriting

Focused freewriting is more concentrated: you start with your question about your subject and answer it without stopping for, say, fifteen minutes or one full page. As in all freewriting, you push to bypass mental blocks and self-consciousness, not debating what to say or editing what you've written. With focused freewriting, though, you let the physical act of writing take you into and around your subject.

An example of focused freewriting can be found in the work of Sara Ling, whose journal entry appears on page 11. In a composition course, Ling's instructor had distributed "Welcome to Cyberbia," an essay by M. Kadi about communication on the Internet. The instructor then gave the following assignment:

> *Response to a reading*. M. Kadi's "Welcome to Cyberbia" holds that the Internet will do little to bridge differences among people because its users gravitate toward other users who are like themselves in most respects. A decade after Kadi wrote, do her concerns seem valid? Can the Internet serve as a medium for positive change in the way people of diverse backgrounds relate to each other? If so, how? If not, why not? In an essay of 500–700 words, respond to Kadi's essay with a limited and well-supported opinion of your own. The first draft is due Monday, April 4, for class discussion.

On first reading Kadi's essay, Ling had been impressed with its tight logic but had found unconvincing its pessimistic view of the Internet's potential. She reread the essay and realized that some of Kadi's assertions did not correspond to her own Internet experiences. This discovery prompted the following focused freewriting:

> Kadi says we only meet people like ourselves on the Internet, but I've met lots who have very different backgrounds and interests—or "turned out to have" is more like it, since I didn't know anything about them at first. There's the anonymity thing, but Kadi ignores it. You can be anyone or no one. People can get to know me and my ideas without knowing I'm female or Asian American or a student. Then they can find out the facts about me, but the facts will be less likely to get in the way of communication. Communication without set identity, especially physical appearance. This could make for more tolerance of others, of difference.

(We will continue to follow Ling's work in this and the next three chapters.)

2d Brainstorm.

A method similar to freewriting is **brainstorming**—focusing intently on a subject for a fixed period (say, fifteen minutes), pushing yourself to list every idea and detail that comes to mind. Like free-writing, brainstorming requires turning off your internal editor so that you keep moving ahead. (The technique of invisible writing on a computer, described on p. 12, can help you move forward.)

Here is an example of brainstorming by a student, Johanna Abrams, on what a summer job can teach:

summer work teaches—
  how to look busy while doing nothing
  how to avoid the sun in summer
  seriously: discipline, budgeting money, value of money
which job? Burger King cashier? baby-sitter? mail-room clerk?
mail room: how to sort mail into boxes: this is learning??
how to survive getting fired—humiliation, outrage
Mrs. King! the mail-room queen as learning experience
the shock of getting fired: what to tell parents, friends?
Mrs. K was so rigid—dumb procedures
initials instead of names on the mail boxes—confusion!
Mrs. K's anger, resentment: the disadvantages of being smarter than your boss
The odd thing about working in an office: a world with its own rules for how to act
what Mr. D said about the pecking order—big chick (Mrs. K) pecks on little chick (me)
a job can beat you down—make you be mean to other people

(A later phase of Abrams's writing process appears on p. 24, and her final essay appears in Exercise 5.2, pp. 49–50.)

Working on a computer makes it fairly easy to edit and shape a brainstorming list into a preliminary outline of your paper. With a few keystrokes, you can delete weak ideas, expand strong ones, and rearrange items. You can also freewrite from the list if you think some ideas are especially promising and deserve more thought.

2e Cluster.

Like freewriting and brainstorming, **clustering** also draws on free association and rapid, unedited work. But it emphasizes the relations between ideas by combining writing and nonlinear drawing. When clustering, you radiate outward from a center point—your topic. When an idea occurs, you pursue related ideas in a branching structure until they seem exhausted. Then you do the same with other ideas, staying open to connections, continuously branching out or drawing arrows.

The following example of clustering shows how Robert Benday used the technique for ten minutes to expand on the topic of writing as a means of disguise, an idea he arrived at through freewriting (see p. 12).

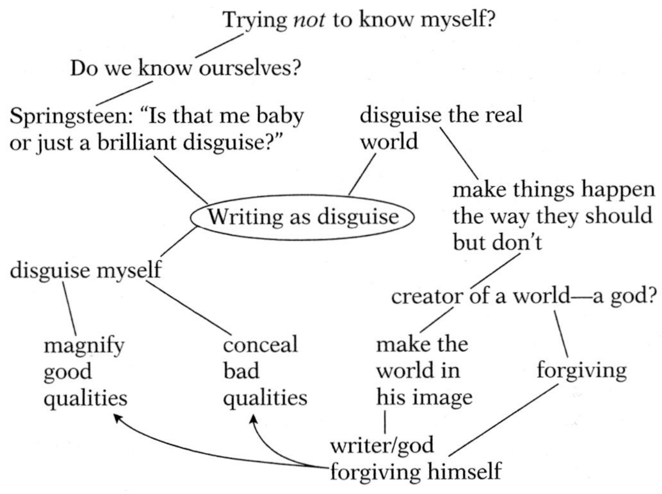

EXERCISE 2.1
Using freewriting, brainstorming, or clustering

If you haven't tried any of them before, experiment with freewriting, brainstorming, or clustering. Continue with one of the topics you selected in Exercise 1.2 (p. 6), or begin with a new topic. Write or draw for at least ten minutes without stopping to reread or edit. When you finish, examine what you have written for ideas and relationships that could help you develop the topic. What do you think of the technique you tried? Did you have any difficulties with it? Did it help you to loosen up and generate ideas?

2f Ask questions.

Asking yourself a set of questions about your subject—and writing out the answers—can help you look at the topic objectively and see fresh possibilities in it.

1 • Journalist's questions

A journalist with a story to report poses a set of questions:

Who was involved?
What happened, and what were the results?
When did it happen?
Where did it happen?
Why did it happen?
How did it happen?

These questions can also be useful in probing an essay subject, especially when you are telling a story or examining causes and effects.

2 • Questions about patterns

We think about and understand a vast range of subjects through patterns such as narration, classification, and comparison and contrast. Asking questions based on the patterns can help you view your topic from many angles. Sometimes you may want to develop an entire essay using just one pattern.

How did it happen? (Narration)
How does it look, sound, feel, smell, taste? (Description)
What are examples of it or reasons for it? (Illustration or support)
What is it? What does it encompass, and what does it exclude? (Definition)
What are its parts or characteristics? (Division or analysis)
What groups or categories can it be sorted into? (Classification)
How is it like, or different from, other things? (Comparison and contrast)
Why did it happen? What results did or could it have? (Cause-and-effect analysis)
How do you do it, or how does it work? (Process analysis)

For more on these patterns, including paragraph-length examples, see pages 61–66.

2g Read.

Many assignments require reading for the purpose of exploring ideas or gathering information. To respond to M. Kadi's essay about the Internet, for instance, Sara Ling had to understand and question Kadi's work. Essays on literary works as well as research papers also demand reading. But even when reading is not required by an assignment, it can help you locate or develop your topic by introducing you to ideas you didn't know and testing or expanding on what you do know.

Say you were writing in favor of amateur athletics, a subject to which you had given a lot of thought. You might be inclined to proceed entirely on your own, drawing on facts, examples, and opinions already in your head. But a little reading might open up more. For instance, an article in *Time* magazine could introduce you to an old rule for amateur status, or a posting to an online newsgroup could suggest a pro-amateurism argument that hadn't occurred to you. (See pp. 415–35 for techniques of library and computer research that you can use to locate sources on a topic.)

People often read passively, absorbing content like blotters, not interacting with it. To read for ideas, you need to be more active, probing text and illustrations with your mind, connecting them and the world you know. Always write while you read so that you can keep notes on content and—just as important—on what the content makes you *think*. See pages 93–95 for specific guidelines on the process of active reading.

Note Whenever you use the information or ideas of others in your writing, you must acknowledge your sources in order to avoid the serious offense of plagiarism. (See p. 459.)

2h Think critically.

Even if you do not read for information and ideas on your topic, you can still think critically about it. Critical thinking (discussed on pp. 91–105) can produce creative ideas by leading you to see what is not obvious. It can also lead you systematically to conclusions about your topic.

Sara Ling, writing about communication on the Internet, used the operations of critical thinking to explore her topic:

- *Analysis:* What are the subject's elements or characteristics? Ling looked at the ways Internet users can communicate because of their anonymity.
- *Interpretation:* What is the meaning or significance of the elements? Ling saw that the anonymity of Internet users could help them transcend their physical differences.
- *Synthesis:* How do the elements relate to each other, or how does this subject relate to another one? Ling perceived important differences between anonymous Internet communication and face-to-face interaction.
- *Evaluation:* What is the value or significance of the subject? Ling concluded that by making people more tolerant of each other, the Internet could help build community out of diversity.

EXERCISE 2.2
Developing a topic

Use at least two of the discovery techniques discussed on the preceding pages to develop one of the topics you worked with in Exercise 1.2 (p. 6).

3 Thesis and Organization

How does writing take shape?

You'll form rough ideas into writing through two main operations: developing a thesis and organizing the ideas and information that support the thesis. Finding your thesis, or main idea, gives you a focus and direction. Organizing your raw material emphasizes your central concerns and helps you clear away unneeded ideas, spot possible gaps, and energize your topic.

3a Develop a thesis statement.

Your readers will expect your essay to be focused on a main idea, or **thesis.** In your final draft you may express this idea in a **thesis statement,** often at the end of your introduction. You can think of a thesis statement as both a claim about your subject and a promise you make to readers about how you approach the subject. The rest of your essay supports the claim and thus delivers on the promise.

Your thesis statement may be the answer to the question you posed in narrowing your subject (pp. 5–6), but it probably will not leap fully formed into your head. You may begin with an idea you want to communicate, but you will need to refine that idea to fit the realities of the paper you write. And often you will have to write and rewrite before you come to a conclusion about what you have. Still, it's wise to try to pin down your thesis when you have a fairly good stock of ideas. Then the thesis can help you start drafting, help keep you focused, and serve as a point of reference when changes inevitably occur.

1 • Functions of the thesis statement

As shown in the box on the facing page, the thesis statement serves three crucial functions and one optional one.

http://www.ablongman.com/littlebrown

➤ The writing process
- ➤ Video tutorials ➤ Outlining with a word processor
- ➤ Web exercises ➤ Exer. 3
- ➤ Downloads ➤ Exer. 3.1 in electronic format
- ➤ Web links ➤ Thesis and organization

The thesis statement

- The thesis statement **narrows your subject** to a single, central idea that you want readers to gain from your essay.
- It **claims something specific and significant** about your subject, a claim that requires support.
- It **conveys your purpose**, your reason for writing.
- It often concisely **previews the arrangement of ideas.**

Here are examples of questions and answering thesis statements. As assertions, the thesis statements each consist of a topic (usually naming the general subject) and a claim about the topic.

Question	Thesis statement
1. What are the advantages of direct distribution of music via the Web?	Because artists can now publish their music directly via the Web, consumers have many more choices than traditional distribution allows. [*Topic:* consumers. *Claim:* have many more choices.]
2. How did Home Inc. survive the scandal over its hiring practices?	After Home Inc.'s hiring practices were exposed in the media, the company avoided a scandal with policy changes and a well-publicized outreach to employees and consumers. [*Topic:* the company. *Claim:* avoided a scandal in two ways.]
3. Why did Abraham Lincoln delay in emancipating the slaves?	Lincoln delayed emancipating any slaves until 1863 because his primary goal was to restore and preserve the Union, with or without slavery. [*Topic:* Lincoln's delay. *Claim:* was caused by his goal of preserving the Union.]
4. Which college students should be entitled to federal aid?	As an investment in its own economy, the United States should provide a tuition grant to any college student who qualifies academically. [*Topic:* United States. *Claim:* should provide a tuition grant to any college student who qualifies academically.]
5. What steps can prevent juvenile crime?	Juveniles can be diverted from crime by active learning programs, full-time sports, and intervention by mentors and role models. [*Topic:* juveniles. *Claim:* can be diverted from crime in three ways.]

Question	Thesis statement
6. Why should strip-mining be controlled?	Strip-mining should be tightly controlled in this region to reduce its pollution of water resources, its destruction of the land, and its devastating effects on people's lives. [*Topic:* strip-mining. *Claim:* should be tightly controlled for three reasons.]

Notice that statements 5 and 6 clearly predict the organization of the essay that will follow.

CULTURE LANGUAGE In some cultures it is considered unnecessary or impolite for a writer to have an opinion or to state his or her main idea outright. When writing in standard American English for school or work, you can assume that your readers expect a clear and early idea of what you think.

2 • Drafting and revision of the thesis statement

While you are developing your thesis statement, ask the questions below about each attempt.

- *Does the statement make a concise* ***claim*** *about your subject?*

Original This new product brought in over $300,000 last year.

The original sentence states a fact, not a claim of significance that requires support. The following revision makes a point about the product's success:

Revised This new product succeeded because of its innovative marketing campaign, including widespread press coverage, in-store entertainment, and a consumer newsletter.

- *Is the claim* ***limited*** *to a single specific idea?*

Original Diets are dangerous.

The original sentence is so broad that it seems insupportable. The revision limits the kinds of diets and their effects:

Revised Fad diets can be dangerous when they deprive the body of essential nutrients or rely on excessive quantities of potentially harmful foods.

The following original sentence is also too general, whereas the revision specifies differences and their significance:

Original Televised sports are different from live sports.

Revised Although television cannot transmit all the excitement of being in a crowd during a game, its close-ups and slow-motion replays reveal much about the players and the strategy of the game.

- *Is the statement **unified** so that its parts clearly relate to each other?*

Original Seat belts can save lives, but carmakers now install air bags.

With two facts linked by *but,* the original sentence moves in two directions, not one. The revision clarifies the relation between the parts and their significance.

Revised If drivers had used lifesaving seat belts more often, carmakers might not have needed to install air bags.

- *Does the statement at least imply your **purpose**?*

Original Educators' motives for using the Internet vary widely.

The original sentence conveys no hint of the writer's reason for exploring the subject. In contrast, the revision implies a purpose of arguing against a mainly financial motivation for using the Internet in education:

Revised Too often, educators' uses of the Internet seem motivated less by teaching and learning than by making or saving money.

EXERCISE 3.1
Evaluating thesis statements

Evaluate the following thesis statements, considering whether each one is sufficiently limited, specific, and unified. Also consider whether each is a claim that implies the essay's purpose. Rewrite the statements as necessary to meet these goals.

1. Aggression usually leads to violence, injury, and even death, and we should use it constructively.
2. Electronic mail is invaluable.
3. One evening of a radio talk show amply illustrates both the appeal of such shows and their silliness.
4. Good manners make our society work.
5. The poem is about motherhood.
6. Television is useful for children and a mindless escape for adults who do not want to think about their problems.
7. I disliked American history in high school, but I like it in college.
8. Drunken drivers, whose perception and coordination are impaired, should receive mandatory suspensions of their licenses.
9. Business is a good major for many students.
10. The state's lenient divorce laws undermine the institution of marriage, which is fundamental to our culture, and they should certainly be made stricter for couples who have children.

3b Organize your ideas.

Most essays share a basic pattern of introduction (states the subject), body (develops the subject), and conclusion (pulls the essay's ideas together). Introductions and conclusions are discussed on pages 67–71. Within the body, every paragraph develops some aspect of the essay's main idea, or thesis. See pages 44–46 for Sara Ling's essay, with annotations highlighting the body's pattern of support for the thesis statement.

CULTURE LANGUAGE If you are not used to reading and writing American academic prose, its pattern of introduction-body-conclusion and the particular schemes discussed here may seem unfamiliar. For instance, instead of introductions that focus quickly on the topic and thesis, you may be used to openings that establish personal connections with readers or that approach the thesis indirectly. And instead of body paragraphs that first emphasize general points and then support those points with specific evidence, you may be used to general statements without support (because writers can assume that readers will supply the evidence themselves) or to evidence without explanation (because writers can assume that readers will infer the general points). When writing American academic prose, you need to take into account readers' expectations for directness and for the statement and support of general points.

1 • The general and the specific

Organizing material for an essay requires that you distinguish general and specific ideas and see the relations between ideas. **General** and **specific** refer to the number of instances or objects included in a group signified by a word. The following "ladder" illustrates a general-to-specific hierarchy:

Most general
↑ life form
plant
rose
↓ Uncle Dan's prize-winning American Beauty rose
Most specific

As you arrange your material, pick out the general ideas and then the specific points that support them. Set aside points that seem irrelevant to your key ideas. On a computer, you can easily experiment with various arrangements of general ideas and supporting information: save the master list, duplicate it, and then use the Cut and Paste functions to move material around or (a little quicker) drag selected text to where you want it.

2 • Schemes for organizing essays

An essay's body paragraphs may be arranged in many ways that are familiar to readers. The choice depends on your subject, purpose, and audience.

- *Spatial:* In describing a person, place, or thing, move through space systematically from a starting point to other features—for instance, top to bottom, near to far, left to right.
- *Chronological:* In recounting a sequence of events, arrange the events as they actually occurred in time, first to last.
- *General to specific:* Begin with an overall discussion of the subject; then fill in details, facts, examples, and other support.
- *Specific to general:* First provide the support; then draw a conclusion from it.
- *Climactic:* Arrange ideas in order of increasing importance to your thesis or increasing interest to the reader.
- *Problem-solution:* First outline a problem that needs solving; then propose a solution.

You can adapt these schemes to the different kinds of writing discussed in Chapters 8–14 of this book. For instance, an argument might take a climactic or a problem-solution approach, building in the key element of a response to probable objections (see pp. 120–21).

3 • Outlines

It's not essential to craft a detailed outline before you begin drafting an essay; in fact, too detailed a plan could prevent you from discovering ideas while you draft. Still, even a rough scheme can show you patterns of general and specific, suggest proportions, and highlight gaps or overlaps in coverage.

There are several different kinds of outlines, some more flexible than others.

Scratch or informal outline

A scratch or informal outline includes key general points in the order they will be covered. It may also suggest specific evidence.

Here is Sara Ling's scratch outline for her essay on Internet communication:

Thesis statement

By lowering the barriers of physical appearance, the unique anonymity of Internet communication could build diversity into community.

Scratch outline

No fear of prejudgment
  Physical attributes unknown—age, race, gender, etc.
  We won't be shut out because of appearance

Inability to prejudge others
  Assumptions based on appearance
  Meeting of minds only
  Finding shared interests and concerns

A scratch or informal outline may be all you need to begin drafting. Sometimes, though, it may prove too skimpy a guide, and you may want to use it as a preliminary to a more detailed outline. Indeed, Sara Ling used her scratch outline as a base for a detailed formal outline that gave her an even more definite sense of direction (see opposite).

Tree diagram

In a tree diagram, ideas and details branch out in increasing specificity. Unlike more linear outlines, this diagram can be supplemented and extended indefinitely, so it is easy to alter. Johanna Abrams developed the following example from her brainstorming about a summer job (p. 14):

Thesis statement

Two months working in a large agency taught me that an office's pecking order should be respected.

Tree diagram

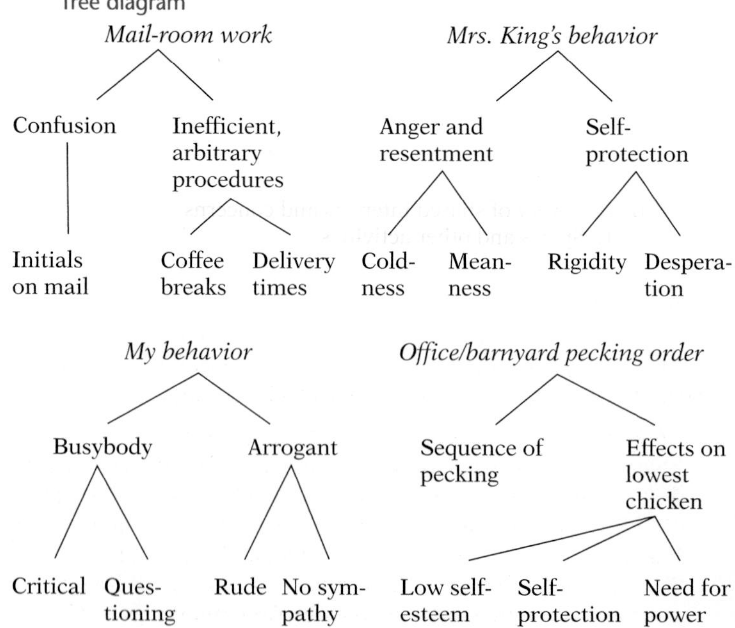

A tree diagram or other visual map can be especially useful for planning a project for the Web. The diagram can help you lay out the organization of your project and its links and then later can serve as a site map for your readers. (For more on composing for the Web, see pp. 139–45.)

Formal outline

A formal outline not only lays out main ideas and their support but also shows the relative importance of all the essay's elements. On the basis of her scratch outline (previous two pages), Sara Ling prepared a formal outline for her essay on the Internet:

Thesis statement

By lowering the barriers of physical appearance, the unique anonymity of Internet communication could build diversity into community.

Formal outline

I. No fear of being prejudged
  A. Unknown physical attributes
    1. Gender
    2. Age
    3. Race
    4. Style
  B. Freer communication
  C. No automatic rejection
II. Inability to prejudge others
  A. No assumptions based on appearance
    1. Body type
    2. Physical disability
    3. Race
  B. Discovery of shared interests and concerns
    1. Sports and other activities
    2. Family values
    3. Political views
  C. Reduction of physical bias

This example illustrates several principles of outlining that can ensure completeness, balance, and clear relationships:

- *All parts are systematically indented and labeled:* Roman numerals (I, II) for primary divisions; indented capital letters (A, B) for secondary divisions; further indented Arabic numerals (1, 2) for supporting examples. (The next level down would be indented further still and labeled with small letters: a, b.)
- *The outline divides the material into several groups.* A long list of points at the same level should be broken up into groups.

- *Topics of equal generality appear in parallel headings,* with the same indention and numbering or lettering.
- *All subdivided headings break into at least two parts.* A topic cannot logically be divided into only one part.
- *All headings are expressed in parallel grammatical form*—in the example, as phrases using nouns plus modifiers. This is a topic outline; in a sentence outline all headings are expressed as full sentences (see pp. 509–10).

Note Because of its structure, a formal outline can be an excellent tool for analyzing a draft before revising it. See pages 31–32.

4 • Unity and coherence

Two qualities of effective writing relate to organization: unity and coherence. When you perceive that someone's writing "flows well," you are probably appreciating these qualities.

To check an outline or draft for **unity,** ask these questions:

- Is each section relevant to the main idea (thesis) of the essay?
- Within main sections, does each example or detail support the principal idea of that section?

To check your outline or draft for **coherence,** ask the following questions:

- Do the ideas follow a clear sequence?
- Are the parts of the essay logically connected?
- Are the connections clear and smooth?

See also pages 52–60 on unity and coherence in paragraphs.

EXERCISE 3.2
Organizing ideas

The following list of ideas was extracted by a student from freewriting he did for a brief paper on soccer in the United States. Using his thesis statement as a guide, pick out the general ideas and arrange the relevant specific points under them. In some cases you may have to infer general ideas to cover specific points in the list.

Thesis statement

Soccer will probably never be the sport in the United States that it is elsewhere because both the potential fans and the potential backers resist it.

List of ideas

Sports seasons are already too crowded for fans.
Soccer rules are confusing to Americans.

A lot of kids play soccer in school, but the game is still "foreign."
Sports money goes where the money is.
Backers are wary of losing money on new ventures.
Fans have limited time to watch.
Fans have limited money to pay for sports.
Backers are concerned with TV contracts.
Previous attempts to start a pro soccer league failed.
TV contracts almost matter more than live audiences.
Failure of the US Football League was costly.
Baseball, football, hockey, and basketball seasons overlap.
Soccer fans couldn't fill huge stadiums.
American soccer fans are too few for TV interest.

4 Drafting

What can I do about writer's block?

Writer's block happens to everyone, even the most experienced writers. To confront it, try to think of drafting as an occasion for exploration. Don't expect to transcribe solid thoughts into polished prose: solidity and polish will come with revision and editing. Instead, let the act of writing help you to find and form your meaning.

4a Start writing.

Beginning a draft often takes courage, even for seasoned professionals. Procrastination may actually help if you let ideas simmer at the same time. At some point, though, you'll have to face the blank paper or computer screen. The following techniques can help you begin:

- *Read over what you've already written*—notes, outlines, and so on—and immediately start your draft with whatever comes to mind.
- *Freewrite* (see p. 12).

http://www.ablongman.com/littlebrown
➤ The writing process
  ➤ Video tutorials ➤ Overcoming writer's block
  ➤ Web links ➤ Drafting

- *Write scribbles or type nonsense* until usable words start coming.
- *Pretend you're writing to a friend about your subject.*
- *Describe an image that represents your subject*—a physical object, a facial expression, two people arguing over something, a giant machine gouging the earth for a mine, whatever.
- *Skip the opening and start in the middle.* Or write the conclusion.
- *Write a paragraph.* Explain what you think your essay will be about when you finish it.
- *Start writing the part that you understand best or feel most strongly about.* Using your outline, divide your essay into chunks—say, one for the introduction, another for the first point, and so on. One of these chunks may call out to be written.

4b Maintain momentum.

Drafting requires momentum: the forward movement opens you to fresh ideas and connections. To keep moving while drafting, try one or more of these techniques:

- *Set aside enough time for yourself.* For a brief essay, a first draft is likely to take at least an hour or two.
- *Work in a quiet place.*
- *Make yourself comfortable.*
- *If you must stop working, write down what you expect to do next.* Then you can pick up where you stopped with minimal disruption.
- *Be as fluid as possible, and don't worry about mistakes.* Spontaneity will allow your attitudes toward your subject to surface naturally in your sentences, and it will also make you receptive to ideas and relations you haven't seen before. Mistakes will be easier to find and correct later, when you're not also trying to create.
- *Keep going.* Skip over sticky spots; leave a blank if you can't find the right word; put alternative ideas or phrasings in brackets so that you can consider them later without bogging down. If an idea pops out of nowhere but doesn't seem to fit in, quickly jot it down on a separate sheet, or write it into the draft and bracket or boldface it for later attention. You can use an asterisk (*) or some other symbol to mark places where you feel blocked or uncertain. On a word processor you can find these places later by using the Find command to locate the symbol.

- *Resist self-criticism.* Don't worry about your style, grammar, spelling, punctuation, and the like. Don't worry about what your readers will think. These are very important matters, but save them for revision. On a word processor help yourself resist self-criticism by turning off automatic spelling or grammar checkers (see p. 41) or by trying invisible writing (p. 12).
- *Use your thesis statement and outline.* They can remind you of your planned purpose, organization, and content.
- *But don't feel constrained by your thesis and outline.* If your writing leads you in a more interesting direction, follow.

If you write on a word processor, frequently save the text you're drafting—at least every ten to fifteen minutes and every time you leave the computer. (Most word processors have an Auto Save function that can be set to save your text automatically as you're writing.) After each writing session, back up your drafts on a separate disk or server. If you can't back up your files, print out paper copies (so-called hard copy).

4c A sample first draft

Sara Ling's first draft on Internet communication appears below. As you read the draft, mark the thesis statement and each key idea developing the thesis. Note places where you think the ideas could be clearer or better supported.

Title?

In "Welcome to Cyberbia," written in 1995, M. Kadi predicts that the Internet will lead to more fragmentation in society because people just seek out others like themselves. But Kadi fails to foresee how the unique anonymity of Internet communication could actually build diversity into community by lowering the barriers of physical appearance.

Anonymity on the Internet. It's one of the best things about technology. No one knows your age or gender or race. Whether your fat or thin or neat or sloppy. What kind of clothes you wear. (Maybe your not wearing clothes at all). People who know you personally don't even know who you are with an invented screen name.

We can make ourselves known without first being prejudged because of our physical attributes. For example, I participate in a snowboarding forum that has mostly men. I didn't realize what I was getting into when I used my full name as my screen name. Before long,

I had received unfriendly responses such as "What does a girl know?" and "Why don't you go back to knitting?" I guess I had run into a male prejudice against female snowboarders. However, another woman on the forum had no such problems. At first she signed on with a screen name that did not reveal her gender, and no one responded negatively to her messages. When she had contributed for a while, she earned respect from the other snowboarders. When she revealed that she was a woman at that point, no one responded negatively in the way I experienced. She posed at first as someone different from who she really was and could make herself heard.

We also cannot prejudge others because of their appearance. Often in face-to-face interaction we assume we know things about people just because of the way they look. Assumptions prevent people from discovering their shared interests and concerns, and this is particularly true where race is concerned. The anonymity of the Internet makes physical barriers irrelevant, and only people's minds meet. Because of this, the Internet could create a world free of physical bias.

Logged on to the Internet, we can become more tolerant of others. We can become a community.

EXERCISE 4.1
Analyzing a first draft

Compare Sara Ling's draft, above, with the previous step in her planning (her formal outline) on page 25. List the places where the act of drafting led Ling to rearrange her information, add or delete material, or explore new ideas.

5 Revising and Editing

Why and how should I revise?

Revising is an essential task in creating an effective piece of writing. During revision (literally "re-seeing") you shift your focus outward from yourself and your subject toward your readers, concentrating on what will help them respond as you want. Many writers revise in two stages, first viewing the work as a whole, evaluating and improving its overall meaning and structure, and then editing sentences for wording, grammar, punctuation, spelling, and so on.

For you as for many writers, overall revision may be more difficult than editing because often you must pull your work apart before you can put it back together and look for sentence-level errors. But knowing that you will edit later also gives you the freedom at first to look beyond the confines of the page or screen to the whole paper.

5a Revise the essay as a whole.

Your first step in revising your writing should be to examine large-scale issues such as whether your purpose and main idea will be clear to readers and whether the draft fully develops the thesis. In revising, you may need to move, combine, or delete whole paragraphs; rethink major points; or flesh out ideas with details or research.

1 • Reading your work critically

To revise your writing, you have to read it critically, and that means you have to create some distance between your draft and yourself. One of the following techniques may help you see your work objectively:

- *Take a break after finishing the draft.* A few hours may be enough; a whole night or day is preferable.
- *Ask someone to read and react to your draft.* If your instructor encourages collaboration among students, by all means take advantage of the opportunity to hear the responses of others. (See pp. 46–48 for more on collaboration.)
- *Type a handwritten draft.* The act of transcription can reveal gaps in content or problems in structure.
- *Outline your draft.* Highlight the main points supporting the thesis, and write these sentences down separately in outline form.

http://www.ablongman.com/littlebrown
➤ The writing process
  ➤ Video tutorials
    ➤ Revising with a word processor
    ➤ Working with text on a word processor
    ➤ Using spelling and grammar/style checkers
  ➤ Downloads
    ➤ Checklist for revision
    ➤ Checklist for editing
  ➤ Web links ➤ Revising and editing

(If you're working on a word processor, you can copy and paste these sentences.) Then examine the outline you've made for logical order, gaps, and digressions. A formal outline can be especially illuminating because of its careful structure (see pp. 25–26).

- *Listen to your draft.* Read the draft out loud to yourself or a friend or classmate, read it into a tape recorder and play the tape, or have someone read the draft to you.
- *Ease the pressure.* Don't try to re-see everything in your draft at once. Use the checklist below, making a separate pass through the draft for each item. (You can download the check-

Checklist for whole-essay revision

Purpose

What is the essay's purpose? Does it conform to the assignment?

Thesis

What is the thesis of the essay? Where does it become clear? How well does the paper deliver on the commitment of the thesis?

Structure

What are the main points supporting the thesis? (List them.) How does the arrangement of these points contribute to the paper's purpose?

Development

How well do details, examples, and other evidence support each main point? Where, if at all, might readers find support skimpy or have trouble understanding the content?

Tone

How appropriate is the paper's tone for the purpose, topic, and intended readers? Where is it most and least successful?

Unity

Which, if any, sentences or paragraphs do not contribute to the thesis? Should these digressions be cut, or can they be rewritten to support the thesis?

Coherence

How clearly and smoothly does the paper flow? Where does it seem rough or awkward? Can any transitions be improved?

Title, introduction, conclusion

Does the title reflect the essay's content and purpose? Is it interesting? How well does the introduction engage and focus readers' attention on the thesis of the essay? How effective is the conclusion in providing a sense of completion?

list from this book's Web site: see the box on p. 31. Make a copy for each writing project, and insert answers to each question with your ideas for changes.)

2 • Writing a title

The revision stage is a good time to consider a title because attempting to sum up your essay in a phrase can focus your attention sharply on your topic, purpose, and audience.

Here are suggestions for titling an essay:

- *A* ***descriptive title*** *is almost always appropriate and is usually expected for academic writing***.** It announces the topic clearly, accurately, and as briefly as possible. Sara Ling's final title—"The Internet: Fragmentation or Community?"—is an example. Other examples are "Images of Lost Identity in *North by Northwest*"; "An Experiment in Small-Group Dynamics"; "Why Lincoln Delayed Emancipating the Slaves"; "Food Poisoning Involving *E. coli* Bacteria: A Review of the Literature."
- *A* ***suggestive title****—the kind often found in popular magazines—may be appropriate for more informal writing.* Examples include "Making Peace" (for an essay on the Peace Corps) and "Anyone for Soup?" (for an essay on working in a soup kitchen). For a more suggestive title, Ling might have chosen something like "What We Don't Know Can Help Us" or "Secrets of the Internet." Such a title conveys the writer's attitude and hints at the topic, thereby pulling readers into the essay to learn more. A source for such a title may be a familiar phrase, a fresh image, or a significant expression from the essay itself.
- *A title tells readers how big the topic is.* For Ling's essay, the title "The Internet" or "Anonymity" would have been too broad, whereas "Lose Your Body" or "Discovering Common Ground" would have been too narrow because each deals with only part of the paper's content.
- *A title should not restate the assignment or the thesis statement,* as in "The Trouble with M. Kadi's Picture of the Internet" or "What I Think About Diversity on the Internet."

For more information on essay titles, see pages 393–94 (capitalizing words in a title), 508 (MLA title format), and 535 (APA title format).

3 • Revising on a word processor

Word processors have removed the mechanical drudgery of revision, but they have also complicated the process in at least two ways. First, you need to decide whether to consider revisions on a paper printout or on screen:

- *Working on paper copy* allows you to see the whole draft at once and may be easier to read accurately, but if your work is stored on a computer you then have to key in your changes.
- *Working on a computer* allows you to see changes as you make them and to experiment with different versions of the same passage, but it can prevent you from seeing your work as a whole.

You may prefer one method over the other, or you may combine methods, reading a paper copy to find problems and then using the computer to try out revisions.

The second complication of revising on a word processor is file management. When revising or editing, you should always work on a duplicate of your latest draft so that the original remains intact until you're truly finished with it. For a single paper, then, you could produce several versions to keep track of. The screen shot below and the following explanations (keyed to each other by number) demonstrate the labeling and organizing that are basic to file management.

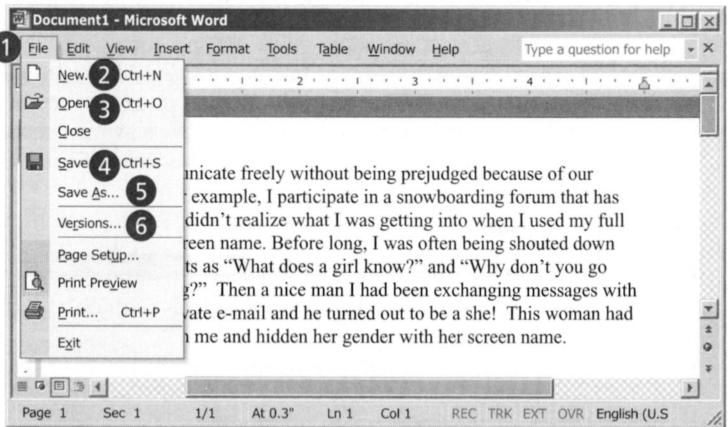

1. From a word processor's File menu, you can create new documents, save and rename them, and open them.
2. Select New to start composing a new document. You'll be able to choose the kind of document, such as a blank word-processing document (for papers) or a letter. Save your new document right away using the Save command (4).

3. Select Open to view or edit a saved document.
4. Select Save to save and name a new document or to save changes you have made to an existing document. A dialog box will let you name the document and decide where to place it in your file structure (see below).
5. Select Save As for either of two file-management purposes: to copy a document and rename the copy, or to copy a document in a new location. As with the Save function, a dialog box will let you rename the file and decide where to place it. The Save As function leaves the original intact, so it's one way to record successive drafts of a paper, each with a different name (for instance, *netcom, netcom2,* and so on). You'll see each name in your file structure.
6. Select Versions to save different stages of a particular document under a single file name. The word processor will store and time-stamp each version, and you'll be able to compare and select revisions.

Using the File menu commands is only part of file management. You can also name documents and use the computer's file spaces to organize your work and make documents easy to retrieve. The next screen shot and following explanations demonstrate this process.

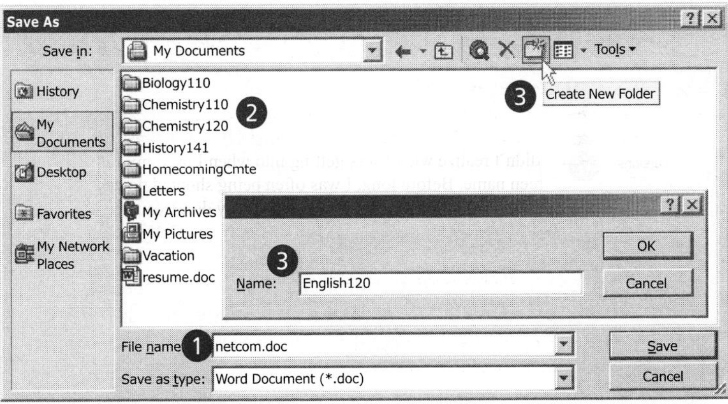

1. When you first save a document or copy one using Save As, the word processor will prompt you to name the document. Give each new document a name that you'll be able to recognize later—perhaps a shortened version of the document's subject (as here: *netcom*), a reference to the assignment (such as *Paper*

1), or a format that matches the file-naming conventions of a course by including your name and other information (such as *LingAsnmnt1* or *Ling.p1d1*). For a copied document, the name might relate to the original—for a revision, say, *netcom2, Paper1.2,* or *Ling.p1d2.*

2. The same dialog box will ask you to decide where to put your file within your file structure. Select an existing folder if the document relates to others in the same folder—for instance, the papers for a particular course or the drafts of a particular paper. Open the folder and then click Save to save your file.
3. Select the New Folder icon to create and name a new folder—if, for instance, you're saving the first paper for a course (as in the screen shot) or you're saving the first draft of a paper (in which case the folder name can reflect the paper's name, such as *NetcomPaper*).

Note Two precautions can prevent significant loss of work if the computer malfunctions:

- *Save your work every ten to fifteen minutes.* Most word processors have an Auto Save function that will save your work automatically as you type, at the interval you specify. Still, get in the habit of saving manually whenever you make major changes.
- *Create backups.* After doing any major work on a project, save a duplicate of the file on a second drive or diskette.

5b A sample revision

In revising her first draft, Sara Ling had the help of her instructor and several of her classmates, to whom she showed the draft as part of her assignment. (See pp. 46–48 for more on this kind of collaboration.) She revised thoroughly in response to others' comments and her own evaluation of the draft's strengths and weaknesses. The first half of the revision begins below. The following notes on the main changes are keyed to the revision by matching numbers in the paper's right margin.

1. With a descriptive title, Ling named her topic and forecast how she would approach it.
2. Ling rewrote and expanded the previous abrupt introduction to draw readers into the question she would explore and to give a fuller summary of Kadi's essay.
3. Ling rewrote the transitions between paragraphs to make each paragraph relate clearly to her thesis statement and to make the essay flow more smoothly.

4. Ling added examples to support her general statements. This and the following two categories of changes occupied most of Ling's attention during revision.
5. Ling condensed the example from her experience and sharpened the point she wanted it to illustrate. Some readers commented that the example overwhelmed the paragraph and her argument.
6. In response to her classmates, Ling added a paragraph to qualify her ideas and acknowledge complexities she had previously ignored.

The Internet: Fragmentation or Community? 1
~~Title~~?

We hear all sorts of predictions about how the Internet will enrich our lives 2
and promote equality, tolerance, and thus community in our society. But are
these promises realistic? In her 1995 essay "Welcome to Cyberbia," M. Kadi
argues that they are not. Instead, she
~~In "Welcome to Cyberbia," written in 1995, M. Kadi~~ predicts that
not community, *users merely*
the Internet will lead to more fragmentation, ~~in society~~ because ~~people~~
with the same biases, needs, and concerns as their own. The point is an interesting
~~just~~ seek out others ~~like themselves.~~ ~~B~~but Kadi fails to foresee *one,*
that
~~how~~ the unique anonymity of Internet communication could actually
build diversity into community by lowering the barriers of physical
appearance.

Writing on the Internet, you can be as anonymous as you like. Unless you
~~Anonymity on the Internet. It's one of the best things about tech-~~ 3
tell them, the people you communicate with do not *you're*
~~nology. No one~~ know~~s~~ your age or gender or race. Whether ~~your~~ fat or
you're
thin or neat or sloppy. What kind of clothes you wear. (Maybe ~~your~~ not
Even p
wearing clothes at all). ~~P~~eople who know you personally don't ~~even~~
if you conceal your identity
know who you are with an invented screen name.

Because of this anonymity, we 3
~~We~~ can make ourselves known without first being prejudged
because of our physical attributes. For example, *a high school student* 4
can participate in a physics discussion group, and not be ignored at first
by professional physicists in the group just because of her age. An adult man
can chat about music with teenagers, who might be inclined to dismiss him until
they hear what he has to say.
~~I participate in a snowboarding forum that has mostly men. I didn't re-~~
~~alize what I was getting into when I used my full name as my screen~~
~~name. Before long, I had received unfriendly responses such as "What~~
~~does a girl know?" and "Why don't you go back to knitting?" I guess I~~

had run into a male prejudice against female snowboarders. However, another woman on the forum had no such problems. At first she signed on with a screen name that did not reveal her gender, and no one responded negatively to her messages. When she had contributed for a while, she earned respect from the other snowboarders. When she revealed that she was a woman at that point, no one responded negatively in the way I experienced. She posed at first as someone different from who she really was and could make herself heard.

When I joined a snowboarding forum using my full name, I received hostile 5
responses such as "What does a girl know?" When a woman I know later joined the same forum, she established herself first before revealing her gender. The absence of hostile responses in her case implies that the male participants had learned not to judge women just for being women.

Granted, concealing or altering identities on the Internet can be a problem, 6
as when adults pose as children to seduce or harm them. These well-publicized occurrences say a great deal about the need to monitor the use of the Internet by children, and being cautious about getting together with Internet correspondents. However, they do not undermine the value of people being able to make themselves heard in situations where normally (in the real world) they would be shut out.

> **EXERCISE 5.1**
> **Analyzing a revised draft**
>
> Compare Ling's revised draft with her first one on pages 29–30. Referring to the discussion of her intentions for revision on pages 36–67, can you see the reasons for most of her changes? Where would you suggest further revisions, and why?

5c Edit the revised draft.

After you've revised your essay so that all the content is in place, then turn to the important work of removing any surface problems that could interfere with a reader's understanding or enjoyment of your ideas.

1 • Discovering what needs editing

Try these approaches to spot possible flaws in your work:

- *Take a break.* Even fifteen or twenty minutes can clear your head.
- *Read the draft slowly, and read what you actually see.* Otherwise, you're likely to read what you intended to write but didn't.

- *Read as if you are encountering the draft for the first time.* Put yourself in the reader's place.
- *Have a classmate, friend, or relative read your work.* Make sure you understand and consider the reader's suggestions, even if eventually you decide not to take them.
- *Read the draft aloud,* preferably into a tape recorder, listening for awkward rhythms, repetitive sentence patterns, and missing or clumsy transitions.
- *Learn from your own experience.* Keep a record of the problems that others have pointed out in your writing. When editing, check your work against this record.

In your editing, work first for clarity and a smooth movement among sentences and then for correctness. Use the questions in the checklist on the next page to guide your editing, referring to the page numbers in parentheses as needed. (You can download this checklist from this book's Web site: see the box on p. 31. Duplicate the list for each writing project, and insert your answers along with notes on specific changes you need or want to make.)

The second paragraph of Sara Ling's edited draft appears below. One change Ling made throughout the essay shows up here: she resolved an inconsistency in references to *you, people,* and *we,* settling on a consistent *we.* In addition, Ling corrected several sentence fragments in the middle of the paragraph.

> Writing on the Internet, ~~you~~ *we* can be as anonymous as ~~you~~ *we* like. Unless ~~you~~ *we* tell them, the people ~~you~~ *we* communicate with do not know ~~your~~ *our* age or gender or race~~.~~, ~~W~~*w*hether ~~you're~~ *we're* fat or thin or neat or sloppy~~.~~, *or* ~~W~~*w*hat kind of clothes ~~you~~ *we* wear~~.~~ (~~Maybe you're not~~ *if we're* wearing clothes at all). Even people who know ~~you~~ *us* personally don't know who ~~you~~ *we* are if ~~you~~ *we* conceal ~~your~~ *our* identit~~y~~*ies* with ~~an~~ invented screen name*s*.

2 • Editing on a word processor

When you work on a word processor, consider these additional approaches to editing:

- *Don't rely on your word processor's spelling or grammar and style checker to find what needs editing.* See the discussion of these checkers on pages 41–43.
- *If possible, work on a double-spaced paper copy.* Most people find it much harder to spot errors on a computer screen than on paper.

Checklist for editing

Clarity

How well do words and sentences convey their intended meanings? Which if any words and sentences are confusing? Check the paper especially for these:

Exact words (pp. 190–200)
Parallelism (pp. 173–77)
Clear modifiers (pp. 307–14)
Clear reference of pronouns (pp. 290–93)
Complete sentences (pp. 315–19)
Sentences separated correctly (pp. 321–25)

Effectiveness

How well do words and sentences engage and direct readers' attention? Where, if at all, does the writing seem wordy, choppy, or dull? Check the paper especially for these:

Emphasis of main ideas (pp. 162–72)
Smooth and informative transitions (pp. 58–60)
Variety in sentence length and structure (pp. 178–81)
Appropriate words (pp. 182–90)
Concise sentences (pp. 202–08)

Correctness

How little or how much do surface errors interfere with clarity and effectiveness? Check the paper especially for these:

Spelling (pp. 382–86)
Verb forms, especially *-s* and *-ed* endings and correct forms of irregular verbs (pp. 236–52)
Verb tenses, especially consistency (pp. 253–61)
Agreement between subjects and verbs, especially when words come between them or the subject is *each, everyone,* or a similar word (pp. 268–75)
Pronoun forms (pp. 277–83)
Agreement between pronouns and the words they refer to (their antecedents), especially when the antecedent contains *or* or it is *everyone, person,* or a similar word (pp. 284–89)
Sentence fragments (pp. 315–19)
Commas, especially with comma splices (pp. 321–25), with *and* or *but* (340–41), with introductory elements (342–43), with nonessential elements (344–48), and with series (348–49)
Apostrophes in possessives but not plural nouns (*Dave's/witches,* pp. 364–67) and in contractions but not possessive personal pronouns (*it's/its,* p. 368)

- *Use the Find command to locate and correct your common problems*—certain misspellings, overuse of *there is,* wordy phrases such as *the fact that,* and so on.
- *Resist overediting.* The ease of editing on a computer can lead to rewriting sentences over and over, stealing the life from your prose. If your grammar and style checker contributes to the temptation, consider turning it off.
- *Take special care with additions and omissions.* Make sure you haven't omitted needed words or left in unneeded words.

3 • Working with spelling and grammar/style checkers

The spelling checker and grammar and style checker that may come with your word processor can be helpful *if* you work within their limitations. The programs miss many problems and may even flag items that are actually correct. Further, they know nothing of your purpose and your audience, so they cannot make important decisions about your writing. Always use these tools critically:

- *Read your work yourself to ensure that it's clear and error-free.*
- *Consider a checker's suggestions carefully, weighing each one against your intentions.* If you aren't sure whether to accept a checker's suggestion, consult a dictionary, writing handbook, or other source. Your version may be fine.

Using a spelling checker

Your word processor's spelling checker can be a great ally: it will flag words that are spelled incorrectly and usually suggest alternative spellings that resemble what you've typed. However, this ally also has the potential to undermine you because of its limitations:

- *The checker may flag a word that you've spelled correctly,* just because the word does not appear in its dictionary.
- *The checker may suggest incorrect alternatives.* In providing a list of alternative spellings for your word, the checker may highlight the one it considers most likely to be correct. You need to verify that this alternative is actually what you intend before selecting it. Consult an online or printed dictionary when you aren't sure of the checker's recommendations (see pp. 190–91).
- *Most important, a spelling checker will not flag misused words.* The jingle shown in the screen shot on the next page has circulated widely as a warning about spelling checkers. Can you spot the thirteen misspellings missed by a spelling checker? (See also p. 387 to use the jingle to test your own spelling checker.)

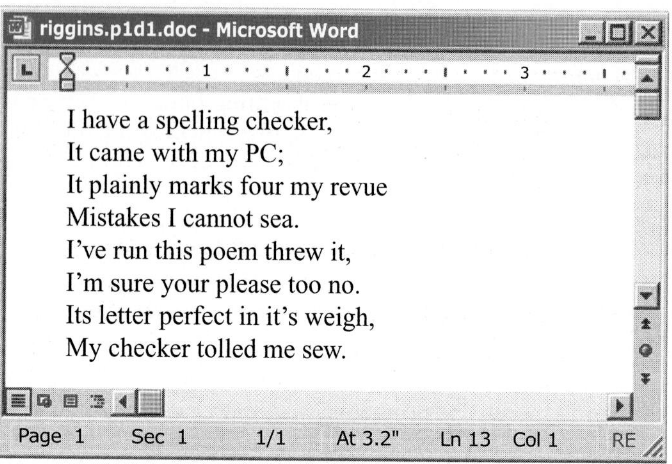

You can supplement a spelling checker by maintaining a file of your frequent misspellings and selecting Find under the Edit menu to check for them. But in the end *the only way to rid your papers of spelling errors is to proofread your papers yourself.* See opposite for proofreading tips. And see Chapter 45 for more advice on spelling.

Using a grammar and style checker

Word processors' grammar and style checkers can flag incorrect grammar or punctuation and wordy or awkward sentences. However, these programs can call your attention only to passages that *may* be faulty. They miss many errors because they are not yet capable of analyzing language in all its complexity (for instance, they can't accurately distinguish a word's part of speech when there are different possibilities, as *light* can be a noun, a verb, or an adjective). And they often question passages that don't need editing, such as an appropriate passive verb or a deliberate and emphatic use of repetition.

In the screen shot opposite, the checker has flagged a direct repetition of *light* in the first sentence but left unflagged the other intrusive repetitions of the word. And the checker has flagged the entire second sentence because it is long, but in fact the sentence is grammatically correct and clear.

You can customize a grammar and style checker to suit your needs and habits as a writer. (Select Options under the Tools menu.) Most checkers allow you to specify whether to check grammar only or grammar and style. Some style checkers can be set to the level

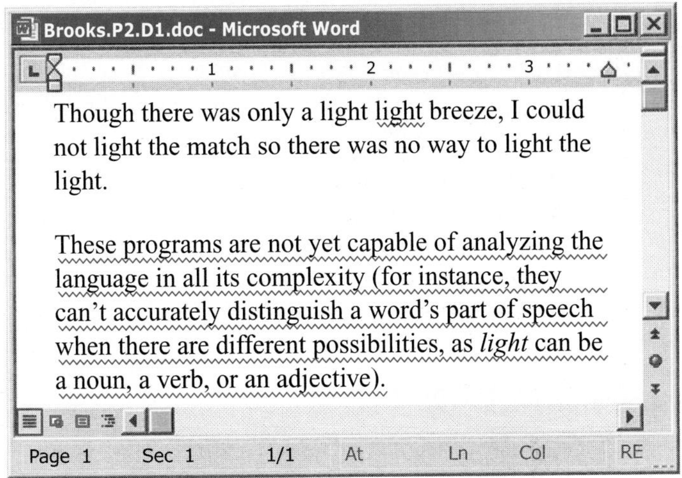

of writing you intend, such as formal, standard, and informal. (For academic writing choose formal.) You can also instruct the checker to flag specific grammar and style problems that tend to bother you, such as mismatched subjects and verbs, apostrophes in plural nouns, and overused passive voice.

5d Format and proofread the final draft.

After editing your essay, retype or print it one last time. Follow your instructor's directions in formatting your document. Two common formats are discussed and illustrated in this book: Modern Language Association (MLA) on pages 507–09 and American Psychological Association (APA) on pages 535–38. In addition, Chapter 7 treats principles and elements of document design.

Be sure to proofread the final essay several times to spot and correct errors. To increase the accuracy of your proofreading, you may need to experiment with ways to keep yourself from relaxing into the rhythm and the content of your prose. Here are a few tricks, including some used by professional proofreaders:

- *Read printed copy,* even if you will eventually submit the paper electronically. Most people proofread more accurately when reading type on paper than when reading it on a computer screen. (At the same time, don't view the printed copy as necessarily error-free just because it's clean. Clean-looking copy may still harbor errors.)

- *Read the paper aloud,* very slowly, and distinctly pronounce exactly what you see.
- *Place a ruler under each line as you read it.*
- *Read "against copy,"* comparing your final draft one sentence at a time against the edited draft.
- *Ignore content.* To keep the content of your writing from distracting you while you proofread, read the essay backward, end to beginning, examining each sentence as a separate unit. Or, taking advantage of a word processor, isolate each paragraph from its context by printing it on a separate page. (Of course, reassemble the paragraphs before submitting the paper.)

5e A sample final draft

Sara Ling's final essay appears below, typed in MLA format except for margins and page numbers. Comments in the margins point out key features of the essay's content.

Sara Ling

Professor Nelson

English 120A

14 April 2004

The Internet:

Fragmentation or Community?

Descriptive title

We hear all sorts of predictions about how the Internet will enrich our individual lives and promote communication, tolerance, and thus community in our society. But are these promises realistic? In her 1995 essay "Welcome to Cyberbia," M. Kadi argues that they are not. Instead, she predicts that the Internet will lead to more fragmentation, not community, because users merely seek out others with the same biases, concerns, and needs as their own. The point is an interesting one, but Kadi fails to foresee that the unique anonymity of Internet communication could actually build diversity into community by lowering the barriers of physical appearance.

Introduction

1. Question to be addressed

2. Summary of Kadi's essay

3. Thesis statement

Writing on the Internet, we can be as anonymous as we like. Unless we tell them, the people we commu-

Explanation of Internet's anonymity

nicate with do not know our age or gender or race, whether we're fat or thin or neat or sloppy, or what kind of clothes we wear (if we're wearing clothes at all). Even people who know us personally don't know who we are if we conceal our identities with invented screen names.

First main point: We are not prejudged by others.

1. Examples

Because of this anonymity, we can make ourselves known without first being prejudged because of our physical attributes. For example, a high school student can establish herself in a physics discussion group without fear of being ignored by the group's professional physicists just because of her age. An adult man can chat about music with teenagers who might be inclined to dismiss him. When I joined a snowboarding forum using my full name, I received hostile responses, such as "What does a girl know?" When a woman I know later joined the same forum, she established herself first before revealing her gender. The absence of hostile responses in her case implies that the male participants had learned not to rush to judge women just for being women.

2. Qualification of first main point

Granted, concealing or altering identities on the Internet can be a problem, as when adults pose as children to seduce or harm them. These well-publicized occurrences say a great deal about the need to monitor the use of the Internet by children and to be cautious about meeting with Internet correspondents.

3. Conclusion of first main point

However, they do not undermine the value of being able to make ourselves heard in situations where normally (in the real world) we would be shut out.

Second main point: We cannot prejudge others.

The Internet's anonymity has a flip side, too: just as we cannot be prejudged, so we cannot prejudge others because of their appearance.

1. Clarification of second main point

Often in face-to-face interaction, we assume we know things about people just because of the way they look.

2. Examples

Someone with an athletic build must be unintelligent. Someone who is heavy must be uninteresting. Someone in a wheelchair must be unapproachable or pathetic. Perhaps most significant, someone of another race must have fixed and contrary views about all kinds of issues, from family values to crime to affirmative action. Assumptions like these prevent us from discovering the interests and concerns we share with people who merely look different. But with the anonymity of the Internet, such physical barriers to understanding are irrelevant.

3. Effects

4. Conclusion of second main point

A world without physical bias may be an unreachable ideal. However, the more we communicate at first with just our minds, the more likely it is that our minds will find common ground and put less emphasis on physical characteristics. Logged on, we can begin to become more accepted and more accepting, more tolerated and more tolerant. We can begin to become a community.

Conclusion, summarizing essay

Work Cited

Kadi, M. "Welcome to Cyberbia." <u>Utne Reader</u> Mar.-Apr. 1995: 57-59.

Work cited in MLA style (see p. 479)

5f Collaborate on revisions.

In many writing courses students work together on writing, most often commenting on each other's work to help with revision. This collaborative writing gives experience in reading written work critically and in reaching others through writing. Collaboration may occur face to face in small groups, via drafts and comments on paper, or on computers.

Whether you collaborate in person, on paper, or on a computer, you will be more comfortable and helpful and will benefit more from others' comments if you follow a few guidelines:

Commenting on others' writing

- *Be sure you know what the writer is saying.* If necessary, summarize the paper to understand its content. (See p. 97.)
- *Address only your most significant concerns with the work.* Use the revision checklist on page 32 as a guide to what is signifi-

cant. Unless you have other instructions, ignore mistakes in grammar, punctuation, spelling, and the like. (The temptation to focus on such errors may be especially strong if the writer is less experienced than you are with standard American English.) Emphasizing mistakes will contribute little to the writer's revision.

- *Remember that you are the reader, not the writer.* Don't edit sentences, add details, or otherwise assume responsibility for the paper.
- *Be specific.* If something confuses you, say *why.* If you disagree with a conclusion, say *why.*
- *Be supportive as well as honest.* Tell the writer what you like about the paper. Word comments positively: instead of *This paragraph doesn't interest me,* say *You have an interesting detail here that I almost missed.* Question the writer in a way that emphasizes the effect of the work on you, the reader: *This paragraph confuses me because. . . .* And avoid measuring the work against a set of external standards: *This essay is poorly organized. Your thesis statement is inadequate.*
- *While reading, make your comments in writing.* Even if you will be delivering your comments in person later on, the written record will help you recall what you thought.
- *Link comments to specific parts of a paper.* Especially if you are reading the paper on a computer, be clear about what in the paper each comment relates to. You can embed your comments directly into the paper, distinguishing them with highlighting or color. If you're reviewing a word-processor document, you may be able to use the Comment function (in the Tools menu) to annotate the paper.
- *Phrase your comments carefully.* Avoid misunderstandings by making sure comments are both clear and respectful. If you are responding on paper or online, not face to face with the writer, remember that the writer has nothing but your written words to go on. He or she can't ask you for immediate clarification and can't infer your attitudes from gestures, facial expressions, and tone of voice.

Benefiting from comments on your writing

- *Think of your readers as counselors or coaches.* They can help you see the virtues and flaws in your work and sharpen your awareness of readers' needs.
- *Read or listen to comments closely.*
- *Know what the critic is saying.* If you need more information, ask for it, or consult the appropriate section of this handbook.

- *Don't become defensive.* Letting comments offend you will only erect a barrier to improvement in your writing. As one writing teacher advises, "Leave your ego at the door."
- *Revise your work in response to appropriate comments.* You will learn more from the act of revision than from just thinking about changes.
- *Remember that you are the final authority on your work.* You should be open to suggestions, but you are free to decline advice when you think it is inappropriate.
- *Keep track of both the strengths and the weaknesses others identify.* Then in later assignments you can build on your successes and give special attention to problem areas.

CULTURE LANGUAGE In some cultures writers do not expect criticism from readers, or readers do not expect to think critically about what they read. If critical responses are uncommon in your native culture, collaboration may at first be uncomfortable for you. As a writer in English, think of a draft or even a final paper as more an exploration of ideas than the last word on your subject; then you may be more receptive to readers' suggestions. As a reader, allow yourself to approach a text skeptically, and know that your tactful questions and suggestions will usually be considered appropriate.

5g Prepare a writing portfolio.

Your writing teacher may ask you to assemble samples of your writing into a portfolio, or folder, once or more during the course. Such a portfolio gives you a chance to consider all your writing over a period and showcase your best work.

Although the requirements for portfolios vary, most teachers are looking for a range of writing that demonstrates your progress and strengths as a writer. You, in turn, see how you have advanced from one assignment to the next, as you've had time for new knowledge to sink in and time for practice. Teachers often allow students to revise papers before placing them in the portfolio, even if the papers have already been submitted earlier. In that case, every paper in the portfolio can benefit from all your learning.

A portfolio assignment will probably also provide guidelines for what to include and how the portfolio will be evaluated. Be sure you understand the purpose of the portfolio and who will read it. For instance, if your composition teacher will be the only reader and his or her guidelines encourage you to show evidence of progress, you might include a paper that took big risks but never entirely succeeded. In contrast, if a committee of teachers will read your work and the guidelines urge you to demonstrate your competence as a writer, you might include only papers that did succeed.

Unless the guidelines specify otherwise, provide error-free copies of your final drafts, label all your samples with your name, and assemble them all in a folder. Add a cover letter or memo that lists the samples, explains why you've included each one, and evaluates your progress as a writer. The self-evaluation involved should be a learning experience for you and will help your readers assess your development as a writer.

EXERCISE 5.2
Analyzing an essay

Johanna Abrams, a student, was asked to write a narrative essay based on a personal experience that turned out to be a significant event or that represented a turning point—big or small—in her life. Read the essay carefully; then answer the following questions.

1. What is Abrams's purpose?
2. Who do you think constitutes Abrams's intended audience? What does the tone reveal about her attitude toward the topic?
3. How well does the thesis statement convey Abrams's purpose and attitude? What claim does the thesis statement make? How specific is the statement? How well does it preview Abrams's ideas and organization?
4. What organization does Abrams use? Is it clear throughout the essay?
5. What details, examples, and reasons does Abrams use to support her ideas? Where is the supporting evidence skimpy?
6. How successful is Abrams in making you care about the topic and her view of it?

Working in the Barnyard

Until two months ago I thought summer jobs occupied time and helped pay the next year's tuition but otherwise provided no useful training. Then I took a temporary job in a large government agency. Two months there taught me the very valuable lesson that the hierarchy of supervisor to employee should be respected.

Last May I was hired by the personnel department of the agency to fill in for vacationing workers in the mail room. I had seven coworkers and a boss, Mrs. King. Our job was to sort the huge morning and afternoon mail shipments into four hundred slots, one for every employee in the agency. Then we delivered the sorted mail out of grocery carts that we wheeled from office to office along assigned corridors, picking up outgoing mail as we went along. Each mail delivery took an entire half-day to sort and deliver.

My trouble began almost as soon as I arrived. Hundreds of pieces of mail were dumped on a shallow table against a wall of mail slots. I was horrified to see that the slots were labeled not with people's names but with their initials—whereas the incoming letters, of course, contained full names. Without thinking, I asked why this was a good idea, only to receive a sharp glance from Mrs. King. So I repeated the question. This time Mrs. King told me not to question what I didn't understand. It was the first of many such exchanges, and I hadn't been on the job a half-hour.

I mastered the initials and the sort and delivery procedures after about a week. But the longer I worked at the job, the more I saw how inefficient all the procedures were, from delivery routes to times for coffee breaks. When I asked Mrs. King about the procedures, however, she always reacted the same way: it was none of my business.

I pestered Mrs. King more and more over the next seven weeks, but my efforts were fruitless, even counterproductive. Mrs. King began calling me snide names. Then she began picking on my work and singling me out for reprimands, even though I did my best and worked faster than most of the others.

Two months after I had started work, the personnel manager called me in and fired me. I objected, of course, calling up all the deficiencies I had seen in Mrs. King and her systems. The manager interrupted to ask if I had ever heard of the barnyard pecking order. As he explained it, the top chicken pecks on the one below it, the second pecks on the third, and so on all the way down the line to the lowliest chicken, whose life is a constant misery. Mrs. King, the manager said, was that lowliest chicken at the bottom of the pecking order in the agency's management. With little education, she had spent her entire adult life building up her small domain, and she had to protect it from everyone, especially the people who worked for her. The arbitrariness of her systems was an assertion of her power, for no one should doubt for a moment that she ruled her roost.

I had a month before school began again to think about my adventure. At first it irritated me that I should be humiliated while Mrs. King continued on as before. But eventually I saw how arrogant, and how unsympathetic, my behavior had been. In my next job, I'll learn the pecking order before I become a crusader, *if* I do.

—JOHANNA ABRAMS (student)

6 Paragraphs

How can paragraphs help me and my readers?

Paragraphs give you a means of developing your essay's central idea (its thesis) step by step, point by point. They help your readers distinguish your ideas and follow your organization, and they give readers a breather from long stretches of text. In the body of an essay, you may use paragraphs for any of these purposes:

- To introduce one of the main points supporting your essay's thesis and to develop the point with examples, facts, or other supporting evidence. (See pp. 18–21 for a discussion of an essay's thesis.)
- Within a group of paragraphs centering on one main point, to introduce and develop a key example or other important evidence.
- To shift approach—for instance, from pros to cons, from problem to solution, from questions to answers.
- To mark movement in a sequence, such as from one reason or step to another.

This chapter discusses the three qualities of an effective body paragraph: the topic sentence and unity (next page), coherence (p. 54), and development (p. 60). It describes two special kinds of paragraphs: introductions and conclusions (pp. 68 and 70). And finally it shows how paragraphs can be linked in an essay (p. 71).

CULTURE LANGUAGE Not all cultures share the paragraphing conventions of American academic writing. The conventions are not universal even among users of standard American English: for instance, US newspaper writers compose very short paragraphs that will break up text in narrow columns. In some other languages, writing moves differently from English—not from left to right, but from right to left or down rows from top to bottom. Even in languages that move as English does, writers may not use paragraphs at all. Or they may use paragraphs but not state their central ideas

http://www.ablongman.com/littlebrown

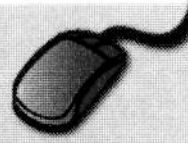

➤ The writing process

➤ Video tutorials ➤ Achieving paragraph unity
➤ Web exercises ➤ Exers. 4–6
➤ Downloads ➤ Chapter 6 exercises in electronic format
➤ Web links ➤ Paragraphs

Checklist for revising paragraphs

- Is the paragraph **unified**? Does it focus on one central idea that is either stated in a **topic sentence** or otherwise apparent? (See section 6a, below.)
- Is the paragraph **coherent**? Do the sentences follow a clear sequence? Are the sentences linked as appropriate by parallelism, repetition or restatement, pronouns, consistency, and transitional expressions? (See p. 54.)
- Is the paragraph **developed**? Is the general idea of the paragraph well supported with specific evidence such as details, facts, examples, and reasons? (See p. 60.)

or provide transitional expressions to show readers how sentences relate. If your native language is not English and you have difficulty with paragraphs, don't worry about paragraphing during drafting. Instead, during a separate step of revision, divide your text into parts that develop your main points. Mark those parts with indentions.

6a Unify the paragraph around a central idea.

An effective paragraph develops one central idea related to the overall thesis of the paper. Often, the central idea is stated up front in a **topic sentence.** The paragraph is **unified** if the rest of the sentences in the paragraph support the topic sentence, as they do in this example:

> Some people really like chili, apparently, but nobody can agree how the stuff should be made. C. V. Wood, twice winner at Terlingua, uses flank steak, pork chops, chicken, and green chilis. My friend Hughes Rudd of CBS News, who imported five hundred pounds of chili powder into Russia as a condition of accepting employment as Moscow correspondent, favors coarse-ground beef. Isadore Bleckman, the cameraman I must live with on the road, insists upon one-inch cubes of stew beef and puts garlic in his chili, an Illinois affectation. An Indian of my acquaintance, Mr. Fulton Batisse, who eats chili for breakfast when he can, uses buffalo meat and plays an Indian drum while it's cooking. I ask you.
>
> —Charles Kuralt, *Dateline America*

Topic sentence: general statement announcing topic of paragraph

Four specific examples, all providing evidence for general statement

Kuralt's paragraph works because it follows through on its central idea, which is stated in the topic sentence. Each of the next four sentences offers an example of a chili concoction. (In the final sentence Kuralt comments on the examples.)

What if instead Kuralt had written his paragraph as follows? Here the topic of chili preparation is forgotten mid-paragraph, as the sentences digress to describe life in Moscow:

> Some people really like chili, apparently, but nobody can agree how the stuff should be made. [Topic sentence: general statement] C. V. Wood, twice winner at Terlingua, uses flank steak, pork chops, chicken, and green chilis. My friend Hughes Rudd, who imported five hundred pounds of chili powder into Russia as a condition of accepting employment as Moscow correspondent, favors coarse-ground beef. [Two examples supporting statement] He had some trouble finding the beef in Moscow, though. He sometimes had to scour all the markets and wait in long lines. For any American used to overstocked supermarkets and department stores, Russia can be quite a shock. [Digression]

Instead of following through on its topic sentence, the paragraph loses its way.

A central idea must always govern a paragraph's content as if it were standing guard at the opening, but in fact paragraphs often do not begin with a topic sentence. You may want to start with a transition from the previous paragraph, not stating the central idea until the second or third sentence. You may want to give the evidence for your idea first and let it build to a topic sentence at the end, as in this example about the Civil War general William Tecumseh Sherman:

> Sherman is considered by some to be the inventor of "total war": the first general in human history to carry the logic of war to its ultimate extreme, the first to scorch the earth, the first to consciously demoralize the hostile civilian population in order to subdue its army, the first to wreck an economy in order to starve its soldiers. He has been called our first "merchant of terror" and seen as the spiritual father of our Vietnam War concepts of "search and destroy," "pacification," [Information supporting and building to topic sentence] "strategic hamlets," and "free-fire zones." As such, he remains a cardboard figure of our history: a monstrous arch-villain to unreconstructed Southerners, and an embarrassment to Northerners. [Topic sentence]
>
> —Adapted from JAMES RESTON, JR., "You Cannot Refine It"

Sometimes you may not state a paragraph's central idea at all, especially in narrative and descriptive writing in which the point becomes clear in the details. But the point must be clear whether it is stated or not.

EXERCISE 6.1
Revising a paragraph for unity

The following paragraph contains ideas or details that do not support its central idea. Identify the topic sentence in the paragraph and delete the unrelated material.

In the southern part of the state, some people still live much as they did a century ago. They use coal- or wood-burning stoves for heating and cooking. Their homes do not have electricity or indoor bathrooms or running water. The towns they live in don't receive adequate funding from the state and federal governments, so the schools are poor and in bad shape. Beside most homes there is a garden where fresh vegetables are gathered for canning. Small pastures nearby support livestock, including cattle, pigs, horses, and chickens. Most of the people have cars or trucks, but the vehicles are old and beat-up from traveling on unpaved roads.

6b Make the paragraph coherent.

When a paragraph is **coherent,** readers can see how it holds together: the sentences seem to flow logically and smoothly into one another. Exactly the opposite happens with this paragraph:

The ancient Egyptians were masters of preserving dead people's bodies by making mummies of them. [Topic sentence] Mummies several thousand years old have been discovered nearly intact. The skin, hair, teeth, finger- and toenails, and facial features of the mummies were evident. It is possible to diagnose the diseases they suffered in life, such as smallpox, arthritis, and nutritional deficiencies. The process was remarkably effective. Sometimes apparent were the fatal afflictions of the dead people: a middle-aged king died from a blow on the head, and polio killed a child king. Mummification consisted of removing the internal organs, applying natural preservatives inside and out, and then wrapping the body in layers of bandages. [Sentences related to topic sentence but disconnected from each other]

The paragraph is hard to read. The sentences lurch instead of gliding from point to point.

The paragraph as it was actually written appears below. It is much clearer because the writer arranged information differently and also built links into his sentences so that they would flow smoothly:

- After stating the central idea in a topic sentence, the writer moves to two more specific explanations and illustrates the second with four sentences of examples.
- Circled words repeat or restate key terms or concepts.
- Boxed words link sentences and clarify relationships.
- Underlined phrases are in parallel grammatical form to reflect their parallel content.

> The ancient Egyptians were masters of preserving dead people's bodies by making mummies of them. Basically, mummification consisted of removing the internal organs, applying natural preservatives inside and out, and then wrapping the body in layers of bandages. And the process was remarkably effective. Indeed, mummies several thousand years old have been discovered nearly intact. Their skin, hair, teeth, finger- and toenails, and facial features are still evident. Their diseases in life, such as smallpox, arthritis, and nutritional deficiencies, are still diagnosable. Even their fatal afflictions are still apparent: a middle-aged king died from a blow on the head; a child king died from polio.
>
> —MITCHELL ROSENBAUM (student), "Lost Arts of the Egyptians"

Topic sentence

Explanation 1: what mummification is

Explanation 2: why the Egyptians were masters

Specific examples of explanation 2

1 • Paragraph organization

A coherent paragraph organizes information so that readers can easily follow along. These are common paragraph schemes:

- *General to specific:* Sentences downshift from more general statements to more specific ones. (See the paragraph above by Mitchell Rosenbaum.)
- *Climactic:* Sentences increase in drama or interest, ending in a climax. (See the paragraph by Lawrence Mayer on the next page.)
- *Spatial:* Sentences scan a person, place, or object from top to bottom, from side to side, or in some other way that approximates the way people actually look at things. (See the paragraph by Virginia Woolf on pp. 61–62.)

- *Chronological:* Sentences present events as they occurred in time, earlier to later. (See the paragraph by Kathleen LaFrank on p. 58.)

2 • Parallelism

Parallelism helps tie sentences together. In the following paragraph the underlined parallel structures of *She* and a verb link all sentences after the first one. Parallelism also appears *within* many of the sentences. Aphra Behn (1640–89) was the first Englishwoman to write professionally.

> In addition to her busy career as a writer, Aphra Behn also found time to briefly marry and spend a little while in debtor's prison. She found time to take up a career as a spy for the English in their war against the Dutch. She made the long and difficult voyage to Suriname [in South America] and became involved in a slave rebellion there. She plunged into political debate at Will's Coffee House and defended her position from the stage of the Drury Lane Theater. She actively argued for women's rights to be educated and to marry whom they pleased, or not at all. She defied the seventeenth-century dictum that ladies must be "modest" and wrote freely about sex. —ANGELINE GOREAU, "Aphra Behn"

3 • Repetition and restatement

Repeating or restating key words helps make a paragraph coherent and also reminds readers what the topic is. In the following paragraph note the underlined repetition of *sleep* and restatement of *adults:*

> Perhaps the simplest fact about sleep is that individual needs for it vary widely. Most adults sleep between seven and nine hours, but occasionally people turn up who need twelve hours or so, while some rare types can get by on three or four. Rarest of all are those legendary types who require almost no sleep at all; respected researchers have recently studied three such people. One of them—a healthy, happy woman in her seventies—sleeps about an hour every two or three days. The other two are men in early middle age, who get by on a few minutes a night. One of them complains about the daily fifteen minutes or so he's forced to "waste" in sleeping.
>
> —LAWRENCE A. MAYER, "The Confounding Enemy of Sleep"

Key term

parallelism The use of similar grammatical structures for similar elements of meaning within or among sentences: *the book caused a stir in the media and aroused debate in Congress.* (See also Chapter 16.)

4 • Pronouns

Because pronouns refer to nouns, they can help relate sentences to each other. In the paragraph on the previous page by Angeline Goreau, *she* works just this way by substituting for *Aphra Behn* in every sentence after the first.

5 • Consistency

Consistency (or the lack of it) occurs primarily in the tense of verbs and in the person and number of nouns and pronouns. Any inconsistencies not required by meaning will interfere with a reader's ability to follow the development of ideas.

In the following paragraphs, inconsistencies appear in the underlined words:

Shifts in tense

In the Hopi religion, water is the driving force. Since the Hopi lived in the Arizona desert, they needed water urgently for drinking, cooking, and irrigating crops. Their complex beliefs are focused in part on gaining the assistance of supernatural forces in obtaining water. Many of the Hopi kachinas, or spirit essences, were directly concerned with clouds, rain, and snow.

Shifts in number

Kachinas represent spiritually the things and events of the real world, such as cumulus clouds, mischief, cornmeal, and even death. A kachina is not worshiped as a god but regarded as an interested friend. They visit the Hopi from December through July in the form of men who dress in kachina costumes and perform dances and other rituals.

Shifts in person

Unlike the man, the Hopi woman does not keep contact with kachinas through costumes and dancing. Instead, one receives a tihu, or small effigy, of a kachina from the man impersonating the

Key terms

pronoun A word that refers to and functions as a noun, such as *I, you, he, she, it, we, they: The patient could not raise her arm.* (See p. 211.)

tense The form of a verb that indicates the time of its action, such as present (*I run*), past (*I ran*), or future (*I will run*). (See p. 213.)

number The form of a noun, pronoun, or verb that indicates whether it is singular (one) or plural (more than one): *boy, boys.*

person The form of a pronoun that indicates whether the subject is speaking (first person: *I, we*), spoken to (second person: *you*), or spoken about (third person: *he, she, it, they*). All nouns are in the third person.

kachina. You are more likely to receive a tihu as a girl approaching marriage, though a child or older woman may receive one, too.

The grammar checker on a word processor cannot help you locate shifts in tense, number, or person among sentences. Shifts are sometimes necessary (as when tenses change to reflect actual differences in time), and even a passage with needless shifts may still consist of sentences that are grammatically correct (as all the sentences are in the above examples). The only way to achieve consistency in your writing is to review it yourself.

6 • Transitional expressions

Transitional expressions such as *therefore, in contrast,* or *meanwhile* can forge specific connections between sentences. Notice the difference in two versions of the same paragraph:

> Medical science has succeeded in identifying the hundreds of viruses that can cause the common cold. It has discovered the most effective means of prevention. One person transmits the cold viruses to another most often by hand. An infected person covers his mouth to cough. He picks up the telephone. His daughter picks up the telephone. She rubs her eyes. She has a cold. It spreads. To avoid colds, people should wash their hands often and keep their hands away from their faces.

Paragraph is choppy and hard to follow

> Medical science has thus succeeded in identifying the hundreds of viruses that can cause the common cold. It has also discovered the most effective means of prevention. One person transmits the cold virus to another most often by hand. For instance, an infected person covers his mouth to cough. Then he picks up the telephone. Half an hour later, his daughter picks up the same telephone. Immediately afterward, she rubs her eyes. Within a few days, she, too, has a cold. And thus, it spreads. To avoid colds, therefore, people should wash their hands often and keep their hands away from their faces. —Kathleen LaFrank (student), "Colds: Myth and Science"

Transitional expressions (boxed) remove choppiness and spell out relationships

Note that transitional expressions can link paragraphs as well as sentences. In the first sentence of LaFrank's paragraph, the word *thus* signals a connection to an effect discussed in the preceding paragraph. See pages 71–73 for more on such transitions.

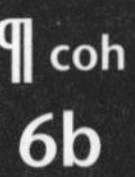

The following box lists many transitional expressions by the functions they perform:

Transitional expressions

To add or show sequence
again, also, and, and then, besides, equally important, finally, first, further, furthermore, in addition, in the first place, last, moreover, next, second, still, too

To compare
also, in the same way, likewise, similarly

To contrast
although, and yet, but, but at the same time, despite, even so, even though, for all that, however, in contrast, in spite of, nevertheless, notwithstanding, on the contrary, on the other hand, regardless, still, though, yet

To give examples or intensify
after all, an illustration of, even, for example, for instance, indeed, in fact, it is true, of course, specifically, that is, to illustrate, truly

To indicate place
above, adjacent to, below, elsewhere, farther on, here, near, nearby, on the other side, opposite to, there, to the east, to the left

To indicate time
after a while, afterward, as long as, as soon as, at last, at length, at that time, before, earlier, formerly, immediately, in the meantime, in the past, lately, later, meanwhile, now, presently, shortly, simultaneously, since, so far, soon, subsequently, then, thereafter, until, until now, when

To repeat, summarize, or conclude
all in all, altogether, as has been said, in brief, in conclusion, in other words, in particular, in short, in simpler terms, in summary, on the whole, that is, therefore, to put it differently, to summarize

To show cause or effect
accordingly, as a result, because, consequently, for this purpose, hence, otherwise, since, then, therefore, thereupon, thus, to this end, with this object

Note Draw carefully on this list of transitional expressions because the ones in each group are not interchangeable. For instance, *besides, finally,* and *second* may all be used to add information, but each has its own distinct meaning.

CULTURE LANGUAGE If transitional expressions are not common in your native language, you may be tempted to compensate when writing in English by adding them to the beginnings of most sentences. But such explicit transitions aren't needed everywhere, and in fact too many can be intrusive and awkward. When inserting transitional expressions, consider the reader's need for a signal: often the connection from sentence to sentence is already clear from the context or can be made clear by relating the content of sentences more closely (see pp. 165–66). When you do need transitional expressions, try varying their positions in your sentences, as illustrated in the sample paragraph on page 58.

EXERCISE 6.2
Arranging sentences coherently

After the topic sentence (sentence 1), the sentences in the student paragraph below have been deliberately scrambled to make the paragraph incoherent. Using the topic sentence and other clues as guides, rearrange the sentences to form a well-organized, coherent unit.

We hear complaints about the Postal Service all the time, but 1
we should not forget what it does *right.* The total volume of mail 2
delivered by the Postal Service each year makes up almost half the
total delivered mail in all the world. Its 70,000 employees handle 3
140 billion pieces of mail each year. And when was the last time 4
they failed to deliver yours? In fact, on any given day the Postal 5
Service delivers almost as much mail as the rest of the world combined. That huge number means over 2 million pieces per em- 6
ployee and over 560 per man, woman, and child in the country.

6c Develop the central idea.

An effective, well-developed paragraph always provides the specific information that readers need and expect in order to understand you and to stay interested in what you say. Paragraph length can be a rough gauge of development: anything much shorter than 75 to 125 words may leave readers with a sense of incompleteness. Take this example:

> Untruths can serve as a kind of social oil when they smooth connections between people. In preventing confrontation and injured feelings, they allow everyone to go on as before.

General statements needing examples to be clear and convincing

This paragraph lacks development, or completeness. It does not provide enough information for us to evaluate or even care about the writer's assertions. To improve the paragraph, the writer needs to support the general statements with specific examples, as in this revision:

> Untruths can serve as a kind of social oil when they smooth connections between people. Assuring a worried friend that his haircut is flattering, claiming an appointment to avoid an aunt's dinner invitation, pretending interest in an acquaintance's children—these lies may protect the liar, but they also protect the person lied to. In preventing confrontation and injured feelings, the lies allow everyone to go on as before.
>
> —JOAN LAR (student), "The Truth of Lies"

Examples specifying kinds of lies and consequences

To develop or shape a paragraph's central idea, one or more of the following patterns may help. (These patterns may also be used to develop entire essays. See p. 16.)

1 • Narration

Narration retells a significant sequence of events, usually in the order of their occurrence (that is, chronologically). A narrator is concerned not just with the sequence of events but also with their consequence, their importance to the whole.

> Jill's story is typical for "recruits" to religious cults. She was very lonely in college and appreciated the attention of the nice young men and women who lived in a house near campus. They persuaded her to share their meals and then to move in with them. Between intense bombardments of "love," they deprived her of sleep and sometimes threatened to throw her out. Jill became increasingly confused and dependent, losing touch with any reality besides the one in the group. She dropped out of school and refused to see or communicate with her family. Before long she, too, was preying on lonely college students.
>
> —HILLARY BEGAS (student), "The Love Bombers"

Important events in chronological order

2 • Description

Description details the sensory qualities of a person, scene, thing, or feeling, using concrete and specific words to convey a dominant mood, to illustrate an idea, or to achieve some other purpose. In the following paragraph, almost every word helps to create a picture in the reader's mind:

> The sun struck straight upon the house, making the white walls glare between the dark win-

dows. Their panes, woven thickly with green branches, held circles of impenetrable darkness. Sharp-edged wedges of light lay upon the window-sill and showed inside the room plates with blue rings, cups with curved handles, the bulge of a great bowl, the criss-cross pattern in the rug, and the formidable corners and lines of cabinets and bookcases. Behind their conglomeration hung a zone of shadow in which might be a further shape to be disencumbered of shadow or still denser depths of darkness.

—VIRGINIA WOOLF, *The Waves*

Specific record of sensory details

3 • Illustration or support

An idea may be developed with several specific examples, like those used by Charles Kuralt on page 52 and by Joan Lar on the previous page. Or it may be developed with a single extended example, as in the next paragraph:

The language problem that I was attacking loomed larger and larger as I began to learn more. When I would describe in English certain concepts and objects enmeshed in Korean emotion and imagination, I became slowly aware of nuances, of differences between two languages even in simple expression. The remark "Kim entered the house" seems to be simple enough, yet, unless a reader has a clear visual image of a Korean house, his understanding of the sentence is not complete. When a Korean says he is "in the house," he may be in his courtyard, or on his porch, or in his small room! If I wanted to give a specific picture of entering the house in the Western sense, I had to say "room" instead of house—sometimes. I say "sometimes" because many Koreans entertain their guests on their porches and still are considered to be hospitable, and in the Korean sense, going into the "room" may be a more intimate act than it would be in the English sense. Such problems!

—KIM YONG IK, "A Book-Writing Venture"

Topic sentence (assertion to be illustrated)

Single detailed example

Sometimes you can develop a paragraph by providing your reasons for stating a general idea. For instance:

There are three reasons, quite apart from scientific considerations, that mankind needs to travel in space. The first reason is the need for garbage disposal: we need to transfer industrial processes into

Topic sentence

> space, so that the earth may remain a green and pleasant place for our grandchildren to live in. The second reason is the need to escape material impoverishment: the resources of this planet are finite, and we shall not forgo forever the abundant solar energy and minerals and living space that are spread out all around us. The third reason is our spiritual need for an open frontier: the ultimate purpose of space travel is to bring to humanity not only scientific discoveries and an occasional spectacular show on television but a real expansion of our spirit.
>
> —FREEMAN DYSON, "Disturbing the Universe"

Three reasons arranged in order of increasing drama and importance

4 • Definition

Defining a complicated, abstract, or controversial term often requires extended explanation. The following definition of the word *quality* comes from an essay asserting that "quality in product and effort has become a vanishing element of current civilization." Notice how the writer pins down her meaning by offering examples and by setting up contrasts with nonquality:

> In the hope of possibly reducing the hail of censure which is certain to greet this essay (I am thinking of going to Alaska or possibly Patagonia in the week it is published), let me say that quality, as I understand it, means investment of the best skill and effort possible to produce the finest and most admirable result possible. Its presence or absence in some degree characterizes every man-made object, service, skilled or unskilled labor—laying bricks, painting a picture, ironing shirts, practicing medicine, shoemaking, scholarship, writing a book. You do it well or you do it half-well. Materials are sound and durable or they are sleazy; method is painstaking or whatever is easiest. Quality is achieving or reaching for the highest standard as against being satisfied with the sloppy or fraudulent. It is honesty of purpose as against catering to cheap or sensational sentiment. It does not allow compromise with the second-rate.
>
> —BARBARA TUCHMAN, "The Decline of Quality"

General definition

Activities in which quality may figure

Contrast between quality and nonquality

5 • Division or analysis

With division or analysis, you separate something into its elements to understand it better—for instance, you might divide a newspaper into its sections, such as national news, regional news, life-style, and so on. As in the paragraph below, you may also interpret the meaning and significance of the elements you identify.

> The surface realism of the soap opera conjures up an illusion of "liveness." The domestic settings and easygoing rhythms encourage the viewer to believe that the drama, however ridiculous, is simply an extension of daily life. The conversation is so slow that some have called it "radio with pictures." (Advertisers have always assumed that busy housewives would listen, rather than watch.) Conversation is casual and colloquial, as though one were eavesdropping on neighbors. There is plenty of time to "read" the character's face; close-ups establish intimacy. The sets are comfortably familiar: well-lit interiors of living rooms, restaurants, offices, and hospitals. Daytime soaps have little of the glamour of their prime-time relations. The viewer easily imagines that the conversation is taking place in real time.
>
> —RUTH ROSEN, "Search for Yesterday"

Topic and focus: how "liveness" seems an extension of daily life

Elements:
- Slow conversation
- Casual conversation
- Intimate close-ups
- Familiar sets
- Absence of glamour
- Appearance of real time

Analysis is a key skill in critical reading. See page 98.

6 • Classification

When you sort many items into groups, you classify the items to see their relations more clearly. The following paragraph identifies three groups, or classes, of parents:

> In my experience, the parents who hire daytime sitters for their school-age children tend to fall into one of three groups. The first group includes parents who work and want someone to be at home when the children return from school. These parents are looking for an extension of themselves, someone who will give the care they would give if they were at home. The second group includes parents who may be home all day themselves but are too disorganized or too frazzled by their children's demands to handle child care alone. They are looking for an organizer and helpmate. The third and final group includes parents who do not want to be bothered by their children, whether they are home all day or not. Unlike the parents in the first two groups, who care for their children whenever and however they can, these parents are looking for a permanent substitute for themselves.
>
> —NANCY WHITTLE (student), "Modern Parenting"

Topic sentence

Three groups:
- Alike in one way (all hire sitters)
- No overlap in groups (each has a different attitude)

Classes arranged in order of increasing drama

7 • Comparison and contrast

Comparison and contrast may be used separately or together to develop an idea. The following paragraph illustrates one of two common ways of organizing a comparison and contrast: **subject by subject,** first one subject and then the other.

> Consider the differences also in the behavior of rock and classical music audiences. At a rock concert, the audience members yell, whistle, sing along, and stamp their feet. They may even stand during the entire performance. The better the music, the more active they'll be. At a classical concert, in contrast, the better the performance, the more *still* the audience is. Members of the classical audience are so highly disciplined that they refrain from even clearing their throats or coughing. No matter what effect the powerful music has on their intellects and feelings, they sit on their hands.
>
> —Tony Nahm (student), "Rock and Roll Is Here to Stay"

Subjects: rock and classical audiences

Rock audience

Classical audience

The next paragraph illustrates the other common organization: **point by point,** with the two subjects discussed side by side and matched feature for feature:

> The first electronic computer, ENIAC, went into operation just over fifty years ago, yet the differences between it and today's home computer are enormous. ENIAC was enormous itself, consisting of forty panels, each two feet wide and four feet deep. Today's PC or Macintosh, by contrast, can fit easily on one's desk or even lap. ENIAC had to be configured by hand, with its programmers taking up to two days to reset switches and cables. Today, the average home user can change programs in an instant. And for all its size and inconvenience, ENIAC was also slow. In its time, its operating speed of 100,000 pulses per second seemed amazingly fast. However, today's home machine can operate at 1 billion pulses per second or faster.
>
> —Shirley Kajiwara (student), "The Computers We Deserve"

Subjects: ENIAC and home computer

Size: ENIAC, home computer

Ease of programming: ENIAC, home computer

Speed: ENIAC, home computer

8 • Cause-and-effect analysis

When you use analysis to explain why something happened or what did or may happen, then you are determining causes or effects. In the following paragraph the author looks at the cause of an effect—Japanese collectivism:

> This *shinkansen* or "bullet train" speeds across the rural areas of Japan giving a quick view of cluster after cluster of farmhouses surrounded by rice paddies. This particular pattern did not develop purely by chance, but as a consequence of the technology peculiar to the growing of rice, the staple of the Japanese diet. The growing of rice requires the construction and maintenance of an irrigation system, something that takes many hands to build. More importantly, the planting and the harvesting of rice can only be done efficiently with the cooperation of twenty or more people. The "bottom line" is that a single family working alone cannot produce enough rice to survive, but a dozen families working together can produce a surplus. Thus the Japanese have had to develop the capacity to work together in harmony, no matter what the forces of disagreement or social disintegration, in order to survive. —WILLIAM OUCHI, *Theory Z*

Effect: pattern of Japanese farming

Causes: Japanese dependence on rice, which requires collective effort

Effect: working in harmony

9 • Process analysis

When you analyze how to do something or how something works, you explain a process. The following example identifies the process, describes the equipment needed, and details the steps in the process:

> As a car owner, you waste money when you pay a mechanic to change the engine oil. The job is not difficult, even if you know little about cars. All you need is a wrench to remove the drain plug, a large, flat pan to collect the draining oil, plastic bottles to dispose of the used oil, and fresh oil. First, warm up the car's engine so that the oil will flow more easily. When the engine is warm, shut it off and remove its oil-filler cap (the owner's manual shows where this cap is). Then locate the drain plug under the engine (again consulting the owner's manual for its location) and place the flat pan under the plug. Remove the plug with the wrench, letting the oil flow into the pan. When the oil stops flowing, replace the plug and, at the engine's filler hole, add the amount and kind of fresh oil specified by the owner's manual. Pour the used oil into the plastic bottles and take it to a waste-oil collector, which any garage mechanic can recommend. —ANTHONY ANDRES (student), "Do-It-Yourself Car Care"

Process: changing the oil

Equipment needed

Steps in process

EXERCISE 6.3
Analyzing and revising skimpy paragraphs

The following paragraphs are not well developed. Rewrite one into a well-developed paragraph, supplying your own concrete details or examples to support general statements.

1. One big difference between successful and unsuccessful teachers is the quality of communication. A successful teacher is sensitive to students' needs and excited by the course subject. In contrast, an unsuccessful teacher seems uninterested in students and bored by the subject.

2. Gestures are one of our most important means of communication. We use them instead of speech. We use them to supplement the words we speak. And we use them to communicate some feelings or meanings that words cannot adequately express.

EXERCISE 6.4
Writing with the patterns of development

Write at least three focused, coherent, and well-developed paragraphs, each one developed with a different pattern. Draw on the topics here or choose your own topics.

1. *Narration:* an experience of public speaking, a disappointment, leaving home, waking up
2. *Description:* your room, a crowded or deserted place, a food, an intimidating person
3. *Illustration or support:* study habits, having a headache, the best sports event, usefulness (or uselessness) of a self-help book
4. *Definition:* humor, an adult, fear, authority
5. *Division or analysis:* a television news show, a barn, a site on the World Wide Web, a piece of music
6. *Classification:* factions in a campus controversy, styles of playing poker, types of Web sites, kinds of teachers
7. *Comparison and contrast:* Surfing the Web and watching TV, AM and FM radio announcers, high school and college football, movies on TV and in a theater
8. *Cause-and-effect analysis:* connection between tension and anger, causes of failing a course, connection between credit cards and debt, causes of a serious accident
9. *Process analysis:* preparing for a job interview, setting up an e-mail account, protecting your home from burglars, making a jump shot

6d Write introductory and concluding paragraphs.

Introductory paragraphs set up your essay, piquing readers' interest in your topic. Concluding paragraphs finish your essay, giving readers a sense of completion.

¶ 6d

1 • Introductions

An introduction draws readers from their world into your world:

- It focuses readers' attention on the topic and arouses their curiosity about what you have to say.
- It specifies your subject and implies your attitude.
- Often it includes your thesis statement (see p. 18).
- It is concise and sincere.

To focus readers' attention, you have a number of options:

Some strategies for introductions

- Ask a question.
- Relate an incident.
- Use a vivid quotation.
- Offer a surprising statistic or other fact.
- State an opinion related to your thesis.
- Provide background.
- Outline the argument your thesis refutes.
- Make a historical comparison or contrast.
- Outline a problem or dilemma.
- Create a visual image that represents your subject.
- Define a word central to your subject.
- In some business or technical writing, simply state your main idea.

CULTURE LANGUAGE These options for an introduction may not be what you are used to if your native language is not English. In other cultures, readers may seek familiarity or reassurance from an author's introduction, or they may prefer an indirect approach to the subject. In academic and business English, however, writers and readers prefer originality and concise, direct expression.

Effective openings

A very common introduction opens with a statement of the essay's general subject, clarifies or limits the subject in one or more sentences, and then asserts the point of the essay in the thesis statement. Here are two examples:

> Can your home or office computer make you sterile? Can it strike you blind or dumb? The answer is, probably not. Nevertheless, reports of side effects relating to computer use should be examined, especially in the area of birth defects, eye

Subject related to reader's experience

Clarification of subject: bridge to thesis statement

complaints, and postural difficulties. Although little conclusive evidence exists to establish a causal link between computer use and problems of this sort, the circumstantial evidence can be disturbing. — Thesis statement

—THOMAS HARTMANN, "How Dangerous Is Your Computer?"

The Declaration of Independence is so widely regarded as a statement of American ideals that its origins in practical politics tend to be forgotten. — Statement about subject
Thomas Jefferson's draft was intensely debated and then revised in the Continental Congress. Jefferson was disappointed with the result. — Clarification of subject: bridge to thesis statement
However, a close reading of both the historical context and the revisions themselves indicates that the Congress improved the document for its intended purpose. — Thesis statement

—ANN WEISS (student), "The Editing of the Declaration of Independence"

In much business writing, it's more important to tell readers immediately what your point is than to try to engage them. This introduction to a brief memo quickly outlines a problem and (in the thesis statement) suggests a way to solve it:

Starting next month, staff vacations will leave our department short-handed. We need to hire two or perhaps three temporary keyboarders to maintain our schedules for the month. — Thesis statement

Additional examples of effective introductions appear in complete writing samples on pages 44, 49, 72, 106, 122, 131, and 133.

Introduction *don'ts*

When writing and revising your introduction, avoid approaches that are likely to bore readers or make them question your sincerity or control:

- *A vague generality or truth.* Don't extend your reach too wide with a line such as *Throughout human history . . .* or *In today's world. . . .* You may have needed a warm-up paragraph to start drafting, but your readers can do without it.
- *A flat announcement.* Don't start with *The purpose of this essay is . . . , In this essay I will . . . ,* or any similar presentation of your intention or topic.
- *A reference to the essay's title.* Don't refer to the title of the essay in the first sentence—for example, *This is a big problem* or *This book is about the history of the guitar.*

- *According to Webster. . . .* Don't start by citing a dictionary definition. A definition can be an effective springboard to an essay, but this kind of lead-in has become dull with overuse.
- *An apology.* Don't fault your opinion or your knowledge with *I'm not sure if I'm right, but I think . . . , I don't know much about this, but . . . ,* or similar lines.

2 • Conclusions

Your conclusion finishes off your essay and tells readers where you think you have brought them. It answers the question "So what?"

Effective conclusions

Usually set off in its own paragraph, the conclusion may consist of a single sentence or a group of sentences. It may take one or more of the following approaches:

Some strategies for conclusions

- Recommend a course of action.
- Summarize the paper if it's long or complicated.
- Echo the approach of the introduction.
- Restate your thesis and reflect on its implications.
- Strike a note of hope or despair.
- Give a symbolic or powerful fact or other detail.
- Give an especially compelling example.
- Create a visual image that represents your subject.

The following paragraph concludes an essay on the Declaration of Independence (the introduction appears on the previous page):

> The Declaration of Independence has come to be a statement of this nation's political philosophy, but that was not its purpose in 1776. Jefferson's passionate expression had to bow to the goals of the Congress as a whole to forge unity among the colonies and to win the support of foreign nations.
>
> —ANN WEISS (student), "The Editing of the Declaration of Independence"

[Echo of introduction: contrast between past and present]

[Restatement and elaboration of thesis]

In the next paragraph the author concludes an essay on environmental protection with a call for action:

> Until we get the answers [about the effects of pollutants], I think we had better keep on building

power plants and growing food with the help of fertilizers and such insect-controlling chemicals as we now have. The risks are well known, thanks to the environmentalists. If they had not created a widespread public awareness of the ecological crisis, we wouldn't stand a chance. But such awareness by itself is not enough. Flaming manifestos and prophecies of doom are no longer much help, and a search for scapegoats can only make matters worse. The time for sensations and manifestos is about over. Now we need rigorous analysis, united effort and very hard work.

—PETER F. DRUCKER,
"How Best to Protect the Environment"

Summary and opinion

Call for action

Conclusions to avoid

Several kinds of conclusions rarely work well:

- *A repeat of the introduction.* Don't simply replay your introduction. The conclusion should capture what the paragraphs of the body have added to the introduction.
- *A new direction.* Don't introduce a subject different from the one your essay has been about.
- *A sweeping generalization.* Don't conclude more than you reasonably can from the evidence you have presented. If your essay is about your frustrating experience trying to clear a parking ticket, you cannot reasonably conclude that *all* local police forces are too tied up in red tape to be of service to the people.
- *An apology.* Don't cast doubt on your essay. Don't say, *Even though I'm no expert* or *This may not be convincing, but I believe it's true* or anything similar. Rather, to win your readers' confidence, display confidence.

6e Link paragraphs within an essay.

Though you may draft paragraphs or groups of paragraphs almost as mini-essays, you will eventually need to stitch them together into a logical, larger whole. The techniques for linking paragraphs mirror those for linking sentences within paragraphs:

- Make sure each paragraph contributes to your thesis.
- Arrange the paragraphs in a clear, logical order. See pages 22–26 for advice on organization.
- Create links between paragraphs. Use repetition and restatement to stress and connect key terms, and use transitional ex-

pressions and transitional sentences to indicate sequence, direction, contrast, and other relationships.

- You will probably use varied patterns of development for individual paragraphs, even when the whole essay is developed and structured by some other pattern. Just be sure to follow through on your overall pattern.

The following essay illustrates the way effective paragraphs can build an effective essay. Linda Devereaux, the student author of the essay, received this assignment to create a profile, or detailed description, of a person:

> Think of a person you know, and then focus on a particular aspect of that person's life or personality—perhaps something the person does especially well, struggles with or has overcome, or has contributed to your life or to the community in which he or she has lived. Be sure to include a thesis statement in the opening paragraph. The overall length should be 500–1000 words.

In her essay, Devereaux chose to write a profile of her son, Eric, who has attention-deficit hyperactivity disorder (ADHD). As an overarching structure, however, she chose to analyze the life of ADHD children generally and to focus on Eric at key points. The overall organization is climactic. Sentences and paragraphs are linked by repetition, restatement, and pronouns (circled words); parallelism among sentences (underlined); transitional expressions (boxed words); and transitional sentences (noted in marginal comments).

Eric: A Picture of Hyperactivity

A hyperactive committee member can contribute to efficiency. A hyperactive salesperson can contribute to profits. When a child is hyperactive, though, people—even parents—may wish he had never been born. A collage of those who must cope with hyperactivity in children is a dark picture of frustration, anger, and loss. [Thesis statement]

The first part of the collage is the doctors. In [Transitional topic sentence] their terminology the word *hyperactivity* has been replaced by *ADHD,* attention-deficit hyperactivity disorder. They apply the term to children like my Eric who are "abnormally or excessively busy." But doctors do not fully understand the problem and thus differ over how to treat it. For example, one of Eric's doctors recommended a special diet; another recommended behavior-modifying drugs;

[Paragraph developed by definition, example, and cause-and-effect analysis]

and still another, who does not consider ADHD to be a medical problem, recommended a psychiatrist for the entire family. The result has been a merry-go-round of tests, confusion, and frustration for Eric and his parents.

As Eric's mother, I can say what ADHD means to the parents who form the second part of the collage. It means worry that is deep and enduring. It means despair that is a companion on dark and sleepless nights. It means fear that is heart-twisting and constant, for Eric is most destructive toward himself. It means a mixture of frustration, guilt, and anger. And finally, since there are times when that anger goes out of control and Eric is in danger from me, it means self-loathing.

Transitional topic sentence

Paragraph developed by definition and cause-and-effect analysis

The weight of ADHD, however, rests not on the doctors, not on my husband, not on me, but on Eric. For him is reserved the final and darkest part of the collage because he is most affected. From early childhood Eric has been dragged from doctor to doctor, attached to strange and frightening machines, and tested or discussed by physicians, neighbors, teachers, and us. His playmates dislike him because of his temper and his unwillingness to follow rules. Even his pets mistrust him because he treats them erratically, often hurting them without meaning to. As time goes on, Eric sees us—his parents—more and more often in tears and anger, and he knows he is the cause. He is highly intelligent, but he does poorly in school because of his short attention span. He is fond of sports and games, but he never joins the other children because he has an uncontrollable temper and poor coordination. Now, at age eight, he is obsessed with one thought: "Mama," he asks me repeatedly, "why do I have to be this way?"

Transitional sentence

Topic sentence

Paragraph developed by narration and cause-and-effect analysis

At last the collage is completed, and it is dark and somber. *ADHD*, as applied to children, is a term with uncertain, unattractive, and bitter associations. But the picture does have a bright spot, for inside every ADHD child like Eric is a lovely, trustful, calm person waiting to be recognized.

Transitional sentence

—Linda Devereaux (student)

7 Document Design

What makes documents clear and attractive?

Page margins, paragraph breaks, headings, illustrations, and other elements of design can clarify and further the purpose of a document. An appropriate, clear, and pleasing design will not transform a poorly written document into a good one, but it will make a strong document even more effective.

This chapter looks at the principles and elements of design that can help you effectively present various academic and business documents. More information on business formats appears in Chapter 13. Information on designing for the World Wide Web appears in Chapter 12.

7a Format academic papers appropriately for each discipline.

Many academic disciplines prefer specific formats for students' papers. This book details two such formats:

- MLA, used in English, foreign languages, and other humanities (pp. 507–09).
- APA, used in the social sciences and some natural and applied sciences (pp. 535–38).

Other academic formats can be found in the style guides listed on page 467.

The design guidelines in this chapter extend the range of elements and options covered by most academic styles. Your instructors may want you to adhere strictly to a particular style or may allow some latitude in design. Ask them for their preferences.

7b Work with the principles of document design.

Most of the principles of design respond to the ways we read. White space, for instance, relieves our eyes and helps to lead us

http://www.ablongman.com/littlebrown

➤ The writing process
  ➤ Video tutorials
    ➤ Formatting documents on a word processor
    ➤ Working with illustrations on a word processor
  ➤ Web links ➤ Document design

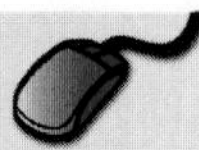

through a document. Groupings or lists help to show relationships. Type sizes, images, and color add variety and help to emphasize important elements.

The sample documents on the next two pages illustrate quite different ways of presenting a report for a marketing course. Even at a glance, the second document is easier to scan and read. It makes better use of white space, groups similar elements, uses bullets and fonts for emphasis, and more successfully integrates the visual data of the chart.

As you design your own documents, think about your purpose, the expectations of your readers, and how readers will move through your document. Also consider the following general principles, noting that they overlap and support one another:

- *Conduct readers through the document.* Establish **flow,** a pattern for the eye to follow, with headings, lists, and other elements.
- *Use white space to ease crowding and focus readers' attention.* Provide ample margins, and give breathing room to headings, lists, and other elements. Even the space indicating new paragraphs (indentions or blank lines) gives readers a break and reassures them that ideas are divided into manageable chunks.
- *Group information to show relationships.* Use headings (like those in this chapter) and lists (like the one you're reading) to convey the similarities and differences among parts of a document.
- *Emphasize important elements.* Establish hierarchies of information with type fonts and sizes, headings, indentions, color, boxes, and white space. In this book, for example, the importance of headings is clear from their size and color and from the presence or absence of decorative devices, such as the rule above 7c below.
- *Standardize to create and fulfill expectations.* Help direct readers through a document by, for instance, using the same size and color for all headings at the same level of importance. Standardizing also reduces clutter, making it easier for readers to determine the significance of the parts.

7c Use the elements of design appropriately for your content and purpose.

Applying the preceding design principles involves seven main elements of document design: print quality; margins; text; lists; headings; tables, figures, and images; and color. You won't use all these elements for every project, however, and in many academic- and

Ineffective design

Ready or Not, Here They Come: College Students and the Internet

College life once meant classrooms of students listening to teachers or groups of students talking over lunch in the union. But the reality today is more complex: students interact with their peers and professors by computer as much as face to face. As these students graduate and enter the workforce, all of society will be affected by their experience.

According to the Pew Internet Research Center (2002), today's college students are practiced computer and Internet users. The Pew Center reports that 20 percent of students in college today started using computers between ages five and eight. By age eighteen all students were using computers. Almost all college students, 86 percent, rely on the Internet, with 66 percent of students using more than one e-mail address. Computer ownership among this group is also very high: 85 percent have purchased or have been given at least one computer.

Students are eager to tap into the Internet's benefits and convenience.

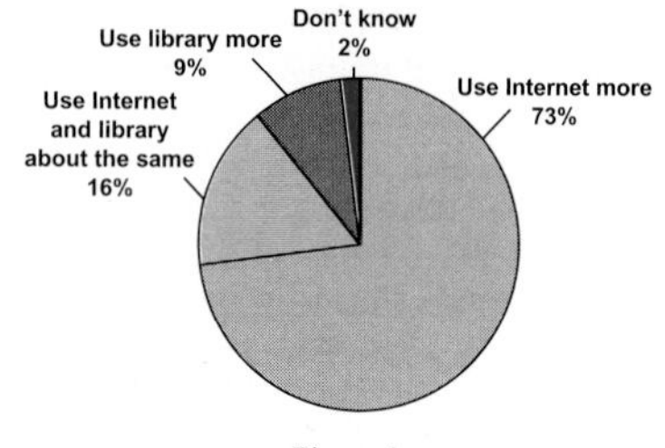

Figure 1

Figure 1, from the Pew Report, shows that the Internet has eclipsed the library as the site of college students' research. In fact, a mere 9 percent of students report relying more on the

Runs title and subtitle together. Does not distinguish title from text.

Crowds the page with minimal margins.

Downplays paragraph breaks with small indentions.

Buries statistics in a paragraph. Obscures relationships with nonparallel wording.

Does not introduce the figure, leaving readers to infer its meaning and purpose.

Leaves large white space that overemphasizes the figure.

Presents the figure undynamically, flat on.

Does not caption the figure to explain what it shows, offering only a figure number and a partial text explanation.

business-writing situations you will be required to follow a prescribed format.

Note Your word processor may provide wizards or templates for many kinds of documents, such as letters, memos, reports, agendas, résumés, and brochures. **Wizards** guide you through setting up and writing complicated documents. **Templates** are preset forms to which you add your own text, headings, and other elements. Wizards and templates can be helpful, but not if they lead you to create cookie-cutter documents no matter what the writing situation. Al-

Effective design

Distinguishes title from subtitle and both from text.

Provides adequate margins

Emphasizes paragraph breaks with white space.

Groups statistics in a bulleted list set off with white space. Uses parallel wording for parallel information.

Introduces the figure to indicate its meaning and purpose.

Reduces white space with shorter labels and a key.

Presents the figure dynamically, emphasizing the most significant segment.

Captions the figure so that it can be read separately from the text.

Ready or Not, Here They Come
College Students and the Internet

College life once meant classrooms of students listening to teachers or groups of students talking over lunch in the union. But the reality today is more complex: students interact with their peers and professors by computer as much as face to face. As these students graduate and enter the workforce, all of society will be affected by their experience.

According to the Pew Internet Research Center (2002), today's college students are practiced computer users and Internet users.

- They started young: 20 percent were using computers between ages five and eight, and all were using them by age eighteen.
- They rely on the Internet: 86 percent have used the network, and 66 percent use more than one e-mail address.
- They own computers: 85 percent have purchased or have been given at least one computer.

Students are eager to tap into the Internet's benefits and convenience. Figure 1, from the Pew Report, shows that the Internet has eclipsed the library as the site of college students' research.

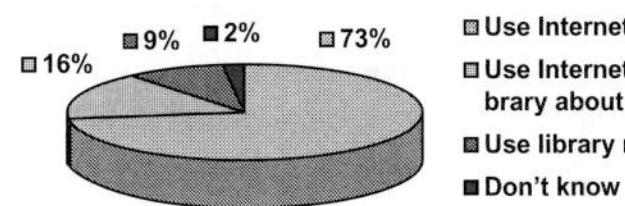

Figure 1. College students' use of the Internet and the library for research

ways keep in mind that a document should be appropriate for your subject, audience, and purpose.

1 • Print quality

The cartridge on your printer should be fresh enough to produce a dark impression. A printer that forms characters out of tiny dots may be acceptable for your academic papers, but make sure the tails on letters such as *j, p,* and *y* fall below the line of type, as they do here. For documents that are complex or that will be distributed to the public, use an inkjet or laser printer, which creates characters more like the ones you see here.

2 • Margins

Margins at the top, bottom, and sides of a page help to prevent the page from overwhelming readers with unpleasant crowding. Most academic and business documents use a minimum one-inch margin on all sides.

3 • Text

A document must be readable. You can make text readable by attending to line spacing, type fonts and sizes, highlighting, word spacing, and line breaks.

Line spacing

Most academic documents are double-spaced, with an initial indention for paragraphs, while most business documents are single-spaced, with an extra line of space between paragraphs. Double or triple spacing sets off headings in both.

Type fonts and sizes

The readability of text also derives from the type fonts (or faces) and their sizes. For academic and business documents, choose a type size of 10 or 12 points, as in these samples:

10-point Courier　　10-point Times New Roman
12-point Courier　　12-point Times New Roman

For text, generally use a font with **serifs**—the small lines finishing the letters in the samples above and in the font you're reading now. **Sans serif** fonts (*sans* means "without" in French) include the one below, found on many word processors:

10-point Arial　　12-point Arial

Though fine for headings, sans serif type can be more difficult than serif type to read in extended text.

Your word processor probably offers many decorative fonts as well:

10-point Corvallis Sans　　10-point Tekton
10-POINT STENCIL　　10-point Park Avenue

Such fonts often appear in publicity documents, such as flyers and brochures, where they can attract attention and reinforce a theme. Decorative fonts are generally inappropriate in academic and much business writing, where letter forms should be conventional and regular.

Note The point size of a type font is often an unreliable guide to its actual size, as the preceding decorative fonts illustrate: all the samples are 10 points, but they vary considerably. Before you use a font, print out a sample to be sure it is the size you want.

Highlighting

Within a document's text, underlined, *italic,* **boldface,** or even color type can emphasize key words or sentences. Underlining is rarest these days, having been replaced by italics in all but a few academic disciplines. (It remains called for in MLA style. See Chapter 56.) Both academic and business writing sometimes use boldface to give strong emphasis—for instance, to a term being defined—and sometimes use color for headings and illustrations. (See p. 84 for more on color in document design.)

No matter what your writing situation, use highlighting selectively to complement your meaning, not merely to decorate your work. Many readers consider type embellishments to be distracting.

Word spacing

In most writing situations, follow these guidelines for spacing within and between words:

- Leave one space between words.
- Leave one space after all punctuation, with these exceptions:

Dash (two hyphens or the so-called em-dash on a computer)	book--its	book—its
Hyphen	one-half	
Apostrophe within a word	book's	
Two or more adjacent marks	book.")	
Opening quotation mark, parenthesis, or bracket	("book	[book

- Leave one space before and after an ellipsis mark. In the examples below, ellipsis marks indicate omissions within a sentence and at the end of a sentence. See pages 377–78 for additional examples.

book . . . in   book. . . . The

Line breaks

Your word processor will generally insert appropriate breaks between lines of continuous text: it will not, for instance, automatically begin a line with a comma or period, and it will not end a line with an opening parenthesis or bracket. However, you will have to prevent it from breaking a two-hyphen dash or a three-dot ellipsis mark by spacing to push the beginning of each mark to the next line.

When you instruct it to do so (usually under the Tools menu), your word processor will also automatically hyphenate words to prevent very short lines. If you must decide yourself where to break words, follow the guidelines on page 389.

4 • Lists

Lists give visual reinforcement to the relations between like items—for example, the steps in a process or the elements of a proposal. A list is easier to read than a paragraph and adds white space to the page.

When wording a list, work for parallelism among items—for instance, all complete sentences or all phrases (see also p. 176). Set the list with space above and below and with numbering or bullets (centered dots or other devices, used in the list below about headings). On most word processors you can format a numbered or bulleted list automatically using the Format menu.

5 • Headings

Headings are signposts: they direct the reader's attention by focusing the eye on a document's most significant content. Most academic and business documents use headings functionally, to divide text, orient readers, and create emphasis. Short academic and business documents, such as a three-page paper or a one-page letter, may not need headings at all. But for longer documents follow these guidelines:

- *Use one, two, or three levels of headings* depending on the needs of your material and the length of your document. Some level of heading every two or so pages will help keep readers on track.
- *Create an outline of your document* to plan where headings should go. Use the first level of heading for the main points (and sections) of your document. Use a second and perhaps a third level of heading to mark subsections of supporting information.
- *Keep headings as short as possible* while making them specific about the material that follows.
- *Word headings consistently*—for instance, all questions (*What Is the Scientific Method?*), all phrases with *-ing* words (*Understanding the Scientific Method*), or all phrases with nouns (*The Scientific Method*).

- *Indicate the relative importance of headings* with type size, positioning, and highlighting, such as capital letters, underlining, or boldface.

First-Level Heading

Second-Level Heading

Third-Level Heading

Generally, you can use the same type font and size for headings as for the text. Avoid very decorative fonts like the Corvallis Sans or Stencil shown on page 78.

- *Don't break a page immediately after a heading.* Push the heading to the next page.

Note Document format in psychology and some other social sciences requires a particular treatment of headings. See page 536.

6 • Tables, figures, and images

Tables, figures, and images can often make a point for you more efficiently than words can. Tables present data. Figures (such as graphs and charts) usually recast data in visual form. Images (such as diagrams, drawings, and photographs) can explain processes, represent what something looks like, add emphasis, or convey a theme.

In academic and many business documents, tables, figures, and images directly reinforce and amplify the text. Follow these guidelines:

- *Focus on a purpose for your illustration*—a reason for including it and a point you want it to make. Otherwise, readers may find it irrelevant or confusing.
- *Provide a source note for someone else's independent material,* whether it's data or an entire illustration (see p. 462). Each discipline has a slightly different style for such source notes: those in the table and figures on the next two pages reflect the style of the social sciences. See also Chapters 56–57.
- *Number figures and images together, and label them as figures:* Figure 1, Figure 2, and so on.
- *Number and label tables separately from figures:* Table 1, Table 2, and so on.
- *Refer to each illustration* (for instance, "See Figure 2") at the point(s) in the text where readers will benefit by consulting it.
- *Place each illustration on a page by itself* immediately after the page that refers to it.

Note Many businesses and academic disciplines have preferred styles for illustrations that differ from those given here. When in doubt about how to prepare and place tables and figures, ask your instructor or supervisor.

Tables

Tables usually summarize raw data, displaying the data concisely and clearly.

- *Provide a self-explanatory title above the table.* Readers should see what the table shows without having to refer to your text.
- *Provide self-explanatory headings for horizontal rows and vertical columns.* Use abbreviations only if you are certain readers will understand them.
- *Lay out rows and columns for maximum clarity.* In the sample below, lines divide the table into parts, headings align with their data, and numbers align vertically down columns.

Table 1

Percentage of Young Adults Living at Home, 1960–2000

	1960	1970	1980	1990	2000
Males					
Age 18–24	52	54	54	58	57
Age 25–34	9	9	10	15	13
Females					
Age 18–24	35	41	43	48	47
Age 25–34	7	7	7	8	8

Note: Data from U.S. Bureau of Census, *Census 2000 Summary Tables,* retrieved July 1, 2003, from http://www.census.gov/servlet/QTTTable?_ts=30543101060

Figures

Figures represent data graphically. They include the three kinds presented on the facing page: pie charts (showing percentages making up a whole), bar graphs (showing comparative data), and line graphs (showing change).

- *Provide a self-explanatory caption or legend below the figure.* Readers should see what the figure shows without having to refer to the body of your document.
- *Provide self-explanatory labels for all parts of the figure.*
- *Draw the figure to reflect its purpose and the visual effect you want it to have.* For instance, shortening the horizontal date axis in Figure 3 opposite emphasizes the dramatic movement of the line over time.

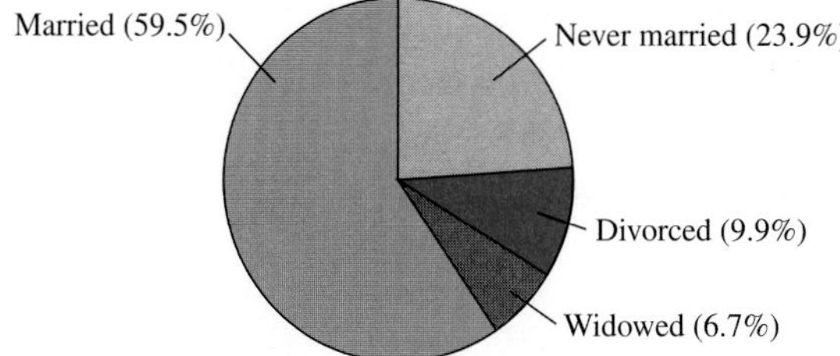

Figure 1. Marital status in 2002 of US adults aged eighteen and over. Data from Statistical Abstract of the United States, 2003.

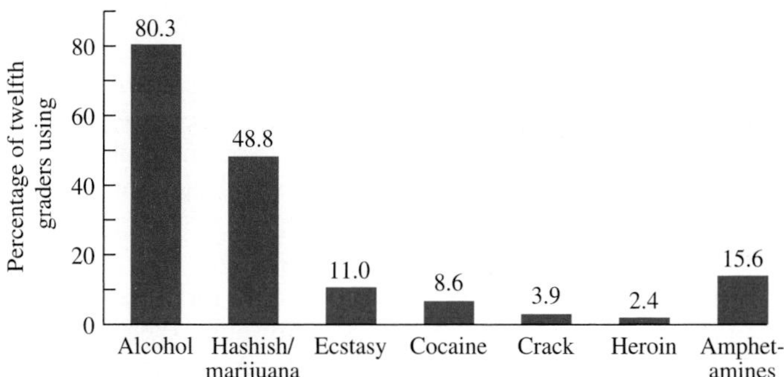

Figure 2. Lifetime prevalence of use of alcohol, compared with other drugs, among twelfth graders. Data from Monitoring the Future, Institute for Social Research, University of Michigan, published in Lloyd D. Johnston et al., Monitoring the Future: National Survey Results on Drug Use, 1975–2000. Vol. 1: Secondary School Students. Bethesda, MD: National Institute on Drug Abuse, 2001.

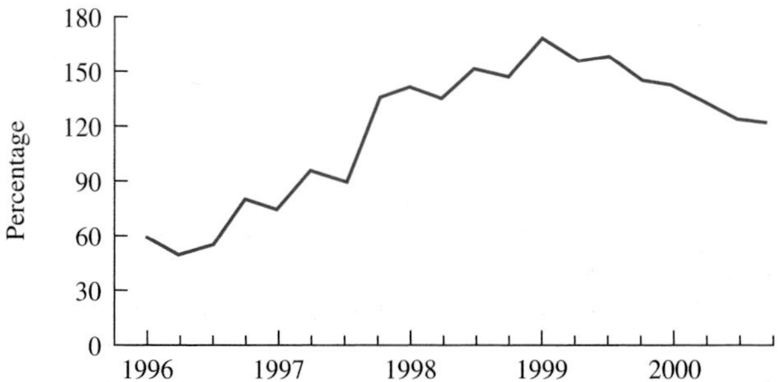

Figure 3. Five-year cumulative return for equities in Standard & Poor's 500 Index, 1996–2000.

- *Take special care with graphs.* Generally make the width greater than the height, and always show a zero point so that the values are clear.

Photographs and other images

Images can either add substance to a document or simply enliven it. In a psychology paper, for instance, a photograph may illustrate a key experiment, while in a brochure a photograph may add the visual interest of, say, people working together. In academic and most business documents, images may include not only photographs but also diagrams and drawings. They cannot represent your ideas by themselves: you need to consider carefully how they relate and add to your text, you need to explain their significance, and you need to label, number, and caption them (see p. 82).

Note When using an image prepared by someone else, such as a photograph downloaded from the Web, you must verify that the source permits reproduction of the image before you use it. In most documents but especially academic papers, you must also cite the source. See pages 464–65 on copyright issues with electronic sources.

7 • Color

With a color printer, most word processors and desktop publishers can produce documents that use color for bullets, headings, borders, boxes, illustrations, and other elements. Ask your instructor or supervisor whether color is appropriate in your documents. If you do use it, follow these guidelines:

- *Employ color to clarify and highlight your content.* Too much color or too many colors on a page will distract rather than focus readers' attention.
- *Make sure that color type is readable.* For text, where type is likely to be relatively small, use only dark colors. For headings, lighter colors may be readable if the type is large and boldfaced.
- *Stick to the same color for all headings at the same level*—for instance, red for main headings, black for secondary headings.
- *Use color for bullets, lines, and other nontext elements.* But use no more than a few colors to keep pages clean.
- *Use color to distinguish the parts of illustrations*—the segments of charts, the lines of graphs, and the parts of diagrams. Use only as many colors as you need to make your illustration clear.

EXERCISE 7.1
Redesigning a paper

Save a duplicate copy of a recent paper or one you are currently working on. Then format the duplicate using appropriate elements of design, such as type fonts, lists, and headings. (For a new paper, be sure your instructor will accept your new design.) When you have finished the redesign, share the work with your instructor.

7d A sample report

You can use the design principles and elements discussed on pages 75–84 to good effect in reports such as the one shown on the next page. This business report outlines a problem and proposes a solution. In keeping with a formal business-writing situation, the document is single-spaced (with double spacing between paragraphs and around the list), and the overall appearance is restrained. Color appears only in headings and the figure. The document uses two type fonts, one for the text and headings and one for the figure. Headings clearly delineate the structure of the page: first a summary, then an outline of the problem, and then a discussion of the solution. The figure is visually pleasing and clear, with a caption and labels that explain its content. A bulleted list emphasizes a group of solutions.

Note In many academic disciplines and business organizations, reports have specific formatting requirements: in psychology, for instance, a report should include an abstract (see pp. 535–36). If you are unsure about the format expectations for your reports, ask your instructor or supervisor.

Canada Geese at ABC Institute: An Environmental Problem

Summary

The flock of Canada geese on and around ABC Institute's grounds has grown dramatically in recent years. What was once a source of pleasure for institute employees and others using the grounds has become a nuisance and an environmental problem. This report reviews the problem, considers the options for reducing the flock, and proposes as a solution the cooperation of ABC Institute, the municipalities around Taylor Lake, and the US Fish and Wildlife Service to reduce the flock by humane means.

The Problem

Canada geese began living at Taylor Lake, adjacent to ABC Institute, when they were relocated there in 1986 by the state game department. As a nonmigratory flock, the geese are present year-round, with the highest population each year occurring in fall, winter, and early spring, after the young have fledged.

In recent years the flock of geese at Taylor Lake has grown dramatically. The Audubon Society's annual Christmas bird census shows a thirty-fold increase from the 37 geese counted in 1988 to the 1150 counted in 2003 (see Figure 1).

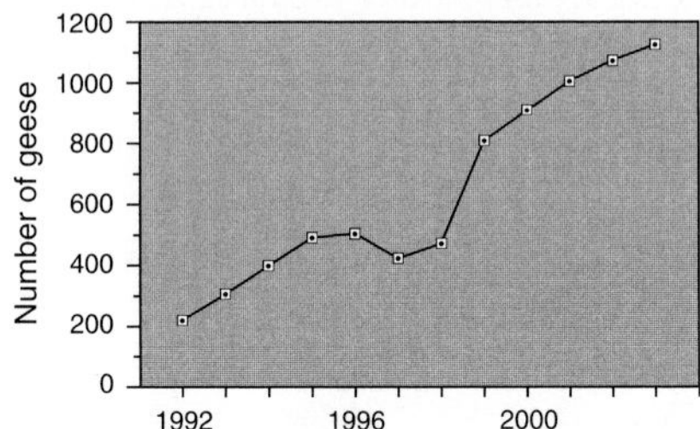

Figure 1. Goose population of Taylor Lake, 1992–2003.

The principal environmental problem caused by the geese is pollution of grass and water by defecation. During high-population months, geese droppings cover the ABC Institute's grounds as well as the park's athletic fields and picnicking areas. The runoff from these droppings into Taylor Lake has substantially affected the quality of the lake's water, so that local authorities have twice (2002 and 2003) issued warnings against swimming.

The Solution

Several possible solutions to the goose overpopulation and resulting environmental problems are *not viable alternatives:*

- Harass the geese with dogs, light, and noise so that the geese choose to leave. This solution is inhumane to the geese and unpleasant for human neighbors.
- Feed the geese a chemical that will weaken the shells of their eggs and thus reduce growth of the flock. This solution is inhumane to the geese and also impractical, because geese are long-lived.
- Kill adult geese. This solution is, obviously, inhumane to the geese.

The most appropriate and humane solution is to thin the goose population by trapping and removing many geese (perhaps 600) to areas less populated by humans, such as wildlife preserves and wilderness areas. Though costly (see figures below), this solution would be efficient and harmless to the geese, provided that sizable netted enclosures are used for traps. [Discussion of solution continues, followed by "Recommendations."]

II

Writing in and out of School

8 Academic Writing

What are the features of writing in academic situations?

8a

When you write for your college courses, you work within a culture of teachers and students who have specific expectations. These expectations and the particular writing assignment will shape your choice of subject and your purpose, as noted in Chapter 1. They should also shape the structure of your writing, the mix of general statements and specific information, the tone you assume, even the fine points of grammar and usage.

CULTURE LANGUAGE Language and culture interact, each influencing the other. American academic prose serves and shapes the culture of US higher education and is in turn influenced by its use in that culture. Its expectations may differ from the ways you are used to speaking, writing, and reading, especially if your first language is not English or if it is a dialect of English besides that used for academic writing. Throughout the handbook, the symbol opening this paragraph highlights common trouble spots in academic writing.

8a Consider the audience represented by the instructor.

Much of your academic writing will have only one reader besides you: the instructor of the course you are writing for. Like everyone else, instructors have preferences and pet peeves, but you'll waste time and energy trying to anticipate them. Do attend to written and spoken directions for assignments, of course. But otherwise view your instructor as a representative of a larger culture whose response will be guided by the culture's expectations.

- *In a composition course the instructor will represent the audience specified by the assignment or (if no audience was specified) the group you evidently intend to address*—perhaps your classmates or the school administration or readers of the town newspaper. The instructor's evaluation of your work will depend on how well you communicate with your target readers.

http://www.ablongman.com/littlebrown
➤ Writing in and out of school
➤ Web links ➤ Academic writing

- *In courses such as literature, psychology, management, and chemistry, the instructor will represent practitioners of the discipline.* He or she will look for your command of the discipline's research methods, principles, and vocabulary, as well as your ability to organize and express ideas appropriately for the discipline.

In each of your courses, your instructor will also be serving as a coach, guiding you toward achieving the goals of the course. But you'll need to do your part, too, presenting yourself as a serious and competent student of your subject, alert to your readers' expectations.

8b Observe academic conventions for content and structure.

Unless you write papers in only one discipline, you will find wide variation in what your instructors expect for the content and structure of your papers. However, you will also find important similarities because all academic writing shares the broad aim of exchanging and often creating knowledge. Mixed with traditions of prose in the United States, this aim results in writing with distinctive features, including the following:

- *The organization and presentation are straightforward,* as simple as the content and purpose allow.
- *A central idea or claim, called a* ***thesis,*** *controls the entire paper.* (See p. 18.)
- *The thesis is clearly stated,* usually near the beginning.
- *The thesis is supported with evidence,* drawn usually from research and sometimes from the writer's own experience.
- *Paragraphs break content into chunks.* Each paragraph usually focuses on a stated idea supporting the thesis and provides specific evidence for the idea.
- *Sentences, paragraphs, and sections are clearly related* so that readers always know where they are in the paper's development.

CULTURE LANGUAGE These features are far from universal. In other cultures, academic writers may be indirect, may expect readers to discover the thesis, or may work mainly from support to thesis instead of the other way around. Recognizing such differences between practices in your native culture and in the United States can help you adapt to US academic writing.

8c Use the language expected in academic writing.

American academic writing relies on a dialect called **standard American English.** The dialect is also used in business, the professions, government, the media, and other sites of social and economic power where people of diverse backgrounds must communicate with one another. It is "standard" not because it is better than other forms of English, but because it is accepted as the common language, much as the dollar bill is accepted as the common currency.

You'll recognize standard American English as the dialect used in this handbook, in magazines and newspapers, and on television news. But you might also notice that the dialect varies a lot, from the formal English of a President's State of the Union address through the middle formality of this handbook to the informal chitchat between anchors on morning TV. Even in academic writing, standard American English allows much room for the writer's own voice, as these two passages on the same topic show:

More formal

One technique for heightening the emotional appeal of advertisements is "color engineering." Adding color to a product or the surrounding advertisement can increase sales despite the fact that the color serves no practical purpose. For example, until the 1920s manufacturers made fountain pens of hard black rubber. When they suddenly introduced colorful pens, sales rose dramatically.

Less formal

"Color engineering" can intensify the emotional appeal of advertisements. New color in a product or the surrounding ad can boost sales even when the color serves no other use. In the 1920s, for example, fountain-pen makers introduced colorful pens along with the familiar ones of hard black rubber. Sales shot up.

Both examples illustrate several principles of standard American English as it is used in academic writing:

- *Follow the rules and conventions of grammar and usage*—those described in guides to the dialect, such as this handbook.
- *Use a standard vocabulary,* not one that only some groups understand, such as slang, an ethnic or regional dialect, or another language. (See pp. 183–88 for more on specialized vocabularies.)
- *Create some distance between writer and reader with the third person (he, she, it, they).* The first person (*I, we*) is sometimes appropriate to express personal opinions or invite readers to

think along, but not with a strongly explanatory purpose (*I discovered that "color engineering" can intensify . . .*). The second person (*you*) is appropriate only in addressing readers directly (as in this handbook), and even then it may seem condescending or too chummy (*You should know that "color engineering" can heighten . . .*).

CULTURE LANGUAGE If your first language is not English or is an English dialect besides standard American, you know well the power of communicating with others who share your language. Learning to write standard American English in no way requires you to abandon your first language. Like most multilingual people, you are probably already adept at switching between languages as the situation demands—speaking one way with your relatives, say, and another way with an employer. As you practice academic writing, you'll develop the same flexibility.

EXERCISE 8.1
Considering your academic writing

Look back at a paper you wrote for a course in high school or college. To what extent does it share the features of academic writing discussed in this chapter? How does it differ?

EXERCISE 8.2
Considering your native language or dialect CULTURE LANGUAGE

What main similarities and differences do you notice between writing in your native language or dialect and writing for US college courses? Consider especially content, structure, and the expression of ideas. Which differences do you think are easiest to bridge? Which are most difficult? Why?

9 Critical Reading and Writing

Why and how should I think critically when I read and write?

Throughout college and beyond, you will be expected to think, read, and write critically—that is, to question, test, and build on what others say and what you yourself think. In daily life, critical thinking helps you figure out why things happen to you or what your experiences mean. In school and at work, critical thinking sharpens your ability to learn and to perform. It helps you understand and discern which information and ideas are useful, fair, and wise—and which are not.

9a Read critically.

In school and at work, much of your critical thinking will focus on written texts (a short story, a journal article, a Web site) or on visual objects (a photograph, a chart, a film). Like all subjects worthy of critical consideration, such works operate on at least three levels: (1) what the creator actually says or shows, (2) what the creator does not say or show but builds into the work (intentionally or not), and (3) what you think. Discovering each level of the work, even if it is visual, involves four main steps: previewing the material, reading actively, summarizing, and forming a critical response.

CULTURE LANGUAGE The idea of reading critically may require you to make some adjustments if readers in your native culture tend to seek understanding or agreement more than engagement from what they read. Readers of English use texts for all kinds of reasons, including pleasure, reinforcement, and information. But they also read skeptically, critically, to see the author's motives, test their own ideas, and arrive at new knowledge.

1 • Preview the material.

When you're reading a work of literature, such as a short story or a poem, it's often best just to plunge right in (see p. 124). But for critical reading of other works, it's worthwhile to form some expectations and even some preliminary questions before you start reading word for word. Your reading will be more informed and fruitful.

Use the following questions as a previewing guide:

- *Length:* Is the material brief enough to read in one sitting, or do you need more time? To gauge the length of an online source such as a Web site, study any menus for an indication of the

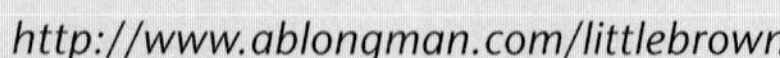

➤ Writing in and out of school
  ➤ Video tutorials ➤ Investigating assumptions
  ➤ Web exercises ➤ Exer. 1
  ➤ Web links
    ➤ Critical reading and writing
    ➤ Visual literacy

source's complexity. Then scroll through a couple of pages and follow a couple of links to estimate the overall length.

- *Facts of publication:* Does the date of publication suggest currency or datedness? Does the publisher or publication specialize in a particular kind of material—scholarly articles, say, or popular books? For a Web source, who or what sponsors the site: an individual? a nonprofit organization? an academic institution? a corporation? a government body? (See pp. 440–41 on reading electronic addresses.)
- *Content cues:* What do the title, summary or abstract, headings, illustrations, and other features tell you? What questions do they raise in your mind?
- *Author:* What does the biographical information tell you about the author's publications, interests, biases, and reputation in the field? For an online message, which may be posted by an unfamiliar or anonymous author, what can you gather about the author from his or her words? If possible, trace unfamiliar authors to learn more about them. (See pp. 441, 444.)
- *Yourself:* Do you anticipate particular difficulties with the content? What biases of your own may influence your response to the text—for instance, anxiety, curiosity, boredom, or an outlook similar or opposed to that of the author?

2 • Read actively.

Reading is itself more than a one-step process. Your primary goal is to understand the first level on which the text operates—what the author actually says.

The first time through new material, read as steadily and smoothly as possible, trying to get the gist of what the author is saying and a sense of his or her tone. Then reread the material *slowly* to grasp its content and how it is constructed. That means stopping to puzzle out a paragraph if you didn't get the point, looking up words in a dictionary, or following links at a Web site.

Use your pen, pencil, or keyboard freely to annotate the text or make separate notes. Below is an example of active reading by a student, Charlene Robinson. She was responding to "Student Loans," an essay by Thomas Sowell reprinted in Exercise 9.1 (pp. 95–96).

> The first lesson of economics is scarcity: There is never enough of anything to fully satisfy all those who want it.
>
> The first lesson of politics is to disregard the first lesson of economics. When politicians discover some group that is being vocal about not

basic contradiction between economics and politics

having as much as they want, the "solution" is to give them more. Where do politicians get this "more"? They rob Peter to pay Paul.

After a while, of course, they discover that Peter doesn't have enough. Bursting with compassion, politicians rush to the rescue. Needless to say, they do not admit that robbing Peter to pay Paul was a dumb idea in the first place. On the contrary, they now rob Tom, Dick, and Harry to help Peter.

The latest chapter in this long-running saga is that politicians have now suddenly discovered that many college students graduate heavily in debt. To politicians it follows, as the night follows the day, that the government should come to their rescue with the taxpayers' money.

biblical reference?

ironic and dismissive language

politicians = fools? or irresponsible?

After reading the text, Robinson wrote about it in the journal she kept on her computer. She divided the journal into two columns, one each for the text and her responses. Here is the portion pertaining to the paragraphs above:

Text	**Responses**
Economics teaches lessons (1), and politics (politicians) and economics are at odds.	Is economics truer or more reliable than politics? More scientific?
Politicians don't accept econ. limits--always trying to satisfy "vocal" voters by giving them more of what they want (2).	Politicians do spend a lot of our money. Is that what they're elected to do, or do they go too far?
"Robbing Peter to pay Paul" (2)--from the Bible (the Apostles)?	
Politicians support student-loan program with taxpayer refunds bec. of "vocal" voters (2-4): another ex. of not accepting econ. limits.	I support the loan program, too. Are politicians being irresponsible when they do? (Dismissive language underlined on copy.)

You should try to answer the questions about meaning that you raise in your annotations and your journal, and that may take another reading or some digging in other sources, such as dictionaries and encyclopedias. Recording in your journal what you think the author means will help you build an understanding of the text, and a focused attempt to summarize will help even more (see p. 97). Such efforts will resolve any confusion you feel, or they will give you the confidence to say that your confusion is the fault of the author, not the reader.

EXERCISE 9.1
Reading

Reprinted below is an essay by Thomas Sowell on the federal government's student-loan program. An economist, Sowell is also a newspaper columnist and the author of many books on economics, politics, and education. This essay appeared in Sowell's collection *Is Reality Optional?*

Read this essay at least twice, until you think you understand what the author is saying. Either on these pages or separately, note your questions and reactions in writing, just as student writer Charlene Robinson did for the first four paragraphs. Look up any words you don't know, and try to answer your questions. You might want to discuss the essay with your classmates as well.

Student Loans

The first lesson of economics is scarcity: There is never enough 1
of anything to fully satisfy all those who want it.

The first lesson of politics is to disregard the first lesson of eco- 2
nomics. When politicians discover some group that is being vocal about not having as much as they want, the "solution" is to give them more. Where do politicians get this "more"? They rob Peter to pay Paul.

After a while, of course, they discover that Peter doesn't have 3
enough. Bursting with compassion, politicians rush to the rescue. Needless to say, they do not admit that robbing Peter to pay Paul was a dumb idea in the first place. On the contrary, they now rob Tom, Dick, and Harry to help Peter.

The latest chapter in this long-running saga is that politicians 4
have now suddenly discovered that many college students graduate heavily in debt. To politicians it follows, as the night follows the day, that the government should come to their rescue with the taxpayers' money.

How big is this crushing burden of college students' debt that 5
we hear so much about from politicians and media deep thinkers? For those students who graduate from public colleges owing money, the debt averages a little under $7000. For those who graduate from private colleges owing money, the average debt is a little under $9000.

Buying a very modestly priced automobile involves more debt 6
than that. And a car loan has to be paid off faster than the ten years that college graduates get to repay their student loans. Moreover, you have to keep buying cars every several years, while one college education lasts a lifetime.

College graduates of course earn higher incomes than other 7
people. Why, then, should we panic at the thought that they have to

repay loans for the education which gave them their opportunities? Even graduates with relatively modest incomes pay less than 10 percent of their annual salary on the first loan the first year—with declining percentages in future years, as their pay increases.

Political hysteria and media hype may focus on the low-income student with a huge debt. That is where you get your heart-rending stories—even if they are not all that typical. In reality, the soaring student loans of the past decade have resulted from allowing high-income people to borrow under government programs. 8

Before 1978, college loans were available through government programs only to students whose family income was below some cut-off level. That cut-off level was about double the national average income, but at least it kept out the Rockefellers and the Vanderbilts. But, in an era of "compassion," Congress took off even those limits. 9

That opened the floodgates. No matter how rich you were, it still paid to borrow money through the government at low interest rates. The money you had set aside for your children's education could be invested somewhere else, at higher interest rates. Then, when the student loan became due, parents could pay it off with the money they had set aside—pocketing the difference in interest rates. 10

To politicians and the media, however, the rapidly growing loans showed what a great "need" there was. The fact that many students welshed when time came to repay their loans showed how "crushing" their burden of debt must be. In reality, those who welsh typically have smaller loans, but have dropped out of college before finishing. People who are irresponsible in one way are often irresponsible in other ways. 11

No small amount of the deterioration of college standards has been due to the increasingly easy availability of college to people who are not very serious about getting an education. College is not a bad place to hang out for a few years, if you have nothing better to do, and if someone else is paying for it. Its costs are staggering, but the taxpayers carry much of that burden, not only for state universities and city colleges, but also to an increasing extent even for "private" institutions. 12

Numerous government subsidies and loan programs make it possible for many people to use vast amounts of society's resources at low cost to themselves. Whether in money terms or in real terms, federal aid to higher education has increased several hundred percent since 1970. That has enabled colleges to raise their tuition by leaps and bounds and enabled professors to be paid more and more for doing less and less teaching. 13

Naturally all these beneficiaries are going to create hype and hysteria to keep more of the taxpayers' money coming in. But we would be fools to keep on writing blank checks for them. 14

When you weigh the cost of things, in economics that's called "trade-offs." In politics, it's called "mean-spirited." Apparently, if we just took a different attitude, scarcity would go away. 15

—THOMAS SOWELL

3 • Summarize the main points.

A good way to master the content of a text and see its strengths and weaknesses is to **summarize** it: distill it to its main points, in your own words. Here is one procedure for summarizing:

- *Understand the meaning*. Look up words or concepts you don't know so that you understand the author's sentences and how they relate to each other.
- *Understand the organization*. Work through the text to identify its sections—single paragraphs or groups of paragraphs focused on a single topic, related pages or links in a Web site. To understand how parts of a work relate to each other, try drawing a tree diagram or creating an outline (pp. 23–26). Although both tools work well for straight text, the tree diagram may work better for nonlinear material such as a Web site.
- *Distill each section*. Write a one- or two-sentence summary of each section you identify. Focus on the main point of the section, omitting examples, facts, and other evidence used to support the point.

Summarizing even a single paragraph can be tricky. Here is one attempt to summarize paragraphs 1–4 of Thomas Sowell's "Student Loans" (p. 95).

Draft summary — As much as politicians would like to satisfy voters by giving them everything they ask for, the government cannot afford a student-loan program.

This sentence "misreads" the four paragraphs because it asserts that the government cannot afford student loans. Sowell's point is more complicated than that. This accurate summary captures it:

Revised summary — As their support of the government's student-loan program illustrates, politicians ignore the economic reality that using resources to benefit one group (students in debt) involves taking the resources from another group (taxpayers).

Using your own words when writing a summary not only helps you understand the meaning but also constitutes the first step in avoiding plagiarism. The second step is to cite the source when you use it in something written for others. See Chapter 54.

Note Many word processors include an AutoSummarize function that can distill a paragraph or a whole document to a few sentences. Do not count on this tool for summarizing texts that you may have copied onto your computer. The summaries are rarely accurate, and you will not gain the experience of interacting with the text on your own.

EXERCISE 9.2
Summarizing

Start where the preceding summary of Thomas Sowell's essay ends (at paragraph 5) to summarize the entire essay. Your summary, in your own words, should not exceed one paragraph. (For additional exercises in summarizing, see pp. 452–53.)

4 • Form a critical response.

Once you've grasped the content of what you're reading—what the author says—then you can turn to understanding what the author does not say outright but suggests or implies or even lets slip. At this stage you are concerned with the purpose or intention of the author and with how he or she carries it out.

Critical thinking and reading consist of four overlapping operations: analyzing, interpreting, synthesizing, and (often) evaluating.

Analyzing

Analysis is the separation of something into its parts or elements, the better to understand it. To see these elements in what you are reading, begin with a question that reflects your purpose in analyzing the text: why you're curious about it or what you're trying to make out of it. This question will serve as a kind of lens that highlights some elements and not others.

Analyzing Thomas Sowell's "Student Loans" (pp. 95–96), you might ask these questions:

Questions for analysis	Elements
What is Sowell's attitude toward politicians?	References to politicians: content, words, tone
How does Sowell support his assertions about the loan program's costs?	Support: evidence, such as statistics and examples

The screen shot on the next page shows the opening page of a Web site that promises relief from student-loan debt. Analyzing this page, you might ask these questions:

Questions for analysis	Elements
What kind of organization is the Federated Loan Consolidation Corporation?	Information about the corporation: address, name, text
What are the intentions of the Federated Loan Consolidation Corporation?	Information about the corporation (as above) as well as features of the site design: type, color, art

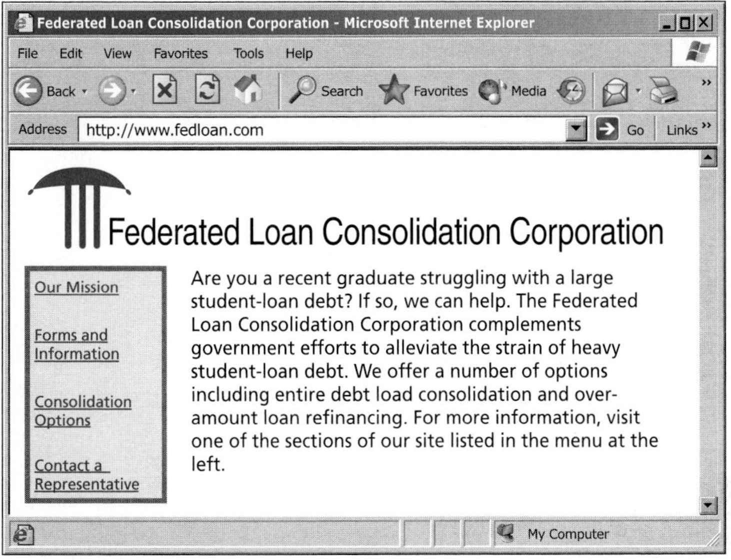

Interpreting

Identifying the elements of something is of course only the beginning: you also need to interpret the meaning or significance of the elements and of the whole. **Interpretation** usually requires you to infer the author's **assumptions**—that is, opinions or beliefs about what is or what could or should be. (*Infer* means to draw a conclusion based on evidence.)

Assumptions are pervasive: we all adhere to certain values, beliefs, and opinions. But assumptions are not always stated outright. Speakers and writers may judge that their audience already understands and accepts their assumptions; they may not even be aware of their assumptions; or they may deliberately refrain from stating their assumptions for fear that the audience will disagree. That is why your job as a critical reader is to interpret what the assumptions are.

For example, Thomas Sowell's "Student Loans" (pp. 95–96) is based on certain assumptions, some obvious, some not so obvious. If you were analyzing Sowell's attitude toward politicians, as suggested earlier, you would focus on his statements about them. Sowell says that they "disregard the first lesson of economics" (paragraph 2), which implies that they ignore important principles (knowing that Sowell is an economist himself makes this a reasonable assumption on your part). Sowell also says that politicians "rob Peter to pay Paul," are "[b]ursting with compassion," "do not admit . . . a dumb idea," are characters in a "long-running saga," and arrive at the solution of spending taxes "as the night follows the day"—that is, inevitably (paragraphs 2–4). From these statements and others, you can infer the following:

> Sowell assumes that politicians become compassionate when a cause is loud and popular, not necessarily just, and they act irresponsibly by trying to solve the problem with other people's (taxpayers') money.

To discover assumptions of the Federated Loan Consolidation Corporation (previous page), you would look at the address of the Web site, where *com* indicates that the organization is a commercial entity. (See pp. 440–41 for more on interpreting electronic addresses.) Yet you might also notice that the page does not resemble those of other corporate sites, which typically have flashier designs incorporating more images, color, and boxes, among other elements. Instead, the page's look is rather plain—the sort of design you might expect from a government site. The prominent "Federated" in the organization's name and "complements government efforts" in the text reinforce the appearance of a government connection. These findings might lead you to infer the following:

> The Federated Loan Consolidation Corporation assumes that its readers (potential customers) will be more willing to explore its refinancing options if they believe that it is a reliable organization somehow affiliated with the government.

Synthesizing

If you stopped at analysis and interpretation, critical reading might leave you with a pile of elements and possible meanings but no vision of the whole. With **synthesis** you make connections among parts *or* among wholes. You create a new whole by drawing conclusions about relationships and implications.

The statement below about Thomas Sowell's essay "Student Loans" connects his assumptions about politicians to a larger idea also implied by the essay:

> Sowell's view that politicians are irresponsible with taxpayers' money reflects his overall opinion that the laws of economics, not politics, should drive government.

The next statement draws on elements of the Federated Loan Consolidation Corporation home page and the inference above about the company's understanding of its readers:

> The Federated Loan Consolidation Corporation uses its name, a mention of the government, and a restrained design to appeal to potential customers who may be wary of commercial lending operations.

With synthesis, you create something different from what you started with. To the uncritical reader (perhaps someone burdened with student loans), the home page of the Federated Loan Consolidation Corporation might seem to offer government-backed relief from debt. To you—after analysis, interpretation, and synthesis—the official-looking page is a kind of mask worn by a commercial lender. The difference depends entirely on the critical reading.

Evaluating

Much critical reading and writing ends at synthesis: you form and explain your understanding of what the work says and doesn't say. If you are also expected to **evaluate** the work, however, you will go further to judge its quality and significance. You may be evaluating a source you've discovered in research (see pp. 437–44), or you may be completing an assignment to state and defend a judgment, a statement such as *Thomas Sowell fails to show consistent and widespread abuse of the student-loan program* or *On the home page of the Federated Loan Consolidation Corporation, a commercial lender attempts to mislead vulnerable customers by wearing the reassuring costume of government.*

Evaluation takes a certain amount of confidence. You may think that you lack the expertise to cast judgment on another's work, especially if the work is difficult or the author well known. True, the more informed you are, the better a critical reader you are. But conscientious reading and analysis will give you the internal authority to judge a work *as it stands* and *as it seems to you,* against your own unique bundle of experiences, observations, and attitudes.

EXERCISE 9.3
Reading an essay critically

Reread Thomas Sowell's "Student Loans" (pp. 95–96) in order to form your own critical response to it. Focus on any elements suggested by your questions about the text: possibilities are assumptions, evidence, organization, use of language, tone, vision of education or students. Be sure to write while reading and thinking; your notes will help your analysis and enhance your creativity, and they will be essential for writing about the selection.

EXERCISE 9.4
Reading a Web site critically

Visit the Web site of a corporation or other commercial organization, such as the manufacturer of a car, television, computer, or other product you own; the bank where you have your account; or the online store where you buy books or music. Examine the site's layout, color, images, sound, video, and interactive features as well as the content of the text. What do the elements tell you about the site's purpose—for instance, does the site aim to sell something, to give advice, to provide services? What assumptions does it make about readers? How well do the elements achieve the site's purpose?

9b View images critically.

Every day we are bombarded with images—pictures on billboards, commercials on television, graphs and charts in newspapers and textbooks, to name just a few examples. Most images slide by without our noticing them, or so we think. But images, sometimes even more than text, can influence us covertly. Their creators have purposes, some worthy, some not, and understanding those purposes requires that we think critically.

The methods of viewing images critically parallel those for reading text critically: preview, analyze, interpret, synthesize, and (often) evaluate. Here we'll apply these methods to the illustration on the next page, an advertisement for *Time* magazine that appeared in the magazine itself.

1 • Preview.

Look at the work as a whole to determine its source, its content, and its overall effect.

The advertisement for *Time*, like most ads, has two significant sources: the site where the ad appeared and the company promoting its product. In this case, the sources are the same: the magazine is advertising itself.

The ad depicts a boy being scanned by an airport security person. A superimposed *Time* cover and text in the white space link the scene to the magazine. Overall, the ad pinpoints the significant controversy over US national security in the aftermath of the terrorist attacks of September 11, 2001, using this controversy to promote the magazine.

2 • Analyze.

Study the work closely to discover the particular elements, their relative importance, and the effects of color, composition, and similar features.

In the *Time* ad the most prominent element is the photograph: the boy, the man, the scanning tool, the "Baggage Claim" sign overhead, the clutter of people and activity in the background. Type and shape form the familiar image of a *Time* cover, with the scanner centered in it like the bull's-eye on a target.

Beneath the visual elements, the ad's text guides readers' impression of the photograph and *Time* cover. Positioned on a white background, the words attract attention even though they are set in small type. They encourage readers to question what they see and to seek (or continue seeking) answers in *Time* magazine.

3 • Interpret.

Consider what the elements convey about the assumptions and intentions of the work's creator.

Time clearly assumes that readers are both emotionally and rationally concerned about national security. On the one hand, the ad appeals to readers' reason: to their interest in current news and opinion, their grasp of the need for national security, their regard for "common sense" solutions and for "conversation" as a way to reach solutions. On the other hand, the ad also appeals strongly to emotion. Treating a boy as if he were a security threat is absurd, even humorous. The boy's innocent, patient, nervous expression arouses sympathy, while the man's serious attention to his work arouses disdain. The disorderly scene behind the main figures evokes the frustration and anxiety of air travel today. Most subtly, the ad plucks feelings about so-called profiling, or singling out people as suspicious solely because of physical characteristics such as gender or hair and skin color. Many people, reluctantly or not, favor profiling over the waste and inconvenience caused by searching everyone, even small boys.

The intentions of the ad are layered: *Time* seems to want to attract readers' notice and to define itself as cutting edge, with the larger purpose of increasing its sales.

4 • Synthesize.

Consider how the work's elements relate to and reinforce one another to achieve an overall meaning or effect.

The *Time* ad represents an image of the magazine: a site of questioning and dialog, up-to-the-minute in its coverage, calm, humorous, alert to readers' concerns, aware that readers may favor profiling but not want to say so outright.

The ultimate aim of this message is complicated by its appearing in *Time:* readers are already holding the magazine they're being urged to buy. Generally, advertisements appear in places where they are likely to attract new customers. This ad seems to assume little permanence in readers: perhaps they picked up the magazine at a newsstand or doctor's office; perhaps even subscribers need selling on the magazine's virtues. The ad tells readers what they can get in *Time,* assures them that the magazine understands their attitudes, and whets their desire for the promised "conversation"—not just in this week's issue but in the issues to come with a paid subscription.

5 • Evaluate.

Judge whether the work achieves its purpose, whether the purpose is worthwhile, and how reasonable, significant, or valuable the work is.

The *Time* ad can be evaluated both as a work of persuasion and, within that category, as a work of advertising. As persuasion, advertising rarely meets high standards of reasonableness and accuracy. Its promotional purpose encourages one-sidedness and selective use of evidence, when evidence is offered. *Time* makes a central claim, that it provides dialog about difficult issues. The claim is not supported directly, although readers could seek support in the rest of the magazine. They would have to decide for themselves whether to be engaged or provoked by the ad's subtle message about profiling.

Judged solely as an advertisement, the *Time* piece fares well. Eye-catching, humorous, and concise, it entices the reader to study the photograph and nod in response to the question. The ad plants a memorable idea about the magazine that may strengthen the loyalty of current subscribers and induce occasional readers to become subscribers.

EXERCISE 9.5
Writing about the *Time* advertisement

In a paragraph, write your own evaluation of the *Time* ad on page 103. Base your evaluation on analysis, interpretation, and synthesis, as outlined on the preceding pages. What do you see in the ad? How effective is it?

EXERCISE 9.6
Viewing an image critically

Look in a magazine or book for an image that interests you. Or search the wide array of images at the Corbis photograph collection (*http://corbis.com*) or the *WebMuseum* (*http://www.ibiblio.org/wm*). Using the approach given on the preceding pages, "read" the image methodically and critically, writing down your responses. (A writing suggestion based on this exercise appears on p. 108.)

9c Write critically.

Critical writing builds on the skills of critical reading. It involves shaping your analysis, interpretation, synthesis, and perhaps evaluation of the work into an essay that states and supports an idea (or thesis) about the work. Critical writing is *not* summarizing, or merely reporting what the author says. You may write a summary to clarify the author's meaning for yourself (p. 97), and you may briefly summarize a work in your own larger piece of writing. But in writing critically you must go further.

In the following essay, Charlene Robinson, a student, writes critically about Thomas Sowell's "Student Loans," one of the essays she read in a composition class. She received the following assignment:

> Form your own critical response to one of the readings assigned so far this term. Then write your response into a well-structured critique of the reading. Feel free to agree or disagree with the author, but do not assume that your readers see the same things in the reading or share your views; be sure to offer evidence of the author's ideas in the form of direct quotations, summaries, and paraphrases. Document any borrowings from the author using the style of the Modern Language Association (MLA). The length should be 500–700 words.

In responding to Sowell's essay, Robinson used a process of critical reading like the one outlined in this chapter, making notes not only on what Sowell says but also on her own questions and ideas. She then focused and organized her ideas, developing her own thesis about Sowell's text, and drafted and revised until she believed she had supported her thesis. She quotes from Sowell's text, documenting borrowed material in MLA style: the numbers in parentheses are page numbers in the book containing Sowell's essay, listed at the end as a work cited. (See Chapter 56 for more on MLA style.)

Weighing the Costs

In his essay "Student Loans," the economist Thomas Sowell challenges the US government's student-loan program for several reasons: a scarce resource (taxpayers' money) goes to many undeserving students, a high number of recipients fail to repay their loans, and the easy availability of money has led to both lower academic standards and higher college tuitions. Sowell wants his readers to "weigh the costs of things" (133) in order to see, as he does, that the loan program should not receive so much government funding. But does he provide the evidence of cost and other problems to lead the reader to agree with him? The answer is no, because hard evidence is less common than debatable and unsupported assumptions about students, scarcity, and the value of education.

Introduction:
1. Summary of Sowell's essay
2. Robinson's critical question
3. Thesis statement

Sowell's portrait of student-loan recipients is questionable. It is based on averages, some statistical and some not, but averages are often deceptive. For example, Sowell cites college graduates' low average debt of $7000 to $9000 (131) without acknowledging the fact that many students' debts are much higher or giving the full range of statistics. Similarly, Sowell dismisses "heart-rending

First main point
Evidence for the first point:
1. Paraphrases and quotations from Sowell's text (with source citations in MLA style)

stories" of "the low-income student with a huge debt" as "not at all typical" (132), yet he invents his own exaggerated version of the typical loan recipient: an affluent slacker ("Rockefellers" and "Vanderbilts") for whom college is a "place to hang out for a few years" sponging off the government, while his or her parents clear a profit from making use of the loan program (132). While such students (and parents) may well exist, are they really typical? Sowell does not offer any data one way or the other—for instance, how many loan recipients come from each income group, what percentage of loan funds go to each group, how many loan recipients receive significant help from their parents, and how many receive none.

2. Sowell's omissions

Another set of assumptions in the essay has to do with "scarcity": "There is never enough of anything to fully satisfy all those who want it," Sowell says (131). This statement appeals to readers' common sense, but does the "lesson" of scarcity necessarily apply to the student-loan program? Sowell omits many important figures needed to prove that the nation's resources are too scarce to support the program, such as the total cost of the program, its percentage of the total education budget and the total federal budget, and its cost compared to the cost of defense, Medicare, and other expensive programs. Moreover, Sowell does not mention the interest paid by loan recipients, even though the interest must offset some of the costs of running the program and covering unpaid loans.

Transition to second main point

Second point

Evidence for second point: Sowell's omissions

The most fundamental and most debatable assumption underlying Sowell's essay is that higher education is a kind of commodity that not everyone is entitled to. In order to diminish the importance of graduates' average debt from education loans, Sowell claims that a car loan will probably be higher (131). This comparison between education and an automobile implies that the two are somehow equal as products and that an affordable higher education is no more a right than a new car is. Sowell also condemns the "irresponsible" students who drop out of school and "the increasingly easy availability of college to people who are not very serious about getting an education" (132). But he overlooks the value of encouraging education, including education of those

Third main point

Evidence for third main point: paraphrases and quotations of Sowell's text (with source citations in MLA style)

who don't finish college or who aren't scholars. For many in the United States, education has a greater value than that of a mere commodity like a car. And even from an economic perspective such as Sowell's, the cost to society of an uneducated public needs to be taken into account.

Sowell writes with conviction, and his concerns are valid: high taxes, waste, unfairness, declining educational standards, obtrusive government. However, the essay's flaws make it unlikely that Sowell could convince readers who do not already agree with him. He does not support his portrait of the typical loan recipient, he fails to demonstrate a lack of resources for the loan program, and he neglects the special nature of education compared to other services and products. Sowell may have the evidence to back up his assumptions, but by omitting it he himself does not truly weigh the costs of the loan program.

Conclusion:
1. Acknowledgment of Sowell's concerns
2. Summary of three main points
3. Return to theme of introduction: weighing costs

Work Cited

Sowell, Thomas. "Student Loans." Is Reality Optional? and Other Essays. Stanford: Hoover, 1993. 131–33.

Reference to complete source for Sowell's essay (in MLA style)

—CHARLENE ROBINSON

EXERCISE 9.7
Writing critically about an essay

Write an essay based on your own critical reading of Thomas Sowell's essay (Exercise 9.3, p. 101). Your critique may be entirely different from Charlene Robinson's, or you may have developed some of the same points. If there are similarities, they should be expressed and supported in your own way, in the context of your own approach.

EXERCISE 9.8
Writing critically about an image

Write an essay based on your critical response to an image (Exercise 9.6, p. 105). Be sure to use specific descriptions of the image to support your ideas about it.

10 Writing Arguments

How do I make a case for an idea?

Making a case for an idea involves opening readers' minds to your opinion, changing readers' own opinions, or moving readers to action. The method is called **argument:** forming and stating an opinion about a debatable issue, gathering and providing support for your idea, organizing logically, expressing yourself reasonably, and acknowledging views different from your own.

10a Use the elements of argument.

In one common view, an argument has four main elements: a subject, claims, evidence, and assumptions. (The last three are adapted from the work of the British philosopher Stephen Toulmin.)

1 • Start with a subject.

An argument starts with a subject and often with an idea about the subject as well—that is, a view that makes you want to write about the subject. For instance, you might think that your school should do more for energy conservation or that the school's chemistry laboratory is a disgrace. (If you don't have a subject or you aren't sure what you think about it, try some of the invention techniques discussed on pages 10–17.)

Your subject should meet several requirements:

- It can be disputed: reasonable people can disagree over it.
- It *will* be disputed: it is controversial.
- It is something you care about and know about or want to research.
- It is narrow enough to argue in the space and time available.

http://www.ablongman.com/littlebrown

➤ Writing in and out of school
  ➤ Video tutorials
    ➤ Finding subjects for argument
    ➤ Answering opposing views
  ➤ Web exercises ➤ Exers. 2–4
  ➤ Downloads ➤ Exer. 10.5 (p. 119) in electronic format
  ➤ Web links
    ➤ Reading arguments
    ➤ Writing arguments

On the flip side of these requirements, some subjects will not work as the starting place of argument because they concern indisputable facts, such as the functions of the human liver; personal preferences or beliefs, such as a moral commitment to vegetarianism; or ideas that few would disagree with, such as the virtues of a secure home.

EXERCISE 10.1
Testing argument subjects

Analyze each subject below to determine whether it is appropriate for argument. Explain your reasoning in each case.

1. Granting of athletic scholarships
2. Care of automobile tires
3. Censoring the Web sites of hate groups
4. History of the town park
5. Housing for the homeless
6. Billboards in urban residential areas or in rural areas
7. Animal testing for cosmetics research
8. Cats versus dogs as pets
9. Ten steps in recycling wastepaper
10. Benefits of being a parent

2 • Formulate claims.

Claims are statements that require support. In an argument you develop your subject into a central claim or **thesis,** asserted outright as the **thesis statement** (p. 18). This central claim is what the argument is about.

A thesis statement is always an **opinion**—that is, a judgment based on facts and arguable on the basis of facts. It may claim something about past or present reality:

> The college's chemistry laboratory is outdated.
> Academic cheating increases with the rate of unemployment.

The thesis statement may make a claim of value:

> The new room fees are unjustified given the condition of the dormitories.
>
> Computer music pirates undermine the system that encourages the very creation of music.

The thesis statement may recommend a course of action, often a solution to a perceived problem:

> The college's outdated chemistry laboratory should be replaced incrementally over the next five years.
>
> Schools and businesses can help to resolve the region's traffic congestion by implementing car pools and rewarding participants.

The backbone of an argument consists of specific claims that support the thesis statement. These may be statements of opinion, too, or they may fall in two other categories:

- Statements of **fact,** including facts that are generally known or are verifiable (such as the cost of tuition at your school) and those that require inference from verifiable facts (such as the monetary value of a college education).
- Statements of **belief,** or convictions based on personal faith or values, such as *The primary goal of government should be to provide equality of opportunity for all.* Although seemingly arguable, a statement of belief is not based on facts and so cannot be contested on the basis of facts.

EXERCISE 10.2
Conceiving a thesis statement

Narrow each arguable subject in Exercise 10.1 to a specific opinion, and draft a tentative thesis statement for each. Or choose five arguable subjects and opinions of your own, and draft a thesis statement for each one. One thesis statement should interest you enough to develop it into a complete argument in later exercises.

3 • Support claims with evidence.

You show the validity of your claims by supporting them with **evidence.** The evidence to support the claim opposite about the outdated chemistry lab might include the present lab's age, an inventory of facilities and equipment, and the testimony of chemistry professors.

There are several kinds of evidence:

- **Facts** whose truth can be verified: *Poland is slightly smaller than New Mexico.*
- **Statistics,** facts expressed as numbers: *Of those polled, 62 percent prefer a flat tax.*
- **Examples,** specific instances of the point being made: *Many groups, such as the elderly and the disabled, would benefit from this policy.*
- **Expert opinions,** the judgments formed by authorities on the basis of their own examination of the facts: *Affirmative action is necessary to right past injustices, a point argued by Howard Glickstein, a past director of the US Commission on Civil Rights.*
- **Appeals** to readers' beliefs or needs, statements that ask readers to accept a claim in part because it states something they already accept as true without evidence: *The shabby, antiquated*

chemistry lab shames the school, making it seem a second-rate institution.

Evidence must be reliable to be convincing. Ask these questions about your evidence:

- *Is it accurate*—trustworthy, exact, and undistorted?
- *Is it relevant*—authoritative, pertinent, and current?
- *Is it representative*—true to its context, neither under- nor over-representing any element of the sample it's drawn from?
- *Is it adequate*—plentiful and specific?

EXERCISE 10.3
Using evidence

Gather and develop evidence for the thesis statement you chose to develop in Exercise 10.2. You may want to begin drafting your argument at this point, testing your evidence as you support your claim.

4 • Be aware of assumptions.

An **assumption** is an opinion, a principle, or a belief that ties evidence to claims: the assumption explains why a particular piece of evidence is relevant to a particular claim. For instance:

Claim: The college's chemistry laboratory is outdated.
Evidence (in part): The testimony of chemistry professors.
Assumption: Chemistry professors are the most capable of evaluating the present lab's quality.

Assumptions are not flaws in arguments but necessities: we all acquire beliefs and opinions that shape our views of the world. Just as interpreting a work's assumptions is a significant part of critical reading (see pp. 99–100), so discovering your own assumptions is a significant part of argumentative critical writing. If your readers do not share your assumptions or if they perceive that you are not forthright about your biases, they will be less receptive to your argument. (See the following discussion of reasonableness.)

CULTURE LANGUAGE The ways of conceiving and writing arguments described here may be initially uncomfortable to you if your native culture approaches such writing differently. In some cultures, for example, a writer is expected to begin indirectly, to avoid asserting his or her opinion outright, to rely for evidence on appeals to tradition, or to establish a compromise rather than argue a position. In American academic and business settings, writers aim for a well-articulated opinion, evidence gathered from many sources, and a direct and concise argument for the opinion.

10b Write reasonably.

To establish common ground between you and your readers, your argument must be reasonable. Readers expect logical thinking, appropriate appeals, fairness toward the opposition, and, combining all of these, writing that is free of fallacies.

1 • Use logic in your thinking.

The thesis of your argument is a conclusion you reach by reasoning about evidence. Two processes of reasoning, induction and deduction, are familiar to you even if you aren't familiar with their names.

Induction

When you're about to buy a used car, you consult friends, relatives, and consumer guides before deciding what kind of car to buy. Using **induction,** or **inductive reasoning,** you make specific observations about cars (your evidence) and you induce, or infer, a **generalization** that Car X is most reliable. The generalization is a claim supported by your observations.

You might also use inductive reasoning in a term paper on print advertising:

Evidence: Advertisements in newspapers and magazines.
Evidence: Comments by advertisers and publishers.
Evidence: Data on the effectiveness of advertising.
Generalization or claim: Print is the most cost-effective medium for advertising.

This reasoning builds from the evidence to the claim, with the assumptions connecting evidence to claim:

Evidence

Data and opinions on advertising media.

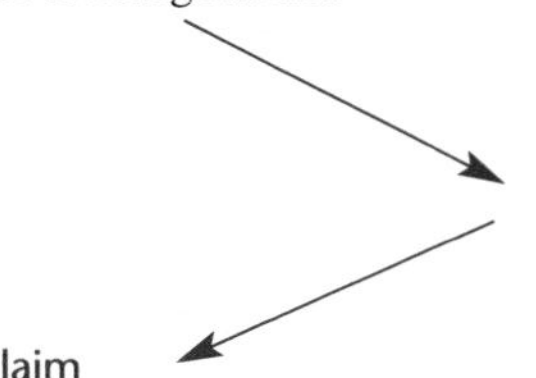

Assumption

What is true in one set of circumstances (one set of print ads) is true in a similar set of circumstances (other print ads).

Claim

Generalization: Print is the most cost-effective advertising medium.

Reasoning inductively, you connect your evidence to your generalization by assuming that what is true in one set of circumstances (the ads you look at) is true in a similar set of circumstances (other ads). With induction you create new knowledge from what is already known.

The more evidence you accumulate, the more probable it is that your generalization is true. Note, however, that absolute certainty is not possible. At some point you must *assume* that your evidence justifies your generalization, for yourself and your readers. Most errors in inductive reasoning involve oversimplifying either the evidence or the generalization. See pages 117–19 on fallacies.

Deduction

You use **deduction,** or **deductive reasoning,** when you proceed from your generalization that Car X is the most reliable used car to your own specific circumstances (you want to buy a used car) to the conclusion that you should buy a Car X. In deduction your assumption is a generalization, principle, or belief that you think is true. You apply it to the evidence (new information) in order to arrive at your claim (the conclusion you draw). The following diagram corresponds to the one for induction on the previous page, picking up the example of print advertising:

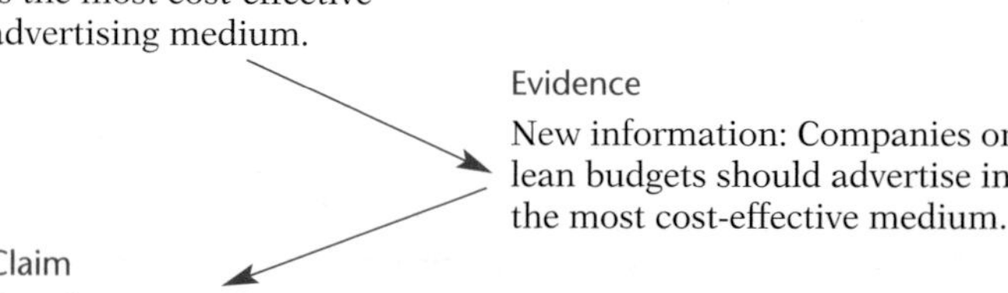

With deduction you apply what is already known to new information in order to draw a conclusion.

The conventional way of displaying a deductive argument is in a **syllogism.** If you want the school administration to postpone new room fees for one dormitory, your deductive argument might be expressed in this syllogism:

Premise: The administration should not raise fees on dorm rooms in poor condition. [A generalization or belief that you assume to be true.]
Premise: The rooms in Polk Hall are in poor condition. [New information: a specific case of the first premise.]
Conclusion: The administration should not raise fees on the rooms in Polk Hall. [Your claim.]

As long as the premises of a syllogism are true, the conclusion derives logically and certainly from them.

The force of deductive reasoning depends on the reliability of the premises and the care taken to apply them in drawing conclusions. The reasoning process is **valid** if the premises lead logically to the conclusion. It is **true** if the premises are believable. Sometimes the reasoning is true but *not* valid:

Premise: The administration should not raise fees on dorm rooms in bad condition.
Premise: Tyler Hall is a dormitory.
Conclusion: The administration should not raise fees on the rooms in Tyler Hall.

Both premises may be true, but the first does not *necessarily* apply to the second, so the conclusion is invalid. Sometimes, too, the reasoning is valid but *not* true:

Premise: All college administrations are indifferent to students' needs.
Premise: The administration of Central State is a college administration.
Premise: The administration of Central State is indifferent to students' needs.

This syllogism is valid but useless: the first premise is an untrue assumption, so the entire argument is untrue. Invalid and untrue syllogisms underlie many of the fallacies discussed on pages 117–19.

A particular hazard of deductive reasoning is the **unstated premise:** the basic assumption linking evidence and conclusion is not stated but implied. Here the unstated premise is believable and the argument is reasonable:

> Ms. Stein has worked with drug addicts for fifteen years, so she knows a great deal about their problems. [Unstated premise: Anyone who has worked fifteen years with drug addicts knows about their problems.]

But when the unstated premise is wrong or unfounded, the argument is false. For example:

> Since Jane Lightbow is a senator, she must receive money illegally from lobbyists. [Unstated premise: All senators receive money illegally from lobbyists.]

2 • Use appropriate appeals.

Rational and emotional appeals

In most arguments you will combine **rational appeals** to readers' capacities for logical reasoning with **emotional appeals** to readers' beliefs and feelings. In the following example, the second sentence makes a rational appeal (to the logic of financial gain), and the third sentence makes an emotional appeal (to the sense of fairness and open-mindedness).

> Advertising should show more physically challenged people. The millions of disabled Americans have considerable buying power, yet so far advertisers have made no attempt to tap that power. Further, by keeping the physically challenged out of the mainstream depicted in ads, advertisers encourage widespread prejudice against disability, prejudice that frightens and demeans those who hold it.

For an emotional appeal to be successful, it must be appropriate for the audience and the argument:

- It must not misjudge readers' actual feelings.
- It must not raise emotional issues that are irrelevant to the claims and the evidence. (See p. 118 for a discussion of specific inappropriate appeals, such as bandwagon and ad hominem.)

Ethical appeal

A third kind of approach to readers, the **ethical appeal,** is the sense you give of being a competent, fair person who is worth heeding. A rational appeal and an appropriate emotional appeal contribute to your ethical appeal, and so does your acknowledging opposing views (see opposite). An argument that is concisely written and correct in grammar, spelling, and other matters will underscore your competence. In addition, a sincere and even tone will assure readers that you are balanced and want to reason with them.

A sincere and even tone need not exclude language with emotional appeal—words such as *frightens* and *demeans* at the end of the above example about advertising. But avoid certain forms of expression that will mark you as unfair:

- Insulting words such as *idiotic* or *fascist*.
- Biased language such as *fags* or *broads* (see pp. 185–88).
- Sarcasm—for instance, using the phrase *What a brilliant idea* to indicate contempt for the idea and its originator.
- Exclamation points! They'll make you sound shrill!

3 • Acknowledge opposing views.

To write a reasonable argument, you must discover and acknowledge views that might be different from your own. Assuming your thesis is indeed arguable, then others can marshal their own evidence to support a different view or views. You need to determine what these other views are and what the support is for them. Then, in your argument, you need to take these views on, refute those you can, grant the validity of others, and demonstrate why, despite their validity, the opposing views are less compelling than your own. (See the sample essay on pp. 121–24 for examples.)

Before you draft your essay, list for yourself all the opposing views you can think of. You'll find them in your research, by talking to friends, and by critically thinking about your own ideas. You can also look for a range of views in a discussion group dealing with your subject. (The archive at *http://groups.google.com* is a place to start.)

To deal with opposing views, figure out which views you can refute (do more research if necessary), and prepare to concede those views you can't refute. It's not a mark of weakness or failure to admit that the opposition has a point or two. Indeed, by showing yourself to be honest and fair, you strengthen your ethical appeal and thus your entire argument.

EXERCISE 10.4
Reaching your readers

Continuing your argument-in-progress from Exercise 10.3 (p. 112), analyze whether your claims are rational or emotional and whether the mix is appropriate for your audience and argument. Analyze your ethical appeal, too, considering whether it can be strengthened. Then make a list of possible opposing views. Think freely at first, not stopping to censor views that seem far-fetched or irrational. When your list is complete, decide which views must be taken seriously and why, and develop a response to each.

4 • Avoid fallacies.

Fallacies—errors in argument—either evade the issue of the argument or treat the argument as if it were much simpler than it is.

Evasions

An effective argument squarely faces the central issue or question it addresses. An ineffective argument may dodge the issue in one of the following ways:

- **Begging the question:** treating an opinion that is open to question as if it were already proved or disproved.

The college library's expenses should be reduced by cutting subscriptions to useless periodicals. [Begged questions: Are some of the library's periodicals useless? Useless to whom?]

- **Non sequitur** (Latin: "It does not follow"): linking two or more ideas that are not necessarily connected.

She uses a wheelchair, so she must be unhappy. [The second clause does not follow from the first.]

- **Red herring:** introducing an irrelevant issue intended to distract readers from the relevant issues.

A campus speech code is essential to protect students, who already have enough problems coping with rising tuition. [Tuition costs and speech codes are different subjects. What protections do students need that a speech code will provide?]

- **Appeal to readers' fear or pity:** substituting emotions for reasoning.

She should not have to pay taxes, because she is an aged widow with no friends or relatives. [Appeals to people's pity. Should age and loneliness, rather than income, determine a person's tax obligation?]

- **Bandwagon:** inviting readers to accept a claim because everyone else does.

As everyone knows, marijuana use leads to heroin addiction. [What is the evidence?]

- **Ad hominem** (Latin: "to the man"): attacking the qualities of the people holding an opposing view rather than the substance of the view itself.

One of the scientists has been treated for emotional problems, so his pessimism about nuclear waste merits no attention. [Do the scientist's previous emotional problems invalidate his current views?]

Oversimplifications

In a vain attempt to create something neatly convincing, an ineffective argument may conceal or ignore complexities in one of the following ways:

- **Hasty generalization:** making a claim on the basis of inadequate evidence.

It is disturbing that several of the youths who shot up schools were users of violent video games. Obviously, these games can breed violence, and they should be banned. [A few cases do not establish the relation between the games and violent behavior. Most youths who play violent video games do not behave violently.]

- **Sweeping generalization:** making an insupportable statement. Many sweeping generalizations are **absolute statements** involving words such as *all, always, never,* and *no one* that allow no exceptions. Others are **stereotypes,** conventional and oversimplified characterizations of a group of people:

  People who live in cities are unfriendly.
  Californians are fad-crazy.
  Women are emotional.
  Men can't express their feelings.

  (See also pp. 185–88 on sexist and other biased language.)
- **Reductive fallacy:** oversimplifying (reducing) the relation between causes and effects.

  Poverty causes crime. [If so, then why do people who are not poor commit crimes? And why aren't all poor people criminals?]

- **Post hoc fallacy** (from Latin *post hoc, ergo propter hoc,* meaning "after this, therefore because of this"): assuming that because *A* preceded *B,* then *A* must have caused *B.*

  The town council erred in permitting the adult bookstore to open, for shortly afterward two women were assaulted. [It cannot be assumed without evidence that the women's assailants visited or were influenced by the bookstore.]

- **Either/or fallacy:** assuming that a complicated question has only two answers—one good and one bad, both good, or both bad.

  Either we permit mandatory drug testing in the workplace or productivity will continue to decline. [Productivity is not necessarily dependent on drug testing.]

EXERCISE 10.5
Identifying and revising fallacies

Identify at least one fallacy illustrated by each of the following sentences. Then revise the sentence to make it more reasonable. Possible answers to starred items appear at the back of the book.

*1. A successful marriage demands a maturity that no one under twenty-five possesses.
*2. Students' persistent complaints about the grading system prove that it is unfair.
*3. The United States got involved in World War II because the Japanese bombed Pearl Harbor.

*4. People watch television because they are too lazy to talk or read or because they want mindless escape from their lives.

*5. Racial tension is bound to occur when people with different backgrounds are forced to live side by side.

6. Emerging nations should not be allowed to use nuclear technology for creating energy because eventually they will use it to wage war.
7. Mountain climbing has more lasting effects than many people think: my cousin blacked out three times after he climbed Pikes Peak.
8. Failing to promote democracy throughout the Middle East will lose the region forever to American influence.
9. She admits to being an atheist, so how could she be a good philosophy teacher?
10. Teenagers are too young to be encouraged to use contraceptives.

10c Organize your argument effectively.

All arguments include the same parts:

- The **introduction** establishes the significance of the subject and provides background. The introduction generally includes the thesis statement, but the statement may come later if you think readers will have difficulty accepting it before they see at least some support. (See pp. 68–70 for more on introductions.)
- The **body** states the claims that support the thesis and, in one or more paragraphs, develops each claim with clearly relevant evidence. See below for more on organizing the body.
- The **response to opposing views** details those views and either demonstrates your argument's greater strengths or concedes the opponents' points. See below for more on organizing this response.
- The **conclusion** restates the thesis, summarizes the argument, and makes a final appeal to readers. (See pp. 70–71 for more on conclusions.)

The structure of the body and the response to opposing views depends on your subject, purpose, audience, and form of reasoning. Here are several possible arrangements:

The traditional scheme	The problem-solution scheme
Claim 1 and evidence	The problem: claims and evidence
Claim 2 and evidence	The solution: claims and evidence
Claim X and evidence	Response to opposing views
Response to opposing views	

Variations on the traditional scheme

Use a variation if you believe your readers will reject your argument without an early or intermittent response to opposing views.

Response to opposing views	Claim 1 and evidence
Claim 1 and evidence	Response to opposing views
Claim 2 and evidence	Claim 2 and evidence
Claim X and evidence	Response to opposing views
	Claim X and evidence
	Response to opposing views

EXERCISE 10.6
Organizing your argument

Continuing from Exercise 10.4 (p. 117), develop a structure for your argument. Consider especially how you will introduce it, how you will arrange your claims, where you will place your responses to opposing views, and how you will conclude.

10d A sample argument

Craig Holbrook, a student, wrote an argument in response to the following assignment:

> Select an issue that can be argued, that you care about, and that you know something about through experience, reading, Web surfing, and so on. As you plan and draft your argument, keep the following in mind:
>
> Narrow and shape your subject into a specific thesis statement.
> Gather and use evidence to support your claim.
> Be aware of assumptions you are making.
> Present your claims and evidence reasonably, attempting to establish common ground with your readers.
> Acknowledge and try to refute opposing views.
> Organize your argument paper straightforwardly and appropriately for your purpose.
>
> The paper should be 900–1200 words in length.

Holbrook's response to this assignment illustrates the principles discussed in this chapter. Note especially the structure, the relation of claims and supporting evidence, the kinds of appeals the author makes, and the ways he addresses opposing views.

TV Can Be Good for You

Television wastes time, pollutes minds, destroys brain cells, and turns some viewers into murderers. Thus runs the prevailing talk about the medium, supported by serious research as well as simple be-

Introduction:

Identification of prevailing view

lief. But television has at least one strong virtue, too, which helps to explain its endurance as a cultural force. In an era when people often have little time to speak with one another, television provides replacement voices that ease loneliness, spark healthful laughter, and even educate young children.

Disagreement with prevailing view

Thesis statement making three claims for television

Most people who have lived alone understand the curse of silence, when the only sound is the buzz of unhappiness or anxiety inside one's own head. Although people of all ages who live alone can experience intense loneliness, the elderly are especially vulnerable to solitude. For example, they may suffer increased confusion or depression when left alone for long periods but then rebound when they have steady companionship (Bondevik and Skogstad 329–30).

Background for claim 1: effects of loneliness

Evidence for effects of loneliness

A study of elderly men and women in New Zealand found that television can actually serve as a companion by assuming "the role of social contact with the wider world," reducing "feelings of isolation and loneliness because it directs viewers' attention away from themselves" ("Television Programming"). Thus television's replacement voices can provide comfort because they distract from a focus on being alone.

Evidence for effects of television on loneliness

Statement of claim 1

The absence of real voices can be most damaging when it means a lack of laughter. Here, too, research shows that television can have a positive effect on health. Laughter is one of the most powerful calming forces available to human beings, proven in many studies to reduce heart rate, lower blood pressure, and ease other stress-related ailments (Burroughs, Mahoney, and Lippman 172; Griffiths 18). Television offers plenty of laughter for all kinds of viewers: the recent listings for a single Friday night included more than twenty comedy programs running on the networks and on basic cable between 6 and 9 PM.

Background for claim 2: effects of laughter

Evidence for effects of laughter

Evidence for comedy on television

A study reported in a health magazine found that laughter inspired by television and video is as healthful as the laughter generated by live comedy. Volunteers laughing at a video comedy routine "showed significant improvements in several immune functions, such as natural killer-cell activity" (Laliberte 78). Further, the effects of the comedy were so profound that "merely anticipating watching a funny video improved mood, depression, and anger as much as two days beforehand" (Laliberte

Evidence for effects of laughter in response to television

Statement of claim 2

79). Even for people with plenty of companionship, television's replacement voices can have healthful effects by causing laughter.

Background for claim 3: educational effects

Evidence for educational programming on television

Television also provides information about the world. This service can be helpful to everyone but especially to children, whose natural curiosity can exhaust the knowledge and patience of their parents and caretakers. While the TV may be baby-sitting children, it can also enrich them. For example, educational programs such as those on the Discovery Channel, the Disney Channel, and PBS offer a steady stream of information at various cognitive levels. Even many cartoons, which are generally dismissed as mindless or worse, familiarize children with the material of literature, including strong characters enacting classic narratives.

Evidence for educational effects of television on children

Statement of claim 3

Two researchers studying children and television found that TV is a source of creative and psychological instruction, inspiring children "to play imaginatively and develop confidence and skills" (Colman and Colman 9). Instead of passively watching, children "interact with the programs and videos" and "sometimes include the fictional characters they've met into reality's play time" (Colman and Colman 8). Thus television's replacement voices both inform young viewers and encourage exchange.

Anticipation of objections

1. Harm of television

2. Need for actual interaction

Qualification of claims in response to objections

The value of these replacement voices should not be oversold. For one thing, almost all observers agree that too much TV does no one any good and may cause considerable harm. Many studies show that excessive TV watching leads to increased violent behavior, especially in children, and can cause, rather than ease, other antisocial behaviors and depression (Reeks 114; Walsh 34). In addition, human beings require the give and take of actual interaction. Steven Pinker, an expert in children's language acquisition, warns that children cannot develop language properly by watching television. They need to interact with actual speakers who respond directly to their specific needs (282). Replacement voices are not real voices and in the end can do only limited good.

Conclusion

But even limited good is something, especially for those who are lonely, angry, or neglected. Television is not an entirely positive force, but neither is it an entirely negative one. Its voices stand by to provide company, laughter, and information whenever they're needed.

Works Cited

Bondevik, Margareth, and Anders Skogstad. "The Oldest Old, ADL, Social Network, and Loneliness." Western Journal of Nursing Research 20.3 (1998): 325–43.

Burroughs, W. Jeffrey, Diana L. Mahoney, and Louis G. Lippman. "Perceived Attributes of Health-Promoting Laughter: Cross-Generational Comparison." Journal of Psychology 136.2 (2002): 171–81.

Colman, Robyn, and Adrian Colman. "Inspirational Television." Youth Studies in Australia 21.3 (2002): 8–10.

Griffiths, Joan. "The Mirthful Brain." Omni Aug. 1996: 18–19.

Laliberte, Richard W. "The Benefits of Laughter." Shape Sept. 2002: 78–79.

Pinker, Steven. The Language Instinct: How the Mind Creates Language. New York: Harper, 1994.

Reeks, Anne. "Kids and TV: A Guide." Parenting Apr. 2002: 110–15.

"Television Programming for Older People, the Perspective of the Older Community: Summary Research Report." NZ on Air. 25 July 2001. 15 Oct. 2002 <http://www.nzonair.gov.nz/media/policyandresearch/oldpeoplesreport.pdf>.

Walsh, Teri. "Too Much TV Linked to Depression." Prevention Feb. 1999: 34–36.

—Craig Holbrook (student)

11 Reading and Writing About Literature

By Sylvan Barnet

What's involved in analyzing a story, poem, or other literary work?

Writers of literature—stories, novels, poems, and plays—are concerned with presenting human experience concretely, with giving a sense of the feel of life rather than telling about it. Reading and writing about literature thus require extremely close attention to the feel of the words. For instance, the word *woods* in Robert Frost's "Stopping by Woods on a Snowy Evening" has a rural, folksy quality that *forest* doesn't have, and many such small distinctions contribute to the poem's effect.

When you read literature, you interpret distinctions like these, forming an idea of the work. When you write about literature, you state your idea as your thesis, and you support the thesis with evidence from the work. (See pp. 18–21 for more on thesis statements.)

Note Writing about literature is not merely summarizing literature. Your thesis is a claim about the meaning or effect of the literary work, not a statement of its plot. And your paper is a demonstration of your thesis, not a retelling of the work's changes or events.

11a Write while reading literature.

You will become more engaged in reading literature if you write while you read. If you own the book you're reading, don't hesitate to underline or highlight passages that especially interest you. Don't hesitate to annotate the margins, indicating your pleasures, displeasures, and uncertainties with remarks such as *Nice detail* or *Do we need this long description?* or *Not believable.* If you don't own the book, make these notes on separate sheets or on your computer.

An effective way to interact with a text is to keep a **reading journal.** A journal is not a diary in which you record your doings; instead, it is a place to develop and store your reflections on what you read, such as an answer to a question you may have posed in the margin of the text or a response to something said in class. You may, for instance, want to reflect on why your opinion is so different from that of another student. You may even make an entry in the form of a letter to the author or from one character to another. (See p. 10 for more on journal keeping.)

11b Read literature critically.

Reading literature critically involves interacting with a text, not in order to make negative judgments but in order to understand the

http://www.ablongman.com/littlebrown
➤ Writing in and out of school
  ➤ Web links ➤ Reading and writing about literature
➤ Research writing
  ➤ Web links ➤ Sources in literature and other humanities

work and evaluate its significance or quality. Such interaction is not passive, like scanning a newspaper or watching television. Instead, it is a process of engagement, of diving into the words themselves.

1 • Meaning in literature

In analyzing any literary work, you face right off the question of *meaning.* Readers disagree all the time over the meanings of works of literature, partly because literature *shows* rather than *tells:* it gives concrete images of imagined human experiences, but it usually does not say how we ought to understand the images. Further, readers bring different experiences to their reading and thus understand images differently. In writing about literature, then, we can offer only our *interpretation* of the meaning rather than *the* meaning. Still, most people agree that there are limits to interpretation: it must be supported by evidence that a reasonable person finds at least plausible if not totally convincing.

2 • Questions for literary analysis

One reason interpretations of meaning differ is that readers approach literary works differently, focusing on certain elements and interpreting those elements distinctively. For instance, some critics look at a literary work mainly as an artifact of the particular time and culture in which it was created, while other critics stress the work's effect on its readers.

This chapter emphasizes so-called formalist criticism, which sees a literary work primarily as something to be understood in itself. This critical framework engages the reader immediately in the work of literature, without requiring extensive historical or cultural background, and it introduces the conventional elements of literature that all critical approaches discuss, even though they view the elements differently. The list below poses questions for each element that can help you think constructively and imaginatively about what you read.

- **Plot:** the relationships and patterns of events. (Even a poem has a plot—for instance, a change in mood from grief to resignation.)

  What actions happen?
  What conflicts occur?
  How do the events connect to each other and to the whole?

- **Characters:** the people the author creates (including the narrator of a story or the speaker of a poem).

Who are the principal people in the work?
How do they interact?
What do their actions, words, and thoughts reveal about their personalities and the personalities of others?
Do the characters stay the same, or do they change? Why?

- **Point of view:** the perspective or attitude of the speaker in a poem or the voice who tells a story. The point of view may be **first person** (a participant, using *I*) or **third person** (an outsider, using *he, she, it, they*). A first-person narrator may be a major or a minor character in the narrative and may be **reliable** or **unreliable** (unable to report events wholly or accurately). A third-person narrator may be **omniscient** (knows what goes on in all characters' minds), **limited** (knows what goes on in the mind of only one or two characters), or **objective** (knows only what is external to the characters).

  Who is the narrator (or the speaker of a poem)?
  How does the narrator's point of view affect the narrative?

- **Tone:** the narrator's or speaker's attitude, perceived through the words (for instance, joyful, bitter, or confident).

  What tone (or tones) do you hear? If there is a change, how do you account for it?
  Is there an ironic contrast between the narrator's tone (for instance, confidence) and what you take to be the author's attitude (for instance, pity for human overconfidence)?

- **Imagery:** word pictures or visual details involving the senses (sight, sound, touch, smell, taste).

  What images does the writer use? What senses do they draw on?
  What patterns are evident in the images (for instance, religious or commercial images)?
  What is the significance of the imagery?

- **Symbolism:** concrete things standing for larger and more abstract ideas (for instance, the American flag may symbolize freedom, or a dead flower may symbolize mortality).

  What symbols does the author use? What do they seem to signify?
  How does the symbolism relate to the theme of the work?

- **Setting:** the place where the action happens.

  What does the locale contribute to the work?
  Are scene shifts significant?

- **Form:** the shape or structure of the work.

  What *is* the form? (For example, a story might divide sharply in the middle, moving from happiness to sorrow.)
  What parts of the work does the form emphasize, and why?

- **Theme:** the central idea, a conception of human experience suggested by the work as a whole. Theme is neither plot (what happens) nor subject (such as youth or marriage). Rather it is what the author says with that plot about that subject.

  Can you state the theme in a sentence? For instance, you might state the following about Kate Chopin's "The Story of an Hour" (opposite): *Happiness depends partly on freedom.*
  Do certain words, passages of dialog or description, or situations seem to represent the theme most clearly?
  How do the work's elements combine to develop the theme?

- **Appeal:** the degree to which the work pleases you.

  What do you especially like or dislike about the work? Why?
  Do you think your responses are unique, or would they be common to most readers? Why?

11c Two literary works and sample papers

The following pages reprint two works of literature (a short story and a poem), each followed by a student paper on the work. In each student paper the author develops a thesis about the work, supporting this main idea with quotations, paraphrases, and summaries from the work being discussed, a primary source. In the second paper (p. 133), the author also draws sparingly on secondary sources (other critics' views), which further support his own views.

Key terms

quotation An exact repetition of an author's words, placed in quotation marks. (See also pp. 369–71, 451–52.)

paraphrase A restatement of an author's words, closely following the author's line of thought but using different words and sentence structures. (See also pp. 450–51.)

summary A condensation of an extended passage into a sentence or more. (See also pp. 97, 449.)

primary source A firsthand account: for instance, a historical document, a work of literature, or your own observations. (See also p. 411.)

secondary source A report on or analysis of other sources, often primary ones: for instance, a historian's account of a battle or a critic's view of a poem. (See also p. 411.)

Note the following features of the students' papers:

- *The writers do not merely summarize the literary works they write about.* Occasionally, they briefly summarize to make their meaning clear, but their essays consist mostly of their own analysis.
- *Each writer uses many quotations from the literary work.* The quotations provide evidence for the writer's ideas and let readers hear the voice of the work.
- *Both writers integrate quotations smoothly into their own sentences* (see pp. 453–58).
- *The writers use the present tense of verbs.* (*Chopin shows; Mrs. Mallard dies*) to describe both the author's work and the action in the work.

For the format of a literature paper, consult several other sections of this handbook:

- *Use MLA document format* for treatment of margins, quotations, and other elements (pp. 507–09).
- *Cite sources in MLA style:* parenthetical text citations and a list of works cited (pp. 471–506).
- *Indicate any editing of quotations.* Use ellipsis marks (. . .) to indicate deletions from quotations (pp. 377–79). Use brackets to indicate additions to or changes in quotations (pp. 379–80).

1 • A short story and an essay about it

Short story

Kate Chopin

The Story of an Hour

Knowing that Mrs. Mallard was afflicted with a heart trouble, great care was taken to break to her as gently as possible the news of her husband's death.

It was her sister Josephine who told her, in broken sentences, veiled hints that revealed in half concealing. Her husband's friend Richards was there, too, near her. It was he who had been in the newspaper office when intelligence of the railroad disaster was received, with Brently Mallard's name leading the list of "killed." He had only taken the time to assure himself of its truth by a second telegram, and had hastened to forestall any less careful, less tender friend in bearing the sad message.

She did not hear the story as many women have heard the same, with a paralyzed inability to accept its significance. She wept at once with sudden, wild abandonment, in her sister's arms. When the storm of grief had spent itself she went away to her room alone. She would have no one follow her.

There stood, facing the open window, a comfortable, roomy armchair. Into this she sank, pressed down by a physical exhaustion that haunted her body and seemed to reach into her soul.

She could see in the open square before her house the tops of trees that were all aquiver with the new spring life. The delicious breath of rain was in the air. In the street below a peddler was crying his wares. The notes of a distant song which some one was singing reached her faintly, and countless sparrows were twittering in the eaves.

There were patches of blue sky showing here and there through the clouds that had met and piled one above the other in the west facing her window.

She sat with her head thrown back upon the cushion of the chair quite motionless, except when a sob came up into her throat and shook her, as a child who has cried itself to sleep continues to sob in its dreams.

She was young, with a fair, calm face, whose lines bespoke repression and even a certain strength. But now there was a dull stare in her eyes, whose gaze was fixed away off yonder on one of those patches of blue sky. It was not a glance of reflection, but rather indicated a suspension of intelligent thought.

There was something coming to her and she was waiting for it, fearfully. What was it? She did not know; it was too subtle and elusive to name. But she felt it creeping out of the sky, reaching toward her through the sounds, the scents, the color that filled the air.

Now her bosom rose and fell tumultuously. She was beginning to recognize this thing that was approaching to possess her, and she was striving to beat it back with her will—as powerless as her two white slender hands would have been.

When she abandoned herself a little whispered word escaped her slightly parted lips. She said it over and over under her breath: "Free, free, free!" The vacant stare and the look of terror that had followed it went from her eyes. They stayed keen and bright. Her pulses beat fast, and the coursing blood warmed and relaxed every inch of her body.

She did not stop to ask if it were not a monstrous joy that held her. A clear and exalted perception enabled her to dismiss the suggestion as trivial.

She knew that she would weep again when she saw the kind, tender hands folded in death; the face that had never looked save with love upon her, fixed and gray and dead. But she saw beyond that bitter moment a long procession of years to come that would belong to her absolutely. And she opened and spread her arms out to them in welcome.

There would be no one to live for her during those coming years; she would live for herself. There would be no powerful will bending her in the blind persistence with which men and women believe they have a right to impose a private will upon a fellow creature. A kind intention or a cruel intention made the act seem no less a crime as she looked upon it in that brief moment of illumination.

And yet she had loved him—sometimes. Often she had not. What did it matter! What could love, the unsolved mystery, count for in face of this possession of self-assertion which she suddenly recognized as the strongest impulse of her being.

"Free! Body and soul free!" she kept whispering.

Josephine was kneeling before the closed door with her lips to the keyhole, imploring for admission. "Louise, open the door! I beg; open the door—you will make yourself ill. What are you doing, Louise? For heaven's sake open the door."

"Go away. I am not making myself [illegible] drinking in the very elixir of life [illegible]

Her [illegible] ad of her. Sp[illegible] would be her[illegible] ng. It was onl[illegible] might be long[illegible]

[illegible] door to her sister's importuni[illegible] ish triumph in her eyes, and she carried herse[illegible] wittingly like a goddess of Victory. She clasped her sister's waist and together they descended the stairs. Richards stood waiting for them at the bottom.

Some one was opening the front door with a latchkey. It was Brently Mallard who entered, a little travel-stained, composedly carrying his grip-sack and umbrella. He had been far from the scene of accident, and did not even know there had been one. He stood amazed at Josephine's piercing cry; at Richards' quick motion to screen him from the view of his wife.

But Richards was too late.

When the doctors came they said she had died of heart disease—of joy that kills.

An essay on fiction (no secondary sources)

Note The parenthetical citations in the following essay refer to page numbers in the source cited at the end of the essay.

Ironies of Life in Kate Chopin's "The Story of an Hour"

Kate Chopin's "The Story of an Hour"—which takes only a few minutes to read—has an ironic ending: Mrs. Mallard dies just when she is beginning to live. On first reading, the ending seems almost too ironic for belief. On rereading the story, however, one sees that the ending is believable partly because it is consistent with other ironies in the story.

After we know how the story turns out, if we reread it we find irony at the very start. Because Mrs. Mallard's friends and her sister assume, mistakenly, that she was deeply in love with her husband, Brently Mallard, they take great care to tell her gently of his death. They mean well, and in fact they do well, bringing her an hour of life, an hour of joyous freedom, but it is ironic that they think their news is sad. True, Mrs. Mallard at first expresses grief when she hears the news, but soon (unknown to her friends) she finds joy in it. So Richards's "sad message" (23), though sad in Richards's eyes, is in fact a happy message.

Among the small but significant ironic details is the statement near the end of the story that when Mallard entered the house, Richards tried to conceal him from Mrs. Mallard, but "Richards was too late" (24). Almost at the start of the story, in the second paragraph, Richards "hastened" (23) to bring his sad news. But if Richards had arrived "too late" at the start, Brently Mallard would have arrived at home first, and Mrs. Mallard's life would not have ended an hour later but would simply have gone on as it had been. Yet another irony at the end of the story is the diagnosis of the doctors. They say she died of "heart disease—of joy that kills" (24). In one sense they are right: Mrs. Mallard has for the last hour experienced a great joy. But of course the doctors totally misunderstand the joy that kills her. It is not joy at seeing her husband alive, but her realization that the great joy she experienced during the last hour is over.

All of these ironic details add richness to the story, but the central irony resides not in the well-intentioned but ironic actions of Richards, or in the unconsciously ironic words of the doctors, but in Mrs. Mallard's own life. She "sometimes" (24) loved her husband, but in a way she has been dead, a body subjected to her husband's will. Now, his apparent death brings her new life. Appropriately, this new life comes to her at the season of the year when "the tops of trees . . . were all aquiver with the new spring life" (24). But, ironically, her new life will last only an hour. She is "Free, free, free" (24), but only until her husband walks through the doorway. She looks forward to "summer days" (24), but she will not see even the end of this spring day. If her years of marriage were ironic, bringing her a sort of living death instead of joy, her new life is ironic too, not only because it grows out of her moment of grief for her supposedly dead husband, but also because her vision of "a long procession of years" (24) is cut short within an hour on a spring day.

Work Cited

Chopin, Kate. "The Story of an Hour." An Introduction to Literature. Ed. Sylvan Barnet, William Burto, and William E. Cain. 13th ed. New York: Longman, 2004. 23–24.

—Janet Vong (student)

2 • A poem and an essay about it

Poem

Gwendolyn Brooks

The Bean Eaters

They eat beans mostly, this old yellow pair.
Dinner is a casual affair.
Plain chipware on a plain and creaking wood,
Tin flatware.

Two who are Mostly Good.
Two who have lived their day,
But keep on putting on their clothes
And putting things away.

And remembering . . .
Remembering, with twinklings and twinges,
As they lean over the beans in their rented back room that
    is full of beads and receipts and dolls and cloths,
    tobacco crumbs, vases and fringes.

An essay on poetry (with secondary sources)

Note The parenthetical citations in this essay refer either to lines of Brooks's poem or to pages in the secondary sources cited at the end of the essay. We know which is which from the context and from the word *line* in the first citation in the second paragraph.

Marking Time Versus Enduring in Gwendolyn Brooks's "The Bean Eaters"

Gwendolyn Brooks's poem "The Bean Eaters" runs only eleven lines. It is written in plain language about very plain people. Yet its meaning is ambiguous. One critic, George E. Kent, says the old couple who eat beans "have had their day and exist now as time-markers" (141). However, another reader, D. H. Melhem, perceives not so much time marking as "endurance" in the old couple (123). Is this poem a despairing picture of old age or a more positive portrait?

"The Bean Eaters" describes an "old yellow pair" who "eat beans mostly" (line 1) off "Plain chipware" (3) with "Tin flatware" (4) in "their rented back room" (11). Clearly, they are poor. Their existence is accompanied not by friends or relatives—children or grandchildren are not mentioned—but by memories and a few possessions (9–11). They are "Mostly Good" (5), words Brooks capitalizes at the end of a line, perhaps to stress the old people's adherence to traditional values as well as their lack of saintliness. They are unexceptional, whatever message they have for readers.

The isolated routine of the couple's life is something Brooks draws attention to with a separate stanza:

> Two who are Mostly Good.
> Two who have lived their day,
> But keep on putting on their clothes
> And putting things away. (5–8)

Brooks emphasizes how isolated the couple is by repeating "Two who." Then she emphasizes how routine their life is by repeating "putting."

A pessimistic reading of this poem seems justified. The critic Harry B. Shaw reads the lines just quoted as perhaps despairing: "they are putting things away as if winding down an operation and readying for withdrawal from activity" (80). However, Shaw observes, the word *But* also indicates that the couple resist slipping away, that they intend to hold on (80). This dual meaning is at the heart of Brooks's poem: the old people live a meager existence, yes, but their will, their self-control, and their connection with another person—their essential humanity—are unharmed.

The truly positive nature of the poem is revealed in the last stanza. In Brooks's words, the old couple remember with some "twinges" perhaps, but also with "twinklings" (10), a cheerful image. As Melhem says, these people are "strong in mutual affection and shared memories" (123). And the final line, which is much longer than all the rest and which catalogs the evidence of the couple's long life together, is almost musically affirmative: "As they lean over the beans in their rented back room that is full of beads and receipts and dolls and cloths, tobacco crumbs, vases and fringes" (11).

What these people have is not much, but it is something.

Works Cited

Brooks, Gwendolyn. "The Bean Eaters." Literature: An Introduction to Fiction, Poetry, and Drama. Ed. X. J. Kennedy and Dana Gioia. 8th ed. New York: Longman, 2002. 823.

Kent, George E. A Life of Gwendolyn Brooks. Lexington: UP of Kentucky, 1990.

Melhem, D. H. Gwendolyn Brooks: Poetry and the Heroic Voice. Lexington: UP of Kentucky, 1987.

Shaw, Harry B. Gwendolyn Brooks. Twayne's United States Authors Ser. 395. Boston: Twayne, 1980.

—Kenneth Scheff (student)

12 Writing Online

How can I communicate effectively through e-mail and Web compositions?

The main forms of online writing, electronic mail and Web compositions, dramatically expand your options as a writer, but they also present distinctive challenges. Some are technical, such as sending attachments with e-mail or mastering the software for creating Web pages. Others are more conceptual, such as taking advantage of e-mail's informality or the Web's unique organization. At the same time, online communication also requires just what traditional writing does: attention to subject, audience, purpose, and other elements of the writing situation.

12a Write effective electronic mail.

You may be using e-mail every day to converse quickly and casually with friends and family. In college you'll also use e-mail for a host of academic reasons, from collaborating with classmates to conducting research, and you'll want to communicate both purposefully and efficiently. This section covers composing and responding to messages and observing Internet etiquette. For more on using e-mail as a research tool, see pages 433–34.

Note The e-mail program at your school may differ from the one used for the screen shots here. If you aren't sure how to use your school's e-mail, ask one of the school's technology advisers.

1 • Composing messages

To use e-mail productively for writing, pause to weigh each element of the message, as illustrated in the screen shot on the next page and the explanations following it.

http://www.ablongman.com/littlebrown

- ➤ Writing in and out of school
  - ➤ Video tutorials
    - ➤ Using e-mail
    - ➤ Balancing Web design and content
  - ➤ Web links
    - ➤ E-mail
    - ➤ Web composition
    - ➤ HTML editors

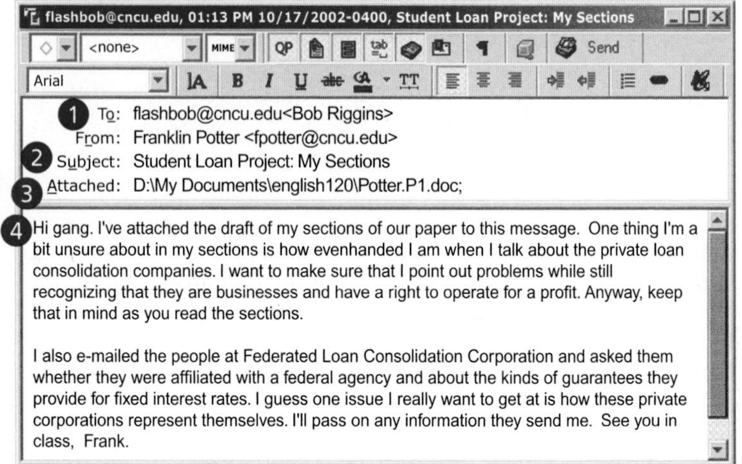

1. *Think about the readers listed in the To or Recipient field.* Consider whether you're addressing an individual or a group, what the audience knows or needs to know about your subject and purpose, and what tone is appropriate for addressing this audience. (See p. 8 for a list of questions to ask about audience.)
2. *Describe the content of your message in the Subject heading.* Then your audience will know what to expect and what priority to assign the message.
3. *Use attachments to share your work and to respond to the writing of others.* In the screen shot, the writer is sending a draft to his classmates for feedback. Be aware that attachments are not always readable: different word processors (such as *WordPerfect* and *Microsoft Word*) use different, often incompatible, file formats; and documents sent over the Internet are sometimes encoded in special formats (such as MIME) that may need to be decoded at the recipient's end. Consult a technology adviser at your school if you have trouble with attachments.
4. *Pitch the content and tone of your message to your audience.* In the message shown in the screen shot, the writer knows the recipients well and yet has serious information to convey to them, so he writes informally but states his points and concerns carefully. Writing to the corporation mentioned in the message, the writer would be more formal in both tone and approach. Although e-mail is typically more casual than printed correspondence, in academic settings a crafted message is more likely to

achieve the intended purpose. Use short paragraphs with blank lines between them. For long messages—which recipients can review only one screen at a time—provide a tight structure, an introduction that forecasts the content, and a clear division into parts (using headings if necessary). Proofread all but the most informal messages for errors in grammar, punctuation, and spelling.

Note Some e-mail programs don't allow underlining, italics, and boldface. Even if you can use such highlighting, you should assume that your recipients will not be able to see it in your messages. For alternatives, use underscores to indicate _underlining_ or asterisks to provide *emphasis*.

2 • Responding to messages

When you respond to a message, rely on the strategies discussed opposite and heed some special concerns.

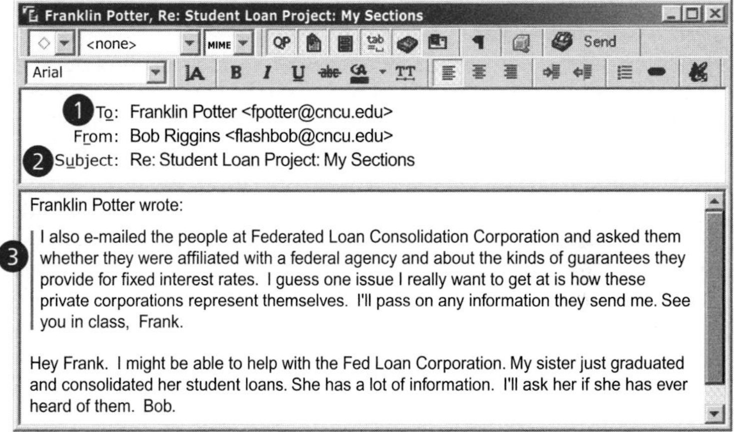

1. *Check that the response addresses the appropriate person or people.* Using the Reply or Respond function can be tricky because some programs address only the original sender while others address all recipients of the original message.
2. *Check that the reply has an appropriate subject heading.* Most e-mail programs label a response with the same subject heading as the original, preceded by *Re:* (from Latin, meaning "In reference to"). If your response indeed continues the same subject,

then *Re:* indicates as much. However, if you raise a new issue, you should rewrite the subject heading to say so.

3. *Use quoted material from earlier messages critically.* Most e-mail programs can copy the original message into your response, setting off the quoted material with a vertical line (as in the screen shot) or some other device. By weaving your replies into the quoted material, you can respond to the author point by point, as you would in conversation. However, delete from the original anything you are not responding to so that your recipient can focus on what you have to say without wading through his or her own words.

3 • Observing netiquette

To communicate effectively online, you'll need to abide by some rules of behavior and simple courtesies. You won't always see others observing this **netiquette,** or Internet etiquette, but you will see that those who do observe it receive the more thoughtful and considerate replies.

Addressing messages

- *Avoid spamming.* With a few keystrokes, you can broadcast a message to many recipients at once—all the students in a course, say, or all the participants in a discussion group. Occasionally you may indeed have a worthwhile idea or important information that everyone on the list will want to know. But flooding whole lists with irrelevant messages—called **spamming**—is rude and irritating.
- *Avoid sending frivolous messages to all the members of a group.* Instead of dashing off "I agree" and distributing the two-word message widely, put some time into composing a thoughtful response and send it only to those who will be interested.

Composing messages

- *Remember that the messages you receive represent individuals.* Don't say or do anything that you wouldn't say or do face to face.
- *Use names.* In the body of your message, address your reader(s) by name if possible and sign off with your own name and information on how to contact you. Your own name is especially important if your e-mail address does not spell it out.
- *Pay careful attention to tone.* Refrain from **flaming,** or attacking, correspondents. Don't use all-capital letters, which SHOUT. And use irony or sarcasm only cautiously: in the absence of facial expressions, they can lead to misunderstandings. To indicate irony and emotions, you can use **emoticons,** such as

the smiley :-). These sideways faces made up of punctuation can easily be overused, though, and should not substitute for thoughtfully worded opinions.

- *Avoid saying anything in e-mail that you would not say in a printed document such as a letter or memo.* E-mail can usually be retrieved from the server, and in business and academic settings it may well be retrieved in disputes over contracts, grades, and other matters.

Reading and responding to messages

- *Be a forgiving reader.* Avoid nitpicking over spelling or other surface errors. And because attitudes are sometimes difficult to convey, give authors an initial benefit of the doubt: a writer who at first seems hostile may simply have tried too hard to be concise; a writer who at first seems unserious may simply have failed at injecting humor into a worthwhile message.
- *Forward messages only with permission.* You may want to send a message you've received to someone else, but do so only if you know that the author of the message won't mind.
- *Avoid participating in flame "wars,"* overheated dialogs that contribute little or no information or understanding. If a war breaks out in a discussion, ignore it: don't rush to defend someone who is being attacked, and don't respond even if you are under attack yourself.

12b Create effective Web compositions.

Creating a Web page or site is sometimes as simple as saving a document in a different format, but more often it means thinking in a new way.

The diagrams on the next page show a key difference between traditional printed documents and Web sites. Most traditional documents are meant to be read in sequence from start to finish. In contrast, most Web sites are intended to be examined in whatever order readers choose as they follow links to pages within the site and to other sites. A Web site thus requires careful planning of the links between pages and thoughtful cues to orient readers.

When you create a composition for the Web, it will likely fall into one of two categories: pages such as class papers that resemble printed documents in being linear and text-heavy and that call for familiar ways of writing and reading (p. 141); or "native" hypertext documents that you build from scratch, which call for screen-oriented writing and reading (p. 142).

Traditional document

VA Literacy Volunteers
Literacy Introduction
2
Resources for Tutors
3
Resources for Students
4
Exercises

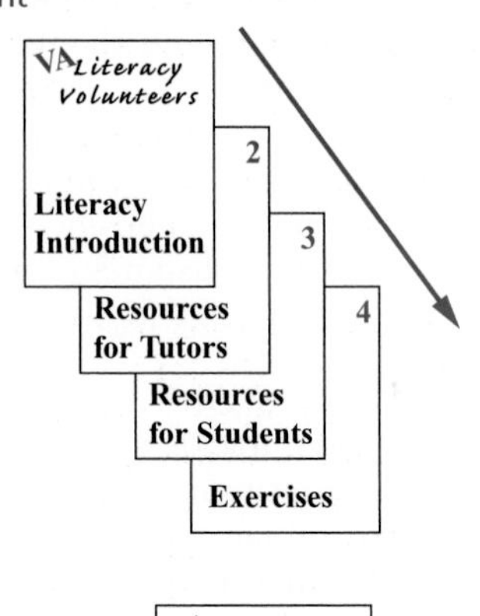

Web site

VA Literacy Volunteers
Home Page
Resources for Students
Resources for Tutors
Writing
Reading
Contact Us
Adult Illiteracy
Teaching
Writing
Reading
Exercises
Writing
Reading

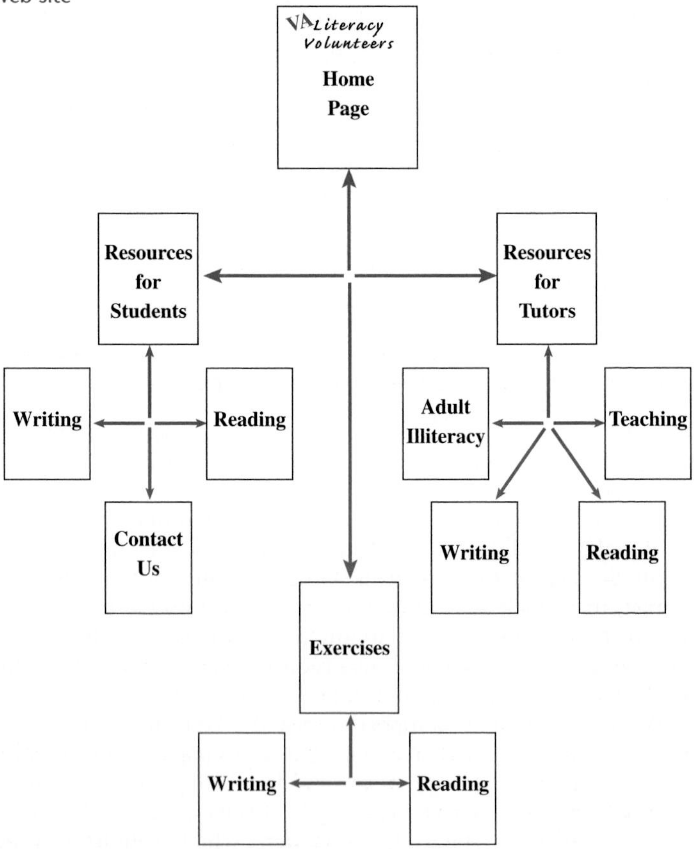

Note It's easy to incorporate material from other sources into a Web site, but you have the same obligation to cite your sources as you do in a printed document (see pp. 459–64). Further, you may need to seek the copyright holder's permission before publishing the material on the Web. See pages 464–65 for more on copyright.

1 • Using HTML

Most Web pages are created using hypertext markup language, or HTML, and an HTML editor. The HTML editing program inserts command codes into your document that achieve the effects you want when the material appears on the Web.

From the user's point of view, most HTML editors work much as word processors do, with similar options for sizing, formatting, and highlighting copy and with a display that shows what you will see in the final version. Indeed, you can compose a Web page without bothering at all about the behind-the-scenes HTML coding. As you gain experience with Web building, however, you may want to create more sophisticated pages by editing the codes themselves.

There are many HTML editors on the market. The Web site for this book (see p. 135) provides links to free or low-cost editors.

2 • Creating online papers

If an instructor asks you to post a paper to a Web site, you can compose it on your word processor and then use the Save As HTML function available on most word processors to translate it into a Web page. After translating the paper, your word processor should allow you to modify some of the elements on the page, or you can open the translated document in an HTML editor.

The illustration on the next page shows the opening screen of a student's project for a composition course. The project incorporates many of the design features that make any text-heavy document more accessible to Web readers:

- *Use a simple white or cream-colored background.* It is more difficult to read text on a computer screen than on paper, and bright or dark background colors compound the problem.
- *Use a standard type font and size.* (See p. 78 on fonts.) With standard fonts, a size of at least 12 points should ensure that pages are readable on most systems.
- *Use a maximum line length of seventy or eighty characters.* Longer lines are hard to read. You may have to increase the margins to create shorter lines.
- *Use headings as signposts* in documents that require scrolling

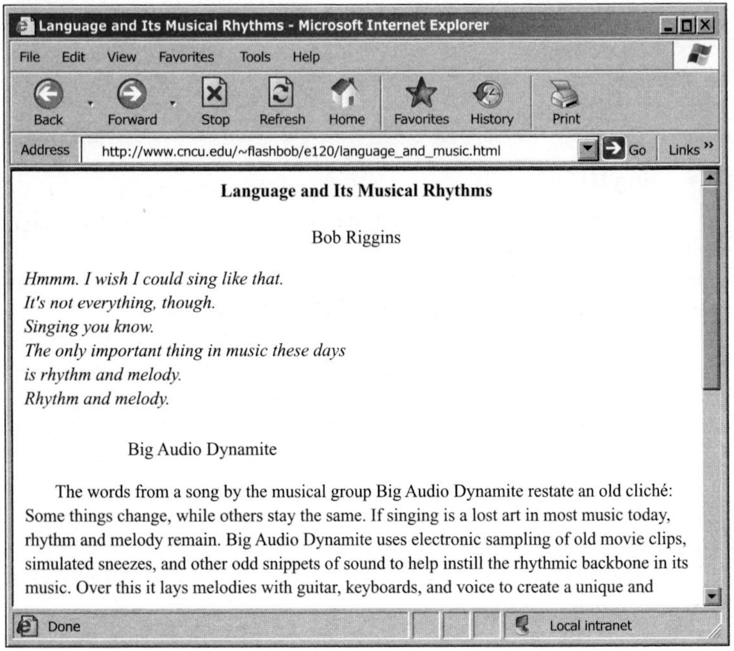

Language and Its Musical Rhythms

Bob Riggins

Hmmm. I wish I could sing like that.
It's not everything, though.
Singing you know.
The only important thing in music these days
is rhythm and melody.
Rhythm and melody.

Big Audio Dynamite

The words from a song by the musical group Big Audio Dynamite restate an old cliché: Some things change, while others stay the same. If singing is a lost art in most music today, rhythm and melody remain. Big Audio Dynamite uses electronic sampling of old movie clips, simulated sneezes, and other odd snippets of sound to help instill the rhythmic backbone in its music. Over this it lays melodies with guitar, keyboards, and voice to create a unique and

through several screens. Otherwise, readers may lose their sense of the document's overall organization.

3 • Creating original sites

When you create an original Web site, you need to be aware that Web readers generally alternate between skimming pages for highlights and focusing intently on sections of text. To facilitate this kind of reading, you'll want to consider the preceding guidelines for handling text and also your site's structure and content, flow, ease of navigation, and use of images, video, and sound.

Structure and content

Your site's organization should be easy to grasp so that it does not disorient readers:

- *Sketch possible site plans before getting started.* (See p. 140 for an example.) Your aim is to develop a sense of the major components of your project and to create a logical space for each component.
- *Consider how menus on the site's pages can provide overviews of*

the organization as well as direct access to the pages (see p. 144). The screen shot below, from the site of a volunteer organization, includes two menus: a box near the top provides an overview of the site, and a set of icons at the bottom of each page directs readers home or elsewhere.

- *Treat the first few sentences of any page as a get-acquainted space for you and your readers.* On the page below, the text hooks readers with an interesting situation and then orients them with general information.
- *Compose descriptive links.* As you create links within your own site or to other sites on the Web, indicate what's at the other locations. Instead of just *Click here,* for instance, say *Click here for writing exercises.* When you provide a list of links to related sites, annotate each one with information about its contents.
- *Distill your text so that it includes only essential information.* Concise prose is essential in any writing situation, of course. But

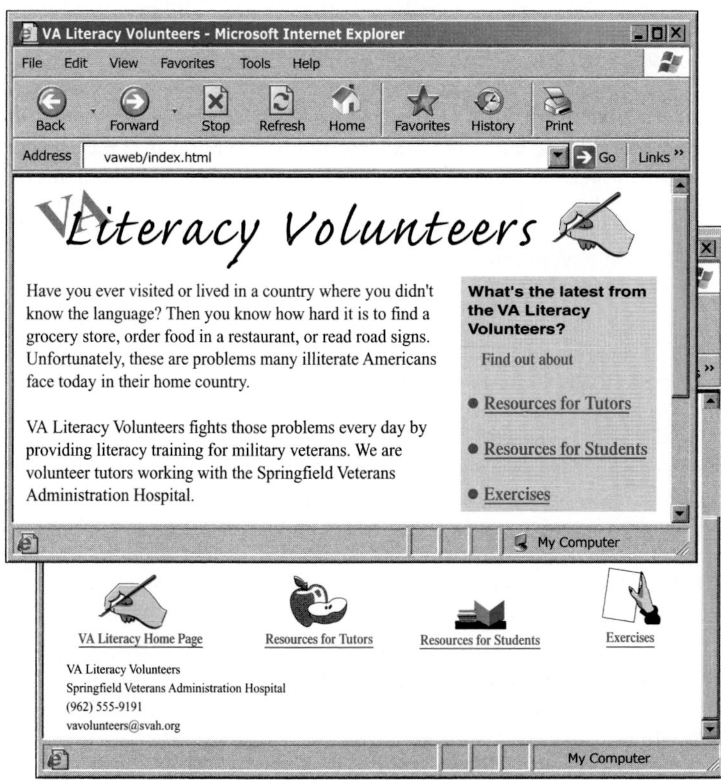

Web readers expect to scan text quickly and, in any event, have difficulty following long text passages on a computer screen. (See pp. 202–08 for advice on writing concisely.)

Flow

Beginning Web authors sometimes start at the top of the page and then add element upon element until information proceeds down the screen much as it would in a printed document. However, by thinking about how information will flow on a page, you can take better advantage of the Web's visual nature.

To achieve flow on your Web pages, follow these guidelines:

- *Standardize elements of your design to create expectations in readers and to fulfill those expectations*. For instance, develop a uniform style for the main headings of pages, for headings within pages, and for menus.
- *Make scanning easy for readers*. Focus readers on crucial text by adding space around it. Use icons and other images to emphasize text. Add headings to break up text and to highlight content. Use lists to reinforce the parallel importance of items. (See pp. 80–81 for more on headings and lists.)
- *Position boxes, illustrations, and other elements to help conduct readers through a page*. Such elements can align in the center or on the left or right of the page. Use space around the elements to keep them from interfering with text and to highlight them.

Ease of navigation

A Web site of more than a couple of pages requires a menu on every page that lists the features of the site, giving its plan at a glance. By clicking on any item in the menu, readers can go directly to a page that interests them. The Web site shown on the previous page uses two kinds of menu: a text box and a set of icons. (Always supplement icons with verbal descriptions of the links to be sure readers understand where each link leads.)

You can embed a menu at the top, side, or bottom of a page. Menus at the top or side are best on short pages because they will not scroll off the screen as readers move down the page. On longer pages menus at the bottom prevent readers from reaching a dead end, a point where they can't easily move forward or backward.

In designing a menu, keep it simple: many different type fonts and colors will overwhelm readers instead of orienting them. And make the menus look the same from one page to the next so that readers recognize them easily.

Images, video, and sound

The Web makes it possible to incorporate multimedia elements such as icons, graphics, photographs, artwork, animation, video clips, and sound clips. Exploring the Web, you'll see that site designers have taken advantage of these capabilities—so much so that Web readers often expect at least some visual enhancement of text.

Images such as icons and photographs are easier to use than video and sound, though they do require some technical expertise. To use images effectively, follow these guidelines:

- *Use visual elements for a purpose*. They should supplement or replace text, highlight important features, and direct the flow of information. Don't use them as mere decoration.
- *Compose captions for images that relate them to your text.* Don't ask the elements to convey your meaning by themselves.
- *Provide alternative descriptions of images* for readers with disabilities or readers whose Web browsers can't display the images.
- *Make the size of your files a central concern* so that readers don't have to wait forever for your site to download. As a rule, don't use images with a file size of more than thirty kilobytes (30k).

You can use your own multimedia elements or obtain them from other sources:

- *Create your own graphs, diagrams, and other illustrations using a graphics program.* Any graphics program requires learning and practice to be used efficiently but can produce professional-looking illustrations.
- *Incorporate your own artwork, photographs, video clips, and sound recordings.* You may be able to find the needed equipment and software at your campus computer lab.
- *Obtain icons, video, and other multimedia elements from CD-ROMs or from the Web itself.* Be sure that you have enough space on your hard drive or a diskette to hold the file.

For more information on working with multimedia, see this book's Web site (box on p. 135).

Note Sometimes CD-ROM and Web multimedia are not restricted by copyright, and you may use them freely as long as you acknowledge your sources. Often, however, these resources are restricted, and you must seek the copyright holders' permission before using them. See pages 464–65 for more on copyright.

13 Business Writing

How can I communicate effectively in the work world?

Writing for business, you are addressing busy people who want to see quickly why you are writing and how they should respond to you. To help them, follow these basic guidelines:

13a

- State your purpose right at the start.
- Be straightforward, clear, concise, objective, and courteous.
- Observe conventions of grammar and usage, which make your writing clear and impress your reader with your care.

This chapter explains and illustrates some business-writing essentials: business letter format, job-application letters, résumés, memos, and electronic communication. See Chapter 7 on document design for pointers on type fonts, page layout, headings, and other elements of business documents. See page 86 in that chapter for a sample of a business report.

CULTURE LANGUAGE Business writing in the United States favors efficiency and may seem abrupt or impolite compared with such writing in your native culture. For instance, business writers elsewhere may be expected to begin with polite questions about the addressee or with compliments for the addressee's company. US business writers, in contrast, get right to the point. See the sample documents in this chapter for examples of appropriate openings and other features of US business writing.

13a Use established formats for business letters and résumés.

1 • Business letter format

For any business letter, use either unlined white paper measuring 8½" by 11" or what is called letterhead stationery with your address printed at the top of the sheet. Type the letter single-

http://www.ablongman.com/littlebrown

➤ Writing in and out of school
  ➤ Video tutorials
    ➤ Using e-mail
    ➤ Designing a *PowerPoint* presentation
  ➤ Web links ➤ Business writing

spaced (with double space between elements) on only one side of a sheet.

A common form for business letters is illustrated on the next page.

- The **return-address heading** gives your address (but not your name) and the date. (If you are using stationery with a printed heading, you need only give the date.) Place your heading at least an inch from the top of the page. Align the heading at the left margin.
- The **inside address** shows the name, title, and complete address of the person you are writing to. Place the address at least two lines below the return-address heading.
- The **salutation** greets the addressee. Position it at the left margin, two lines below the inside address and two lines above the body of the letter. Follow it with a colon. Whenever possible, address your letter to a specific person. (Call the company or department to ask whom to address.) If you can't find a person's name, then use a job title (*Dear Human Resources Manager, Dear Customer Service Manager*) or use a general salutation (*Dear Smythe Shoes*). Use *Ms.* as the title for a woman when she has no other title, when you don't know how she prefers to be addressed, or when you know that she prefers *Ms.*
- The **body** of the letter, containing its substance, begins at the left margin. Instead of indenting the first line of each paragraph, insert an extra line of space between paragraphs.
- The letter's **close** begins two lines below the last line of the body and aligns at the left margin. The close should reflect the level of formality in the salutation: *Respectfully, Cordially, Yours truly,* and *Sincerely* are more formal closes; *Regards* and *Best wishes* are less formal. Capitalize only the first word, and follow the close with a comma.
- The **signature** falls below the close and has two parts: your name typed four lines below the close, and your handwritten signature in the space between. Give your name as you sign checks and other documents.
- Below the signature at the left margin, you may want to include additional information such as *Enc.* (indicating an enclosure with the letter) or *cc: Margaret Zusky* (indicating that a copy is being sent to the person named).

Use an envelope that will accommodate the letter once it is folded horizontally in thirds. The envelope should show your name and address in the upper left corner and the addressee's name, title, and address in the center.

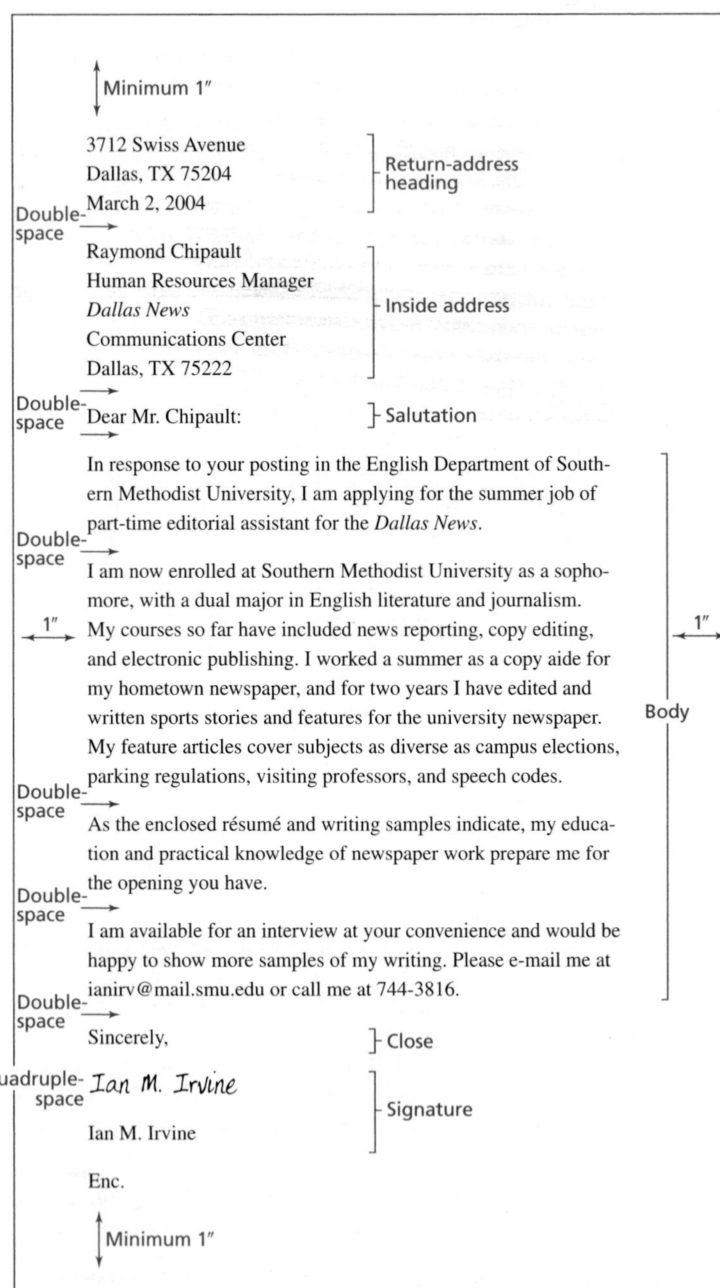

3712 Swiss Avenue
Dallas, TX 75204
March 2, 2004

Raymond Chipault
Human Resources Manager
Dallas News
Communications Center
Dallas, TX 75222

Dear Mr. Chipault:

In response to your posting in the English Department of Southern Methodist University, I am applying for the summer job of part-time editorial assistant for the *Dallas News*.

I am now enrolled at Southern Methodist University as a sophomore, with a dual major in English literature and journalism. My courses so far have included news reporting, copy editing, and electronic publishing. I worked a summer as a copy aide for my hometown newspaper, and for two years I have edited and written sports stories and features for the university newspaper. My feature articles cover subjects as diverse as campus elections, parking regulations, visiting professors, and speech codes.

As the enclosed résumé and writing samples indicate, my education and practical knowledge of newspaper work prepare me for the opening you have.

I am available for an interview at your convenience and would be happy to show more samples of my writing. Please e-mail me at ianirv@mail.smu.edu or call me at 744-3816.

Sincerely,

Ian M. Irvine

Ian M. Irvine

Enc.

2 • Job-application letter

The sample on the facing page illustrates the key features of a job-application letter:

- *Interpret your résumé for the particular job.* Don't detail your entire résumé, reciting your job history. Instead, highlight and reshape only the relevant parts.
- *Announce at the outset what job you seek and how you heard about it.*
- *Include any special reason you have for applying,* such as a specific career goal.
- *Summarize your qualifications for this particular job,* including relevant facts about education and employment history and emphasizing notable accomplishments. Mention that additional information appears in an accompanying résumé.
- *Describe your availability.* At the end of the letter, mention that you are free for an interview at the convenience of the addressee, or specify when you will be available (for instance, when your current job or classes leave your free, or when you could travel to the employer's city).

3 • Print or electronic résumé

For the résumé that accompanies your letter of application, you can use the guidelines below and the samples on the next two pages. (The samples illustrate only one possible organization; another arranges employment history not by job but by functions and skills.)

- *Provide the appropriate information in table form:* your name, postal address, phone number, and e-mail address; career objective; education; employment history; any special skills or awards; and information about how to obtain your references.
- *Use headings to mark the various sections of the résumé.* Space around the headings and within sections so that important information stands out.
- *Use capital letters conventionally.* Keep in mind that passages with many capitals can be hard to read. Do use capitals for proper nouns (pp. 392–93), but consider dropping them for job titles, course names, department names, and the like.
- *Limit your résumé to one page* so that it can be quickly reviewed. However, if your experience and education are extensive, a two-page résumé is preferable to a single cramped, unreadable page.
- *For a printed résumé, use techniques of document design.* Readable type fonts, lists, and some other elements discussed on pages 75–85 can make your résumé clearer and more attractive.

Résumé (traditional design)

Ian M. Irvine
3712 Swiss Avenue
Dallas, TX 75204
214-744-3816
ianirv@mail.smu.edu

POSITION DESIRED

Part-time editorial assistant.

EDUCATION

Southern Methodist University, 2002 to present.
Current standing: sophomore.
Major: English literature and journalism.
Journalism courses: news reporting, copy editing, electronic publishing, communications arts, broadcast journalism.

Abilene (Texas) Senior High School, 1998-2002.
Graduated with academic, college-preparatory degree.

EMPLOYMENT HISTORY

2002 to present. Reporter, *Daily Campus*, student newspaper of Southern Methodist University.
Write regular coverage of baseball, track, and soccer teams.
Write feature stories on campus policies and events. Edit sports news, campus listings, features.

Summer 2003. Copy aide, *Abilene Reporter-News*.
Routed copy, ran errands, and assisted reporters with research.

Summer 2002. Painter, Longhorn Painters, Abilene.
Prepared and painted exteriors and interiors of houses.

SPECIAL SKILLS

Fluent in Spanish.
Proficient in Internet research and word processing.

REFERENCES

Available on request:

Placement Office
Southern Methodist University
Dallas, TX 75275

Résumé (contemporary design)

Ian M. Irvine

3712 Swiss Avenue
Dallas, TX 75204
214-744-3816
ianirv@mail.smu.edu

Position desired	Part-time editorial assistant.
Education	*Southern Methodist University*, 2002 to present. Current standing: sophomore. Major: English literature and journalism. Journalism courses: news reporting, copy editing, electronic publishing, communications arts, broadcast journalism. *Abilene (Texas) Senior High School*, 1998-2002. Graduated with academic, college-preparatory degree.
Employment history	2002 to present. Reporter, *Daily Campus*, student newspaper of Southern Methodist University. Write regular coverage of baseball, track, and soccer teams. Write feature stories on campus policies and events. Edit sports news, campus listings, features. Summer 2003. Copy aide, *Abilene Reporter-News*. Routed copy, ran errands, and assisted reporters with research. Summer 2002. Painter, Longhorn Painters, Abilene. Prepared and painted exteriors and interiors of houses.
Special skills	Fluent in Spanish. Proficient in Internet research and word processing.
References	Available on request: Placement Office Southern Methodist University Dallas, TX 75275

13a

Employers often want an electronic version of a résumé so that they can add it to a computerized database of applicants. The employers may scan your printed résumé to convert it to an electronic file, or they may request electronic copy from you in the first place. If you think a potential employer may use an electronic version of your résumé, follow these additional guidelines:

- *Keep the design simple for accurate scanning or electronic transmittal.* Avoid images, unusual type, more than one column, vertical or horizontal lines, and highlighting (boldface, italic, or underlining). If its highlighting were removed, the traditionally designed sample on page 150 could probably be scanned or transmitted electronically. The two-column sample on page 151 perhaps could not.
- *Use concise, specific words to describe your skills and experience.* The employer's computer may use keywords (often nouns) to identify the résumés of suitable job candidates, and you want to ensure that your résumé includes the appropriate keywords. Name your specific skills—for example, the computer programs you can operate—and write concretely with words like *manager* (not *person with responsibility for*) and *reporter* (not *staff member who reports*). Look for likely keywords in the employer's description of the job you seek.

13b Write focused business memos.

Business memorandums (memos, for short) address people within the same organization. Most memos deal briefly with a specific topic, such as an answer to a question, a progress report, or an evaluation.

Both the form and the structure of a memo are designed to get to the point and dispose of it quickly (see the sample opposite). State your reason for writing in the first sentence. Devote the first paragraph to a concise presentation of your answer, conclusion, or evaluation. In the rest of the memo explain your reasoning or evidence. Use headings or lists as appropriate to highlight key information.

Most companies have their own conventions for memo formats. The heading usually consists of the company name, the addressee's name, the writer's name (initialed in handwriting), the date, and a subject description or title. The body of the memo is usually single-spaced, with double spacing between paragraphs and no paragraph indentions. An indication of who receives copies of the memo can be given two spaces below the last line of the body.

Bigelow Wax Company

TO: Aileen Rosen, Director of Sales
FROM: Patricia Phillips, Territory 12 PP
DATE: March 17, 2004
SUBJECT: 2003 sales of Quick Wax in Territory 12

Since it was introduced in January of 2003, Quick Wax has been unsuccessful in Territory 12 and has not affected the sales of our Easy Shine. Discussions with customers and my own analysis of Quick Wax suggest three reasons for its failure to compete with our product.

1. Quick Wax has not received the promotion necessary for a new product. Advertising—primarily on radio—has been sporadic and has not developed a clear, consistent image for the product. In addition, the Quick Wax sales representative in Territory 12 is new and inexperienced; he is not known to customers, and his sales pitch (which I once overheard) is weak. As far as I can tell, his efforts are not supported by phone calls or mailings from his home office.

2. When Quick Wax does make it to the store shelves, buyers do not choose it over our product. Though priced competitively with our product, Quick Wax is poorly packaged. The container seems smaller than ours, though in fact it holds the same eight ounces. The lettering on the Quick Wax package (red on blue) is difficult to read, in contrast to the white-on-green lettering on the Easy Shine package.

3. Our special purchase offers and my increased efforts to serve existing customers have had the intended effect of keeping customers satisfied with our product and reducing their inclination to stock something new.

Copies: L. Mendes, Director of Marketing
L. MacGregor, Customer Service Manager

13c Use the tools of electronic communication effectively.

Communicating via electronic devices, especially electronic mail and fax machines, speeds up correspondence but also creates new challenges. E-mail now plays such a prominent role in communication of all sorts that it is discussed separately (see pp. 135–39). Generally, the standards for business e-mail are the same as for other business correspondence.

Faxes follow closely the formats of print documents, whether letters or memos. But there are unique concerns:

- *Consider legibility.* Small type, photographs, horizontal lines, and other elements that look fine on your copy may not be legible to the addressee.
- *Include a cover sheet.* Most faxes require a cover sheet with fax-specific information: the addressee's name, company, and fax number; the date, time, and subject; your own name and fax and telephone numbers (the telephone number is important in case something goes wrong with the transmission); and the total number of pages (including the cover sheet) in the fax.
- *Advise your addressee to expect a fax.* Fax transmissions can go astray. Advice is essential if the fax is confidential, because the machine is often shared.
- *Consider urgency.* Transmission by fax can imply that the correspondence is urgent. If yours isn't, you may want to use the mail instead. (Swamping your correspondents with needless faxes can make you the child who cried wolf when you really have an urgent message to transmit.)

14 Making Oral Presentations

How can I speak effectively to a group?

Oral presentation is partly writing, involving the same consideration of subject, audience, and purpose. Yet speechmaking and writing also differ, notably in that a listener cannot stop to rehear a section the way a reader can reread. Effective speakers use organization, voice, body language, and other techniques to help their audience listen.

http://www.ablongman.com/littlebrown

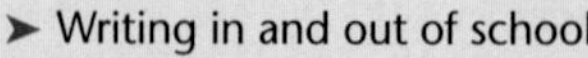

➤ Writing in and out of school

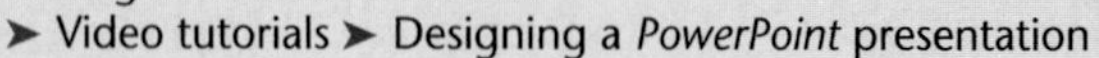

➤ Video tutorials ➤ Designing a *PowerPoint* presentation

➤ Web links ➤ Oral presentations

14a Consider purpose and audience.

The most important step in developing an oral presentation is to identify your purpose: what do you want your audience to know or do as a result of your speech? In school and work settings, you're likely to be speaking for the same reasons that you write: to explain something to listeners or to persuade listeners to accept your opinion or take an action. See page 9 for more on these purposes.

Adapting to your audience is a critical task in public speaking as well as in writing. You'll want to consider the questions about audience on page 8. But a listening audience requires additional considerations as well:

- *Why is your audience assembled?* Listeners who are required to attend may be more difficult to interest and motivate than listeners who attend because they want to hear you and your ideas.
- *How large is your audience?* With a small group you can be informal. If you are speaking to a hundred or more people, you may need a public address system, a lectern, special lighting, and audiovisual equipment.
- *Where will you speak?* Your approach should match the setting—more casual for a small classroom, more formal for an auditorium.
- *How long are you scheduled to speak and when?* A long speech early in the morning or late in the afternoon may find your audience too sleepy to listen well.

When speaking, unlike when writing, you can see and hear your audience's responses during your presentation. Thus you have the luxury and challenge of adapting your presentation to an audience as you speak. If you sense that an audience is bored, try to spice up your presentation. If an audience is restless, check your watch to make sure you have not gone overtime.

14b Organize the presentation.

An effective oral presentation, like an effective essay, has a recognizable shape that guides listeners and helps them see how ideas and details relate to each other. To the advice in Chapter 3 on organizing and outlining an essay, add the following guidelines for the introduction, conclusion, and supporting material.

1 • The introduction

First impressions count. The beginning of an oral presentation should try to accomplish three goals:

- *Gain the audience's attention and interest.* Begin with a question, an unusual example or statistic, or a short, relevant story.
- *Put yourself in the speech.* If you demonstrate your expertise, experience, or concern, your audience will be more interested in what you say and more trusting of you.
- *Introduce and preview your topic and purpose.* By the time your introduction is over, listeners should know what your subject is and the direction you'll take to develop your ideas. This information will give them expectations for your speech on which they can pin the specific points that follow.

In addition to these guidelines for beginning a speech, there are important pitfalls to avoid:

- *Don't try to cram too much into your introduction.* Giving only a sneak preview of your speech can pique your audience's curiosity about what you have to say.
- *Don't begin with an apology.* A statement such as *I wish I'd been given more time to get ready for this presentation* will only undermine your listeners' confidence in you.
- *Don't begin with "My speech is about. . . ."* The statement is dull and does little to clarify purpose.

2 • Supporting material

Just as you do when writing, you can and should use facts, statistics, examples, and expert opinions to support spoken arguments (see pp. 111–12). In addition, as a speaker you can draw on other kinds of supporting material:

- *Use vivid description.* Paint a mental image of a scene, a concept, an event, or a person.
- *Use well-chosen quotations.* They can add an emotional or humorous moment to your speech.
- *Use true or fictional stories.* A narrative can rivet the audience's attention and illustrate your point. Most listeners remember a good story long after they have forgotten other details from a speech.
- *Use analogies.* Comparisons between essentially unlike things, such as a politician and a tightrope walker, link concepts memorably.

3 • The conclusion

Last impressions count as much as first impressions. You may hope that listeners will remember every detail of your speech, but they are more likely to leave with a general impression and a few ideas about you and your message. You want your conclusion to be clear, of course, but you also want it to be memorable. Remind listeners of how your topic and main idea connect to their needs and interests. If your speech was motivational, tap an emotion that matches your message. If your speech was informational, give some tips on how to remember important details.

14c Deliver the presentation.

1 • Methods of delivery

An oral presentation may be delivered impromptu, extemporaneously, from a text, or from memory. No one technique is best for all speeches; indeed, a single speech may include all four.

Speaking impromptu

Impromptu means "without preparation": an impromptu presentation is one you deliver off-the-cuff, with no planning or practice. For instance, you may be called on in a class to express your opinion or to summarize something you've written. The only way to prepare for such incidents is to be well prepared in general.

Speaking extemporaneously

Extemporaneous speaking—that done with some preparation, but without reading from a text—is the most common form of presentation, typical of class lectures and business briefings. With extemporaneous speaking, you have time to prepare and practice in advance. Then, instead of following a script of every word, you speak from notes that guide you through the presentation. You can look and sound natural while still covering all the material you want to convey.

Speaking from a text

Delivering a presentation from a text involves writing the text out in advance and then reading aloud from it. With a text in front of you, you're unlikely to lose your way. However, a reading speaker can be dull for an audience. Try to avoid this form of delivery for an entire presentation.

If you do use a text, write it so that it sounds spoken (less formal) rather than written (more formal): for instance, the sentence *Although costs rose, profits remained steady* would sound fine in writing but stiff and awkward in speech. In addition, rehearse thoroughly so that you can read with expression and can look up frequently to make eye contact with listeners (see the facing page).

Speaking from memory

A memorized presentation has a distinct advantage: complete freedom from notes or a text. That means you can look at your audience every minute and can move away from a lectern and even into the audience. However, you may be like most speakers in seeming less relaxed, not more relaxed, when presenting from memory: your mind is too busy retrieving the next words to attend to the responses of the audience. Further, you risk forgetting your place or a whole passage.

For these reasons, many experts discourage memorization. At least reserve the method for the introduction, perhaps, or some other part with which you want to make a strong impression. Rehearse not only to memorize the words but, beyond that, to deliver the words fresh, as if for the first time.

2 • Vocal delivery

The sound of your voice will influence how your listeners receive you. When rehearsing, consider volume, speed, and articulation.

- *Speak loudly.* In a meeting with five other people, you can speak in a normal volume. As your audience grows in size, so should your volume. Most speakers can project to as many as a hundred people, but a larger audience may require a microphone. If you can rehearse in the room where you'll be speaking, ask a friend or colleague to sit at the back and tell you what volume is easy to hear.
- *Speak slowly enough to be understandable.* Most audiences prefer speech that's a little fast, around 150 words a minute; but they have difficulty following too-rapid speech at, say, 190 words a minute.
- *Speak clearly and correctly.* To avoid mumbling or slurring words, practice articulating. Sometimes it helps to open your mouth a little wider than usual.

3 • Physical delivery

You are more than your spoken words when you make an oral presentation. Your face and body also play a role in how your speech is received.

- *Make eye contact with listeners.* Looking directly in your listeners' eyes conveys your honesty, your confidence, and your control of your material. Move your gaze around the entire room, settle on someone, and establish direct eye contact; then move on to someone else.
- *Stand up.* Always stand for a presentation, unless it takes place in a small room where standing would be inappropriate. You can see more audience members when you stand, and they in turn can hear your voice and see your gestures more clearly.
- *Stand straight, and move around.* Turn your body toward one side of the room and the other, step out from behind any lectern or desk, and gesture appropriately, as you would in conversation.

4 • Visual aids

You can supplement an oral presentation with visual aids such as posters, models, slides, or videos.

- *Use visual aids to underscore your points.* Short lists of key ideas, illustrations such as graphs or photographs, or objects such as models can make your presentation more interesting and memorable. But use visual aids judiciously: a battery of illustrations or objects will bury your message rather than amplify it.
- *Match visual aids and setting.* An audience of five people may be able to see a photograph and share a chart; an audience of a hundred will need projected images.
- *Coordinate visual aids with your message.* Time each visual aid to reinforce a point you're making. Tell listeners what they're looking at—what they should be getting from the aid. Give them enough viewing time so they don't mind turning their attention back to you.
- *Show visual aids only while they're needed.* To regain your audience's attention, remove or turn off any aid as soon as you have finished with it.

With the *PowerPoint* software program, you can integrate visual aids with your speaking notes distilled as pointers for the audience. (Learn about using *PowerPoint* at this book's Web site: see the box on p. 154.)

5 • Practice

Practicing an oral presentation is the speechmaker's equivalent of editing and proofreading a written text. You won't gain much by practicing silently in your head; instead, you need to rehearse out loud, with the notes you will be using. For your initial rehearsals, you can gauge your performance by making an audio- or videotape of yourself or by practicing in front of a mirror. Practicing out loud will also tell you if your presentation is running too long or too short.

If you plan to use visual aids, you'll need to practice with them, too, preferably in the room where you'll make the presentation and certainly with the help of anyone who will be assisting you. Your goal is to eliminate hitches (upside-down slides, missing charts) and to weave the visuals seamlessly into your presentation.

6 • Stage fright

Many people report that speaking in front of an audience is their number-one fear. Even many experienced and polished speakers have some anxiety about delivering an oral presentation, but they use this nervous energy to their advantage, letting it propel them into working hard on each presentation, preparing well in advance, and rehearsing until they're satisfied with their delivery. They know that the symptoms of anxiety are usually imperceptible to listeners, who cannot see or hear a racing heart, upset stomach, cold hands, and worried thoughts.

Several techniques can help you reduce your level of anxiety:

- *Use simple relaxation exercises.* Deep breathing or tensing and relaxing your stomach muscles can ease some of the physical symptoms of speech anxiety—stomachache, rapid heartbeat, and shaky hands, legs, and voice.
- *Think positively.* Instead of worrying about the mistakes you might make, concentrate on how well you've prepared and practiced your presentation and how significant your ideas are.
- *Don't avoid opportunities to speak in public.* Practice and experience build speaking skills and offer the best insurance for success.

III

Clarity and Style

15 Emphasis

How can my sentences stress the meanings I intend?

To write exactly what you mean, edit to emphasize the main ideas in your sentences. You can gain emphasis by attending to your subjects and verbs (below), using sentence beginnings and endings (p. 165), coordinating equally important ideas (p. 167), and subordinating less important ideas (p. 170). In addition, emphatic writing is concise writing, the subject of Chapter 20.

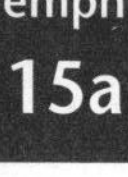

Note Many grammar and style checkers can spot some problems with emphasis, such as nouns made from verbs, passive voice, wordy phrases, and long sentences that may also be flabby and unemphatic. However, the checkers cannot help you identify the important ideas in your sentences or tell you whether those ideas receive appropriate emphasis for your meaning.

15a Use subjects and verbs for key actors and actions.

The heart of every sentence is its subject, which usually names the actor, and its verb, which usually specifies the subject's action: *Children* [subject] *grow* [verb]. When these elements do not identify the key actor and action in the sentence, readers must find that information elsewhere and the sentence may be wordy and unemphatic.

In the next sentences, the subjects and verbs are underlined.

Unemphatic The <u>intention</u> of the company <u>was</u> to expand its workforce. A <u>proposal</u> <u>was</u> also <u>made</u> to diversify the backgrounds and abilities of employees.

These sentences are unemphatic because their key ideas (the com-

Key terms

subject Who or what a sentence is about: *<u>Biologists</u> often study animals.* (See p. 219.)

verb The part of a sentence that asserts something about the subject: *Biologists often <u>study</u> animals.* (See p. 212.)

http://www.ablongman.com/littlebrown
➤ Sentences and words
➤ Web exercises ➤ Exers. 1–4
➤ Downloads ➤ Chapter 15 exercises in electronic format
➤ Web links ➤ Emphasis

pany's intending and proposing) do not appear in their subjects and verbs. Revised, the sentences are not only clearer but more concise:

Revised — The company intended to expand its workforce. It also proposed to diversify the backgrounds and abilities of employees.

The constructions discussed below and on the next page usually drain meaning from a sentence's subject and verb.

Nouns made from verbs

Nouns made from verbs can obscure the key actions of sentences and add words. These nouns include *intention* (from *intend*), *proposal* (from *propose*), *decision* (from *decide*), *expectation* (from *expect*), *persistence* (from *persist*), *argument* (from *argue*), and *inclusion* (from *include*).

Unemphatic — After the company made a decision to hire more disabled workers, its next step was the construction of wheelchair ramps and other facilities.

Revised — After the company decided to hire more disabled workers, it next constructed wheelchair ramps and other facilities.

Weak verbs

Weak verbs, such as *made* and *was* in the unemphatic sentence above, tend to stall sentences just where they should be moving and often bury key actions:

Unemphatic — The company is now the leader among businesses in complying with the 1990 disabilities act. Its officers make frequent speeches on the act to business groups.

Revised — The company now leads other businesses in complying with the 1990 disabilities act. Its officers frequently speak on the act to business groups.

Forms of *be, have,* and *make* are often weak, but don't try to eliminate every use of them: *be* and *have* are essential as helping verbs (*is going, has written*); *be* links subjects and words describing

Key terms

noun A word that names a person, thing, quality, place, or idea: *student, desk, happiness, city, democracy.* (See p. 211.)

helping verb A verb used with another verb to convey time, obligation, and other meanings: *was drilling, would have been drilling.* (See p. 213.)

them (*Planes are noisy*); and *have* and *make* have independent meanings (among them "possess" and "force," respectively). But do consider replacing forms of *be, have,* and *make* when one of the words following the verb could be made into a strong verb itself, as in the following examples.

Unemphatic	Emphatic
was influential	influenced
is a glorification	glorifies
have a preference	prefer
had the appearance	appeared, seemed
made a claim	claimed

emph 15a

Passive voice

Verbs in the passive voice state actions received by, not performed by, their subjects. Thus the passive de-emphasizes the true actor of the sentence, sometimes omitting it entirely. Generally, prefer the active voice, in which the subject performs the action. (See also pp. 266–67 for help with editing the passive voice.)

Unemphatic The 1990 law is seen by most businesses as fair, but the costs of complying have sometimes been exaggerated.

Revised Most business see the 1990 law as fair, but some opponents have exaggerated the costs of complying.

EXERCISE 15.1
Revising: Emphasis of subjects and verbs

Rewrite the following sentences so that their subjects and verbs identify their key actors and actions. Answers to starred items appear at the end of the book.

Example:

The issue of students making a competition over grades is a reason why their focus on learning may be lost.

Students who compete over grades may lose their focus on learning.

*1. The work of many heroes was crucial in helping to emancipate the slaves.

Key terms

passive voice The verb form when the subject names the *receiver* of the verb's action: *The house was destroyed by the tornado.*

active voice The verb form when the subject names the *performer* of the verb's action: *The tornado destroyed the house.*

*2. The contribution of Harriet Tubman, an escaped slave herself, included the guidance of hundreds of other slaves to freedom on the Underground Railroad.
3. A return to slavery was risked by Tubman or possibly death.
4. During the Civil War she was also a carrier of information from the South to the North.
5. After the war, money was raised by Tubman for former slaves who needed help.

15b Use sentence beginnings and endings.

Readers automatically seek a writer's principal meaning in the main clause of a sentence—essentially, in the subject that names the actor and the verb that usually specifies the action (see p. 162). Thus you can help readers understand your intended meaning by controlling the information in your subjects and the relation of the main clause to any modifiers attached to it.

Old and new information

Generally, readers expect the beginning of a sentence to contain information that they already know or that you have already introduced. They then look to the ending for new information. In the unemphatic passage below, the subjects of the second and third sentences both begin with new topics (underlined) while the old topics (the controversy and education) appear at the ends of the sentences:

Unemphatic Education almost means controversy these days, with rising costs and constant complaints about its inadequacies. But the value of schooling should not be obscured by the controversy. The single best means of economic advancement, despite its shortcomings, remains education.

In the more emphatic revision on the next page, the underlined old information begins each sentence and new information ends the sentence. The passage follows the pattern A→B. B→C. C→D.

Key terms

main clause A word group that can stand alone as a sentence, containing a subject and a verb and not beginning with a subordinating word: *The books were expensive.* (See p. 230.)

modifier A word or word group that describes another word or word group—for example, *sweet candy, running in the park.* (See pp. 214 and 295.)

Revised — Education almost means controversy these days, with rising costs and constant complaints about its inadequacies. But the controversy should not obscure the value of schooling. Education remains, despite its shortcomings, the single best means of economic advancement.

Cumulative and periodic sentences

You can call attention to information by placing it first or last in a sentence, reserving the middle for incidentals:

Unemphatic — Education remains the single best means of economic advancement, despite its shortcomings. [Emphasizes shortcomings.]

Revised — Despite its shortcomings, education remains the single best means of economic advancement. [Emphasizes advancement more than shortcomings.]

Revised — Education remains, despite its shortcomings, the single best means of economic advancement. [De-emphasizes shortcomings.]

A sentence that begins with the main clause and then adds modifiers is called **cumulative** because it accumulates information as it proceeds:

Cumulative — Education has no equal in opening minds, instilling values, and creating opportunities.

Cumulative — Most of the Great American Desert is made up of bare rock, rugged cliffs, mesas, canyons, mountains, separated from one another by broad flat basins covered with sun-baked mud and alkali, supporting a sparse and measured growth of sagebrush or creosote or saltbush, depending on location and elevation.
—EDWARD ABBEY

The opposite kind of sentence, called **periodic,** saves the main clause until just before the end (the period) of the sentence. Everything before the main clause points toward it:

Periodic — In opening minds, instilling values, and creating opportunities, education has no equal.

Periodic — With people from all over the world—Korean grocers, Jamaican cricket players, Vietnamese fishers, Haitian cabdrivers, Chinese doctors—the American mosaic is continually changing.

The periodic sentence creates suspense by reserving important information for the end. But readers should already have an idea of the sentence's subject—because it appeared in the preceding sentence—so that they know what the opening modifiers describe.

EXERCISE 15.2
Sentence combining: Beginnings and endings

Locate the main idea in each group of sentences below. Then combine each group into a single sentence that emphasizes that idea by placing it at the beginning or the end. For sentences 2–5, determine the position of the main idea by considering its relation to the previous sentences: if the main idea picks up a topic that's already been introduced, place it at the beginning; if it adds new information, place it at the end. Possible answers to starred items appear at the end of the book.

Example:

The storm blew roofs off buildings. It caused extensive damage. It knocked down many trees. It severed power lines.

Main idea at beginning: The storm caused extensive damage, blowing roofs off buildings, knocking down many trees, and severing power lines.

Main idea at end: Blowing roofs off buildings, knocking down many trees, and severing power lines, the storm caused extensive damage.

*1. Pat Taylor strode into the room. The room was packed. He greeted students called "Taylor's Kids." He nodded to their parents and teachers.

*2. This was a wealthy Louisiana oilman. He had promised his "Kids" free college educations. He was determined to make higher education available to all qualified but disadvantaged students.

3. The students welcomed Taylor. Their voices joined in singing. They sang "You Are the Wind Beneath My Wings." Their faces beamed with hope. Their eyes flashed with self-confidence.
4. The students had thought a college education was beyond their dreams. It seemed too costly. It seemed too demanding.
5. Taylor had to ease the costs and the demands of getting to college. He created a bold plan. The plan consisted of scholarships, tutoring, and counseling.

15c Use coordination to relate equal ideas.

Use **coordination** to show that two or more elements in a sentence are equally important in meaning and thus to clarify the relation between them:

- Link two main clauses with a comma and a coordinating conjunction, such as *and* or *but*.

  equally important

  Independence Hall in Philadelphia is now restored, <u>but</u> fifty years ago it was in bad shape.

- Link two main clauses with a semicolon alone or with a semicolon and a conjunctive adverb, such as *however*.

  equally important

  The building was standing; <u>however</u>, it suffered from decay.

- Within clauses, link words and phrases with a coordinating conjunction, such as *and* or *or*.

  equally important

  The people <u>and</u> officials of the nation were indifferent to Independence Hall <u>or</u> took it for granted.

- Link main clauses, words, or phrases with a correlative conjunction such as *not only . . . but also*.

  equally important

  People <u>not only</u> took the building for granted <u>but also</u> neglected it.

For the punctuation of coordinate elements, see pages 339–41 (comma and coordinating conjuction), 353 (coordinating conjuction alone), and 356–57 (semicolon alone or with a conjunctive adverb).

Note Grammar and style checkers may spot some errors in punctuating coordinated elements, and they can flag long sentences that may contain excessive coordination. But otherwise they provide little help with coordination because they cannot recognize the relations among ideas in sentences. You'll need to weigh and clarify those relations yourself.

1 • Coordinating to smooth sentences

Coordination shows the equality between elements, as illustrated above. At the same time as it clarifies meaning, it can also help smooth choppy sentences:

Key terms

coordinating conjunctions *And, but, or, nor,* and sometimes *for, so, yet.* (See p. 217.)

conjunctive adverbs Modifiers that describe the relation of the ideas in two clauses, such as *hence, however, indeed,* and *thus.* (See p. 325.)

correlative conjunctions Pairs of connecting words, such as *both . . . and, either . . . or, not only . . . but also.* (See p. 217.)

Choppy sentences — We should not rely so heavily on oil. Coal and uranium are also overused. We have a substantial energy resource in the moving waters of our rivers. Smaller streams add to the total volume of water. The resource renews itself. Coal and oil are irreplaceable. Uranium is also irreplaceable. The cost of water does not increase much over time. The costs of coal, oil, and uranium rise dramatically.

The following revision groups coal, oil, and uranium and clearly opposes them to water (the connecting words are underlined):

Ideas coordinated — We should not rely so heavily on coal, oil, and uranium, for we have a substantial energy resource in the moving waters of our rivers and streams. Coal, oil, and uranium are irreplaceable and thus subject to dramatic cost increases; water, however, is self-renewing and more stable in cost.

2 • Coordinating effectively

Use coordination only to express the *equality* of ideas or details. A string of coordinated elements—especially main clauses—implies that all points are equally important:

Excessive coordination — The weeks leading up to the resignation of President Nixon were eventful, and the Supreme Court and the Congress closed in on him, and the Senate Judiciary Committee voted to begin impeachment proceedings, and finally the President resigned on August 9, 1974.

Such a passage needs editing to stress the important points (underlined below) and to de-emphasize the less important information:

Revised — The weeks leading up to the resignation of President Nixon were eventful, as the Supreme Court and the Congress closed in on him and the Senate Judiciary Committee voted to begin impeachment proceedings. Finally, the President resigned on August 9, 1974.

Even within a single sentence, coordination should express a logical equality between ideas:

Faulty — John Stuart Mill was a nineteenth-century utilitarian, and he believed that actions should be judged by their usefulness or by the happiness they cause. [The two clauses are not separate and equal: the second expands on the first by explaining what a utilitarian such as Mill believed.]

Revised — John Stuart Mill, a nineteenth-century utilitarian, believed that actions should be judged by their usefulness or by the happiness they cause.

EXERCISE 15.3
Revising: Excessive or faulty coordination

Revise the following sentences to eliminate excessive or faulty co-ordination. Relate ideas effectively to achieve proper emphasis by adding or subordinating information or by forming more than one sentence. Each item has more than one answer. Possible answers to starred items appear at the end of the book.

Example:

My dog barks, and I have to move out of my apartment.

Because my dog's barking disturbs my neighbors, I have to move out of my apartment.

*1. Often soldiers admired their commanding officers, and they gave them nicknames, and these names frequently contained the word *old,* but not all of the commanders were old.

*2. General Thomas "Stonewall" Jackson was also called "Old Jack," and he was not yet forty years old.

3. Another Southern general in the Civil War was called "Old Pete," and his full name was James Longstreet.
4. The Union general Henry W. Halleck had a reputation as a good military strategist, and he was an expert on the work of a French military authority, Henri Jomini, and Halleck was called "Old Brains."
5. General William Henry Harrison won the Battle of Tippecanoe, and he received the nickname "Old Tippecanoe," and he used the name in his presidential campaign slogan, "Tippecanoe and Tyler, Too," and he won the election in 1840, but he died of pneumonia a month after taking office.

15d Use subordination to emphasize ideas.

Use **subordination** to indicate that some elements in a sentence are less important than others for your meaning. Usually, the main idea appears in the main clause, and supporting details appear in subordinate structures:

- Use a subordinate clause beginning with *although, because, if, who (whom), that, which,* or another subordinating word:

less important (subordinate clause) | more important (main clause)

Although production costs have declined, they are still high.

Key term

subordinate clause A word group that contains a subject and a verb, begins with a subordinating word such as *because* or *who,* and is not a question: *Words can do damage when they hurt feelings.* (See p. 230.)

less important (subordinate clause)

Costs, which include labor and facilities, are difficult to control.

more important (main clause)

- Use a phrase:

less important (phrase) — more important (main clause)

Despite some decline, production costs are still high.

less important (phrase)

Costs, including labor and facilities, are difficult to control.

more important (main clause)

- Use a single word:

Declining costs have not matched prices.
Labor costs are difficult to control.

For punctuating subordinate elements, see pages 342–43 (comma with introductory elements) and 344–47 (commas with interrupting elements).

Note Grammar and style checkers may spot some errors in punctuating subordinated elements, and they can flag long sentences that may contain excessive subordination. But otherwise they provide little help with subordination because they cannot recognize the relations among ideas in sentences. You'll need to weigh and clarify those relations yourself.

1 • Subordinating to distinguish important ideas

A string of main clauses can make everything in a passage seem equally important:

String of main clauses	Computer prices have dropped, and production costs have dropped more slowly, and computer manufacturers have struggled, for their profits have been shrinking.

Emphasis comes from keeping the important information in the main clause (underlined) and subordinating less important details:

Revised	Because production costs have dropped more slowly than prices, computer manufacturers have struggled with shrinking profits.

2 • Subordinating effectively

Subordinate only the less important information in a sentence.

Key term

phrase A word group that lacks a subject or verb or both: *Words can do damage by hurting feelings.* (See p. 227.)

Faulty — Ms. Angelo was in her first year of teaching, although she was a better instructor than others with many years of experience.

The sentence above suggests that Angelo's inexperience is the main idea, whereas the writer intended to stress her skill *despite* her inexperience. Subordinating the inexperience and elevating the skill to the main clause (underlined) gives appropriate emphasis:

Revised — Although Ms. Angelo was in her first year of teaching, she was a better instructor than others with many years of experience.

Subordination loses its power to organize and emphasize when too much loosely related detail crowds into one long sentence:

Overloaded — The boats that were moored at the dock when the hurricane, which was one of the worst in three decades, struck were ripped from their moorings, because the owners had not been adequately prepared, since the weather service had predicted the storm would blow out to sea, as storms do at this time of year.

The revision stresses important information in the main clauses:

Revised — Struck by one of the worst hurricanes in three decades, the boats at the dock were ripped from their moorings. The owners were unprepared because the weather service had said that hurricanes at this time of year blow out to sea.

EXERCISE 15.4
Revising: Faulty or excessive subordination

Revise the following sentences to eliminate faulty or excessive subordination and to achieve proper emphasis. Correct faulty subordination by reversing main and subordinate structures. Correct excessive subordination by coordinating equal ideas or by making separate sentences. Possible answers to starred items appear at the end of the book.

Example:

Terrified to return home, he had driven his mother's car into a cornfield.

Having driven his mother's car into a cornfield, he was terrified to return home.

*1. Genaro González is a talented writer, which means that his stories and novels have been published to critical acclaim.

*2. He loves to write, although he has also earned a doctorate in psychology.

3. His first story, which reflects his growing consciousness of his Aztec heritage and place in the world, is titled "Un Hijo del Sol."
4. González, who writes equally well in English and Spanish, received a large fellowship that enabled him to take a leave of absence from the University of Texas–Pan American, where he teaches psychology, so that for a year he could write full-time.
5. González wrote the first version of "Un Hijo del Sol" while he was a sophomore at Pan American, which is in the Rio Grande valley of southern Texas, which González calls "el Valle" in the story.

EXERCISE 15.5
Revising: Coordination and subordination

The following paragraph consists entirely of simple sentences. Use coordination and subordination to combine sentences in the way you think most effective to emphasize main ideas. Possible answers to starred sentences appear at the end of the book.

*Sir Walter Raleigh personified the Elizabethan Age. *That was the period of Elizabeth I's rule of England. *The period occurred in the last half of the sixteenth century. *Raleigh was a courtier and poet. *He was also an explorer and entrepreneur. *Supposedly, he gained Queen Elizabeth's favor. *He did this by throwing his cloak beneath her feet at the right moment. *She was just about to step over a puddle. There is no evidence for this story. It does illustrate Raleigh's dramatic and dynamic personality. His energy drew others to him. He was one of Elizabeth's favorites. She supported him. She also dispensed favors to him. However, he lost his queen's goodwill. Without her permission he seduced one of her maids of honor. He eventually married the maid of honor. Elizabeth died. Then her successor imprisoned Raleigh in the Tower of London. Her successor was James I. The king falsely charged Raleigh with treason. Raleigh was released after thirteen years. He was arrested again two years later on the old treason charges. At the age of sixty-six he was beheaded.

16 Parallelism

How can I make connections plain within sentences?

When ideas within sentences have the same function and importance, you can show their connection using parallelism, or parallel structure, as shown in the following example:

The air is dirtied by factories belching smoke and cars spewing exhaust.

With **parallelism,** you use the same grammatical forms to express equally important ideas. In the example above, the two underlined phrases have the same function and importance (both specify sources of air pollution), so they also have the same grammatical construction.

Note A grammar and style checker cannot recognize faulty parallelism because it cannot recognize the relations among ideas. You will need to find problems with parallelism on your own.

16a Use parallelism with *and, but, or, nor, yet.*

The coordinating conjunctions *and, but, or, nor,* and *yet* always signal a need for parallelism:

The industrial base was shifting and shrinking. [Parallel words.]

Politicians rarely acknowledged the problem or proposed alternatives. [Parallel phrases.]

Industrial workers were understandably disturbed that they were losing their jobs and that no one seemed to care. [Parallel clauses.]

When sentence elements linked by coordinating conjunctions are not parallel in structure, the sentence is awkward and distracting:

Nonparallel The reasons steel companies kept losing money were that their plants were inefficient, high labor costs, and foreign competition was increasing.

Revised The reasons steel companies kept losing money were inefficient plants, high labor costs, and increasing foreign competition.

Nonparallel Success was difficult even for efficient companies be-

Key term

coordinating conjunctions Words that connect elements of the same kind and importance: *and, but, or, nor,* and sometimes *for, so, yet.* (See p. 217.)

http://www.ablongman.com/littlebrown
➤ Sentences and words
  ➤ Video tutorials ➤ Achieving parallelism
  ➤ Web exercises ➤ Exers. 5 and 6
  ➤ Downloads ➤ Chapter 16 exercises in electronic format
  ➤ Web links ➤ Parallelism

cause of the shift away from all manufacturing in the United States and the fact that steel production was shifting toward emerging nations.

Revised — Success was difficult even for efficient companies because of the shift away from all manufacturing in the United States and toward steel production in emerging nations.

All the words required by idiom or grammar must be stated in compound constructions (see also p. 201):

Faulty — Given training, workers can acquire the skills and interest in other jobs. [Idiom dictates different prepositions with *skills* and *interest*.]

Revised — Given training, workers can acquire the skills for and interest in other jobs.

16b Use parallelism with *both . . . and, not . . . but,* or another correlative conjunction.

Correlative conjunctions stress equality and balance between elements. Parallelism confirms the equality.

> It is not a tax bill but a tax relief bill, providing relief not for the needy but for the greedy. —Franklin Delano Roosevelt

With correlative conjunctions, the element after the second connector must match the element after the first connector:

Nonparallel — Huck Finn learns not only that human beings have an enormous capacity for folly but also enormous dignity. [The first element includes *that human beings have;* the second element does not.]

Revised — Huck Finn learns that human beings have not only an enormous capacity for folly but also enormous dignity. [Repositioning *that human beings have* makes the two elements parallel.]

16c Use parallelism in comparisons.

Parallelism confirms the likeness or difference between two elements being compared using *than* or *as*.

Key term

correlative conjunctions Pairs of words that connect elements of the same kind and importance, such as *both . . . and, either . . . or, neither . . . nor, not . . . but, not only . . . but also.* (See p. 217.)

Nonparallel	Huck Finn proves less a bad boy than to be an independent spirit. In the end he is every bit as determined in rejecting help as he is to leave for "the territory."
Revised	Huck Finn proves less a bad boy than an independent spirit. In the end he is every bit as determined to reject help as he is to leave for "the territory."

(See also pp. 298–99 on making comparisons logical.)

16d Use parallelism with lists, headings, and outlines.

// 16d

The items in a list or outline are coordinate and should be parallel. Parallelism is essential in the headings that divide a paper into sections (see pp. 80–81) and in a formal topic outline (pp. 25–26).

Nonparallel	Revised
Changes in Renaissance England	Changes in Renaissance England
1. Extension of trade routes	1. Extension of trade routes
2. Merchant class became more powerful	2. Increased power of the merchant class
3. The death of feudalism	3. Death of feudalism
4. Upsurging of the arts	4. Upsurge of the arts
5. Religious quarrels began	5. Rise of religious quarrels

EXERCISE 16.1
Revising: Parallelism

Revise the following sentences to create parallelism wherever it is required for grammar and coherence. Add or delete words or rephrase as necessary. Answers to starred items appear at the end of the book.

Example:

After emptying her bag, searching the apartment, and she called the library, Jennifer realized she had lost the book.

After emptying her bag, searching the apartment, and calling the library, Jennifer realized she had lost the book.

*1. The ancient Greeks celebrated four athletic contests: the Olympic Games at Olympia, the Isthmian Games were held near Corinth, at Delphi the Pythian Games, and the Nemean Games were sponsored by the people of Cleonae.

*2. Each day the games consisted of either athletic events or holding ceremonies and sacrifices to the gods.

*3. In the years between the games, competitors were taught wrestling, javelin throwing, and how to box.

*4. Competitors participated in running sprints, spectacular chariot and horse races, and running long distances while wearing full armor.
*5. The purpose of such events was developing physical strength, demonstrating skill and endurance, and to sharpen the skills needed for war.

6. Events were held for both men and for boys.
7. At the Olympic Games the spectators cheered their favorites to victory, attended sacrifices to the gods, and they feasted on the meat not burned in offerings.
8. The athletes competed less to achieve great wealth than for gaining honor both for themselves and their cities.
9. Of course, exceptional athletes received financial support from patrons, poems and statues by admiring artists, and they even got lavish living quarters from their sponsoring cities.
10. With the medal counts and flag ceremonies, today's Olympians sometimes seem to be proving their countries' superiority more than to demonstrate individual talent.

EXERCISE 16.2
Sentence combining: Parallelism

Combine each group of sentences below into one concise sentence in which parallel elements appear in parallel structures. You will have to add, delete, change, and rearrange words. Each item has more than one possible answer. Answers to starred items appear at the end of the book.

Example:

The new process works smoothly. It is efficient, too.
The new process works smoothly and efficiently.

*1. People can develop post-traumatic stress disorder (PTSD). They develop it after experiencing a dangerous situation. They will also have felt fear for their survival.
*2. The disorder can be triggered by a wide variety of events. Combat is a typical cause. Similarly, natural disasters can result in PTSD. Some people experience PTSD after a hostage situation.

3. PTSD can occur immediately after the stressful incident. Or it may not appear until many years later.
4. Sometimes people with PTSD will act irrationally. Moreover, they often become angry.
5. Other symptoms include dreaming that one is reliving the experience. They include hallucinating that one is back in the terrifying place. In another symptom one imagines that strangers are actually one's former torturers.

17 Variety and Details

What makes sentences interesting?

Writing that is interesting as well as clear has at least two features: the sentences vary in length and structure, and they are well textured with details.

Note Some grammar and style checkers will flag long sentences, and you can check for appropriate variety in a series of such sentences. But generally these programs cannot help you see where variety may be needed because they cannot recognize the relative importance and complexity of your ideas. Nor can they suggest where you should add details. To edit for variety and detail, you need to listen to your sentences and determine whether they clarify your meaning.

17a Vary sentence length.

In most contemporary writing, sentences tend to vary from about ten to about forty words, with an average of between fifteen and twenty-five words. If your sentences are all at one extreme or the other, your readers may have difficulty focusing on main ideas and seeing the relations among them:

- If most of your sentences contain thirty-five words or more, your main ideas may not stand out from the details that support them. Break some of the long sentences into shorter, simpler ones.
- If most of your sentences contain fewer than ten or fifteen words, all your ideas may seem equally important and the links between them may not be clear. Try combining them with coordination (p. 167) and subordination (p. 170) to show relationships and stress main ideas over supporting information.

17b Vary sentence structure.

A passage will be monotonous if all its sentences follow the same pattern, like soldiers marching in a parade. To vary structure,

http://www.ablongman.com/littlebrown
➤ Sentences and words
➤ Video tutorials ➤ Achieving variety
➤ Downloads ➤ Chapter 17 exercise in electronic format
➤ Web links ➤ Variety

try subordination, sentence combining, varying sentence beginnings, and varying word order.

1 • Subordination

A string of main clauses in simple or compound sentences can be especially plodding:

Monotonous The moon is now drifting away from the earth. It moves away at the rate of about one inch a year. This movement is lengthening our days. They increase a thousandth of a second every century. Forty-seven of our present days will someday make up a month. We might eventually lose the moon altogether. Such great planetary movement rightly concerns astronomers, but it need not worry us. It will take 50 million years.

Enliven such writing—and make the main ideas stand out—by expressing the less important information in subordinate clauses and phrases. In the revision below, underlining indicates subordinate structures that used to be main clauses:

Revised The moon is now drifting away from the earth <u>about one inch a year</u>. <u>At a thousandth of a second every century</u>, this movement is lengthening our days. Forty-seven of our present days will someday make up a month, <u>if we don't eventually lose the moon altogether</u>. Such great planetary movement rightly concerns astronomers, but it need not worry us. It will take 50 million years.

2 • Sentence combining

As the preceding example shows, subordinating to achieve variety often involves combining short, choppy sentences into longer units that link related information and stress main ideas. Another example of such sentence combining follows on the next page.

Key terms

main clause A word group that contains a subject and a verb and does not begin with a subordinating word: *Tourism is an industry. It brings in over $2 billion a year.* (See p. 230.)

subordinate clause A word group that contains a subject and verb, begins with a subordinating word such as *because* or *who,* and is not a question: *Tourism is an industry <u>that brings in over $2 billion a year</u>.* (See p. 230.)

phrase A word group that lacks a subject or verb or both: *Tourism is an industry <u>valued at over $2 billion a year</u>.* (See p. 227.)

Monotonous — Astronomy may seem a remote science. It may seem to have little to do with people's daily lives. Many astronomers find otherwise. They see their science as soothing. It gives perspective to everyday routines and problems.

Combining five sentences into one, the revision is both clearer and easier to read. Underlining highlights the changes:

Revised — Astronomy may seem a remote science having little to do with people's daily lives, but many astronomers find their science soothing because it gives perspective to everyday routines and problems.

3 • Varying sentence beginnings

An English sentence often begins with its subject, which generally captures old information from a preceding sentence (see p. 167):

> The defendant's lawyer was determined to break the prosecution's witness. He relentlessly cross-examined the stubborn witness for a week.

However, an unbroken sequence of sentences beginning with the subject quickly becomes monotonous:

Monotonous — The defendant's lawyer was determined to break the prosecution's witness. He relentlessly cross-examined the witness for a week. The witness had expected to be dismissed within an hour and was visibly irritated. She did not cooperate. She was reprimanded by the judge.

Beginning some of these sentences with other expressions improves readability and clarity:

Revised — The defendant's lawyer was determined to break the prosecution's witness. For a week he relentlessly cross-examined the witness. Expecting to be dismissed within an hour, the witness was visibly irritated. She did not cooperate. Indeed, she was reprimanded by the judge.

The underlined expressions represent the most common choices for varying sentence beginnings:

- Adverb modifiers, such as *For a week* (modifies the verb *cross-examined*).
- Adjective modifiers, such as *Expecting to be dismissed within an hour* (modifies *witness*).

- Transitional expressions, such as *Indeed.* (See p. 59 for a list.)

CULTURE LANGUAGE In standard American English, placing certain adverb modifiers at the beginning of a sentence requires you to change the normal subject-verb order as well. The most common of these modifiers are negatives, including *seldom, rarely, in no case, not since,* and *not until.*

Faulty — Seldom [adverb] a witness [subject] has held [verb phrase] the stand so long.

Revised — Seldom [adverb] has [helping verb] a witness [subject] held [main verb] the stand so long.

4 • Varying word order

Occasionally, you can vary a sentence and emphasize it at the same time by inverting the usual order of parts:

> A dozen witnesses testified for the prosecution, and the defense attorney barely questioned eleven of them. The twelfth, however, he grilled. [Normal word order: *He grilled the twelfth, however.*]

Inverted sentences used without need are artificial. Use them only when emphasis demands.

17c Add details.

Relevant details such as facts and examples create the texture and life that keep readers awake and help them grasp your meaning. Notice the difference in the next two examples:

Flat — Constructed after World War II, Levittown, New York, consisted of thousands of houses in two basic styles. Over the decades, residents have altered the houses so dramatically that the original styles are often unrecognizable.

Detailed — Constructed on potato fields after World War II, Levittown, New York, consisted of more than seventeen thousand houses in Cape Cod and ranch styles. Over the decades, residents have added expansive front porches, punched dormer windows through roofs, converted garages to sun porches,

Key terms

adverb A word or word group that describes a verb, an adjective, another adverb, or a whole sentence: *dressed sharply, clearly unhappy, soaring from the mountain.* (See p. 214.)

adjective A word or word group that describes a noun or pronoun: *sweet smile, certain someone.* (See p. 214.)

and otherwise altered the houses so dramatically that the original styles are often unrecognizable.

EXERCISE 17.1
Revising: Variety

The following paragraph consists entirely of simple sentences that begin with their subjects. Use the techniques discussed in this chapter to vary the sentences. Delete, add, change, and rearrange words to make the paragraph more readable and to make important ideas stand out clearly. Answers to starred sentences appear at the end of the book.

*The Italian volcano Vesuvius had been dormant for many years. *It then exploded on August 24 in the year AD 79. *The ash, pumice, and mud from the volcano buried two busy towns. *Herculaneum is one. *The more famous is Pompeii. Both towns lay undiscovered for many centuries. Herculaneum and Pompeii were discovered in 1709 and 1748, respectively. The excavation of Pompeii was the more systematic. It was the occasion for initiating modern methods of conservation and restoration. Herculaneum was simply looted of its more valuable finds. It was then left to disintegrate. Pompeii appears much as it did before the eruption. A luxurious house opens onto a lush central garden. An election poster decorates a wall. A dining table is set for breakfast.

18 Appropriate and Exact Words

Is this the right word?

The choice of the "right" word depends partly on whether the word is appropriate for your writing situation (below) and partly on whether it expresses your meaning exactly (p. 190).

18a Choose appropriate words.

Appropriate words suit your writing situation—your subject, purpose, and audience. In most college and career writing you

http://www.ablongman.com/littlebrown

➤ Sentences and words
- ➤ Video tutorials ➤ Using appropriate language
- ➤ Web exercises ➤ Exers. 7–10
- ➤ Downloads ➤ Chapter 18 exercises in electronic format
- ➤ Web links ➤ Appropriate and exact language

should rely on what's called **standard American English,** the dialect of English normally expected and used in schools, businesses, government, and the communications media.

The vocabulary of standard American English is huge, allowing expression of an infinite range of ideas and feelings; but it does exclude words that only some groups of people use, understand, or find inoffensive. Some of these more limited vocabularies should be avoided altogether; others should be used cautiously and in relevant situations, as when aiming for a special effect with an audience you know will appreciate it. Whenever you doubt a word's status, consult a dictionary (see p. 190).

Note Many grammar and style checkers can be set to flag potentially inappropriate words, such as nonstandard language, slang, colloquialisms, and gender-specific terms (*manmade, mailman*). However, the checker can flag only words listed in its dictionary of questionable words. For example, a checker flagged *businessman* as potentially sexist in *A successful businessman puts clients first,* but the checker did not flag *his* in *A successful businessperson listens to his clients*. If you use a checker to review your language, you'll need to determine whether a flagged word is or is not appropriate for your writing situation, and you'll still need to hunt for possibly inappropriate words on your own.

1 • Nonstandard dialect CULTURE LANGUAGE

Like many countries, the United States includes scores of regional, social, or ethnic groups with their own distinct **dialects,** or versions of English. Standard American English is one of those dialects, and so are Black English, Appalachian English, Creole, and the English of coastal Maine. All the dialects of English share many features, but each also has its own vocabulary, pronunciation, and grammar.

If you speak a dialect of English besides standard American English, be careful about using your dialect in situations where standard English is the norm, such as in academic or business writing. Dialects are not wrong in themselves, but forms imported from one dialect into another may still be perceived as unclear or incorrect. When you know standard English is expected in your writing, edit to eliminate expressions in your dialect that you know (or have been told) differ from standard English. These expressions may include *theirselves, hisn, them books,* and others labeled "nonstandard" by a dictionary. They may also include verb forms, as discussed on pages 241–48. For help identifying and editing nonstandard language, see the "Guide to CULTURE LANGUAGE Topics" just before the back endpapers of this book.

Your participation in the community of standard American English does not require you to abandon your own dialect. You may want to use it in writing you do for yourself, such as journals, notes, and drafts, which should be composed as freely as possible. You may want to quote it in an academic paper, as when analyzing or reporting conversation in dialect. And, of course, you will want to use it with others who speak it.

2 • Slang

Slang is the language used by a group, such as musicians or computer programmers, to reflect common experiences and to make technical references efficient. The following example is from an essay on the slang of "skaters" (skateboarders):

> Curtis slashed ultra-punk crunchers on his longboard, while the Rube-man flailed his usual Gumbyness on tweaked frontsides and lofty fakie ollies. —Miles Orkin, "Mucho Slingage by the Pool"

Among those who understand it, slang may be vivid and forceful. It often occurs in dialog, and an occasional slang expression can enliven an informal essay. But most slang is too flippant and imprecise for effective communication, and it is generally inappropriate for college or business writing. Notice the gain in seriousness and precision achieved in the following revision:

Slang — Many students start out pretty together but then get weird.

Revised — Many students start out with clear goals but then lose their direction.

3 • Colloquial language

Colloquial language is the everyday spoken language, including expressions such as *get together, go crazy,* and *do the dirty work.*

When you write informally, colloquial language may be appropriate to achieve the casual, relaxed effect of conversation. An occasional colloquial word dropped into otherwise more formal writing can also help you achieve a desired emphasis. But most colloquial language is not precise enough for college or career writing. In such writing you should generally avoid any words and expressions labeled "informal" or "colloquial" in your dictionary.

Colloquial — According to a Native American myth, the Great Creator had a dog hanging around with him when he created the earth.

Revised — According to a Native American myth, the Great Creator was accompanied by a dog when he created the earth.

4 • Technical words

All disciplines and professions rely on specialized language that allows the members to communicate precisely and efficiently with each other. Chemists, for instance, have their *phosphatides,* and literary critics have their *motifs* and *subtexts.* Without explanation technical words are meaningless to nonspecialists. When you are writing for nonspecialists, avoid unnecessary technical terms and carefully define terms you must use.

5 • Indirect and pretentious writing

Small, plain, and direct words are almost always preferable to big, showy, or evasive words. Take special care to avoid euphemisms, double-talk, and pretentious writing.

A **euphemism** is a presumably inoffensive word that a writer or speaker substitutes for a word deemed potentially offensive or too blunt, such as *passed away* for *died* or *misspeak* for *lie.* Use euphemisms only when you know that blunt, truthful words would needlessly hurt or offend members of your audience.

A kind of euphemism that deliberately evades the truth is **double-talk** (also called **doublespeak** or **weasel words**): language intended to confuse or to be misunderstood. Today double-talk is unfortunately common in politics and advertising—the *revenue enhancement* that is really a tax, the *peace-keeping function* that is really war making, the *biodegradable* bags that last decades. Double-talk has no place in honest writing.

Euphemism and sometimes double-talk seem to keep company with **pretentious writing,** fancy language that is more elaborate than its subject requires. Choose your words for their exactness and economy. The big, ornate word may be tempting, but pass it up. Your readers will be grateful.

Pretentious To perpetuate our endeavor of providing funds for our elderly citizens as we do at the present moment, we will face the exigency of enhanced contributions from all our citizens.

Revised We cannot continue to fund Social Security and Medicare for the elderly unless we raise taxes.

6 • Sexist and other biased language

Even when we do not mean it to, our language can reflect and perpetuate hurtful prejudices toward groups of people. Such biased language can be obvious—words such as *nigger, honky, mick, kike, fag, dyke,* or *broad.* But it can also be subtle, generalizing about groups in ways that may be familiar but that are also inaccurate or unfair.

Biased language reflects poorly on the user, not on the person or persons whom it mischaracterizes or insults. Unbiased language does not submit to false generalizations. It treats people respectfully as individuals and labels groups as they wish to be labeled.

Stereotypes of race, ethnicity, religion, age, and other characteristics

A **stereotype** is a generalization based on poor evidence, a kind of formula for understanding and judging people simply because of their membership in a group:

Men are uncommunicative.
Women are emotional.
Liberals want to raise taxes.
Conservatives are affluent.

At best, stereotypes betray a noncritical writer, one who is not thinking beyond notions received from others. In your writing, be alert for statements that characterize whole groups of people.

Stereotype: Elderly drivers should have their licenses limited to daytime driving only. [Asserts that all elderly people are poor night drivers.]

Revised: Drivers with impaired night vision should have their licenses limited to daytime driving only.

Some stereotypes have become part of the language, but they are still potentially offensive:

Stereotype: The administrators are too blind to see the need for a new gymnasium.

Revised: The administrators do not understand the need for a new gymnasium.

Sexist language

Among the most subtle and persistent biased language is that expressing narrow ideas about men's and women's roles, position, and value in society. Like other stereotypes, this **sexist language** can wound or irritate readers, and it indicates the writer's thoughtlessness or unfairness. The box opposite suggests some ways of eliminating sexist language.

CULTURE LANGUAGE Forms of address vary widely from culture to culture. In some cultures, for instance, one shows respect by referring to all older women as if they were married, using the equivalent of *Mrs.* Usage in the United States is changing toward making no assumptions about marital status, rank, or other characteristics—for instance, addressing a woman as *Ms.* unless she is known to prefer *Mrs.* or *Miss.*

Eliminating sexist language

- Avoid demeaning and patronizing language:

Sexist Dr. Keith Kim and Lydia Hawkins coauthored the article.
Revised Dr. Keith Kim and Dr. Lydia Hawkins coauthored the article.
Revised Keith Kim and Lydia Hawkins coauthored the article.

Sexist Ladies are entering almost every occupation formerly filled by men.
Revised Women are entering almost every occupation formerly filled by men.

- Avoid occupational or social stereotypes:

Sexist The considerate doctor commends a nurse when she provides his patients with good care.
Revised The considerate doctor commends a nurse who provides good care for patients.

Sexist The grocery shopper should save her coupons.
Revised Grocery shoppers should save their coupons.

- Avoid referring needlessly to gender:

Sexist Marie Curie, a woman chemist, discovered radium.
Revised Marie Curie, a chemist, discovered radium.

Sexist The patients were tended by a male nurse.
Revised The patients were tended by a nurse.

- Avoid using *man* or words containing *man* to refer to all human beings. Here are a few alternatives:

businessman	businessperson
chairman	chair, chairperson
congressman	representative in Congress, legislator
craftsman	craftsperson, artisan
layman	layperson
mankind	humankind, humanity, human beings, humans
manmade	handmade, manufactured, synthetic, artificial
manpower	personnel, human resources
policeman	police officer
salesman	salesperson, sales representative

Sexist Man has not reached the limits of social justice.
Revised Humankind [or Humanity] has not reached the limits of social justice.

Sexist The furniture consists of manmade materials.
Revised The furniture consists of synthetic materials.

(continued)

appr
18a

Eliminating sexist language

(continued)

- Avoid the **generic *he,*** the male pronoun used to refer to both genders. (See also pp. 287–88.)

  Sexist — The newborn child explores his world.

  Revised — Newborn children explore their world. [Use the plural for the pronoun and the word it refers to.]

  Revised — The newborn child explores the world. [Avoid the pronoun altogether.]

  Revised — The newborn child explores his or her world. [Substitute male and female pronouns.]

  Use the last option sparingly—only once in a group of sentences and only to stress the singular individual.

Appropriate labels

We often need to label groups: *swimmers, politicians, mothers, Christians, Westerners, students.* But labels can be shorthand stereotypes, slighting the person labeled and ignoring the preferences of the group members themselves. Although sometimes dismissed as "political correctness," showing sensitivity about labels hurts no one and helps gain your readers' trust and respect.

- *Avoid labels that (intentionally or not) disparage the person or group you refer to.* A person with emotional problems is not a *mental patient.* A person with cancer is not a *cancer victim.* A person using a wheelchair is not *wheelchair-bound.*
- *Use names for racial, ethnic, and other groups that reflect the preferences of each group's members,* or at least many of them. Examples of current preferences include *African American* or *black, latino/latina* (for Americans and American immigrants of Spanish-speaking descent), and *disabled* (rather than *handicapped*). But labels change often. To learn how a group's members wish to be labeled, ask them directly, attend to usage in reputable periodicals, or check a recent dictionary.

A helpful reference is *Guidelines for Bias-Free Writing,* by Marilyn Schwartz and the Task Force on Bias-Free Language of the Association of American University Presses.

EXERCISE 18.1
Revising: Appropriate words

Rewrite the following sentences as needed for standard written English, focusing on inappropriate slang, technical or pretentious language, and biased language. Consult a dictionary to determine whether particular words are appropriate and to find suitable substitutes. Answers to starred items appear at the end of the book.

Example:

If negotiators get hyper during contract discussions, they may mess up chances for a settlement.

If negotiators become excited or upset during contract discussions, they may harm chances for a settlement.

*1. Acquired immune deficiency syndrome (AIDS) is a major deal all over the world.
*2. The disease gets around primarily by sexual intercourse, exchange of bodily fluids, shared needles, and blood transfusions.
*3. Those who think the disease is limited to homos and druggies are quite mistaken.
*4. Stats suggest that in the United States one in every five hundred college kids carries the virus.
*5. A person with AIDS does not deserve to be subjected to exclusionary behavior or callousness on the part of his fellow citizens. Instead, he has the necessity for all the compassion, medical care, and financial assistance due those who are in the extremity of illness.

6. An AIDS victim often sees a team of doctors or a single doctor with a specialized practice.
7. The doctor may help his patients by obtaining social services for them as well as by providing medical care.
8. The AIDS sufferer who loses his job may need public assistance.
9. For someone who is very ill, a full-time nurse may be necessary. She can administer medications and make the sick person as comfortable as possible.
10. Some people with AIDS have insurance, but others lack the bread for premiums.

EXERCISE 18.2
Revising: Sexist language

Revise the following sentences to eliminate sexist language. If you change a singular noun or pronoun to plural, be sure to make any needed changes in verbs or other pronouns. Answers to starred items appear at the end of the book.

Example:

The career placement officer at most colleges and universities spends part of his time advising students how to write successful résumés.

Career placement officers at most colleges and universities spend part of their time advising students how to write successful résumés.

*1. When a person applies for a job, he should represent himself with the best possible résumé.
*2. A person applying for a job as a mailman should appear to be honest and responsible.
*3. A girl applying for a position as an in-home nurse should also represent herself as honest and responsible.
*4. Of course, she should also have a background of capable nursing.
*5. The businessman who is scanning a stack of résumés will, of necessity, read them all quickly.

6. The person who wants his résumé to stand out will make sure it highlights his best points.
7. The computer programmer will highlight his experience with computers.
8. Volunteer work may be appropriate, too, such as being chairman of a student organization.
9. If the student has been secretary for a campus organization, she could include that volunteer experience in her résumé.
10. If everyone writing a résumé would keep in mind the man who will be reading it, the applicant might know better what he should include and how he should format that information.

18b Choose exact words.

To write clearly and effectively, you will want to find the words that fit your meaning exactly and convey your attitude precisely.

Note A grammar and style checker can provide some help with inexact language. For instance, you can set it to flag commonly confused words (such as *continuous/continual*), misused prepositions in idioms (such as *accuse for* instead of *accuse of*), and clichés. But the checker can flag only words stored in its dictionary. It can't help you at all in using words with appropriate connotations, making abstract words concrete, or solving other problems discussed in this section. You'll need to read your work carefully on your own.

1 • Word meanings and synonyms

For writing exactly, a dictionary is essential and a thesaurus can be helpful.

Desk dictionaries

A desk dictionary defines about 150,000 to 200,000 words and provides pronunciation, grammatical functions, history, and other information. Here is a sample from *Merriam-Webster's Collegiate Dictionary:*

Good desk dictionaries, in addition to *Merriam-Webster's,* include the *American Heritage College Dictionary,* the *Random House Webster's College Dictionary,* and *Webster's New World Dictionary.* Most of these are available in both print and electronic form (CD-ROM or online). In addition, several Web sites provide online dictionaries or links to online dictionaries. This book's Web site provides links: see the box on page 182.

CULTURE LANGUAGE If English is not your native language, you probably should have a dictionary prepared especially for students using English as a second language (ESL). Such a dictionary contains special information on prepositions, count versus noncount nouns, and many other matters. Reliable ESL dictionaries include *COBUILD English Language Dictionary, Longman Dictionary of Contemporary English,* and *Oxford Advanced Learner's Dictionary.*

Thesauruses

To find a word with the exact shade of meaning you intend, you may want to consult a thesaurus, or book of **synonyms**—words with approximately the same meaning. A thesaurus such as *Roget's International Thesaurus* lists most imaginable synonyms for thousands of words. The word *news,* for instance, has half a page of synonyms in *Roget's International,* including *tidings, dispatch, gossip,* and *journalism.*

Since a thesaurus aims to open up possibilities, its lists of synonyms include approximate as well as precise matches. The thesaurus does not define synonyms or distinguish among them, however, so you need a dictionary to discover exact meanings. In general, don't use a word from a thesaurus—even one you like the sound of—until you are sure of its appropriateness for your meaning.

Note This book's Web site provides links to online thesauruses: see the box on page 182. Your word processor may also include a thesaurus, making it easy to look up synonyms and insert the chosen word into your text. But still you should consult a dictionary unless you are certain of the word's meaning and appropriateness.

2 • The right word for your meaning

All words have one or more basic meanings (called **denotations**)—the meanings listed in the dictionary, without reference to emotional associations. If readers are to understand you, you must use words according to their established meanings.

- Consult a dictionary whenever you are unsure of a word's meaning.
- Distinguish between similar-sounding words that have widely different denotations:

  Inexact Older people often suffer <u>infirmaries</u> [places for the sick].
  Exact Older people often suffer <u>infirmities</u> [disabilities].

  Some words, called **homonyms,** sound exactly alike but differ in meaning: for example, *principal/principle* or *rain/reign/rein.* (See pp. 383–84 for a list of commonly confused homonyms.)
- Distinguish between words with related but distinct meanings:

  Inexact Television commercials <u>continuously</u> [unceasingly] interrupt programming.
  Exact Television commercials <u>continually</u> [regularly] interrupt programming.

In addition to their emotion-free meanings, many words also carry associations with specific feelings. These **connotations** can shape readers' responses and are thus a powerful tool for writers. The following word pairs have related denotations but very different connotations:

pride: sense of self-worth
vanity: excessive regard for oneself

firm: steady, unchanging, unyielding
stubborn: unreasonable, bullheaded

lasting: long-lived, enduring
endless: without limit, eternal

enthusiasm: excitement
mania: excessive interest or desire

A dictionary can help you track down words with the exact connotations you want. Besides providing meanings, your dictionary may also list and distinguish synonyms to guide your choices. A thesaurus can also help if you use it carefully, as discussed on the previous page.

EXERCISE 18.3
Using a dictionary

Look up five of the following words in a dictionary. First, find out whether the dictionary lists the oldest or most common meanings first in its entries. Then, for each word, write down (*a*) the division into syllables, (*b*) the pronunciation, (*c*) the grammatical functions and forms, (*d*) the etymology, (*e*) each meaning, and (*f*) any special uses indicated by labels. Finally, use the word in two sentences of your own.

1. depreciation
2. secretary
3. grammar
4. manifest
5. assassin
6. astrology
7. toxic
8. steal
9. plain (*adjective*)
10. ceremony

EXERCISE 18.4
Revising: Denotation

Revise any underlined word below that is used incorrectly. Consult a dictionary if you are uncertain of a word's precise meaning. Answers to starred items appear at the end of the book.

Example:

Sam and Dave are going to Bermuda and Hauppage, respectfully, for spring vacation.

Sam and Dave are going to Bermuda and Hauppage, respectively, for spring vacation.

*1. Maxine Hong Kingston was rewarded many prizes for her first two books, *The Woman Warrior* and *China Men*.
*2. Kingston sites her mother's tales about ancestors and ancient Chinese customs as the sources of these memoirs.
*3. Two of Kingston's progeny, her great-grandfathers, are focal points of *China Men*.
*4. Both men led rebellions against suppressive employers: a sugarcane farmer and a railroad-construction engineer.
*5. In her childhood Kingston was greatly effected by her mother's tale about a pregnant aunt who was ostracized by villagers.
6. The aunt gained avengeance by drowning herself in the village's water supply.
7. Kingston decided to make her nameless relative infamous by giving her immortality in *The Woman Warrior*.
8. Kingston's novel *Tripmaster Monkey* has been called the premiere novel about the 1960s.
9. Her characters embody the principles that led to her own protest against the Vietnam War.
10. Kingston's innovative books infer her opposition to racism and sexism both in the China of the past and in the United States of the present.

EXERCISE 18.5
Considering the connotations of words

Fill in the blank in each sentence below with the most appropriate word from the list in parentheses. Consult a dictionary to be sure of your choice. Answers to starred items appear at the end of the book.

Example:

Channel 5 _________ Oshu the winner before the polls closed. (*advertised, declared, broadcast, promulgated*)

Channel 5 declared Oshu the winner before the polls closed.

*1. AIDS is a serious health _________. (*problem, worry, difficulty, plight*)

*2. Once the virus has entered the blood system, it _________ T-cells. (*murders, destroys, slaughters, executes*)

3. The _________ of T-cells is to combat infections. (*ambition, function, aim, goal*)
4. Without enough T-cells, the body is nearly _________ against infections. (*defenseless, hopeless, desperate*)
5. To prevent exposure to the disease, one should be especially _________ in sexual relationships. (*chary, circumspect, cautious, calculating*)

3 • Concrete and specific words

Clear, exact writing balances abstract and general words, which outline ideas and objects, with concrete and specific words, which sharpen and solidify.

- **Abstract words** name qualities and ideas: *beauty, inflation, management, culture, liberal.* **Concrete words** name things we can know by our five senses of sight, hearing, touch, taste, and smell: *sleek, humming, brick, bitter, musty.*
- **General words** name classes or groups of things, such as *buildings, weather,* or *birds,* and include all the varieties of the class. **Specific words** limit a general class, such as *buildings,* by naming one of its varieties, such as *skyscraper* or *hut.*

Abstract and general words are useful in the broad statements that set the course for your writing:

> The wild horse in America has a romantic history.
>
> Relations between the sexes today are more relaxed than they were in the past.

But such statements need development with concrete and specific detail. Detail can turn a vague sentence into an exact one:

Vague The size of his hands made his smallness real. [How big were his hands? How small was he?]

Exact Not until I saw his delicate, doll-like hands did I realize that he stood a full head shorter than most other men.

If you write on a computer, you can use its Find function to help you find and revise abstract and general words that you tend to overuse. Examples of such words include *nice, interesting, things, very, good, a lot, a little,* and *some.*

EXERCISE 18.6
Revising: Concrete and specific words

Make the following paragraph vivid by expanding the sentences with appropriate details of your own choosing. Substitute concrete and specific words for the abstract and general ones that are underlined.

I remember clearly how awful I felt the first time I attended Mrs. Murphy's second-grade class. I had recently moved from a small town in Missouri to a crowded suburb of Chicago. My new school looked big from the outside and seemed dark inside as I walked down the long corridor toward the classroom. The class was noisy as I neared the door; but when I entered, everyone became quiet and looked at me. I felt uncomfortable and wanted a place to hide. However, in a loud voice Mrs. Murphy directed me to the front of the room to introduce myself.

4 • Idioms

Idioms are expressions in any language that do not fit the rules for meaning or grammar—for instance, *put up with, plug away at, make off with.*

Idiomatic combinations of verbs or adjectives and prepositions can be confusing for both native and nonnative speakers of English. A number of these pairings are listed on the next page. (More appear on pp. 251–52.)

CULTURE LANGUAGE If you are learning standard American English, you are justified in stumbling over its prepositions: their meanings can shift depending on context, and they have many idiomatic uses. In mastering English prepositions, you probably can't avoid memorization. But you can help yourself by memorizing related groups, such as *at/in/on* and *for/since.*

At, in, or *on* in expressions of time

- Use *at* before actual clock time: *at* 8:30.
- Use *in* before a month, year, century, or period: *in April, in 2007, in the twenty-first century, in the next month.*
- Use *on* before a day or date: *on Tuesday, on August 3, on Labor Day.*

exact
18b

Idioms with prepositions

abide by a rule
abide in a place or state

according to
accords with

accuse of a crime

accustomed to

adapt from a source
adapt to a situation

afraid of

agree on a plan
agree to a proposal
agree with a person

angry with

aware of

based on

capable of

certain of

charge for a purchase
charge with a crime

concur in an opinion
concur with a person

contend for a principle
contend with a person

dependent on

differ about or over a question
differ from in some quality
differ with a person

disappointed by or in a person
disappointed in or with a thing

familiar with

identical with or to

impatient at her conduct
impatient for a raise
impatient of restraint
impatient with a person

independent of

infer from

inferior to

involved in a task
involved with a person

oblivious of or to one's surroundings
oblivious of something forgotten

occupied by a person
occupied in study
occupied with a thing

opposed to

part from a person
part with a possession

prior to

proud of

related to

rewarded by the judge
rewarded for something done
rewarded with a gift

similar to

superior to

wait at a place
wait for a train, a person
wait in a room
wait on a customer

At, in, or *on* in expressions of place

- Use *at* before a specific place or address: *at the school, at 511 Iris Street.*
- Use *in* before a place with limits or before a city, state, country, or continent: *in the house, in a box, in Oklahoma City, in China, in Asia.*

- Use *on* to mean "supported by" or "touching the surface of": *on the table, on Iris Street, on page 150.*

For or *since* in expressions of time

- Use *for* before a period of time: *for an hour, for two years.*
- Use *since* before a specific point in time: *since 1999, since Friday.*

A dictionary of English as a second language is the best source for the meanings of prepositions; see the suggestions on page 191.

EXERCISE 18.7
Using prepositions in idioms

In the sentences below, insert the preposition that correctly completes each idiom. Consult the box on the previous page or a dictionary as needed. Answers to starred items appear at the end of the book.

Example:

I disagree ______ many feminists who say women should not be homemakers.

I disagree with many feminists who say women should not be homemakers.

*1. The friend who introduced Mark and Lana was proud ______ his matchmaking.
*2. They had fallen ______ love ______ their first date.
*3. Mark and Lana had become so dependent ______ each other that they talked ______ the phone several times every day.
*4. Certain ______ their love, Mark and Lana decided to get married.
*5. Now, as Mark and Lana waited ______ the justice of the peace, they seemed oblivious ______ the other people in the lobby.
6. But Mark inferred ______ Lana's glance at a handsome man that she was no longer occupied ______ him alone.
7. Angry ______ Lana, Mark charged her ______ not loving him enough to get married.
8. Impatient ______ Mark's childish behavior, Lana disagreed ______ his interpretation of her glance.
9. They decided that if they could differ so violently ______ a minor incident, they should part ______ each other.
10. They agreed ______ think things over and meet again in one week.

EXERCISE 18.8
Using prepositions in idioms CULTURE LANGUAGE

Complete the following sentences by filling in the blanks with the appropriate prepositions from this list: *at, by, for, from, in, of, on, to, with.* Answers to starred items appear at the end of the book.

exact 18b

Example:

The most recent amendment to the US Constitution, ratified _______ May 18, 1992, was first proposed _______ 1789.

The most recent amendment to the US Constitution, ratified on May 18, 1992, was first proposed in 1789.

*1. The Eighteenth Amendment _______ the Constitution _______ the United States was ratified _______ 1919.

*2. It prohibited the "manufacture, sale, or transportation _______ intoxicating liquors."

3. It was adopted _______ response _______ a nationwide crusade _______ temperance groups.

4. The amendment did not prevent Americans _______ drinking, and the sale _______ alcoholic beverages was taken over _______ organized crime.

5. Wide-scale smuggling and bootlegging came _______ the demand _______ liquor.

5 • Figurative language

Figurative language (or a **figure of speech**) departs from the literal meanings of words, usually by comparing very different ideas or objects:

Literal	As I try to write, I can think of nothing to say.
Figurative	As I try to write, my mind is a slab of black slate.

Imaginatively and carefully used, figurative language can capture meaning more precisely and feelingly than literal language. Here is a figure of speech at work in technical writing (paraphrasing the physicist Edward Andrade):

> The molecules in a liquid move continuously like couples on an overcrowded dance floor, jostling each other.

The two most common figures of speech are the simile and the metaphor. Both compare two things of different classes, often one abstract and the other concrete. A **simile** makes the comparison explicit and usually begins with *like* or *as:*

> Whenever we grow, we tend to feel it, as a young seed must feel the weight and inertia of the earth when it seeks to break out of its shell on its way to becoming a plant. —ALICE WALKER

A **metaphor** claims that the two things are identical, omitting such words as *like* and *as:*

> A school is a hopper into which children are heaved while they are young and tender; therein they are pressed into certain standard shapes and covered from head to heels with official rubber stamps. —H. L. MENCKEN

Successful figurative language is fresh and unstrained, calling attention not to itself but to the writer's meaning. Be wary of mixed metaphors, which combine two or more incompatible figures:

Mixed Various thorny problems that we try to sweep under the rug continue to bob up all the same.

Improved Various thorny problems that we try to weed out continue to thrive all the same.

EXERCISE 18.9
Using figurative language

Invent appropriate similes or metaphors of your own to describe each scene or quality below, and use the figure in a sentence.

Example:

The attraction of a lake on a hot day
The small waves like fingers beckoned us irresistibly.

1. The sound of a kindergarten classroom
2. People waiting in line to buy tickets to a rock concert
3. The politeness of strangers meeting for the first time
4. A streetlight seen through dense fog
5. The effect of watching television for ten hours straight

6 • Trite expressions

Trite expressions, or **clichés,** are phrases so old and so often repeated that they have become stale. They include the following:

add insult to injury
better late than never
cool, calm, and collected
crushing blow
easier said than done
face the music
few and far between
green with envy
hard as a rock
heavy as lead
hit the nail on the head
hour of need
a needle in a haystack
point with pride
pride and joy
ripe old age
rude awakening
sadder but wiser
shoulder the burden
shoulder to cry on
sneaking suspicion
stand in awe
strong as an ox
thin as a rail
tried and true
wise as an owl

Clichés may slide into your drafts while you are trying to find the words for your meaning. To edit clichés, listen to your writing for any expressions that you have heard or used before. You can also supplement your efforts with a computerized style checker, which may include a cliché detector. When you find a cliché, substitute fresh words of your own or restate the idea in plain language.

EXERCISE 18.10
Revising: Trite expressions

Revise the following sentences to eliminate trite expressions. Answers to starred items appear at the end of the book.

Example:

The basketball team had almost seized victory, but it faced the test of truth in the last quarter of the game.

The basketball team seemed about to win, but the real test came in the last quarter of the game.

*1. The disastrous consequences of the war have shaken the small nation to its roots.
*2. Prices for food have shot sky high, and citizens have sneaking suspicions that others are making a killing on the black market.
*3. Medical supplies are so few and far between that even civilians who are as sick as dogs cannot get treatment.
*4. With most men fighting or injured or killed, women have had to bite the bullet and bear the men's burden in farming and manufacturing.
*5. Last but not least, the war's heavy drain on the nation's pocketbook has left the economy in shambles.

6. Our reliance on foreign oil to support our driving habit has hit record highs in recent years.
7. Gas-guzzling sport-utility vehicles are responsible for part of the increase.
8. In the near future, we may have to bite the bullet and make use of public transportation or drive more fuel-efficient cars.
9. Both solutions are easier said than done.
10. But it stands to reason that we cannot go on using the world's oil reserves at such a rapid rate.

19 Completeness

Are all needed words in place?

Sometimes, omitting even a little word like *of* or *in* can make a sentence unclear. In editing, check your sentences to be sure you've included all the words they need. For additional help with complete sentences, see Chapter 35 on sentence fragments.

Note Grammar and style checkers will not flag most kinds of incomplete sentences discussed in this section. Only your own careful proofreading can ensure that sentences are complete.

19a Write complete compounds.

You may omit words from a compound construction when the omission will not confuse readers:

> Environmentalists have hopes for alternative fuels and [for] public transportation.
>
> Some cars will run on electricity and some [will run] on methane.

Such omissions are possible only when the words omitted are common to all the parts of a compound construction. When the parts differ in any way, all words must be included in all parts.

> One new car gets eighty miles per gallon; some old cars get as little as five miles per gallon. [One verb is singular, the other plural.]
>
> Environmentalists believe in and work for fuel conservation. [Idiom requires different prepositions with *believe* and *work.*]

19b Add needed words.

In haste or carelessness, do not omit small words that are needed for clarity:

Incomplete	Regular payroll deductions are a type painless savings. You hardly notice missing amounts, and after period of years the contributions can add a large total.
Revised	Regular payroll deductions are a type of painless savings. You hardly notice the missing amounts, and after a period of years the contributions can add up to a large total.

Attentive proofreading is the only insurance against this kind of omission. *Proofread all your papers carefully.* See pages 43–44 for suggestions.

Key term

compound construction Two or more elements (words, phrases, clauses) that are equal in importance and that function as a unit: *Rain fell, streams overflowed* (clauses); *dogs and cats* (words).

http://www.ablongman.com/littlebrown

➤ Sentences and words
  ➤ Web exercises ➤ Exer. 11
  ➤ Downloads ➤ Chapter 19 exercise in electronic format
  ➤ Web links ➤ Complete sentences

CULTURE LANGUAGE If your native language is not English, you may have difficulty knowing when to use the English articles *a, an,* and *the.* For guidelines on using articles, see pages 301–04.

EXERCISE 19.1
Revising: Completeness

Add words to the following sentences so that the sentences are complete and clear. Possible answers to starred items appear at the end of the book.

Example:

Our house is closer to the courthouse than the subway stop.
Our house is closer to the courthouse than it is to the subway stop.
Our house is closer to the courthouse than the subway stop is.

*1. The first ice cream, eaten China in about 2000 BC, was lumpier than modern ice cream.
*2. The Chinese made their ice cream of milk, spices, and overcooked rice and packed in snow to solidify.
3. In the fourteenth century ice milk and fruit ices appeared in Italy and the tables of the wealthy.
4. At her wedding in 1533 to the king of France, Catherine de Médicis offered several flavors fruit ices.
5. Modern sherbets resemble her ices; modern ice cream her soft dessert of thick, sweetened cream.

20 Conciseness

Have I deleted all unneeded words?

Unnecessary words pad your sentences without adding to your meaning, and they can make your writing unclear. You want to make every word count. Bear in mind, however, that writing concisely is not the same as writing briefly: detail and originality should not be cut with needless words. Rather, the length of the expression should be appropriate to the thought.

http://www.ablongman.com/littlebrown

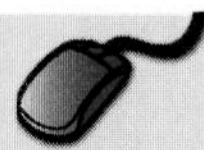

➤ Sentences and words
➤ Video tutorials ➤ Sentence combining
➤ Web exercises ➤ Exers. 12 and 13
➤ Downloads ➤ Chapter 20 exercises in electronic format
➤ Web links ➤ Writing concisely

Ways to achieve conciseness

Wordy (87 words)

The highly pressured nature of critical-care nursing is due to the fact that the patients have life-threatening illnesses. Critical-care nurses must have possession of steady nerves to care for patients who are critically ill and very sick. The nurses must also have possession of interpersonal skills. They must also have medical skills. It is considered by most health-care professionals that these nurses are essential if there is to be improvement of patients who are now in critical care from that status to the status of intermediate care.

Focus on subject and verb, and cut or shorten empty words and phrases.

Avoid nouns made from verbs.

Cut unneeded repetition.

Combine sentences.

Change passive voice to active voice.

Eliminate *there is* constructions.

Cut unneeded repetition, and reduce clauses and phrases.

Concise (37 words)

Critical-care nursing is highly pressured because the patients have life-threatening illnesses. Critical-care nurses must possess steady nerves and interpersonal and medical skills. Most health-care professionals consider these nurses essential if patients are to improve to intermediate care.

You may find yourself writing wordily when you are unsure of your subject or when your thoughts are tangled. It's fine, even necessary, to stumble and grope while drafting. But straighten out your ideas and aim for conciseness during revision and editing.

Note Any grammar and style checker will identify at least some wordy structures, such as repeated words, weak verbs, passive voice, and *there is* and *it is* constructions. No checker can identify all these structures, however, nor can it tell you whether the structure is appropriate for your ideas. In short, a checker can't substitute for your own careful reading and editing.

CULTURE LANGUAGE Wordiness is not a problem of incorrect grammar. A sentence may be perfectly grammatical but still contain unneeded words that interfere with the clarity and force of your idea.

20a Focus on the subject and verb.

Using the subjects and verbs of your sentences for the key actors and actions will reduce words and emphasize important ideas. (See pp. 162–64 for more on this topic.)

Wordy The reason why most of the country shifts to daylight savings time is that winter days are much shorter than summer days.

Concise Most of the country shifts to daylight savings time because winter days are much shorter than summer days.

Focusing on subjects and verbs will also help you avoid several other causes of wordiness discussed further on pages 162–64:

Nouns made from verbs

Wordy The occurrence of the winter solstice, the shortest day of the year, is an event taking place about December 22.

Concise The winter solstice, the shortest day of the year, occurs about December 22.

Weak verbs

Wordy The earth's axis has a tilt as the planet is in orbit around the sun so that the northern and southern hemispheres are alternately in alignment toward the sun.

Concise The earth's axis tilts as the planet orbits around the sun so that the northern and southern hemispheres alternately align toward the sun.

Passive voice

Wordy During its winter the northern hemisphere is tilted farthest away from the sun, so the nights are made longer and the days are made shorter.

Concise During its winter the northern hemisphere tilts away from the sun, making the nights longer and the days shorter.

See also pages 264–65 on changing the passive voice to the active voice, as in the example above.

20b Cut empty words.

Empty words walk in place, gaining little or nothing in meaning. Many of them can be cut entirely. The following are just a few examples.

Key terms

passive voice The verb form when the subject names the *receiver* of the verb's action: *The house was destroyed by the tornado.* (See p. 265.)

active voice The verb form when the subject names the *performer* of the verb's action: *The tornado destroyed the house.* (See p. 265.)

all things considered	in a manner of speaking
as far as I'm concerned	in my opinion
for all intents and purposes	last but not least
for the most part	more or less

Other empty words can also be cut, usually along with some of the words around them:

area	element	kind	situation
aspect	factor	manner	thing
case	field	nature	type

Still others can be reduced from several words to a single word:

For	Substitute
at all times	always
at the present time	now, yet
at this point in time	now
because of the fact that	because
by virtue of the fact that	because
due to the fact that	because
for the purpose of	for
in order to	to
in the event that	if
in the final analysis	finally

Cutting or reducing such words and phrases will make your writing move faster and work harder:

Wordy As far as I am concerned, because of the fact that a situation of discrimination continues to exist in the field of medicine, women have not at the present time achieved equality with men.

Concise Because of continuing discrimination in medicine, women have not yet achieved equality with men.

20c Cut unneeded repetition.

Deliberate repetition and restatement can make writing more coherent by linking sentences (see p. 56). But unnecessary repetition weakens sentences:

Wordy Many unskilled workers without training in a particular job are unemployed and do not have any work.

Concise Many unskilled workers are unemployed.

Be especially alert to phrases that say the same thing twice. In the examples below, the unneeded words are underlined:

circle around	important [basic] essentials
consensus of opinion	puzzling in nature
continue on	repeat again
cooperate together	return again
final completion	revert back
frank and honest exchange	square [round] in shape
the future to come	surrounding circumstances

CULTURE LANGUAGE The preceding phrases are redundant because the main word already implies the underlined word or words. A dictionary will tell you what meanings a word implies. *Assassinate,* for instance, means "murder someone well known," so the following sentence is redundant: *Julius Caesar was assassinated and killed.*

20d Tighten clauses and phrases.

Modifiers can be expanded or contracted depending on the emphasis you want to achieve. (Generally, the longer a construction, the more emphasis it has.) When editing your sentences, consider whether any modifiers can be reduced without loss of emphasis or clarity:

Wordy The Channel Tunnel, which runs between Britain and France, bores through a bed of solid chalk that is twenty-three miles across.

Concise The Channel Tunnel between Britain and France bores through twenty-three miles of solid chalk.

20e Cut *there is* or *it is* constructions.

You can postpone the sentence subject with the words *there is* (*there are, there was, there were*) and *it is* (*it was*): *There is a good reason to vote. It is your vote that counts.* These **expletive constructions** can be useful to emphasize the subject (as when introducing it for the first time) or to indicate a change in direction. But often they just add words and weaken sentences:

Wordy There were delays and cost overruns that plagued construction of the Channel Tunnel. It is the expectation of investors to earn profits at last, now that there are trains passing daily through the tunnel.

Key term

modifier A word or word group that limits or qualifies another word: *slippery road.* (See p. 295)

Concise — Delays and cost overruns plagued construction of the Channel Tunnel. Investors expect to earn profits at last, now that trains pass daily through the tunnel.

CULTURE LANGUAGE When you must use an expletive construction, be careful to include *there* or *it*. Only commands and some questions can begin with verbs.

20f Combine sentences.

Often the information in two or more sentences can be combined into one tight sentence:

Wordy — An unexpected problem with the Channel Tunnel is stowaways. The stowaways are mostly illegal immigrants. They are trying to smuggle themselves into England. They cling to train roofs and undercarriages.

Concise — An unexpected problem with the Channel Tunnel is stowaways, mostly illegal immigrants who are trying to smuggle themselves into England by clinging to train roofs and undercarriages.

(See also pp. 179–80 on combining sentences to achieve variety.)

20g Avoid jargon.

Jargon can refer to the special vocabulary of any discipline or profession (see p. 185). But it has also come to describe vague, inflated language that is overcomplicated, even incomprehensible. When it comes from government or business, we call it *bureaucratese*. It sounds almost as if the writer deliberately ignored every suggestion for clear, concise writing:

Jargon — The necessity for individuals to become separate entities in their own right may impel children to engage in open rebelliousness against parental authority or against sibling influence, with resultant bewilderment of those being rebelled against.

Translation — Children's natural desire to become themselves may make them rebel against bewildered parents or siblings.

EXERCISE 20.1
Revising: Writing concisely

Make the following sentences more concise. Combine sentences when doing so reduces wordiness. Answers to starred items appear at the end of the book.

Example:

It is thought by some people that there is gain from exercise only when it involves pain.

Some people think that gain comes from exercise only with pain.

*1. If sore muscles after exercising are a problem for you, there are some measures that can be taken by you to ease the discomfort.
*2. First, the immediate application of cold will help to reduce inflammation.
*3. Blood vessels are constricted by cold. Blood is kept away from the injured muscles.
*4. It is advisable to avoid heat for the first day.
*5. The application of heat within the first twenty-four hours can cause an increase in muscle soreness and stiffness.

6. There are two ways the application of cold can be made: you can take a cold shower or use an ice pack.
7. Inflammation of muscles can also be reduced with aspirin, ibuprofen, or another anti-inflammatory medication.
8. There is the idea that muscle soreness can be worsened by power lifting.
9. While healing is occurring, you need to take it easy.
10. A day or two after overdoing exercise, it is advisable for you to get some light exercise and gentle massage.

EXERCISE 20.2
Revising: Conciseness

Make the following paragraph as concise as possible. Be merciless. Answers to starred sentences appear at the end of the book.

*At the end of a lengthy line of reasoning, he came to the conclusion that the situation with carcinogens [cancer-causing substances] should be regarded as similar to the situation with the automobile. *Instead of giving in to an irrational fear of cancer, we should consider all aspects of the problem in a balanced and dispassionate frame of mind, making a total of the benefits received from potential carcinogens (plastics, pesticides, and other similar products) and measuring said total against the damage done by such products. This is the nature of most discussions about the automobile. Instead of responding irrationally to the visual, aural, and air pollution caused by automobiles, we have decided to live with them (while simultaneously working to improve on them) for the benefits brought to society as a whole.

IV

Sentence Parts and Patterns

Basic Grammar

How are sentences constructed?

Every language constructs sentences by arranging the words of the language into patterns and sometimes by altering the words as well. The **grammar** of a language describes how it works, and understanding the grammar of English can help you create clear and accurate sentences. This section explains the kinds of words in sentences (Chapter 21) and how to build basic sentences (22), expand them (23), and classify them (24).

Note Grammar and style checkers can both offer assistance and cause problems as you compose sentences. Look for the cautions and tips for using such checkers in this and the next two parts of this book. For more information about grammar and style checkers, see pages 42–43.

gram 21

21 Parts of Speech

What are the kinds of words, and how do they work?

All English words fall into eight groups, or **parts of speech,** such as nouns, verbs, adjectives, and adverbs. A word's part of speech determines its form and its position in a sentence. The same word may even serve as different parts of speech in different sentences, as these examples show:

> The government sent aid to the city. [*Aid* is a noun.]
> Governments aid citizens. [*Aid* is a verb.]

The *function* of a word in a sentence always determines its part of speech in that sentence.

http://www.ablongman.com/littlebrown

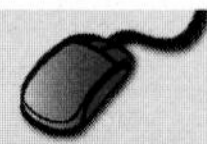

➤ Sentences and words
- ➤ Web exercises ➤ Exer. 14
- ➤ Downloads ➤ Chapter 21 exercises in electronic format
- ➤ Web links ➤ Basic grammar

21a Learn to recognize nouns.

Nouns name. They may name a person (*Rosie O'Donnell, Jesse Jackson, astronaut*), a thing (*chair, book, Mt. Rainier*), a quality (*pain, mystery, simplicity*), a place (*city, Washington, ocean, Red Sea*), or an idea (*reality, peace, success*).

The forms of nouns depend partly on where they fit in certain groups. As the examples indicate, the same noun may appear in more than one group.

- **Common nouns** name general classes of things and do not begin with capital letters: *earthquake, citizen, earth, fortitude, army.*
- **Proper nouns** name specific people, places, and things and begin with capital letters: *Helen Hunt, Washington Monument, El Paso, US Congress.*
- **Count nouns** name things considered countable in English. Most add *-s* or *-es* to distinguish between singular (one) and plural (more than one): *citizen, citizens; city, cities.* Some count nouns form irregular plurals: *woman, women; child, children.*
- **Noncount nouns** name things that aren't considered countable in English (*earth, sugar*), or they name qualities (*chaos, fortitude*). Noncount nouns do not form plurals.
- **Collective nouns** are singular in form but name groups: *army, family, herd, US Congress.*

In addition, most nouns form the **possessive** by adding *-'s* to show ownership (*Nadia's books, citizen's rights*), source (*Auden's poems*), and some other relationships.

21b Learn to recognize pronouns.

Most **pronouns** substitute for nouns and function in sentences as nouns do: *Susanne Ling enlisted in the Navy when she graduated.*

Pronouns fall into several subclasses depending on their form or function:

- **Personal pronouns** refer to a specific individual or to individuals: *I, you, he, she, it, we,* and *they.*
- **Indefinite pronouns**, such as *everybody* and *some,* do not substitute for any specific nouns, though they function as nouns (*Everybody speaks*).
- **Relative pronouns**—*who, whoever, which, that*—relate groups of words to nouns or other pronouns (*The book that won is a novel*).

- **Interrogative pronouns**, such as *who, which,* and *what,* introduce questions (*Who will contribute?*).
- **Demonstrative pronouns**, including *this, that,* and *such,* identify or point to nouns (*This is the problem*).
- **Intensive pronouns**—a personal pronoun plus *-self* or *-selves* (*himself, ourselves*)—emphasize a noun or other pronoun (*He himself asked that question*).
- **Reflexive pronouns** have the same form as intensive pronouns but indicate that the sentence subject also receives the action of the verb (*They injured themselves*).

The personal pronouns *I, he, she, we,* and *they* and the relative pronouns *who* and *whoever* change form depending on their function in the sentence. (See Chapter 30.)

21c Learn to recognize verbs.

gram 21c

Verbs express an action (*bring, change, grow, consider*), an occurrence (*become, happen, occur*), or a state of being (*be, seem, remain*).

1 • Forms of verbs

Verbs have five distinctive forms. If the form can change as described here, the word is a verb:

- The **plain form** is the dictionary form of the verb. When the subject is a plural noun or the pronoun *I, we, you,* or *they,* the plain form indicates action that occurs in the present, occurs habitually, or is generally true.

  A few artists live in town today.
  They hold classes downtown.

- The ***-s* form** ends in *-s* or *-es*. When the subject is a singular noun, a pronoun such as *everyone,* or the personal pronoun *he, she,* or *it,* the *-s* form indicates action that occurs in the present, occurs habitually, or is generally true.

  The artist lives in town today.
  She holds classes downtown.

- The **past-tense form** indicates that the action of the verb occurred before now. It usually adds *-d* or *-ed* to the plain form, although most irregular verbs create it in different ways (see pp. 236–39).

  Many artists lived in town before this year.
  They held classes downtown. [Irregular verb.]

- The **past participle** is usually the same as the past-tense form, except in most irregular verbs. It combines with forms of *have* or *be* (*has climbed, was created*), or by itself it modifies nouns and pronouns (*the sliced apples*).

  Artists have lived in town for decades.
  They have held classes downtown. [Irregular verb.]

- The **present participle** adds *-ing* to the verb's plain form. It combines with forms of *be* (*is buying*), modifies nouns and pronouns (*the boiling water*), or functions as a noun (*Running exhausts me*).

  A few artists are living in town today.
  They are holding classes downtown.

The verb *be* has eight forms rather than the five forms of most other verbs:

Plain form	be		
Present participle	being		
Past participle	been		
	I	*he, she, it*	*we, you, they*
Present tense	am	is	are
Past tense	was	was	were

2 • Helping verbs

Some verb forms combine with **helping verbs** to indicate time, possibility, obligation, necessity, and other kinds of meaning: *can run, was sleeping, had been working*. In these **verb phrases** *run, sleeping,* and *working* are **main verbs**—they carry the principal meaning.

	Verb phrase	
	Helping	*Main*
Artists	can	train others to draw.
The techniques	have	changed little.

These are the most common helping verbs:

be able to	had better	must	used to
be supposed to	have to	ought to	will
can	may	shall	would
could	might	should	

Forms of *be:* be, am, is, are, was, were, been, being
Forms of *have:* have, has, had, having
Forms of *do:* do, does, did

See pages 243–48 for more on helping verbs.

EXERCISE 21.1
Identifying nouns, pronouns, and verbs

Identify the words that function as nouns, pronouns, and verbs in the following sentences, using the initials *N, P,* or *V*. Answers to starred items appear at the end of the book.

Example:

The gingko tree (N) has (V) another name (N): it (P) is (V) the maidenhair tree (N).

*1. Ancestors of the gingko tree, a relic from the age of the dinosaurs, lived 175 to 200 million years ago.
*2. The tree sometimes grows to over a hundred feet in height.
*3. It has fan-shaped leaves about three inches wide.
*4. A deciduous tree, the gingko loses its leaves in the fall after they turn bright yellow.
*5. The gingko tree is esteemed in the United States and Europe as an ornamental tree.

6. Because the gingko shows tolerance for smoke, low temperatures, and low rainfall, it appears in many cities.
7. A shortcoming, however, is the foul odor of its fruit.
8. The fruit of the gingko looks something like a plum.
9. Inside the fruit lies a large white seed that some Asians value as a food.
10. Because only the female gingko bears fruit, the male is more common as an ornamental tree.

gram 21d

21d Learn to recognize adjectives and adverbs.

Adjectives describe or modify nouns and pronouns. They specify which one, what quality, or how many.

old (adjective) → city (noun)   generous (adjective) → one (pronoun)   two (adjective) → pears (noun)

Adverbs describe or modify verbs, adjectives, other adverbs, and whole groups of words. They specify when, where, how, and to what extent.

nearly (adverb) → destroyed (verb)   too (adverb) → quickly (adverb)

very (adverb) → generous (adjective)   Unfortunately, (adverb) → taxes will rise. (word group)

An *-ly* ending often signals an adverb, but not always: *friendly* is an adjective; *never* is an adverb. The only way to tell whether a word is an adjective or an adverb is to determine what it modifies.

Adjectives and adverbs appear in three forms: **positive** (*green, angrily*), **comparative** (*greener, more angrily*), and **superlative** (*greenest, most angrily*).

See Chapter 33 for more on adjectives and adverbs.

EXERCISE 21.2
Identifying adjectives and adverbs

Identify the adjectives (*ADJ*) and adverbs (*ADV*) in the following sentences. Mark *a, an,* and *the* as adjectives. Answers to starred items appear at the end of the book.

Example:

Stress can hit people when they least [ADV] expect it.

*1. You can reduce stress by making a few simple changes.
*2. Get up fifteen minutes earlier than you ordinarily do.
*3. Eat a healthy breakfast, and eat it slowly so that you enjoy it.
*4. Do your unpleasant tasks early in the day.
*5. Every day, do at least one thing you really enjoy.
6. If waiting in lines is stressful for you, carry a book or magazine when you know you'll have to wait.
7. Make promises sparingly and keep them faithfully.
8. Plan ahead to prevent stressful situations.
9. For example, carry spare keys so you won't be locked out of your car or house.
10. See a doctor and dentist regularly.

gram 21e

21e Learn to recognize connecting words: Prepositions and conjunctions.

Connecting words are mostly small words that link parts of sentences. They never change form.

1 • Prepositions

Prepositions form nouns or pronouns (plus any modifiers) into word groups called **prepositional phrases:** *about love, down the stairs.* These phrases usually serve as modifiers in sentences, as in *The plants trailed down the stairs.* (See also p. 227.) A list of prepositions appears on the next page.

CULTURE LANGUAGE The meanings and uses of English prepositions can be difficult to master. See pages 195–97 for a discussion of prepositions in idioms. See pages 251–52 for uses of prepositions in two-word verbs such as *look after* or *look up.*

Common prepositions

about	before	except for	of	throughout
above	behind	excepting	off	till
according to	below	for	on	to
across	beneath	from	onto	toward
after	beside	in	on top of	under
against	between	in addition to	out	underneath
along	beyond	inside	out of	unlike
along with	by	inside of	outside	until
among	concerning	in spite of	over	up
around	despite	instead of	past	upon
as	down	into	regarding	up to
aside from	due to	like	round	with
at	during	near	since	within
because of	except	next to	through	without

2 • Subordinating conjunctions

Subordinating conjunctions form sentences into word groups called **subordinate clauses,** such as *when the meeting ended.* These clauses serve as parts of sentences: *Everyone was relieved when the meeting ended.* (See p. 230 for more on subordinate clauses.)

Common subordinating conjunctions

after	even if	rather than	until
although	even though	since	when
as	if	so that	whenever
as if	if only	than	where
as long as	in order that	that	whereas
as though	now that	though	wherever
because	once	till	whether
before	provided	unless	while

CULTURE LANGUAGE Subordinating conjunctions convey meaning without help from other function words, such as the coordinating conjunctions *and, but, for,* or *so:*

Faulty Even though the parents are illiterate, but their children may read well. [*Even though* and *but* have the same meaning, so both are not needed.]

Revised Even though the parents are illiterate, their children may read well.

3 • Coordinating and correlative conjunctions

Coordinating and correlative conjunctions connect words or word groups of the same kind, such as nouns, adjectives, or sentences.

Coordinating conjunctions consist of a single word:

Coordinating conjunctions

and	nor	for	yet
but	or	so	

Biofeedback or simple relaxation can relieve headaches.
Relaxation works well, and it is inexpensive.

Correlative conjunctions are combinations of coordinating conjunctions and other words:

Common correlative conjunctions

both . . . and	neither . . . nor
not only . . . but also	whether . . . or
not . . . but	as . . . as
either . . . or	

Both biofeedback and relaxation can relieve headaches.

The headache sufferer learns not only to recognize the causes of headaches but also to control those causes.

EXERCISE 21.3
Adding connecting words

Fill each blank in the following sentences with the appropriate connecting word: a preposition, a subordinating conjunction, or a coordinating conjunction. Consult the lists on these two pages if you need help. Answers to starred items appear at the end of the book.

Example:

A Trojan priest warned, "Beware ______ Greeks bearing gifts." *(preposition)*

A Trojan priest warned, "Beware of Greeks bearing gifts."

*1. Just about everyone has heard the story ______ the Trojan Horse. (*preposition*)
*2. This incident happened at the city of Troy ______ was planned by the Greeks. (*coordinating conjunction*)

*3. The Greeks built a huge wooden horse; ______ it was a hollow space big enough to hold many men. (*preposition*)

*4. At night, they rolled the horse to the gate of Troy ______ left it there before sailing their ships out to sea. (*coordinating conjunction*)

*5. ______ the morning, the Trojans were astonished to see the enormous horse. (*preposition*)

6. ______ they were amazed when they saw that the Greeks were gone. (*coordinating conjunction*)

7. ______ they were curious to examine this gift from the Greeks, they dragged the horse into the city and left it outside the temple. (*subordinating conjunction*)

8. In the middle of the night, the hidden Greeks emerged ______ the horse and began setting fires all over town. (*preposition*)

9. ______ the Trojan soldiers awoke and came out of their houses, the Greeks killed them one by one. (*subordinating conjunction*)

10. By the next morning, the Trojan men were dead ______ the women were slaves to the Greeks. (*coordinating conjunction*)

gram
22

21f Learn to recognize interjections.

Interjections express feeling or command attention. They are rarely used in academic or business writing.

Oh, the meeting went fine.
They won seven thousand dollars! Wow!

22 The Sentence

What makes a sentence a sentence?

The essential elements of any sentence are the subject and the predicate. Usually naming an actor and an action, the subject and predicate together form a complete thought.

http://www.ablongman.com/littlebrown

➤ Sentences and words
  ➤ Web exercises ➤ Exers. 15 and 16
  ➤ Downloads ➤ Chapter 22 exercises in electronic format
  ➤ Web links ➤ Basic grammar

22a Learn to recognize subjects and predicates.

Most sentences make statements. First the **subject** names something; then the **predicate** makes an assertion about the subject or describes an action by the subject.

Subject	Predicate
Art	thrives.

The **simple subject** consists of one or more nouns or pronouns, whereas the **complete subject** also includes any modifiers. The **simple predicate** consists of one or more verbs, whereas the **complete predicate** adds any words needed to complete the meaning of the verb plus any modifiers.

Sometimes, as in the short example *Art thrives,* the simple and complete subject and predicate are the same. More often, they are different:

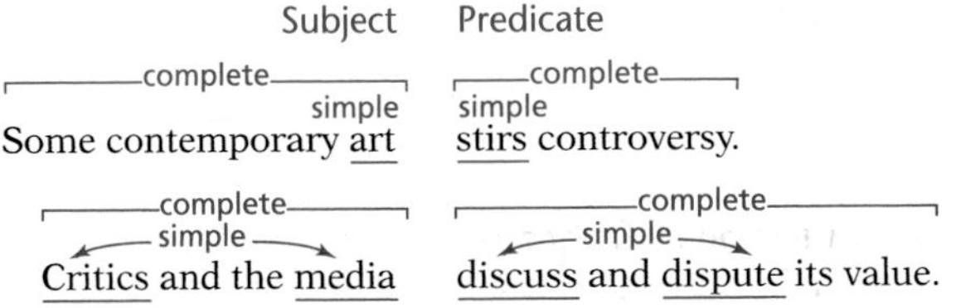

In the second example, the simple subject and simple predicate are both **compound:** in each, two words joined by a coordinating conjunction (*and*) serve the same function.

Sometimes a sentence's subject and the verb of the predicate may be hard to identify, so that you can't tell whether the sentence is complete or whether subject and verb match grammatically. The tests below for finding the subject and the predicate verb use the following example:

> Art that makes it into established museums has often survived controversy.

To identify the simple subject, these tests will work for most sentences:

- Ask *who* or *what* is acting or being described in the sentence. In the example the thing acting is *art that makes it into established museums.* This is the complete subject.
- Delete from the complete subject any modifiers—words or word groups that don't name the actor of the sentence but give information about it. In the example, the actor and simple subject is

art. The word group *that makes it into established museums* adds information to, or modifies, this simple subject.

To identify the simple predicate, the verb or verbs of the sentence, use these tests:

- Ask what the sentence asserts about the subject: what is its action, or what state is it in? In the example sentence, the assertion about *art* is that it *has often survived controversy.* This is the complete predicate.
- Isolate the verb, the simple predicate, by locating the word or words that would change if you changed the number of the subject or the time of the subject's action. For instance:

Example	Art . . . has often survived controversy.
Plural	Arts . . . have often survived controversy.
Present	Art . . . often survives controversy.
Future	Art . . . often will survive controversy.

As the underlining indicates, *has survived* would change and thus forms the simple predicate. (See p. 316 for more on identifying sentence verbs.)

Note If a sentence contains a word group such as *that makes it into established museums* or *because viewers finally agree about its quality,* you may be tempted to mark the subject and verb in the word group as the subject and verb of the sentence. But these word groups are subordinate clauses, made into modifiers by the words they begin with: *that* and *because.* See pages 230–32 for more on subordinate clauses.

CULTURE LANGUAGE The subject of an English sentence may be a noun (*art*) or a pronoun that refers to the noun (*it*), but not both. (See p. 332.)

Faulty	Some art it stirs controversy.
Revised	Some art stirs controversy.

EXERCISE 22.1
Identifying subjects and predicates

In the following sentences, draw a vertical line between the complete subject and the complete predicate. Underline each simple subject once and each simple predicate twice. Answers to starred items appear at the end of the book.

Example:

The pony, the light horse, and the draft horse | are the three main types of domestic horses.

*1. The horse has a long history of serving humanity but today is mainly a show and sport animal.
*2. A member of the genus *Equus*, the domestic horse is related to the wild Przewalski's horse, the ass, and the zebra.
*3. The domestic horse and its relatives are all plains-dwelling herd animals.
*4. An average-sized adult horse may require twenty-six pounds or more of pasture feed or hay per day.
*5. Racehorses require grain for part of their forage.

6. Oddly, the modern horse evolved in North America and then became extinct here after spreading to other parts of the world.
7. It was reintroduced here by the Spaniards, profoundly affecting the culture of Native Americans.
8. The North American animals called wild horses are actually descended from escaped domesticated horses that reproduced in the wild.
9. According to records, horses were hunted and domesticated as early as four to five thousand years ago.
10. The earliest ancestor of the modern horse may have been eohippus, approximately 55 million years ago.

22b Learn the basic predicate patterns.

English sentences usually follow one of five patterns, each differing in the complete predicate (the verb and any words following it).

CULTURE LANGUAGE The word order in English sentences may not correspond to word order in the sentences of your native language or dialect. English, for instance, strongly prefers subject first, then verb, then any other words, whereas some other languages prefer the verb first.

Pattern 1: The earth trembled.

In the simplest pattern the predicate consists only of an **intransitive verb,** a verb that does not require a following word to complete its meaning.

Subject	Predicate
	Intransitive verb
The earth	trembled.
The hospital	may close.

Pattern 2: The earthquake destroyed the city.

In pattern 2 the verb is followed by a **direct object,** a noun or pronoun that identifies who or what receives the action of the verb. A verb that requires a direct object to complete its meaning is called **transitive.**

Subject	Predicate	
	Transitive verb	*Direct object*
The earthquake	destroyed	the city.
Education	opens	doors.

CULTURE LANGUAGE Only transitive verbs can be used in the passive voice: *The city was destroyed*. Your dictionary will indicate whether a verb is transitive or intransitive. For some verbs (*begin, learn, read, write,* and others), it will indicate both uses.

Pattern 3: The result was chaos.

In pattern 3 the verb is followed by a **subject complement,** a word that renames or describes the subject. A verb in this pattern is called a **linking verb** because it links its subject to the description following. The linking verbs include *be, seem, appear, become, grow, remain, stay, prove, feel, look, smell, sound,* and *taste.* Subject complements are usually nouns or adjectives.

Subject	Predicate	
	Linking verb	*Subject complement*
The result	was	chaos.
The man	became	an accountant.

Pattern 4: The government sent the city aid.

In pattern 4 the verb is followed by a direct object and an **indirect object,** a word identifying to or for whom the action of the verb is performed. The direct object and indirect object refer to different things, people, or places.

Subject	Predicate		
	Transitive verb	*Indirect object*	*Direct object*
The government	sent	the city	aid.
One company	offered	its employees	bonuses.

A number of verbs can take indirect objects, including *allow, bring, buy, deny, find, get, give, leave, make, offer, pay, read, sell, send, show, teach,* and *write.*

CULTURE LANGUAGE Some verbs are never followed by an indirect object—*admit, announce, demonstrate, explain, introduce, mention,*

Key term

passive voice The verb form when the subject names the receiver of the verb's action: *Bad weather was predicted.* (See pp. 265–67.)

prove, recommend, say, and some others. However, the direct objects of these verbs may be followed by *to* or *for* and a noun or pronoun that specifies to or for whom the action was done: *The manual explains the new procedure to workers. A video demonstrates the procedure for us.*

Pattern 5: The citizens considered the earthquake a disaster.

In pattern 5 the verb is followed by a direct object and an **object complement,** a word that renames or describes the direct object. Object complements may be nouns or adjectives.

Subject	Predicate		
	Transitive verb	*Direct object*	*Object complement*
The citizens	considered	the earthquake	a disaster.
Success	makes	some people	nervous.

EXERCISE 22.2
Identifying sentence parts

In the following sentences identify the subject (*S*) and verb (*V*) as well as any direct objects (*DO*), indirect objects (*IO*), subject complements (*SC*), or object complements (*OC*). Answers to starred items appear at the end of the book.

Example:

Crime statistics (S) can (V) cause (V) surprise (DO).

*1. The number of serious crimes in the United States decreased.
*2. A decline in serious crimes occurred each year.
*3. The Crime Index measures serious crime.
*4. The FBI invented the index.
*5. The four serious violent crimes are murder, robbery, forcible rape, and aggravated assault.
6. Auto theft, burglary, arson, and larceny-theft are the four serious crimes against property.
7. The Crime Index gives the FBI a measure of crime.
8. The index shows trends in crimes and the people who commit them.
9. The nation's largest cities showed the largest decline in crime.
10. Smaller cities, where crime did not decrease, proved that the decline in crime is unrepresentative of the nation.

22c Learn alternative sentence patterns.

Most English sentences first name the actor in the subject and then assert something about the actor in the predicate. But four kinds of sentences alter this basic pattern.

1 • Questions

The following are the most common ways of forming questions from statements. Remember to end a question with a question mark (p. 339).

- Move the verb or a part of it to the beginning of the question. These questions may be answered yes or no. The verb may be a form of *be:*

  The rate is high. Is the rate high?

  Or the verb may consist of a helping verb and a main verb. Then move the helping verb—or the first helping verb if there's more than one—to the front of the question:

  Rates can rise. Can rates rise?
  Rates have been rising. Have rates been rising?

- If the verb consists of only one word and is not a form of *be,* start the question with a form of *do* and use the plain form of the verb. These questions can also be answered yes or no.

  Interest rates rose. Did interest rates rise?

- Add a question word—*how, what, who, when, where, which, why*—to the beginning of a yes-or-no question. Such a question requires an explanatory answer.

  Did rates rise today? Why did rates rise today?
  Is the rate high? Why is the rate high?

- Add *who, what,* or *which* to the beginning of a question as the subject. Then the subject-verb order remains the same as in a statement:

  Something is the answer. What is the answer?
  Someone can answer. Who can answer?

gram
22c

Key terms

helping verb A verb such as *can, may, be, have,* or *do* that forms a verb phrase with another verb to show time, permission, and other meanings. (See p. 213.)

main verb The verb that carries the principal meaning in a verb phrase: has *walked,* could be *happening*. (See p. 213.)

plain form The dictionary form of the verb: I *walk*. You *forget*. (See p. 212.)

2 • Commands

Construct a command simply by deleting the subject of the sentence, *you:*

Think of options. Eat your spinach.
Watch the news. Leave me alone.

3 • Passive sentences

In the basic subject-predicate pattern, the subject performs the action of the verb. The verb is in the **active voice:**

subject (Kyong) — active verb (wrote) — object (paper)

Kyong wrote the paper.

In the **passive voice,** the subject *receives* the action of the verb:

subject (paper) — passive verb (was written)

The paper was written by Kyong.

In the passive voice, the object of the active verb (*paper*) becomes the subject of the passive verb.

Passive verbs always consist of a form of *be* plus the past participle of the main verb (*paper was written, absences were excused*). The actual actor (the person or thing performing the action of the verb) may be expressed in a phrase (as in the example above: *by Kyong*) or may be omitted entirely if it is unknown or unimportant: *The house was flooded.*

For more on the formation and uses of the passive voice, see pages 265–67.

4 • Sentences with postponed subjects

Two kinds of sentences state the subject after the predicate. In one, the normal word order reverses for emphasis:

The cause of the problem lies here. [Normal order.]
Here lies the cause of the problem. [Reversed order.]

The second kind of sentence starts with *there* or *it* and postpones the subject:

verb (will be) — subject (people)

There will be eighteen people at the meeting. [Normal order: *Eighteen people will be at the meeting.*]

verb (was) — subject (that Marinetti was nominated)

It was surprising that Marinetti was nominated. [Normal order: *That Marinetti was nominated was surprising.*]

gram 22c

The words *there* and *it* in such sentences are **expletives.** Their only function is to postpone the sentence subject. Expletive sentences do have their uses (see p. 207), but they are often just wordy.

CULTURE LANGUAGE When you use an expletive construction, be careful to include *there* or *it*. Only commands and some questions can begin with verbs (see the previous two pages).

Faulty No one predicted the nomination. Were no polls showing Marinetti ahead.

Revised No one predicted the nomination. There were no polls showing Marinetti ahead.

EXERCISE 22.3
Rewriting passives and expletives

Rewrite each passive sentence below as active, and rewrite each expletive construction to restore normal subject-predicate order. Answers to the starred items appear at the end of the book. (For additional exercises with the passive voice and with expletives, see pp. 164, 208, and 268.)

Example:

The doctor's groundbreaking work was recognized by other medical professionals.

Other medical professionals recognized the doctor's groundbreaking work.

*1. The screenplay for *Born on the Fourth of July* was cowritten by Ron Kovic.
*2. The film was directed by Oliver Stone.
3. Tom Cruise was nominated for an Oscar by the Academy of Motion Picture Arts and Sciences.
4. It was a surprise to some critics that Tom Cruise could excel in such a meaty role.
5. There are few such roles available to actors.

23 Phrases and Subordinate Clauses

How do word groups work within sentences?

Word groups within sentences serve as modifiers (adjectives or adverbs) or as nouns. Most word groups are one of the following:

- A **phrase,** which lacks either a subject or a predicate or both: *fearing an accident; in a panic.*

- A **subordinate clause,** which contains a subject and a predicate (like a sentence) but begins with a subordinating word: *when prices rise; whoever laughs.*

Because they function as parts of speech (adjectives, adverbs, or nouns), phrases and subordinate clauses cannot stand alone as complete sentences (see Chapter 35 on sentence fragments).

23a Learn to recognize phrases.

1 • Prepositional phrases

A **prepositional phrase** consists of a preposition plus a noun, pronoun, or word group serving as a noun, called the **object of the preposition.** Prepositions include *about, at, by, for, to, under,* and *with.* A fuller list appears on page 216.

Preposition	Object
of	spaghetti
on	the surface
with	great satisfaction
upon	entering the room
from	where you are standing

Prepositional phrases usually function as adjectives or adverbs, adding details and making sentences more interesting for readers. An adjective phrase usually falls immediately after the word it modifies, but an adverb phrase need not.

Life on a raft was an opportunity for adventure.
noun adjective phrase noun adjective phrase

Huck Finn rode the raft by choice.
verb adverb phrase

With his companion, Jim, Huck met many types of people.
adverb phrase verb noun adjective phrase

http://www.ablongman.com/littlebrown
➤ Sentences and words
➤ Web exercises ➤ Exers. 17–20
➤ Downloads ➤ Chapter 23 exercises in electronic format
➤ Web links ➤ Basic grammar

2 • Verbal phrases

Certain forms of verbs, called **verbals,** can serve as modifiers or nouns. Often these verbals appear with their own modifiers and objects in **verbal phrases.**

Note Verbals cannot serve as verbs in sentences. *The sun rises over the dump* is a sentence; *The sun rising over the dump* is a sentence fragment. (See p. 315.)

Participial phrases

Present participles (ending in *-ing*), **past participles** (usually ending in *-d* or *-ed*), and phrases made from them serve as adjectives. They usually fall just before or after the word they modify.

Strolling shoppers fill the malls.
adjective noun

They make selections determined by personal taste.
noun adjective phrase

Note With irregular verbs, the past participle may have a different ending—for instance, *hidden funds.* (See p. 236.)

CULTURE LANGUAGE For verbs expressing feeling, the present and past participles have different meanings: *It was a boring lecture. The bored students slept.* (See p. 300.)

Gerund phrases

A **gerund** is the *-ing* form of a verb when it serves as a noun. Gerunds and gerund phrases replace nouns and can do whatever nouns can do.

sentence subject
Shopping satisfies personal needs.
noun

object of preposition
Malls are good at creating such needs.
noun phrase

Infinitive phrases

An **infinitive** is the plain form of a verb plus *to: to hide.* Infinitives and infinitive phrases serve as adjectives, adverbs, or nouns. A noun or noun phrase replaces a noun:

sentence subject — subject complement
To design a mall is to create an artificial environment.
noun phrase — noun phrase

An adverb or adverb phrase modifies a verb, adjective, other adverb, or entire word group and may fall near or away from the word it modifies:

To achieve this goal, designers emphasize the familiar.
adverb phrase — verb

Malls are designed to make shoppers feel safe.
verb — adverb phrase

An adjective or adjective phrase modifies a noun or pronoun and usually falls immediately after the word it modifies:

The environment supports the impulse to shop.
noun — adjective

CULTURE LANGUAGE Infinitives and gerunds may follow some verbs and not others and may differ in meaning after a verb: *The singer stopped to sing. The singer stopped singing.* (See pp. 249–51.)

3 • Absolute phrases

An **absolute phrase** consists of a noun or pronoun and a participle, plus any modifiers. It modifies the rest of its sentence and may fall in more than one place in the sentence.

Their own place established, many ethnic groups are making way for new arrivals.
absolute phrase

Unlike a participial phrase (opposite), an absolute phrase always contains a noun that serves as its subject:

Learning English, many immigrants discover American culture.
participial phrase

Immigrants having learned English, their opportunities widen.
absolute phrase

4 • Appositive phrases

An **appositive** is usually a noun that renames another noun. An appositive phrase includes modifiers as well. Both appositives and appositive phrases usually fall immediately after the nouns they rename.

Bizen ware, a dark stoneware, is produced in Japan.
noun — appositive phrase

Appositives and appositive phrases sometimes begin with *that is, such as, for example,* or *in other words.*

Bizen ware is used in the Japanese tea ceremony, that is, the Zen Buddhist observance that links meditation and art.
noun — appositive phrase

EXERCISE 23.1
Identifying phrases

In each sentence below, identify every verbal, appositive, and verbal, appositive, prepositional, and absolute phrase. (Some sentences contain more than one such word or phrase.) Answers to starred items appear at the end of the book.

Example:

participial phrase: borrowed from many sources

Modern English contains words borrowed from many sources.

prepositional phrase: from many sources

*1. Because of its many synonyms, or words with similar meanings, English can make it difficult to choose the exact word.

*2. Borrowing words from other languages such as French and Latin, English acquired an unusual number of synonyms.

*3. Having so many choices, how does a writer decide between *motherly* and *maternal* or among *womanly, feminine,* and *female?*

*4. Some people prefer longer and more ornate words to avoid the flatness of shortened words.

*5. During the Renaissance a heated debate occurred between the Latinists, favoring Latin words, and the Saxonists, preferring native Anglo-Saxon words.

6. Students in writing classes are often told to choose the shorter word, generally an Anglo-Saxon derivative.
7. Better advice, wrote William Hazlitt, is the principle of choosing "the best word in common use."
8. Keeping this principle in mind, a writer would choose either *womanly*, the Anglo-Saxon word, or *feminine*, a French deriva- [illegible] uation.

[illegible] same meaning, usage having

[illegible], for example, has a slightly

[illegible] h derivative *manual*, a close

23b Learn to recognize subordinate clauses.

A **clause** is any group of words that contains both a subject and a predicate. There are two kinds of clauses, and the distinction between them is important:

- A **main clause** makes a complete statement and can stand alone as a sentence: *The sky darkened.*
- A **subordinate clause** is just like a main clause *except* that it begins with a subordinating word: *when the sky darkened; whoever calls.* The subordinating word reduces the clause from a com-

plete statement to a single part of speech: an adjective, adverb, or noun.

Note A subordinate clause punctuated as a sentence is a sentence fragment. (See pp. 315–18.)

Adjective clauses

An **adjective clause** modifies a noun or pronoun. It usually begins with the relative pronoun *who, whom, whose, which,* or *that* but may also begin with *where, when,* or *why.* The clause ordinarily falls immediately after the word it modifies.

Parents who are illiterate may have bad memories of school.
noun adjective clause

Children whom the schools fail sometimes have illiterate parents.
noun adjective clause

One school, which is open year-round, helps parents learn to read.
noun adjective clause

The school is in a city where the illiteracy rate is high.
noun adjective clause

In the first three examples, the relative pronouns *who, whom,* and *which* refer to the nouns modified by the clause (*Parents, Children, school*). The relative pronoun serves as the subject of its clause (*who are illiterate, which is open year-round*) or as an object (*whom the schools fail*). In the last example, *where* substitutes for *in which* (*a city in which the illiteracy rate is high*).

See pages 344–46 for advice on punctuating adjective clauses.

Adverb clauses

An **adverb clause** modifies a verb, an adjective, another adverb, or a whole word group. It always begins with a subordinating conjunction, such as *after, although, because, how, if, until, when,* or *while.* (See p. 216 for a fuller list.) The clause may fall in more than one place in its sentence (but see pp. 308–09 for limitations).

The school began teaching parents when adult illiteracy gained national attention.
verb adverb clause

At first the program was not as successful as its founders had hoped.
adjective adverb clause

Because it was directed at people who could not read, advertising had to be inventive.
adverb clause — main clause

Noun clauses

A **noun clause** replaces a noun in a sentence and serves as a subject, object, or complement. It begins with *that, what, whatever, who, whom, whoever, whomever, when, where, whether, why,* or *how.*

Whether the program would succeed depended on door-to-door advertising.
sentence subject — noun clause

Teachers explained in person how the program would work.
direct object — noun clause

Whoever seemed slightly interested was invited to an open meeting.
sentence subject — noun clause

A few parents were anxious about what their children would think.
object of preposition — noun clause

The children's needs were what the parents asked most about.
subject complement — noun clause

EXERCISE 23.2
Identifying clauses

Underline the subordinate clauses in the following sentences and identify each one as adjective (*ADJ*), adverb (*ADV*), or noun (*N*) by determining how it functions in its sentence. Answers to starred items appear at the end of the book.

Example:

N
Whoever follows the Koran refers to God as *Allah,* the Arabic word for his name.

*1. The Prophet Muhammad, who was born about AD 570 in the city of Mecca, was the founder of Islam.
*2. He grew up in the care of his grandfather and an uncle because both of his parents had died.

Key terms

object A noun, pronoun, or word group that receives the action of or is influenced by a transitive verb, a verbal, or a preposition. An object may be a *direct object,* an *indirect object,* or an *object of a preposition.* (See pp. 221–22 and 227.)

complement A word or word group that completes the sense of a subject, an object, or a verb. (See pp. 222 and 223.)

*3. His family was part of a powerful Arab tribe that lived in western Arabia.

*4. When he was about forty years old, he had a vision in a cave outside Mecca.

*5. He believed that God had selected him to be the prophet of a true religion for the Arabs.

6. Throughout his life he continued to have revelations, which have been written in the Koran.
7. The Koran is the sacred book of Muslims, who as adherents of Islam view Muhammad as God's messenger.
8. When he no longer had the support of the clans of Mecca, Muhammad and his followers moved to Medina.
9. There they established an organized Muslim community that soon had armed clashes with the Meccans and Jewish clans.
10. Muhammad continued as the religious, political, and military leader of Islam, which spread in Asia and Africa.

24 Sentence Types

How can classifying sentences help me construct them?

Understanding the ways of structuring sentences can be helpful for managing the flow and emphasis of information. One useful classification indentifies four sentence types: simple, compound, complex, and compound-complex.

24a Learn to recognize simple sentences.

A **simple sentence** consists of a single main clause and no subordinate clause:

main clause

Last summer was unusually hot.

main clause

The summer made many farmers leave the area for good or reduced them to bare existence.

http://www.ablongman.com/littlebrown

➤ Sentences and words
  ➤ Web exercises ➤ Exer. 21
  ➤ Downloads ➤ Chapter 24 exercises in electronic format
  ➤ Web links ➤ Basic grammar

24b Learn to recognize compound sentences.

A **compound sentence** consists of two or more main clauses and no subordinate clause:

main clause — main clause
Last July was hot, but August was even hotter.

main clause — main clause
The hot sun scorched the earth, and the lack of rain killed many crops.

24c Learn to recognize complex sentences.

A **complex sentence** consists of one main clause and one or more subordinate clauses:

main clause — subordinate clause
Rain finally came, although many had left the area by then.

main clause — subordinate clause — subordinate clause
Those who remained were able to start anew because the government came to their aid.

24d Learn to recognize compound-complex sentences.

A **compound-complex sentence** has the characteristics of both the compound sentence (two or more main clauses) and the complex sentence (at least one subordinate clause):

subordinate clause — main clause — main clause
Even though government aid finally came, many people had already been reduced to poverty, and others had been forced to move.

EXERCISE 24.1
Identifying sentence structures

Mark the main clauses and subordinate clauses in the following sentences. Then identify each sentence as simple, compound, complex, or compound-complex. Answers to starred items appear at the end of the book.

Example:

main clause — subordinate clause
The human voice is produced in the larynx, a section of the throat that has two bands called vocal chords. [Complex.]

*1. Our world has many sounds, but they all have one thing in common.
*2. The one thing that all sounds share is that they are produced by vibrations.
*3. The vibrations make the air move in waves, and these sound waves travel to the ear.
*4. When sound waves enter the ear, the brain has to interpret them.
*5. Sound waves can also travel through other material, such as water and even the solid earth.

6. Some sounds are pleasant, and others, which we call noise, are not.
7. Most noises are produced by irregular vibrations at irregular intervals; an example is the barking of a dog.
8. Sounds have frequency and pitch.
9. When an object vibrates rapidly, it produces high-frequency, high-pitched sounds.
10. People can hear sounds over a wide range of frequencies; dogs and cats can hear sounds with higher frequencies.

Verbs

How and why do verbs change?

Verbs change in many ways to indicate differences in time, subject, and other aspects of sentences. The following chapters explain and solve the most common problems with verbs' forms (Chapter 25), tenses (26), mood (27), voice (28), and agreement with their subjects (29).

25 Verb Forms

What's wrong with *throwed* and *have went?*

Throwed and *have went* are forms of the verbs *throw* and *go* that are considered incorrect in standard American English. (The standard forms are *threw* or *thrown* and *have gone*.) Errors like these in verb forms can frustrate or confuse readers who expect standard English.

This chapter focuses on the verb forms most likely to cause difficulty: irregular verbs (below), *-s* and *-ed* endings (p. 241), helping verbs (p. 243), verbs followed by *-ing* or *to* words (p. 249), and two-word verbs (p. 251).

25a Use the correct forms of *sing/sang/sung* and other irregular verbs.

Most verbs are **regular:** they form their past tense and past participle by adding *-d* or *-ed* to the plain form (next page).

http://www.ablongman.com/littlebrown

➤ Sentences and words
- ➤ Video tutorials ➤ Using irregular verbs
- ➤ Web exercises ➤ Exers. 22–26
- ➤ Downloads ➤ Chapter 25 exercises in electronic format
- ➤ Web links ➤ Verbs

Plain form	Past tense	Past participle
live	lived	lived
act	acted	acted

About two hundred English verbs are **irregular:** they form their past tense and past participle in some irregular way. Check a dictionary under the verb's plain form if you have any doubt about its other forms. If the verb is irregular, the dictionary will list the plain form, the past tense, and the past participle in that order (*go, went, gone*). If the dictionary gives only two forms (as in *think, thought*), then the past tense and the past participle are the same.

Common irregular verbs

Plain form	Past tense	Past participle
arise	arose	arisen
become	became	become
begin	began	begun
bite	bit	bitten, bit
blow	blew	blown
break	broke	broken
bring	brought	brought
burst	burst	burst
buy	bought	bought
catch	caught	caught
choose	chose	chosen
come	came	come
cut	cut	cut
dive	dived, dove	dived
do	did	done
draw	drew	drawn
dream	dreamed, dreamt	dreamed, dreamt
drink	drank	drunk
drive	drove	driven
eat	ate	eaten
fall	fell	fallen

(continued)

Key terms

plain form The dictionary form of the verb: *I walk. You forget.* (See p. 212.)

past-tense form The verb form indicating action that occurred in the past: *I walked. You forgot.* (See p. 212.)

past participle The verb form used with *have, has,* or *had: I have walked.* It may also serve as a modifier: *This is a forgotten book.* (See p. 213.)

Common irregular verbs

(continued)

Plain form	Past tense	Past participle
find	found	found
fly	flew	flown
forget	forgot	forgotten, forgot
freeze	froze	frozen
get	got	got, gotten
give	gave	given
go	went	gone
grow	grew	grown
hang (suspend)	hung	hung
hang (execute)	hanged	hanged
hear	heard	heard
hide	hid	hidden
hold	held	held
keep	kept	kept
know	knew	known
lay	laid	laid
lead	led	led
leave	left	left
let	let	let
lie	lay	lain
lose	lost	lost
pay	paid	paid
ride	rode	ridden
ring	rang	rung
rise	rose	risen
run	ran	run
say	said	said
see	saw	seen
set	set	set
shake	shook	shaken
shrink	shrank, shrunk	shrunk, shrunken
sing	sang, sung	sung
sink	sank, sunk	sunk
sit	sat	sat
sleep	slept	slept
speak	spoke	spoken
stand	stood	stood
steal	stole	stolen
swim	swam	swum
swing	swung	swung
take	took	taken
throw	threw	thrown
wear	wore	worn
write	wrote	written

Note A grammar and style checker may flag incorrect forms of irregular verbs, but it may also fail to do so. For example, a checker flagged *The runner stealed second base* (*stole* is correct) but not *The runner had steal second base* (*stolen* is correct). When in doubt about the forms of irregular verbs, refer to the preceding list, consult a dictionary, or consult the links at this book's Web site (see the box on p. 236).

CULTURE LANGUAGE Some English dialects use distinctive verb forms that differ from those of standard American English: for instance, *drug* for *dragged, growed* for *grew, come* for *came*, or *went* for *gone*. In situations requiring standard American English, use the forms in the preceding list or in a dictionary.

EXERCISE 25.1
Using irregular verbs

For each irregular verb in parentheses, supply either the past tense or the past participle, as appropriate, and identify the form you used. Answers to starred items appear at the end of the book.

Example:

Though we had [hide] the cash box, it was [steal].

Though we had hidden the cash box, it was stolen. [Two past participles.]

*1. The world population has [grow] by two-thirds of a billion people in less than a decade.
*2. Recently it [break] the 6 billion mark.
*3. Experts have [draw] pictures of a crowded future.
*4. They predict that the world population may have [slide] up to as much as 10 billion by the year 2050.
*5. Though the food supply [rise] in the last decade, the share to each person [fall].
6. At the same time the water supply, which had actually [become] healthier in the twentieth century, [sink] in size and quality.
7. The number of species on earth [shrink] by 20 percent.
8. Changes in land use [run] nomads and subsistence farmers off the land.
9. Yet all has not been [lose].
10. Recently human beings have [begin] to heed these and other problems and to explore how technology can be [drive] to help the earth and all its populations.
11. Some new techniques for waste processing have [prove] effective.
12. Crop management has [take] some pressure off lands with poor soil, allowing their owners to produce food.
13. Genetic engineering could replenish food supplies that have [shrink].

14. Population control has [find] adherents all over the world.
15. Many endangered species have been [give] room to thrive.

25b Distinguish between *sit* and *set, lie* and *lay,* and *rise* and *raise.*

The forms of *sit* and *set, lie* and *lay,* and *rise* and *raise* are easy to confuse.

Plain form	Past tense	Past participle
sit	sat	sat
set	set	set
lie	lay	lain
lay	laid	laid
rise	rose	risen
raise	raised	raised

In each of these confusing pairs, one verb is intransitive (it does not take an object) and one is transitive (it does take an object). (See p. 231 for more on this distinction.)

Intransitive

The patients lie in their beds. [*Lie* means "recline" and takes no object.]

Visitors sit with them. [*Sit* means "be seated" or "be located" and takes no object.]

Patients' temperatures rise. [*Rise* means "increase" or "get up" and takes no object.]

Transitive

Orderlies lay the dinner trays on tables. [*Lay* means "place" and takes an object, here *trays.*]

Orderlies set the trays down. [*Set* means "place" and takes an object, here *trays.*]

Nursing aides raise the shades. [*Raise* means "lift" or "bring up" and takes an object, here *shades.*]

EXERCISE 25.2
Distinguishing between *sit/set, lie/lay, rise/raise*

Choose the correct verb from the pair given in brackets. Then supply the past tense or past participle, as appropriate. Answers to starred items appear at the end of the book.

Example:

After I washed all the windows, I [lie, lay] down the squeegee and then I [sit, set] the table.

After I washed all the windows, I laid down the squeegee and then I set the table.

*1. Yesterday afternoon the child [lie, lay] down for a nap.
*2. The child has been [rise, raise] by her grandparents.
3. Most days her grandfather has [sit, set] with her, reading her stories.
4. She has [rise, raise] at dawn most mornings.
5. Her toys were [lie, lay] on the floor.

25c Use the -*s* and -*ed* forms of the verb when they are required. CULTURE LANGUAGE

Speakers of some English dialects and nonnative speakers of English sometimes omit the -*s* and -*ed* verb endings when they are required in standard American English.

Note A grammar and style checker will flag many omitted -*s* and -*ed* endings from verbs, as in *he ask* and *was ask*. But it will miss many omissions, too. You'll need to proofread your papers carefully to catch missing endings.

1 • Required -*s* ending

Use the -*s* form of a verb when *both* of these situations hold:

- The subject is a singular noun (*boy*), an indefinite pronoun (*everyone*), or *he, she,* or *it*. (These subjects are **third person,** used when someone or something is being spoken about.)
- The verb's action occurs in the present.

The letter asks [not ask] for a quick response.
Delay costs [not cost] money.

Be especially careful with the -*s* forms of *be* (*is*), *have* (*has*), and *do* (*does, doesn't*). These forms should always be used to indicate present time with third-person singular subjects.

The company is [not be] late in responding.
It has [not have] problems.
It doesn't [not don't] have the needed data.
The contract does [not do] depend on the response.

In addition, *be* has an -*s* form in the past tense with *I* and third-person singular subjects:

The company was [not were] in trouble before.

I, you, and plural subjects do *not* take the -*s* form of verbs:

I am [not is] a student.
You are [not is] also a student.
They are [not is] students, too.

2 • Required -*ed* or -*d* ending

The -*ed* or -*d* verb form is required in *any* of these situations:

- The verb's action occurred in the past:

The company asked [not ask] for more time.

- The verb form functions as a modifier:

The data concerned [not concern] should be retrievable.

- The verb form combines with a form of *be* or *have:*

The company is supposed [not suppose] to be the best.
It has developed [not develop] an excellent reputation.

Watch especially for a needed -*ed* or -*d* ending when it isn't pronounced clearly in speech, as in *asked, discussed, mixed, supposed, walked,* and *used*.

EXERCISE 25.3
Using -*s* and -*ed* verb endings CULTURE LANGUAGE

Supply the correct form of each verb in parentheses. Be careful to include -*s* and -*ed* (or -*d*) endings where they are needed for standard English. Answers to starred items appear at the end of the book.

Example:

Unfortunately, the roof on our new house already [leak].
Unfortunately, the roof on our new house already leaks.

*1. A teacher sometimes [ask] too much of a student.
*2. In high school I was once [punish] for being sick.
*3. I had [miss] a week of school because of a serious case of the flu.
*4. I [realize] that I would fail a test unless I had a chance to make up the class work.
*5. I [discuss] the problem with the teacher.
6. He said I was [suppose] to make up the work while I was sick.
7. At that I [walk] out of the class.
8. I [receive] a failing grade then, but it did not change my attitude.

9. I [work] harder in the courses that have more understanding teachers.
10. Today I still balk when a teacher [make] unreasonable demands or [expect] miracles.

25d Use helping verbs with main verbs appropriately. CULTURE LANGUAGE

Helping verbs combine with main verbs in verb phrases: *The line should have been cut. Who was calling?*

Note Grammar and style checkers often spot omitted helping verbs and incorrect main verbs with helping verbs, but sometimes they do not. A checker flagged *Many been fortunate, She working,* and *Her ideas are grow more complex* but overlooked other examples on the following pages, such as *The conference will be occurred.* Careful proofreading is the only insurance against missing helping verbs and incorrect main verbs.

vb 25d

1 • Required helping verbs

Standard American English requires helping verbs in certain situations:

- The main verb ends in *-ing:*

  Researchers are conducting fieldwork all over the world. [Not Researchers conducting. . . .]

- The main verb is *been* or *be:*

  Many have been fortunate in their discoveries. [Not Many been. . . .]

  Some could be real-life Indiana Joneses. [Not Some be. . . .]

- The main verb is a past participle, such as *talked, begun,* or *thrown.*

Key terms

helping verb A verb such as *can, may, be, have,* or *do* that forms a verb phrase with another verb to show time, permission, and other meanings. (See p. 213.)

main verb The verb that carries the principal meaning in a verb phrase: *has walked, could be happening.* (See p. 213.)

verb phrase A helping verb plus a main verb: *will be singing, would speak.* (See p. 213.)

Their discoveries were covered in newspapers and magazines. [Not Their discoveries covered. . . .]

The researchers have given interviews on TV. [Not The researchers given. . . .]

The omission of a helping verb may create an incomplete sentence, or **sentence fragment,** because a present participle (*conducting*), an irregular past participle (*been*), or the infinitive *be* cannot stand alone as the only verb in a sentence (see p. 316). To work as sentence verbs, these verb forms need helping verbs.

2 • Combination of helping verb + main verb

Helping verbs and main verbs combine into verb phrases in specific ways.

Note The main verb in a verb phrase (the one carrying the main meaning) does not change to show a change in subject or time: *she has sung, you had sung*. Only the helping verb may change.

Form of *be* + present participle

The progressive tenses indicate action in progress. Create them with *be, am, is, are, was, were,* or *been* followed by the main verb's present participle, as in the following example.

She is working on a new book.

Be and *been* require additional helping verbs to form the progressive tenses:

can	might	should		have	
could	must	will	be working	has	been working
may	shall	would		had	

When forming the progressive tenses, be sure to use the *-ing* form of the main verb:

Faulty Her ideas are grow more complex. She is developed a new approach to ethics.

Revised Her ideas are growing more complex. She is developing a new approach to ethics.

Key terms

present participle The *-ing* form of the verb: *flying, writing.* (See p. 213.)

progressive tenses Verb tenses expressing action in progress—for instance, *I am flying* (present progressive), *I was flying* (past progressive), *I will be flying* (future progressive). (See pp. 256–57.)

Form of *be* + past participle

The passive voice of the verb indicates that the subject *receives* the action of the verb. Create the passive voice with *be, am, is, are, was, were, being,* or *been* followed by the past participle of a transitive verb:

Her latest book was completed in four months.

Be, being, and *been* require additional helping verbs to form the passive voice:

have / has / had	been completed	am / is / are / was / were	being completed

will be completed

Be sure to use the main verb's past participle for the passive voice:

Faulty Her next book will be publish soon.
Revised Her next book will be published soon.

Note Only transitive verbs may form the passive voice:

Faulty A philosophy conference will be occurred in the same week. [*Occur* is not a transitive verb.]
Revised A philosophy conference will occur in the same week.

See pages 265–67 for advice on when to use and when to avoid the passive voice.

vb
25d

Forms of *have*

Four forms of *have* serve as helping verbs: *have, has, had, having.* One of these forms plus the main verb's past participle creates one of the perfect tenses, those expressing action completed before another specific time or action.

Key terms

past participle The *-d* or *-ed* form of a regular verb: *hedged, walked.* Most irregular verbs have distinctive past participles: *eaten, swum.* (See p. 213.)

passive voice The verb form when the subject names the receiver of the verb's action: *An essay was written by every student.* (See p. 265.)

transitive verb A verb that requires an object to complete its meaning: *Every student completed an essay* (*essay* is the object of *completed*). (See p. 221.)

perfect tenses Verb tenses expressing an action completed before another specific time or action: *We have eaten* (present perfect), *We had eaten* (past perfect), *We will have eaten* (future perfect). (See p. 256.)

> Some students have complained about the laboratory.
> Others had complained before.

Will and other helping verbs sometimes accompany forms of *have* in the perfect tenses:

> Several more students will have complained by the end of the week.

Forms of *do*

Do, does, and *did* have three uses as helping verbs, always with the plain form of the main verb:

- To pose a question: *How did the trial end?*
- To emphasize the main verb: *It did end eventually.*
- To negate the main verb, along with *not* or *never: The judge did not withdraw.*

Be sure to use the main verb's plain form with any form of *do:*

Faulty	The judge did remained in court.
Revised	The judge did remain in court.

Modals

The modal helping verbs include *can, could, may,* and *might,* along with several two- and three-word combinations, such as *have to, be able to, be supposed to,* and *had better.* (See p. 213 for a list of modals.)

Modals convey various meanings, with these being most common:

- **Ability:** *can, could, be able to*

  The equipment can detect small vibrations. [Present.]

  The equipment could detect small vibrations. [Past.]

  The equipment is able to detect small vibrations. [Present. Past: *was able to.* Future: *will be able to.*]

- **Possibility:** *could, may, might, could/may/might have* + past participle

  The equipment could fail. [Present.]

  The equipment may fail. [Present and future.]

  The equipment might fail. [Present and future.]

  The equipment may have failed. [Past.]

- **Necessity or obligation:** *must, have to, be supposed to*

  The lab must purchase a backup machine. [Present or future.]

  The lab has to purchase a backup machine. [Present or future. Past: *had to.*]

The lab will have to purchase a backup machine. [Future.]

The lab is supposed to purchase a backup machine. [Present. Past: *was supposed to.*]

- **Permission:** *may, can, could*

  The lab may spend the money. [Present or future.]

  The lab can spend the money. [Present or future.]

  The lab could spend the money if it received a grant. [Present or future, more tentative.]

  The school then announced that the lab could spend the money. [Past.]

- **Intention:** *will, shall, would*

  The lab will spend the money. [Future.]

  Shall we offer advice? [Future. Use *shall* for questions requesting opinion or consent.]

  We knew we would offer advice. [Past.]

- **Request:** *could, can, would*

  Could [or can or would] you please obtain a bid? [Present or future.]

- **Advisability:** *should, had better, ought to, should have* + past participle

  You should obtain three bids. [Present or future.]

  You had better obtain three bids. [Present or future.]

  You ought to obtain three bids. [Present or future.]

  You should have obtained three bids. [Past.]

- **Past habit:** *would, used to*

  In years past we would obtain five bids.

  We used to obtain five bids.

The following conventions govern the combination of modals and main verbs shown in the examples:

- One-word modals do not change form to show a change in subject: *I could run, she could run.* Most two- and three-word modals do change form, like other helping verbs: *I have to run, she has to run.*
- Modals can sometimes indicate past, present, or future time, occasionally with a word change (*can* to *could,* for instance), with a form change in a two- or three-word modal (such as *is/was able to*), or with *have* before the past participle of the main verb (*might have driven*).

- Don't use *to* between a one-word modal and the main verb: *can drive,* not *can to drive.* (Most of the two- and three-word modals do include *to: ought to drive.*)
- Don't use two one-word modals together: *I will be able to drive,* not *I will can drive.*

EXERCISE 25.4
Using helping verbs CULTURE LANGUAGE

Add helping verbs to the following sentences where they are needed for standard American English. Answers to starred items appear at the end of the book.

Example:

The school be opened to shelter storm victims.
The school will be opened to shelter storm victims.

*1. Each year thousands of new readers been discovering Agatha Christie's mysteries.
*2. The books written by a prim woman who had worked as a nurse during World War I.
3. Christie never expected that her play *The Mousetrap* be performed for decades.
4. During her life Christie always complaining about movie versions of her stories.
5. Readers of her stories been delighted to be baffled by her.

EXERCISE 25.5
Revising: Helping verbs plus main verbs CULTURE LANGUAGE

Revise the following sentences so that helping verbs and main verbs are used correctly. If a sentence is correct as given, circle the number preceding it. Answers to starred items appear at the end of the book.

Example:

The college testing service has test as many as five hundred students at one time.

The college testing service has tested as many as five hundred students at one time.

*1. A report from the Bureau of the Census has confirm a widening gap between rich and poor.
*2. As suspected, the percentage of people below the poverty level did increased over the last decade.
3. More than 17 percent of the population is make 5 percent of all the income.
4. About 1 percent of the population will keeping an average of $500,000 apiece after taxes.
5. The other 99 percent all together will may retain about $300,000.

25e Use a gerund or an infinitive after a verb as appropriate. CULTURE LANGUAGE

Gerunds and infinitives may follow certain verbs but not others. And sometimes the use of a gerund or infinitive with the same verb changes the meaning of the verb.

Note A grammar and style checker will spot some but not all errors in matching gerunds or infinitives with verbs. For example, a checker flagged *I adore to shop* but not *I practice to swim* or *I promise helping out*. Use the lists given here and a dictionary of English as a second language to determine whether an infinitive or a gerund is appropriate. (See p. 197 for a list of ESL dictionaries.)

1 • Either gerund or infinitive

A gerund or an infinitive may come after the following verbs with no significant difference in meaning:

begin	continue	intend	prefer
can't bear	hate	like	start
can't stand	hesitate	love	

The pump began working. The pump began to work.

2 • Meaning change with gerund or infinitive

With four verbs, a gerund has quite a different meaning from an infinitive:

forget	remember	stop	try

The engineer stopped eating. [He no longer ate.]
The engineer stopped to eat. [He stopped in order to eat.]

3 • Gerund, not infinitive

Do not use an infinitive after these verbs:

admit	avoid	detest	enjoy
adore	consider	discuss	escape
appreciate	deny	dislike	finish

Key terms

gerund The *-ing* form of the verb used as a noun: *Smoking is unhealthful.* (See p. 228.)

infinitive The plain form of the verb usually preceeded by *to: to smoke.* An infinitive may serve as an adjective, adverb, or noun. (See p. 228.)

imagine
keep
mind
miss
postpone
practice
put off
quit
recall
recollect
resent
resist
risk
suggest
tolerate
understand

Faulty He finished to eat lunch.
Revised He finished eating lunch.

4 • Infinitive, not gerund

Do not use a gerund after these verbs:

agree
appear
arrange
ask
assent
beg
claim
consent
decide
expect
have
hope
manage
mean
offer
plan
prepare
pretend
promise
refuse
say
wait
want
wish

Faulty He decided checking the pump.
Revised He decided to check the pump.

5 • Noun or pronoun + infinitive

Some verbs may be followed by an infinitive alone or by a noun or pronoun and an infinitive. The presence of a noun or pronoun changes the meaning.

ask
beg
choose
dare
expect
help
need
promise
want
wish
would like

He expected to watch.
He expected his workers to watch.

Some verbs *must* be followed by a noun or pronoun before an infinitive:

admonish
advise
allow
cause
challenge
command
convince
encourage
forbid
force
hire
instruct
invite
oblige
order
permit
persuade
remind
request
require
teach
tell
train
urge
warn

He instructed his workers to watch.

Do not use *to* before the infinitive when it follows one of the next verbs and a noun or pronoun:

feel	make ("force")
have	see
hear	watch
let	

He let his workers learn by observation.

EXERCISE 25.6
Revising: Verbs plus gerunds or infinitives CULTURE LANGUAGE

Revise the following sentences so that gerunds or infinitives are used correctly with verbs. Circle the number preceding any sentence that is already correct. Answers to starred items appear at the end of the book.

Example:

A politician cannot avoid to alienate some voters.
A politician cannot avoid alienating some voters.

*1. A program called HELP Wanted tries to encourage citizens take action on behalf of American competitiveness.
*2. Officials working on this program hope improving education for work.
3. American businesses find that their workers need learning to read.
4. In the next ten years the United States expects facing a shortage of 350,000 scientists.
5. HELP Wanted suggests creating a media campaign.

vb 25f

25f Use the appropriate particles with two-word verbs. CULTURE LANGUAGE

Standard American English includes some verbs that consist of two words: the verb itself and a **particle,** a preposition or adverb that affects the meaning of the verb. For example:

Look up the answer. [Research the answer.]
Look over the answer. [Examine the answer.]

Key terms

preposition A word such as *about, for,* or *to* that takes a noun or pronoun as its object: *at the house, in the woods.* (See p. 216 for a list of prepositions.)

adverb A word that modifies a verb (*went down*), adjective (*very pretty*), another adverb (*too sweetly*), or a whole word group (*Eventually, the fire died*). (See p. 214.)

The meanings of these two-word verbs are often quite different from the meanings of the individual words that make them up. (There are some three-word verbs, too, such as *put up with* and *run out of.*)

A dictionary of English as a second language will define two-word verbs for you and say whether the verbs may be separated in a sentence, as explained below. (See p. 197 for a list of ESL dictionaries.) A grammar and style checker will recognize few if any misuses of two-word verbs. You'll need to proofread on your own to catch and correct errors.

Note Many two-word verbs are more common in speech than in more formal academic or business writing. For formal writing, consider using *research* instead of *look up, examine* or *inspect* instead of *look over.*

1 • Inseparable two-word verbs

Verbs and particles that may not be separated by any other words include the following:

catch on	go over	play around	stay away
come across	grow up	run into	stay up
get along	keep on	run out of	take care of
give in	look into	speak up	turn up at

Faulty Children grow quickly up.
Revised Children grow up quickly.

2 • Separable two-word verbs

Most two-word verbs that take direct objects may be separated by the object.

Parents help out their children.
Parents help their children out.

If the direct object is a pronoun, the pronoun *must* separate the verb from the particle.

Faulty Parents help out them.
Revised Parents help them out.

The separable two-word verbs include the following:

bring up	give back	make up	throw out
call off	hand in	point out	try on
call up	hand out	put away	try out
drop off	help out	put back	turn down
fill out	leave out	put off	turn on
fill up	look over	take out	turn up
give away	look up	take over	wrap up

EXERCISE 25.7
Revising: Verbs plus particles CULTURE LANGUAGE

The two- and three-word verbs in the sentences below are underlined. Some are correct as given, and some are not because they should or should not be separated by other words. Revise the verbs and other words that are incorrect. Consult the lists on these two pages or an ESL dictionary if necessary to determine which verbs are separable. Answers to starred items appear at the end of the book.

Example:

Hollywood producers never seem to come up with entirely new plots, but they also never run new ways out of to present old ones.

Hollywood producers never seem to come up with [correct] entirely new plots, but they also never run out of new ways to present old ones.

*1. American movies treat everything from going out with someone to making up an ethnic identity, but few people look their significance into.

*2. While some viewers stay away from topical films, others turn at the theater up simply because a movie has sparked debate.

3. Some movies attracted rowdy spectators, and the theaters had to throw out them.

4. Filmmakers have always been eager to point their influence out to the public.

5. Everyone agrees that filmmakers will keep creating controversy on, if only because it can fill up theaters.

26 Verb Tenses

How do *walked* and *has walked* differ?

Walked and *has walked* illustrate different **tenses** of the verb *to walk*. That is, they show the action of the verb to be occurring at different times, one (*has walked*) before the other (*walked*) and both

http://www.ablongman.com/littlebrown
➤ Sentences and words
➤ Web exercises ➤ Exers. 27–29
➤ Downloads ➤ Chapter 26 exercises in electronic format
➤ Web links ➤ Verbs

before the present. The table opposite illustrates the tense forms for a regular verb. (Irregular verbs have some different forms. See pp. 236–39.)

Note Grammar and style checkers can provide little help with incorrect verb tenses and tense sequences because correctness usually depends on meaning. Proofread carefully yourself to catch errors in tense or tense sequence.

CULTURE LANGUAGE In standard American English, a verb conveys time and sequence through its form. In some other languages and English dialects, various markers besides verb form may indicate the time of a verb. For instance, in African American dialect *I be attending class on Friday* means that the speaker attends class every Friday. To a speaker of standard American English, however, the sentence may be unclear: last Friday? this Friday? every Friday? The intended meaning must be indicated by verb tense. *I attended class on Friday. I will attend class on Friday. I attend class on Friday.*

26a Observe the special uses of the present tense (*sing*).

Most academic and business writing uses the past tense (*the rebellion occurred*), but the present tense has several distinctive uses.

Action occurring now
She understands the problem.
We define the problem differently.

Habitual or recurring action
Banks regularly undergo audits.
The audits monitor the banks' activities.

A general truth
The mills of the gods grind slowly.
The earth is round.

Discussion of literature, film, and so on
Huckleberry Finn has adventures we all envy.
In that article the author examines several causes of crime.

Future time
Next week we draft a new budget.
Funding ends in less than a year.

(Future time is really indicated here by *Next week* and *in less than a year.*)

Tenses of a regular verb (active voice)

Present Action that is occurring now, occurs habitually, or is generally true

Simple present Plain form or *-s* form	**Present progressive** *Am, is,* or *are* plus *-ing* form
I walk. You/we/they walk. He/she/it walks.	I am walking. You/we/they are walking. He/she/it is walking.

Past Action that occurred before now

Simple past Past-tense form (*-d* or *-ed*)	**Past progressive** *Was* or *were* plus *-ing* form
I/he/she/it walked. You/we/they walked.	I/he/she/it was walking. You/we/they were walking.

Future Action that will occur in the future

Simple future Plain form plus *will*	**Future progressive** *Will be* plus *-ing* form
I/you/he/she/it/we/they will walk.	I/you/he/she/it/we/they will be walking.

Present perfect Action that began in the past and is linked to the present

Present perfect *Have* or *has* plus past participle (*-d* or *-ed*)	**Present perfect progressive** *Have been* or *has been* plus *-ing* form
I/you/we/they have walked. He/she/it has walked.	I/you/we/they have been walking. He/she/it has been walking.

Past perfect Action that was completed before another past action

Past perfect *Had* plus past participle (*-d* or *-ed*)	**Past perfect progressive** *Had been* plus *-ing* form
I/you/he/she/it/we/they had walked.	I/you/he/she/it/we/they had been walking.

Future perfect Action that will be completed before another future action

Future perfect *Will have* plus past participle (*-d* or *-ed*)	**Future perfect progressive** *Will have been* plus *-ing* form
I/you/he/she/it/we/they will have walked.	I/you/he/she/it/we/they will have been walking.

26b Observe the uses of the perfect tenses (*have/had/will have sung*).

The **perfect tenses** consist of a form of *have* plus the verb's past participle (*closed, hidden*). They indicate an action completed before another specific time or action. The present perfect tense also indicates action begun in the past and continued into the present.

> present perfect
> The dancer has performed here only once. [The action is completed at the time of the statement.]

> present perfect
> Critics have written about the performance ever since. [The action began in the past and continues now.]

> past perfect
> The dancer had trained in Asia before his performance. [The action was completed before another past action.]

> future perfect
> He will have performed here again by next month. [The action begins now or in the future and will be completed by a specified time in the future.]

CULTURE LANGUAGE With the present perfect tense, the words *since* and *for* are followed by different information. After *since,* give a specific point in time: *The United States has been a member of the United Nations since 1945.* After *for,* give a span of time: *The United States has been a member of the United Nations for over half a century.*

26c Observe the uses of the progressive tenses (*is/was/will be singing*). CULTURE LANGUAGE

The **progressive tenses** indicate continuing (therefore progressive) action. They consist of a form of *be* plus the verb's *-ing* form (present participle). (The words *be* and *been* must be combined with other helping verbs. See p. 244.)

> present progressive
> The economy is improving.

> past progressive
> Last year the economy was stagnating.

> future progressive
> Economists will be watching for signs of growth.

present perfect progressive
The government has been expecting an upturn.

past perfect progressive
Various indicators had been suggesting improvement.

future perfect progressive
By the end of this year, investors will have been watching interest rates nervously for nearly a decade.

Note Verbs that express unchanging states (especially mental states) rather than physical actions do not usually appear in the progressive tenses. These verbs include *adore, appear, believe, belong, care, hate, have, hear, know, like, love, mean, need, own, prefer, remember, see, sound, taste, think, understand,* and *want.*

Faulty — She is wanting to study ethics.
Revised — She wants to study ethics.

26d Keep tenses consistent.

Within a sentence, the tenses of verbs and verb forms need not be identical as long as they reflect actual changes in time: *Ramon will graduate from college thirty years after his father arrived in America.* But needless shifts in tense will confuse or distract readers:

Inconsistent — Immediately after Booth shot Lincoln, Major Rathbone threw himself upon the assassin. But Booth pulls a knife and plunges it into the major's arm.

Revised — Immediately after Booth shot Lincoln, Major Rathbone threw himself upon the assassin. But Booth pulled a knife and plunged it into the major's arm.

Inconsistent — The main character in the novel suffers psychologically because he has a clubfoot, but he eventually triumphed over his disability.

Revised — The main character in the novel suffers psychologically because he has a clubfoot, but he eventually triumphs over his disability. [Use the present tense when discussing the content of literature, film, and so on.]

26e Use the appropriate sequence of verb tenses.

The **sequence of tenses** is the relation between the verb tense in a main clause and the verb tense in a subordinate clause. The tenses are often different, as in the following sentence:

Ramon's father arrived in the United States thirty years ago, after he had married, and now Ramon has decided that he will return to his father's homeland.

English tense sequence can be tricky for native speakers and especially challenging for nonnative speakers. The main difficulties are discussed below.

1 • Past or past perfect tense in main clause

When the verb in the main clause is in the past or past perfect tense, the verb in the subordinate clause must also be past or past perfect:

The researchers discovered [main clause: past] that people varied [subordinate clause: past] widely in their knowledge of public events.

The variation occurred [main clause: past] because respondents had been born [subordinate clause: past perfect] in different decades.

None of them had been born [main clause: past perfect] when Eisenhower was [subordinate clause: past] President.

Exception Always use the present tense for a general truth, such as *The earth is round:*

Most understood [main clause: past] that popular Presidents are [subordinate clause: present] not necessarily good Presidents.

2 • Conditional sentences

A **conditional sentence** states a factual relation between cause and effect, makes a prediction, or speculates about what might happen. Such a sentence usually consists of a subordinate clause beginning with *if, when,* or *unless* and a main clause stating the result. The three kinds of conditional sentences use distinctive verbs.

Key terms

main clause A word group that contains a subject and a verb and does not begin with a subordinating word: *Books are valuable.* (See p. 230.)

subordinate clause A word group that contains a subject and a verb, begins with a subordinating word such as *because* or *who,* and is not a question: *Books are valuable when they enlighten.* (See p. 230.)

Factual relation

For statements asserting that something always or usually happens whenever something else happens, use the present tense in both clauses:

subordinate clause: present — main clause: present

When a voter casts a ballot, he or she has complete privacy.

If the linked events occurred in the past, use the past tense in both clauses:

subordinate clause: past — main clause: past

When voters registered in some states, they had to pay a poll tax.

Prediction

For a prediction, generally use the present tense in the subordinate clause and the future tense in the main clause:

subordinate clause: present — main clause: future

Unless citizens regain faith in politics, they will not vote.

Sometimes the verb in the main clause consists of *may, can, should,* or *might* plus the verb's plain form: *If citizens regain faith, they may vote.*

Speculation

Speculations are mainly of two kinds, each with its own verb pattern. For events that are possible in the present but unlikely, use the past tense in the subordinate clause and *would, could,* or *might* plus the verb's plain form in the main clause:

subordinate clause: past — main clause: *would* + verb

If voters had more confidence, they would vote more often.

Use *were* instead of *was* when the subject is *I, he, she, it,* or a singular noun. (See p. 263 for more on this distinctive verb form.)

subordinate clause: past — main clause: *would* + verb

If the voter were more confident, he or she would vote more often.

For events that are impossible now, that are contrary to fact, use the same forms as above (including the distinctive *were* when applicable):

subordinate clause: past — main clause: *might* + verb

If Lincoln were alive, he might inspire confidence.

For events that were impossible in the past, use the past perfect tense in the subordinate clause and *would, could,* or *might* plus the present perfect tense in the main clause:

subordinate clause: past perfect — main clause: *might* + present perfect

If Lincoln had lived past the Civil War, he might have helped stabilize the country.

3 • Indirect quotations

An **indirect quotation** reports what someone said or wrote but not in the exact words and not in quotation marks: *Lincoln said that events had controlled him* (quotation: "Events have controlled me"). An indirect quotation generally appears in a subordinate clause (underlined above), with certain conventions governing verb tense in most cases:

- When the verb in the main clause is in the present tense, the verb in the indirect quotation (subordinate clause) is in the same tense as the original quotation:

  main clause: present — subordinate clause: present

  Haworth says that Lincoln is our noblest national hero. [Quotation: "Lincoln is our noblest national hero."]

  main clause: present — subordinate clause: past

  He says that Lincoln was a complicated person. [Quotation: "Lincoln was a complicated person."]

- When the verb in the main clause is in the past tense, the verb in the indirect quotation usually changes tense from the original quotation. Present tense changes to past tense:

  main clause: past — subordinate clause: past

  An assistant to Lincoln said that the President was always generous. [Quotation: "The President is always generous."]

  Past tense and present perfect tense change to past perfect tense. (Past perfect tense does not change.)

  main clause: past — subordinate clause: past perfect

  Lincoln said that events had controlled him. [Quotation: "Events have controlled me."]

- When the direct quotation states a general truth or reports a situation that is still true, use the present tense in the indirect quotation regardless of the verb in the main clause:

  main clause: past — subordinate clause: present

  Lincoln said that right makes might. [Quotation: "Right makes might."]

Note As several of the examples show, an indirect quotation differs in at least two additional ways from the original quotation: (1) the indirect quotation is usually preceded by *that,* and (2) the indirect quotation changes pronouns, especially from forms of *I* or *we* to forms of *he, she,* or *they.*

EXERCISE 26.1
Adjusting tense sequence: Past or past perfect tense

The tenses in each sentence below are in correct sequence. Change the tense of one verb as instructed. Then change the tenses of other verbs as needed to restore correct sequence. Some items have more than one possible answer. Answers to starred items appear at the end of the book.

Example:

Delgado will call when he reaches his destination. (*Change will call to called.*)

Delgado called when he reached [or had reached] his destination.

t seq
26e

*1. Diaries that Adolf Hitler is supposed to have written have surfaced in Germany. (*Change have surfaced to had surfaced.*)
*2. Many people believe that the diaries are authentic because a well-known historian has declared them so. (*Change believe to believed.*)
3. However, the historian's evaluation has been questioned by other authorities, who call the diaries forgeries. (*Change has been questioned to was questioned.*)
4. They claim, among other things, that the paper is not old enough to have been used by Hitler. (*Change claim to claimed.*)
5. Eventually, the doubters will win the debate because they have the best evidence. (*Change will win to won.*)

EXERCISE 26.2
Revising: Tense sequence with conditional sentences

Supply the appropriate tense for each verb in brackets below. Answers to starred items appear at the end of the book.

Example:

If Babe Ruth or Jim Thorpe [be] athletes today, they [remind] us that even sports heroes must contend with a harsh reality.

If Babe Ruth or Jim Thorpe were athletes today, they might [or could or would] remind us that even sports heroes must contend with a harsh reality.

*1. When an athlete [turn] professional, he or she commits to a grueling regimen of mental and physical training.

*2. If athletes [be] less committed, they [disappoint] teammates, fans, and themselves.
*3. If professional athletes [be] very lucky, they may play until age forty.
*4. Unless an athlete achieves celebrity status, he or she [have] few employment choices after retirement.
*5. If professional sports [be] less risky, athletes [have] longer careers and more choices after retirement.

6. If you think you [be] exposed to the flu in the winter, you [get] a flu shot.
7. If you are allergic to eggs, you [have] an allergic reaction to the flu shot.
8. If you get the flu after having a flu shot, your illness [be] milder.
9. If you had had a flu shot last year, you [avoid] the illness.
10. If you [be] not so afraid of shots, you [will] get a flu shot every year.

EXERCISE 26.3
Changing verb tense in indirect quotations

Change each quotation into an indirect quotation, deleting quotation marks and changing verbs as necessary so that they are in the correct tense sequence. As needed, also change capital letters to small letters and add *that* or *whether* to each indirect quotation. You may also have to change *I* to *he* or *she.* Answers to starred items appear at the end of the book.

Example:

Friedrich Nietzsche said, "Woman was God's second mistake."

Friedrich Nietzsche said that woman was God's second mistake.

*1. In his speech accepting the Nobel Prize, William Faulkner said, "I believe that man will not merely endure: he will prevail."
*2. Cornelia Otis Skinner commented cynically, "Woman's virtue is man's greatest invention."

3. Just as cynically, Ogden Nash declared, "Women would rather be right than reasonable."
4. Nietzsche asked, "Is man only a blunder of God, or God only a blunder of man?"
5. Mistinguett, the French dancer, commented teasingly: "A kiss can be a comma, a question mark, or an exclamation point."

27 Verb Mood

When is it right to say *he were?*

The odd-sounding construction *he were* illustrates a particular **mood** of the verb *is,* a particular attitude on the writer's or speaker's part toward what he or she is saying. In the sentence *I wish he were going,* the *were* reinforces the writer's expression of a desire.

English verbs express three possible moods. The **indicative mood** states a fact or opinion or asks a question: *The theater needs help. Can you help the theater?* The **imperative mood** expresses a command or gives a direction, and it omits the subject of the sentence, *you: Help the theater.* The more complicated **subjunctive mood** expresses wishes, suggestions, and other attitudes, using *he were* and other distinctive verb forms described below.

Note A grammar and style checker may spot some simple errors in the subjunctive mood, but it may miss others. For example, a checker flagged *I wish I was home* (should be *were home*) but not *If I had a hammer, I will hammer in the morning* (should be *would hammer*). Instead of relying on the checker to find and correct problems, proofread your work looking for appropriate uses of subjunctive verbs.

27a Use the subjunctive verb forms appropriately, as in *I wish I were.*

The subjunctive mood expresses a suggestion, requirement, or desire, or it states a condition that is contrary to fact (that is, imaginary or hypothetical).

- Verbs such as *ask, insist, urge, require, recommend,* and *suggest* indicate request or requirement. They often precede a subordinate clause beginning with *that* and containing the substance of the request or requirement. For all subjects, the verb in the *that* clause is the plain form:

  Rules require that every donation be mailed. [plain form: be]

http://www.ablongman.com/littlebrown

➤ Sentences and words
  ➤ Web exercises ➤ Exer. 30
  ➤ Downloads ➤ Chapter 27 exercise in electronic format
  ➤ Web links ➤ Verbs

- Contrary-to-fact clauses state imaginary or hypothetical conditions and usually begin with *if* or *unless* or follow *wish*. For present contrary-to-fact clauses, use the verb's past-tense form (for *be*, use the past-tense form *were*):

  If the theater were [past] in better shape and had [past] more money, its future would be assured.

  I wish I were [past] able to donate money.

  For past contrary-to-fact clauses, use the verb's past perfect form (*had* + past participle):

  The theater would be better funded if it had been [past perfect] better managed last year.

  Note Do not use the helping verb *would* or *could* in a contrary-to-fact clause beginning with *if:*

Not	Many people would have helped if they would have known.
But	Many people would have helped if they had known.

See also pages 259–60 for more on verb tenses in contrary-to-fact sentences like these.

27b Keep mood consistent.

Shifts in mood within a sentence or among related sentences can be confusing. Such shifts occur most frequently in directions.

Inconsistent	Cook the mixture slowly, and you should stir it until the sugar is dissolved. [Mood shifts from imperative to indicative.]
Revised	Cook the mixture slowly, and stir it until the sugar is dissolved. [Consistently imperative.]

EXERCISE 27.1
Revising: Subjunctive mood

Revise the following sentences with appropriate subjunctive verb forms. Answers to starred items appear at the end of the book.

Example:

I would help the old man if I was able to reach him.
I would help the old man if I were able to reach him.

*1. If John Hawkins would have known of all the dangerous side effects of smoking tobacco, would he have introduced the dried plant to England in 1565?

*2. Hawkins noted that if a Florida Indian man was to travel for several days, he would have smoked tobacco to satisfy his hunger and thirst.

3. Early tobacco growers feared that their product would not gain acceptance unless it was perceived as healthful.
4. To prevent fires, in 1646 the General Court of Massachusetts passed a law requiring that a colonist smoked tobacco only if he was five miles from any town.
5. To prevent decadence, in 1647 Connecticut passed a law mandating that one's smoking of tobacco was limited to once a day in one's own home.

28 Verb Voice

Which is better: *The book was written by her* or *She wrote the book?*

Generally, you should prefer the **active voice** of *She wrote the book,* in which the subject (*She*) performs the action of the verb (*wrote*). In the **passive voice** of *The book was written by her,* the subject (*book*) receives the action of the verb (*was written*) and the actual actor appears in a trailing phrase (*by her*). (Naming the actual actor is optional in the passive voice.) The passive voice does have its uses (see the next page), but the active voice is usually more direct and concise.

CULTURE LANGUAGE A passive verb always consists of a form of *be* plus the past participle of the main verb: *rents are controlled, people were inspired.* Other helping verbs must also be used with the words *be, being,* and *been: rents have been controlled, people would have been inspired.* Only a transitive verb (one that takes an object) may be used in the passive voice. (See pp. 221, 245.)

http://www.ablongman.com/littlebrown
- Sentences and words
  - Web exercises ➤ Exers. 31–33
  - Downloads ➤ Chapter 28 exercises in electronic format
  - Web links ➤ Verbs

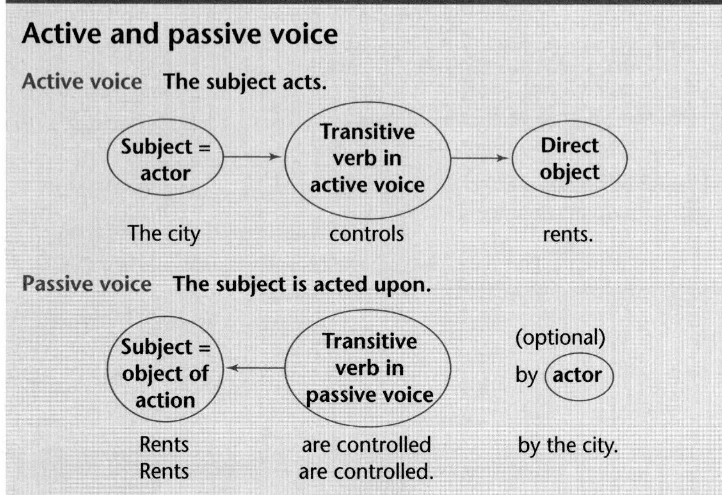

28a Prefer the active voice. Use the passive voice when the actor is unknown or unimportant.

The active voice is usually clearer, more concise, and more forthright than the passive voice.

Weak passive: The Internet is used for research by many scholars, and its expansion to the general public has been criticized by some.

Strong active: Many scholars use the Internet for research, and some have criticized its expansion to the general public.

The passive voice is useful in two situations: when the actor is unknown and when the actor is unimportant or less important than the object of the action.

> The Internet was established in 1969 by the US Department of Defense. The network has now been extended internationally to governments, universities, foundations, corporations, and private individuals. [In the first sentence the writer wishes to stress the Internet rather than the Department of Defense. In the second sentence the actor is unknown or too complicated to name.]

> After the solution had been cooled to 10°C, the acid was added. [The person who cooled and added, perhaps the writer, is less important than the facts that the solution was cooled and acid was added. Passive sentences are common in scientific writing.]

Note Most grammar and style checkers can be set to spot the passive voice. But they will also flag appropriate uses of the passive voice (such as when the actor is unknown). Use the checker to help you see the passive voice in your writing, but decide for yourself whether flagged verbs are appropriate.

28b Keep voice consistent.

Shifts in voice that involve shifts in subject are usually unnecessary and confusing.

Inconsistent Internet newsgroups cover an enormous range of topics for discussion. Forums for meeting people with like interests are provided in these groups.

Revised Internet newsgroups cover an enormous range of topics for discussion and provide forums for meeting people with like interests.

A shift in voice is appropriate when it helps focus the reader's attention on a single subject, as in *The candidate campaigned vigorously and was nominated on the first ballot.*

EXERCISE 28.1
Revising: Using the active voice

Rewrite the following passive sentences into the active voice, adding a subject as necessary. Possible answers to starred items appear at the end of the book.

Example:

Contaminants are removed from water by treatment plants.

Treatment plants remove contaminants from water.

*1. Water quality is determined by many factors.
*2. Suspended and dissolved substances are contained in all natural waters.
*3. The amounts of the substances are controlled by the environment.
*4. Some dissolved substances are produced by pesticides.
*5. Sediment is deposited in water by fields, livestock feedlots, and other sources.

6. The bottom life of streams and lakes is affected by sediment.
7. Light penetration is reduced by sediment, and bottom-dwelling organisms may be smothered.
8. The quality of water in city systems is measured frequently.
9. If legal levels are exceeded by pollutants, the citizens must be notified by city officials.
10. The chlorine taste of water is disliked by many people.

EXERCISE 28.2
Converting between active and passive voices

To practice using the two voices of the verb, convert the verbs in the following sentences from active to passive or from passive to active. (In converting from passive to active, you may need to add a subject.) Which version of the sentence seems more effective and why? Answers to starred items appear at the end of the book.

Example:

The aspiring actor was discovered in a nightclub.

A talent scout discovered the actor in a nightclub.

*1. When the Eiffel Tower was built in 1889, it was thought by the French to be ugly.
*2. At the time, many people still resisted industrial technology.
3. The tower's naked steel construction typified this technology.
4. Beautiful ornament was expected to grace fine buildings.
5. Further, a structure without solid walls could not even be called a building.

29 Agreement of Subject and Verb

Does the verb of this sentence match the subject?

A verb and its subject should match, or **agree,** in number and person: a singular subject takes a singular verb, and a plural subject takes a plural verb, as in the examples below:

Daniel Inouye was the first Japanese American in Congress.
subject verb

More Japanese Americans live in Hawaii and California than elsewhere.
subject verb

Most problems of subject-verb agreement arise when endings are omitted from subjects or verbs or when the relation between

http://www.ablongman.com/littlebrown

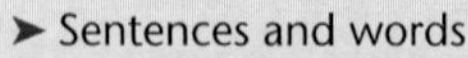
➤ Sentences and words

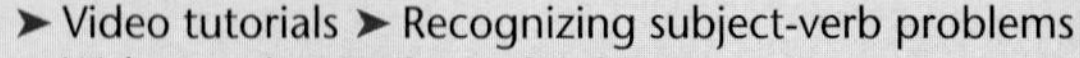
➤ Video tutorials ➤ Recognizing subject-verb problems
➤ Web exercises ➤ Exers. 34–37
➤ Downloads ➤ Chapter 29 exercises in electronic format
➤ Web links ➤ Subject-verb agreement

sentence parts is uncertain. This chapter covers these tricky situations.

Note A grammar and style checker will look for problems with subject-verb agreement. Most checkers also allow you to customize settings so that you can turn off other options and look just for agreement problems. Checkers will catch all simple errors, such as *Addie and John is late* and many more complicated sentences such as *Is Margaret and Tom going with us?* (should be *Are*). But a checker failed to flag *The old group has gone their separate ways* (should be *have*) and offered a wrong correction for *The old group have gone their separate ways*, which is already correct. Do not automatically accept a checker's points, and proofread your work carefully on your own.

29a The *-s* and *-es* endings work differently for nouns and verbs.

An *-s* or *-es* ending does opposite things to nouns and verbs: it usually makes a noun *plural*, but it always makes a present-tense verb *singular*. Thus a singular-noun subject will not end in *-s*, but its verb will. A plural-noun subject will end in *-s*, but its verb will not. Between them, subject and verb use only one *-s* ending.

Singular subject	Plural subject
The boy play**s**.	The boy**s** play.
The bird soar**s**.	The bird**s** soar.

The only exceptions to these rules involve the nouns that form irregular plurals, such as *child/children, woman/women*. The irregular plural still requires a plural verb: *The children play. The women read.*

CULTURE LANGUAGE If your first language or dialect is not standard American English, subject-verb agreement may be problematic, especially for the following reasons:

- Some English dialects follow different rules for subject-verb agreement, such as omitting the *-s* ending for singular verbs or using the *-s* ending for plural verbs.

Key terms

	Number	
Person	**Singular**	**Plural**
First	I eat.	We eat.
Second	You eat.	You eat.
Third	He/she/it eats.	They eat.
	The bird eats.	Birds eat.

Nonstandard	The voter resist change.
Standard	The voter resist**s** change.
Standard	The voter**s** resist change.

The verb *be* changes spelling for singular and plural in both present and past tense. (See also p. 213.)

Nonstandard	Taxes is high. They was raised just last year.
Standard	Taxes are high. They were raised just last year.

Have also has a distinctive *-s* form, *has:*

Nonstandard	The new tax have little chance of passing.
Standard	The new tax ha**s** little chance of passing.

- *Be, have,* and also *do* change form with different subjects when they serve as helping verbs:

Singular subject	Plural subject
A traffic light wa**s** installed.	Traffic light**s** were installed.
The new light doe**s** not [or doe**s**n't] help.	The new light**s** do not [or don't] help.
Traffic ha**s** worsened.	Accident**s** have increased.

- No other helping verbs change form with singular or plural subjects:

Singular subject	Plural subject
The light should help.	The light**s** should help.

- As the above examples show, the main verb in a verb phrase (*installed, help, worsened, increased*) does not change with different subjects.

vb agr
29b

29b Subject and verb should agree even when other words come between them.

The catalog of course requirements often baffles [not baffle] students.

The requirements stated in the catalog are [not is] unclear.

Key term

helping verb A verb such as *be, have,* and *can* that combines with another verb to show time, permission, and other meanings: *The family has been gone. You can rent the house.* (See p. 213.)

Note Phrases beginning with *as well as, together with, along with,* and *in addition to* do not change the number of the subject:

> The president, as well as the deans, has [not have] agreed to revise the catalog.

29c Subjects joined by *and* usually take plural verbs.

> Frost and Roethke were contemporaries.

Exceptions When the parts of the subject form a single idea or refer to a single person or thing, they take a singular verb:

> Avocado and bean sprouts is a California sandwich.

When a compound subject is preceded by the adjective *each* or *every,* the verb is usually singular:

> Each man, woman, and child has a right to be heard.

29d When parts of a subject are joined by *or* or *nor,* the verb agrees with the nearer part.

> Either the painter or the carpenter knows the cost.

> The cabinets or the bookcases are too costly.

When one part of the subject is singular and the other plural, avoid awkwardness by placing the plural part closer to the verb so that the verb is plural:

Awkward Neither the owners nor the contractor agrees.

Revised Neither the contractor nor the owners agree.

29e With *everyone* and other indefinite pronouns, use a singular or plural verb as appropriate.

Most indefinite pronouns are singular in meaning (they refer to a single unspecified person or thing), and they take a singular verb:

> Something smells. Neither is right.

> None of them has any money.

The plural indefinite pronouns refer to more than one unspecified thing, and they take a plural verb:

Both are correct. Several were invited.

The other indefinite pronouns take a singular or a plural verb depending on whether the word they refer to is singular or plural:

All of the money is reserved for emergencies.

All of the funds are reserved for emergencies.

CULTURE LANGUAGE See page 305 for the distinction between *few* ("not many") and *a few* ("some").

29f Collective nouns such as *team* take singular or plural verbs depending on meaning.

vb agr 29f

Use a singular verb with a collective noun when the group acts as a unit:

The group agrees that action is necessary.

But when the group's members act separately, not together, use a plural verb:

The old group have gone their separate ways.

The collective noun *number* may be singular or plural. Preceded by *a,* it is plural; preceded by *the,* it is singular:

A number of people are in debt.

The number of people in debt is very large.

Key terms

indefinite pronoun A pronoun that does not refer to a specific person or thing:

Singular			*Singular or plural*	*Plural*
anybody	everyone	no one	all	both
anyone	everything	nothing	any	few
anything	much	one	more	many
each	neither	somebody	most	several
either	nobody	someone	some	
everybody	none	something		

collective noun A noun with singular form that names a group of individuals or things—for instance, *army, audience, committee, crowd, family, group, team.*

CULTURE LANGUAGE Some noncount nouns (nouns that don't form plurals) are collective nouns because they name groups: for instance, *furniture, clothing, mail.* These noncount nouns usually take singular verbs: *Mail arrives daily.* But some of these nouns take plural verbs, including *clergy, military, people, police,* and any collective noun that comes from an adjective, such as *the poor, the rich, the young, the elderly.* If you mean one representative of the group, use a singular noun such as *police officer* or *poor person.* If you are unsure whether a noun takes a singular or plural verb, consult a dictionary of English as a second language. (See p. 197 for a list.)

29g *Who, which,* and *that* take verbs that agree with their antecedents.

When used as subjects, *who, which,* and *that* refer to another word in the sentence, called the **antecedent.** The verb agrees with the antecedent.

Mayor Garber ought to listen to the people who work for her.

Bardini is the only aide who has her ear.

Agreement problems often occur with *who, which,* or *that* when the sentence includes *one of the* or *the only one of the:*

Bardini is one of the aides who work unpaid. [Of the aides who work unpaid, Bardini is one.]

Bardini is the only one of the aides who knows the community. [Of the aides, only one, Bardini, knows the community.]

CULTURE LANGUAGE In phrases like those above involving *one of the,* be sure the noun is plural: *Bardini is one of the aides* [not *aide*] *who work unpaid.*

29h *News* and other singular nouns ending in *-s* take singular verbs.

Singular nouns ending in *-s* include *athletics, economics, linguistics, mathematics, measles, mumps, news, physics, politics,* and *statistics,* as well as place names such as *Athens, Wales,* and *United States.*

After so long a wait, the news has to be good.

Statistics is required of psychology majors.

A few of these words also take plural verbs, but only when they describe individual items rather than whole bodies of activity or knowledge: *The statistics prove him wrong.*

Measurements and figures ending in *-s* may also be singular when the quantity they refer to is a unit.

Three years is a long time to wait.

Three-fourths of the library consists of reference books.

29i The verb agrees with the subject even when the normal word order is inverted.

Inverted subject-verb order occurs mainly in questions and in constructions beginning with *there* or *it* and a form of *be.*

Is voting a right or a privilege?

Are a right and a privilege the same thing?

There are differences between them.

29j *Is, are,* and other linking verbs agree with their subjects, not subject complements.

Make a linking verb agree with its subject, usually the first element in the sentence, not with the noun or pronoun serving as a subject complement.

The child's sole support is her court-appointed guardians.

Her court-appointed guardians are the child's sole support.

29k Use singular verbs with titles and with words being defined.

Hakada Associates is a new firm.

Key terms

linking verb A verb that connects or equates the subject and subject complement: for example, *seem, become,* and forms of *be.* (See p. 222.)

subject complement A word that describes or renames the subject: *They became chemists.* (See p. 222.)

Dream Days remains a favorite book.

Folks is a down-home word for *people*.

EXERCISE 29.1
Revising: Subject-verb agreement

Revise the verbs in the following sentences as needed to make subjects and verbs agree in number. If the sentence is already correct as given, circle the number preceding it. Answers to starred items appear at the end of the book.

Example:

Each of the job applicants type sixty words per minute.
Each of the job applicants types sixty words per minute.

*1. Weinstein & Associates are a consulting firm that try to make businesspeople laugh.
*2. Statistics from recent research suggests that humor relieves stress.
*3. Reduced stress in businesses in turn reduce illness and absenteeism.
*4. Reduced stress can also reduce friction within an employee group, which then work together more productively.
*5. In special conferences held by one consultant, each of the participants practice making others laugh.

6. "Isn't there enough laughs within you to spread the wealth?" the consultant asks his students.
7. The consultant quotes Casey Stengel's rule that the best way to keep your management job is to separate the underlings who hate you from the ones who have not decided how they feel.
8. Such self-deprecating comments in public is uncommon among business managers, the consultant says.
9. Each of the managers in a typical firm take the work much too seriously.
10. The humorous boss often feels like the only one of the managers who have other things in mind besides profits.
11. One consultant to many companies suggest cultivating office humor with practical jokes such as a rubber fish in the water cooler.
12. When a manager or employees regularly posts cartoons on the bulletin board, office spirit usually picks up.
13. When someone who has seemed too easily distracted is entrusted with updating the cartoons, his or her concentration often improves.
14. In the face of levity, the former sourpuss becomes one of those who hides bad temper.
15. Every one of the consultants caution, however, that humor has no place in life-affecting corporate situations such as employee layoffs.

EXERCISE 29.2
Adjusting for subject-verb agreement

Rewrite the following paragraphs to change the underlined words from plural to singular. (You will sometimes need to add *a* or *the* for the singular, as in the example below.) Then change verbs as necessary so that they agree with their new subjects. Answers to the first paragraph appear at the end of the book.

Example:

Siberian tigers are an endangered subspecies.
The Siberian tiger is an endangered subspecies.

*Siberian tigers are the largest living cats in the world, much bigger than their relative the Bengal tiger. *They grow to a length of nine to twelve feet, including their tails, and to a height of about three and a half feet. *They can weigh over six hundred pounds. *These carnivorous hunters live in northern China and Korea as well as in Siberia. *During the long winter of this Arctic climate, the yellowish striped coats get a little lighter in order to blend with the snow-covered landscape. *The coats also grow quite thick, since the tigers have to withstand temperatures as low as –50°F.

Siberian tigers sometimes have to travel great distances to find food. They need about twenty pounds of food a day because of their size and the cold climate, but when they have fresh food they may eat as much as a hundred pounds at one time. They hunt mainly deer, boars, and even bears, plus smaller prey such as fish and rabbits. They pounce on their prey and grab them by the back of the neck. Animals that are not killed immediately are thrown to the ground and suffocated with a bite to the throat. Then the tigers feast.

Pronouns

How can I use words such as *he, it,* and *you* clearly?

Pronouns—words such as *she* and *who* that refer to nouns—merit special care because all their meaning comes from the other words they refer to. To show their function in a sentence and their relation to other words, pronouns may change form (for instance, *I, me*), person (*you, she*), number (*I, we*), and gender (*he, she*). This section discusses changing pronoun case (below), matching pronouns and the words they refer to (Chapter 31), and making sure pronouns refer clearly to their nouns (Chapter 32).

30 Pronoun Case

Is it *she and I* or *her and me*? Is it *who* or *whom*?

Choosing the right **case** of a pronoun—the right form, such as *she* or *her*—requires understanding how the pronoun functions in its sentence.

- The **subjective case** indicates that the pronoun is a subject or subject complement.

Key terms

subject Who or what a sentence is about: *Biologists often study animals. They often work in laboratories.* (See p. 219.)

subject complement A word that renames or describes the sentence subject: *Biologists are scientists. The best biologists are she and Scoggins.* (See p. 222.)

http://www.ablongman.com/littlebrown

➤ Sentences and words
  ➤ Video tutorials ➤ Understanding pronouns
  ➤ Web exercises ➤ Exers. 38–40
  ➤ Downloads ➤ Chapter 30 exercises in electronic format
  ➤ Web links ➤ Case of nouns and pronouns

- The **objective case** indicates that the pronoun is an object of a verb or preposition.
- The **possessive case** indicates that the pronoun owns or is the source of a noun in the sentence.

Subjective	Objective	Possessive
I	me	my, mine
you	you	your, yours
he	him	his
she	her	her, hers
it	it	its
we	us	our, ours
you	you	your, yours
they	them	their, theirs
who	whom	whose
whoever	whomever	—

Note Some grammar and style checkers can't spot any problems with pronoun case. Others do flag mistakes, but they also miss a lot. For instance, one checker spotted the error in *We asked whom would come* (should be *who would come*), but it overlooked *We dreaded them coming* (should be *their coming*). To be sure you catch possible errors in case, review your sentences on your own, deciding for yourself which are correct.

CULTURE LANGUAGE In standard American English, *-self* pronouns do not change form to show function. Their only forms are *myself, yourself, himself, herself, itself, ourselves, yourselves, themselves*. Avoid nonstandard forms such as *hisself, ourself,* and *theirselves*.

30a Distinguish between compound subjects and compound objects: *she and I* vs. *her and me.*

Compound subjects or objects—those consisting of two or more nouns or pronouns—have the same case forms as they would if one noun or pronoun stood alone.

Key terms

object of verb The receiver of the verb's action (**direct object**): *Many biologists study animals. The animals teach them.* Or the person or thing the action is performed for (**indirect object**): *Some biologists give animals homes. The animals give them pleasure.* (See pp. 221–22.)

object of preposition The word linked by *with, for,* or another preposition to the rest of the sentence: *Many biologists work in a laboratory. For them the lab often provides a second home.* (See p. 227.)

compound subject
She and Novick discussed the proposal.

compound object
The proposal disappointed her and him.

If you are in doubt about the correct form, try the test below.

A test for case forms in compound constructions

- **Identify a compound construction** (one connected by *and, but, or, nor*):

  [He, Him] and [I, me] won the prize.
  The prize went to [he, him] and [I, me].

- **Write a separate sentence for each part of the compound:**

  [He, Him] won the prize. [I, Me] won the prize.
  The prize went to [he, him]. The prize went to [I, me].

- **Choose the pronouns that sound correct:**

  He won the prize. I won the prize. [Subjective.]
  The prize went to him. The prize went to me. [Objective.]

- **Put the separate sentences back together:**

  He and I won the prize.
  The prize went to him and me.

30b Use the subjective case for subject complements: *It was she.*

After a linking verb, a pronoun renaming the subject (a subject complement) should be in the subjective case:

subject complement
The ones who care most are she and Novick.

subject complement
It was they whom the mayor appointed.

Key term

linking verb A verb, such as a form of *be,* that connects a subject and a word that renames or describes the subject (subject complement): *They are biologists.* (See p. 222.)

If this construction sounds stilted to you, use the more natural order: *She and Novick are the ones who care most. The mayor appointed them.*

EXERCISE 30.1
Choosing between subjective and objective pronouns

From the pairs in brackets, select the appropriate subjective or objective pronoun(s) for each of the following sentences. Answers to starred items appear at the end of the book.

Example:

"Between you and [I, me]," the seller said, "this deal is a steal."
"Between you and me," the seller said, "this deal is a steal."

*1. Jody and [I, me] had been hunting for jobs.
*2. The best employees at our old company were [she, her] and [I, me], so [we, us] expected to find jobs quickly.
3. Between [she, her] and [I, me] the job search had lasted two months, and still it had barely begun.
4. Slowly, [she, her] and [I, me] stopped sharing leads.
5. It was obvious that Jody and [I, me] could not be as friendly as [we, us] had been.

case
30c

30c The use of *who* vs. *whom* depends on the pronoun's function in its clause.

1 • Questions

At the beginning of a question use *who* for a subject and *whom* for an object:

subject → Who wrote the policy? object ← Whom does it affect?

To find the correct case of *who* in a question, follow the steps below:

- Pose the question:

  [Who, Whom] makes that decision?
  [Who, Whom] does one ask?

- Answer the question, using a personal pronoun. Choose the pronoun that sounds correct, and note its case:

  [She, Her] makes that decision. She makes that decision. [Subjective.]

  One asks [she, her]. One asks her. [Objective.]

- Use the same case (*who* or *whom*) in the question:

  Who makes that decision? [Subjective.]
  Whom does one ask? [Objective.]

2 • Subordinate clauses

In subordinate clauses use *who* and *whoever* for all subjects, *whom* and *whomever* for all objects.

subject
Give old clothes to whoever needs them.

object
I don't know whom the mayor appointed.

To determine which form to use, try the test below:

- Locate the subordinate clause:

  Few people know [who, whom] they should ask.
  They are unsure [who, whom] makes the decision.

- Rewrite the subordinate clause as a separate sentence, substituting a personal pronoun for *who, whom.* Choose the pronoun that sounds correct, and note its case:

  They should ask [she, her]. They should ask her. [Objective.]

  [She, her] usually makes the decision. She usually makes the decision. [Subjective.]

- Use the same case (*who* or *whom*) in the subordinate clause:

  Few people know whom they should ask. [Objective.]
  They are unsure who makes the decision. [Subjective.]

Note Don't let expressions such as *I think* and *she says* mislead you into using *whom* rather than *who* for the subject of a clause.

subject
He is the one who I think is best qualified.

To choose between *who* and *whom* in such constructions, delete the interrupting phrase so that you can see the true relation between parts: *He is the one who is best qualified.*

Key term

subordinate clause A word group that contains a subject and a verb and also begins with a subordinating word, such as *who, whom,* or *because.* (See p. 230.)

EXERCISE 30.2
Choosing between *who* and *whom*

From the pairs in brackets, select the appropriate form of the pronoun in each of the following sentences. Answers to starred items appear at the end of the book.

Example:

My mother asked me [who, whom] I was meeting.
My mother asked me whom I was meeting.

*1. The school administrators suspended Jurgen, [who, whom] they suspected of setting the fire.
*2. Jurgen had been complaining to other custodians, [who, whom] reported him.
*3. He constantly complained of unfair treatment from [whoever, whomever] happened to be passing in the halls, including pupils.
*4. "[Who, Whom] here has heard Mr. Jurgen's complaints?" the police asked.
*5. "[Who, Whom] did he complain most about?"
6. His coworkers agreed that Jurgen seemed less upset with the staff or students, most of [who, whom] he did not even know, than with the building itself.
7. "He took out his aggression on the building," claimed one coworker [who, whom] often witnessed Jurgen's behavior.
8. "He cursed and kicked the walls and [whoever, whomever] he saw nearby."
9. The coworker thought that Jurgen might have imagined people [who, whom] instructed him to behave the way he did.
10. "He's someone [who, whom] other people can't get next to," said the coworker.

30d Use the appropriate case in other constructions.

1 • *We* or *us* with a noun

The choice of *we* or *us* before a noun depends on the use of the noun:

object of preposition
Freezing weather is welcomed by us skaters.

subject
We skaters welcome freezing weather.

2 • Pronoun in an appositive

In an appositive the case of a pronoun depends on the function of the word the appositive describes or identifies:

appositive identifies object
The class elected two representatives, DeShawn and me.

appositive identifies subject
Two representatives, DeShawn and I, were elected.

3 • Pronoun after *than* or *as*

When a pronoun follows *than* or *as* in a comparison, the case of the pronoun indicates what words may have been omitted. A subjective pronoun must be the subject of the omitted verb:

subject
Some critics like Glass more than he [does].

An objective pronoun must be the object of the omitted verb:

object
Some critics like Glass more than [they like] him.

4 • Subject and object of infinitive

Both the object *and* the subject of an infinitive are in the objective case:

subject of infinitive
The school asked him to speak.

object of infinitive
Students chose to invite him.

5 • Case before a gerund

Ordinarily, use the possessive form of a pronoun or noun immediately before a gerund:

The coach disapproved of their lifting weights.

The coach's disapproving was a surprise.

Key terms

appositive A noun or noun substitute that renames another noun immediately before it. (See p. 229.)

infinitive The plain form of the verb plus *to: to run.* (See p. 228.)

gerund The *-ing* form of a verb used as a noun: *Running is fun.* (See p. 228.)

EXERCISE 30.3
Revising: Pronoun case

Revise all inappropriate case forms in the sentences below. If a sentence is already correct as given, circle the number preceding it. Answers to starred items appear at the end of the book.

Example:

Convincing we veterans to vote yes will be difficult.
Convincing <u>us</u> veterans to vote yes will be difficult.

*1. Written four thousand years ago, *The Epic of Gilgamesh* tells of a bored king who his people thought was too harsh.
*2. Gilgamesh found a source of entertainment when he met Enkidu, a wild man who had lived with the animals in the mountains.
*3. Immediately, him and Gilgamesh wrestled to see whom was more powerful.
*4. After hours of struggle, Enkidu admitted that Gilgamesh was stronger than he.
*5. The friendship of the two strong men was sealed by them fighting.
6. Gilgamesh said, "Between you and I, mighty deeds will be accomplished, and our fame will be everlasting."
7. Among their glorious acts, Enkidu and him defeated the giant bull, Humbaba, and cut down the bull's cedar forests.
8. Their bringing back cedar logs to Gilgamesh's treeless land won great praise from the people.
9. When Enkidu died, Gilgamesh mourned his death, realizing that no one had been a better friend than him.
10. When Gilgamesh himself died many years later, his people raised a monument praising Enkidu and he for their friendship and their mighty deeds of courage.

31 Agreement of Pronoun and Antecedent

Is this the right pronoun?

The right pronoun is the one that matches its **antecedent**—the word to which it refers—in person, number, and gender. This chapter focuses on agreement in number: singular and plural antecedents and the pronouns that replace them.

<u>Homeowners</u> fret over <u>their</u> tax bills.
antecedent — pronoun

<u>Its</u> constant increases make the tax <u>bill</u> a dreaded document.
pronoun antecedent

Note Grammar and style checkers cannot help with agreement between pronoun and antecedent because they cannot recognize the intended relation between the two. You'll need to check for errors on your own.

CULTURE LANGUAGE The gender of a pronoun should match its antecedent, not a noun that the pronoun may modify: *Sara Young invited <u>her</u>* [not <u>*his*</u>] *son to join the company's staff.* Also, nouns in English have only neuter gender unless they specifically refer to males or females. Thus nouns such as *book, table, sun,* and *earth* take the pronoun *it.*

31a Antecedents joined by *and* usually take plural pronouns.

pn agr
31a

Mr. Bartos and I cannot settle <u>our</u> dispute.

The dean and my adviser have offered <u>their</u> help.

Exceptions When the compound antecedent refers to a single idea, person, or thing, then the pronoun is singular (see next page).

Key terms

	Number	
Person	**Singular**	**Plural**
First	*I*	*we*
Second	*you*	*you*
Third	*he, she, it,* indefinite pronouns, singular nouns	*they,* plural nouns
Gender		
Masculine	*he,* nouns naming males	
Feminine	*she,* nouns naming females	
Neuter	*it,* all other nouns	

http://www.ablongman.com/littlebrown

➤ Sentences and words

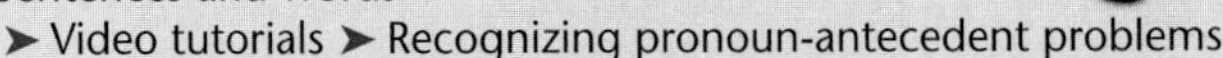
➤ Video tutorials ➤ Recognizing pronoun-antecedent problems
➤ Web exercises ➤ Exers. 41–43
➤ Downloads ➤ Chapter 31 exercise in electronic format
➤ Web links ➤ Pronoun-antecedent agreement

My friend and adviser offered her help.

When the compound antecedent follows *each* or *every,* the pronoun is singular.

Every girl and woman took her seat.

31b When parts of an antecedent are joined by *or* or *nor,* the pronoun agrees with the nearer part.

Tenants or owners must present their grievances.

Either the tenant or the owner will have her way.

When one subject is plural and the other singular, the sentence will be awkward unless you put the plural subject second.

Awkward Neither the tenants nor the owner has yet made her case.
Revised Neither the owner nor the tenants have yet made their case.

31c With *everyone, person,* and other indefinite words, use a singular or plural pronoun as appropriate.

Indefinite words—indefinite pronouns and generic nouns—do not refer to any specific person or thing. Most indefinite pronouns and all generic nouns are singular in meaning. When they serve as antecedents of pronouns, the pronouns should be singular.

Key terms

indefinite pronoun A noun that does not refer to a specific person or thing:

Singular			*Singular or plural*	*Plural*
anybody	everyone	no one	all	both
anyone	everything	nothing	any	few
anything	much	one	more	many
each	neither	somebody	most	several
either	nobody	someone	some	
everybody	none	something		

generic noun A singular noun such as *person, individual,* and *student* when it refers to a typical member of a group, not to a particular individual: *The individual has rights.*

Everyone on the women's team now has her own locker.
indefinite pronoun

Every person on the women's team now has her own locker.
generic noun

Five indefinite pronouns—*all, any, more, most, some*—may be singular or plural in meaning depending on what they refer to:

Few women athletes had changing spaces, so most had to change in their rooms.

Most of the changing space was dismal, its color a drab olive green.

Four indefinite pronouns—*both, few, many, several*—are always plural in meaning:

Few realize how their athletic facilities have changed.

Most agreement problems arise with the singular indefinite words. We often use these words to mean something like "many" or "all" rather than "one" and then refer to them with plural pronouns, as in *Everyone has their own locker* or *A person can padlock their locker.* Often, too, we mean indefinite words to include both masculine and feminine genders and thus resort to *they* instead of the **generic *he***—the masculine pronoun referring to both genders, as in *Everyone deserves his privacy.* (For more on the generic *he,* which many readers view as sexist, see p. 188.)

Although some experts accept *they, them,* and *their* with singular indefinite words, most do not, and many teachers and employers regard the plural as incorrect. To be safe, work for agreement between singular indefinite words and the pronouns that refer to them. You have several options:

Ways to correct agreement with indefinite words

- **Change the indefinite word to a plural, and use a plural pronoun to match:**

  Faulty Every athlete deserves their privacy.

  Revised Athletes deserve their privacy.

(continued)

Ways to correct agreement with indefinite words

(continued)

- **Rewrite the sentence to omit the pronoun:**

  Faulty Everyone is entitled to their own locker.
  Revised Everyone is entitled to a locker.

- **Use *he or she* (*him or her, his or her*) to refer to the indefinite word:**

  Faulty Now everyone has their private space.
  Revised Now everyone has his or her private space.

  However, used more than once in several sentences, *he or she* quickly becomes awkward. (Many readers do not accept the alternative *he/she.*) In most cases, using the plural or omitting the pronoun will not only correct agreement problems but also create more readable sentences.

31d Collective nouns such as *team* take singular or plural pronouns depending on meaning.

Use a singular pronoun with a collective noun when referring to the group as a unit:

> The committee voted to disband itself.

When referring to the individual members of the group, use a plural pronoun:

> The old group have gone their separate ways.

CULTURE LANGUAGE In standard American English, collective nouns that are noncount nouns (they don't form plurals) usually take singular pronouns: *The mail sits in its own basket.* A few noncount nouns take plural pronouns, including *clergy, military, police, the rich,* and *the poor: The police support their unions.*

EXERCISE 31.1
Revising: Pronoun-antecedent agreement

Revise the following sentences so that pronouns and their antecedents agree in person and number. Some items have more than

Key term

collective noun A noun with singular form that names a group of individuals or things—for instance, *army, audience, committee, crowd, family, group, team.*

one possible answer. Try to avoid the generic *he* (see p. 287). If you change the subject of a sentence, be sure to change the verb as necessary for agreement. If a sentence is already correct as given, circle the number preceding it. Answers to starred items appear at the end of the book.

Example:

Each of the Boudreaus' children brought their laundry home at Thanksgiving.

All of the Boudreaus' children brought their laundry home at Thanksgiving. *Or:* Each of the Boudreaus' children brought laundry home at Thanksgiving. *Or:* Each of the Boudreaus' children brought his or her laundry home at Thanksgiving.

*1. Each girl raised in a Mexican American family in the Rio Grande Valley of Texas hopes that one day they will be given a *quinceañera* party for their fifteenth birthday.
*2. Such celebrations are very expensive because it entails a religious service followed by a huge party.
*3. A girl's immediate family, unless they are wealthy, cannot afford the party by themselves.
*4. Her parents will ask each close friend or relative if they can help with the preparations.
*5. Surrounded by her family and attended by her friends and their escorts, the *quinceañera* is introduced as a young woman eligible for fashionable Mexican American society.

6. Almost any child will quickly astound observers with their capabilities.
7. Despite their extensive research and experience, neither child psychologists nor parents have yet figured out how children work.
8. Of course, the family has a tremendous influence on the development of a child in their midst.
9. Each member of the immediate family exerts their own unique pull on the child.
10. Other relatives, teachers, and friends also can affect the child's view of the world and of themselves.
11. The workings of genetics also strongly influence the child, but it may never be fully understood.
12. The psychology community cannot agree in its views of whether nurture or nature is more important in a child's development.
13. Another debated issue is whether the child's emotional development or their intellectual development is more central.
14. Just about everyone has their strong opinion on these issues, often backed up by evidence.
15. Neither the popular press nor scholarly journals devote much of their space to the wholeness of the child.

32 Reference of Pronoun to Antecedent

Is it clear what this pronoun refers to?

A pronoun should refer clearly to its **antecedent,** the noun or nouns it refers to. Otherwise, readers will have difficulty grasping the pronoun's meaning. In editing your writing, make sure that each pronoun refers to an obvious, close, and specific antecedent.

Note Grammar and style checkers are not sophisticated enough to recognize unclear pronoun reference. For instance, a checker did not flag any of the confusing examples on the next page. You must proofread your work to spot unclear pronoun reference.

CULTURE LANGUAGE In standard American English, a pronoun needs a clear antecedent nearby, but don't use both a pronoun and its antecedent as the subject of the same clause: *Jim* [not *Jim he*] *told Mark to go alone.* (See also p. 332.)

ref 32a

32a Make a pronoun refer clearly to one antecedent.

When either of two nouns can be a pronoun's antecedent, the reference will not be clear.

Confusing Emily Dickinson is sometimes compared with Jane Austen, but she was quite different.

Revise such a sentence in one of two ways:

- Replace the pronoun with the appropriate noun.

Clear Emily Dickinson is sometimes compared with Jane Austen, but Dickinson [or Austen] was quite different.

- Avoid repetition by rewriting the sentence. If you use the pronoun, make sure it has only one possible antecedent.

Clear Despite occasional comparison, Emily Dickinson and Jane Austen were quite different.

http://www.ablongman.com/littlebrown
➤ Sentences and words
➤ Video tutorials ➤ Recognizing pronoun-reference problems
➤ Web exercises ➤ Exers. 44 and 45
➤ Downloads ➤ Chapter 32 exercise in electronic format
➤ Web links ➤ Pronoun reference

Clear Though sometimes compared with her, Emily Dickinson was quite different from Jane Austen.

32b Place a pronoun close enough to its antecedent to ensure clarity.

A clause beginning with *who, which,* or *that* should generally fall immediately after the word to which it refers:

Confusing Jody found a dress in the attic that her aunt had worn.

Clear In the attic Jody found a dress that her aunt had worn.

32c Make a pronoun refer to a specific antecedent, not an implied one.

A pronoun should refer to a specific noun or other pronoun. A reader can only guess at the meaning of a pronoun when its antecedent is implied by the context, not stated outright.

1 • Vague *this, that, which,* or *it*

This, that, which, or *it* should refer to a specific noun, not to a whole word group expressing an idea or situation.

Confusing The faculty agreed on changing the requirements, but it took time.

Clear The faculty agreed on changing the requirements, but the agreement took time.

Clear The faculty agreed on changing the requirements, but the change took time.

Confusing The British knew little of the American countryside, and they had no experience with the colonists' guerrilla tactics. This gave the colonists an advantage.

Clear The British knew little of the American countryside, and they had no experience with the colonists' guerrilla tactics. This ignorance and inexperience gave the colonists an advantage.

2 • Implied nouns

A noun may be implied in some other word or phrase, such as an adjective (*happiness* implied in *happy*), a verb (*driver* implied in *drive*), or a possessive (*mother* implied in *mother's*). But a pronoun cannot refer clearly to an implied noun, only to a specific, stated one.

Confusing	Cohen's report brought her a lawsuit.
Clear	Cohen was sued over her report.
Confusing	Her reports on psychological development generally go unnoticed outside it.
Clear	Her reports on psychological development generally go unnoticed outside the field.

32d Use *it* and *they* to refer to definite antecedents.

It and *they* should have definite noun antecedents. Rewrite the sentence if the antecedent is missing.

Confusing	In Chapter 4 of this book it describes the early flights of the Wright brothers.
Clear	Chapter 4 of this book describes the early flights of the Wright brothers.
Confusing	In the average television drama they present a false picture of life.
Clear	The average television drama presents a false picture of life.

32e Use *you* only to mean "you, the reader."

In all but very formal writing, *you* is acceptable when the meaning is clearly "you, the reader." But the context must be appropriate for such a meaning:

Inappropriate	In the fourteenth century you had to struggle simply to survive.
Revised	In the fourteenth century one [or a person] had to struggle simply to survive.

Writers sometimes drift into *you* because *one, a person,* or a similar indefinite word can be difficult to sustain. Sentence after sentence, the indefinite word may sound stuffy, and it requires *he* or *he or she* for pronoun-antecedent agreement (see pp. 286–88). To avoid these problems, try using plural nouns and pronouns:

Original — In the fourteenth century one had to struggle simply to survive.

Revised — In the fourteenth century people had to struggle simply to survive.

32f Keep pronouns consistent.

Within a sentence or a group of related sentences, pronouns should be consistent. Partly, consistency comes from making pronouns and their antecedents agree (see Chapter 31). In addition, the pronouns within a passage should match each other.

Inconsistent — One finds when reading that your concentration improves with practice, so that I now comprehend more in less time.

Revised — I find when reading that my concentration improves with practice, so that I now comprehend more in less time.

EXERCISE 32.1
Revising: Pronoun reference

Many of the pronouns in the following sentences do not refer to specific, appropriate antecedents. Revise the sentences as necessary to make them clear. Answers to starred items appear at the end of the book.

Example:

In Grand Teton National Park they have moose, elk, and trumpeter swans.

Moose, elk, and trumpeter swans live in Grand Teton National Park.

*1. "Life begins at forty" is a cliché many people live by, and this may or may not be true.
*2. Living successfully or not depends on one's definition of it.
*3. When she was forty, Pearl Buck's novel *The Good Earth* won the Pulitzer Prize.
*4. Buck was raised in a missionary family in China, and she wrote about it in her novels.
*5. In *The Good Earth* you have to struggle, but fortitude is rewarded.
6. Buck received much critical praise and earned over $7 million, but she was very modest about it.

7. Pearl Buck donated most of her earnings to a foundation for Asian American children that proves her generosity.
8. Kenneth Kaunda, past president of Zambia, was elected to it in 1964, when he was forty.
9. When Catherine I became Empress of Russia at age forty, they feared more than loved her.
10. At forty, Paul Revere made his famous ride to warn American revolutionary leaders that the British were going to arrest them. This gave the colonists time to prepare for battle.
11. In the British House of Commons they did not welcome forty-year-old Nancy Astor as the first female member when she entered in 1919.
12. In AD 610 Muhammad, age forty, began to have a series of visions that became the foundation of the Muslim faith. Since then, millions of people have become one.
13. In the *Book of Romance* it reserves a chapter for the story of Elizabeth Barrett, who at forty married Robert Browning against her father's wishes.
14. In the 1840s they did not normally defy their fathers, but Elizabeth was too much in love to obey.
15. She left a poetic record of her love for Robert, and readers still enjoy reading them.

Modifiers

What do modifiers do?

Modifiers describe or limit other words in a sentence. They are adjectives, adverbs, or word groups serving as adjectives or adverbs. This section shows you how to identify and solve problems in the forms of modifiers (Chapter 33) and in their relation to the rest of the sentence (Chapter 34).

33 Adjectives and Adverbs

Should I use *bad* or *badly*?

Choosing between *bad* and *badly* means choosing whether to use an adjective (*bad*) or an adverb (*badly*). The choice depends on how the word functions in its sentence. An **adjective** modifies nouns (*bad weather*) and pronouns (*bad one*). An **adverb** modifies verbs (*The fans behaved badly*), adjectives (*badly wrong*), other adverbs (*not badly*), and whole word groups (*Otherwise, the room was empty*).

Note Grammar and style checkers will spot some but not all problems with misused adjectives and adverbs. For instance, a checker flagged *Some children suffer bad* and *Chang was the most wisest person in town* and *Jenny did not feel nothing*. But it did not flag *Educating children good is everyone's focus.* You'll need to proofread your work on your own to be sure you've used adjectives and adverbs appropriately.

CULTURE LANGUAGE In standard American English, an adjective does not change along with the noun it modifies to show plural number: *white* [not *whites*] *shoes, square* [not *squares*] *spaces, better* [not *betters*] *chances.* Only nouns form plurals.

http://www.ablongman.com/littlebrown

➤ Sentences and words
- ➤ Web exercises ➤ Exers. 46–51
- ➤ Downloads ➤ Chapter 33 exercises in electronic format
- ➤ Web links ➤ Adjectives and adverbs

33a Use adjectives only to modify nouns and pronouns.

Using adjectives instead of adverbs to modify verbs, adverbs, or other adjectives is nonstandard:

Nonstandard	Educating children good is everyone's focus.
Standard	Educating children well is everyone's focus.
Nonstandard	Some children suffer bad.
Standard	Some children suffer badly.

CULTURE LANGUAGE To negate a verb or an adjective, use the adverb *not:*

They are not learning. They are not stupid.

To negate a noun, use the adjective *no:*

No child should fail to read.

EXERCISE 33.1
Revising: Adjectives and adverbs

Revise the sentences below to use adjectives and adverbs appropriately. If any sentence is already correct as given, circle the number preceding it. Answers to starred items appear at the end of the book.

Example:

The announcer warned that traffic was moving very slow.
The announcer warned that traffic was moving very slowly.

*1. The eighteenth-century essayist Samuel Johnson suffered bad in his early life.
*2. Johnson's family was poor, his hearing was bad, and he received little education.
*3. After failing as a schoolmaster, Johnson moved to London, where he did good.
*4. Johnson was taken serious as a critic and dictionary maker.
*5. Johnson was real surprised when he received a pension from King George III.

6. Thinking about his meeting with the king, Johnson felt proudly.
7. Johnson was relieved that he had not behaved badly in the presence of the king.
8. If he had been more diligent, Johnson might have made money quicker.

9. After living cheap for over twenty years, Johnson finally had enough money from the pension to eat and dress good.
10. With the pension, Johnson could spend time writing and live stylish.

33b Use an adjective after a linking verb to modify the subject. Use an adverb to modify a verb.

Some verbs may or may not be linking verbs, depending on their meaning in the sentence. When the word after the verb modifies the subject, the verb is linking and the word should be an adjective: *He looked happy. The milk turned sour.* When the word modifies the verb, however, it should be an adverb: *He looked carefully. The car turned suddenly.*

Two word pairs are especially tricky. One is *bad* and *badly:*

The weather grew bad. (grew = linking verb; bad = adjective)

She felt bad. (felt = linking verb; bad = adjective)

Flowers grow badly in such soil. (grow = verb; badly = adverb)

The other tricky pair is *good* and *well. Good* serves only as an adjective. *Well* may serve as an adverb with a host of meanings or as an adjective meaning only "fit" or "healthy."

Decker trained well. (trained = verb; well = adverb)

She felt well. (felt = linking verb; well = adjective)

Her health was good. (was = linking verb; good = adjective)

ad
33c

33c Use the comparative and superlative forms of adjectives and adverbs appropriately.

Adjectives and adverbs can show degrees of quality or amount with the endings *-er* and *-est* or with the words *more* and *most* or *less* and *least.* Most modifiers have the three forms shown on the next page.

Key term

linking verb A verb that connects a subject and a word that describes the subject: *They are golfers.* Linking verbs are forms of *be,* the verbs of our five senses (*look, sound, smell, feel, taste*), and *appear, seem, become, grow, turn, prove, remain, stay.* (See p. 222.)

	Adjectives	Adverbs
Positive The basic form listed in the dictionary	red awful	soon quickly
Comparative A greater or lesser degree of the quality named	redder more/less awful	sooner more/less quickly
Superlative The greatest or least degree of the quality named	reddest most/least awful	soonest most/least quickly

If sound alone does not tell you whether to use *-er/-est* or *more/most,* consult a dictionary. If the endings can be used, the dictionary will list them. Otherwise, use *more* or *most.*

1 • Irregular adjectives and adverbs

The irregular modifiers change the spelling of their positive form to show comparative and superlative degrees.

Positive	Comparative	Superlative
Adjectives		
good	better	best
bad	worse	worst
little	littler, less	littlest, least
many some much	more	most
Adverbs		
well	better	best
badly	worse	worst

2 • Double comparisons

A double comparative or double superlative combines the *-er* or *-est* ending with the word *more* or *most.* It is redundant.

> Chang was the wisest [not most wisest] person in town.
> He was smarter [not more smarter] than anyone else.

3 • Logical comparisons

Absolute modifiers

Some adjectives and adverbs cannot logically be compared—for instance, *perfect, unique, dead, impossible, infinite.* These absolute words can be preceded by adverbs like *nearly* or *almost* that mean "approaching," but they cannot logically be modified by *more* or *most* (as in *most perfect*).

Not He was the most unique teacher we had.
But He was a unique teacher.

Completeness

To be logical, a comparison must also be complete in the following ways:

- The comparison must state a relation fully enough for clarity.

Unclear Carmakers worry about their industry more than environmentalists.
Clear Carmakers worry about their industry more than environmentalists do.
Clear Carmakers worry about their industry more than they worry about environmentalists.

- The items being compared should in fact be comparable.

Illogical The cost of an electric car is greater than a gasoline-powered car. [Illogically compares a cost and a car.]
Revised The cost of an electric car is greater than the cost of [or that of] a gasoline-powered car.

See also pages 175–76 on parallelism with comparisons.

Any vs. *any other*

Use *any other* when comparing something with others in the same group. Use *any* when comparing something with others in a different group.

Illogical Los Angeles is larger than any city in California. [Since Los Angeles is itself a city in California, the sentence seems to say that Los Angeles is larger than itself.]
Revised Los Angeles is larger than any other city in California.

Illogical Los Angeles is larger than any other city in Canada. [The cities in Canada constitute a group to which Los Angeles does not belong.]
Revised Los Angeles is larger than any city in Canada.

33d Watch for double negatives.

A **double negative** is a nonstandard construction in which two negative words such as *no, not, none, barely, hardly,* or *scarcely* cancel each other out. Some double negatives are intentional: for instance, *She was not unhappy* indicates with understatement that she was indeed happy. But most double negatives say the opposite of what is intended: *Jenny did not feel nothing* asserts that Jenny felt other than nothing, or something. For the opposite meaning, one of the negatives must be eliminated (*She felt nothing*) or one of them must be changed to a positive (*She did not feel anything*).

Faulty The IRS cannot hardly audit all tax returns. None of its audits never touch many cheaters.

Revised The IRS cannot audit all tax returns. Its audits never touch many cheaters.

33e Distinguish between present and past participles as adjectives. CULTURE LANGUAGE

Both present participles and past participles may serve as adjectives: *a burning building, a burned building.* As in the examples, the two participles usually differ in the time they indicate.

But some present and past participles—those derived from verbs expressing feeling—can have altogether different meanings. The present participle modifies something that causes the feeling: *That was a frightening storm* (the storm frightens). The past participle modifies something that experiences the feeling: *They quieted the frightened horses* (the horses feel fright).

The following participles are among those likely to be confused:

amazing/amazed
amusing/amused
annoying/annoyed
astonishing/astonished
boring/bored
confusing/confused
depressing/depressed
embarrassing/embarrassed
exciting/excited
exhausting/exhausted
fascinating/fascinated
frightening/frightened
frustrating/frustrated
interesting/interested
pleasing/pleased
satisfying/satisfied
shocking/shocked
surprising/surprised
tiring/tired
worrying/worried

EXERCISE 33.2
Revising: Present and past participles CULTURE LANGUAGE

Revise the adjectives in the following sentences as needed to distinguish between present and past participles. If the sentence is al-

Key terms

present participle The *-ing* form of a verb: *flying, writing.* (See p. 213.)

past participle The *-d* or *-ed* form of a regular verb: *slipped, walked.* Most irregular verbs have distinctive past participles, such as *eaten* or *swum.* (See p. 213.)

ready correct as given, circle the number preceding it. Answers to starred items appear at the end of the book.

Example:

The subject was embarrassed to many people.
The subject was embarrassing to many people.

*1. Several critics found Alice Walker's *The Color Purple* to be a fascinated book.
*2. One confused critic wished that Walker had deleted the scenes set in Africa.
*3. Another critic argued that although the book contained many depressed episodes, the overall effect was excited.
*4. Since other readers found the book annoyed, this critic pointed out its many surprising qualities.
*5. In the end most critics agreed that the book was a satisfied novel about the struggles of an African American woman.

6. The movie made from the book was less interested for many.
7. Some viewers found the entire movie irritated.
8. They criticized the movie for relying on tired feelings.
9. Other viewers thought that Whoopi Goldberg did an amazed job of creating Celie, the central character.
10. Some critics congratulated Steven Spielberg, the director, for creating a fulfilling movie.

33f Use *a, an, the,* and other determiners appropriately. CULTURE LANGUAGE

Determiners are special kinds of adjectives that mark nouns because they always precede nouns. Some common determiners are *a, an,* and *the* (called **articles**) and *my, their, whose, this, these, those, one, some,* and *any.*

Native speakers of standard American English can rely on their intuition when using determiners, but speakers of other languages and dialects often have difficulty with them. In standard American English, the use of determiners depends on the context they appear in and the kind of nouns they precede:

- A **proper noun** names a particular person, place, or thing and begins with a capital letter: *February, Joe Allen, Red River.* Most proper nouns are not preceded by determiners.
- A **count noun** names something that is countable in English and can form a plural: *girl/girls, apple/apples, child/children.* A singular count noun is always preceded by a determiner; a plural count noun sometimes is.
- A **noncount noun** names something not usually considered countable in English, and so it does not form a plural. A non-

count noun is sometimes preceded by a determiner. Here is a sample of noncount nouns, sorted into groups by meaning:

Abstractions: confidence, democracy, education, equality, evidence, health, information, intelligence, knowledge, luxury, peace, pollution, research, success, supervision, truth, wealth, work

Food and drink: bread, candy, cereal, flour, meat, milk, salt, water, wine

Emotions: anger, courage, happiness, hate, joy, love, respect, satisfaction

Natural events and substances: air, blood, dirt, gasoline, gold, hair, heat, ice, oil, oxygen, rain, silver, smoke, weather, wood

Groups: clergy, clothing, equipment, furniture, garbage, jewelry, junk, legislation, machinery, mail, military, money, police, vocabulary

Fields of study: accounting, architecture, biology, business, chemistry, engineering, literature, psychology, science

A dictionary of English as a second language will tell you whether a noun is a count noun, a noncount noun, or both. (See p. 197 for recommended dictionaries.)

Note Many nouns are sometimes count nouns and sometimes noncount nouns:

The library has a room for readers. [*Room* is a count noun meaning "walled area."]

The library has room for reading. [*Room* is a noncount noun meaning "space."]

Partly because the same noun may fall into different groups, grammar and style checkers are unreliable guides to missing or misused articles and other determiners. For instance, a checker flagged the omitted *a* before *Scientist* in *Scientist developed new processes;* it did not flag the omitted *a* before *new* in *A scientist developed new process;* and it mistakenly flagged the correctly omitted article *the* before *Vegetation* in *Vegetation suffers from drought.* To correct omitted or misused articles, you will need to read and edit carefully on your own.

1 • *A, an,* and *the*

With singular count nouns

A or *an* precedes a singular count noun when the reader does not already know its identity, usually because you have not mentioned it before:

> A scientist in our chemistry department developed a process to strengthen metals. [*Scientist* and *process* are being introduced for the first time.]

The precedes a singular count noun that has a specific identity for the reader, for one of the following reasons:

- You have mentioned the noun before:

  > A scientist in our chemistry department developed a process to strengthen metals. The scientist patented the process. [*Scientist* and *process* were identified in the preceding sentence.]

- You identify the noun immediately before or after you state it:

  > The most productive laboratory is the research center in the chemistry department. [*Most productive* identifies *laboratory. In the chemistry department* identifies *research center*. And *chemistry department* is a shared facility—see below.]

- The noun names something unique—the only one in existence:

  > The sun rises in the east. [*Sun* and *east* are unique.]

- The noun names an institution or facility that is shared by the community of readers:

  > Many men and women aspire to the presidency. [*Presidency* is a shared institution.]
  >
  > The fax machine has changed business communication. [*Fax machine* is a shared facility.]

The is not used before a singular noun that names a general category:

> Wordsworth's poetry shows his love of nature [not the nature].
>
> General Sherman said that war is hell. [*War* names a general category.]
>
> The war in Croatia left many dead. [*War* names a specific war.]

With plural count nouns

A or *an* never precedes a plural noun. *The* does not precede a plural noun that names a general category. *The* does precede a plural noun that names specific representatives of a category.

> Men and women are different. [*Men* and *women* name general categories.]
>
> The women formed a team. [*Women* refers to specific people.]

With noncount nouns

A or *an* never precedes a noncount noun. *The* does precede a noncount noun that names specific representatives of a general category.

Vegetation suffers from drought. [*Vegetation* names a general category.]

The vegetation in the park withered or died. [*Vegetation* refers to specific plants.]

With proper nouns

A or *an* never precedes a proper noun. *The* generally does not precede proper nouns.

Garcia lives in Boulder.

There are exceptions, however. For instance, we generally use *the* before plural proper nouns (*the Murphys, the Boston Celtics*) and before the names of groups and organizations (*the Department of Justice, the Sierra Club*), ships (*the Lusitania*), oceans (*the Pacific*), mountain ranges (*the Alps*), regions (*the Middle East*), rivers (*the Mississippi*), and some countries (*the United States, the Netherlands*).

2 • Other determiners

The uses of English determiners besides articles also depend on context and kind of noun. The following determiners may be used as indicated with singular count nouns, plural count nouns, or noncount nouns.

With any kind of noun (singular count, plural count, noncount)
my, our, your, his, her, its, their, possessive nouns (*boy's, boys'*)
whose, which(ever), what(ever)
some, any, the other
no

Their account is overdrawn. [Singular count.]
Their funds are low. [Plural count.]
Their money is running out. [Noncount.]

Only with singular nouns (count and noncount)
this, that

This account has some money. [Count.]
That information may help. [Noncount.]

Only with noncount nouns and plural count nouns
most, enough, other, such, all, all of the, a lot of

Most funds are committed. [Plural count.]
Most money is needed elsewhere. [Noncount.]

Only with singular count nouns

one, every, each, either, neither, another

One car must be sold. [Singular count.]

Only with plural count nouns

these, those
both, many, few, a few, fewer, fewest, several
two, three, and so forth

Two cars are unnecessary. [Plural count.]

Note *Few* means "not many" or "not enough." *A few* means "some" or "a small but sufficient quantity."

Few committee members came to the meeting.
A few members can keep the committee going.

Do not use *much* with a plural count noun.

Many [not much] members want to help.

Only with noncount nouns

much, more, little, a little, less, least, a large amount of

Less luxury is in order. [Noncount.]

Note *Little* means "not many" or "not enough." *A little* means "some" or "a small but sufficient quantity."

Little time remains before the conference.
The members need a little help from their colleagues.

Do not use *many* with a noncount noun.

Much [not many] work remains.

EXERCISE 33.3
Revising: Articles CULTURE LANGUAGE

For each blank, indicate whether *a, an, the,* or no article should be inserted. Answers to starred sentences appear at the end of the book.

Example:

On our bicycle trip across _______ country, we carried _______ map and plenty of _______ food and _______ water.

On our bicycle trip across the country, we carried a map and plenty of food and water.

*From _____ native American Indians who migrated from _____ Asia 20,000 years ago to _____ new arrivals who now come by _____ planes, _____ United States is _____ nation of foreigners. *It is _____ country of immigrants who are all living under _____ single flag.

*Back in _____ seventeenth and eighteenth centuries, at least 75 percent of the population came from _____ England. *However, between 1820 and 1975 more than 38 million immigrants came to this country from elsewhere in _____ Europe. Many children of _____ immigrants were self-conscious and denied their heritage; many even refused to learn _____ native language of their parents and grandparents. They tried to "Americanize" themselves. The so-called Melting Pot theory of _____ social change stressed _____ importance of blending everyone together into _____ kind of stew. Each nationality would contribute its own flavor, but _____ final stew would be something called "American."

This Melting Pot theory was never completely successful. In the last half of the twentieth century, _____ ethnic revival changed _____ metaphor. Many people now see _____ American society as _____ mosaic. Americans are once again proud of their heritage, and _____ ethnic differences make _____ mosaic colorful and interesting.

EXERCISE 33.4
Revising: Adjectives and adverbs

Revise the sentences below to correct errors in the use of adjectives and adverbs. If a sentence is already correct as given, circle the number preceding it. Answers to starred items appear at the end of the book.

Example:

Sports fans always feel happily when their team wins.
Sports fans always feel happy when their team wins.

*1. Americans often argue about which professional sport is better: basketball, football, or baseball.
*2. Basketball fans contend that their sport offers more action because the players are constant running and shooting.
*3. Because it is played indoors in relative small arenas, basketball allows fans to be more closer to the action than the other sports do.
*4. Football fanatics say they don't hardly stop yelling once the game begins.
*5. They cheer when their team executes a real complicated play good.
6. They roar more louder when the defense stops the opponents in a goal-line stand.

7. They yell loudest when a fullback crashes in for a score.
8. In contrast, the supporters of baseball believe that it might be the most perfect sport.
9. It combines the one-on-one duel of pitcher and batter struggling valiant with the tight teamwork of double and triple plays.
10. Because the game is played slow and careful, fans can analyze and discuss the manager's strategy.

34 Misplaced and Dangling Modifiers

Where can a modifier go in a sentence? When does a modifier dangle?

A modifier needs to relate clearly to the word it describes, and that need limits its possible positions in a sentence. A **misplaced modifier** does not relate to the intended word (see below). A **dangling modifier** does not relate sensibly to anything in the sentence (see p. 313).

Note Grammar and style checkers do not recognize many problems with modifiers. For instance, a checker failed to flag the misplaced modifiers in *Gasoline high prices affect usually car sales* or the dangling modifier in *The vandalism was visible passing the building*. Proofread your work on your own to find and correct problems with modifiers.

34a Reposition misplaced modifiers.

A misplaced modifier falls in the wrong place in a sentence. It is usually awkward or confusing. It may even be unintentionally funny.

http://www.ablongman.com/littlebrown
➤ Sentences and words
 ➤ Video tutorials ➤ Repairing misplaced modifiers
 ➤ Web exercises ➤ Exers. 52–55
 ➤ Downloads ➤ Chapter 34 exercises in electronic format
 ➤ Web links ➤ Misplaced and dangling modifiers

1 • Clear placement

Readers tend to link a modifier to the nearest word it could modify. Any other placement can link the modifier to the wrong word.

Confusing He served steak to the men on paper plates.

Clear He served the men steak on paper plates.

Confusing According to the police, many dogs are killed by automobiles and trucks roaming unleashed.

Clear According to the police, many dogs roaming unleashed are killed by automobiles and trucks.

2 • *Only* and other limiting modifiers

mm 34a

Limiting modifiers include *almost, even, exactly, hardly, just, merely, nearly, only, scarcely,* and *simply*. For clarity, place such a modifier immediately before the word or word group you intend it to limit.

Unclear The archaeologist only found the skull on her last dig.

Clear The archaeologist found only the skull on her last dig.

Clear The archaeologist found the skull only on her last dig.

3 • Adverbs with grammatical units

Adverbs can often move around in sentences, but some will be awkward if they interrupt certain grammatical units:

- A single-word adverb can interrupt subject and verb: *Bo gladly accepted*. But a longer adverb stops the flow of the sentence:

subject — adverb — verb

Awkward Kuwait, after the Gulf War ended in 1991, began returning to normal.

adverb — subject — verb

Revised After the Gulf War ended in 1991, Kuwait began returning to normal.

Key term

adverb A word or word group that describes a verb, adjective, other adverb, or whole word group, specifying how, when, where, or to what extent: *quickly see, solid like a boulder.*

- Any adverb is awkward between a verb and its direct object:

  verb adverb object
  Awkward The war had damaged badly many of Kuwait's oil fields.

  verb object
  Revised The war had badly damaged many of Kuwait's oil fields.
  adverb

- A **split infinitive**—an adverb placed between *to* and the verb—annoys many readers:

  infinitive
  Awkward The weather service expected temperatures to not rise.

  infinitive
  Revised The weather service expected temperatures not to rise.

  A split infinitive may sometimes be natural and preferable, though it may still bother some readers.

  infinitive
  Several US industries expect to more than triple their use of robots.

  Here the split infinitive is more economical than the alternatives, such as *Several US industries expect to increase their use of robots by more than three times.*

- A single-word adverb may interrupt a verb phrase after the first helping verb: *Scientists have lately been using spacecraft to study the sun.* But a longer adverb is usually awkward inside a verb phrase:

  helping verb adverb
  Awkward The spacecraft *Ulysses* will after traveling near the sun
  main verb
  report on the sun's energy fields.

  adverb
  Revised After traveling near the sun, the spacecraft *Ulysses*
  verb phrase
  will report on the sun's energy fields.

mm 34a

CULTURE LANGUAGE In a question, place a one-word adverb after the first helping verb and subject:

helping verb subject adverb rest of verb phrase
Will spacecraft ever be able to leave the solar system?

Key terms

direct object The receiver of the verb's action: *The car hit a tree.* (See p. 222.)

infinitive A verb form consisting of *to* plus the verb's plain (or dictionary) form: *to produce, to enjoy.* (See p. 228.)

verb phrase A verb consisting of a helping verb and a main verb that carries the principal meaning: *will have begun, can see.* (See p. 213.)

4 • Other adverb positions CULTURE LANGUAGE

A few adverbs are subject to special conventions for placement:

- Adverbs of frequency include *always, never, often, rarely, seldom, sometimes,* and *usually.* They generally appear at the beginning of a sentence, before a one-word verb, or after the helping verb in a verb phrase:

  helping verb — adverb — main verb
  Robots have sometimes put humans out of work.

  adverb — verb phrase
  Sometimes robots have put humans out of work.

  Adverbs of frequency always follow the verb *be:*

  verb adverb
  Robots are often helpful to workers.

- Adverbs of degree include *absolutely, almost, certainly, completely, definitely, especially, extremely, hardly,* and *only.* They fall just before the word modified (an adjective, another adverb, sometimes a verb):

  mm 34a

  adverb adjective
  Robots have been especially useful in making cars.

- Adverbs of manner include *badly, beautifully, openly, sweetly, tightly, well,* and others that describe how something is done. They usually fall after the verb:

  verb adverb
  Robots work smoothly on assembly lines.

- The position of the adverb *not* depends on what it modifies. When it modifies a verb, place it after the helping verb (or the first helping verb if more than one):

  helping verb — main verb
  Robots do not think.

  When *not* modifies another adverb or an adjective, place it before the other modifier:

  adjective
  Robots are not sleek machines.

5 • Order of adjectives CULTURE LANGUAGE

English follows distinctive rules for arranging two or three adjectives before a noun. (A string of more than three adjectives before a noun is rare.) The adjectives follow this order:

Determiner	Opinion	Size or shape	Color	Origin	Material	Noun used as adjective	Noun
many						state	**laws**
	lovely		green	Thai			**birds**
a		square			wooden		**table**
all						business	**reports**
the			blue		litmus		**paper**

See page 349 on punctuating adjectives before a noun.

EXERCISE 34.1
Revising: Misplaced modifiers

Revise the following sentences so that modifiers clearly and appropriately describe the intended words. Answers to starred items appear at the end of the book.

Example:

Although at first I feared the sensation of flight, I came to enjoy flying over time.

Although at first I feared the sensation of flight, over time I came to enjoy flying.

*1. People dominate in our society who are right-handed.
*2. Hand tools, machines, and doors even are designed for right-handed people.
*3. However, nearly 15 percent may be left-handed of the population.
*4. Children often when they begin school prefer one hand or the other.
*5. Parents and teachers should not try to deliberately change a child's preference for the left hand.

6. Women have contributed much to American culture of great value.
7. For example, Elizabeth Pinckney during the colonial era introduced indigo, the source of a valuable blue dye.
8. Emma Willard founded the Troy Female Seminary, the first institution to provide a college-level education for women in 1821.

Key term

adjective A word that describes a noun or pronoun, specifying which one, what quality, or how many: *good one, three cars*. (See p. 214.)

mm 34a

9. Mary Lyon founded Mount Holyoke Female Seminary as the first true women's college with directors and a campus who would sustain the college even after Lyon's death.
10. *Una* was the first US newspaper, which was founded by Pauline Wright Davis in 1853, that was dedicated to gaining women's rights.
11. Mitchell's Comet was discovered in 1847, which was named for Maria Mitchell.
12. Mitchell was the first American woman astronomer who lived from 1818 to 1889.
13. She was a member at Vassar College of the first faculty.
14. She was when elected to the American Academy of Arts and Sciences in 1848 the first woman to join the prestigious organization.
15. Mitchell said that she was persistent rather than especially capable when asked about her many accomplishments.

EXERCISE 34.2
Arranging adjectives CULTURE LANGUAGE

A group of adjectives follows each sentence below. Arrange the adjectives as needed for appropriate order in English, and place them in the sentence. Answers to starred items appear at the end of the book.

Example:

Programs for computer graphics perform _________ chores. (*drafting, many, tedious*)

Programs for computer graphics perform <u>many tedious drafting</u> chores.

*1. _________ specialist developed image controls. (*computer, a, Chinese, young*)
*2. _________ engineer assisted the specialist. (*a* or *an, American, skeptical*)
*3. _________ researchers are carrying out further study. (*several, university*)
*4. The controls depend on _________ object connected by wires to the computer. (*T-shaped, hand-sized, a*)
*5. The image allows a biochemist to walk into _________ display of a molecule. (*holographic, gigantic, a*)
6. Using _________ gestures, the biochemist can rotate and change the entire image. (*simple, hand*)
7. _________ games also depend on computer graphics. (*computer, all, video*)
8. Even _________ games operate this way. (*sophisticated, simulation, flight*)
9. One game is played with _________ racquets. (*rectangular, thin, two*)
10. In the early years of computers, scientists made _________ drawings to simulate motion. (*crude, some, animated*)

34b Connect dangling modifiers to their sentences.

A **dangling modifier** does not sensibly modify anything in its sentence.

Dangling Passing the building, the vandalism became visible. [The modifying phrase seems to describe *vandalism,* but vandalism does not pass buildings. Who was passing the building? Who saw the vandalism?]

Dangling modifiers usually introduce sentences, contain a verb form, and imply but do not name a subject: in the example above, the implied subject is the someone or something passing the building. Readers assume that this implied subject is the same as the subject of the sentence (*vandalism* in the example). When it is not, the modifier "dangles" unconnected to the rest of the sentence. Here is another example:

Dangling Although intact, graffiti covered every inch of the walls and windows. [The walls and windows, not the graffiti, were intact.]

To revise a dangling modifier, you have to rewrite the sentence. (Revising just by moving the modifier will leave it dangling: *The vandalism became visible passing the building.*) Choose a revision method depending on what you want to emphasize in the sentence:

- Rewrite the dangling modifier as a complete clause with its own stated subject and verb. Readers can accept that the new subject and the sentence subject are different.

Identifying and revising dangling modifiers

- **Find a subject.** If the modifier lacks a subject of its own (e.g., *when in diapers*), identify what it describes.
- **Connect the subject and modifier.** Verify that what the modifier describes is in fact the subject of the main clause. If it is not, the modifier is probably dangling:

  modifier / subject
  Dangling When in diapers, my mother remarried.

- **Revise as needed.** Revise a dangling modifier (*a*) by recasting it with a subject of its own or (*b*) by changing the subject of the main clause:

  Revision *a* When I was in diapers, my mother remarried.
  Revision *b* When in diapers, I attended my mother's second wedding.

Dangling Passing the building, the vandalism became visible.

Revised As we passed the building, the vandalism became visible.

- Change the subject of the sentence to a word the modifier properly describes.

Dangling Trying to understand the causes, vandalism has been extensively studied.

Revised Trying to understand the causes, researchers have extensively studied vandalism.

EXERCISE 34.3
Revising: Dangling modifiers

Revise the following sentences to eliminate any dangling modifiers. Each item has more than one possible answer. If a sentence is already correct as given, circle the number preceding it. Answers to starred items appear at the end of the book.

Example:
Driving north, the vegetation became more sparse.

Driving north, we noticed that the vegetation became more sparse. *Or:* As we drove north, the vegetation became more sparse.

*1. After accomplishing many deeds of valor, Andrew Jackson's fame led to his election to the presidency in 1828 and 1832.
*2. While still very young, both of Jackson's parents had died.
*3. To aid the American Revolution, service as a mounted courier was Jackson's choice.
*4. After being struck with a saber by a British officer, Jackson's craggy face bore a scar.
*5. Though not well educated, a successful career as a lawyer and judge proved Jackson's ability.
6. Winning many military battles, the American public believed in Jackson's leadership.
7. Earning the nicknames "Old Hickory" and "Sharp Knife," the War of 1812 established Jackson's military prowess.
8. Losing only six dead and ten wounded, the triumph of the Battle of New Orleans burnished Jackson's reputation.
9. After putting down raiding parties from Florida, Jackson's victories helped pressure Spain to cede that territory.
10. While briefly governor of Florida, the US presidency became Jackson's goal.

Sentence Faults

When is a sentence not a sentence?

Readers have definite (if unconscious) expectations for how sentences should be constructed. If a word group is punctuated as a sentence but does not meet these expectations, readers will likely be confused or annoyed. Such word groups may lack needed elements, include too many elements, or contain elements that do not fit together.

35 Sentence Fragments

frag 35

How can I tell if my sentences are complete?

A complete sentence meets three requirements: it has a subject, the subject has a verb, and it is not merely a subordinate clause (a word group beginning with *because, who,* or a similar word). A **sentence fragment,** in contrast, is a word group that looks like a whole sentence with an initial capital letter and a final period or other end punctuation. Although writers occasionally use fragments deliberately and effectively (see p. 319), readers perceive most fragments as serious errors. To prevent sentence fragments, first test each word group punctuated as a sentence to be sure it is complete (next three pages) and then revise as needed (pp. 318–19).

Note A grammar and style checker can spot many but not all sentence fragments, and it may flag sentences that are actually complete, such as *Continue reading*. Repair any fragments that your checker does find, but proofread your work yourself to ensure that it's fragment-free.

http://www.ablongman.com/littlebrown

➤ Sentences and words
- ➤ Video tutorials ➤ Recognizing sentence fragments
- ➤ Web exercises ➤ Exers. 56–58
- ➤ Downloads ➤ Chapter 35 exercises in electronic format
- ➤ Web links ➤ Sentence fragments

35a Test your sentences for completeness.

A word group punctuated as a sentence should pass *all three* of the following tests. If it does not, it is a fragment and needs revision.

Test 1: Find the verb.

Look for a verb in the group of words:

Fragment — Uncountable numbers of sites on the World Wide Web. [Compare a complete sentence: *Uncountable numbers of sites make up the World Wide Web.*]

Any verb form you find must be a **finite verb,** one that changes form as indicated below. A verbal does not change; it cannot serve as a sentence verb without the aid of a helping verb.

	Finite verbs in complete sentences	Verbals in sentence fragments
Singular	The network grows.	The network growing.
Plural	Networks grow.	Networks growing.
Present	The network grows.	The network growing.
Past	The network grew.	
Future	The network will grow.	

frag 35a

CULTURE LANGUAGE Some languages allow forms of *be* to be omitted as helping verbs or linking verbs. But English requires stating forms of *be:*

Fragments — The network growing. It already larger than its developers anticipated. [Compare complete sentences: *The network is growing. It is already larger than its developers anticipated.*]

Key terms

verb The part of a sentence that asserts something about the subject: *Ducks swim*. Also called *predicate*. (See p. 212.)

verbal A verb form that can serve as a noun, a modifier, or a part of a sentence verb, but not alone as the only verb of a sentence: *drawing, to draw, drawn*. (See p. 228.)

helping verb A verb such as *is, were, have, might,* and *could* that combines with various verb forms to indicate time and other kinds of meaning: for instance, *were drawing, might draw*. (See p. 213.)

linking verb A verb that connects a subject and a word that describes the subject: *They are golfers*. Linking verbs are forms of be, the verbs of our five senses (*look, sound, smell, feel, taste*), and *appear, seem, become, grow, turn, prove, remain, stay*. (See p. 222.)

Complete sentence versus sentence fragment

A complete sentence or main clause

1. contains a subject and a verb (*The wind blows*)
2. and is not a subordinate clause (beginning with a word such as *because* or *who*).

A sentence fragment

1. lacks a verb (*The wind blowing*),
2. or lacks a subject (*And blows*),
3. or is a subordinate clause not attached to a complete sentence (*Because the wind blows*).

Test 2: Find the subject.

The subject of the sentence will usually come before the verb. If there is no subject, the word group is probably a fragment:

Fragment And has enormous popular appeal. [Compare a complete sentence: *And the Web has enormous popular appeal.*]

In one kind of complete sentence, a command, the subject *you* is understood: [*You*] *Experiment with the Web.*

CULTURE LANGUAGE Some languages allow the omission of the sentence subject, especially when it is a pronoun. But in English, except in commands, the subject is stated:

Fragment Web commerce is expanding dramatically. Is threatening traditional stores. [Compare a complete sentence: *It is threatening traditional stores.*]

Test 3: Make sure the clause is not subordinate.

A subordinate clause usually begins with a subordinating word, such as one of those on the next page.

Key terms

subject The part of a sentence that names who or what performs the action or makes the assertion of the verb: *Ducks swim.* (See p. 219.)

subordinate clause A word group that contains a subject and a verb, begins with a subordinating word such as *because* or *who,* and is not a question: *Ducks can swim when they are young.* A subordinate clause may serve as a modifier or as a noun. (See p. 230.)

Subordinating conjunctions			Relative pronouns
after	provided	until	that
although	since	when	which
as	so that	whenever	who/whom
because	than	where	whoever/whomever
even if	that	whereas	
even though	though	whether	
if	till	while	
once	unless		

Subordinate clauses serve as parts of sentences (nouns or modifiers), not as whole sentences:

Fragment When the government devised the Internet. [Compare a complete sentence: *The government devised the Internet.* Or: *When the government devised the Internet, no expansive computer network existed.*]

Fragment The reason that the government devised the Internet. [This fragment is a noun (*reason*) plus its modifier (*that . . . Internet*). Compare a complete sentence: *The reason that the government devised the Internet was to provide secure links among departments and defense contractors.*]

Note Questions beginning with *how, what, when, where, which, who, whom, whose,* and *why* are not sentence fragments: *Who was responsible? When did it happen?*

35b Revise sentence fragments.

Correct sentence fragments in one of two ways depending on the importance of the information in the fragment and thus how much you want to stress it:

- Rewrite the fragment as a complete sentence. The information in the fragment will then have the same importance as that in other complete sentences.

Fragment A major improvement of the Internet occurred with the World Wide Web. Which allows users to move easily between sites.

Revised A major improvement of the Internet occurred with the World Wide Web. It allows users to move easily between sites.

Fragment The Web is a boon to researchers. A vast and accessible library.

Revised The Web is a boon to researchers. It forms a vast and accessible library.

- Combine the fragment with the appropriate main clause. The information in the fragment will then be subordinated to that in the main clause.

Fragment The Web is easy to use. Loaded with links and graphics.
Revised The Web, loaded with links and graphics, is easy to use.

Fragment With the links, users can move to other Web sites. That they want to consult.
Revised With the links, users can move to other Web sites that they want to consult.

35c Be aware of the acceptable uses of incomplete sentences.

A few word groups lacking the usual subject-predicate combination are incomplete sentences, but they are not fragments because they conform to the expectations of most readers. They include exclamations (*Oh no!*); questions and answers (*Where next? To Kansas.*); and commands (*Move along. Shut the window.*).

Experienced writers sometimes use sentence fragments when they want to achieve a special effect. Such fragments appear more in informal than in formal writing. Unless you are experienced and thoroughly secure in your own writing, however, you should avoid all fragments and concentrate on writing clear, well-formed sentences.

EXERCISE 35.1
Revising: Sentence fragments

Correct any sentence fragment below either by combining it with a complete sentence or by making it a complete sentence. If an item contains no sentence fragment, circle the number preceding it. Answers to starred items appear at the end of the book.

Example:

Jujitsu is good for self-protection. Because it enables one to overcome an opponent without the use of weapons.

Jujitsu is good for self-protection because it enables one to overcome an opponent without the use of weapons. *Or:* Jujitsu is good for self-protection. It enables one to overcome an opponent without the use of weapons.

*1. Human beings who perfume themselves. They are not much different from other animals.
*2. Animals as varied as insects and dogs release pheromones. Chemicals that signal other animals.

*3. Human beings have a diminished sense of smell. And do not consciously detect most of their own species' pheromones.
*4. The human substitute for pheromones may be perfumes. Most common in ancient times were musk and other fragrances derived from animal oils.
*5. Some sources say that people began using perfume to cover up the smell of burning flesh. During sacrifices to the gods.
6. Perfumes became religious offerings in their own right. Being expensive to make, they were highly prized.
7. The earliest historical documents from the Middle East record the use of fragrances. Not only in religious ceremonies but on the body.
8. In the nineteenth century, chemists began synthesizing perfume oils. Which previously could be made only from natural sources.
9. The most popular animal oil for perfume today is musk. Although some people dislike its heavy, sweet odor.
10. Synthetic musk oil would help conserve a certain species of deer. Whose gland is the source of musk.

EXERCISE 35.2
Revising: Sentence fragments

Revise the following paragraphs to eliminate sentence fragments by combining them with main clauses or rewriting them as main clauses. Answers to the first paragraph appear at the end of the book.

Example:

Gymnosperms, the most advanced of nonflowering plants. They thrive in diverse environments.

Gymnosperms, the most advanced of nonflowering plants, thrive in diverse environments. *Or:* Gymnosperms are the most advanced of nonflowering plants. They thrive in diverse environments.

*People generally avoid eating mushrooms except those they buy in stores. *But in fact many varieties of mushrooms are edible. *Mushrooms are members of a large group of vegetation called nonflowering plants. *Including algae, mosses, ferns, and coniferous trees. *Even the giant redwoods of California. *Most of the nonflowering plants prefer moist environments. *Such as forest floors, fallen timber, and still water. *Mushrooms, for example. *They prefer moist, shady soil. *Algae grow in water.

Most mushrooms, both edible and inedible, are members of a class called basidium fungi. A term referring to their method of reproduction. The basidia produce spores. Which can develop into mushrooms. This classification including the prized meadow mushroom, cultivated commercially, and the amanitas. The amanita group contains both edible and poisonous species. Another familiar group of mushrooms, the puffballs. They are easily identified by their round shape. Their spores are contained under a thick skin. Which eventually ruptures to release the spores. The famous morels are in still another group. These pitted, spongy mushrooms called sac fungi because the spores develop in sacs.

Anyone interested in mushrooms as food should heed the US Public Health Service warning. Not to eat any wild mushrooms unless their identity and edibility are established without a doubt.

36 Comma Splices and Fused Sentences

Should a new sentence begin here?

The kernel of a sentence is the main clause consisting of a subject and its verb. To know that one main clause is ending and another is beginning, readers expect one of these signals:

- A period, creating two separate sentences:

  The ship was huge. Its mast stood eighty feet high.

- A comma and a coordinating conjunction, linking two clauses in one sentence:

  The ship was huge, <u>and</u> its mast stood eighty feet high.

- A semicolon, separating two clauses within one sentence:

  The ship was huge; its mast stood eighty feet high.

Key terms

main clause A word group that contains a subject and a verb and does not begin with a subordinating word: *A dictionary is essential.*

coordinating conjunction *And, but, or, nor, for, so, yet.* (See p. 217.)

http://www.ablongman.com/littlebrown

➤ Sentences and words

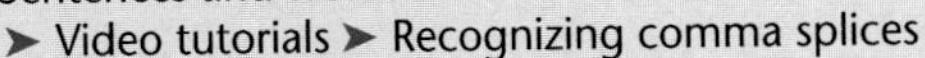

➤ Video tutorials ➤ Recognizing comma splices
➤ Web exercises ➤ Exers. 59–61
➤ Downloads ➤ Chapter 36 exercises in electronic format
➤ Web links ➤ Comma splices and fused sentences

cs/fs
36

Punctuation of two or more main clauses

The following steps can help you identify and revise comma splices and fused sentences.

1. **Underline the main clauses in your draft.**

   Sailors trained on the ship. They learned about wind and sails. Trainees who took the course ranged from high school students to Navy officers. The ship was built in 1910, it had sailed ever since. In almost a century, it had circled the globe forty times. It burned in 2001 its cabins and decks were destroyed.

2. **Are consecutive main clauses separated by periods?**

   If **yes,** OK.
   If **no,** go to question 3.

Comma splice	The ship was built in 1910, it had sailed ever since.
Fused sentence	It burned in 2001 its cabins and decks were destroyed.

3. **Are consecutive main clauses linked by a comma?**

   If **yes,** go to question 4.

Comma splice	The ship was built in 1910, it had sailed ever since.

   If **no,** go to question 5.

Fused sentence	It burned in 2001 its cabins and decks were destroyed.

4. **Does a coordinating conjuction follow the comma between main clauses?**

   If **yes,** OK.
   If **no,** add a coordinating conjuction: *and, but, or, nor, for, so, yet.*

Revised	The ship was built in 1910, and it had sailed ever since.

5. **Are consecutive main clauses separated by a semicolon?**

   If **yes,** OK.
   If **no,** add a semicolon.

Revised	It burned in 2001; its cabins and decks were destroyed.

As an alternative to these revision methods, you can also subordinate one clause to a another:

Revised	When it burned in 2001, its cabins and decks were destroyed.

Readers may be confused if two main clauses run together in a sentence *without* the second or third signal. The result may be a **comma splice,** in which the clauses are joined (or spliced) *only* with a comma.

Comma splice
The ship was huge, its mast stood eighty feet high.

Or the result may be a **fused sentence** (or **run-on sentence**), in which no punctuation or conjunction appears between the clauses.

Fused sentence
The ship was huge its mast stood eighty feet high.

The usual repairs for comma splices and fused sentences are shown in the box opposite and discussed below.

Note Grammar and style checkers can detect many comma splices, but they will miss most fused sentences. For example, a checker flagged *Money is tight, we need to spend carefully* but not *Money is tight we need to spend carefully.* A checker may also question sentences that are actually correct, such as *Money being tighter now than before, we need to spend carefully*. Verify that revision is actually needed on any flagged sentence, and read your work carefully to be sure it is correct.

CULTURE LANGUAGE In standard American English, a sentence may not include more than one main clause unless the clauses are separated by a comma and a coordinating conjunction or by a semicolon. If your native language does not have such a rule or has accustomed you to writing long sentences, you may need to edit your English writing especially for comma splices and fused sentences.

36a Separate main clauses not joined by *and, but,* or another coordinating conjunction.

If your readers point out comma splices or fused sentences in your writing, you're not creating enough separation between main clauses in your sentences. The following guidelines can help you repair the problem.

Separate sentences

Make the clauses into separate sentences when the ideas expressed are only loosely related:

Comma splice Chemistry has contributed much to our understanding of foods, many foods such as wheat and beans can be produced in the laboratory.

Revised Chemistry has contributed much to our understanding of foods. Many foods such as wheat and beans can be produced in the laboratory.

CULTURE LANGUAGE Making separate sentences may be the best option if you are used to writing very long sentences in your native language but often write comma splices in English.

Coordinating conjunction

Insert a coordinating conjunction in a comma splice when the ideas in the main clauses are closely related and equally important:

Comma splice Some laboratory-grown foods taste good, they are nutritious.

Revised Some laboratory-grown foods taste good, and they are nutritious.

In a fused sentence insert a comma and a coordinating conjunction:

Fused Chemists have made much progress they still have a way to go.

Revised Chemists have made much progress, but they still have a way to go.

Semicolon

Insert a semicolon between clauses if the relation between the ideas is very close and obvious without a conjunction:

Comma splice Good taste is rare in laboratory-grown vegetables, they are usually bland.

Revised Good taste is rare in laboratory-grown vegetables; they are usually bland.

Subordination

Subordinate one clause to the other when one idea is less important than the other:

Comma splice The vitamins are adequate, the flavor is deficient.

Revised Even though the vitamins are adequate, the flavor is deficient.

36b Separate main clauses related by *however, for example,* and so on.

Two groups of words that are not conjunctions describe how one main clause relates to another: **conjunctive adverbs** and other **transitional expressions.**

Common conjunctive adverbs and transitional expressions

accordingly	for instance	in the meantime	otherwise
anyway	further	in the past	similarly
as a result	furthermore	likewise	so far
at last	hence	meanwhile	still
at length	however	moreover	that is
besides	incidentally	namely	then
certainly	in contrast	nevertheless	thereafter
consequently	indeed	nonetheless	therefore
even so	in fact	now	thus
finally	in other words	of course	to this end
for all that	in short	on the contrary	undoubtedly
for example	instead	on the whole	until now

(See p. 59 for a longer list of transitional expressions.)

When two main clauses are related by a conjunctive adverb or another transitional expression, they must be separated by a period or by a semicolon. The adverb or expression is also generally set off by a comma or commas.

Comma splice	Most Americans refuse to give up unhealthful habits, consequently our medical costs are higher than those of many other countries.
Revised	Most Americans refuse to give up unhealthful habits. Consequently, our medical costs are higher than those of many other countries.
Revised	Most Americans refuse to give up unhealthful habits; consequently, our medical costs are higher than those of many other countries.

Conjunctive adverbs and transitional expressions are different from coordinating conjunctions (*and, but,* and so on) and subordinating conjunctions (*although, because,* and so on):

- Unlike conjunctions, conjunctive adverbs and transitional expressions do not join two clauses into a grammatical unit but merely describe the way two clauses relate in meaning.
- Thus, unlike conjunctions, conjunctive adverbs and transitional expressions can be moved from one place to another in a clause. No matter where in the clause an adverb or expression falls, though, the clause must be separated from another main clause by a period or semicolon:

  Most Americans refuse to give up unhealthful habits; our medical costs, consequently, are higher than those of many other countries.

EXERCISE 36.1
Sentence combining: Comma splices and fused sentences

Using the method suggested in parentheses, combine each pair of sentences below into one sentence without creating a comma splice or fused sentence. Answers to starred items appear at the end of the book.

Example:

The sun sank lower in the sky. The colors gradually faded. (*Subordinate one clause to the other.*)

As the sun sank lower in the sky, the colors gradually faded.

*1. Some people think that dinosaurs were the first living vertebrates. Fossils of turtles go back 40 million years further. (*Supply a comma and coordinating conjunction.*)

*2. Most other reptiles exist mainly in tropical regions. Turtles inhabit a variety of environments worldwide. (*Subordinate one clause to the other.*)

*3. Turtles do not have teeth. Their jaws are covered with a sharp, horny sheath. (*Supply a semicolon.*)

*4. Turtles cannot expand their lungs to breathe air. They make adjustments in how space is used within the shell. (*Supply a semicolon and a conjunctive adverb or transitional expression.*)

*5. Some turtles can get oxygen from water. They don't need to breathe air. (*Supply a semicolon and a conjunctive adverb or transitional expression.*)

6. The exact origin of paper money is unknown. It has not survived as coins, shells, and other durable objects have. (*Subordinate one clause to the other.*)
7. Scholars disagree over where paper money originated. Many believe it was first used in Europe. (*Subordinate one clause to the other.*)
8. Perhaps goldsmiths were also bankers. Thus they held the gold of their wealthy customers. (*Supply a semicolon.*)
9. The goldsmiths probably gave customers receipts for their gold. These receipts were then used in trade. (*Supply a comma and coordinating conjunction.*)
10. The goldsmiths were something like modern-day bankers. Their receipts were something like modern-day money. (*Supply a semicolon.*)
11. The goldsmiths became even more like modern-day bankers. They began issuing receipts for more gold than they actually held in their vaults. (*Subordinate one clause to the other.*)
12. Today's bankers owe more to their customers than they actually have in reserve. They keep enough assets on hand to meet reasonable withdrawals. (*Supply a semicolon and a conjunctive adverb or transitional expression.*)

cs/fs
36

13. In economic crises, bank customers sometimes fear the loss of their money. Consequently, they demand their deposits. (*Supply a semicolon.*)
14. Depositors' demands may exceed a bank's reserves. The bank may collapse. (*Supply a comma and coordinating conjunction.*)
15. The government now regulates banks to protect depositors. Bank failures are less frequent than they once were. (*Supply a semicolon and a conjunctive adverb or transitional expression.*)

EXERCISE 36.2
Revising: Comma splices and fused sentences

Correct each comma splice or fused sentence below in two of the following ways: (1) make separate sentences of the main clauses; (2) insert an appropriate coordinating conjunction or both a comma and a coordinating conjunction between the main clauses; (3) insert a semicolon and a conjunctive adverb or transitional expression between the main clauses; (4) subordinate one clause to another. If an item contains no comma splice or fused sentence, circle the number preceding it. Answers to starred items appear at the end of the book.

Example:

Carolyn still had a headache, she could not get the child-proof cap off the aspirin bottle.

Carolyn still had a headache because she could not get the child-proof cap off the aspirin bottle. (*Subordination.*)

Carolyn still had a headache, for she could not get the child-proof cap off the aspirin bottle. (*Coordinating conjunction.*)

*1. Money has a long history, it goes back at least as far as the earliest records.

*2. Many of the earliest records concern financial transactions, indeed, early history must often be inferred from commercial activity.

*3. Every known society has had a system of money, though the objects serving as money have varied widely.

*4. Sometimes the objects have had real value, in modern times their value has been more abstract.

*5. Cattle, fermented beverages, and rare shells have served as money each one had actual value for the society.

6. As money, these objects acquired additional value they represented other goods.
7. Today money may be made of worthless paper, it may even consist of a bit of data in a computer's memory.
8. We think of money as valuable only our common faith in it makes it valuable.

9. That faith is sometimes fragile, consequently, currencies themselves are fragile.
10. Economic crises often shake the belief in money, indeed, such weakened faith helped cause the Great Depression of the 1930s.
11. Throughout history money and religion were closely linked, there was little distinction between government and religion.
12. The head of state and the religious leader were often the same person so that all power rested in one ruler.
13. These powerful leaders decided what objects would serve as money, their backing encouraged public faith in the money.
14. Coins were minted of precious metals the religious overtones of money were then strengthened.
15. People already believed the precious metals to be divine, their use in money intensified its allure.

EXERCISE 36.3
Revising: Comma splices and fused sentences

Revise each comma splice and fused sentence in the following paragraphs using the technique that seems most appropriate for the meaning. Answers to the first paragraph appear at the end of the book.

*What many call the first genocide of modern times occurred during World War I, the Armenians were deported from their homes in Anatolia, Turkey. *The Turkish government assumed that the Armenians were sympathetic to Russia, with whom the Turks were at war. *Many Armenians died because of the hardships of the journey, many were massacred. *The death toll was estimated at between 600,000 and 1 million.

Many of the deported Armenians migrated to Russia, in 1918 they established the Republic of Armenia, they continued to be attacked by Turkey, in 1920 they became the Soviet Republic of Armenia rather than surrender to the Turks. Like other Soviet republics, Armenia became independent in 1991, about 3.4 million Armenians live there now.

The Armenians have a long history of conquest by others. As a people, they formed a centralized state in the seventh century BC then they were ruled by the Persian empire until it was conquered by Alexander the Great. Greek and Roman rule followed, internal clan leadership marked by disunity and strife was next. In AD 640 the country was invaded by the Arabs in the eleventh century it was conquered by the Byzantines and then by the Turks, under whose control it remained.

Conflict for the Armenians continues Armenia has territorial disputes with its neighbor Azerbaijan, where many Armenians have settled.

37 Mixed Sentences

How can I untangle sentences?

Tangled sentences often come from **mixed constructions:** the sentences contain parts that do not fit together in either grammar or meaning. Usually the misfit lies in the subject and predicate, so most repairs focus on these essential elements.

Note Grammar and style checkers may recognize a simple mixed construction such as *reason is because,* but they will fail to flag most mixed sentences. A checker was unable to recognize almost all of the mixed sentences in this chapter. Proofread your own work carefully to locate and revise problem sentences.

37a Match subjects and predicates in meaning.

In a sentence with mixed meaning, the subject is said to do or be something illogical. Such a mixture is sometimes called **faulty predication** because the predicate conflicts with the subject.

1 • Illogical equation with *be*

When a form of *be* connects a subject and a word that describes the subject (a complement), the subject and complement must be logically related:

Mixed A compromise between the city and the country would be the ideal place to live.

Revised A community that offered the best qualities of both city and country would be the ideal place to live.

Key terms

subject The part of a sentence that names who or what performs the action or makes the assertion of the verb: *Geese fly.* (See p. 219.)

predicate The part of a sentence containing the verb and asserting something about the subject: *Geese fly.* (See p. 219.)

http://www.ablongman.com/littlebrown
➤ Sentences and words
➤ Web exercises ➤ Exer. 62
➤ Downloads ➤ Chapter 37 exercises in electronic format
➤ Web links ➤ Mixed sentences

2 • *Is when, is where*

Definitions require nouns on both sides of *be.* Clauses that define and begin with *when* or *where* are common in speech but should be avoided in writing.

Mixed An examination is when you are tested on what you know.

Revised An examination is a test of what you know.

3 • *Reason is because*

The commonly heard construction *reason is because* is redundant since *because* means "for the reason that":

Mixed The reason the temple requests donations is because the school needs expansion.

Revised The reason the temple requests donations is that the school needs expansion.

Revised The temple requests donations because the school needs expansion.

4 • Other mixed meanings

Faulty predications are not confined to sentences with *be:*

Mixed The use of emission controls was created to reduce air pollution.

Revised Emission controls were created to reduce air pollution.

37b Untangle sentences that are mixed in grammar.

Many mixed sentences start with one grammatical plan or construction but end with a different one:

Mixed By paying more attention to impressions than facts [modifier (prepositional phrase)] leads [verb] us to misjudge others.

This mixed sentence makes a prepositional phrase work as the subject of *leads,* but prepositional phrases function as modifiers, not as nouns, and thus not as sentence subjects.

Revised By paying more attention to impressions than facts, [modifier (prepositional phrase)] we misjudge [subject + verb] others.

Mixed sentences are especially likely on a computer when you connect parts of two sentences or rewrite half a sentence but not the other half. Mixed sentences may also occur when you don't make the subject and verb of a sentence carry the principal meaning. (See p. 162.) Here is another example:

Mixed (subject; modifier (subordinate clause)) The fact that someone may be considered guilty just for associating with someone guilty.

Revised (subject + verb) The fact is that someone may be considered guilty just for associating with someone guilty.

EXERCISE 37.1
Revising: Mixed sentences

Revise the following sentences so that their parts fit together both in grammar and in meaning. Each item has more than one possible answer. If a sentence is already correct as given, circle the number preceding it. Answers to starred items appear at the end of the book.

Example:

When they found out how expensive pianos are is why they were discouraged.

When they found out how expensive pianos are, they were discouraged. *Or:* They were discouraged because they found out how expensive pianos are.

*1. A hurricane is when the winds in a tropical depression rotate counterclockwise at more than seventy-four miles per hour.
*2. Because hurricanes can destroy so many lives and so much property is why people fear them.
*3. Through high winds, storm surge, floods, and tornadoes is how hurricanes have killed thousands of people.
*4. Storm surge is where the hurricane's winds whip up a tide that spills over seawalls and deluges coastal islands.
*5. Among the hurricanes in history, they have become less deadly since 1950.
6. The reason for the lower death rates is because improved communication systems and weather satellites warn people early enough to escape the hurricane.
7. By simply boarding up a house's windows will not protect a family from a major hurricane.
8. The immediate danger of a hurricane is in how strong its winds are.
9. A hurricane that packs winds of 150 to 200 miles per hour can inflict terrible damage even on inland towns.
10. However, the worst damage to inland areas is when tornadoes and floods strike.

37c State parts of clauses, such as subjects, only once. CULTURE LANGUAGE

In some languages other than English, certain parts of sentences may be repeated. These include the subject in any kind of clause or an object or adverb in an adjective clause. In English, however, these parts are stated only once in a clause.

1 • Repetition of subject

You may be tempted to restate a subject as a pronoun before the verb. But the subject needs stating only once in its clause:

Faulty The liquid it reached a temperature of 180°F.
Revised The liquid reached a temperature of 180°F.

Faulty Gases in the liquid they escaped.
Revised Gases in the liquid escaped.

2 • Repetition in an adjective clause

Adjective clauses begin with *who, whom, whose, which, that, where,* and *when* (see also p. 231). The beginning word replaces another word: the subject (*He is the person who called*), an object of a verb or preposition (*He is the person whom I mentioned*), or a preposition and pronoun (*He knows the office where* [*in which*] *the conference will occur*).

Do not state the word being replaced in an adjective clause:

Faulty The technician whom the test depended on her was burned. [*Whom* should replace *her.*]
Revised The technician whom the test depended on was burned.

Adjective clauses beginning with *where* or *when* do not need an adverb such as *there* or *then:*

Faulty Gases escaped at a moment when the technician was unprepared then.
Revised Gases escaped at a moment when the technician was unprepared.

Note *Whom, which,* and similar words are sometimes omitted but are still understood by the reader. Thus the word being replaced should not be stated.

Key term

clause A group of words containing both a subject and a verb. (See p. 230.)

Faulty Accidents rarely happen to technicians the lab has trained *them*. [*Whom* is understood: . . . *technicians whom the lab has trained.*]

Revised Accidents rarely happen to technicians the lab has trained.

EXERCISE 37.2
Revising: Repeated subjects and other parts CULTURE LANGUAGE

Revise the following sentences to eliminate any unneeded words. If a sentence is already correct as given, circle the number preceding it. Answers to starred items appear at the end of the book.

Example:

Scientists they use special instruments for measuring the age of artifacts.

Scientists use special instruments for measuring the age of artifacts.

*1. Archaeologists and other scientists they can often determine the age of their discoveries by means of radiocarbon dating.
*2. This technique it can be used on any material that once was living.
*3. This technique is based on the fact that all living organisms they contain carbon.
*4. The most common isotope is carbon 12, which it contains six protons and six neutrons.
*5. A few carbon atoms are classified as the isotope carbon 14, where the nucleus consists of six protons and eight neutrons there.

6. Because of the extra neutrons, the carbon 14 atom it is unstable and radioactive.
7. What is significant about the carbon 14 atom is its half-life of 5700 years.
8. Scientists they measure the proportion of carbon 14 to carbon 12 and estimate the age of the specimen.
9. This kind of dating is most accurate when a specimen is between 500 and 50,000 years old then.
10. With younger specimens too little carbon 14 has decayed, and with older ones too little is left that the scientists can measure it.

mixed 37c

V

Punctuation

38 End Punctuation

What punctuation goes at the end of a sentence?

End a sentence with one of three punctuation marks: a period (.), a question mark (?), or an exclamation point (!).

Note Do not rely on a grammar and style checker to identify missing or misused end punctuation. Although a checker may flag missing question marks after direct questions or incorrect combinations of marks (such as a question mark and a period at the end of a sentence), it cannot do much else.

38a Use a period after most sentences and in many abbreviations.

1 • Statements, mild commands, and indirect questions

Statement

The airline went bankrupt. It no longer flies.

Mild command

Think of the possibilities. Please consider others.

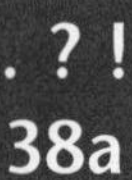

Indirect question

An **indirect question** reports what someone asked but not in the exact form or words of the original question:

The judge asked why I had been driving with my lights off.
No one asked how we got home.

CULTURE LANGUAGE In standard American English, an indirect question uses the wording and subject-verb order of a statement: *The reporter asked why the negotiations failed* [not *why did the negotiations fail*].

Note A period always falls inside a closing quotation mark: *She said, "The play will close tonight."* (See also p. 372.)

http://www.ablongman.com/littlebrown
➤ Punctuation, spelling, and mechanics
➤ Web exercises ➤ Exer. 1
➤ Downloads ➤ Chapter 38 exercise in electronic format
➤ Web links ➤ End punctuation

2 • Abbreviations

Use periods with abbreviations that consist of or end in small letters. Otherwise, omit periods from abbreviations.

Dr.	Mr., Mrs.	e.g.	Feb.	ft.
St.	Ms.	i.e.	p.	a.m., p.m.
PhD	BC, AD	USA	IBM	JFK
BA	AM, PM	US	USMC	AIDS

Note When an abbreviation falls at the end of a sentence, use only one period: *My first class is at 8 a.m.*

38b Use a question mark after a direct question and sometimes to indicate doubt.

1 • Direct questions

Who will follow her?
What is the difference between these two people?

After indirect questions, use a period: *We wondered who would follow her.* (See the facing page.)

Questions in a series are each followed by a question mark:

The officer asked how many times the suspect had been arrested. Three times? Four times? More than that?

Note A question mark falls inside or outside a closing quotation mark depending on whether it is part of a quoted question or part of the larger sentence. (See also p. 373.)

He asked, "Who will go?" [Question mark part of the quoted question.]

Did he say, "I will go"? [Question mark part of the larger sentence, a question.]

2 • Doubt

A question mark within parentheses can indicate doubt about a number or date.

The Greek philosopher Socrates was born in 470 (?) BC and died in 399 BC. [Socrates's birthdate is not known for sure.]

Use sentence structure and words, not a question mark, to express sarcasm or irony.

Not Stern's friendliness (?) bothered Crane.
But Stern's insincerity bothered Crane.

38c Use an exclamation point after an emphatic statement, interjection, or command.

No! We must not lose this election!
Come here immediately!

Follow mild interjections and commands with commas or periods, as appropriate: *Oh, call whenever you can.*

Use exclamation points sparingly, even in informal writing. Overused, they'll fail to impress readers, and they may make you sound overemphatic.

Note An exclamation point falls inside or outside a closing quotation mark depending on whether it is part of the quotation or part of the larger sentence. (See also p. 373.)

EXERCISE 38.1
Revising: End punctuation

Insert appropriate end punctuation (periods, question marks, or exclamation points) where needed in the following paragraph. Answers to the starred lines appear at the end of the book.

*When visitors first arrive in Hawaii, they often encounter an
*unexpected language barrier Standard English is the language of
*business and government, but many of the people speak Pidgin
*English Instead of an excited "Aloha" the visitors may be greeted
*with an excited Pidgin "Howzit" or asked if they know "how fo' find
*one good hotel" Many Hawaiians question whether Pidgin will hold children back because it prevents communication with *haoles,* or Caucasians, who run businesses Yet many others feel that Pidgin is a last defense of ethnic diversity on the islands To those who want to make standard English the official language of the state, these Hawaiians may respond, "Just 'cause I speak Pidgin no mean I dumb" They may ask, "Why you no listen" or, in standard English, "Why don't you listen"

Key term

interjection A word that expresses feeling or commands attention, either alone or within a sentence: *Oh! Hey! Wow!* (See p. 218.)

39 The Comma

What do commas do (and not do)?

The most common punctuation mark within sentences, commas do mainly the following:

- Separate main clauses linked by *and, but,* and other coordinating conjunctions (below).
- Set off most introductory elements (p. 342).
- Set off nonessential elements (p. 345).
- Separate items in a series (p. 348).
- Separate coordinate adjectives (p. 349).
- Separate parts of dates, addresses, place names, and long numbers (p. 350).
- Separate signal phrases and quotations (p. 351).

Commas can be easy to misuse. For guidance on when *not* to use a comma, see page 352.

Note Grammar and style checkers will ignore many comma errors. For example, a checker failed to catch the missing commas in *We cooked lasagna spinach and apple pie* and the misused commas in *The trip was short but, the weather was perfect* and *The travelers were tempted by, the many shops.* Revise any errors that your checker does catch, but you'll have to proofread your work on your own to find and correct most errors.

39a Use a comma before *and, but,* or another coordinating conjunction linking main clauses.

When a coordinating conjunction links words or phrases, do not use a comma: *Dugain plays and sings Irish and English folk songs*. However, *do* use a comma when a coordinating conjunction joins main clauses, as in the examples on page 341.

http://www.ablongman.com/littlebrown
➤ Punctuation, spelling, and mechanics
➤ Video tutorials
➤ Using a grammar checker to spot comma problems
➤ Web exercises ➤ Exers. 2–7
➤ Downloads ➤ Chapter 39 exercises in electronic format
➤ Web links ➤ Commas

Main uses of the comma

- **Separate main clauses linked by a coordinating conjunction** (opposite).

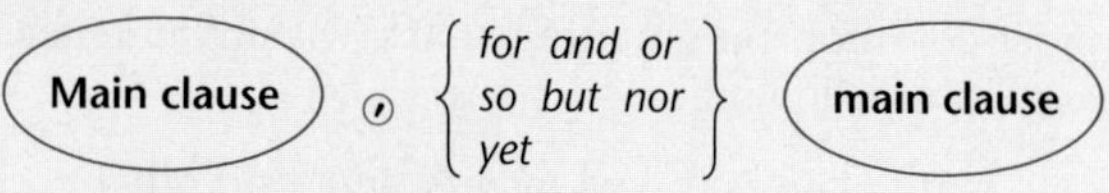

The building is finished, but it has no tenants.

- **Set off most introductory elements** (p. 342).

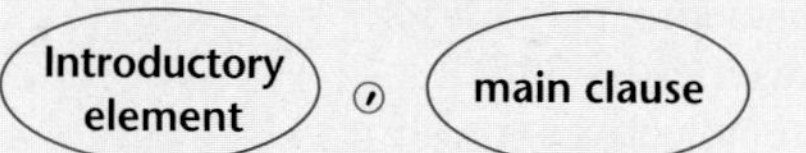

Unfortunately, the only tenant pulled out.

- **Set off nonessential elements** (p. 345).

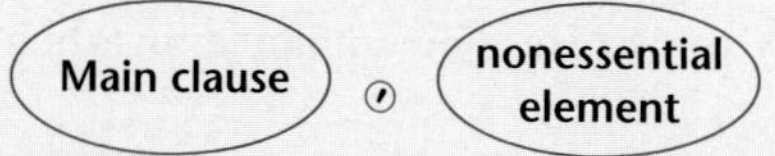

The empty building symbolizes a weak local economy, which affects everyone.

Beginning of main clause , **nonessential element** , **end of main clause** .

The primary cause, the decline of local industry, is not news.

- **Separate items in a series** (p. 348).

The city needs healthier businesses, new schools, and improved housing.

- **Separate coordinate adjectives** (p. 349).

A tall, sleek skyscraper is not needed.

Other uses of the comma:

Separate parts of dates, addresses, long numbers (p. 350).
Separate quotations and signal phrases (p. 351).

See also page 352 for when *not* to use the comma.

39a

Caffeine can keep coffee drinkers alert, and it may elevate their mood.

Caffeine was once thought to be safe, but now researchers warn of harmful effects.

Coffee drinkers may suffer sleeplessness, for the drug acts as a stimulant to the nervous system.

Note The comma goes *before,* not after, the coordinating conjunction: *Caffeine increases heart rate, and it* [not *and, it*] *constricts blood vessels.*

Exception Some writers omit the comma between main clauses that are very short and closely related in meaning: *Caffeine helps but it also hurts.* If you are in doubt about whether to use the comma in such a sentence, use it. It will always be correct.

EXERCISE 39.1
Punctuating linked main clauses

Insert a comma before each coordinating conjunction that links main clauses in the following sentences. If a sentence is already correct as given, circle the number preceding it. Answers to starred items appear at the end of the book.

Example:

I would have attended the concert and the reception but I had to baby-sit for my niece.

I would have attended the concert and the reception, but I had to baby-sit for my niece.

*1. Parents once automatically gave their children the father's last name but some no longer do.
*2. Parents were once legally required to give their children the father's last name but these laws have been contested in court.
*3. Parents may now give their children any last name they choose and the arguments for choosing the mother's last name are often strong and convincing.
*4. Parents who choose the mother's last name may do so because they believe that the mother's importance should be recognized or because the mother's name is easier to pronounce.

Key terms

coordinating conjunctions *And, but, or, nor,* and sometimes *for, so, yet.* (See p. 217.)

main clause A word group that contains a subject and a verb and does not begin with a subordinating word: *Water freezes at temperatures below 32°F.* (See p. 230.)

*5. The child's last name may be just the mother's or it may link the mother's and the father's with a hyphen.
6. Sometimes the first and third children will have the mother's last name and the second child will have the father's.
7. Occasionally, the mother and father combine parts of their names and a new last name is formed.
8. Critics sometimes point out that unusual names confuse others and can create difficulties for children.
9. Children with last names different from their fathers' may feel embarrassed or have identity problems since most children in the United States still bear their fathers' names.
10. Hyphenated names are awkward and difficult to pass on so some observers think they will die out in a generation or two.

39b Use a comma to set off most introductory elements.

An **introductory element** begins a sentence and modifies a word or words in the main clause that follows. It is usually followed by a comma.

Subordinate clause

Even when identical twins are raised apart, they grow up very like each other.

Verbal or verbal phrase

Explaining the similarity, some researchers claim that one's genes are one's destiny.

Concerned, other researchers deny the claim.

Prepositional phrase

In a debate that has lasted centuries, scientists use identical twins to argue for or against genetic destiny.

Key terms

subordinate clause A word group that contains a subject and a verb, begins with a subordinating word such as *because* or *who,* and is not a question: *When water freezes, crystals form.* (See p. 230.)

verbal A verb form used as an adjective, adverb, or noun. A verbal plus any object or modifier is a **verbal phrase:** *frozen water, ready to freeze, rapid freezing.* (See p. 228.)

prepositional phrase A word group consisting of a preposition, such as *for* or *in,* followed by a noun or pronoun plus any modifiers: *in a jar, with a spoon.* (See p. 227.)

Transitional expression

Of course, scientists can now look directly at the genes themselves to answer questions.

You may omit the comma after a short subordinate clause or prepositional phrase if its omission does not create confusion: *When snow falls the city collapses*. *By the year 2000 the world population had topped 6 billion*. But the comma is never wrong.

Note Take care to distinguish *-ing* words used as modifiers from *-ing* words used as subjects. The former almost always take a comma; the latter never do.

modifier — subject — verb
Studying identical twins, geneticists learn about inheritance.

subject — verb
Studying identical twins helps geneticists learn about inheritance.

EXERCISE 39.2
Punctuating introductory elements

In the following sentences, insert commas where needed after introductory elements. If a sentence is already correct as given, circle the number preceding it. Answers to starred items appear at the end of the book.

Example:

After the new library opened the old one became a student union.

After the new library opened, the old one became a student union.

*1. Veering sharply to the right a large flock of birds neatly avoids a high wall.
*2. Moving in a fluid mass is typical of flocks of birds and schools of fish.
*3. With the help of complex computer simulations zoologists are learning more about this movement.
*4. Because it is sudden and apparently well coordinated the movement of flocks and schools has seemed to be directed by a leader.
*5. Almost incredibly the group could behave with more intelligence than any individual seemed to possess.

Key term

transitional expression A word or phrase that shows the relationship between sentences: *for example, however, in fact, of course, in contrast.* (See p. 59.)

6. However new studies have discovered that flocks and schools are leaderless.
7. As it turns out evading danger is really an individual response.
8. When each bird or fish senses a predator it follows individual rules for fleeing.
9. To keep from colliding with its neighbors each bird or fish uses other rules for dodging.
10. Multiplied over hundreds of individuals these responses look as if they have been choreographed.

39c Use a comma or commas to set off nonessential elements.

Commas around part of a sentence often signal that the element is not essential to the meaning. This **nonessential element** may modify or rename the word it refers to, but it does not limit the word to a particular individual or group. The meaning of the word would still be clear if the element were deleted:

Nonessential element

The company, which is located in Oklahoma, has an excellent reputation.

(Because it does not restrict meaning, a nonessential element is also called a **nonrestrictive element.**)

In contrast, an **essential** (or **restrictive**) **element** *does* limit the word it refers to: the element cannot be omitted without leaving the meaning too general. Because it is essential, such an element is *not* set off with commas.

Essential element

The company rewards employees who work hard.

Omitting the underlined words would distort the meaning: the company doesn't necessarily reward *all* employees, only the hardworking ones.

The same element in the same sentence may be essential or nonessential depending on your meaning and the context:

Essential

Not all the bands were equally well received, however. The band playing old music held the audience's attention. The other groups created much less excitement. [*Playing old music* distinguishes a particular band from all possible bands, so the information is essential.]

A test for nonessential and essential elements

1. **Identify the element:**

   Hai Nguyen who emigrated from Vietnam lives in Denver.
   Those who emigrated with him live elsewhere.

2. **Remove the element.** Does the fundamental meaning of the sentence change?

   Hai Nguyen lives in Denver. **No.**
   Those live elsewhere. **Yes.** [Who are *Those?*]

3. **If *no,* the element is *nonessential* and *should* be set off with punctuation:**

   Hai Nguyen, who emigrated from Vietnam, lives in Denver.

   If *yes,* the element is *essential* and should *not* be set off with punctuation:

   Those who emigrated with him live elsewhere.

Nonessential
A new band called Fats made its debut on Saturday night. The band, playing old music, held the audience's attention. If this performance is typical, the group has a bright future. [*Playing old music* adds information about a band already named and thus already familiar to readers, so the phrase is nonessential.]

Note When a nonessential element falls in the middle of a sentence, be sure to set it off with a pair of commas, one *before* and one *after* the element.

1 • Nonessential phrases and clauses

Most nonessential phrases and subordinate clauses function as adjectives to modify nouns or pronouns. In each of the following examples, the underlined words could be omitted with no loss of clarity:

Elizabeth Blackwell was the first woman to graduate from an American medical school, in 1849. [Phrase.]

Key terms

phrase A word group lacking a subject or a verb or both: *in Duluth, carrying water.* (See p. 227.)

subordinate clause A word group that contains a subject and a verb, begins with a subordinating word such as *who* or *although,* and is not a question: *Samson, who won a gold medal, coaches in Utah.* (See p. 230.)

She was a medical pioneer, helping to found the first medical college for women. [Phrase.]

She taught at the school, which was affiliated with the New York Infirmary. [Clause.]

Blackwell, who published books and papers on medicine, practiced pediatrics and gynecology. [Clause.]

Note Use *that* only in an essential clause, never in a nonessential clause: . . . *school, which* [not *that*] *was affiliated*. . . . Many writers reserve *which* for nonessential clauses.

2 • Nonessential appositives

Appositives may also be essential or nonessential, depending on meaning and context. A nonessential appositive merely adds information about the word it refers to:

Toni Morrison's fifth novel, *Beloved*, won the Pulitzer Prize in 1988. [The word *fifth* identifies the novel, so the book's title simply adds a detail.]

In contrast, an essential appositive limits or defines the word it refers to:

Morrison's novel *The Bluest Eye* is about an African American girl who longs for blue eyes. [Morrison has written more than one novel, so the title is essential to identify the intended one.]

3 • Other nonessential elements

Like nonessential modifiers or appositives, many other elements contribute to texture, tone, or overall clarity but are not essential to the meaning. Unlike nonessential modifiers or appositives, these other nonessential elements generally do not refer to any specific word in the sentence.

Note Use a pair of commas—one before, one after—when any of these elements falls in the middle of a sentence.

Absolute phrases

Domestic recycling having succeeded, the city now wants to extend the program to businesses.

Many businesses, their profits already squeezed, resist recycling.

Key terms

appositive A noun that renames another noun immediately before it: *His wife, Kyra Sedgwick, is also an actor.* (See p. 229.)

absolute phrase A phrase modifying a whole main clause and consisting of a participle and its subject: *Their homework completed, the children watched TV.* (See p. 229.)

Parenthetical and transitional expressions

Generally, set off parenthetical and transitional expressions with commas:

> The world's most celebrated holiday is, perhaps surprisingly, New Year's Day. [Parenthetical expression.]
>
> Interestingly, Americans have relatively few holidays. [Parenthetical expression.]
>
> American workers, for example, receive fewer holidays than European workers do. [Transitional expression.]

(Dashes and parentheses may also set off parenthetical expressions. See pp. 375–76.)

When a transitional expression links main clauses, precede it with a semicolon and follow it with a comma (see p. 357):

> European workers often have long paid vacations; indeed, they may receive a full month after just a few years with a company.

Note The conjunctions *and* and *but,* sometimes used as transitional expressions, are not followed by commas (see p. 353). Nor are commas required after some transitional expressions that we read without pauses, such as *also, hence, next, now,* and *thus.* A few transitional expressions, notably *therefore* and *instead,* do not need commas when they fall inside or at the ends of clauses.

> American workers thus put in more work days. But the days themselves may be shorter.

Phrases of contrast

> The substance, not the style, is important.
> Substance, unlike style, cannot be faked.

Tag questions

> Jones should be allowed to vote, should he not?
> They don't stop to consider others, do they?

Yes and *no*

> Yes, the editorial did have a point.
> No, that can never be.

Key terms

parenthetical expression An explanatory or supplemental word or phrase, such *as all things considered, to be frank,* or a brief example or fact. (See p. 376.)

transitional expression A word or phrase that shows the relationship between sentences: *for example, however, in fact.* (See p. 59.)

tag question A question at the end of a statement, consisting of a pronoun, a helping verb, and sometimes *not: It isn't wet, is it?*

Words of direct address
Cody, please bring me the newspaper.
With all due respect, sir, I will not.

Mild interjections
Well, you will never know who did it.
Oh, they forgot all about the baby.

EXERCISE 39.3
Punctuating essential and nonessential elements

Insert commas in the following sentences to set off nonessential elements, and delete any commas that incorrectly set off essential elements. If a sentence is already correct as given, circle the number preceding it. Answers to starred items appear at the end of the book.

Example:

Elizabeth Blackwell who attended medical school in the 1840s was the first American woman to earn a medical degree.

Elizabeth Blackwell, who attended medical school in the 1840s, was the first American woman to earn a medical degree.

*1. Italians insist that Marco Polo the thirteenth-century explorer did not import pasta from China.
*2. Pasta which consists of flour and water and often egg existed in Italy long before Marco Polo left for his travels.
*3. A historian who studied pasta says that it originated in the Middle East in the fifth century.
*4. Most Italians dispute this account although their evidence is shaky.
*5. Wherever it originated, the Italians are now the undisputed masters, in making and cooking pasta.
6. Marcella Hazan, who has written several books on Italian cooking, insists that homemade and hand-rolled pasta is the best.
7. Most cooks buy dried pasta lacking the time to make their own.
8. The finest pasta is made from semolina, a flour from hard durum wheat.
9. Pasta manufacturers choose hard durum wheat, because it makes firmer cooked pasta than common wheat does.
10. Pasta, made from common wheat, gets soggy in boiling water.

39d Use commas between items in a series.

A **series** consists of three or more items of equal importance. The items may be words, phrases, or clauses.

Key term

interjection A word that expresses feeling or commands attention: *Oh, must we?*

^ ; 39d

Anna Spingle married at the age of seventeen, had three children by twenty-one, and divorced at twenty-two.

She worked as a cook, a baby-sitter, and a crossing guard.

Some writers omit the comma before the coordinating conjunction in a series (*Breakfast consisted of coffee, eggs and kippers*). But the final comma is never wrong, and it always helps the reader see the last two items as separate.

39e Use commas between two or more adjectives that equally modify the same word.

Adjectives that equally modify the same word—**coordinate adjectives**—may be separated either by *and* or by a comma.

Spingle's scratched and dented car is an eyesore, but it gets her to work.

She has dreams of a sleek, shiny car.

Adjectives are not coordinate—and should not be separated by commas—when the one nearer the noun is more closely related to the noun in meaning. (See the examples on the next page.)

Tests for commas with adjectives

1. **Identify the adjectives:**

   She was a faithful sincere friend.

   They are dedicated medical students.

2. **Can the adjectives be reversed without changing meaning?**

   She was a sincere faithful friend. **Yes.**

   They are medical dedicated students. **No.**

3. **Can the word *and* be inserted between the adjectives without changing meaning?**

   She was a faithful and sincere friend. **Yes.**

   They are dedicated and medical students. **No.**

4. **If *yes* to both questions, the adjectives *should* be separated by a comma:**

   She was a faithful, sincere friend.

5. **If *no* to both questions, the adjectives should *not* be separated by a comma:**

   They are dedicated medical students.

Spingle's children work at various odd jobs.
They all expect to go to a nearby community college.

EXERCISE 39.4
Punctuating series and coordinate adjectives

Insert commas in the following sentences to separate coordinate adjectives or elements in a series. If a sentence is already correct as given, circle the number preceding it. Answers to starred items appear at the end of the book.

Example:

Although quiet by day, the club became a noisy smoky dive at night.

Although quiet by day, the club became a noisy, smoky dive at night.

*1. Shoes with high heels were originally designed to protect feet from mud garbage and animal waste in the streets.
*2. The first known high heels worn strictly for fashion appeared in the sixteenth century.
*3. The heels were worn by men and made of colorful silk fabrics soft suedes or smooth leathers.
*4. High-heeled shoes became popular when the short powerful King Louis XIV of France began wearing them.
*5. Louis's influence was so strong that men and women of the court priests and cardinals and even household servants wore high heels.

6. Eventually only wealthy fashionable French women wore high heels.
7. In the seventeenth and eighteenth centuries, French culture represented the one true standard of elegance and refinement.
8. High-heeled shoes for women spread to other courts of Europe among the Europeans of North America and to almost all social classes.
9. Now high heels are common, though depending on the fashion they range from short squat thick heels to tall skinny spikes.
10. A New York boutique recently showed a pair of purple satin pumps with tiny jeweled bows and four-inch stiletto heels.

^, 39f

39f Use commas in dates, addresses, place names, and long numbers.

When they appear within sentences, elements punctuated with a comma also end with a comma, as in the following examples.

Dates

July 4, 1776, is the date the Declaration was signed.

The bombing of Pearl Harbor on Sunday, December 7, 1941, prompted American entry into World War II.

Do not use commas between the parts of a date in inverted order (*15 December 1992*) or in dates consisting of a month or season and a year (*December 1941*).

Addresses and place names

Use the address 220 Cornell Road, Woodside, California 94062, for all correspondence.

Columbus, Ohio, is the location of Ohio State University.

Do not use a comma between a state name and a zip code.

Long numbers

Use the comma to separate the figures in long numbers into groups of three, counting from the right. With numbers of four digits, the comma is optional.

The new assembly plant cost $7,525,000.
A kilometer is 3,281 feet [*or* 3281 feet].

CULTURE LANGUAGE Usage in standard American English differs from that in some other languages, which use a period, not a comma, to separate the figures in long numbers.

39g Use commas with quotations according to standard practice.

The words *she said, he writes,* and so on identify the source of a quotation. These **signal phrases** should be separated from the quotation by punctuation, usually a comma or commas.

Eleanor Roosevelt said, "You must do the thing you think you cannot do."

"Knowledge is power," wrote Francis Bacon.

"The shore has a dual nature," observes Rachel Carson, "changing with the swing of the tides." [The signal phrase interrupts the quotation at a comma and thus ends with a comma.]

Exceptions When a signal phrase interrupts a quotation between main clauses, follow the signal phrase with a semicolon or a period. The choice depends on the punctuation of the original.

Not "That part of my life was over," she wrote, "his words had sealed it shut."

But "That part of my life was over," she wrote. "His words had sealed it shut." [*She wrote* interrupts the quotation at a period.]

Or "That part of my life was over," she wrote; "his words had sealed it shut." [*She wrote* interrupts the quotation at a semicolon.]

Do not use a comma when a signal phrase follows a quotation ending in an exclamation point or a question mark:

"Claude!" Mrs. Harrison called.
"Why must I come home?" he asked.

Do not use a comma with a quotation that is integrated into your sentence structure, including one introduced by *that:*

James Baldwin insists that "one must never, in one's life, accept . . . injustices as commonplace."

Baldwin thought that the violence of a riot "had been devised as a corrective" to his own violence.

Do not use a comma with a quoted title unless it is a nonessential appositive:

The Beatles recorded "She Loves You" in the early 1960s.

See Exercise 43.1, page 373, for practice with punctuating quotations.

no ^ ,
39h

39h Delete commas where they are not required.

Commas can make sentences choppy and even confusing if they are used more often than needed. The most common spots for misused commas are discussed below.

1 • Not between subject and verb, verb and object, or preposition and object

Not The returning soldiers, received a warm welcome. [Separated subject and verb.]

But The returning soldiers received a warm welcome.

Not They had chosen, to fight for their country despite, the risks. [Separated verb *chosen* and its object; separated preposition *despite* and its object.]

But They had chosen to fight for their country despite the risks.

Key term

nonessential appositive A word or words that rename an immediately preceding noun but do not limit or define the noun: *The author's first story, "Biloxi," won a prize.* (See p. 346.)

2 • Not in most compound constructions

Compound constructions consisting of two elements almost never require a comma. The only exception is the sentence consisting of two main clauses linked by a coordinating conjunction: *The computer failed, but employees kept working* (see p. 339).

compound subject

Not Banks, and other financial institutions have helped older

compound object of preposition

people with money management, and investment.

But Banks and other financial institutions have helped older people with money management and investment.

compound predicate

Not One bank created special accounts for older people, and held

compound object of verb

classes, and workshops.

But One bank created special accounts for older people and held classes and workshops.

3 • Not after a conjunction

Not Parents of adolescents notice increased conflict at puberty, and, they complain of bickering.

But Parents of adolescents notice increased conflict at puberty, and they complain of bickering.

Not Although, other primates leave the family at adolescence, humans do not.

But Although other primates leave the family at adolescence, humans do not.

4 • Not around essential elements

Not Hawthorne's work, *The Scarlet Letter,* was the first major American novel. [The title is essential to distinguish the novel from the rest of Hawthorne's work.]

But Hawthorne's work *The Scarlet Letter* was the first major American novel.

Key terms

compound construction Two or more words, phrases, or clauses connected by a coordinating conjunction, usually *and, but, or, nor: man and woman, old or young, leaking oil and spewing steam.*

conjunction A connecting word such as a **coordinating conjunction** (*and, but, or,* and so on) or a **subordinating conjunction** (*although, because, when,* and so on). (See pp. 216–17.)

Not The symbols, that Hawthorne uses, have influenced other novelists. [The clause identifies which symbols were influential.]

But The symbols that Hawthorne uses have influenced other novelists.

5 • Not around a series

Commas separate the items *within* a series (p. 348) but do not separate the series from the rest of the sentence.

Not The skills of, hunting, herding, and agriculture, sustained the Native Americans.

But The skills of hunting, herding, and agriculture sustained the Native Americans.

6 • Not before an indirect quotation

Not The report concluded, that dieting could be more dangerous than overeating.

But The report concluded that dieting could be more dangerous than overeating.

EXERCISE 39.5
Revising: Needless and misused commas

Revise the following sentences to eliminate needless or misused commas. If a sentence is already correct as given, circle the number preceding it. Answers to starred items appear at the end of the book.

Example:

Aquifers can be recharged by rainfall, but, the process is slow.
Aquifers can be recharged by rainfall, but the process is slow.

*1. An important source of water, is underground aquifers.
*2. Underground aquifers are deep, and sometimes broad layers of water, that are trapped between layers of rock.
*3. Porous rock, or sediment holds the water.
*4. Deep wells drilled through the top layers of solid rock, produce a flow of water.
*5. Such wells are sometimes called, artesian wells.
6. One of the largest aquifers in North America, the Ogallala aquifer, is named after the Ogallala Indian tribe, which once lived in the region and hunted buffalo there.

Key term

essential element Limits the word it refers to and thus can't be omitted without leaving the meaning too general. (See p. 344.)

7. The Ogallala aquifer underlies a region from western Texas through northern Nebraska, and has a huge capacity of fresh water, that is contained in a layer of sand and gravel.
8. But, the water in the Ogallala is being removed at a rate faster than it is being replaced.
9. Water is pumped from the aquifer for many purposes, such as, drinking and other household use, industrial use, and, agricultural use.
10. The great plains area above the Ogallala, often lacks enough rainfall for the crops, that are grown there.
11. As a consequence, the crops in the great plains are watered by irrigation systems, that pump water from the Ogallala, and distribute it from half-mile-long sprinkler arms.
12. Scientists estimate that, at the present consumption rate the Ogallala will be depleted in forty years.
13. Water table levels are receding from six inches to three feet a year, the amount depending on location.
14. Some areas are experiencing water shortages already, and the pumping continues.
15. Without federal regulation and conservation, the Ogallala will one day, be depleted.

EXERCISE 39.6
Revising: Commas

Insert commas in the following paragraphs wherever they are needed, and eliminate any misused or needless commas. Answers to the first paragraph appear at the end of the book.

*Ellis Island New York reopened for business in 1990 but now the customers are tourists not immigrants. *This spot which lies in New York Harbor was the first American soil seen, or touched by many of the nation's immigrants. *Though other places also served as ports of entry for foreigners none has the symbolic power of, Ellis Island. *Between its opening in 1892 and its closing in 1954, over 20 million people about two-thirds of all immigrants were detained there before taking up their new lives in the United States. *Ellis Island processed over 2000 newcomers a day when immigration was at its peak between 1900 and 1920.

As the end of a long voyage and the introduction to the New World Ellis Island must have left something to be desired. The "huddled masses" as the Statue of Liberty calls them indeed were huddled. New arrivals were herded about kept standing in lines for hours or days yelled at and abused. Assigned numbers they submitted their bodies to the pokings and proddings of the silent nurses and doctors, who were charged with ferreting out the slightest sign, of sickness disability or insanity. That test having been passed the immigrants faced interrogation by an official through an interpreter. Those, with names deemed inconveniently long or difficult to pronounce, often found themselves permanently labeled with abbreviations, of their names, or with the names, of their hometowns. But, millions survived the examination humiliation and confusion, to take the last short boat ride to New York City. For many of them and especially for their descendants Ellis Island eventually became not a nightmare but the place where a new life began.

40 The Semicolon

When is a semicolon needed?

Use a semicolon (;) to separate equal and balanced sentence elements—usually main clauses (below) and occasionally items in a series (p. 359).

Note A grammar and style checker can spot a few errors in the use of semicolons. For example, a checker suggested using a semicolon after *perfect* in *The set was perfect, the director had planned every detail,* thus correcting a comma splice. But it missed the incorrect semicolon in *The set was perfect; deserted streets, dark houses, and gloomy mist* (a colon would be correct; see pp. 360–62). To find semicolon errors, you'll need to proofread on your own.

40a Use a semicolon between main clauses not joined by *and, but,* or another coordinating conjunction.

When no coordinating conjunction links two main clauses, the clauses should be separated by a semicolon.

Key terms

main clause A word group that contains a subject and a verb and does not begin with a subordinating word: *Parks help cities breathe.*

coordinating conjunctions *And, but, or, nor,* and sometimes *for, so, yet.*

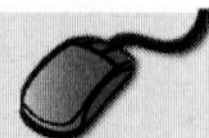

http://www.ablongman.com/littlebrown
➤ Punctuation, spelling, and mechanics
  ➤ Web exercises ➤ Exer. 8
  ➤ Downloads ➤ Chapter 40 exercises in electronic format
  ➤ Web links ➤ Semicolons

A new ulcer drug arrived on the market with a mixed reputation; doctors find that the drug works but worry about its side effects.

The side effects are not minor; some leave the patient quite uncomfortable or even ill.

Note This rule prevents the errors known as comma splice and fused sentence. (See pp. 321–25.)

40b Use a semicolon between main clauses related by *however, for example,* and so on.

When a conjunctive adverb or another transitional expression relates two main clauses in a single sentence, the clauses should be separated with a semicolon:

An American immigrant, Levi Strauss, invented blue jeans in the 1860s; eventually, his product clothed working men throughout the West.

The position of the semicolon between main clauses never changes, but the conjunctive adverb or transitional expression may move around within the second clause. Wherever the adverb or expression falls, it is usually set off with a comma or commas.

Blue jeans have become fashionable all over the world; however, the American originators still wear more jeans than anyone else.

Blue jeans have become fashionable all over the world; the American originators, however, still wear more jeans than anyone else.

Blue jeans have become fashionable all over the world; the American originators still wear more jeans than anyone else, however.

Note This rule prevents the errors known as comma splice and fused sentence. (See pp. 321–25.)

Key terms

conjunctive adverb A modifier that describes the relation of the ideas in two clauses, such as *anyway, besides, consequently, finally, furthermore, hence, however, indeed, instead, meanwhile, moreover, namely, otherwise, still, then, therefore, thus.* (See p. 325.)

transitional expression A word or phrase that shows the relationship between ideas. Transitional expressions include conjunctive adverbs as well as *as a result, at last, even so, for example, in contrast, in fact, in other words, in the meantime, of course, on the whole, until now,* and many other words and phrases. (See p. 59.)

EXERCISE 40.1
Sentence combining: Related main clauses

Combine each set of three sentences below into one sentence containing only two main clauses. As indicated in parentheses, connect the clauses with a semicolon alone or with a semicolon plus a conjunctive adverb or transitional expression followed by a comma. You will have to add, delete, change, and rearrange words. Each item has more than one possible answer. Answers to starred items appear at the end of the book.

Example:

The Albanians censored their news. We got little news from them. And what we got was unreliable. (*Therefore and semicolon.*)

The Albanians censored their news; therefore, the little news we got from them was unreliable.

*1. Electronic instruments are prevalent in jazz. They are also prevalent in rock music. They are less common in classic music. (*However and semicolon.*)

*2. Jazz and rock change rapidly. They nourish experimentation. They nourish improvisation. (*Semicolon alone.*)

*3. The notes and instrumentation of traditional classical music were established by a composer. The composer was writing decades or centuries ago. Such music does not change. (*Therefore and semicolon.*)

*4. Contemporary classical music not only can draw on tradition. It can also respond to innovations. These are innovations such as jazz rhythms and electronic sounds. (*Semicolon alone.*)

*5. Much contemporary electronic music is more than just one type of music. It is more than just jazz, rock, or classical. It is a fusion of all three. (*Semicolon alone.*)

6. Most music computers are too expensive for the average consumer. Digital keyboard instruments can be inexpensive. They are widely available. (*However and semicolon.*)

7. Inside the keyboard is a small computer. The computer controls a sound synthesizer. The instrument can both process and produce music. (*Consequently and semicolon.*)

8. The person playing the keyboard presses keys or manipulates other controls. The computer and synthesizer convert these signals. The signals are converted into vibrations and sounds. (*Semicolon alone.*)

9. The inexpensive keyboards can perform only a few functions. To the novice computer musician, the range is exciting. The range includes drum rhythms and simulated instruments. (*Still and semicolon.*)

10. Would-be musicians can orchestrate whole songs. They start from just the melody lines. They need never again play "Chopsticks." (*Semicolon alone.*)

40c Use semicolons between main clauses or series items containing commas.

Normally, commas separate main clauses linked by coordinating conjunctions (*and, but, or, nor*) and separate items in a series. But when the clauses or series items contain commas, a semicolon between them makes the sentence easier to read.

> Lewis and Clark led the men of their party with consummate skill, inspiring and encouraging them, doctoring and caring for them; and they kept voluminous journals. —PAGE SMITH

> The custody case involved Amy Dalton, the child; Ellen and Mark Dalton, the parents; and Ruth and Hal Blum, the grandparents.

40d Delete or replace unneeded semicolons.

Semicolons are often misused in certain constructions that call for other punctuation or no punctuation.

1 • Not between a main clause and subordinate clause or phrase

The semicolon does not separate unequal parts, such as main clauses and subordinate clauses or phrases.

Not Pygmies are in danger of extinction; because of encroaching development.

But Pygmies are in danger of extinction because of encroaching development.

Not According to African authorities; only about 35,000 Pygmies exist today.

But According to African authorities, only about 35,000 Pygmies exist today.

2 • Not before a series or explanation

Colons and dashes, not semicolons, introduce series, explanations, and so forth. (See pp. 361 and 375.)

Not Teachers have heard all sorts of reasons why students do poorly; psychological problems, family illness, too much work, too little time.

But Teachers have heard all sorts of reasons why students do poorly: psychological problems, family illness, too much work, too little time.

; 40d

EXERCISE 40.2
Revising: Semicolons

Insert semicolons in the following paragraph wherever they are needed. Eliminate any misused or needless semicolons, substituting other punctuation as appropriate. Answers to starred sentences appear at the end of the book.

*The set, sounds, and actors in the movie captured the essence of horror films. *The set was ideal; dark, deserted streets, trees dipping their branches over the sidewalks, mist hugging the ground and creeping up to meet the trees, looming shadows of unlighted, turreted houses. *The sounds, too, were appropriate, especially terrifying was the hard, hollow sound of footsteps echoing throughout the film. But the best feature of the movie was its actors; all of them tall, pale, and thin to the point of emaciation. With one exception, they were dressed uniformly in gray and had gray hair. The exception was an actress who dressed only in black; as if to set off her pale yellow, nearly white, long hair; the only color in the film. The glinting black eyes of another actor stole almost every scene, indeed, they were the source of the film's mischief.

: 41

41 The Colon

What does a colon do?

The colon (:) is mainly a mark of introduction: it signals that the words following it will explain or amplify. It also has several conventional uses, such as in expressions of time.

Note Most grammar and style checkers cannot recognize missing or misused colons. For example, a checker failed to flag *The President promised the following, lower taxes, stronger schools, and greater prosperity* (a colon, not a comma, should come after *following*). You'll have to check for colon errors yourself.

http://www.ablongman.com/littlebrown
➤ Punctuation, spelling, and mechanics
➤ Web exercises ➤ Exer. 12
➤ Downloads ➤ Chapter 41 exercise in electronic format
➤ Web links ➤ Colons

41a Use a colon to introduce a concluding explanation, series, appositive, or long or formal quotation.

As an introducer, a colon is always preceded by a complete main clause. It may or may not be followed by a main clause. This is one way the colon differs from the semicolon, which generally separates main clauses only. (See pp. 356–57.)

Explanation

Soul food has a deceptively simple definition: the ethnic cooking of African Americans.

Sometimes a concluding explanation is preceded by *the following* or *as follows* and a colon:

A more precise definition might be the following: soul food draws on dishes originating in Africa, brought to the New World by slaves, and modified in the Caribbean and the American South.

Note A complete sentence *after* a colon may begin with a capital letter or a small letter. Just be consistent throughout an essay.

Series

At least three soul food dishes are familiar to most Americans: fried chicken, barbecued spareribs, and sweet potatoes.

Appositive

Soul food has one disadvantage: fat.

Namely, that is, and other expressions that introduce appositives *follow* the colon: *Soul food has one disadvantage: namely, fat.*

Long or formal quotation

One soul food chef has a solution: "Instead of using ham hocks to flavor beans, I use smoked turkey wings. The soulful, smoky taste remains, but without all the fat of pork."

When a complete sentence introduces a quotation, as above, a colon generally ends the sentence.

Key terms

main clause A word group that contains a subject and a verb and does not begin with a subordinating word: *Soul food is varied.* (See p. 230.)

appositive A noun or noun substitute that renames another noun immediately before it: *my brother, Jack.* (See p. 229.)

: 41a

41b Use a colon after the salutation of a business letter, between a title and subtitle, and between divisions of time.

Salutation of business letter

Dear Ms. Burak:

Title and subtitle

Charles Dickens: An Introduction to His Novels

Time

12:26 AM   6:00 PM

41c Delete or replace unneeded colons.

Use the colon only at the end of a main clause, not in the following situations.

- Delete a colon after a verb:

  Not The best-known soul food dishes are: fried chicken and barbecued spareribs.

  But The best-known soul food dishes are fried chicken and barbecued spareribs.

- Delete a colon after a preposition:

  Not Soul food recipes can be found in: mainstream cookbooks as well as specialized references.

  But Soul food recipes can be found in mainstream cookbooks as well as specialized references.

- Delete a colon after *such as* or *including:*

  Not Many Americans have not tasted delicacies such as: chitlins and black-eyed peas.

  But Many Americans have not tasted delicacies such as chitlins and black-eyed peas.

EXERCISE 41.1
Revising: Colons and semicolons

In the following sentences, use colons or semicolons where they are needed, and delete or replace them where they are incorrect. If

Key term

preposition *In, on, outside,* or another word that takes a noun or pronoun as its object: *in the house.* (See p. 215.)

a sentence is already correct as given, circle the number preceding it. Answers to starred items appear at the end of the book.

Example:

Mix the ingredients as follows sift the flour and salt together, add the milk, and slowly beat in the egg yolk.

Mix the ingredients as follows: sift the flour and salt together, add the milk, and slowly beat in the egg yolk.

*1. Sunlight is made up of three kinds of radiation; visible rays; infrared rays, which we cannot see; and ultraviolet rays, which are also invisible.

*2. Especially in the ultraviolet range; sunlight is harmful to the eyes.

*3. Ultraviolet rays can damage the retina: furthermore, they can cause cataracts on the lens.

*4. Infrared rays are the longest; measuring 700 nanometers and longer, while ultraviolet rays are the shortest; measuring 400 nanometers and shorter.

*5. The lens protects the eye by: absorbing much of the ultraviolet radiation and thus protecting the retina.

6. By protecting the retina, however, the lens becomes a victim; growing cloudy and blocking vision.
7. The best way to protect your eyes is: to wear hats that shade the face and sunglasses that screen out the ultraviolet rays.
8. Many sunglass lenses have been designed as ultraviolet screens; many others are extremely ineffective.
9. If sunglass lenses do not screen out ultraviolet rays and if people can see your eyes through them, they will not protect your eyes, and you will be at risk for cataracts later in life.
10. People who spend much time outside in the sun; really owe it to themselves to buy a pair of sunglasses that will shield their eyes.

42 The Apostrophe

Where do apostrophes go (and not go)?

The apostrophe (’) appears as part of a word to indicate possession (pp. 364–66), the omission of one or more letters (p. 368), and sometimes plural number (p. 368).

Apostrophes are easy to misuse. For safety’s sake, check your drafts to be sure that all words ending in *-s* neither omit needed apostrophes nor add unneeded ones.

Uses and misuses of the apostrophe

Uses of the apostrophe

- **Use an apostrophe to form the possessives of nouns and indefinite pronouns** (opposite).

Singular	Plural
Ms. Park's	the Parks'
lawyer's	lawyers'
everyone's	two weeks'

- **Use an apostrophe to form contractions** (p. 368).

it's a girl	shouldn't
you're	won't

- **The apostrophe is optional for plurals of abbreviations, dates, and words or characters named as words** (p. 368).

MAs or MA's	*C*s or *C*'s
1960s or 1960's	*if*s or *if*'s

Misuses of the apostrophe

- **Do not use an apostrophe plus *-s* to form the possessives of plural nouns** (p. 366). Instead, use an apostrophe alone after the *-s* that forms the plural.

Not	But
the Kim's car	the Kims' car
boy's fathers	boys' fathers
babie's care	babies' care

- **Do not use an apostrophe to form plurals of nouns** (p. 367).

Not	But
book's are	books are
the Freed's	the Freeds

- **Do not use an apostrophe with verbs ending in *-s*** (p. 367).

Not	But
swim's	swims

- **Do not use an apostrophe to form the possessives of personal pronouns** (p. 367).

Not	But
it's toes	its toes
your's	yours

√ 42

Note Grammar and style checkers have mixed results in recognizing apostrophe errors. For instance, most flag missing apostrophes in contractions (as in *isnt*), but many cannot distinguish between *its* and *it's, their* and *they're, your* and *you're, whose* and *who's*. The checkers can identify some apostrophe errors in possessives but will overlook others and may flag correct plurals. Instead of relying on your checker, try using your word processor's Search or Find function to hunt for all words you have ended in *-s*. Then check them to ensure that they correctly omit or include apostrophes and that needed apostrophes are correctly positioned.

42a Use the apostrophe and sometimes *-s* to form possessive nouns and indefinite pronouns.

A noun or indefinite pronoun shows possession with an apostrophe and, usually, an *-s: the dog's hair, everyone's hope*. Remember that the apostrophe or apostrophe-plus-*s* is an *addition*. Before this addition, always spell the name of the owner or owners without dropping or adding letters.

1 • Singular words: Add *-'s*.

Bill Boughton's skillful card tricks amaze children.
Anyone's eyes would widen.
Most tricks will pique an adult's curiosity, too.

The *-'s* ending for singular words pertains also to singular words ending in *-s*, as the next examples show.

Henry James's novels reward the patient reader.
The business's customers filed suit.

Key term

indefinite pronoun A pronoun that does not refer to a specific person or thing, such as *anyone, no one,* or *something*. (See p. 271.)

http://www.ablongman.com/littlebrown
➤ Punctuation, spelling, and mechanics
➤ Video tutorials ➤ Recognizing apostrophe problems
➤ Web exercises ➤ Exers. 9 and 10
➤ Downloads ➤ Chapter 42 exercises in electronic format
➤ Web links ➤ Apostrophes

Exception An apostrophe alone may be added to a singular word ending in *-s* when another *s* would make the word difficult to say:

Moses' mother concealed him in the bulrushes.
Joan Rivers' jokes offend many people.

However, the added *-s* is never wrong (*Moses's, Rivers's*).

2 • Plural words ending in *-s:* Add -' only.

Workers' incomes have fallen slightly over the past year.
Many students benefit from several years' work after high school.
The Jameses' talents are extraordinary.

Note the difference in the possessives of singular and plural words ending in *-s*. The singular form usually takes *-s: James's*. The plural takes only the apostrophe: *Jameses'*.

3 • Plural words not ending in *-s:* Add -'s.

Children's educations are at stake.
We need to attract the media's attention.

4 • Compound words: Add -'s only to the last word.

The brother-in-law's business failed.
Taxes are always somebody else's fault.

5 • Two or more owners: Add -'s depending on possession.

Individual possession
Zimbale's and Mason's comedy techniques are similar. [Each comedian has his own technique.]

Joint possession
The child recovered despite her mother and father's neglect. [The mother and father were jointly neglectful.]

EXERCISE 42.1
Forming possessives

Form the possessive of each word or word group in brackets. Answers to starred items appear at the end of the book.

Example:
The [men] blood pressures were higher than the [women].
The men's blood pressures were higher than the women's.

*1. In the myths of the ancient Greeks, the [goddesses] roles vary widely.
*2. [Demeter] responsibility is the fruitfulness of the earth.

*3. [Athena] role is to guard the city of Athens.
*4. [Artemis] function is to care for wild animals and small children.
*5. [Athena and Artemis] father, Zeus, is the king of the gods.

6. Even a single [goddess] responsibilities are often varied.
7. Over several [centuries] time, Athena changes from a [mariner] goddess to the patron of crafts.
8. Athena is also concerned with fertility and with [children] well-being, since the strength of Athens depended on a large and healthy population.
9. Athena often changes into [birds] forms.
10. In [Homer] *Odyssey* she assumes a [sea eagle] form.
11. In ancient Athens the myths of Athena were part of [everyone] knowledge and life.
12. A cherished myth tells how Athena fights to retain possession of her [people] land when the god Poseidon wants it.
13. [Athena and Poseidon] skills are different, and each promises a special gift to the Athenians.
14. At the [contest] conclusion, Poseidon has given water and Athena has given an olive tree, for sustenance.
15. The other gods decide that the [Athenians] lives depend more on Athena than on Poseidon.

42b Delete or replace any apostrophe in a plural noun, a singular verb, or a possessive personal pronoun.

√ 42b

1 • Plural nouns

The plurals of nouns are generally formed by adding *-s* or *-es*: *boys, families, Joneses.* Don't add an apostrophe to form the plural:

Not The Jones' controlled the firm's until 1999.
But The Joneses controlled the firms until 1999.

2 • Singular verbs

Verbs ending in *-s never* take an apostrophe:

Not The subway break's down less often now.
But The subway breaks down less often now.

3 • Possessives of personal pronouns

His, hers, its, ours, yours, theirs, and *whose* are possessive forms of *he, she, it, we, you, they,* and *who.* They do not take apostrophes:

Not The house is her's. It's roof leaks.
But The house is hers. Its roof leaks.

Don't confuse possessive pronouns with contractions (next page).

42c Use the apostrophe to form contractions.

A **contraction** replaces one or more letters, numbers, or words with an apostrophe, as in the following examples:

it is	it's	cannot	can't
they are	they're	does not	doesn't
you are	you're	were not	weren't
who is	who's	class of 2001	class of '01

Note Don't confuse contractions with personal pronouns:

Contractions	Personal pronouns
It's a book.	Its cover is green.
They're coming.	Their car broke down.
You're right.	Your idea is good.
Who's coming?	Whose party is it?

42d Increasingly, the apostrophe does not mark plurals of abbreviations, dates, and words and characters named as words.

You'll sometimes see apostrophes used to form the plurals of abbreviations (*BA's*), dates (*1900's*), and words or characters named as words (*but's*). However, most current style guides recommend against the apostrophe in these cases.

BAs	PhDs
1990s	2000s

The sentence has too many *but*s [or buts].
Two *3*s [or 3s] end the zip code.

Note Underline or italicize a word or character named as a word (see p. 397), but not the added *-s*.

EXERCISE 42.2
Revising: Apostrophes

In the following paragraph, correct any mistakes in the use of apostrophes or any confusion between contractions and possessive personal pronouns. Answers to starred sentences appear at the end of the book.

*Landlocked Chad is among the worlds most troubled countries. *The people's of Chad are poor: they're average per capita income equals $1000 per year. *Just over 30 percent of Chads population is literate, and every five hundred people must share only two teacher's. The natural resources of the nation have never been plentiful, and now, as it's slowly being absorbed into the growing Sahara Desert, even water is scarce. Chads political conflicts go back to the nineteenth century, when the French colonized the land by brutally subduing it's people. The rule of the French—who's inept government of the colony did nothing to ease tensions among racial, tribal, and religious group's—ended with independence in 1960. But since then the Chadians experience has been one of civil war and oppression, and their also threatened with invasions from they're neighbors.

43 Quotation Marks

How do quotation marks work?

Quotation marks—either double (" ") or single (' ')—mainly enclose direct quotations from speech or writing, enclose certain titles, and highlight words used in a special sense. These are the uses covered in this chapter, along with placing quotation marks outside or inside other punctuation marks. Additional issues with quotations are discussed elsewhere in this book:

- Punctuating *she said* and other signal phrases with quotations (p. 351).
- Altering quotations using the ellipsis mark (p. 377) or brackets (p. 379).
- Quoting sources versus paraphrasing or summarizing them (pp. 449–52).
- Avoiding plagiarism when quoting (pp. 459–65).
- Integrating quotations into your text (pp. 453–58).
- Formatting long prose quotations and poetry quotations in MLA style (pp. 508–09) or in APA style (pp. 537–38).

http://www.ablongman.com/littlebrown
➤ Punctuation, spelling, and mechanics
  ➤ Web exercises ➤ Exer. 11
  ➤ Downloads ➤ Chapter 43 exercise in electronic format
  ➤ Web links ➤ Quotation marks

Note Always use quotation marks in pairs, one at the beginning of a quotation and one at the end. Some grammar and style checkers will help you use quotation marks in pairs by flagging a lone mark. Most checkers can also be set to ignore other punctuation with quotations or to look for punctuation inside or outside quotation marks. If you set your checker to expect punctuation inside quotation marks, it may not detect errors when punctuation should actually fall outside quotation marks. For example, a checker flagged *She said, "I must go".* (the period should fall inside the quotation mark), but it missed *Who said, "I am here?"* (the question mark should fall outside the quotation mark). Proofread carefully to catch errors in punctuating quotations that a checker cannot recognize.

43a Use double quotation marks to enclose direct quotations.

A **direct quotation** reports what someone said or wrote, in the exact words of the original:

> "Life," said the psychoanalyst Karen Horney, "remains a very efficient therapist."

" " 43b

Do not use quotation marks with an **indirect quotation,** which reports what someone said or wrote but not in the exact words.

> The psychoanalyst Karen Horney claimed that life is a good therapist.

When quoting dialog, begin a new paragraph for each speaker.

> "What shall I call you? Your name?" Andrews whispered rapidly, as with a high squeak the latch of the door rose.
>
> "Elizabeth," she said. "Elizabeth."
>
> —GRAHAM GREENE, *The Man Within*

When you quote a single speaker for more than one paragraph, put quotation marks at the beginning of each paragraph but at the end of only the last paragraph.

43b Use single quotation marks to enclose a quotation within a quotation.

> "In formulating any philosophy," Woody Allen writes, "the first consideration must always be: What can we know? Descartes hinted at

the problem when he wrote, 'My mind can never know my body, although it has become quite friendly with my leg.'"

Notice that two different quotation marks appear at the end of the sentence—one single (to finish the interior quotation) and one double (to finish the main quotation).

43c Put quotation marks around the titles of works that are parts of other works.

Use quotation marks to enclose the titles of works that are published or released within larger works. (See the box below.) Use single quotation marks for a quotation within a quoted title, as in the article title and essay title in the box. And enclose all punctuation in the title within the quotation marks, as in the article title.

Titles to be enclosed in quotation marks

Other titles should be underlined or italicized. (See p. 396.)

Song
"The Star-Spangled Banner"

Short story
"The Gift of the Magi"

Short poem
"Mending Wall"

Article in a periodical
"Does 'Scaring' Work?"

Essay
"Joey: A 'Mechanical Boy'"

Page or document on a Web site
"Readers' Page" (on the site Friends of Prufrock)

Episode of a television or radio program
"The Mexican Connection" (on Sixty Minutes)

Subdivision of a book
"The Mast Head" (Chapter 35 of Moby-Dick)

Note Some academic disciplines do not require quotation marks for titles within source citations. See page 523 on the style of the American Psychological Association (APA).

43d Quotation marks may enclose words being used in a special sense.

On movie sets movable "wild walls" make a one-walled room seem four-walled on film.

Note Use underlining or italics for words you are defining. (See p. 397.)

43e Delete quotation marks where they are not required.

Title of your paper

Not "The Death Wish in One Poem by Robert Frost"

But The Death Wish in One Poem by Robert Frost

Or The Death Wish in "Stopping by Woods on a Snowy Evening"

Common nickname

Not As President, "Jimmy" Carter preferred to use his nickname.

But As President, Jimmy Carter preferred to use his nickname.

Slang or trite expression

Quotation marks will not excuse slang or a trite expression that is inappropriate to your writing. If slang is appropriate, use it without quotation marks.

Not We should support the President in his "hour of need" rather than "wimp out on him."

But We should give the President the support he needs rather than turn away like cowards.

" "

43f

43f Place other punctuation marks inside or outside quotation marks according to standard practice.

1 • Commas and periods: Inside quotation marks

Swift uses irony in his essay "A Modest Proposal."

Many first-time readers are shocked to see infants described as "delicious."

"'A Modest Proposal,'" wrote one critic, "is so outrageous that it cannot be believed."

Exception When a parenthetical source citation immediately follows a quotation, place any period or comma *after* the citation:

One critic calls the essay "outrageous" (Olms 26).

Partly because of "the cool calculation of its delivery" (Olms 27), Swift's satire still chills a modern reader.

2 • Colons and semicolons: Outside quotation marks

A few years ago the slogan in elementary education was "learning by playing"; now educators are concerned with teaching basic skills.

We all know the meaning of "basic skills": reading, writing, and arithmetic.

3 • Dashes, question marks, and exclamation points: Inside quotation marks only if part of the quotation

When a dash, question mark, or exclamation point is part of the quotation, place it *inside* quotation marks. Don't use any other punctuation, such as a period or comma:

"But must you—" Marcia hesitated, afraid of the answer.

"Go away!" I yelled.

Did you say, "Who is she?" [When both your sentence and the quotation would end in a question mark or exclamation point, use only the mark in the quotation.]

When a dash, question mark, or exclamation point applies only to the larger sentence, not to the quotation, place it *outside* quotation marks—again, with no other punctuation:

One evocative line in English poetry—"After many a summer dies the swan"—comes from Alfred, Lord Tennyson.

Who said, "Now cracks a noble heart"?

The woman called me "stupid"!

" "
43f

EXERCISE 43.1
Revising: Quotation marks

Insert quotation marks as needed in the following paragraph. Answers to starred sentences appear at the end of the book.

*In one class we talked about a passage from I Have a Dream, the speech delivered by Martin Luther King, Jr., on the steps of the Lincoln Memorial on August 28, 1963:

> *When the architects of our republic wrote the magnificent words of the Constitution and the Declaration of Independence, they were signing a promissory note to which every American was to feel heir. *This note was a promise that all men would be guaranteed the unalienable rights of life, liberty, and the pursuit of happiness.

*What did Dr. King mean by this statement? the teacher asked. *Perhaps we should define promissory note first. Then she explained that a person who signs such a note agrees to pay a specific sum of money on a particular date or on demand by the holder of the note. One student suggested, Maybe Dr. King meant that the writers of the Constitution and Declaration promised that all people in America should be equal. He and over 200,000 people had gathered in Washington, DC, added another student. Maybe their purpose was to demand payment, to demand those rights for African Americans. The whole discussion was an eye-opener for those of us (including me) who had never considered that those documents make promises that we should expect our country to fulfill.

44 Other Marks

How do writers use the dash, parentheses, the ellipsis mark, brackets, and the slash?

Each of these punctuation marks has distinctive uses:

- The dash (—) sets off interruptions (below).
- Parentheses (**( )**) enclose some nonessential information and labels for lists within sentences (p. 376).
- The ellipsis mark (. . .) indicates an omission from a quotation (p. 377).
- Brackets (**[ ]**) mainly indicate changes in quotations (p. 379).
- The slash (**/**) separates options, lines of poetry, and the parts of electronic addresses (p. 380).

Note Many grammar and style checkers will flag a lone parenthesis or bracket so that you can match it with another parenthesis or bracket. But most checkers cannot recognize other misuses of the marks covered here and instead simply ignore the marks. You'll need to proofread your papers carefully for errors.

44a Use the dash or dashes to indicate shifts and to set off some sentence elements.

The **dash** is mainly a mark of interruption: it signals a shift, insertion, or break. In your papers, form a dash with two hyphens

http://www.ablongman.com/littlebrown
➤ Punctuation, spelling, and mechanics
➤ Web exercises ➤ Exers. 12 and 13
➤ Downloads ➤ Chapter 44 exercises in electronic format
➤ Web links ➤ Other punctuation marks

(--) or use the character called an em dash on your word processor. Do not add extra space around or between the hyphens or around the em dash.

Note When an interrupting element starting with a dash falls in the middle of a sentence, be sure to add the closing dash to signal the end of the interruption. See the first example below.

1 • Shifts and hesitations

The novel—if one can call it that—appeared in 1999.

If the book had a plot—but a plot would be conventional.

"I was worried you might think I had stayed sway because I was influenced by—" He stopped and lowered his eyes.

Astonished, Howe said, "Influenced by what?"

"Well, by—" Blackburn hesitated and for an answer pointed to the table. —LIONEL TRILLING

2 • Nonessential elements

Dashes may be used instead of commas to set off and emphasize modifiers, parenthetical expressions, and other nonessential elements:

Though they are close together—separated by only a few blocks—the two neighborhoods could be in different countries.

Dashes are especially useful when a nonessential element contains punctuation of its own:

The qualities Monet painted—sunlight, rich shadows, deep colors—abounded near the rivers and gardens he used as subjects.

3 • Introductory series and concluding series and explanations

Shortness of breath, skin discoloration or the sudden appearance of moles, persistent indigestion, the presence of small lumps—all these may signify cancer. [Introductory series.]

The patient undergoes a battery of tests—CAT scan, bronchoscopy, perhaps even biopsy. [Concluding series.]

Many patients are disturbed by the CAT scan—by the need to keep still for long periods in an exceedingly small space. [Concluding explanation.]

A colon could be used instead of a dash in the last two examples. The dash is more informal.

Key term

nonessential element Gives added information but does not limit the word it refers to. (See p. 344.)

— 44a

4 • Overuse

Too many dashes can make writing jumpy or breathy:

Not In all his life—eighty-seven years—my great-grandfather never allowed his picture to be taken—not even once. He claimed the "black box"—the camera—would steal his soul.

But In all his eighty-seven years, my great-grandfather did not allow his picture to be taken even once. He claimed the "black box"—the camera—would steal his soul.

44b Use parentheses to enclose parenthetical expressions and labels for lists within sentences.

Note Parentheses *always* come in pairs, one before and one after the punctuated material.

1 • Parenthetical expressions

Parenthetical expressions include explanations, facts, digressions, and examples that may be helpful or interesting but are not essential to meaning. Parentheses de-emphasize parenthetical expressions. (Commas emphasize them more and dashes still more.)

The population of Philadelphia (now about 1.5 million) has declined since 1950.

Note Don't put a comma before a parenthetical expression enclosed in parentheses. Punctuation after the parenthetical expression should be placed outside the closing parenthesis.

Not Philadelphia's population compares with Houston's, (just over 1.6 million.)

But Philadelphia's population compares with Houston's (just over 1.6 million).

When it falls between other complete sentences, a complete sentence enclosed in parentheses begins with a capital letter and ends with a period.

In general, coaches will tell you that scouts are just guys who can't coach. (But then, so are brain surgeons.) —Roy Blount

2 • Labels for lists within sentences

Outside the Middle East, the countries with the largest oil reserves are (1) Venezuela (63 billion barrels), (2) Russia (57 billion barrels), and (3) Mexico (51 billion barrels).

When you set a list off from your text, do not enclose such labels in parentheses.

44c Use the ellipsis mark to indicate omissions from quotations.

The **ellipsis mark,** consisting of three spaced periods (. . .), generally indicates an omission from a quotation. The following examples quote from or refer to this passage about environmentalism:

Original quotation

"At the heart of the environmentalist world view is the conviction that human physical and spiritual health depends on sustaining the planet in a relatively unaltered state. Earth is our home in the full, genetic sense, where humanity and its ancestors existed for all the millions of years of their evolution. Natural ecosystems—forests, coral reefs, marine blue waters—maintain the world exactly as we would wish it to be maintained. When we debase the global environment and extinguish the variety of life, we are dismantling a support system that is too complex to understand, let alone replace, in the foreseeable future."

—EDWARD O. WILSON, "Is Humanity Suicidal?"

1. Omission of the middle of a sentence

Wilson writes, "Natural ecosystems . . . maintain the world exactly as we would wish it to be maintained."

2. Omission of the end of a sentence, without source citation

Wilson writes, "Earth is our home. . . ." [The sentence period, closed up to the last word, precedes the ellipsis mark.]

3. Omission of the end of a sentence, with source citation

Wilson writes, "Earth is our home . . ." (27). [The sentence period follows the source citation.]

4. Omission of parts of two or more sentences

Wilson writes, "At the heart of the environmentalist world view is the conviction that human physical and spiritual health depends on sustaining the planet . . . where humanity and its ancestors existed for all the millions of years of their evolution."

5. Omission of one or more sentences

As Wilson puts it, "At the heart of the environmentalist world view is the conviction that human physical and spiritual health depends on sustaining the planet in a relatively unaltered state. . . . When we debase the global environment and extinguish the variety of life, we are dismantling a support system that is too complex to understand, let alone replace, in the foreseeable future."

6. Omission from the middle of a sentence through the end of another sentence

"Earth is our home. . . . When we debase the global environment and extinguish the variety of life, we are dismantling a support system that is too complex to understand, let alone replace, in the foreseeable future."

7. Omission of the beginning of a sentence, leaving a complete sentence

a. Bracketed capital letter

"[H]uman physical and spiritual health," Wilson writes, "depends on sustaining the planet in a relatively unaltered state." [No ellipsis mark is needed because the brackets around the *H* indicate that the letter was not capitalized originally and thus that the beginning of the sentence has been omitted.]

b. Small letter

According to Wilson, "human physical and spiritual health depends on sustaining the planet in a relatively unaltered state." [No ellipsis mark is needed because the small *h* indicates that the beginning of the sentence has been omitted.]

c. Capital letter from the original

Hami comments, ". . . Wilson argues eloquently for the environmentalist world view." [An ellipsis mark *is* needed because the quoted part of the sentence begins with a capital letter and it is not clear that the beginning of the original sentence has been omitted.]

8. Use of a word or phrase

Wilson describes the earth as "our home." [No ellipsis mark needed.]

Note these features of the examples:

- Use an ellipsis mark when it is not otherwise clear that you have left out material from the source, as when you omit one or more sentences (examples 5 and 6) or when the words you quote form a complete sentence that is different in the original (examples 1–4 and 7c).
- You don't need an ellipsis mark when it is obvious that you have omitted something, such as when capitalization indicates omission (examples 7a and 7b) or when a phrase clearly comes from a larger sentence (example 8).
- After a grammatically complete sentence, an ellipsis mark follows the sentence period (examples 2, 5, and 6) *except* when a parenthetical source citation follows the quotation (example 3). Then the sentence period falls after the citation.

If you omit one or more lines of poetry or paragraphs of prose from a quotation, use a separate line of ellipsis marks across the full width of the quotation to show the omission:

> In "Song: Love Armed" from 1676, Aphra Behn contrasts two lovers' experiences of a romance:

Love in fantastic triumph sate,
  Whilst bleeding hearts around him flowed,

. . . .

But my poor heart alone is harmed,
  Whilst thine the victor is, and free. (lines 1-2, 15-16)

(See pp. 508–09 for the format of displayed quotations like this one.)

EXERCISE 44.1
Using ellipsis marks

Use ellipsis marks and any other needed punctuation to follow the numbered instructions for quoting from the following paragraph. The answer to the starred item appears at the end of the book.

Women in the sixteenth and seventeenth centuries were educated in the home and, in some cases, in boarding schools. Men were educated at home, in grammar schools, and at the universities. The universities were closed to female students. For women, "learning the Bible," as Elizabeth Joceline puts it, was an impetus to learning to read. To be able to read the Bible in the vernacular was a liberating experience that freed the reader from hearing only the set passages read in the church and interpreted by the church. A Protestant woman was expected to read the scriptures daily, to meditate on them, and to memorize portions of them. In addition, a woman was expected to instruct her entire household in "learning the Bible" by holding instructional and devotional times each day for all household members, including the servants.

—CHARLOTTE F. OTTEN, *English Women's Voices, 1540–1700*

*1. Quote the fifth sentence, but omit everything from *that freed the reader* to the end.
2. Quote the fifth sentence, but omit the words *was a liberating experience that.*
3. Quote the first and sixth sentences.

44d Use brackets to indicate changes in quotations.

Brackets have specialized uses in mathematical equations, but their main use for all kinds of writing is to indicate that you have altered a quotation to explain, clarify, or correct it.

"That Texaco station [just outside Chicago] is one of the busiest in the nation," said a company spokesperson.

The word *sic* (Latin for "in this manner") in brackets indicates that an error in the quotation appeared in the original and was not made by you. Do not underline or italicize *sic* in brackets.

According to the newspaper report, "The car slammed thru [sic] the railing and into oncoming traffic."

Do not use *sic* to make fun of a writer or to note errors in a passage that is clearly nonstandard.

44e Use the slash between options, between lines of poetry run into the text, and in electronic addresses.

Option

Some teachers oppose pass/fail courses.

Poetry

Many readers have sensed a reluctant turn away from death in Frost's lines "The woods are lovely, dark and deep, / But I have promises to keep" (13–14).

When separating lines of poetry in this way, leave a space before and after the slash. (See pp. 508–09 for more on quoting poetry.)

Electronic address

http://www.stanford.edu/depts/spc/spc.html

See pages 440–41 for more on electronic addresses.

EXERCISE 44.2

Revising: Dashes, parentheses, ellipsis marks, brackets, slashes

Insert dashes, parentheses, ellipsis marks, brackets, or slashes as needed in the following paragraph. In some cases, two or more different marks could be correct. Answers to starred sentences appear at the end of the book.

*"Let all the learned say what they can, 'Tis ready money makes the man." *These two lines of poetry by the Englishman William Somerville 1645–1742 may apply to a current American economic problem. *Non-American investors with "ready money" pour some of it as much as $1.3 trillion in recent years into the United States. *Stocks and bonds, savings deposits, service companies, factories, artworks, political campaigns the investments of foreigners are varied and grow more numerous every day. Proponents of foreign investment argue that it revives industry, strengthens the economy, creates jobs more than 3 million, they say, and encourages free trade among nations. Opponents caution that the risks associated with heavy foreign investment namely decreased profits at home and increased political influence from outside may ultimately weaken the economy. On both sides, it seems, "the learned say, 'Tis ready money makes the man or country." The question is, whose money theirs or ours?

VI

Spelling and Mechanics

45 Spelling

What can a poor speller do?

You can train yourself to spell better by following this chapter's tips for pinpointing and fixing your spelling problems. But you can improve your spelling instantly by adopting three habits:

- Carefully proofread all of your writing.
- Be suspicious of your spellings.
- Check a dictionary *every time* you doubt a spelling.

Note A word processor's spelling checker can help you find and track spelling errors in your papers. But its usefulness is limited, mainly because it can't spot the confusion of words with similar spellings, such as *their/they're/there* and *principal/principle.* A grammar and style checker may flag such words, but only the ones listed in its dictionary, and you still must select the correct spelling. Proofread your papers yourself to catch spelling errors. See pages 41–43 for more on spelling checkers and grammar and style checkers.

45a Anticipate typical spelling problems.

Misspellings often result from misleading pronunciation, different forms of the same word, and the confusion of British and American spellings.

1 • Pronunciation

In English, unlike some other languages, pronunciation of words is an unreliable guide to their spelling. The same letter or combination of letters may have different sounds in different words. (Say aloud these different ways of pronouncing the letters *ough: tough, dough, cough, through, bough.*) In addition, some words contain letters that are not pronounced clearly or at all, such as the *ed* in *asked,* the silent *e* in *swipe,* or the unpronounced *gh* in *tight*. Pronunciation is especially misleading with **homonyms,** words that are pronounced the same but spelled differently. Some homonyms and near-homonyms appear in the opposite box.

http://www.ablongman.com/littlebrown
➤ Punctuation, spelling, and mechanics
➤ Web exercises ➤ Exer. 14
➤ Downloads ➤ Chapter 45 exercises in electronic format
➤ Web links ➤ Spelling

Words commonly confused

accept (to receive)
except (other than)

affect (to have an influence on)
effect (result)

all ready (prepared)
already (by this time)

allusion (indirect reference)
illusion (erroneous belief or perception)

ascent (a movement up)
assent (agreement)

bare (unclothed)
bear (to carry, or an animal)

board (a plane of wood)
bored (uninterested)

brake (stop)
break (smash)

buy (purchase)
by (next to)

cite (to quote an authority)
sight (the ability to see)
site (a place)

desert (to abandon)
dessert (after-dinner course)

discreet (reserved, respectful)
discrete (individual, distinct)

fair (average, or lovely)
fare (a fee for transportation)

forth (forward)
fourth (after *third*)

hear (to perceive by ear)
here (in this place)

heard (past tense of *hear*)
herd (a group of animals)

hole (an opening)
whole (complete)

its (possessive of *it*)
it's (contraction of *it is*)

know (to be certain)
no (the opposite of *yes*)

meat (flesh)
meet (encounter)

passed (past tense of *pass*)
past (after, or a time gone by)

patience (forbearance)
patients (persons under medical care)

peace (the absence of war)
piece (a portion of something)

plain (clear)
plane (a carpenter's tool, or an airborne vehicle)

presence (the state of being at hand)
presents (gifts)

principal (most important, or the head of a school)
principle (a basic truth or law)

rain (precipitation)
reign (to rule)
rein (a strap for an animal)

right (correct)
rite (a religious ceremony)
write (to make letters)

road (a surface for driving)
rode (past tense of *ride*)

scene (where an action occurs)
seen (past participle of *see*)

stationary (unmoving)
stationery (writing paper)

their (possessive of *they*)
there (opposite of *here*)
they're (contraction of *they are*)

to (toward)
too (also)
two (following *one*)

waist (the middle of the body)
waste (discarded material)

weak (not strong)
week (Sunday through Saturday)

(continued)

Words commonly confused
(continued)

weather (climate)
whether (*if,* or introducing a choice)

which (one of a group)
witch (a sorcerer)

who's (contraction of *who is*)
whose (possessive of *who*)

your (possessive of *you*)
you're (contraction of *you are*)

2 • Different forms of the same word

Spellings often differ for the same word's noun and verb forms or noun and adjective forms: for example, *advice* (noun) and *advise* (verb); *height* (noun) and *high* (adjective). Similar changes occur in the parts of some irregular verbs (*know, knew, known*) and the plurals of irregular nouns (*man, men*).

3 • American vs. British spellings CULTURE LANGUAGE

If you learned English outside the United States, you may be accustomed to British rather than American spellings. Here are the chief differences:

American	British
color, humor	colour, humour
theater, center	theatre, centre
canceled, traveled	cancelled, travelled
judgment	judgement
realize, civilize	realise, civilise
connection	connexion

Your dictionary may list both spellings, but it will specially mark the British one with *chiefly Brit* or a similar label.

45b Follow spelling rules.

1 • *ie* vs. *ei*

To distinguish between *ie* and *ei,* use the familiar jingle:

I before *e,* except after *c,* or when pronounced "ay" as in *neighbor* and *weigh.*

i **before** ***e***	believe	thief	hygiene
ei **after** ***c***	ceiling	conceive	perceive
ei **sounded as "ay"**	sleigh	eight	beige

Exceptions For some exceptions, remember this sentence:

The weird foreigner neither seizes leisure nor forfeits height.

2 • Final *e*

When adding an ending to a word with a final *e,* drop the *e* if the ending begins with a vowel:

advise + able = advisable surprise + ing = surprising

Keep the *e* if the ending begins with a consonant:

care + ful = careful like + ly = likely

Exceptions Retain the *e* after a soft *c* or *g,* to keep the sound of the consonant soft rather than hard: *courageous, changeable.* And drop the *e* before a consonant when the *e* is preceded by another vowel: *argue + ment = argument, true + ly = truly.*

3 • Final *y*

When adding an ending to a word with a final *y,* change the *y* to *i* if it follows a consonant:

beauty, beauties worry, worried supply, supplies

But keep the *y* if it follows a vowel, if it ends a proper name, or if the ending is *-ing:*

day, days Minsky, Minskys cry, crying

4 • Final consonants

When adding an ending to a one-syllable word ending in a consonant, double the final consonant when it follows a single vowel. Otherwise, don't double the consonant.

slap, slapping park, parking pair, paired

In words of more than one syllable, double the final consonant when it follows a single vowel *and* ends a stressed syllable once the new ending is added. Otherwise, don't double the consonant.

refer, referring refer, reference relent, relented

5 • Prefixes

When adding a prefix, do not drop a letter from or add a letter to the original word:

unnecessary disappoint misspell

6 • Plurals

Most nouns form plurals by adding *s* to the singular form. Add *es* for the plural of nouns ending in *s, sh, ch,* or *x.*

boy, boys   kiss, kisses   church, churches

Nouns ending in *o* preceded by a vowel usually form the plural with *s.* Those ending in *o* preceded by a consonant usually form the plural with *es.*

ratio, ratios   hero, heroes

Some very common nouns form irregular plurals.

child, children   woman, women   mouse, mice

Some English nouns that were originally Italian, Greek, Latin, or French form the plural according to their original language:

analysis, analyses	criterion, criteria	piano, pianos
basis, bases	datum, data	thesis, theses
crisis, crises	medium, media	

A few such nouns may form irregular *or* regular plurals: for instance, *index, indices, indexes; curriculum, curricula, curriculums.* The regular plural is more contemporary.

With compound nouns, add *s* to the main word of the compound. Sometimes this main word is not the last word.

city-states   fathers-in-law   passersby

CULTURE LANGUAGE Noncount nouns do not form plurals, either regularly (with an added *s*) or irregularly. Examples of noncount nouns are *equipment, intelligence,* and *wealth.* See pages 301–02.

sp 45b

EXERCISE 45.1
Using correct spellings

Select the correct spelling from the choices in brackets, referring as needed to the list of words on pages 383–84, the preceding rules, or a dictionary. Answers to starred items appear at the end of the book.

Example:

The boat [passed, past] us so fast that we rocked violently in [its, it's] wake.

The boat passed us so fast that we rocked violently in its wake.

*1. Science [affects, effects] many [important, importent] aspects of our lives.
*2. Many people have a [pore, poor] understanding of the [role, roll] of scientific breakthroughs in [their, they're] health.
*3. Many people [beleive, believe] that [docters, doctors], more than science, are [responsable, responsible] for [improvements, improvments] in health care.
*4. But scientists in the [labratory, laboratory] have made crucial steps in the search for [knowlege, knowledge] about health and [medecine, medicine].
*5. For example, one scientist [who's, whose] discoveries have [affected, effected] many people is Ulf Von Euler.

6. In the 1950s Von Euler's discovery of certain hormones [lead, led] to the invention of the birth control pill.
7. Von Euler's work was used by John Rock, who [developed, developped] the first birth control pill and influenced family [planing, planning].
8. Von Euler also discovered the [principal, principle] neurotransmitter that controls the heartbeat.
9. Another scientist, Hans Selye, showed what [affect, effect] stress can have on the body.
10. His findings have [lead, led] to methods of [baring, bearing] stress.

EXERCISE 45.2
Working with a spelling checker

Try your computer's spelling checker on the following jingle, drawn from the *Bulletin of the Missouri Council of Teachers of Mathematics.* Type the jingle or download it from this book's Web site (see the box on p. 382), and run it through your spelling checker. Then proofread the jingle to correct the errors missed by the checker. Answers to the starred lines appear at the end of the book. (Hint: There are thirteen errors in all.)

* I have a spelling checker,
* It came with my PC;
* It plainly marks four my revue
* Mistakes I cannot sea.
I've run this poem threw it,
I'm sure your please too no.
Its letter perfect in it's weigh,
My checker tolled me sew.

sp 45

46 The Hyphen

Where do hyphens go?

Hyphens belong in some compound words and with some prefixes and suffixes. They also divide words at the ends of lines.

46a Use the hyphen in some compound words.

hyph 46a

1 • Compound adjectives

When two or more words serve together as a single modifier before a noun, a hyphen forms the modifying words clearly into a unit.

> She is a well-known actor.
> Some Spanish-speaking students work as translators.

When such a compound adjective follows the noun, the hyphen is unnecessary.

> The actor is well known.
> Many students are Spanish speaking.

The hyphen is also unnecessary in a compound modifier containing an *-ly* adverb, even before the noun: *clearly defined terms.*

When part of a compound adjective appears only once in two or more parallel compound adjectives, hyphens indicate which words the reader should mentally join with the missing part.

> School-age children should have eight- or nine-o'clock bedtimes.

2 • Fractions and compound numbers

Hyphens join the numerator and denominator of fractions: *one-half, three-fourths*. Hyphens also join the parts of the whole numbers *twenty-one* to *ninety-nine*.

Key term

compound word A word expressing a combination of ideas, such as *cross-reference* or *crossroad.*

http://www.ablongman.com/littlebrown

➤ Punctuation, spelling, and mechanics
 ➤ Web exercises ➤ Exer. 15
 ➤ Downloads ➤ Chapter 46 exercise in electronic format
 ➤ Web links ➤ Hyphens

3 • Prefixes and suffixes

Do not use hyphens with prefixes except as follows:

- With the prefixes *self-*, *all-*, and *ex-*: *self-control, all-inclusive, ex-student.*
- With a prefix before a capitalized word: *un-American.*
- With a capital letter before a word: *T-shirt.*
- To prevent misreading: *de-emphasize, re-create a story.*

The only suffix that regularly requires a hyphen is *-elect,* as in *president-elect.*

46b Use the hyphen to divide words at the ends of lines.

You can avoid very short lines in your documents by dividing some words between the end of one line and the beginning of the next. You can set a word processor to divide words automatically at appropriate breaks (in the Tools menu, select Language and then Hyphenation). To divide words manually, follow these guidelines:

- Divide words only between syllables—for instance, *win-dows,* not *wi-ndows.* Check a dictionary for correct syllable breaks.
- Never divide a one-syllable word.
- Leave at least two letters on the first line and three on the second line. If a word cannot be divided to follow this rule (for instance, *a-bus-er*), don't divide it.

If you must break an electronic address—for instance, in a source citation—do so only after a slash. Do not hyphenate, because readers may perceive any added hyphen as part of the address.

Not http://www.library.miami.edu/staff/lmc/soc-
race.html

But http://www.library.miami.edu/staff/lmc/
socrace.html

EXERCISE 46.1
Using hyphens

Insert hyphens wherever they are needed, and delete them where they are not needed. If a sentence is already correct as given, circle the number preceding it. Answers to starred items appear at the end of the book.

Example:

Elephants have twelve inch long teeth, but they have only four of them.

Elephants have twelve-inch-long teeth, but they have only four of them.

*1. The African elephant is well known for its size.
*2. Both male and female African elephants can grow to a ten-foot height.
*3. The non African elephants of south central Asia are somewhat smaller.
*4. A fourteen or fifteen year old elephant has reached sexual maturity.
*5. The elephant life span is about sixty five or seventy years.
6. A newborn elephant calf weighs two to three hundred pounds.
7. It stands about thirty three inches high.
8. A two hundred pound, thirty three inch baby is quite a big baby.
9. Unfortunately, elephants are often killed for their ivory tusks, and partly as a result they are an increasingly-endangered species.
10. African governments have made tusk and ivory selling illegal.

47 Capital Letters

Is it *South* or *south?*

Although mostly straightforward, the rules for capital letters can sometimes be tricky: it's *South* for a specific geographical region (*I am from the South*) but *south* for a direction (*Birds fly south*).

The conventions described in this chapter and a desk dictionary can help you decide whether to capitalize a particular word in most writing. The social, natural, and applied sciences often require specialized capitalization for terminology, such as *Conditions A and B* or *Escherichia coli*. Consult the style guides listed on page 467 for the requirements of the disciplines.

http://www.ablongman.com/littlebrown

➤ Punctuation, spelling, and mechanics
➤ Web exercises ➤ Exer. 16
➤ Downloads ➤ Chapter 47 exercise in electronic format
➤ Web links ➤ Capitals

Note A grammar and style checker will flag overused capital letters and missing capitals at the beginnings of sentences. It will also spot missing capitals at the beginnings of proper nouns and adjectives—*if* the nouns and adjectives are in the checker's dictionary. For example, a checker caught *christianity* and *europe* but not *china* (for the country) or *Stephen king*. You'll need to proofread for capital letters on your own as well.

CULTURE LANGUAGE Conventions of capitalization vary from language to language. English, for instance, is the only language to capitalize the first-person singular pronoun (*I*), and its practice of capitalizing proper nouns but not most common nouns also distinguishes it from some other languages.

47a Capitalize the first word of every sentence.

Every writer should own a good dictionary.

When quoting other writers, you should reproduce the capital letters beginning their sentences or indicate that you have altered the source's capitalization. Whenever possible, integrate the quotation into your own sentence so that its capitalization coincides with yours. The following examples quote from the sentence "Psychotherapists often overlook the benefits of self-deception."

> "Psychotherapists often overlook the benefits of self-deception," the author argues.
>
> The author argues that "the benefits of self-deception" are not always recognized by psychotherapists. [Do not capitalize a phrase quoted from inside a sentence.]

If you need to alter the capitalization in the source, indicate the change with brackets:

> "[T]he benefits of self-deception" are not always recognized by psychotherapists, the author argues.
>
> The author argues that "[p]sychotherapists often overlook the benefits of self-deception."

Note Capitalization of questions in a series is optional. Both of the following examples are correct:

> Is the population a hundred? Two hundred? More?
> Is the population a hundred? two hundred? more?

Also optional is capitalization of the first word in a complete sentence after a colon.

47b Capitalize proper nouns, proper adjectives, and words used as essential parts of proper nouns.

1 • Proper nouns and proper adjectives

Proper nouns name specific persons, places, and things: *Shakespeare, California, World War I.* **Proper adjectives** are formed from some proper nouns: *Shakespearean, Californian.* Capitalize all proper nouns and proper adjectives but not the articles (*a, an, the*) that precede them.

Proper nouns and adjectives to be capitalized

Specific persons and things

Stephen King	Boulder Dam
Napoleon Bonaparte	the Empire State Building

Specific places and geographical regions

New York City	the Mediterranean Sea
China	the Northeast, the South

But: northeast of the city, going south

Days of the week, months, holidays

Monday	Yom Kippur
May	Christmas

Government offices or departments and institutions

House of Representatives	Polk Municipal Court
Department of Defense	Northeast High School

Political, social, athletic, and other organizations and associations and their members

Democratic Party, Democrats	League of Women Voters
Sierra Club	Boston Celtics
B'nai B'rith	Chicago Symphony Orchestra

Races, nationalities, and their languages

Native American	Germans
African American	Swahili
Caucasian	Italian

But: blacks, whites

Religions, their followers, and terms for the sacred

Christianity, Christians	God
Catholicism, Catholics	Allah
Judaism, Orthodox Jews	the Bible [*but* biblical]
Islam, Muslims	the Koran, the Qur'an

Historical events, documents, periods, movements

the Vietnam War
the Constitution
the Renaissance
the Romantic Movement

2 • Common nouns used as essential parts of proper nouns

Capitalize the common nouns *street, avenue, park, river, ocean, lake, company, college, county,* and *memorial* when they are part of proper nouns naming specific places or institutions:

Main Street
Central Park
Mississippi River
Ford Motor Company
Madison College
George Washington Memorial

3 • Compass directions

Capitalize compass directions only when they name a specific region instead of a general direction:

Students from the West often melt in eastern humidity.

4 • Relationships

Capitalize the names of relationships only when they precede or replace proper names:

Our aunt scolded us for disrespecting Father and Uncle Jake.

5 • Titles with persons' names

Before a person's name, capitalize his or her title. After or apart from the name, do not capitalize the title.

Professor Otto Osborne
Doctor Jane Covington
Governor Ella Moore
Otto Osborne, a professor
Jane Covington, a doctor
Ella Moore, the governor

Note Many writers capitalize a title denoting very high rank even when it follows a name or is used alone: *Lyndon Johnson, past President of the United States.*

47c Capitalize most words in titles and subtitles of works.

Within your text, capitalize all the words in a title *except* the following: articles (*a, an, the*); *to* in infinitives; and connecting words (prepositions and conjunctions) of fewer than five letters. Capitalize even these short words when they are the first or last word in a title or when they fall after a colon or semicolon.

"Courtship Through the Ages"
A Diamond Is Forever
"Knowing Whom to Ask"
Learning from Las Vegas
"On the Town"
Management: A New Theory
"Once More to the Lake"
An End to Live For
"The Origins of Laughter"
File Under Architecture

Note The style guides of the academic disciplines have their own rules for capitals in titles. For instance, MLA style for English and some other humanities capitalizes all subordinating conjunctions but no prepositions. In addition, APA style for the social sciences capitalizes only the first word and proper names in book and article titles within source citations (see p. 523).

47d Use capitals according to convention in online communication.

Although common in electronic mail and other online communication, passages or whole messages written in all-capital letters or with no capital letters are difficult to read. Further, messages in all-capital letters may be taken as overly insistent, even rude (see also p. 138). Use capital letters according to rules 47a–47c in all your online communication.

EXERCISE 47.1
Revising: Capitals

Edit the following sentences to correct errors in capitalization. Consult a dictionary if you are in doubt. If a sentence is already correct as given, circle the number preceding it. Answers to starred items appear at the end of the book.

Example:

The first book on the reading list is mark twain's *a connecticut yankee in king arthur's court.*

The first book on the reading list is Mark Twain's *A Connecticut Yankee in King Arthur's Court.*

*1. San Antonio, texas, is a thriving city in the southwest.
*2. The city has always offered much to tourists interested in the roots of spanish settlement in the new world.
*3. The alamo is one of five Catholic Missions built by Priests to convert native americans and to maintain spain's claims in the area.
*4. But the alamo is more famous for being the site of an 1836 battle that helped to create the republic of Texas.

*5. Many of the nearby Streets, such as Crockett street, are named for men who died in that Battle.
6. The Hemisfair plaza and the San Antonio river link tourist and convention facilities.
7. Restaurants, Hotels, and shops line the River. the haunting melodies of "Una paloma blanca" and "malagueña" lure passing tourists into Casa rio and other mexican restaurants.
8. The university of Texas at San Antonio has expanded, and a Medical Center lies in the Northwest part of the city.
9. Sea World, on the west side of San Antonio, entertains grandparents, fathers and mothers, and children with the antics of dolphins and seals.
10. The City has attracted high-tech industry, creating a corridor between san antonio and austin.

48 Underlining or Italics

Is it Hamlet or *Hamlet* or "Hamlet"?

As a work that appears independently—a play—*Hamlet* should be italicized or underlined, depending on the preference of your instructor or the discipline you're writing in. (Quotation marks are used for shorter works; see p. 371.) This chapter provides general guidelines for using underlining or italics.

If you underline two or more words in a row, underline the space between the words, too: Criminal Statistics: Misuses and Numbers.

Note Grammar and style checkers cannot recognize problems with underlining or italics. Check your work yourself to ensure that you have used highlighting appropriately.

48a Use underlining or italics consistently and appropriately for your writing situation.

Word processors have made italic type possible in papers and other documents, and it is now used almost universally in business

http://www.ablongman.com/littlebrown
➤ Punctuation, spelling, and mechanics
  ➤ Web exercises ➤ Exer. 17
  ➤ Downloads ➤ Chapter 48 exercise in electronic format
  ➤ Web links ➤ Underlining or italics

and academic writing. Still, some academic style guides, notably the *MLA Handbook,* continue to prefer underlining, especially in source citations. Ask your instructor for his or her preference. (Underlining is used for the examples in this chapter because it is easier to see than italics.)

Depending on your instructor's preferences, use either italics or underlining consistently throughout a document. For instance, if you are writing an English paper and following MLA style for underlining in source citations, use underlining in the body of your paper as well.

48b Underline or italicize the titles of works that appear independently.

Within your text underline or italicize the titles of works, such as books and periodicals, that are published, released, or produced separately from other works. (See the box below.) Use quotation marks for all other titles, such as songs, essays, short stories, articles in periodicals, and pages of Web sites. (See p. 371.)

Titles to be underlined or italicized

Other titles should be placed in quotation marks (see p. 371).

Books
War and Peace
And the Band Played On

Plays
Hamlet
The Phantom of the Opera

Web sites
Friends of Prufrock
Google

Computer software
Microsoft Internet Explorer
Acrobat Reader

Pamphlets
The Truth About Alcoholism

Long musical works
Tchaikovsky's Swan Lake
But: Symphony in C

Television and radio programs
The Shadow
NBC Sports Hour

Long poems
Beowulf
Paradise Lost

Periodicals
Time
Philadelphia Inquirer

Published speeches
Lincoln's Gettysburg Address

Movies and videos
Schindler's List
How to Relax

Works of visual art
Michelangelo's David
the Mona Lisa

Exceptions Legal documents, the Bible, the Koran, and their parts are generally not underlined or italicized:

We studied the Book of Revelation in the Bible.

48c Underline or italicize the names of ships, aircraft, spacecraft, and trains.

Challenger	*Orient Express*	*Queen Elizabeth 2*
Apollo XI	*Montrealer*	*Spirit of St. Louis*

48d Underline or italicize foreign words that are not part of the English language.

A foreign expression should be underlined or italicized when it has not been absorbed into our language. A dictionary will say whether a word is still considered foreign to English.

The scientific name for the brown trout is *Salmo trutta*. [The Latin scientific names for plants and animals are always underlined or italicized.]

The Latin *De gustibus non est disputandum* translates roughly as "There's no accounting for taste."

48e Underline or italicize words or characters named as words.

Use underlining or italics to indicate that you are citing a character or word as a word rather than using it for its meaning. Words you are defining fall under this convention.

The word *syzygy* refers to a straight line formed by three celestial bodies, as in the alignment of the earth, sun, and moon.

Some people say *th*, as in *thought*, with a faint *s* or *f* sound.

48f Occasionally, underlining or italics may be used for emphasis.

Underlining or italics can stress an important word or phrase, especially in reporting how someone said something. But use such emphasis very rarely, or your writing may sound immature or hysterical.

48g In online communication, use alternatives for underlining or italics.

Electronic mail and other forms of online communication often do not allow conventional highlighting such as underlining or italics for the purposes described in this chapter. The program may not be able to produce the highlighting or may reserve it for a special function. (On Web sites, for instance, underlining indicates a link to another site.)

To distinguish book titles and other elements that usually require underlining or italics, type an underscore before and after the element: *Measurements coincide with those in _Joule's Handbook_.* You can also emphasize words with asterisks before and after: *I *will not* be able to attend.*

Don't use all-capital letters for emphasis; they yell too loudly. (See also p. 138.)

EXERCISE 48.1
Revising: Underlining or italics

Underline or italicize words and phrases as needed in the following sentences, or delete underlining from any words or phrases that are underlined unnecessarily. Note that some highlighting is correct as given. Answers to starred sentences appear at the end of the book.

Example:

Of Hitchcock's movies, Psycho is the scariest.
Of Hitchcock's movies, <u>Psycho</u> is the scariest.

*1. Of the many Vietnam veterans who are writers, Oliver Stone is perhaps the most famous for writing and directing the films Platoon and Born on the Fourth of July.

*2. Tim O'Brien has written short stories for Esquire, GQ, and Massachusetts Review.

*3. Going After Cacciato is O'Brien's dreamlike novel about the horrors of combat.

*4. The word Vietnam is technically two words (<u>Viet</u> and <u>Nam</u>), but most American writers spell it as <u>one</u> word.

*5. American writers use words or phrases borrowed from Vietnamese, such as di di mau ("go quickly") or dinky dau ("crazy").

6. Philip Caputo's <u>gripping</u> account of his service in Vietnam appears in the book A Rumor of War.

7. Caputo's book was made into a television movie, also titled <u>A Rumor of War</u>.

8. <u>David Rabe's</u> plays—including The Basic Training of Pavlo Hummel, Streamers, and Sticks and Bones—depict the effects of the war <u>not only</u> on the soldiers <u>but</u> on their families.

9. Called the <u>poet laureate of the Vietnam war</u>, Steve Mason has

published two collections of poems: Johnny's Song and Warrior for Peace.
10. The Washington Post published rave reviews of Veteran's Day, an autobiography by Rod Kane.

49 Abbreviations

Is it *in.* or *inch?* Is it *dr.* or *doctor?*

In academic writing, appropriate abbreviations depend partly on the discipline: *in.* might be a suitable abbreviation in the text of a technical document, but not in a nontechnical document. Appropriate abbreviations also depend on context: *dr.* is okay before a noun (*Dr. Jones*) but not otherwise (*The doctor is in*).

The guidelines in this chapter pertain to the text of a nontechnical document. Consult one of the style guides listed on page 467 for the requirements of the discipline you are writing in.

Usage varies, but writers increasingly omit periods from abbreviations of two or more words written in all-capital letters: *US, BA, USMC.* See page 337 on punctuating abbreviations.

Note A grammar and style checker may flag some abbreviations, such as *ft.* (for *foot*) and *st.* (for *street*). A spelling checker will flag abbreviations it does not recognize. But neither checker can judge whether an abbreviation is appropriate for your writing situation.

49a Use standard abbreviations for titles immediately before and after proper names.

ab 49a

Before the name	After the name
Dr. James Hsu	James Hsu, MD
Mr., Mrs., Ms., Hon.,	DDS, DVM, PhD,
St., Rev., Msgr., Gen.	EdD, OSB, SJ, Sr., Jr.

Do not use abbreviations such as *Rev., Hon., Prof., Rep., Sen., Dr.,* and *St.* (for *Saint*) unless they appear before a proper name.

http://www.ablongman.com/littlebrown
➤ Punctuation, spelling, and mechanics
➤ Web exercises ➤ Exer. 18
➤ Downloads ➤ Chapter 49 exercise in electronic format
➤ Web links ➤ Abbreviations

49b Familiar abbreviations and acronyms are acceptable in most writing.

An **acronym** is an abbreviation that spells a pronounceable word, such as WHO, NATO, and AIDS. These and other abbreviations using initials are acceptable in most writing as long as they are familiar to readers.

Institutions	LSU, UCLA, TCU
Organizations	CIA, FBI, YMCA, AFL-CIO
Corporations	IBM, CBS, ITT
People	JFK, LBJ, FDR
Countries	US, USA

Note If a name or term (such as *operating room*) appears often in a piece of writing, then its abbreviation (*OR*) can cut down on extra words. Spell out the full term at its first appearance, indicate its abbreviation in parentheses, and then use the abbreviation.

49c Use *BC, AD, AM, PM, no.,* and *$* only with specific dates and numbers.

44 BC	11:26 AM (*or* a.m.)	no. 36 (*or* No. 36)
AD 1492	8:05 PM (*or* p.m.)	$7.41

The abbreviation BC ("before Christ") always follows a date, whereas AD (*anno Domini,* Latin for "in the year of the Lord") precedes a date.

Note BCE ("before the common era") and CE ("common era") are increasingly replacing BC and AD, respectively. Both follow the date: *44 BCE, 1492 CE.*

49d Generally reserve Latin abbreviations for source citations and comments in parentheses.

i.e.	*id est:* that is
cf.	*confer:* compare
e.g.	*exempli gratia:* for example
et al.	*et alii:* and others
etc.	*et cetera:* and so forth
NB	*nota bene:* note well

He said he would be gone a fortnight (i.e., two weeks).
Bloom et al., editors, *Anthology of Light Verse*
Trees, too, are susceptible to disease (e.g., Dutch elm disease).

(Note that the preceding abbreviations are generally not italicized or underlined.)

49e Use *Inc., Bros., Co.,* or & (for *and*) only in official names of business firms.

Not The Santini bros. operate a large moving firm in New York City & environs.

But The Santini brothers operate a large moving firm in New York City and environs.

Or Santini Bros. is a large moving firm in New York City and environs.

49f Generally spell out units of measurement and names of places, calendar designations, people, and courses.

In most academic, general, and business writing, the types of words listed below should always be spelled out. (In source citations and technical writing, however, the first three categories are more often abbreviated.)

Units of measurement

The dog is thirty inches [not in.] high.

Geographical names

The publisher is in Massachusetts [not Mass. or MA].

Names of days, months, and holidays

The truce was signed on Tuesday [not Tues.], April [not Apr.] 16.

Names of people

Robert [not Robt.] Frost writes accessible poems.

Courses of instruction

I'm majoring in political science [not poli. sci.].

EXERCISE 49.1
Revising: Abbreviations

Revise the following sentences as needed to correct inappropriate use of abbreviations for nontechnical writing. If a sentence is already correct as given, circle the number preceding it. Answers to starred items appear at the end of the book.

Example:

One prof. lectured for five hrs.
One professor lectured for five hours.

*1. In an issue of *Science* magazine, Dr. Virgil L. Sharpton discusses a theory that could help explain the extinction of dinosaurs.
*2. About 65 mill. yrs. ago, a comet or asteroid crashed into the earth.
*3. The result was a huge crater about 10 km. (6.2 mi.) deep in the Gulf of Mex.
*4. Sharpton's new measurements suggest that the crater is 50 pct. larger than scientists had previously believed.
*5. Indeed, 20-yr.-old drilling cores reveal that the crater is about 186 mi. wide, roughly the size of Conn.

6. The space object was traveling more than 100,000 miles per hour and hit earth with the impact of 100 to 300 megatons of TNT.
7. On impact, 200,000 cubic km. of rock and soil were vaporized or thrown into the air.
8. That's the equivalent of 2.34 bill. cubic ft. of matter.
9. The impact would have created 400-ft. tidal waves across the Atl. Ocean, temps. higher than 20,000 degs., and powerful earthquakes.
10. Sharpton theorizes that the dust, vapor, and smoke from this impact blocked the sun's rays for mos., cooled the earth, and thus resulted in the death of the dinosaurs.

50 Numbers

Is it *28* or *twenty-eight?*

num 50

Expressing numbers in numerals (*28*) or in words (*twenty-eight*) is often a matter of style in a discipline: the technical disciplines more often prefer numerals, and the nontechnical disciplines more often prefer words. All disciplines use many more numerals in source citations than in the document text.

Note Grammar and style checkers will flag numerals beginning sentences and can be customized to ignore or to look for numerals. But they can't tell you whether numerals or spelled-out numbers are appropriate for your writing situation.

http://www.ablongman.com/littlebrown

➤ Punctuation, spelling, and mechanics
➤ Web exercises ➤ Exer. 19
➤ Downloads ➤ Chapter 50 exercise in electronic format
➤ Web links ➤ Numbers

50a Use numerals according to standard practice in the field you are writing in.

Always use numerals for numbers that require more than two words to spell out:

> The leap year has 366 days.
> The population of Minot, North Dakota, is about 32,800.

In nontechnical academic writing, spell out numbers of one or two words:

> Twelve nations signed the treaty.
>
> The ball game drew forty-two thousand people. [A hyphenated number may be considered one word.]

In much business writing, use numerals for all numbers over ten: *five reasons, 11 participants.* In technical academic and business writing, such as in science and engineering, use numerals for all numbers over ten, and use numerals for zero through nine when they refer to exact measurements: *2 liters, 1 hour.* (Consult one of the style guides listed on p. 467 for more details.)

Note Use a combination of numerals and words for round numbers over a million: *26 million, 2.45 billion.* And use either all numerals or all words when several numbers appear together in a passage, even if convention would require a mixture.

CULTURE LANGUAGE In standard American English, a comma separates the numerals in long numbers (*26,000*), and a period functions as a decimal point (*2.06*).

num 50b

50b Use numerals according to convention for dates, addresses, and other information.

Days and years

June 18, 1985 AD 12 456 BC 1999

Pages, chapters, volumes, acts, scenes, lines

Chapter 9, page 123
Hamlet, act 5, scene 3

Decimals, percentages, and fractions

22.5 $3\frac{1}{2}$
48% (*or* 48 percent)

Addresses

355 Clinton Avenue
Washington, DC 20036

Scores and statistics

21 to 7 a ratio of 8 to 1
a mean of 26

Exact amounts of money

$3.5 million $4.50

The time of day

9:00 AM 3:45 PM

Exceptions Round dollar or cent amounts of only a few words may be expressed in words: *seventeen dollars; sixty cents.* When the word *o'clock* is used for the time of day, also express the number in words: *two o'clock* (not *2 o'clock*).

50c Spell out numbers that begin sentences.

For clarity, spell out any number that begins a sentence. If the number requires more than two words, reword the sentence so that the number falls later and can be expressed as a numeral.

Not 3.7 billion people live in Asia.
But The population of Asia is 3.7 billion.

EXERCISE 50.1
Revising: Numbers

Revise the following sentences so that numbers are used appropriately for nontechnical writing. If a sentence is already correct as given, circle the number preceding it. Answers to starred items appear at the end of the book.

Example:

Addie paid two hundred and five dollars for used scuba gear.
Addie paid $205 for used scuba gear.

*1. The planet Saturn is nine hundred million miles, or nearly one billion five hundred million kilometers, from the sun.
*2. A year on Saturn equals almost thirty of our years.
*3. Thus, Saturn orbits the sun only two and four-tenths times during the average human life span.
*4. It travels in its orbit at about twenty-one thousand six hundred miles per hour.
*5. 15 to 20 times denser than Earth's core, Saturn's core measures 17,000 miles across.
6. The temperature at Saturn's cloud tops is minus one hundred seventy degrees Fahrenheit.
7. In nineteen hundred thirty-three, astronomers found on Saturn's surface a huge white spot 2 times the size of Earth and 7 times the size of Mercury.
8. Saturn's famous rings reflect almost seventy percent of the sunlight that approaches the planet.
9. The ring system is almost forty thousand miles wide, beginning 8,800 miles from the planet's visible surface and ending forty-seven thousand miles from that surface.
10. Saturn generates about one hundred thirty trillion kilowatts of electricity.

VII

Research and Documentation

51 Research Strategy

How should I approach and manage a research project?

Like many writers, you may find it helpful to approach research writing as a detective approaches a new case. The mystery is the answer to a question you care about. The search for an answer leads you to consider what others think about your subject, but you do more than simply report their views. You build on them to develop and support your own opinion.

Your investigation will be more productive and enjoyable if you take some steps described in this chapter: plan your work (below), keep a research journal (facing page), find an appropriate subject and research question (p. 408), set goals for your research (p. 410), and keep a working bibliography (p. 412).

51a Plan the research process.

Research writing is a *writing* process:

- You work within a particular situation of subject, purpose, audience, and other factors (see Chapter 1).
- You gather ideas and information about your subject (Chapter 2).
- You focus and arrange your ideas (Chapter 3).
- You draft to explore your meaning (Chapter 4).
- You revise and edit to develop, shape, and polish (Chapter 5).

Although the process seems neatly sequential in this list, you know from experience that the stages overlap—that, for instance, you may begin drafting before you've gathered all the information you expect to find, and then while drafting you may discover a source that causes you to rethink your approach. Anticipating the process of research writing can free you to be flexible in your search and open to discoveries.

http://www.ablongman.com/littlebrown
➤ Research writing
  ➤ Video tutorials ➤ Finding source information
  ➤ Web exercises ➤ Exer. 1
  ➤ Downloads
    ➤ Scheduling steps in research writing
    ➤ Information for a working bibliography
  ➤ Web links ➤ Planning a research project

A thoughtful plan and systematic procedures can help you follow through on the diverse activities of research writing. One step is to make a schedule like the one below that apportions the available time to the necessary work. You can estimate that each segment marked off by a horizontal line will occupy *roughly* one-quarter of the total time—for example, a week in a four-week assignment. The most unpredictable segments are the first two, so it's wise to get started early enough to accommodate the unexpected.

Complete by:

______ 1. Setting a schedule and beginning a research journal (here and below)
______ 2. Finding a researchable subject and question (next page)
______ 3. Setting goals for sources (p. 410)
______ 4. Finding sources, both print and electronic (p. 415), and making a working bibliography (p. 412)

______ 5. Evaluating and synthesizing sources (pp. 437, 445)
______ 6. Gathering information from sources, often using summary, paraphrase, and direct quotation (p. 447)
______ 7. Taking steps to avoid plagiarism (p. 459)

______ 8. Developing a thesis statement and creating a structure (p. 468)
______ 9. Drafting the paper (p. 469), integrating summaries, paraphrases, and direct quotations into your ideas (p. 453)

______ 10. Revising and editing the paper (p. 470)
______ 11. Citing sources in your text (p. 466)
______ 12. Preparing the list of works cited or references (p. 466)
______ 13. Preparing the final manuscript (p. 470)
______ Final paper due

(You can download the schedule from this book's Web site: see the box on the previous page. Use a duplicate to plan and time the specific steps of each research project you work on.)

51b Keep a research journal.

While working on a research project, carry index cards or a notebook with you at all times to use as a **research journal**, a place to record your activities and ideas. (See p. 10 on journal keeping.)

In the journal's dated entries, you can write about the sources you consult, the leads you want to pursue, any difficulties you encounter, and, most important, your thoughts about sources, leads, difficulties, new directions, relationships, and anything else that strikes you. The very act of writing in the journal can expand and clarify your thinking.

Note The research journal is the place to track and develop your own ideas. To avoid mixing up your thoughts and those of others, keep separate notes on what your sources actually say, using one of the methods discussed on pages 447–48.

51c Find a researchable subject and question.

Before reading this section, you may want to review the suggestions given in Chapter 1 for finding and narrowing a writing subject (pp. 4–6). Generally, the same procedure applies to writing any kind of research paper. However, selecting and limiting a subject for a research paper can present special opportunities and problems. And before you proceed with your subject, you'll want to transform it into a question that can guide your search for sources.

1 • Appropriate subject

Seek a research subject that interests you and that you care about. (It may be a subject you've already written about without benefit of research.) Starting with your own views will motivate you, and you will be a participant in a dialog when you begin examining sources.

When you settle on a subject, ask the following questions about it. For each requirement, there are corresponding pitfalls.

- Are ample sources of information available on the subject?

  Avoid very recent subjects, such as a newly announced medical discovery or a breaking story in today's newspaper.

- Does the subject encourage research in the kinds and number of sources required by the assignment?

  Avoid (*a*) subjects that depend entirely on personal opinion and experience, such as the virtues of your hobby, and (*b*) subjects that require research in only one source, such as a straight factual biography.

- Will the subject lead you to an objective assessment of sources and to defensible conclusions?

Avoid subjects that rest entirely on belief or prejudice, such as when human life begins or why women (or men) are superior. Your readers are unlikely to be swayed from their own beliefs.

- Does the subject suit the length of paper assigned and the time given for research and writing?

  Avoid broad subjects that have too many sources to survey adequately, such as a major event in history.

2 • Research question

Asking a question about your subject can give direction to your research by focusing your thinking on a particular approach. To discover your question, consider what about your subject intrigues or perplexes you, what you'd like to know more about. (See the next page for suggestions on using your own knowledge.)

Try to narrow your research question so that you can answer it in the time and space you have available. The question *How will the Internet affect business?* is very broad, encompassing issues as diverse as electronic commerce, information management, and employee training. In contrast, the question *How will Internet commerce benefit consumers?* or *How, if at all, should Internet commerce be taxed?* is much narrower. Each question also requires more than a simple yes-or-no answer, so that answering, even tentatively, demands thought about pros and cons, causes and effects.

As you read and write, your question will undoubtedly evolve to reflect your increasing knowledge of the subject, and eventually its answer will become your main idea, or thesis statement (see pp. 468–69).

EXERCISE 51.1
Finding a subject and question

Choose three of the following broad subjects (or three subjects of your own), and narrow each of them to at least one subject and question suitable for beginning work on a research paper. For more sample subjects, see Chapter 1, page 6.

1. Business espionage
2. The effect of television on professional sports
3. Computer piracy
4. The European exploration of North America before Columbus
5. Hazardous substances in the workplace
6. Science fiction
7. Water pollution
8. Successes in cancer research
9. Comic film actors

10. An unsolved crime
11. Immunization of children
12. Male and female heroes in modern fiction
13. Computers and the privacy of the individual
14. Gothic or romance novels in the nineteenth and twentieth centuries
15. The social responsibility of business

51d Set goals for your sources.

Before you start looking for sources, consider what you already know about your subject and where you are likely to find information on it.

1 • Your own knowledge

Discovering what you already know about your subject will guide you in discovering what you don't know and need to research. Take some time to spell out facts you have learned, opinions you have heard or read elsewhere, and of course your own opinions. Use one or more of the discovery techniques discussed in Chapter 2 to explore and develop your ideas: keeping a journal, observing your surroundings, freewriting, brainstorming, clustering, asking questions, and thinking critically.

When you've explored your thoughts, make a list of questions for which you don't have answers, whether factual (*What laws govern taxes in Internet commerce?*) or more open-ended (*Who benefits from a tax-free Internet? Who doesn't benefit?*). These questions will give you clues about the sources you need to look for first.

2 • Kinds of sources

For many research projects, you'll want to consult a mix of sources, as described below. You may start by seeking the outlines of your subject—the range and depth of opinions about it—in reference works and articles in popular periodicals or through a Web search. Then, as you refine your views and your research question, you'll move on to more specialized sources, such as scholarly books and periodicals and your own interviews or surveys. (See pp. 419–36 for more on each kind of source.)

51d

Library and Internet sources

The print and electronic sources available through your library—mainly reference works, periodicals, and books—have two big advantages over most of what you'll find on the Internet: they are cataloged and indexed for easy retrieval; and they are generally reliable, having been screened first by their publishers and then by the library's staff. In contrast, the Internet's retrieval systems are more difficult to use effectively, and Internet sources tend to be less reliable because most do not pass through any screening before being posted. (There are many exceptions, such as online scholarly journals and reference works. But these sources may be available through your library's Web site as well.)

Most instructors expect research writers to consult library sources. But they'll accept Internet sources, too, if you have used them judiciously. Even with its disadvantages, the Internet can be a valuable resource for primary sources, current information, and a diversity of views. For guidelines on evaluating both library and Internet sources, see pages 437–44.

Primary and secondary sources

As much as possible, you should rely on **primary sources**, or firsthand accounts: historical documents (letters, speeches, and so on), eyewitness reports, works of literature, reports on experiments or surveys conducted by the writer, or your own interviews, experiments, observations, or correspondence.

In contrast, **secondary sources** report and analyze information drawn from other sources, often primary ones: a reporter's summary of a controversial issue, a historian's account of a battle, a critic's reading of a poem, a physicist's evaluation of several studies. Secondary sources may contain helpful summaries and interpretations that direct, support, and extend your own thinking. However, most research-writing assignments expect your own ideas to go beyond those in such sources.

Scholarly and popular sources

The scholarship of acknowledged experts is essential for depth, authority, and specificity. Generally your instructors will expect you to emphasize scholarly sources in your research. But the general-interest views and information of popular sources can help you apply more scholarly approaches to daily life.

- *Check the publisher.* Is it a scholarly journal (such as *Education Forum*) or a publisher of scholarly books (such as Harvard University Press), or is it a popular magazine (such as *Time* or *Newsweek*) or a publisher of popular books (such as Little, Brown)?
- *Check the author.* Have you seen the name elsewhere, which might suggest that the author is an expert?
- *Check the title.* Is it technical, or does it use a general vocabulary?

- *Check the electronic address.* Addresses for Internet sources often include an abbreviation that tells you something about the source: *edu* means the source comes from an educational institution, *gov* from a government body, *org* from a nonprofit organization, *com* from a commercial organization such as a corporation. (See p. 440 for more on interpreting electronic addresses.)

Older and newer sources

Check the publication date. For most subjects a combination of older, established sources (such as books) and current sources (such as newspaper articles, interviews, or Web sites) will provide both background and up-to-date information. Only historical subjects or very current subjects require an emphasis on one extreme or another.

Impartial and biased sources

Seek a range of viewpoints. Sources that attempt to be impartial can offer an overview of your subject and trustworthy facts. Sources with clear biases can offer a diversity of opinion. Of course, to discover bias, you may have to read the source carefully (see pp. 437–44); but even a bibliographical listing can be informative.

- *Check the author.* You may have heard of the author as a respected researcher (thus more likely to be objective) or as a leading proponent of a certain view (less likely to be objective).
- *Check the title.* It may reveal something about point of view. (Consider these contrasting titles: "Keep the Internet Tax-Free" and "Taxation of Internet Commerce: Issues and Questions.")

Note Sources you find on the Internet must be approached with particular care. See pages 439–44.

Sources with helpful features

Depending on your topic and how far along your research is, you may want to look for sources with features such as illustrations (which can clarify important concepts), bibliographies (which can direct you to other sources), and indexes (which can help you develop keywords for electronic searches; see p. 416).

51e Keep a working bibliography.

To track where sources are and what they are, make a **working bibliography,** a file of books, articles, Web sites, and other possibilities. When you have a substantial file—say, ten to thirty sources—you can decide which ones seem most promising and look them up first.

1 • Source information

When you turn in your paper, you will be expected to attach a list of the sources you have used. So that readers can check or follow up on your sources, your list must include all the information needed to find the sources, in a format readers can understand. (See pp. 466–67.) The box below shows the information to record for each type of source so that you will not have to retrace your steps later. (You can download the lists in the box from this book's Web site: see the box on p. 406. Copy the list for each source you're considering, and fill in the appropriate information.)

Note Whenever possible, record source information in the correct format for the documentation style you will be using. Then you

Information for a working bibliography

For books

Library call number
Name(s) of author(s), editor(s), translator(s), or others listed
Title and subtitle
Publication data:
  Place of publication
  Publisher's name
  Date of publication
Other important data, such as edition or volume number

For periodical articles

Name(s) of author(s)
Title and subtitle of article
Title of periodical
Publication data:
  Volume number and issue number (if any) in which article appears
  Date of issue
  Page numbers on which article appears

For electronic sources

Name(s) of author(s)
Title and subtitle
Publication data for books and articles (see above)
Date of release, online posting, or latest revision
Medium (online, CD-ROM, etc.)
Format of online source (Web site, Web page, e-mail, etc.)
Date you consulted the source
Complete electronic address (unless source was obtained through a subscription service and has no permanent address)
For sources obtained through a subscription service:
  Name of database
  Name of service
  Electronic address of the service's home page *or* search terms used to reach the source

For other sources

Name(s) of author(s), government department, recording artist, or others listed
Title of the work
Format, such as unpublished letter or live performance
Publication or production data:
  Publisher's or producer's name
  Date of publication, release, or production
  Identifying numbers (if any)

will be less likely to omit needed information or to confuse numbers, dates, and other data when it's time to write your citations. This book describes two styles: MLA (p. 471) and APA (p. 517). For others, consult one of the guides listed on page 467.

2 • Bibliographic information for online sources

Unlike that for printed materials, publication information for online sources can be difficult to find and make sense of. The screen shot below shows the first page of a Web site. Circled numbers refer to the numbered explanations on the facing page:

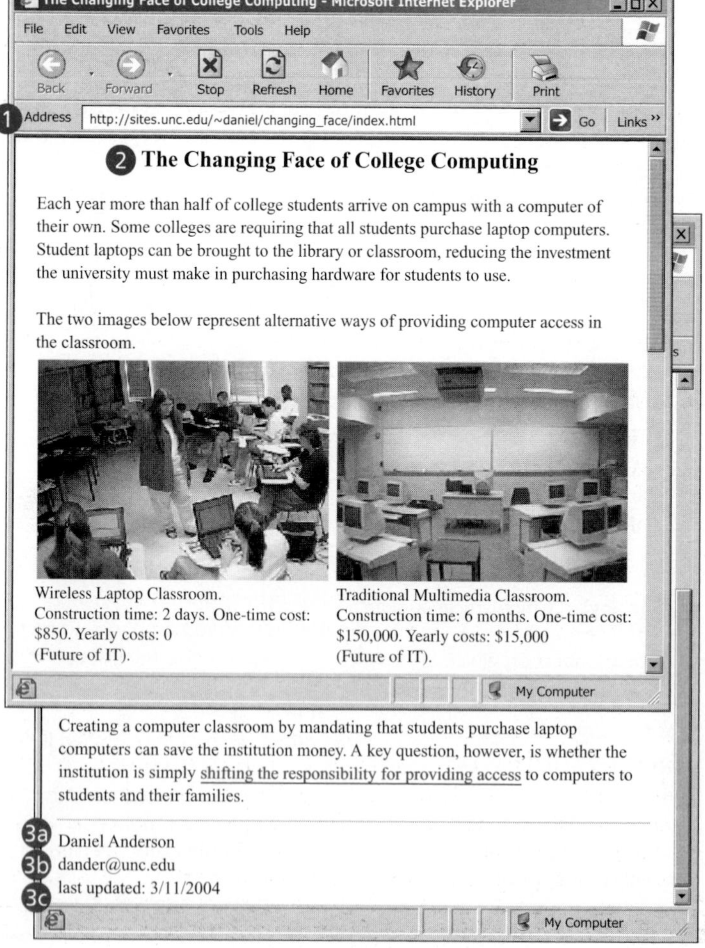

51e

1. *The source's address, or URL, usually appears in the Address or Location field of the Web browser,* near the top of the screen. If the field does not appear, adjust the settings of the browser so that it displays the field.
2. *Use as the source title the title of the page you are consulting.* This information usually appears as a heading at the top of the page or in the bar along the top of the browser window.
3. *Publication information often appears at the end of each page.* Look here for (*a*) the name of the author or the sponsoring organization, (*b*) an address for reaching the sponsor or author directly, and (*c*) the publication date or the date of the last revision.

If the page you are reading does not list publication information, look for it on the site's home page. There may be a link to the home page, or you can find it by editing the address in the Address or Location field: working backward, delete the end of the address up to the preceding slash; then hit Enter. (For the address in the screen shot, you would delete *index.html*.) If that doesn't take you to the home page, delete the end of the remaining address up to the preceding slash and hit Enter. Editing the address in this way, you'll eventually reach the home page.

When scouting a discussion list, Web forum, or newsgroup, save messages that may serve as sources, and keep track of when and where they were posted. You may be able to discover information about the author of a message from the list's archive or from an archive site such as *http://groups.google.com.* See page 434 for more on using discussion groups.

52 Finding Sources

How can I locate ideas and information about my research subject?

Your library and a computer connected to the Internet give you access to an almost infinite range of sources. The challenge, of course, is to find the most worthy and appropriate sources for your needs and then to use them effectively. This chapter shows you how to conduct electronic searches (next page) and take advantage of the print and electronic sources available to you: reference works (p. 419), books (p. 424), periodicals (p. 424), the Web (p. 428), other online sources (p. 433), pamphlets and government publications (p. 435), and your own interviews, surveys, and other primary sources (p. 435). Judging the appropriateness of sources and using them effectively are covered in Chapters 53–54.

52a Use keywords for electronic searches.

As you conduct research, the World Wide Web will be your gateway to ideas and information. You will use the Web to find many of your library's extensive resources, such as books, periodicals, and reference works. And you may use the Web to reach nonlibrary resources, such as a discussion among experts in a field or the reports of a political or environmental group. Some of these resources are trustworthy; others are not. You need to be able to recognize both the type of source you're using and its likely validity.

Note Always begin your academic research on your library's Web site, not with a search engine such as *Google*. Although a direct Web search can be productive, you'll find a higher concentration of relevant and reliable sources through the library.

1 • Kinds of electronic sources

Your school's library and the Web offer several kinds of electronic resources that are suitable for academic research:

- *The library's catalog of holdings* is a database that lists all the resources that the library owns or subscribes to: books, journals, magazines, newspapers, reference works, and more. The catalog may include not only your library's holdings but also those of other schools nearby or in your state.
- *Online databases* include indexes, bibliographies, and other reference works. They are your main route to listings of specific journal articles and book chapters. Your library subscribes to the databases and makes them available through its Web site. (You may also discover databases directly on the Web, but, again, the library is a more productive starting place.)

http://www.ablongman.com/littlebrown
➤ Research writing
  ➤ Video tutorials ➤ Using keywords with a search engine
  ➤ Web exercises ➤ Exer. 2
  ➤ Web links
    ➤ Finding sources
    ➤ General online resources
    ➤ Sources in literature and other humanities
    ➤ Sources in the social sciences
    ➤ Sources in the natural and applied sciences

Two tips for researchers

- **A reference librarian can help.** If you are unsure of how to locate or use your library, either via the Web or at the library itself, consult a reference librarian. This person is very familiar with all the library's resources and with general and specialized research techniques. It is his or her job to help you and others with research. Even very experienced researchers often consult reference librarians.
- **You may be able to borrow from other libraries.** If sources you need are not available from your library, you may be able to obtain them from another library by mail, fax, or Internet. Ask your librarian for help, and plan ahead: interlibrary loans can take a week or longer.

- *Databases on CD-ROM,* or compact disk, include the same information as online databases, but they must be read at a library computer terminal. Increasingly, libraries are providing CD-ROM databases through their Web sites or are moving away from CD-ROMs in favor of online databases.
- *Full-text resources* contain the entire contents of articles, book chapters, even whole books. Some of the library's online or CD-ROM databases provide access to the full text of listed sources. In addition, the Web sites of many periodicals and organizations, such as government agencies, offer the full text of articles, reports, and other publications.

2 • Keyword searches

Probably the most important element in an electronic search is appropriate **keywords,** or **descriptors,** that name your subject for databases and Web search engines.

Databases vs. the Web

To develop keywords it helps to understand what they do when you use them for a search. Most databases index sources by authors, titles, and publication years and also by subject headings found in each database's directory or thesaurus. Electronic databases can usually search among their listings and subjects for uses of your keywords, but they work more efficiently when you use their subject headings for keywords. You can find a database's headings for your subject in two ways: consult its directory, or first use your own keywords to locate a promising source and then use the subject headings given with the source record to find more sources.

The Web has no overall directory of keywords. Some Web search engines do categorize sites into subject directories, but they include only a small portion of the Web's offerings. Other search engines, so-called crawlers, seek your keywords in the titles, summaries, and texts of sites. Their performance depends on how well your keywords describe your subject and anticipate the words used in sources. If you describe your subject too broadly or describe it specifically but don't match the vocabulary in relevant sources, your search will turn up few relevant sources and probably many that aren't relevant.

Keyword refinement

Every database and search engine provides a system that you can use to refine your keywords for a productive search. The basic operations appear in the box below, but resources do differ. For instance, some assume that *AND* should link two or more keywords, while others provide options specifying "Must contain all the words," "May contain any of the words," and other equivalents for the operations described in the box.

Ways to refine keywords

Most databases and search engines work with **Boolean operators,** terms or symbols that allow you to expand or limit your keywords and thus your search.

- **Use *AND* or + to narrow the search** by including only sources that use all the given words. The keywords *Internet AND tax* request only the sources in the shaded area:

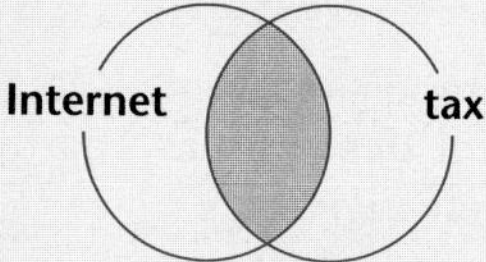

- **Use *NOT* or – ("minus") to narrow the search** by excluding irrelevant words. *Internet AND tax NOT access* excludes sources that use the word *access.*

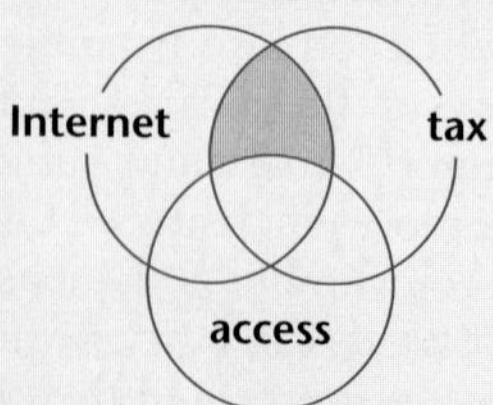

- **Use *OR* to broaden the search** by giving alternative keywords. *Internet OR (electronic commerce) AND tax* allows for sources that use *Internet* or *electronic commerce* (or both) along with *tax.*

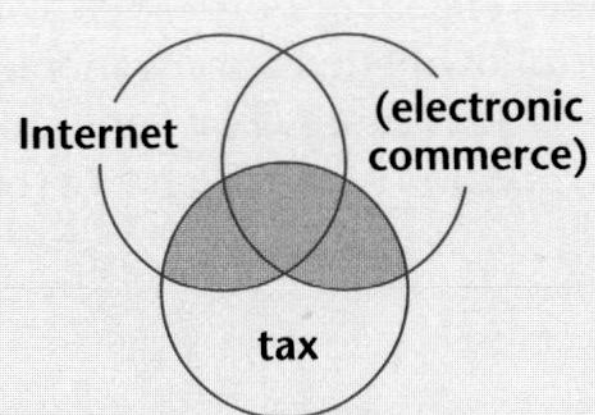

- **Use parentheses or quotation marks to form search phrases.** For instance, *(electronic commerce)* requests the exact phrase, not the separate words.
- **Use *NEAR* to narrow the search** by requiring the keywords to be close to each other—for instance, *Internet NEAR tax.* Depending on the resource you're using, the words could be directly next to each other or many words apart. Some resources use *WITHIN* __ so that you can specify the exact number of words apart—for instance, *Internet WITHIN 10 tax.*
- **Use wild cards to permit different versions of the same word.** In *child**, for instance, the wild card * indicates that sources may include *child, children, childcare, childhood, childish, childlike,* and *childproof.* If a wild card opens up your search too much (as with the example *child**), you may be better off using *OR* to limit the options: *child OR children.* (Note that some systems use ?, :, or + for a wild card instead of *.)
- **Be sure to spell your keywords correctly.** Some search tools will look for close matches or approximations, but correct spelling gives you the best chance of finding relevant sources.

Trial and error

You will probably have to use trial and error in developing your keywords, sometimes turning up few or no sources and sometimes turning up thousands of mostly irrelevant sources. But the process is not busywork—far from it. It can teach you a great deal about your subject: how you can or should narrow it, how it is and is not described by others, what others consider interesting or debatable about it, and what the major arguments are.

See pages 432–33 for a sample keyword search of the Web.

52b Consult reference works.

Reference works, often available online or on CD-ROM, include encyclopedias, dictionaries, bibliographies, indexes, and handbooks. Your research *must* go beyond these sources, but they can help you decide whether your topic really interests you and meets the requirements for a research paper (p. 408), what your keywords might be, and where to go for more detailed sources.

You'll find many reference works through your library and directly on the Web. The following lists give general and specific Web references for a range of disciplines. For additional references and updates of those below, see this book's Web site (box on p. 416).

All disciplines

Internet Public Library
http://www.ipl.org
Library of Congress
http://lcweb.loc.gov
LSU Libraries Webliography
http://www.lib.lsu.edu/weblio.html
World Wide Web Virtual Library
http://vlib.org/Overview.html

Humanities

General

BUBL Humanities Resources
http://bubl.ac.uk/link/hum.html
EDSITEment
http://edsitement.neh.gov
Voice of the Shuttle Humanities Gateway
http://vos.ucsb.edu

Art

artnet.com
http://www.artnet.com
World Wide Arts Resources
http://wwar.com/browse.html

Dance

BUBL Dance Resources
http://bubl.ac.uk/link/d/dance.htm
Google Web Directory Dance Links
http://directory.google.com/Top/Arts/Performing_Arts/Dance

Film

Definitive Online Film Resource
http://www.tdfilm.com
Internet Movie Database
http://www.imdb.com

52b

History

Best of History Web Sites
http://www.besthistorysites.net
Librarians' Index History Links
http://lii.org/search/file/history

Literature

EServer
http://eserver.org

Voice of the Shuttle Drama, Theater, and Performance Art Studies
http://vos.ucsb.edu/browse.asp?id=782
Voice of the Shuttle Literature (in English)
http://vos.ucsb.edu/browse.asp?id=3
Voice of the Shuttle Literatures (Other than English)
http://vos.ucsb.edu/browse.asp?id=2719

Music

American Music Resource
http://www.uncg.edu/~flmccart/amrhome.html
Web Resources for Study and Research in Music
http://www.ucc.ie/ucc/depts/music/online

Philosophy

Guide to Philosophy on the Internet
http://www.earlham.edu/~peters/philinks.htm
Social Science Information Gateway Philosophy Resources
http://www.sosig.ac.uk/roads/subject-listing/World-cat/philos.html

Religion

Internet Resources for the Academic Study of Religion
http://www.academicinfo.net/religindex.html
Virtual Religion Index
http://religion.rutgers.edu/vri

Theater

McCoy's Guide to Theater and Performance Studies
http://www.stetson.edu/departments/csata/thr_guid.html
Theater Connections
http://www.uncc.edu/jvanoate/theater

Social sciences

General

Social Science Data on the Internet
http://odwin.ucsd.edu/idata
Social Science Information Gateway
http://www.sosig.ac.uk
Virtual Library: Social Sciences
http://www.vlib.org/SocialSciences.html

Anthropology

Anthro.Net
http://www.anthro.net
Anthropology Resources on the Internet
http://www.anthropologie.net

Business and economics

Resources for Economics on the Internet
http://rfe.wustl.edu/EconFAQ.html
Virtual International Business and Economic Sources
http://library.uncc.edu/display/?dept=reference&format=open&page=68

Education

AskERIC
http://www.askeric.org
US Department of Education
http://www.ed.gov

Ethnic and gender studies

Diversity and Ethnic Studies Websites and Guides
http://www.public.iastate.edu/~savega/divweb2.htm
Voice of the Shuttle Gender Studies Page
http://vos.ucsb.edu/browse.asp?id=2711

Political science and law

Librarians' Index Law Resources
http://lii.org/search/file/law
Political Science Resources
http://www.psr.keele.ac.uk

Psychology

Psychology Online Resource Central
http://www.psych-central.com
Psych Web
http://www.psywww.com

Sociology

SocioWeb
http://www.socioweb.com/~markbl/socioweb
WWW Virtual Library: Sociology
http://socserv2.mcmaster.ca/w3virtsoclib

Natural and applied sciences

General

Google Web Directory Science Links
http://directory.google.com/Top/Science
Librarians' Index Science Resources
http://lii.org/search/file/scitech
Virtual Library: Science
http://www.vlib.org/Science.html

Biology

Biology Online
http://biology-online.org
National Biological Information Infrastructure
http://www.nbii.gov/index.html

Chemistry

Chemistry.org
http://www.chemistry.org/portal/Chemistry
University of Houston's Chemistry Resources
http://info.lib.uh.edu/indexes/chem.htm

Computer science

IEEE Computer Society
http://www.computer.org
University of Texas Virtual Computer Library
http://www.utexas.edu/computer/vcl

Engineering

BUBL Engineering Resources
http://link.bubl.ac.uk/engineering
Engineering Virtual Library
http://www.eevl.ac.uk

Environmental science

EE-link
http://eelink.net
EnviroLink
http://www.envirolink.org

Geology

American Geological Institute
http://www.agiweb.org
USGS Library
http://library.usgs.gov

Health sciences

Hardin Medical Information Hub
http://www.lib.uiowa.edu/hardin/md
World Health Organization
http://www.who.int

Mathematics

AMS Math on the Web
http://www.ams.org
BUBL Mathematics Resources
http://link.bubl.ac.uk/mathematics

Physics and astronomy

American Institute of Physics
http://www.aip.org
PhysicsWeb
http://www.physicsweb.org

52c Consult books.

Your library's catalog is probably stored on computer, so you can search it either at a terminal in the library or via the library's Web site. Verify with the librarian that the electronic catalog includes all the available books.

You can search the library's catalog by author or title, of course, and by your own keywords or the headings found in *Library of Congress Subject Headings* (*LCSH*). The screen shot below shows the complete record for a book, including the *LCSH* headings that can be used to find similar sources.

Full record for a book

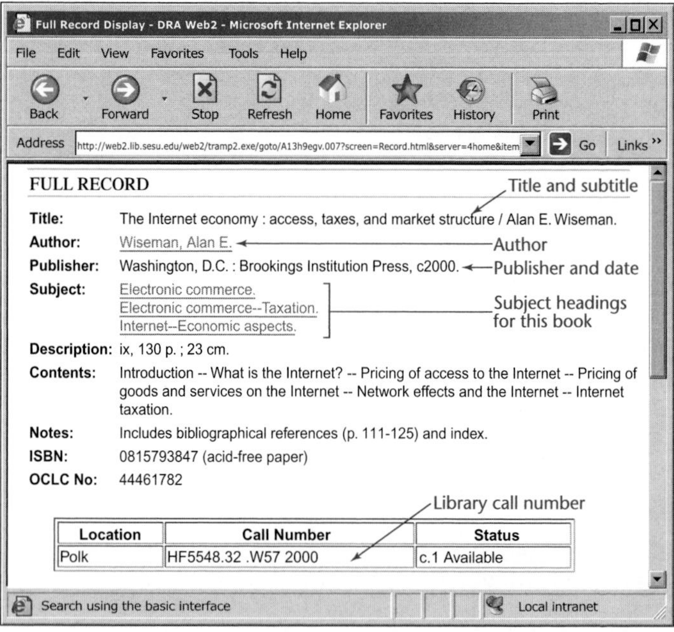

52d

52d Consult periodicals.

Periodicals include newspapers, journals, and magazines. Newspapers, the easiest to recognize, are useful for detailed accounts of past and current events. Journals and magazines can be harder to distinguish, but their differences are important. Most college instructors expect students' research to rely more on journals than on magazines.

Journals	Magazines
Examples: *American Anthropologist, Journal of Black Studies, Journal of Chemical Education*	Examples: *The New Yorker, Time, Rolling Stone, People*
Articles are intended to advance knowledge in a particular field.	Articles are intended to express opinion, inform, or entertain.
Writers and readers are specialists in the field.	Writers may or may not be specialists in their subjects. Readers are members of the general public or a subgroup with a particular interest.
Articles always include source citations.	Articles rarely include source citations.
Appearance is bland, with black-only type, little or no decoration, and only illustrations that directly amplify the text, such as graphs.	Appearance varies but is generally lively, with color, decoration (headings, sidebars, and other elements), and illustrations (drawings, photographs).
Issues may appear quarterly or less often.	Issues may appear weekly, biweekly, or monthly.
Issues may be paged separately (like a magazine) or may be paged sequentially throughout an annual volume, so that issue 3 (the third issue of the year) could open on page 327. (The method of pagination affects source citations. See p. 489.)	Issues are paged separately, each beginning on page 1.

1 • Indexes to periodicals

How indexes work

Indexes provide information on the articles in journals, magazines, and newspapers. Often these indexes include abstracts, or summaries, of the articles, and they may offer the full text of the articles as well. Your library subscribes to periodical indexes and to large databases that include multiple indexes. (See p. 428 for a list.)

The screen shots on the next two pages illustrate a sample database search. Check the library's list of indexes to find the ones that seem most appropriate for your subject. (The library's Web site may include a search function to help you with this step.) Search the indexes themselves as discussed on pages 416–19.

Note Many databases allow you to limit your search to so-called peer-reviewed or refereed journals—that is, scholarly journals whose articles have been reviewed before publication by

1. Initial keyword search of periodical database

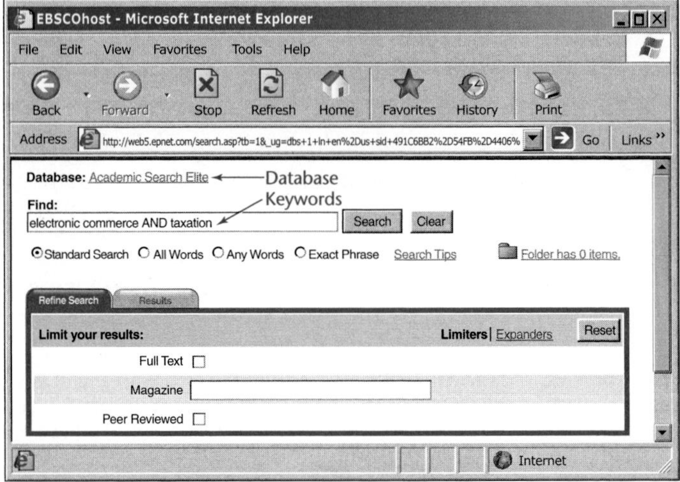

2. Partial search results

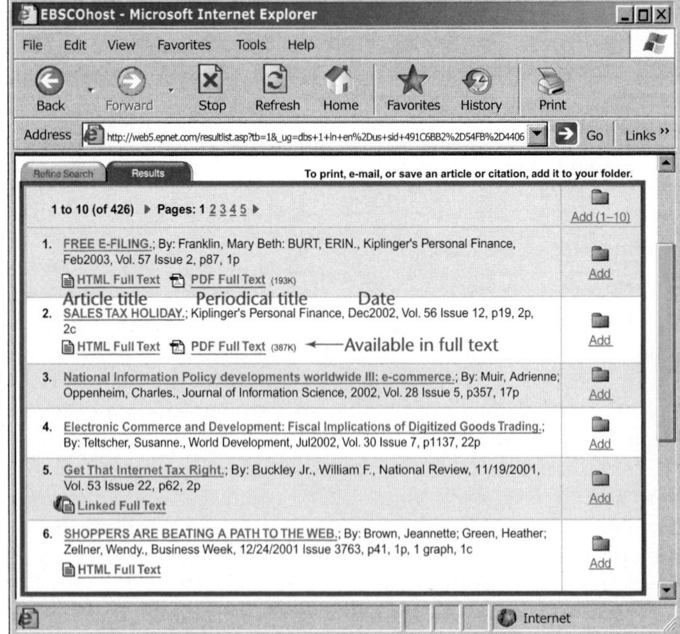

3. Full record with abstract

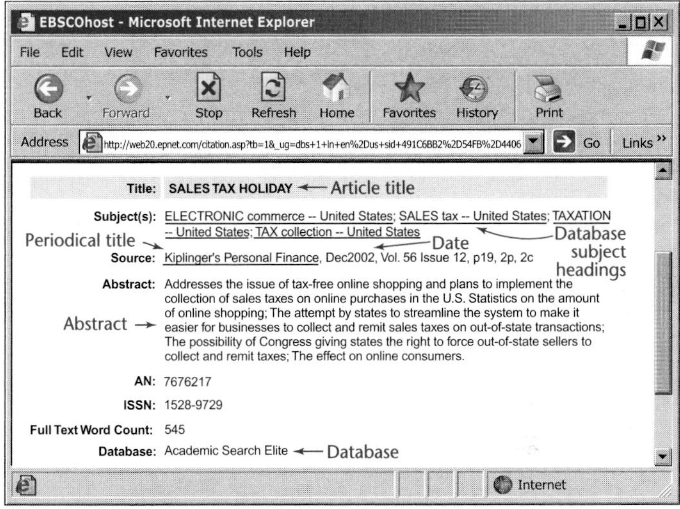

4. Full text of article

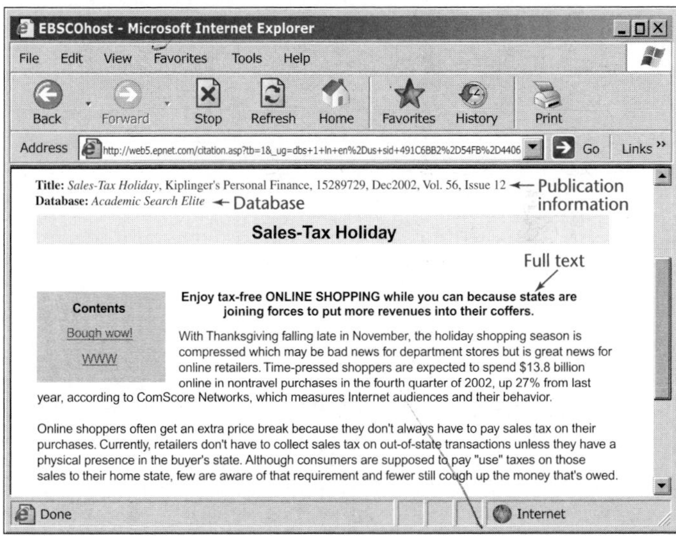

52d

experts in the field and then revised by the author. Limiting your search to peer-reviewed journals can help you navigate huge databases that might otherwise return scores of unusable articles.

The use of abstracts

In screen 3 on the previous page, the full article record shows a key feature of many databases' periodical listings: an **abstract** that summarizes the article. By describing research methods, conclusions, and other information, an abstract can tell you whether you want to pursue an article and thus save you time. However, the abstract cannot replace the actual article. If you want to use the work as a source, you must consult the full text.

Helpful databases

The list below includes databases to which academic libraries commonly subscribe. Some of these databases cover much the same material, so your library may subscribe to several of them but not all.

EBSCOhost Academic Search. A periodical index covering magazines and journals in the social sciences, sciences, arts, and humanities. Many articles are available full-text.

InfoTrac Expanded Academic. The Gale Group's general periodical index covering the social sciences, sciences, arts, and humanities as well as national news periodicals. It includes full-text articles.

LexisNexis Academic. An index of news and business, legal, and reference information, with full-text articles. *LexisNexis* includes international, national, and regional newspapers, news magazines, and legal and business publications.

Nineteenth-Century Masterfile. Perhaps the only electronic database for periodicals from the nineteenth century.

ProQuest Research Library. A periodical index covering the sciences, social sciences, arts, and humanities, including many full-text articles.

Wilson Databases. A collection of indexes, often provided in a package, including *Business Periodicals Index, Education Index, General Science Index, Humanities Index, Readers' Guide to Periodical Literature,* and *Social Sciences Index.*

2 • Locations of periodicals

If an index listing does not include or link directly to the full text of an article, you'll need to consult the periodical itself. Recent issues of periodicals are probably held in the library's periodical room. Back issues are usually stored elsewhere, either in bound volumes or on film that requires a special machine to read. A librarian will show you how to operate the machine.

52e Search the Web.

As an academic researcher, you enter the World Wide Web in two ways: through your library's Web site, and through public search engines such as *Yahoo!* and *Google*. The library entrance, covered in the preceding sections, is your main path to the books and periodicals that, for most subjects, should make up most of your sources. The public entrance, discussed here, can lead to a wealth of information and ideas, but it also has a number of disadvantages:

- *The Web is a wide-open network.* Anyone with the right hardware and software can place information on the Internet, and even a carefully conceived search can turn up sources with widely varying reliability: journal articles, government documents, scholarly data, term papers written by high school students, sales pitches masked as objective reports, wild theories. You must be especially diligent about evaluating Internet sources (see p. 439).
- *The Web changes constantly.* No search engine can keep up with the Web's daily additions and deletions, and a source you find today may be different or gone tomorrow. Some sites are designed and labeled as archives: they do not change except with additions. But generally you should not put off consulting an online source that you think you may want to use.
- *The Web provides limited information on the past.* Sources dating from before the 1980s or even more recently probably will not appear on the Web.
- *The Web is not all-inclusive.* Most books and many periodicals are available only via the library, not directly via the Web.

Clearly, the Web warrants cautious use. It should not be the only resource you work with.

1 • Search engines

To find sources on the Web, you use a **search engine** that catalogs Web sites in a series of directories and conducts keyword searches (see p. 417). Generally, use a directory when you haven't yet refined your topic or you want a general overview. Use keywords when you have refined your topic and you seek specific information.

Current search engines

The box on the next page lists the currently most popular search engines. To reach any one of them, enter its address in the Address or Location field of your Web browser.

Note For a good range of reliable sources, try out more than a single search engine, perhaps as many as four or five. No search engine can catalog the entire Web—indeed, even the most powerful engine may not include half the sites available at any given time, and most engines include only a fifth or less. In addition, most search engines accept paid placements, giving higher billing to sites that pay a fee. These so-called sponsored links are usually marked

Web search engines

The features of search engines change often, and new ones appear constantly. For the latest on search engines, see the links collected by Search Engine Watch at *http://www.searchenginewatch.com/links.*

Directories that review sites

BUBL Link
http://bubl.ac.uk/link

Internet Public Library
http://www.ipl.org/div/subject

Internet Scout Project
http://scout.wisc.edu/archives

Librarians' Index to the Internet
http://lii.org

Most advanced and efficient engines

AlltheWeb
http://www.alltheweb.com

One of the fastest and most comprehensive engines, *AlltheWeb* updates its database frequently so that it returns more of the Web's most recent sites. It allows searches for news, pictures, and audio and video files.

Google
http://www.google.com

Also fast and comprehensive, *Google* ranks a site based not only on its content but also on the other sites that are linked to it, thus providing a measure of a site's usefulness. *Google* also allows searches for news, discussion groups, and images.

Other engines

AltaVista
http://www.altavista.com

Ask Jeeves
http://www.ask.com

Dogpile
http://www.dogpile.com

Excite
http://www.excite.com

Lycos
http://www.lycos.com

MetaCrawler
http://www.metacrawler.com

Yahoo!
http://www.yahoo.com

as such, but they can compromise a search engine's method for arranging sites in response to your keywords.

A sample search engine

The screen shot below, from the *Google* search engine, shows the features common to most engines. The circled numbers are keyed to numbered comments below the screen shot.

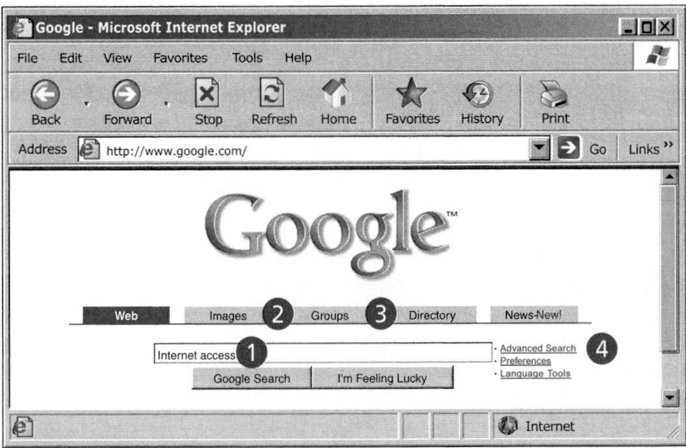

1. To search by keywords, type them into the Search field. (See pp. 417–19 on developing keywords.)
2. Click on listings for specific kinds of sources and information —for instance, images or postings to discussion groups.
3. Instead of searching by keywords, browse a subject directory to zero in on your general subject and perhaps your specific subject.
4. Click Advanced Search for limiting a search and for help using the search engine. Each engine has its own method of ranking **hits,** or sites that match your search criteria, such as the number of times your keywords appear within a site or page, whether the terms appear in the title or the address, and (in *Google*'s case) which other sites have links to the site or page.

Search records

Your Web browser includes functions that allow you to keep track of Web sources and your search:

- ***Favorites*** *or* ***Bookmarks*** *save site addresses as links.* Click one of these terms near the top of the browser screen to add a site you want to return to. A favorite or bookmark remains on file until you delete it.

- *A browser's search history records the sites you visited over a certain period,* such as a single online session or a week's sessions. (After that period, the history is deleted.) If you forgot to bookmark a site, you can click History or Go to locate your search history and recover the site.

2 • A sample search

The following sample Web search illustrates how the refinement of keywords can narrow a search to maximize the relevant hits and minimize the irrelevant ones. Kisha Alder, a student researching the feasibility of Internet taxes, first used the keywords *Internet taxes* on *Google.* But, as shown in the screen shot below, the search produced more than 2 million hits, an unusably large number and a sure sign that Alder's keywords needed revision.

1. First *Google* results

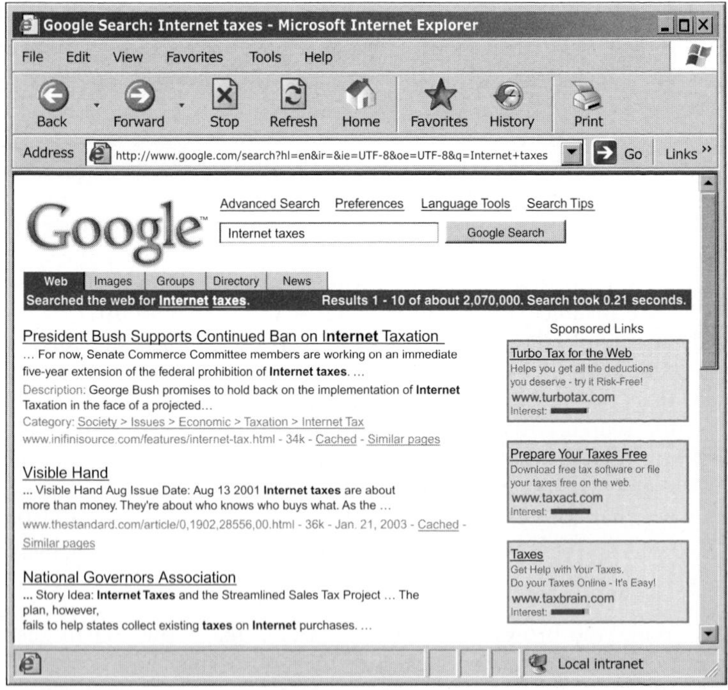

After several tries, Alder arrived at two phrases, *sales tax* and *electronic commerce,* to describe her subject more precisely. Taking advantage of a feature described on *Google*'s Advanced Search help, she added *site:.gov* at the end of her keywords, specifying government-sponsored sites. Narrowed in this way, Alder's search produced a more manageable 533 hits—still a large number but including many potential sources on the first few screens. (See screen 2, below.)

2. Second Google results

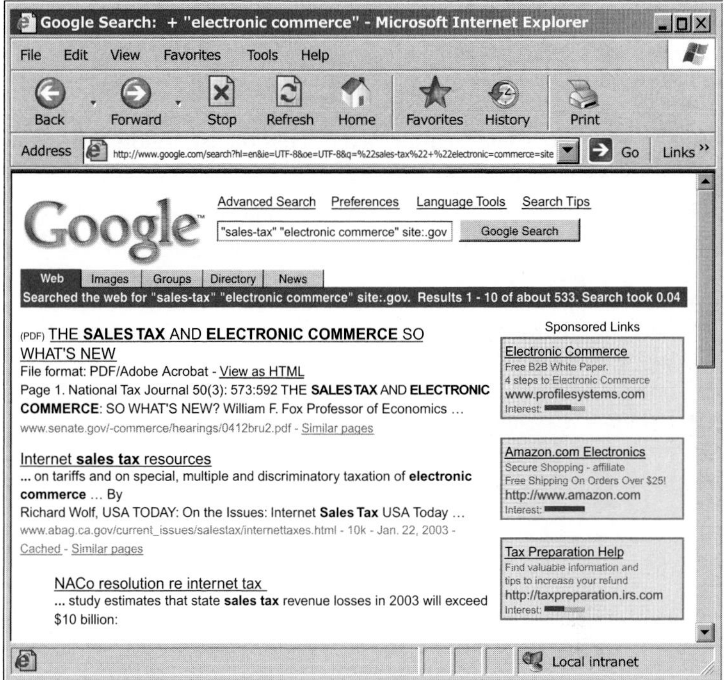

52f Explore other online sources.

Several online sources can put you directly in touch with experts and others whose ideas and information may inform your research. Because these sources, like Web sites, are unfiltered, you must always evaluate them carefully. (See pp. 443–44.)

1 • Using electronic mail

As a research tool, e-mail allows you to communicate with others who are interested in your topic. You may, for instance, carry on an e-mail conversation with a teacher at your school or with other students. Or you may interview an expert in another state to follow up on a scholarly article he or she published. (See pp. 138–39 on e-mail etiquette and the next page on conducting interviews.)

2 • Using discussion lists

A **discussion list** (sometimes called a **listserv** or just a **list**) uses e-mail to connect individuals who are interested in a common subject, often with a scholarly or technical focus. By sending a question to an appropriate list, you may be able to reach scores of people who know something about your topic. For an index of discussion lists, see *http://tile.net/lists* or *http://www.topica.com.*

When conducting research on a discussion list, follow the guidelines for e-mail etiquette on pages 138–39 as well as these:

- ***Lurk*** *for a while*—read without posting messages. Make sure the discussion is relevant to your topic, and get a sense of how the group interacts.
- *Don't ask for information you can find elsewhere.* Most list members are glad to help with legitimate questions but resent messages that rehash familiar debates or that ask them to do someone else's work.
- *Evaluate messages carefully.* Many list subscribers are passionate experts with fair-minded approaches to their topics, but almost anyone with an Internet connection can post a message to a list. See pages 443–44 on evaluating online sources.

3 • Using Web forums and newsgroups

Web forums and newsgroups are more open and less scholarly than discussion lists, so their messages require even more diligent evaluation. **Web forums** allow participants to join a conversation simply by selecting a link on a Web page. For a directory of forums, see *http://www.delphiforums.com.* **Newsgroups** are organized under subject headings such as *soc* for social issues and *biz* for business. For a directory of newsgroups, see *http://groups.google.com.*

4 • Using synchronous communication

With e-mail and discussion groups, there's a delay between a message you send and any response you receive. But with **synchronous** (or simultaneous) **communication,** you and others can converse in real time, the way you talk on the phone. Synchronous programs include instant-messaging applications, Web courseware, Internet relay chat (IRC), and virtual environments called MOOs.

Synchronous communication can be used to conduct interviews or hold debates. Your instructor may ask you to use it for your coursework or research and will provide the software and instructions to get you started. You can also find out more about synchronous communication at the Web site for this book: see the box on page 416.

52g Consult pamphlets and government publications.

Organizations such as social-service groups, professional societies, and all branches of government publish pamphlets, compilations of data, and other sources that usually cannot be retrieved through the library's book catalog or periodicals listings.

Libraries store pamphlets and other loose materials in file drawers, called **vertical files.** To find out what is available in pamphlet form, consult the *Vertical File Index: A Subject and Title Index to Selected Pamphlet Materials.*

Government publications provide a vast array of data, public records, and other historical and contemporary information. For US government publications, consult the *Monthly Catalog of US Government Publications,* available online. Many federal, state, and local government agencies post important publications—legislation, reports, press releases—on their own Web sites. You can find lists of sites for various federal agencies by using the keywords *United States federal government* with a search engine. In addition, several Web sites are useful resources, such as *http://www.fedstats.gov* (government statistics), *http://www.gpoaccess.gov/index.html* (listings of the Government Printing Office), and *http://infoplease.com/us.html* (links to information on federal, state, and local governments).

52h Generate your own sources.

Academic writing will often require you to conduct primary research for information of your own. For instance, you may need to analyze a poem, conduct an experiment, survey a group of people, or interview an expert.

An interview can be especially helpful for a research project because it allows you to ask questions precisely geared to your topic. You can conduct an interview in person, over the telephone, or online using electronic mail (see p. 433) or a form of synchronous communication (see the previous page). A personal interview is preferable if you can arrange it, because you can see the person's expressions and gestures as well as hear his or her tone and words.

Here are a few guidelines for interviews:

- *Call or write for an appointment.* Tell the person exactly why you are calling, what you want to discuss, and how long you expect the interview to take. Be true to your word on all points.
- *Prepare a list of open-ended questions to ask*—perhaps ten or twelve for a one-hour interview. Plan on doing some research for these questions to discover background on the issues and your subject's published views on the issues.
- *Give your subject time to consider your questions.* Don't rush into silences with more questions.
- *Pay attention to your subject's answers* so that you can ask appropriate follow-up questions and pick up on unexpected but worthwhile points.
- *Take care in interpreting answers,* especially if you are online and thus can't depend on facial expressions, gestures, and tone of voice to convey the subject's attitudes.
- *Keep thorough notes.* Take notes during an in-person or telephone interview, or tape-record the interview if you have the equipment and your subject agrees. For online interviews, save the discussion in a file of its own. (A synchronous discussion may require that you activate a Log or Archive function before you begin your interview in order to save it afterward.)
- *Verify quotations.* Before you quote your subject in your paper, check with him or her to ensure that the quotations are accurate.
- *Send a thank-you note immediately after the interview.* Promise your subject a copy of your finished paper, and send the paper promptly.

EXERCISE 52.1
Finding sources

Using your library and three Web search engines, locate at least ten promising sources for one of the topics you selected in the previous chapter (Exercise 51.1, p. 409). Begin by developing a list of keywords, revising it as needed to focus your research. Consider the sources "promising" if they seem directly to address your central research question. Following the guidelines on pages 412–15, make a working bibliography of the sources. Be sure to include all the information you would need to acknowledge the sources in a final paper.

53 Working with Sources

How can I use sources critically and effectively?

Research writing is much more than finding sources and reporting their contents. The challenge and interest come from *interacting* with sources, reading them critically to discover their meanings, judge their relevance and reliability, and create relationships among them.

This chapter offers help with this crucial phase of research writing. It discusses evaluating and synthesizing sources (below and p. 445); gathering information from sources (p. 447); using summary, paraphrase, and direct quotation when borrowing from sources (p. 449); and integrating source material into your text (p. 453). The next chapter (p. 459) discusses avoiding plagiarism and documenting sources.

CULTURE LANGUAGE Interacting with sources requires thinking critically about them and developing independent ideas. These goals may at first be uncomfortable for you if your native culture emphasizes understanding and respecting established authority over questioning and enlarging it. The information here will help you work with sources so that you can become an expert in your own right and convincingly convey your expertise to others.

53a Evaluate sources.

Before you gather ideas and information from your sources, scan them to evaluate what they offer and how you might use it.

Note In evaluating sources, you need to consider how they come to you. The sources you find through the library, both print and online, have been previewed for you by their publishers and by

http://www.ablongman.com/littlebrown

➤ Research writing
- ➤ Video tutorials ➤ Evaluating online sources
- ➤ Web exercises ➤ Exers. 3–8
- ➤ Downloads
  - ➤ Questions for evaluating sources
  - ➤ Questions for evaluating Web sites
  - ➤ Questions for evaluating online discussions
- ➤ Web links ➤ Working with sources

the library's staff. They still require your critical reading, but you can have some confidence in the information they contain. With online sources you reach directly, however, you can't assume similar previewing, so your critical reading must be especially rigorous. Special tips for evaluating Web sites and postings to discussion groups appear on pages 439–44.

1 • Relevance and reliability

Not all the sources you find will prove worthwhile: some may be irrelevant to your topic, and others may be unreliable. Gauging the relevance and reliability of sources is the essential task of evaluating them.

If you haven't already done so, read this book's Chapter 9 on critical reading and writing. It provides a foundation for answering the questions in the box below. (You can download these questions from this book's Web site: see the box on p. 437. Make a copy for each source you're evaluating, and provide written answers between the questions.)

Questions for evaluating sources

For online sources, supplement these guidelines with those opposite and on p. 443.

Relevance

- **Does the source devote some attention to your subject?** Check whether the source focuses on your subject or covers it marginally, and compare the source's coverage to that in other sources.
- **Is the source appropriately specialized for your needs?** Check the source's treatment of a topic you know something about, to ensure that it is neither too superficial nor too technical.
- **Is the source up to date enough for your subject?** Check the publication date. If your subject is current, your sources should be, too.

Reliability

- **Where does the source come from?** It matters whether you found the source through your library or directly on the Internet. (If the latter, see pp. 439–44.) Check whether a library source is popular or scholarly. Scholarly sources, such as refereed journals and university press books, are generally deeper and more reliable.
- **Is the author an expert in the field?** The authors of scholarly publications tend to be experts. To verify expertise, check an author's credentials in a biography (if the source includes one), in a biographical reference, or by a keyword search of the Web.

- **What is the author's bias?** Every author has a point of view that influences the selection and interpretation of evidence. How do the author's ideas relate to those in other sources? What areas does the author emphasize, ignore, or dismiss? When you're aware of sources' biases, you can attempt to balance them.
- **Is the source fair and reasonable?** Even a strongly biased work should present sound reasoning, adequate evidence, and a fair picture of opposing views—all in an objective, calm tone. The absence of any of these qualities should raise a warning flag.
- **Is the source well written?** A logical organization and clear, error-free sentences indicate a careful author.

2 • Web sites

To a great extent, the same critical reading that helps you evaluate library sources will help you evaluate Web sites. But most Web sites have not undergone prior screening by editors and librarians. On your own, you must distinguish scholarship from corporate promotion, valid data from invented statistics, well-founded opinion from clever propaganda.

The following strategy can help you make such distinctions. (You can download the summary questions below from this book's Web site: see the box on p. 437.) We'll apply the strategy to the Web site shown on the next page, *Global Warming Information Center,* which turned up in a search for views and data on global warming.

Questions for evaluating Web sites

Supplement these questions with those opposite and above.

- **What does the URL lead you to expect about the site?** Are those expectations fulfilled?
- **Who is the author or sponsor?** How credible is the person or group responsible for the site?
- **What is the purpose of the site?** What does the site's author or sponsor intend to achieve?
- **What does context tell you?** What do you already know about the site's subject that can inform your evaluation? What kinds of support or other information do the site's links provide?
- **What does presentation tell you?** Is the site's design well thought out and effective? Is the writing clear and error-free?
- **How worthwhile is the content?** Are the site's claims well supported by evidence? Is the evidence from reliable sources?

The Global Warming Information Center - Microsoft Internet Explorer

File Edit View Favorites Tools Help

Back Forward Stop Refresh Home Favorites History Print

Address http://www.nationalcenter.org/Kyoto.html Go Links

Global Warming Information Center

A project of the John P. McGovern M.D. Center for Environmental and Regulatory Affairs of The National Center for Public Policy Research

Bonn Global Warming Earth Summit Fact Kit

(published July 2001 relating to the Bonn Summit)

Summary of the circumstances leading up to the Bonn meeting

A refutation of the most pervasive charges relating to the theory of man-made global warming

Local intranet

Check the electronic address.

Every file on the Web has a unique address called a **uniform resource locator,** or **URL.** In the screen shot here, the URL (seen in the Address field) is *http://www.nationalcenter.org/Kyoto.html.* For purposes of evaluation, the most important part of any URL is the domain name—here, *nationalcenter.org*—which generally contains the name of the organization that sponsors the site (*nationalcenter*) and an abbreviation that describes the type of organization (*org*). *Org* designates a nonprofit organization. The other major abbreviations are *edu* (educational institution), *gov* (government body), *mil* (military), and *com* (commercial organization).

The domain abbreviation can inform your evaluation to some extent: a *com* site usually reflects the company's commercial purposes, an *edu* site usually supports and distributes scholarly pursuits, and an *org* site usually centers on the public interest. But the abbreviation should not unduly influence your evaluation. A *com*

site may offer reliable data, an *edu* site may contain unfiltered student work, and an *org* site may promote a bigoted agenda.

Identify the author or sponsor.

A reputable site will list the author or group responsible for the site and will provide information or a link for contacting the author or group. If none of this information is provided, you should not use the source. If you have only the author or group name, you may be able to discover more in a biographical dictionary or through a keyword search. You should also look for mentions of the author or group in your other sources.

The Web site *Global Warming Information Center* names its sponsor right up front: the John P. McGovern M.D. Center for Environmental and Regulatory Affairs, which is part of the National Center for Public Policy Research (the *nationalcenter* of the site's domain name). The McGovern Center sounds like an organization involved in research about the environment, but discovering more about it proves difficult. The site includes no links to the McGovern Center, so locating it involves following links to the National Center. When finally reached, the McGovern Center home page links to an informative explanation of the center's mission and activities, as described below.

Gauge purpose.

A Web site's purpose determines what ideas and information it offers. Inferring that purpose tells you how to interpret what you see on the site. If a site is intended to sell a product or an opinion, it will likely emphasize favorable ideas and information while ignoring or even distorting what is unfavorable. In contrast, if a site is intended to build knowledge—for instance, a scholarly project or journal—it will likely acknowledge diverse views and evidence.

Determining the purpose of a site often requires looking beneath the surface of words and images and beyond the first page. The elements of the *Global Warming* page—the title, the green background, the photo of a child carrying a globe through a field of grass—suggest an environmentalist purpose of informing readers about the theory and consequences of rising earth temperatures caused by pollution. The site's purpose is actually different, though. Below the title box, a link to the "Bonn Global Warming Earth Summit Fact Kit" promises "A refutation of the most pervasive charges relating to the theory of man-made global warming." Explanations elsewhere on the site express an intention to inform readers about the evidence against global warming in the interest of reducing or overturning environmental regulations.

Consider context.

Your evaluation of a Web site should be informed by considerations outside the site itself. Chief among these is your own knowledge: What do you already know about the site's subject and the prevailing views of it? In addition, you can follow some of the site's links to see how they support, or don't support, the site's credibility. For instance, links to scholarly sources lend authority to a site—but *only if* the scholarly sources actually relate to and back up the site's claims.

Examining the *Global Warming* site, you might register the anti-regulatory bias but also recognize that this view is a significant one in the debates over global warming. That is, the bias does not necessarily disqualify the site as a source on global warming. The question then is the reliability of its information: does it come from trustworthy, less-biased sources? All the site's links lead to the McGovern Center's publications or the parent organization, the National Center for Public Policy Research. Because the links do not go outside the National Center, the question of reliability remains open, to be answered only by further examination of the site.

Look at presentation.

Considering both the look of a site and the way it's written can illuminate its intentions and reliability. Are the site's elements all functional and well integrated, or is the site cluttered with irrelevant material and graphics? Does the design reflect the apparent purpose of the site, or does it undercut or conceal that purpose in some way? Is the text clearly written, or is it difficult to understand? Is it error-free, or does it contain typos and grammatical errors?

At first glance, as noted earlier, the *Global Warming* site casts a pro-environmentalist image that turns out not to coincide with its purpose. Otherwise, the site is cleanly designed, with minimal elements laid out clearly. The text is straightforward and readable. Together, design and readability indicate that the sponsor takes its purpose seriously and has thought out its presentation.

Analyze content.

With information about a site's author, purpose, and context, you're in a position to evaluate its content. Are the ideas and information slanted and, if so, in what direction? Are the views and data authoritative, or do you need to balance them—or even reject them? These questions require close reading of the text and its sources.

The *Global Warming* site links to a wealth of information on the issue it addresses, mostly reports and fact kits like the one listed on the home page. These documents offer statistics and quotations to support skepticism about global warming, with footnotes detailing sources. The footnotes are the crux of the site's reliability: the listed sources should be scholarly and should explain the methods of gathering and interpreting the cited data. Instead, however, they are newspaper and magazine articles and reports from the National Center and groups with similar views.

The public controversy on global warming reflects disagreement among scholars over whether the earth's temperatures are rising significantly, whether human-made pollution is an important cause, how serious the consequences may be, and how to solve the problem. Because the *Global Warming* site does not offer or refer to the scholarly research, its claims and evidence must be viewed suspiciously and probably rejected for use in a research paper. A usable source need not be less biased, but it must be more substantial.

3 • Online discussions

The contributions to online discussions require the same critical scrutiny as Web sites do. On an e-mail discussion list, whose subscribers are likely to be professionals in the field, you will still find wrong or misleading data and skewed opinions. On more accessible Web forums and newsgroups, messages are even more suspect. A reliable discussion-group message may provide very current information or eyewitness testimony, but it will not have the authority of a scholarly publication.

Use the following strategy for evaluating messages in online discussions. You can download the summary questions below from this book's Web site: see the box on page 437.

Questions for evaluating online discussions

Supplement these questions with those on pp. 438–39.

- **Who is the author?** How credible is the person writing?
- **What is the context of the message?** What do the other messages in the discussion thread tell you about the reliability of this message?
- **How worthwhile is the content?** Are the message's claims supported by evidence? Is the evidence from reliable sources? Is the tone moderate?
- **How does the message compare with other sources?** Do the author's claims seem accurate given what you've seen in sources you know to be reliable?

Identify the author.

As with a Web site, checking out the author of an online message can help you judge the reliability of the message. If the author uses a screen name, write directly to him or her requesting full name and credentials. Do not use the message as a source if the author fails to respond. Once you know an author's name, you may be able to obtain background information from a keyword search of the Web or a biographical dictionary.

Consider messages in context.

Messages are often more difficult to evaluate in isolation than in the context of the overall thread of conversation. By returning to the initial posting in the thread and reading forward, you can see how a message relates to other postings. Does the message respond fairly to others' views? Do others object to the message or confirm it?

Analyze content.

A reliable online message will offer evidence for claims and sources for evidence. If you don't see such supporting information, ask the author for it. (If the author does not respond, ignore the message.) Then verify the sources with your own research: are they reputable?

The tone of a message can also be a clue to its reliability. Online discussions are generally more rushed and heated than other kinds of dialog, but look askance at a message that's contemptuous, dismissive, or shrill.

Compare with other sources.

Always consider discussion-group messages in the context of other sources so that you can distinguish singular, untested views from more mainstream views that have been subject to verification.

Be wary of postings that reproduce periodical articles, reports, or other publications. Try to locate the original version of the publication to be sure it has been reproduced fully and accurately, not quoted selectively or distorted. If you can't locate the original version, then don't use the publication as a source.

EXERCISE 53.1
Evaluating Web sites

Find and evaluate three Web sites: a commercial site, such as Microsoft's or Apple's; a site for a nonprofit organization, such as the American Medical Association or Greenpeace; and the personal site of an individual. What do you know or can you infer about each site's author or sponsor? What seems to be the site's purpose or purposes? What do the site's links contribute? How effective is the site's design? How reliable do you judge the site's information to be? How do the three types of sites differ in these respects?

EXERCISE 53.2
Evaluating an online discussion

Using *Google*'s newsgroup site (*http://groups.google.com*), locate a newsgroup on a subject that interests you. (If you already participate in an online discussion group, you can use it instead.) Pick one series of at least ten related messages on a single topic. Write a brief summary of each message (see p. 97 on summarizing). Then analyze and synthesize the messages to develop a one- or two-paragraph evaluation of the discussion. Which messages seem reliable? Which don't? Why?

53b Synthesize sources.

When you begin to locate the differences and similarities among sources, you move into the most significant part of research writing: forging relationships for your own purpose. This **synthesis** is an essential step in reading sources critically and continues through the drafting and revision of a research paper. As you infer connections—say, between one writer's opinions and another's or between two works by the same author—you create new knowledge.

Your synthesis of sources will grow more detailed and sophisticated as you proceed through the research-writing process. Unless you are analyzing primary sources such as the works of a poet, at first read your sources quickly and selectively to obtain an overview of your topic and a sense of how the sources approach it. Don't get bogged down in taking detailed notes, but *do* record your ideas about sources in your research journal (p. 407).

Respond to sources.

Write down what your sources make you think. Do you agree or disagree with the author? Do you find his or her views narrow, or do they open up new approaches for you? Is there anything in the source that you need to research further before you can understand it? Does the source prompt questions that you should keep in mind while reading other sources?

Connect sources.

When you notice a link between sources, jot it down. Do two sources differ in their theories or their interpretations of facts? Does one source illuminate another—perhaps commenting or clarifying or supplying additional data? Do two or more sources report studies that support a theory you've read about or an idea of your own?

Heed your own insights.

Apart from ideas prompted by your sources, you are sure to come up with independent thoughts: a conviction, a point of confusion that suddenly becomes clear, a question you haven't seen anyone else ask. These insights may occur at unexpected times, so it's good practice to keep a notebook handy to record them.

Use sources to support your own ideas.

As your research proceeds, the responses, connections, and insights you form through synthesis will lead you to answer your starting research question with a statement of your thesis (see pp. 468–69). They will also lead you to the main ideas supporting your thesis—conclusions you have drawn from your synthesis of sources, forming the main divisions of your paper. When drafting the paper, make sure each paragraph focuses on an idea of your own, with the support for the idea coming from your sources. In this way, your paper will synthesize the others' work into something wholly your own.

EXERCISE 53.3
Synthesizing sources

The three passages below address the same issue, the legalization of drugs. What similarities do you see in the authors' ideas? What differences? Write a paragraph of your own in which you use these authors' views as a point of departure for your own view about drug legalization.

Perhaps the most unfortunate victims of drug prohibition laws have been the residents of America's ghettos. These laws have proved largely futile in deterring ghetto-dwellers from becoming drug abusers, but they do account for much of what ghetto residents identify as the drug problem. Aggressive, gun-toting drug dealers often upset law-abiding residents far more than do addicts nodding out in doorways. Meanwhile other residents perceive the drug dealers as heroes and successful role models. They're symbols of success to children who see no other options. At the same time the increasingly harsh criminal penalties imposed on adult drug dealers have led drug traffickers to recruit juveniles. Where once children started dealing drugs only after they had been using them for a few years, today the sequence is often reversed. Many children start using drugs only after working for older drug dealers for a while.

> Legalization of drugs, like legalization of alcohol in the 1930s, would drive the drug-dealing business off the streets and out of apartment buildings and into government-regulated, tax-paying stores. It also would force many of the gun-toting dealers out of the business and convert others into legitimate businessmen.
>
> —ETHAN A. NADELMANN, "Shooting Up"
>
> Statistics argue against legalization. The University of Michigan conducts an annual survey of twelfth graders, asking the students about their drug consumption. In 1980, 50 percent of those polled said they had used marijuana in the past twelve months, whereas in 2002 only 37 percent had done so. Cocaine use was halved in the same period (12 percent to 6 percent). At the same time, twelve-month use of legally available drugs—alcohol and nicotine-containing cigarettes—remained constant at about 75 percent and 55 percent, respectively. The numbers of illegal drug users haven't declined nearly enough: those teenaged marijuana and cocaine users are still vulnerable to addiction and even death, and they threaten to infect their impressionable peers. But clearly the prohibition of illegal drugs has helped, while the legal status of alcohol and cigarettes has not made them less popular.
>
> —SYLVIA RUNKLE, "The Case Against Legalization"
>
> I have to laugh at the debate over what to do about the drug problem. Everyone is running around offering solutions—from making drug use a more serious criminal offense to legalizing it. But there isn't a real solution. I know that. I used and abused drugs, and people, and society, for two decades. Nothing worked to get me to stop all that behavior except just plain being sick and tired. Nothing. Not threats, not ten-plus years in prison, not anything that was said to me. I used until I got through. Period. And that's when you'll win the war. When all the dope fiends are done. Not a minute before.
>
> —MICHAEL W. POSEY, "I Did Drugs Until They Wore Me Out. Then I Stopped."

53c Gather information from sources.

You can accomplish a great deal of synthesis while gathering information from your sources. This information gathering is not a mechanical process. Rather, as you read you assess and organize the information in your sources.

Researchers vary in their methods for working with sources, but all methods share the same goals:

- *Keep accurate records of what sources say.* Accuracy helps prevent misrepresentation and plagiarism.

- *Keep accurate records of how to find sources.* These records are essential for retracing steps and for citing sources in the final paper. (See pp. 412–15 on keeping a working bibliography.)
- *Interact with sources.* Reading sources critically leads to an understanding of them, the relationships among them, and their support for one's own ideas.

To achieve these goals, you can take handwritten notes, type notes into your computer, annotate photocopies or printouts of sources, or annotate downloaded documents. On any given project, you may use all the methods. Each has advantages and disadvantages.

- *Handwritten notes:* Taking notes by hand is especially useful if you come across a source with no computer or photocopier handy. But handwritten notes can be risky. It's easy to introduce errors as you work from source to note card. And it's possible to copy source language and then later mistake and use it as your own, thus plagiarizing the source. Always take care to make accurate notes and to place big quotation marks around any passage you quote.
- *Notes on computer:* Taking notes on your computer can streamline the path of source to note to paper, because you can import the notes into your draft as you write. However, computer notes have the same disadvantages as handwritten notes: the risk of introducing errors and the risk of plagiarizing. As with handwritten notes, strive for accuracy, and use quotation marks for quotations.
- *Photocopies and printouts:* Photocopying from print sources or printing out online sources each has the distinct advantages of convenience and reduction in the risks of error and plagiarism during information gathering. But each method has disadvantages, too. The busywork of copying or printing can distract you from the crucial work of interacting with sources. And you have to make a special effort to annotate copies and printouts with the publication information for sources. If you don't have this information for your final paper, you can't use the source.
- *Downloads:* Researching online, you can usually download full-text articles, Web pages, discussion-group messages, and other materials into your word processor. While drafting, you can import source information from one file into another. Like photocopies and printouts, though, downloads can distract you from interacting with sources and can easily become separated from the publication information you must have in order to use the sources. Even more important, directly importing source material creates a high risk of plagiarism. You must keep clear boundaries between your own ideas and words and those of others.

53d Use summary, paraphrase, and quotation.

As you take notes from sources or work source material into your draft, you can summarize, paraphrase, quote, or combine methods. The choice should depend on why you are using a source.

Note *Summaries, paraphrases, and quotations all require source citations. A summary or paraphrase without a source citation or a quotation without quotation marks is plagiarism.* (See pp. 459–65 for more on plagiarism.)

1 • Summary

When you **summarize,** you condense an extended idea or argument into a sentence or more in your own words. (See also p. 97.) Summary is most useful when you want to record the gist of an author's idea without the background or supporting evidence. The sample computer note below shows a summary of the following passage from a government report on the so-called digital divide between US residents with and without access to the Internet:

Original quotation

> The following examples highlight the breadth of the digital divide today:
>
> - Those with a college degree are more than *eight times* as likely to have a computer at home, and nearly *sixteen times* as likely to have home Internet access, as those with an elementary school education.
> - A high-income household in an urban area is more than *twenty times* as likely as a rural, low-income household to have Internet access.
> - A child in a low-income white family is *three times* as likely to have Internet access as a child in a comparable black family, and *four times* as likely to have access as children in a comparable Hispanic household.
>
> —US Department of Commerce, *Falling Through the Net: Toward Digital Inclusion,* p. 7

Summary

> Digital divide
>
> Dept. of Commerce 7
>
> US residents who are urban, white, college educated, and affluent are much more likely to be connected to the Internet than those who are rural, black or Hispanic, not educated past elementary school, and poor.

2 • Paraphrase

When you **paraphrase,** you follow much more closely the author's original presentation, but you still restate it in your own words and sentence structures. Paraphrase is most useful when you want to present or examine an author's line of reasoning but don't feel the original words merit direct quotation. Here is a paraphrase of the quotation from the Department of Commerce report on the previous page:

Paraphrase

> Digital divide
>
> Dept. of Commerce 7
>
> Likelihood of being connected to the Internet among US groups:
>
> Home connection, elementary education vs. college education: 1/16 as likely.
>
> Any access, rural setting and low-income household vs. urban setting and affluent household: 1/20 as likely.
>
> Any access, low-income black child vs. low-income white child: 1/3 as likely.
>
> Any access, low-income Hispanic child vs. low-income white child: 1/4 as likely.

Notice that the paraphrase follows the original but uses different words and different sentence structures. The paraphrase needs a source citation because it borrows ideas from the source, but it does not need quotation marks. In contrast, an unsuccessful paraphrase—one that plagiarizes—copies the author's words or sentence

Paraphrasing a source

- **Read the relevant material several times to be sure you understand it.**
- **Restate the source's ideas in your own words and sentence structures.** You need not put down in new words the whole passage or all the details. Select what is relevant to your topic, and restate only that. If complete sentences seem too detailed or cumbersome, use phrases, as in the example above.
- **Be careful not to distort meaning.** Don't change the source's emphasis or omit connecting words, qualifiers, and other material whose absence will confuse you later or cause you to misrepresent the source.

structures or both *without quotation marks*. The words and sentence structures belong to the original author as much as the ideas do. (See p. 463 for examples of unsuccessful paraphrases.)

CULTURE LANGUAGE If English is your second language, you may have difficulty paraphrasing the ideas in sources because synonyms don't occur to you or you don't see how to restructure sentences. Before attempting a paraphrase, read the original passage several times. Then, instead of "translating" line by line, try to state the gist of the passage without looking at it. Check your effort against the original to be sure you have captured the source author's meaning and emphasis without using his or her words and sentence structures. If you need a synonym for a word, look it up in a dictionary.

3 • Direct quotation

Your notes from sources may include many quotations, especially if you rely on photocopies, printouts, or downloads. Whether to use a quotation in your draft, instead of a summary or paraphrase, depends on whether the source is primary or secondary and on how important the exact words are:

- *Quote extensively when you are analyzing primary sources,* such as literary works and historical documents. The quotations will often be both the target of your analysis and the chief support for your ideas.
- *Quote selectively when you are drawing on secondary sources.* Favor summaries and paraphrases over quotations, and put every quotation to each test in the box below. Most papers of

Tests for direct quotations from secondary sources

The author's original satisfies one of these requirements:

- The language is unusually vivid, bold, or inventive.
- The quotation cannot be paraphrased without distortion or loss of meaning.
- The words themselves are at issue in your interpretation.
- The quotation represents and emphasizes a body of opinion or the view of an important expert.
- The quotation emphatically reinforces your own idea.
- The quotation is a graph, diagram, or table.

The quotation is as short as possible:

- It includes only material relevant to your point.
- It is edited to eliminate examples and other unneeded material, using brackets (pp. 379–80, 391) and ellipsis marks (pp. 377–79.)

ten or so pages should not need more than two or three quotations that are longer than a few lines each.

When you quote a source, either in your notes or in your draft, take precautions to avoid plagiarism or misrepresentation of the source:

- *Copy the material carefully.* Take down the author's exact wording, spelling, capitalization, and punctuation.
- *Proofread every direct quotation at least twice.*
- *Use quotation marks around the quotation* so that later you won't confuse it with a paraphrase or summary.
- *Use brackets* to add words for clarity or to change the capitalization of letters (see pp. 379–80, 391).
- *Use ellipsis marks* to omit irrelevant material (see pp. 377–79).

EXERCISE 53.4
Summarizing and paraphrasing

Prepare two source notes, one summarizing the entire paragraph below and the other paraphrasing the first four sentences (ending with the word *autonomy*). Use the format for a note illustrated on pages 449 and 450, omitting only the heading.

> Federal organization [of the United States] has made it possible for the different states to deal with the same problems in many different ways. One consequence of federalism, then, has been that people are treated differently, by law, from state to state. The great strength of this system is that differences from state to state in cultural preferences, moral standards, and levels of wealth can be accommodated. In contrast to a unitary system in which the central government makes all important decisions (as in France), federalism is a powerful arrangement for maximizing regional freedom and autonomy. The great weakness of our federal system, however, is that people in some states receive less than the best or the most advanced or the least expensive services and policies that government can offer. The federal dilemma does not invite easy solution, for the costs and benefits of the arrangement have tended to balance out.
>
> —PETER K. EISINGER ET AL., *American Politics,* p. 44

EXERCISE 53.5
Combining summary, paraphrase, and direct quotation

Prepare a source note containing a combination of paraphrase or summary and direct quotation that states the main idea of the passage below. Use the format for a note illustrated on pages 449 and 450, omitting only the heading.

> Most speakers unconsciously duel even during seemingly casual conversations, as can often be observed at social gatherings where they show less concern for exchanging information with other guests than for asserting their own dominance. Their verbal dueling often employs very subtle weapons like mumbling, a hostile act which defeats the listener's desire to understand what the speaker claims he is trying to say (but is really not saying because he is mumbling!). Or the verbal dueler may keep talking after someone has passed out of hearing range—which is often an aggressive challenge to the listener to return and acknowledge the dominance of the speaker.
>
> —PETER K. FARB, *Word Play,* p. 107

53e Integrate sources into your text.

The evidence of others' information and opinions should back up, not dominate, your own ideas. To synthesize evidence, you need to smooth the transitions between your ideas and words and those of your sources, and you need to give the reader a context for interpreting the borrowed material.

Note Integrating source material into your sentences involves punctuating signal phrases such as *he insists* (pp. 351–52) and may involve using ellipsis marks for omissions (pp. 377–79) and using brackets for additions and changes (pp. 379–80, 391). The examples in this section use the MLA style of source documentation and also present-tense verbs (such as *disagrees* and *claims*), which are typical of writing in the humanities. For specific variations in documentation style and verb tense within the academic disciplines, see pages 456–58.

Conventions for handling quotations

- For guidelines on when to quote from sources, see pp. 451–52.
- For the punctuation of signal phrases such as *he insists,* see pp. 351–52.
- For guidelines on when to run quotations into your text and when to display them separately from your text, see pp. 508–09 (MLA style) and 537–38 (APA style).
- For the use of brackets around your changes or additions in quotations, see pp. 379–80, 391.
- For the use of the ellipsis mark (. . .) to indicate omissions from quotations, see pp. 377–79.

1 • Introduction of borrowed material

Readers will be distracted from your point if borrowed material does not fit into your sentence. In the passage below, the writer has not meshed the structures of her own and her source's sentences:

Awkward — One editor disagrees with this view and "a good reporter does not fail to separate opinions from facts" (Lyman 52).

In the following revision the writer adds words to integrate the quotation into her sentence:

Revised — One editor disagrees with this view, maintaining that "a good reporter does not fail to separate opinions from facts" (Lyman 52).

To mesh your own and your source's words, you may sometimes need to make a substitution or addition to the quotation, signaling your change with brackets:

Words added — "The tabloids [of England] are a journalistic case study in bad reporting," claims Lyman (52).

Verb form changed — A bad reporter, Lyman implies, is one who "[fails] to separate opinions from facts" (52). [The bracketed verb replaces *fail* in the original.]

Capitalization changed — "[T]o separate opinions from facts" is the work of a good reporter (Lyman 52). [In the original, *to* is not capitalized.]

Noun supplied for pronoun — The reliability of a news organization "depends on [reporters'] trustworthiness," says Lyman (52). [The bracketed noun replaces *their* in the original.]

2 • Interpretation of borrowed material

Even when it does not conflict with your own sentence structure, borrowed material will be ineffective if you merely dump it in readers' laps without explaining how you intend it to be understood. Reading the following passage, we must figure out for ourselves that the writer's sentence and the quotation state opposite points of view:

Dumped — Many news editors and reporters maintain that it is impossible to keep personal opinions from influencing the selection and presentation of facts. "True, news reporters, like everyone else, form impressions of what they see and hear. However, a good reporter does not fail to separate opinions from facts" (Lyman 52).

In the following revision, the underlined additions tell us how to interpret the quotation:

Revised Many news editors and reporters maintain that it is impossible to keep personal opinions from influencing the selection and presentation of facts. Yet not all authorities agree with this view. One editor grants that "news reporters, like everyone else, form impressions of what they see and hear." But, he insists, "a good reporter does not fail to separate opinions from facts" (Lyman 52).

Signal phrases

The words *One editor grants* and *he insists* in the preceding revised passage are **signal phrases:** they tell readers who the source is and what to expect in the quotations that follow. Signal phrases usually contain (1) the source author's name (or a substitute for it, such as *One editor* and *he*) and (2) a verb that indicates the source author's attitude or approach to what he or she says.

Some verbs for signal phrases appear below. These verbs are in the present tense, typical of writing in the humanities. But in the social and natural sciences, past or present perfect is more common. See pages 456–58.

Author is neutral	Author infers or suggests	Author argues	Author is uneasy or disparaging
comments	analyzes	claims	belittles
describes	asks	contends	bemoans
explains	assesses	defends	complains
illustrates	concludes	holds	condemns
notes	considers	insists	deplores
observes	finds	maintains	deprecates
points out	predicts	Author agrees	derides
records	proposes	admits	disagrees
relates	reveals	agrees	laments
reports	shows	concedes	warns
says	speculates	grants	
sees	suggests		
thinks	supposes		
writes			

Vary your signal phrases to suit your interpretation of borrowed material and also to keep readers' interest. A signal phrase may precede, interrupt, or follow the borrowed material:

Precedes Lyman insists that "a good reporter does not fail to separate opinions from facts" (52).

Interrupts	"However," Lyman insists, "a good reporter does not fail to separate opinions from facts" (52).
Follows	"[A] good reporter does not fail to separate opinions from facts," Lyman insists (52).

Background information

You can add information to a signal phrase to inform readers why you are using a source. In most cases, provide the author's name in the text, especially if the author is an expert or readers will recognize the name:

Author named	Harold Lyman grants that "news reporters, like everyone else, form impressions of what they see and hear." But, Lyman insists, "a good reporter does not fail to separate opinions from facts" (52).

If the source title contributes information about the author or the context of the quotation, you can provide it in the text:

Title given	Harold Lyman, in his book *The Conscience of the Journalist*, grants that "news reporters, like everyone else, form impressions of what they see and hear." But, Lyman insists, "a good reporter does not fail to separate opinions from facts" (52).

If the quoted author's background and experience reinforce or clarify the quotation, you can provide these credentials in the text:

Credentials given	Harold Lyman, a newspaper editor for more than forty years, grants that "news reporters, like everyone else, form impressions of what they see and hear." But, Lyman insists, "a good reporter does not fail to separate opinions from facts" (52).

You need not name the author, source, or credentials in your text when you are simply establishing facts or weaving together facts and opinions from varied sources. In the following passage, the information is more important than the source, so the name of the source is confined to a parenthetical acknowledgment:

> To end the abuses of the British, many colonists were urging three actions: forming a united front, seceding from Britain, and taking control of their own international relations (Wills 325–36).

3 • Discipline styles for integrating sources

The preceding guidelines for introducing and interpreting borrowed material apply generally across academic disciplines, but there are differences in verb tenses and documentation style.

English and some other humanities

Writers in English, foreign languages, and related disciplines use MLA style for documenting sources (see Chapter 56) and generally use the present tense of verbs in signal phrases. In discussing sources other than works of literature, the present perfect tense is also sometimes appropriate:

> Lyman insists . . . [present].
> Lyman has insisted . . . [present perfect].

In discussing works of literature, use only the present tense to describe both the work of the author and the action in the work:

> Kate Chopin builds irony into every turn of "The Story of an Hour." For example, Mrs. Mallard, the central character, finds joy in the death of her husband, whom she loves, because she anticipates "the long procession of years that would belong to her absolutely" (23).

Avoid shifting tenses in writing about literature. You can, for instance, shorten quotations to avoid their past-tense verbs.

Shift	Her freedom elevates her, so that "she carried herself unwittingly like a goddess of victory" (24).
No shift	Her freedom elevates her, so that she walks "unwittingly like a goddess of victory" (24).

History and other humanities

Writers in history, art history, philosophy, and related disciplines generally use the present tense or present perfect tense of verbs in signal phrases.

> Lincoln persisted, as Haworth has noted, in "feeling that events controlled him."[3]
>
> What Miller calls Lincoln's "severe self-doubt"[6] undermined his effectiveness on at least two occasions.

The raised numbers after the quotations are part of the Chicago documentation style, used in history and other disciplines. See this book's Web site (*http://www.ablongman.com/littlebrown*) for information on Chicago style.

Social and natural sciences

Writers in the sciences generally use a verb's present tense just for reporting the results of a study (*The data suggest . . .*). Otherwise, they use a verb's past tense or present perfect tense in a signal phrase, as when introducing an explanation, interpretation, or other commentary. (Thus when you are writing for the sciences generally convert the list of signal-phrase verbs on p. 455 from the present to the past or present perfect tense.)

> Lin (1999) has suggested that preschooling may significantly affect children's academic performance through high school (pp. 22–23).
>
> In an exhaustive survey of the literature published between 1990 and 2000, Walker (2001) found "no proof, merely a weak correlation, linking place of residence and rate of illness" (p. 121).

These passages conform to APA documentation style, discussed in Chapter 57. APA style, or one quite similar to it, is also used in sociology, education, nursing, biology, and many other social and natural sciences.

EXERCISE 53.6
Introducing and interpreting borrowed material

Drawing on the ideas in the following paragraph and using examples from your own observations and experiences, write a paragraph about anxiety. Integrate at least one direct quotation and one paraphrase from the following paragraph into your own sentences. In your paragraph identify the author by name and give his credentials: he is a professor of psychiatry and a practicing psychoanalyst.

> There are so many ways in which human beings are different from all the lower forms of animals, and almost all of them make us uniquely susceptible to feelings of anxiousness. Our imagination and reasoning powers facilitate anxiety; the anxious feeling is precipitated not by an absolute impending threat—such as the worry about an examination, a speech, travel—but rather by the symbolic and often unconscious representations. We do not have to be experiencing a potential danger. We can experience something related to it. We can recall, through our incredible memories, the original symbolic sense of vulnerability in childhood and suffer the feeling attached to that. We can even forget the original memory and be stuck with the emotion—which is then compounded by its seemingly irrational quality at this time. It is not just the fear of death which pains us, but the anticipation of it; or the anniversary of a specific death; or a street, a hospital, a time of day, a color, a flower, a symbol associated with death.
>
> —WILLARD GAYLIN, "Feeling Anxious," p. 23

54 Avoiding Plagiarism and Documenting Sources

How can I use sources honestly?

Using sources honestly means clearly distinguishing others' work from your own. **Plagiarism** (from a Latin word for "kidnapper") is the opposite: presenting someone else's words or ideas as if they were yours. Whether deliberate or accidental, plagiarism is a serious and often punishable offense.

- *Deliberate* plagiarism:

  Copying or downloading a phrase, a sentence, or a longer passage from a source and passing it off as your own by omitting quotation marks and a source citation.

  Summarizing or paraphrasing someone else's ideas without acknowledging your debt in a source citation.

  Handing in as your own work a paper you have bought, copied off the Web, had a friend write, or accepted from another student.

- *Accidental* plagiarism:

  Forgetting to place quotation marks around another writer's words.

  Carelessly omitting a source citation for a paraphrase.

  Omitting a source citation for another's idea because you are unaware of the need to acknowledge the idea.

In most schools a code of academic honesty calls for severe consequences for deliberate or accidental plagiarism: a failing grade, suspension from school, or even expulsion.

The way to avoid plagiarism is to acknowledge your sources by documenting them. This chapter discusses plagiarism and the Internet, shows how to distinguish what doesn't require acknowledgment from what does, and provides an overview of source documentation.

http://www.ablongman.com/littlebrown

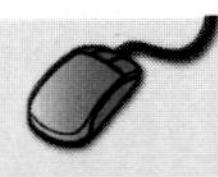

- ➤ Research writing
  - ➤ Video tutorials ➤ Avoiding plagiarism
  - ➤ Web exercises ➤ Exer. 9
  - ➤ Downloads
    - ➤ Checklist for avoiding plagiarism
    - ➤ Chapter 54 exercise in electronic format
  - ➤ Web links ➤ Avoiding plagiarism
- ➤ Documentation in the disciplines

CULTURE LANGUAGE More than in many other cultures, teachers in the United States value students' original thinking and writing. In some other cultures, for instance, students may be encouraged to copy the words of scholars without acknowledgment, in order to demonstrate their mastery of or respect for the scholars' work. In the United States, however, the writing of an author is considered his or her property, and using that writing without a source citation is considered theft. When in doubt about the guidelines in this chapter, ask your instructor for advice.

Checklist for avoiding plagiarism

Type of source

Are you using

- your own independent material,
- common knowledge, or
- someone else's independent material?

You must acknowledge someone else's material.

Quotations

- Do all quotations exactly match their sources? Check them.
- Have you inserted quotation marks around quotations that are run into your text?
- Have you shown omissions with ellipsis marks and additions with brackets?
- Does every quotation have a source citation?

Paraphrases and summaries

- Have you used your own words and sentence structures for every paraphrase and summary? If not, use quotation marks around the original author's words.
- Does every paraphrase and summary have a source citation?

The Web

- Have you obtained any necessary permission to use someone else's material on your Web site?

Source citations

- Have you acknowledged every use of someone else's material in the place where you use it?
- Does your list of works cited include all the sources you have used?

You can download this checklist from this book's Web site: see the box on the previous page. Working with a copy of the list, question every use you make of someone else's material.

54a Beware of plagiarism from the Internet.

The Internet has made it easier to plagiarize than ever before, but it has also made plagiarism easier to catch.

Even honest students risk accidental plagiarism by downloading sources and importing portions into their drafts. Dishonest students may take advantage of downloading to steal others' work. They may also use the term-paper businesses on the Web, which offer both ready-made research and complete papers, usually for a fee. *Paying for research or a paper does not make it the buyer's work.* Anyone who submits someone else's work as his or her own is a plagiarist.

Students who plagiarize from the Internet both deprive themselves of an education in honest research and expose themselves to detection. Teachers can use search engines to locate specific phrases or sentences anywhere on the Web, including among scholarly publications, all kinds of Web sites, and term-paper collections. They can search the term-paper sites as easily as students can, looking for similarities with papers they've received. Increasingly, teachers can use special detection programs that compare students' work with other work anywhere on the Internet, seeking matches as short as a few words.

Some instructors suggest that their students use plagiarism-detection programs to verify that their own work does not include accidental plagiarism, at least not from the Internet. This book's Web site includes links to such programs: see the box on page 459.

54b Know what you need not acknowledge.

1 • Your independent material

Your own observations, thoughts, compilations of facts, or experimental results—expressed in your words and format—do not require acknowledgment. You should describe the basis for your conclusions so that readers can evaluate your thinking, but you need not cite sources for them.

plag
54b

2 • Common knowledge

Common knowledge consists of the standard information on a subject as well as folk literature and commonsense observations.

- *Standard information* includes the major facts of history, such as the dates of Charlemagne's rule as emperor of Rome (800–14). It does not include interpretations of facts, such as a historian's opinion that Charlemagne was sometimes needlessly cruel in extending his power.

- *Folk literature,* such as the fairy tale "Snow White," is popularly known and cannot be traced to a particular writer. Literature traceable to a writer is not folk literature, even if it is very familiar.
- A *commonsense observation* is something most people know, such as that inflation is most troublesome for people with low and fixed incomes. However, an economist's argument about the effects of inflation on Chinese immigrants is not a commonsense observation.

If you do not know a subject well enough to determine whether a piece of information is common knowledge, make a record of the source as you would for any other quotation, paraphrase, or summary. As you read more about the subject, the information may come up in other people's work without any source citation, in which case it is probably common knowledge. But if you are still in doubt when you finish your research, always acknowledge the source.

54c Know what you *must* acknowledge.

You must always acknowledge other people's independent material—that is, any facts or ideas that are not common knowledge or your own. The source may be anything, including a book, an article, a movie, an interview, a microfilmed document, a Web page, a newsgroup posting, or an opinion expressed on the radio. You must acknowledge summaries or paraphrases of ideas or facts as well as quotations of the language and format in which ideas or facts appear: wording, sentence structures, arrangement, and special graphics (such as a diagram). You must acknowledge another's material no matter how you use it, how much of it you use, or how often you use it.

1 • Using copied language: Quotation marks and a source citation

The following example baldly plagiarizes the original quotation from Jessica Mitford's *Kind and Usual Punishment,* page 9. Without quotation marks or a source citation, the example matches Mitford's wording (underlined) and closely parallels her sentence structure:

Original — The character and mentality of the keepers may be of more importance in understanding prisons than the character and mentality of the kept.

Plagiarism — But <u>the character</u> of prison officials (<u>the keepers</u>) is more important <u>in understanding prisons than the character</u> of prisoners (<u>the kept</u>).

To avoid plagiarism, the writer has two options: (1) paraphrase and cite the source (see the examples labeled "Revision (paraphrase)" below) or (2) use Mitford's actual words *in quotation marks* and *with a source citation* (here, in MLA style):

Revision (quotation) According to one critic of the penal system, "The character and mentality of the keepers may be of more importance in understanding prisons than the character and mentality of the kept" (Mitford 9).

Even with a source citation and with a different sentence structure, the next example is still plagiarism because it uses some of Mitford's words (underlined) without quotation marks:

Plagiarism According to one critic of the penal system, the psychology of the kept may say less about prisons than the psychology of the keepers (Mitford 9).

Revision (quotation) According to one critic of the penal system, the psychology of "the kept" may say less about prisons than the psychology of "the keepers" (Mitford 9).

2 • Using paraphrase or summary: Your own words and sentence structure and a source citation

The example below changes the sentence structure of the original Mitford quotation, but it still uses Mitford's words (underlined) without quotation marks and without a source citation:

Plagiarism In understanding prisons, we should know more about the character and mentality of the keepers than of the kept.

To avoid plagiarism, the writer has two options: (1) use quotation marks and cite the source (see above) or (2) *use his or her own words* and still *cite the source* (because the idea is Mitford's, not the writer's):

Revision (paraphrase) Mitford holds that we may be able to learn more about prisons from the psychology of the prison officials than from that of the prisoners (9).

Revision (paraphrase) We may understand prisons better if we focus on the personalities and attitudes of the prison workers rather than those of the inmates (Mitford 9).

In the next example, the writer cites Mitford and does not use her words but still plagiarizes her sentence structure:

Plagiarism One critic of the penal system maintains that the psychology of prison officials may be more informative about prisons that the psychology of prisoners (Mitford 9).

Revision (paraphrase)	One critic of the penal system maintains that we may be able to learn less from the psychology of prisoners than from the psychology of prison officials (Mitford 9).

54d Take care with online sources.

Online sources are so accessible and so easy to download into your own documents that it may seem they are freely available, exempting you from the obligation to acknowledge them. They are not. Acknowledging online sources is somewhat trickier than acknowledging print sources, but no less essential. Further, if you are publishing your work online, you need to take account of sources' copyright restrictions as well.

1 • Online sources in an unpublished project

When you use material from an online source in a print or online document to be distributed just to your class, your obligation to cite sources does not change: you must acknowledge someone else's independent material in whatever form you find it. With online sources, that obligation can present additional challenges:

- *Record complete publication information each time you consult an online source.* Online sources may change from one day to the next or even disappear entirely. See page 413 for the information to record, such as the electronic address and the publication date. Without the proper information, you *may not* use the source.
- *Acknowledge linked sites.* If you use not only a Web site but also one or more of its linked sites, you must acknowledge the linked sites as well. The fact that one person has used a second person's work does not release you from the responsibility to cite the second work.
- *Seek the author's permission before using an e-mail message or a contribution to a discussion group.* (See p. 441 for advice on tracing online authors.) Obtaining permission advises the author that his or her ideas are about to be distributed more widely and lets the author verify that you have not misrepresented the ideas.

2 • Print and online sources in a Web composition

When you use material from print or online sources in a composition for the Web, you must not only acknowledge your sources but also take the additional precaution of observing copyright restrictions. A Web site is a form of publication just as a book or magazine is and so involves the same responsibility to obtain reprint permission from copyright holders.

The legal convention of fair use allows an author to quote a small portion of copyrighted material without obtaining the copyright holder's permission, as long as the author acknowledges the source. The online standards of fair use differ for print and online sources and are not fixed in either case. The guidelines below are conservative:

- *Print sources:* Quote without permission fewer than fifty words from an article or fewer than three hundred words from a book. You'll need the copyright holder's permission to use any longer quotation from an article or book; any quotation at all from a play, poem, or song; and any use of an entire work, such as a photograph, chart, or other illustration.
- *Online sources:* Quote without permission text that represents just a small portion of the whole—say, forty words out of three hundred. Follow the print guidelines above for plays, poems, songs, and illustrations, adding multimedia elements (audio or video clips) to the list of works that require reprint permission for any use.
- *Links:* You may need to seek permission to link your site to another one—for instance, if you rely on the linked site to substantiate your claims or to provide a multimedia element.

Generally, you can find information about a site's copyright on the home page or at the bottoms of other pages: look for a notice using the symbol ©. Most worthwhile sites also provide information for contacting the author or sponsor. (See p. 414 for an illustration.) If you don't find a copyright notice, you *cannot* assume that the work is unprotected by copyright. Only if the site explicitly says it is not copyrighted or is available for free use can you exceed fair use without permission.

EXERCISE 54.1
Recognizing plagiarism

The numbered items on the next page show various attempts to quote or paraphrase the following passage. Carefully compare each attempt with the original passage. Which attempts are plagiarized, inaccurate, or both, and which are acceptable? Why?

I would agree with the sociologists that psychiatric labeling is dangerous. Society can inflict terrible wounds by discrimination, and by confusing health with disease and disease with badness.

—GEORGE E. VAILLANT, *Adaptation to Life,* p. 361

1. According to George Vaillant, society often inflicts wounds by using psychiatric labeling, confusing health, disease, and badness (361).
2. According to George Vaillant, "psychiatric labeling [such as 'homosexual' or 'schizophrenic'] is dangerous. Society can inflict terrible wounds by . . . confusing health with disease and disease with badness" (361).
3. According to George Vaillant, when psychiatric labeling discriminates between health and disease or between disease and badness, it can inflict wounds on those labeled (361).
4. Psychiatric labels can badly hurt those labeled, says George Vaillant, because they fail to distinguish among health, illness, and immorality (361).
5. Labels such as "homosexual" and "schizophrenic" can be hurtful when they fail to distinguish among health, illness, and immorality.
6. "I would agree with the sociologists that society can inflict terrible wounds by discrimination, and by confusing health with disease and disease with badness" (Vaillant 361).

54e Document sources carefully.

Every time you borrow the words, facts, or ideas of others, you must **document** the source—that is, supply a reference (or document) telling readers that you borrowed the material and where you borrowed it from.

Editors and teachers in most academic disciplines require special documentation formats (or styles) in their scholarly journals and in students' papers. All the styles share common features:

- A citation in the text serves two purposes: it signals that material is borrowed, and it refers readers to detailed information about the source so that they can locate both the source and the place in the source where the borrowed material appears.
- Detailed source information, either in footnotes or at the end of the paper, tells readers precisely how to find the source.

Aside from these essential similarities, the disciplines' documentation styles differ markedly in citation form, arrangement of source information, and other particulars. Each discipline's style reflects the needs of its practitioners for certain kinds of information presented in certain ways. For instance, the currency of a source is important in the social sciences, where studies build on and correct each other; thus in-text citations in the social sciences include a source's date of publication. In the humanities, however, currency is less important, so in-text citations do not include date of publication.

The disciplines' documentation formats are described in style guides, including those in the following list. This book presents the styles of the guides marked *: the *MLA Handbook* and the *APA Publication Manual*. In addition, the styles of two of the other guides are detailed on this book's Web site: *The Chicago Manual of Style* (for the humanities) and *Scientific Style and Format: The CBE Manual for Authors, Editors, and Publishers* (for the biological and other sciences). See the box on page 459.

Humanities

The Chicago Manual of Style. 15th ed. 2003. (See this book's Web site.)

*Gibaldi, Joseph. *MLA Handbook for Writers of Research Papers*. 6th ed. 2003. (See pp. 471–517.)

Turabian, Kate L. *A Manual for Writers of Term Papers, Theses, and Dissertations*. 6th ed. Rev. John Grossman and Alice Bennett. 1996.

Social sciences

American Anthropological Association. "AAA Style Guide." 2002. *http://www.aaanet.org/pubs/style_guide.htm*.

American Management Association. *The AMA Style Guide for Business Writing*. 1996.

American Political Science Association. *Style Manual for Political Science*. 2001.

*American Psychological Association. *Publication Manual of the American Psychological Association*. 5th ed. 2001. (See pp. 517–42.)

American Sociological Association. *ASA Style Guide*. 2nd ed. 1997.

A Uniform System of Citation (law). 16th ed. 1996.

Sciences and mathematics

American Chemical Society. *ACS Style Guide: A Manual for Authors and Editors*. 2nd ed. 1997.

American Institute of Physics. *Style Manual for Guidance in the Preparation of Papers*. 4th ed. 1990.

American Mathematical Society. *The AMS Author Handbook: General Instructions for Preparing Manuscripts*. Rev. ed. 1996.

American Medical Association Manual of Style. 9th ed. 1998.

Bates, Robert L., Rex Buchanan, and Marla Adkins-Heljeson, eds. *Geowriting: A Guide to Writing, Editing, and Printing in Earth Science*. 5th ed. 1995.

Council of Biology Editors. *Scientific Style and Format: The CBE Manual for Authors, Editors, and Publishers*. 6th ed. 1994. (CBE is now called the Council of Science Editors.) (See this book's Web site.)

Always ask your instructor which documentation style you should use. If your instructor does not require a particular style, use the one in this book that's appropriate for the discipline you're writing in. Do follow a single system for citing sources so that you provide all the necessary information in a consistent format.

Note Bibliography software, such as *BiblioCite* and *Endnote,* can help you format your source citations in the style of your choice. The programs prompt you for needed information (author's name, book title, date of publication, and so on) and then arrange, capitalize, and punctuate the information as required by the style. But no program can anticipate all varieties of source information or substitute for your own care and attention in giving your sources accurate and complete acknowledgment in the required form.

55 Writing the Paper

What are the stages of writing research?

Like other kinds of writing, research writing involves focusing on a main idea, organizing ideas, expressing ideas in a draft, revising and editing drafts, and formatting the final paper. Because research writing draws on others' work, however, its stages also require attention to interpreting, integrating, and citing sources.

This chapter complements and extends the detailed discussion of the writing situation and the writing process in Chapters 1–5, which also include many tips for using a word processor and more links to this book's Web site. If you haven't already done so, you may want to read Chapters 1–5 before this one.

55a Focus and organize the paper.

Before you begin using your source notes in a draft, give some thought to your main idea and your organization.

1 • Thesis statement

You began research with a question about your subject (see p. 408). Though that question may have evolved during research, you

http://www.ablongman.com/littlebrown
➤ Research writing
➤ Downloads ➤ Checklist for revising a research paper
➤ Web links ➤ Writing the paper
➤ Writing process ➤ Web exercises ➤ Exer. 3

should be able to answer it once you've consulted most of your sources. Try to state that answer in a **thesis statement,** a claim that narrows your subject to a single idea. Here, for example, are the research question and thesis statement of Kisha Alder, whose final paper appears on pages 511–17:

> Research question
>
> How, if at all, should the Internet be taxed?
>
> Thesis statement
>
> To improve equity between online and traditional stores and between consumers with and without Internet access, tax laws should be revised to allow collection of sales taxes on Internet purchases.

A precise thesis statement will give you a focus as you organize and draft your paper. For more on thesis statements, see pages 18–21.

2 • Organization

To structure your paper, you'll need to synthesize, or forge relationships among ideas (see pp. 445–46). Here is one approach:

- *Arrange source information in categories.* Each group should correspond to a main section of your paper: a key idea of your own that supports the thesis.
- *Review your research journal* for connections between sources and other thoughts that can help you organize your paper.
- *Look objectively at your categories.* If some are skimpy, with little information, consider whether you should drop the categories or conduct more research to fill them out. If most of your information falls into one or two categories, consider whether they are too broad and should be divided. (If any of this rethinking affects your thesis statement, revise it accordingly.)
- *Within each group, distinguish between the main idea and the supporting ideas and evidence.* Only the support should come from your sources. The main idea should be your own.

See pages 22–26 for more on organizing a paper, including samples of both informal and formal outlines.

55b Draft, revise, and format the paper.

1 • First draft

In drafting your paper, you do not have to proceed methodically from introduction to conclusion. Here are some tips for writing a draft:

- *Work section by section.* Draft your paper in sections, beginning with the one you feel most confident about. Each section should center on a principal idea contributing to your thesis, a conclusion you have drawn from reading and responding to sources. Start the section by stating the idea; then support it with information, summaries, paraphrases, and quotations from your notes. Remember to insert source information from your notes as well.

  If you have kept your notes on a computer, you can import them (and source information) directly into your draft and then rewrite and edit them so that they work for your ideas and fit into your sentences.
- *Weave the sections together with transitions and other signposts.* As the sections of your paper develop, you will see relationships emerging among them. Spell these relationships out, and highlight them with transitions (see pp. 59 and 71–73). Headings may be appropriate to highlight your organization and signal direction. These signposts will help create a coherent whole.
- *Track source citations.* As you draft your paper, insert the source of each summary, paraphrase, and quotation in parentheses in the text—for instance, "(Frankel 42)" referring to page 42 in a work by Frankel. If you are conscientious about inserting these notes and carrying them through successive drafts, you will be less likely to plagiarize accidentally and you will have little difficulty documenting your sources in the final paper.

2 • Revision and editing

For a complex project like a research paper, you'll certainly want to revise in at least two stages—first for thesis, structure, and other whole-paper issues, and then for clarity, grammar, and similar sentence-level issues. Chapter 5 supports this two-stage approach with checklists for revision (p. 32) and editing (p. 40). The box opposite provides additional steps to take when revising a research paper. (You can download this checklist from this book's Web site: see the box on p. 468. Copy the checklist for each research paper, answering the questions in writing.)

3 • Format

The final draft of your paper should conform to the document format recommended by your instructor or by the style guide of the discipline in which you are writing (see p. 467). This book details two common formats: Modern Language Association (opposite) and American Psychological Association (p. 517).

Checklist for revising a research paper

Thesis statement

How well does your thesis statement describe your subject and your perspective as they emerged during drafting?

Structure

(Outlining your draft as suggested on p. 31 can help you see structure at a glance.)

How consistently does borrowed material illuminate and support—not lead and dominate—your own ideas? How well is the importance of ideas reflected in the emphasis they receive? Will the arrangement of ideas be clear to readers?

Evidence

Where might supporting evidence seem weak or irrelevant to readers?

Reasonableness and clarity

How reasonable will readers find your argument? (See pp. 113–19.) Where do you need to define terms or concepts that readers may not know or may dispute?

In any discipline you can use a word processor to present your ideas effectively and attractively with readable type fonts, headings, illustrations, and other elements. See pages 75–85 for ideas.

56 MLA Documentation and Format

How do I cite sources and format papers in English and other humanities?

The style guide for English, foreign languages, and some other humanities is the *MLA Handbook for Writers of Research Papers* (6th

http://www.ablongman.com/littlebrown

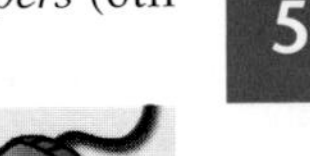

➤ Research writing
  ➤ Web exercises ➤ Exer. 10
  ➤ Downloads ➤ Chapter 56 exercise in electronic format
➤ Documentation in the disciplines ➤ MLA style

ed., 2003), published by the Modern Language Association. In the MLA documentation system, you twice acknowledge each quotation, paraphrase, or summary:

- In your text, a brief parenthetical citation next to the borrowed material directs readers to a complete list of all the works you cite.
- At the end of your paper, the list of works cited includes complete bibliographical information for every source.

Every entry in the list of works cited has at least one corresponding citation in the text, and every in-text citation has a corresponding entry in the list of works cited.

This chapter describes MLA documentation in detail: writing text citations (below), placing citations (p. 477), using supplementary notes (p. 479), and preparing the list of works cited (p. 479). A detailed discussion of MLA document format (p. 509) and a sample MLA paper (p. 511) conclude the chapter.

56a Use MLA parenthetical citations in your text.

1 • Citation formats

In-text citations of sources have two requirements:

- They must include just enough information for the reader to locate the appropriate source in the list of works cited at the end of your paper.
- They must include just enough information for the reader to locate the place in the source where the borrowed material appears.

For any kind of source, you can usually meet both these requirements by providing the author's last name and (if the source uses them) the page numbers where the borrowed material appears. The reader can find the source in your list of works cited and find the borrowed material in the source itself.

The following models illustrate the basic text-citation forms and also forms for more unusual sources, such as those with no named author or no page numbers.

Note Models 1 and 2 opposite show the direct relationship between what you include in your text and what you include in a parenthetical citation. If you do *not* name the author in your text, you include the name in parentheses before the page reference (model 1). If you *do* name the author in your text, you do not include the name in parentheses (model 2).

MLA parenthetical text citations

1. Author not named in your text

When you have not already named the author in your sentence, provide the author's last name and the page number(s), with no punctuation between them, in parentheses:

> One researcher concludes that "women impose a distinctive construction on moral problems, seeing moral dilemmas in terms of conflicting responsibilities" (Gilligan 105).

2. Author named in your text

If the author's name is already given in your text, you need not repeat it in the parenthetical citation. The citation gives just the page number(s):

> One researcher, Carol Gilligan, concludes that "women impose a distinctive construction on moral problems, seeing moral dilemmas in terms of conflicting responsibilities" (105).

3. A work with two or three authors

If the source has two or three authors, give all their last names in the text or in the citation. Separate two authors' names with "and":

> As Frieden and Sagalyn observe, "The poor and the minorities were the leading victims of highway and renewal programs" (29).

> According to one study, "The poor and the minorities were the leading victims of highway and renewal programs" (Frieden and Sagalyn 29).

With three authors, add commas and also "and" before the final name:

> The text by Wilcox, Ault, and Agee discusses the "ethical dilemmas in public relations practice" (125).

> One text discusses the "ethical dilemmas in public relations practice" (Wilcox, Ault, and Agee 125).

4. A work with more than three authors

If the source has more than three authors, you may list all their last names or use only the first author's name followed by "et al." (the abbreviation for the Latin "and others"). The choice depends on what you do in your list of works cited (see p. 482).

> It took the combined forces of the Americans, Europeans, and Japanese to break the rebel siege of Beijing in 1900 (Lopez et al. 362).

> It took the combined forces of the Americans, Europeans, and Japanese to break the rebel siege of Beijing in 1900 (Lopez, Blum, Cameron, and Barnes 362).

5. A work with numbered paragraphs or screens instead of pages

Some electronic sources number each paragraph or screen instead of each page. In citing passages in these sources, give the paragraph or screen number(s) and distinguish them from page numbers: after the author's name, put a comma, a space, and the abbreviation "par." (one paragraph), "pars." (more than one paragraph), "screen," or "screens."

> Twins reared apart report similar feelings (Palfrey, pars. 6-7).

6. An entire work or a work with no page or other reference numbers

When you cite an entire work rather than a part of it, the citation will not include any page or paragraph number. Try to work the author's name into your text, in which case you will not need a parenthetical citation. But remember that the source must appear in the list of works cited.

> Boyd deals with the need to acknowledge and come to terms with our fear of nuclear technology.

Use the same format when you cite a specific passage from a work that has no page, paragraph, or other reference numbers, such as an online source.

If the author's name does not appear in your text, put it in a parenthetical citation:

> Almost 20 percent of commercial banks have been audited for the practice (Friis).

7. A multivolume work

If you consulted only one volume of a multivolume work, your list of works cited will indicate as much (see p. 485), and you can treat the volume as any book.

If you consulted two or more volumes of a multivolume work, your citation must indicate which one you are referring to. In the example the number 5 indicates the volume from which the quotation was taken; the number 438 indicates the page number in that volume.

> After issuing the Emancipation Proclamation, Lincoln said, "What I did, I did after very full deliberations, and under a very heavy and solemn sense of responsibility" (5: 438).

8. A work by an author of two or more cited works

If your list of works cited includes two or more works by the same author, then your citation must tell the reader which of the author's works you are referring to. Give the title either in the text or in a parenthetical citation. In a parenthetical citation, give the full title only if it is brief; otherwise, shorten the title to the first one or two main words (excluding *A, An,* or *The*). For the following source, the full book title is *The Arts and Human Development:*

> At about age seven, most children begin to use appropriate gestures to reinforce their stories (Gardner, Arts 144-45).

9. An anonymous work

Anonymous works are alphabetized by title in the list of works cited. In the text they are referred to by full or shortened title. The next citation refers to an unsigned article titled "The Right to Die." (A page number is omitted because the article is only one page.)

> One article notes that a death-row inmate may demand his own execution to achieve a fleeting notoriety ("Right").

If two or more anonymous works have the same title, distinguish them with additional information in the text citation, such as the publication date, periodical title, or online site title.

10. A government publication or a work with a corporate author

If the author of the work is listed as a government body or a corporation, cite the work by that organization's name. If the name is long, work it into the text to avoid an intrusive citation.

A 2002 report by the Hawaii Department of Education predicts an increase in enrollments (6).

11. An indirect source

When you want to use a quotation that is already in quotation marks—indicating that the author you are reading is quoting someone else—try to find the original source and quote directly from it. If you can't find the original source, then your citation must indicate that your quotation of it is indirect. In the following citation, "qtd. in" ("quoted in") says that Davino was quoted by Boyd:

George Davino maintains that "even small children have vivid ideas about nuclear energy" (qtd. in Boyd 22).

The list of works cited then includes only Boyd (the work consulted), not Davino.

12. A literary work

Novels, plays, and poems are often available in many editions, so your instructor may ask you to provide information that will help readers find the passage you cite no matter what edition they consult. For novels, the page number comes first, followed by a semicolon and then information on the appropriate part or chapter of the work.

Toward the end of James's novel, Maggie suddenly feels "the thick breath of the definite--which was the intimate, the immediate, the familiar, as she hadn't had them for so long" (535; pt. 6, ch. 41).

For poems that are not divided into parts, you can omit the page number and supply the line number(s) for the quotation. To prevent confusion with page numbers, precede the number(s) with "line" or "lines" in the first citation; then just use the number(s).

In Shakespeare's Sonnet 73 the speaker identifies with the trees of late autumn, "Bare ruined choirs, where late the sweet birds sang" (line 4). "In me," Shakespeare writes, "thou seest the glowing of such fire / That on the ashes of his youth doth lie . . ." (9-10).

For verse plays and poems that are divided into parts, omit a page number and cite the appropriate part—act (and scene, if any), canto, book, and so on—plus the line number(s). Use Arabic numerals for parts, including acts and scenes (3.4 in the example).

Later in King Lear the disguised Edgar says, "The prince of darkness is a gentleman" (3.4.147).

For prose plays, provide the page number followed by the act and scene, if any (see the citation of *Death of a Salesman* on p. 479).

13. The Bible

When you cite passages of the Bible in parentheses, abbreviate the title of any book longer than four letters—for instance, "Gen." (Genesis), "1 Sam." (1 Samuel), "Ps." (Psalms), "Matt." (Matthew). Then give the chapter and verse(s) in Arabic numerals.

> According to the Bible, at Babel God "did . . . confound the language of all the earth" (Gen. 11.9).

14. An electronic source

Cite an electronic source as you would any other source: usually by author's name or, if there is no author, by title.

> Business forecasts for the fourth quarter tended to be optimistic (White 4).

This example cites a source with page numbers. For a source with paragraph or screen numbers or no numbering, see models 5 and 6 (p. 474).

15. Two or more works in the same citation

If you use a single parenthetical citation to refer to more than one work, separate the references with a semicolon.

> Two recent articles point out that a computer badly used can be less efficient than no computer at all (Gough and Hall 201; Richards 162).

Since long citations in the text can distract the reader, you may choose to cite several or more works in an endnote or footnote rather than in the text. See page 479.

2 • Placement and punctuation of parenthetical citations

Where to place citations

Position text citations to accomplish two goals: (1) make it clear exactly where your borrowing begins and ends; (2) keep the citation as unobtrusive as possible. You can accomplish both goals by placing the parenthetical citation at the end of the sentence element containing the borrowed material. This sentence element may be a phrase or a clause, and it may begin, interrupt, or conclude the sentence. Usually, as in the following examples, the element ends with a punctuation mark.

> The inflation rate might climb as high as 30 percent (Kim 164), an increase that could threaten the small nation's stability.

> The inflation rate, which might climb as high as 30 percent (Kim 164), could threaten the small nation's stability.

> The small nation's stability could be threatened by its inflation rate, which, one source predicts, might climb as high as 30 percent (Kim 164).

In the last example the addition of *one source predicts* clarifies that Kim is responsible only for the inflation-rate prediction, not for the statement about stability.

When your paraphrase or summary of a source runs longer than a sentence, clarify the boundaries by using the author's name in the first sentence and placing the parenthetical citation at the end of the last sentence.

> Juliette Kim studied the effects of acutely high inflation in several South American and African countries since World War II. She discovered that a major change in government accompanied or followed the inflationary period in 56 percent of cases (22-23).

How to punctuate citations

Generally place a parenthetical citation *before* any punctuation required by your sentence, as in the preceding examples. If the borrowed material is a quotation, place the citation *between* the closing quotation mark and the punctuation.

> Spelling argues that during the 1970s American automobile manufacturers met consumer needs "as well as could be expected" (26), but not everyone agrees with him.

The exception is a quotation ending in a question mark or exclamation point. Then use the appropriate punctuation inside the closing quotation mark, and follow the quotation with the text citation and a period.

> "Of what use is genius," Emerson asks, "if the organ . . . cannot find a focal distance within the actual horizon of human life?" ("Experience" 60). Mad genius is no genius.

When a citation appears at the end of a quotation set off from the text, place it one space *after* the punctuation ending the quotation. No additional punctuation is needed.

> In Arthur Miller's Death of a Salesman, the most poignant defense of Willie Loman comes from his wife, Linda:
>
> > He's not the finest character that ever lived. But he's a human being, and a terrible thing is happening to him. So attention must be paid. He's not to be allowed to fall into his grave like an old dog. Attention, attention must finally be paid to such a person. (56; act 1)

(This citation of a play includes the act number as well as the page number. See pp. 476–77.)

3 • Footnotes or endnotes in special circumstances

Footnotes or endnotes may replace parenthetical citations when you cite several sources at once, when you comment on a source, or when you provide information that does not fit easily in the text. Signal a footnote or endnote in your text with a numeral raised above the appropriate line. Then write a note with the same numeral.

Text At least five studies have confirmed these results.[1]

Note [1] Abbott and Winger 266-68; Casner 27; Hoyenga 78-79; Marino 36; Tripp, Tripp, and Walk 179-83.

In a note the raised numeral is indented one-half inch or five spaces and is followed by a space. If the note appears as a footnote, place it at the bottom of the page on which the citation appears, set it off from the text with quadruple spacing, and single-space the note itself. If the note appears as an endnote, place it in numerical order with the other endnotes on a page between the text and the list of works cited. Double-space all the endnotes.

56b Prepare the MLA list of works cited.

At the end of your paper, a list titled Works Cited includes all the sources you quoted, paraphrased, or summarized in your paper. (If your instructor asks you to include sources you examined but did not cite, title the list Works Consulted.)

The list of works cited always begins a new page, numbered in sequence with the preceding pages. Format the list as in the sample on the next page. Arrange all your sources in alphabetical order by the last name of the author—or by the last name of the first author if there is more than one. If a source has no named author, alphabetize it by the first main word of the title (excluding *A, An,* or *The*).

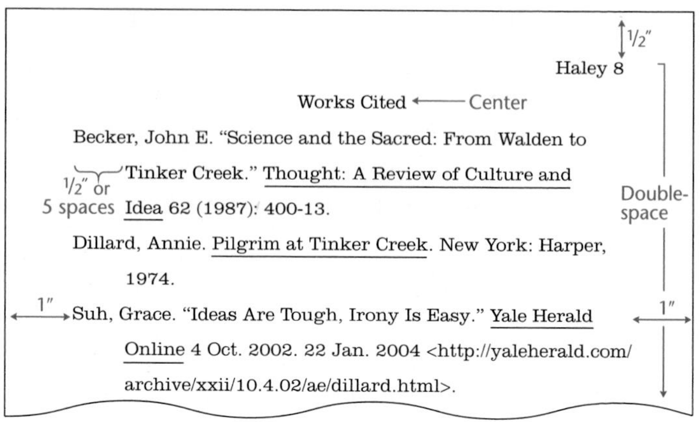
Haley 8

Works Cited

Becker, John E. "Science and the Sacred: From Walden to Tinker Creek." Thought: A Review of Culture and Idea 62 (1987): 400-13.

Dillard, Annie. Pilgrim at Tinker Creek. New York: Harper, 1974.

Suh, Grace. "Ideas Are Tough, Irony Is Easy." Yale Herald Online 4 Oct. 2002. 22 Jan. 2004 <http://yaleherald.com/archive/xxii/10.4.02/ae/dillard.html>.

Use *only* alphabetical order to arrange sources, not another principle such as type of source or date of publication.

The box on these two pages directs you to the MLA formats for works-cited entries. Use your best judgment in adapting the models to your particular sources. If you can't find a model that exactly matches a source you used, locate and follow the closest possible match. You will certainly need to combine formats—for instance, drawing on model 2 ("A book with two or three authors") and model 26 ("An article in a daily newspaper") for a newspaper article with two authors.

MLA works-cited models

Books

1 • Books

The basic format for a book includes the following elements:

① ② ③a ③b ③c

Gilligan, Carol. In a Different Voice: Psychological Theory and Women's Development. Cambridge: Harvard UP, 1982.

1. *Author.* Use the author's full name: the last name first, followed by a comma, and then the first name and any middle name or initial. End the name with a period and one space.
2. *Title.* Give the full title, including any subtitle. Underline the title unless your instructor specifically calls for italics. Capitalize all important words (see pp. 393–94), separate the main title and the subtitle with a colon and one space, and end the title with a period and one space.
3. *Publication information.* You can usually find this information on the book's title page or on the back of the title page.
   a. *The city of publication,* followed by a colon and one space.
   b. *The name of the publisher,* followed by a comma. Shorten most publishers' names—in many cases to a single word. For instance, use "Little" for Little, Brown or "Random" for Random House. For university presses, use the abbreviations "U" and "P," as in the example.
   c. *The date of publication,* ending with a period. Use the latest copyright date if the publication year does not appear on the title page.

When other information is required for a reference, it generally falls either between the author's name and the title or between the title and the publication information, as in the following models.

1. A book with one author

Gilligan, Carol. <u>In a Different Voice: Psychological Theory and Women's Development</u>. Cambridge: Harvard UP, 1982.

2. A book with two or three authors

Lifton, Robert Jay, and Greg Mitchell. <u>Who Owns Death: Capital Punishment, the American Conscience, and the End of Executions</u>. New York: Morrow, 2000.

Wilcox, Dennis L., Phillip H. Ault, and Warren K. Agee. <u>Public Relations: Strategies and Tactics</u>. 4th ed. New York: Harper, 1999.

Give the authors' names in the order provided on the title page. Reverse the first and last names of the first author *only,* not of any other authors. Separate two authors' names with a comma and "and"; separate three authors' names with commas and with "and" before the third name.

3. A book with more than three authors

Lopez, Robert S., Susan Blum, Susan Cameron, and William J. Barnes. <u>Civilizations: Western and World</u>. Boston: Little, 1995.

Lopez, Robert S., et al. Civilizations: Western and World. Boston: Little, 1995.

You may, but need not, give all authors' names if the work has more than three authors. If you choose not to give all names, provide the name of the first author only, and follow the name with a comma and the abbreviation "et al." (for the Latin *et alii,* meaning "and others").

4. Two or more works by the same author(s)

Gardner, Howard. The Arts and Human Development. New York: Wiley, 1973.

---. The Quest for Mind: Piaget, Lévi-Strauss, and the Structuralist Movement. New York: Knopf, 1973.

Give the author's name only in the first entry. For the second and any subsequent works by the same author, substitute three hyphens for the author's name, followed by a period. (If you are citing two or more works by the same editor, editors, or translator, follow the hyphens with a comma and "ed.," "eds.," or "trans." as appropriate. See models 5, 6, and 7.) Note that the three hyphens stand for *exactly* the same name or names. If the second source above were by Gardner and somebody else, both names would have to be given in full.

Place an entry or entries using three hyphens immediately after the entry that names the author. Within the set of entries by the same author, arrange the sources alphabetically by the first main word of the title, as in the preceding examples (Arts, then Quest).

5. A book with an editor

Holland, Merlin, and Rupert Hart-Davis, eds. The Complete Letters of Oscar Wilde. New York: Holt, 2000.

Handle editors' names like authors' names (models 1–3), but add a comma and the abbreviation "ed." (one editor) or "eds." (two or more editors) after the last editor's name.

6. A book with an author and an editor

Mumford, Lewis. The City in History. Ed. Donald L. Miller. New York: Pantheon, 1986.

When citing the work of the author, give his or her name first, and give the editor's name after the title, preceded by "Ed." (singular only, meaning "Edited by"). When citing the work of the editor, use model 5 for a book with an editor, and give the author's name after the title preceded by "By": Miller, Donald L., ed. The City in History. By Lewis Mumford.

7. A translation

Alighieri, Dante. The Inferno. Trans. John Ciardi. New York: NAL, 1971.

When citing the work of the author, give his or her name first, and give the translator's name after the title, preceded by "Trans." ("Translated by"). When citing the work of the translator, give his or her name first, followed by a comma and "trans."; then follow the title with "By" and the author's name: Ciardi, John, trans. The Inferno. By Dante Alighieri.

When a book you cite by author has a translator and an editor, give the translator's *and* editor's names in the order used on the book's title page. For a translated selection from an edited book, see model 18, page 486.

8. A book with a corporate author

Lorenz Research, Inc. Research in Social Studies Teaching. Baltimore: Arrow, 2004.

List the name of the corporation, institution, or other body as author.

9. An anonymous book

The Dorling Kindersley World Reference Atlas. London: Dorling, 2003.

List an anonymous book by its full title. Alphabetize the book by the title's first main word (here Dorling), omitting *A, An,* or *The.*

10. The Bible

The Bible. King James Version.

The New English Bible. London: Oxford UP and Cambridge UP, 1970.

When citing a standard version of the Bible (first example), do not underline the title or the name of the version, and you need not provide publication information. For an edition of the Bible (second example), underline the title and give full publication information.

11. A later edition

Bollinger, Dwight L. Aspects of Language. 2nd ed. New York: Harcourt, 1975.

For any edition after the first, place the edition number after the title. (If an editor's name follows the title, place the edition number after the name. See model 18.) Use the appropriate designation for editions that are named or dated rather than numbered—for instance, "Rev. ed." for "Revised edition."

12. A republished book

James, Henry. The Golden Bowl. 1904. London: Penguin, 1966.

Republished books include paperbound editions of books originally released in hard bindings and books reissued under new titles. Place the original date of publication (but not the place of publication or the publisher's name) after the title, and then provide the full publication information for the source you are using. If the book was originally published under a different title, add this title at the end of the entry and move the original publication date to follow the title—for example, Rpt. of Thomas Hardy: A Life. 1941.

13. A book with a title in its title

Eco, Umberto. Postscript to The Name of the Rose. Trans. William Weaver. New York: Harcourt, 1983.

When a book's title contains another book title (as here: *The Name of the Rose*), do not underline the second title. When a book's title contains a quotation or the title of a work normally placed in quotation marks, keep the quotation marks and underline both titles: Critical Response to Henry James's "Beast in the Jungle." (Note that the underlining extends under the closing quotation mark.)

14. A work in more than one volume

Lincoln, Abraham. The Collected Works of Abraham Lincoln. Ed. Roy P. Basler. 8 vols. New Brunswick: Rutgers UP, 1953.

Lincoln, Abraham. The Collected Works of Abraham Lincoln. Ed. Roy P. Basler. Vol. 5. New Brunswick: Rutgers UP, 1953. 8 vols.

If you use two or more volumes of a multivolume work, give the work's total number of volumes before the publication information ("8 vols." in the first example). Your text citation will indicate which volume you are citing (see p. 475). If you use only one volume, give that volume number before the publication information ("Vol. 5" in the second example). You may add the total number of volumes to the end of the entry ("8 vols." in the second example).

If you cite a multivolume work published over a period of years, give the inclusive years as the publication date: for instance, Cambridge: Harvard UP, 1978-90.

15. A work in a series

Bergman, Ingmar. The Seventh Seal. Mod. Film Scripts Ser. 12. New York: Simon, 1968.

Place the name of the series (not quoted or underlined) just before the publication information. Abbreviate common words such as *modern* and *series*. Add any series number after the series title.

16. Published proceedings of a conference

Watching Our Language: A Conference Sponsored by the Program in Architecture and Design Criticism. 6-8 May 2002. New York: Parsons School of Design, 2002.

Whether in or after the title of the conference, supply information about who sponsored the conference, when it was held, and who published the proceedings. Treat a particular presentation at the conference like a selection from an anthology (model 18).

17. An anthology

Kennedy, X. J., and Dana Gioia, eds. Literature: An Introduction to Fiction, Poetry, and Drama. 9th ed. New York: Longman, 2005.

Cite an entire anthology only when citing the work of the editor or editors or when your instructor permits cross-referencing like that shown in model 19. Give the name of the editor or editors (followed by "ed." or "eds.") and then the title of the anthology.

18. A selection from an anthology

Allende, Isabel. "The Judge's Wife." Trans. Margaret Sayers Peden. Literature: An Introduction to Fiction, Poetry, and Drama. Ed. X. J. Kennedy and Dana Gioia. 9th ed. New York: Longman, 2005. 479-84.

The essentials of this listing are these: author of selection; title of selection (in quotation marks); title of anthology (underlined); editors' names preceded by "Ed." (meaning "Edited by"); publication information for the anthology; and inclusive page numbers for the selection (without the abbreviation "pp."). In addition, this source requires a translator for the selection and an edition number for the anthology. If you wish, you may also supply the original date of publication for the work you are citing, after its title. See model 12 on page 485.

If the work you cite comes from a collection of works by one author and with no editor, use the following form:

Auden, W. H. "Family Ghosts." The Collected Poetry of W. H. Auden. New York: Random House, 1945. 132-33.

If the work you cite is a scholarly article that was previously printed elsewhere, provide the complete information for the earlier publication of the piece, followed by "Rpt. in" ("Reprinted in") and the information for the source in which you found the piece:

Molloy, Francis C. "The Suburban Vision in John O'Hara's Short Stories." Critique: Studies in Modern Fiction 25.2 (1984): 101-13. Rpt. in Short Story Criticism: Excerpts from Criticism of the Works of Short Fiction Writers. Ed. David Segal. Vol. 15. Detroit: Gale, 1989. 287-92.

San Juan, E. "Theme Versus Imitation: D. H. Lawrence's 'The Rocking-Horse Winner.'" D. H. Lawrence Review 3 (1970): 136-40. Rpt. in From Fiction to Film: D. H. Lawrence's "The Rocking-Horse Winner." Ed. Gerald R. Barrett and Thomas L. Erskine. Dickenson Literature and Film Ser. Encino: Dickenson, 1974. 70-74.

19. Two or more selections from the same anthology

Chopin, Kate. "The Storm." Kennedy and Gioia 552-53.

Kennedy, X. J., and Dana Gioia, eds. Literature: An Introduction to Fiction, Poetry, and Drama. 9th ed. New York: Longman, 2005.

O'Connor, Flannery. "Revelation." Kennedy and Gioia 443-58.

When you are citing more than one selection from the same source, you may avoid repetition by giving the source in full (as in the Kennedy and Gioia entry) and then simply cross-referencing it in entries for the works you used. Thus, instead of full information for the Chopin and O'Connor works, give Kennedy and Gioia and the appropriate pages in that book. Note that each entry appears in its proper alphabetical place among other works cited.

20. An introduction, preface, foreword, or afterword

Donaldson, Norman. Introduction. The Claverings. By Anthony Trollope. New York: Dover, 1977. vii-xv.

An introduction, foreword, or afterword is often written by someone other than the book's author. When citing such a piece, give its name without quotation marks or underlining. (But if the piece has a title of its own, provide it, in quotation marks, between the name of the author and the name of the piece.) Follow the title of the book with its author's name preceded by "By." Give the inclusive page numbers of the part you cite. (In the preceding example, the small Roman numerals indicate that the cited work is in the front matter of the book, before page 1.)

When the author of a preface or introduction is the same as the author of the book, give only the last name after the title:

> Gould, Stephen Jay. Prologue. The Flamingo's Smile: Reflections in Natural History. By Gould. New York: Norton, 1985. 13-20.

21. An article in a reference work

> Mark, Herman F. "Polymers." The New Encyclopaedia Britannica: Macropaedia. 15th ed. 1991.
>
> "Reckon." Merriam-Webster's Collegiate Dictionary. 11th ed. 2003.

List an article in a reference work by its title (second example) unless the article is signed (first example). For works with entries arranged alphabetically, you need not include volume or page numbers. For well-known works like those listed above, you may also omit the editors' names and all publication information except any edition number and the year of publication. For works that are not well known, give full publication information:

> "Hungarians in America." The Ethnic Almanac. Ed. Stephanie Bernardo. New York: Doubleday, 1991. 109-11.

2 • Periodicals: Journals, magazines, and newspapers

The basic format for an article from a periodical includes the following information:

> Lever, Janet. "Sex Differences in the Games Children Play." Social Problems 23 (1996): 478-87.

1. *Author.* Use the author's full name: last name first, followed by a comma, and then the first name and any middle name or initial. Omit any title or degree attached to the author's name on the source, such as Dr. or PhD. End the name with a period and one space.
2. *Title of the article.* Give the full title, including any subtitle. Place the title in quotation marks, capitalize all important words in the title (see pp. 393–94), and end the title with a period (inside the final quotation mark) and one space.

3. *Publication information:*
   a. *The title of the periodical,* underlined, followed by a space. Omit any *A, An,* or *The* from the beginning of the title.
   b. *The volume and/or issue number* (in Arabic numerals), followed by a space. See the note following.
   c. *The date of publication,* followed by a colon and a space. See the note following.
   d. *The inclusive page numbers of the article* (without the abbreviation "pp."). For the second number in inclusive page numbers over 100, provide only as many digits as needed for clarity (usually two): 87–88, 100–01, 398–401, 1026–36, 1190–206. If the article does not run on consecutive pages, provide only the first page number followed by a plus sign: 16+. (See also model 26, next page.) See pages 497–498 on electronic periodicals that lack page or other reference numbers.

Note The treatment of volume and issue numbers and publication dates varies depending on the kind of periodical being cited, as the models indicate. For the distinction between journals and magazines, see page 425.

22. An article in a journal with continuous pagination throughout the annual volume

Lever, Janet. "Sex Differences in the Games Children Play." Social Problems 23 (1996): 478-87.

Some journals number the pages of issues consecutively throughout a year, so that each issue after the first in a year begins numbering where the previous issue left off—say, at page 416. For this kind of journal, give the volume number after the title ("23" in the example above) and place the year of publication in parentheses. The page numbers will be enough to guide readers to the issue you used.

23. An article in a journal that pages issues separately or that numbers only issues, not volumes

Dacey, June. "Management Participation in Corporate Buy-Outs." Management Perspectives 7.4 (1998): 20-31.

Some journals page each issue separately (starting each issue at page 1). For these journals, give the volume number, a period, and the issue number (as in "7.4" in the Dacey entry above). Then readers know which issue of the periodical to consult. When citing an article in a journal that numbers only issues, not annual volumes, treat the issue number as if it were a volume number, as in model 22.

24. An article in a monthly or bimonthly magazine

Garber, Marjorie. "Our Genius Problem." Atlantic Monthly Dec. 2002: 46-53.

Follow the magazine title with the month and the year of publication. (Abbreviate all months except May, June, and July.) Don't place the date in parentheses, and don't provide a volume or issue number.

25. An article in a weekly or biweekly magazine

Auletta, Ken. "The Media Mogul." New Yorker 27 Jan. 2003: 26-30.

Follow the magazine title with the day, the month (abbreviated), and the year of publication. (Abbreviate all months except May, June, and July.) Don't place the date in parentheses, and don't provide a volume or issue number.

26. An article in a daily newspaper

Kolata, Gina. "Kill All the Bacteria!" New York Times 7 Jan. 2004, natl. ed.: B1+.

Give the name of the newspaper as it appears on the first page (but without *A*, *An*, or *The*). If the name of the city is not in the title of a local newspaper, add the city name in brackets after the title, without underlining: Gazette [Chicago]. Then follow model 25, with two differences: (1) If the newspaper lists an edition at the top of the first page, include that information after the date and a comma. (See "natl. ed." above.) (2) If the newspaper is divided into lettered or numbered sections, provide the section designation before the page number when the newspaper does the same (as in "B1+" above); otherwise, provide the section designation before the colon —for instance, sec. 1: 1+. The plus sign here and with "B1+" in the preceding model indicates that the articles do not run on consecutive pages but start on page 1 or B1 and continue later.

27. An anonymous article

"The Right to Die." Time 11 Oct. 1996: 101.

For an article with no named author, begin the entry with the title of the article. In the list of works cited, alphabetize an anonymous source by the first main word of the title ("Right" in this model).

28. An editorial or letter to the editor

"Dualing Power Centers." Editorial. New York Times 14 Jan. 2004, natl. ed.: A16.

Add the word "Editorial" or "Letter"—but without quotation marks—after the title if there is one or after the author's name, as follows:

Dowding, Michael. Letter. Economist 5-11 Jan. 1995: 4.

(The numbers "5-11" in this entry are the publication days of the periodical: the issue spans January 5 through 11.)

29. A review

Nelson, Cary. "Between Anonymity and Celebrity." Rev. of Anxious Intellects: Academic Professionals, Public Intellectuals, and Enlightenment Values, by John Michael. College English 64 (2002): 710-19.

"Rev." is an abbreviation for "Review." The name of the author of the work being reviewed follows the title of the work, a comma, and "by." If the review has no title of its own, then "Rev. of . . ." (without quotation marks) immediately follows the name of the reviewer.

30. An abstract of a dissertation or article

Steciw, Steven K. "Alterations to the Pessac Project of Le Corbusier." Diss. U of Cambridge, England, 1986. DAI 46 (1986): 565C.

For an abstract appearing in *Dissertation Abstracts* (*DA*) or *Dissertation Abstracts International* (*DAI*), give the author's name and the title, "Diss." (for "Dissertation"), the institution granting the author's degree, the date of the dissertation, and the publication information.

For an abstract of an article, first provide the publication information for the article itself, followed by the information for the abstract. If the abstract publisher lists abstracts by item rather than page number, add "item" before the number.

Lever, Janet. "Sex Differences in the Games Children Play." Social Problems 23 (1996): 478-87. Psychological Abstracts 63 (1996): item 1431.

3 • Electronic sources

Electronic sources include those available on CD-ROM and those available online, either through your library's Web site or directly over the Internet. Like citations of print sources, citations of electronic sources require available information such as author, title, and date of publication. CD-ROMs require additional information such as vendor name (see models 31 and 32). Online sources require even more additional information, as shown in the sample below. If you need help with finding authors, titles, dates, and other features of online sources, see pages 414–15.

> Sagoff, Mark. "Do We Consume Too Much?" Environmental Challenges to Business. Ed. Joel Reichart and Patricia H. Werhane. Washington, DC: Soc. for Business Ethics, 2000. 106-16. Olsson Center for Applied Ethics. 18 Feb. 2004. U of Virginia. 4 Mar. 2004 <http://www.ocae.virginia.edu/ruffin2/sagoff.html>.

1. *Author.* Use the author's full name: last name first, followed by a comma, and then the first name and any middle name or initial. If you don't see the author's name at the top of the source, look at the end of the document page. If no author is listed, begin with the title.
2. *Title.* Use quotation marks around the title of a periodical article, a part of a book, or an individual document or page on a site. Use underlining for the title of an entire site.
3. *Publication information for the print version, if any.* Many online sources also appear in print, though often in a different format and sometimes with different content. If the source gives information about a print version, provide it after the source title, following an appropriate model from the previous pages. The source here, a selection from an anthology, follows model 18 (p. 486): anthology title, editors' names, place of publication, publisher, date of publication, and inclusive page numbers for the selection.
4. *Publication information for the online version:*
   a. *Title of the site,* underlined.
   b. *Date of electronic publication or last update.* This date is important even if the source has a print version.
   c. *Name of the organization or institution sponsoring the site.*

   If the site has an editor or a version number, add that information immediately after the site title.
5. *Date of your access.* Since online sources can and often do change, providing the date you last consulted the source tells readers which version you consulted. Do not add a period or other punctuation between the access date and the electronic address.

6. *Electronic address, or URL,* enclosed in angle brackets (< >). Usually you'll find the URL in the Location or Address field near the top of your browser screen. To ensure that you get the complete and accurate URL, use Copy and Paste to copy it from the browser into a word-processing file or an e-mail to yourself. In your list of works cited, break a URL *only* after a slash. Do not hyphenate.

Note A URL does not always provide a usable route to a source. The URL may be too long to copy accurately or conveniently, it may be unique to a particular search, or it may be unique to a particular library. In such a case, you may provide the URL of the site's search page, from which the reader can locate your source by author or title, or you may provide the URL of the site's home page along with any keywords or sequence of links you used to reach the source. For a subscription service, you may give just the home page URL or omit the URL; see models 33 and 34 (next two pages).

Try to locate all the information required in the following models. However, if you search for and still cannot find some information, then give what you can find.

31. A source on a periodical CD-ROM database

Kolata, Gina. "Kill All the Bacteria!" New York Times 7 Jan. 2004, natl. ed.: B1+. New York Times Ondisc. CD-ROM. UMI-ProQuest. Mar. 2004.

Databases on CD-ROM are issued periodically—for instance, every six months or every year. The journals, newspapers, and other publications included in such a database are generally available in print as well, so your works-cited entry should give the information for both formats: ① Information for the print version, following models on pages 489–91. ② Title of the CD-ROM, underlined. ③ Medium, "CD-ROM," without quotation marks or underlining. ④ Name of the vendor (or distributor) of the CD-ROM. ⑤ Date of electronic publication.

32. A source on a nonperiodical CD-ROM

Shelley, Mary Wollstonecraft. Frankenstein. Classic Library. CD-ROM. Alameda: Andromeda, 1993.

If you cite a single-issue CD-ROM, use this format: ① Author. ② Title. Underline titles of books or similarly long works. Use quotation marks for short works such as stories or chapters in books. ③ Title of the entire CD-ROM, if any, underlined. ④ Medium, "CD-ROM," without quotation marks or underlining. ⑤ CD-ROM's place of publication, publisher, and date of publication.

If the work you cite or the entire disk has a version or edition number, add it at the appropriate place, as shown in the model below:

> "Sugar." Concise Columbia Encyclopedia. 3rd ed. Microsoft Bookshelf. CD-ROM. 2003-04 ed. Redmond: Microsoft, 2003.

This model also shows citation of a part of a work (in quotation marks) with no author.

33. A work from an online service to which your library subscribes

> ①Netchaeva, Irina. "E-Government and E-Democracy." ②International Journal for Communication Studies 64 (2002): 467-78. ③Academic Search Elite. ④EBSCOhost. ⑤Santa Clara U, Orradre Lib. ⑥20 Dec. 2003 ⑦<http://www.epnet.com>.

Your library subscribes to a number of online services—such as EBSCOhost, ProQuest, and LexisNexis—that often provide access to the full text of articles in periodicals, reference works, and other sources. These services sometimes provide source URLs that you can use to direct your readers to the sources (see the next paragraph). More often, however, the services provide URLs that readers can't follow because they are too long (extending even beyond the browser's Location or Address field), are temporary (generated for each search), or are unique to the subscribing library. In this case follow the model above, if possible, giving the following information: ① Author and title. ② Information for print publication if any, following the appropriate model for a book or article (pp. 482–91). ③ Name of the database, underlined. (The database is the specific index or other reference you consulted.) ④ Name of the service, not underlined. ⑤ Names of the subscribing institution and library. (Add city and state if necessary to identify the library location.) ⑥ Date of your access. ⑦ URL of the service's home page, if known, so that readers can locate information about the service. If you can't find this URL, you may end the entry with the date of your access.

If the service provides a usable URL for a source, follow one of models 38–46. For the Netchaeva example (a journal article), you would use model 40.

34. A work from an online service to which you subscribe

"China--Dragon Kings." The Encyclopedia Mythica. America Online. 6 Jan. 2004. Path: Research and Learn; Encyclopedia; More Encyclopedias; Encyclopedia Mythica.

If you find a source through America Online, MSN, or another personal online service, you may not see a usable URL or any URL for the source. In that case, provide the path you used to get to the source, as in the example above: ① Title of source, in quotation marks, and title of larger work, underlined. ② Name of the service, neither underlined nor quoted. ③ Date of your access, followed by a period. ④ "Path:" (without quotation marks) and the sequence of topics required to reach the source, with the topics separated by semicolons.

If you used a keyword instead of a path to reach the source, give that information instead: Keyword: Chinese dragon kings.

If the online service provides a usable URL for the source, use one of models 38–46. For the source above (an article in an encyclopedia), you would use model 45 for an information database.

35. An entire online site (scholarly project, professional site, personal site, etc.)

A scholarly project or professional site:

Scots Teaching and Research Network. Ed. John Corbett. 2 Feb. 2003. U of Glasgow. 5 Mar. 2004 <http://www.arts.gla.ac.uk/www/english/comet/starn/htm>.

When citing an academic site, include the following: ① Title of the site, underlined. ② Name of any editor(s) of the site, preceded by "Ed." ③ Date of publication or most recent update. ④ Name of any organization or institution that sponsors the site. ⑤ Date of your access. ⑥ URL.

A personal site:

Lederman, Leon. Topics in Modern Physics--Lederman. 28 Aug. 2003. 12 Dec. 2003 <http://www-ed.fnal.gov/samplers/hsphys/people/lederman.html>.

Cite a personal site with this information: ① Author's name, if any. ② Title, if any, underlined. If the site has no title, describe it with a label such as Home page, without quotation marks or underlining. ③ Date of last revision. ④ Date of your access. ⑤ URL.

36. A short work from an online site

> Barbour, John. "The Brus." Scots Teaching and Research Network. Ed. John Corbett. 2 Feb. 2003. U of Glasgow. 5 Mar. 2004 <http://www.arts.gla.ac.uk/www/english/comet/starn/poetry/brus/contents/htm>.

For a poem, an article, or another short work appearing on a site, give the following: ① Author's name. ② Title of the short work, in quotation marks. ③ Title, editor, and publication information for the entire site, as in model 35 on the previous page. ④ Date of your access. ⑤ URL for the short work.

37. The home page for a course

> Anderson, Daniel. Business Communication. Course home page. Jan.-June 2004. Dept. of English, U of North Carolina. 16 Feb. 2004 <http://sites.unc.edu/daniel/eng32/index.html>.

For the home page of a course, provide this information: ① Instructor's name. ② Course title, without quotation marks or underlining. ③ The description Course home page, without quotation marks or underlining. ④ Inclusive dates of the course. ⑤ Names of the department and the school, separated by a comma. ⑥ Date of your access. ⑦ URL for the home page.

38. An online book

An entire book:

> Austen, Jane. Emma. Ed. Ronald Blythe. Harmondsworth: Penguin, 1972. Oxford Text Archive. 1998. Oxford U. 15 Dec. 2003 <http://ota.ox.ac.uk/pub/ota/public/english/Austen/emma.1519>.

For a book published online, give the following information: ① Author and title. ② Name of any editor or translator. ③ Any publication information for the original print version of the book, following one of models 1–17 (pp. 482–86). ④ Title of the site, underlined. ⑤ Date of electronic publication. ⑥ Name of any sponsoring organization or institution. ⑦ Date of your access. ⑧ URL for the book. If the site has an editor, add the name after the site's title (see model 35, previous page).

A part of a book:

> Conrad, Joseph. "A Familiar Preface." Modern Essays. Ed. Christopher Morley. New York: Harcourt, 1921. Bartleby.com: Great Books Online. Ed. Steven van Leeuwan. Nov. 2000. 16 Feb. 2004 <http://www.bartleby.com/237/8.html>.

For a part of a book published online, provide this information: ① Author of the part. ② Title of the part, in quotation marks. (Do not use quotation marks for Introduction, Foreword, or another standard part. See model 20, p. 487.) ③ Title of the book (underlined), editor of the book (if any), and publication information for the print version of the book. ④ Title of the site (underlined) and editor of the site (if any). ⑤ Date of electronic publication. ⑥ Date of your access. ⑦ URL for the part of the book. If the site as a whole has a sponsoring organization, give the name between the date of electronic publication and the date of your access (see the Austen model opposite).

39. An online government publication

> United States. Dept. of Commerce. National Telecommunications and Information Admin. Falling through the Net: Toward Digital Inclusion. Oct. 2001. 1 Mar. 2004 <http://www.ntia.doc.gov/ntiahome/fttn00/contents00.html>.

See page 502 for models of government publications in print. Provide the same information for online publications, and add facts of electronic publication. The model above includes the following: ① Names of government, department, and agency. ② Title of publication, underlined. ③ Date of publication. ④ Date of your access. ⑤ URL.

40. An article in an online journal

> Palfrey, Andrew. "Choice of Mates in Identical Twins." Modern Psychology 4.1 (1996): 26-40. 25 Feb. 2004 <http://www.liasu.edu/modpsy/palfrey4(1).htm>.

Give the following information for an online scholarly article that you reach directly: ① Author, article title, journal title, volume and any issue numbers, and publication date, as in model 22 or 23 (p. 489). ② Page numbers in the journal or total number of pages, paragraphs, or sections, if any of these are given. Omit reference numbers if the source does. ③ Date of your access. ④ URL for the article.

For a journal article reached through a subscription service, see model 33 (p. 494).

41. An online abstract

Palfrey, Andrew. “Choice of Mates in Identical Twins.” Modern Psychology 4.1 (1996): 26-40. Abstract. 25 Feb. 2004 <http://www.liasu.edu/modpsy/abstractpalfrey4(1).htm>.

Treat an online abstract like an online journal article (model 40), but add “Abstract” (without quotation marks or underlining) between the publication information and the date of your access.

42. An article in an online newspaper or on a newswire

Still, Lucia. “On the Battlefields of Business, Millions of Casualties.” New York Times on the Web 3 Mar. 2002. 17 Aug. 2003 <http://www.nytimes.com/specials/downsize/03down1.html>.

Provide the following information for an online newspaper article that you reach directly: ① Author, article title, newspaper title, and publication date as in model 26 (p. 490). Give section, page, or paragraph numbers if the newspaper does. ② Date of your access. ③ URL for the article.

Treat a newswire article similarly, substituting the title of the wire service for the newspaper title (this article is anonymous):

“Film, Fashion Asked to Stop Glamorizing Smoking.” Reuters 18 Feb. 2004. 28 Feb. 2004 <http://www.reuters.com/newsArticle.jhtml?type=industryNewsID2246811>.

See model 33 (p. 494) when citing a newspaper or newswire article that you reached through a subscription service.

43. An article in an online magazine

Lewis, Ricki. “The Return of Thalidomide.” Scientist 22 Jan. 2001: 5. 24 Jan. 2004 <http://www.the-scientist.com/yr2001/jan/lewis_pl_010122.html>.

Provide the following information for an online magazine article that you reach directly: ① Author's name, article title, magazine title, and publication date, as in model 24 or 25 on page 490. ② Any page, paragraph, or other reference numbers. ③ Date of your access. ④ URL for the article.

See model 33 (p. 494) when citing a magazine article that you reached through a subscription service.

44. An online review

Detwiler, Donald S., and Chu Shao-Kang. Rev. of Important Documents of the Republic of China, ed. Tan Quon Chin. Journal of Military History 56.4 (1992): 669-84. 16 Sept. 2002 <http://www.jstor.org/fcgi-bin/jstor/viewitem.fcg/08993718/96p0008x>.

Cite an online review as follows: ① Author, any review title, "Rev. of" and the title of the reviewed book, author or editor of the reviewed book, and publication information—all as in model 29 (p. 491). ② Date of your access. ③ URL for the review.

See model 33 (p. 494) when citing a review that you reached through a subscription service.

45. An article in an online information database

Pull, Jack L. "Wu-ti." Encyclopaedia Britannica Online. Vers. 99.1. 2003. Encyclopaedia Britannica. 23 Dec. 2003 <http://www.eb.com:80>.

For an article in an information database, such as an encyclopedia, provide the following: ① Author's name, if any is given. ② Title of the article, in quotation marks. ③ Title of the database, underlined. ④ Version number, if any is given. ⑤ Date of electronic publication. ⑥ Name of sponsoring organization or publisher. ⑦ Date of your access. ⑧ URL for the article.

See models 33 and 34 (pp. 494–95) when citing an information database that you reached through a library or personal subscription service.

46. An online graphic, video, or audio source

In general, you can base citations of online visual or audio sources on models 55–58 and 63 (pp. 503–04, 505), adding information for the online source, particularly site title, date of your access, and complete URL. The following examples show a range of possibilities:

A work of art:

Pollock, Jackson. Shimmering Substance. 1946. Museum of Modern Art, New York. WebMuseum. 12 Mar. 2004 <http://www.ibiblio.org/wm/paint/auth/Pollock/pollock.shimmering.jpg>.

A map or other illustration:

Hamilton, Calvin J. "Components of Comets." Diagram. Space Art. 2001. 20 Dec. 2003 <wysisiwyg://94/http://spaceart.com/solar/eng/comet.htm>.

A television or radio program:

Terry Gross, host. Fresh Air. National Public Radio. 11 Feb. 2004. 12 Feb. 2004 <http://discover.npr.org/freshair/day_fa.html?display=February/11/2004>.

A sound recording or clip:

Reagan, Ronald W. State of the Union address. 26 Jan. 1982. Vincent Voice Library. Digital and Multimedia Center, U of Michigan. 6 May 2004 <http://www.lib.msu.edu/vincent/presidents/reagan.htm>.

A film or film clip:

Stewart, Leslie J. 96 Ranch Rodeo and Barbecue. 1951. Library of Congress. 7 Jan. 2004 <http://memory.loc.gov/cgi-bin/query/ammem/ncr:@field(DocID+@lit(nv034))>.

47. Electronic mail

①Millon, Michele. ②"Re: Grief Therapy." ③E-mail to the author. ④4 May 2004.

For e-mail, give the following: ① Writer's name. ② Title, if any, from the e-mail's subject heading, in quotation marks. ③ Description of the transmission, including to whom it was sent. ④ Date of posting.

48. A posting to an e-mail discussion list

①Tourville, Michael. ②"European Currency Reform." ③Online posting. ④6 Jan. 2004. ⑤International Finance Discussion List. ⑥12 Jan. 2004 ⑦<http://www.weg.isu/finance-dl/archive/46732>.

Whenever possible, cite an archived version of a posting to an e-mail discussion list so that readers can find it without difficulty. Give this information for the posting: ① Author's name. ② Title, if any, from the e-mail's subject heading, in quotation marks. ③ Online posting, without quotation marks or underlining. ④ Date of posting. ⑤ Name of the discussion list, without quotation marks or underlining. ⑥ Date of your access. ⑦ URL, if known, or e-mail address for the moderator or supervisor of the list.

49. A posting to a newsgroup or Web forum

A newsgroup:

Cramer, Sherry. "Recent Investment Practices in U.S. Business." Online posting. 26 Mar. 2004. 3 Apr. 2004 <news:biz.investment.current.2700>.

For a posting to a newsgroup, give the following: ① Author's name. ② Title from the subject heading, in quotation marks. ③ Online posting, without quotation marks or underlining. ④ Date of posting. ⑤ Date of your access. ⑥ Group's name preceded by "news:"—both enclosed in angle brackets.

A Web forum:

Dente, Robert. "The Abandoned House." Online posting. 25 Jan. 2004. The Creative Process. 27 Jan. 2004 <http://forums/nytimes.com/webin/WebX?1418294@ea7>.

For a posting to a Web forum, provide this information: ① Author's name. ② Title, if any, in quotation marks. ③ Online posting, without quotation marks or underlining. ④ Date of posting. ⑤ Name of the forum, without quotation marks or underlining. ⑥ Date of your access. ⑦ URL.

50. A synchronous communication

Bruckman, Amy. MediaMOO Symposium: Virtual Worlds for Business? 20 Jan. 2004. MediaMOO. 26 Feb. 2004 <http://www.co.gatech.edu/fac/Amy.Bruckman/MediaMOO/cscw-symposium-02.html>.

Whenever possible, cite an archived version of a synchronous communication so that readers can find it without difficulty. Provide this information: ① Speaker's name. ② Description of the event, without quotation marks or underlining. ③ Date of the event. ④ Forum, without quotation marks or underlining. ⑤ Date of your access. ⑥ URL.

51. Computer software

Project Scheduler 9000. Vers. 5.1. Orlando: Scitor, 2004.

For software, provide the following: ① Title, underlined. ② Version number. ③ Publication information, including place of publication, publisher, and date. If the software has a listed author, give his or her name first in the entry. If you consulted or obtained the software online, replace the publication information with the date of your access and the URL, as in previous examples.

4 • Other sources

52. A government publication

Board of Governors. US Federal Reserve System. Federal Reserve Bulletin Aug. 2003: 20-21.

Hawaii. Dept. of Education. Kauai District Schools, Profile 2002-03. Honolulu: Hawaii Dept. of Education, 2004.

Stiller, Ann. Historic Preservation and Tax Incentives. US Dept. of Interior. Washington: GPO, 1996.

United States. Cong. House. Committee on Ways and Means. Medicare Payment for Outpatient Occupational Therapy Services. 107th Cong., 1st sess. Washington: GPO, 2001.

If an author is not listed for a government publication, give the appropriate agency as author, as in the second and last examples. Provide information in the order illustrated, separating elements with a period and a space: the name of the government, the name of the agency (which may be abbreviated), and the title and publication information. For a congressional publication (last example), give the house and committee involved before the title, and give the number and session of Congress after the title. In the last two examples, "GPO" stands for the US Government Printing Office.

53. A pamphlet

Medical Answers About AIDS. New York: Gay Men's Health Crisis, 2004.

Most pamphlets can be treated as books. In the example above, the pamphlet has no listed author, so the title comes first. If the pamphlet has an author, list his or her name first, followed by the title and publication information as given here.

54. An unpublished dissertation or thesis

Wilson, Stuart M. "John Stuart Mill as a Literary Critic." Diss. U of Michigan, 1990.

The title is quoted rather than underlined. "Diss." stands for "Dissertation." "U of Michigan" is the institution that granted the author's degree.

55. A film or video recording

Schindler's List. Dir. Steven Spielberg. Perf. Liam Neeson and Ben Kingsley. Universal, 1993.

Start with the title of the work you are citing, unless you are citing the contribution of a particular individual (see the next model). Give additional information (writer, lead performers, and so on) as you judge appropriate. For a film, end with the distributor and date.

For a videocassette, DVD, filmstrip, or slide program, include the original release date (if any) and the medium (without underlining or quotation marks) before the distributor's name:

George Balanchine, chor. Serenade. Perf. San Francisco Ballet. Dir. Hilary Bean. 1981. Videocassette. PBS Video, 1987.

56. A sound recording

Springsteen, Bruce. "Empty Sky." The Rising. Columbia, 2002.

Brahms, Johannes. Piano Concerto no. 2 in B-flat, op. 83. Perf. Artur Rubinstein. Cond. Eugene Ormandy. Philadelphia Orch. LP. RCA, 1972.

Begin with the name of the individual whose work you are citing. If you're citing a song or song lyrics, give the title in quotation marks. Then provide the title of the recording, underlining the title (first example) unless it identifies a composition by form, number, and key (second example). After the title, provide the names of any other artists it seems appropriate to mention, the manufacturer of the recording, and the date of release. If the medium is other than compact disk, provide it immediately before the manufacturer's name—for instance, LP (as in the second example) or Audiocassette.

57. A television or radio program

"I'm Sorry, I'm Lost." By Alan Ball. Dir. Jill Soloway. Six Feet Under. HBO. 2 Apr. 2003.

Kushner, Tony. Angels in America. Dir. Mike Nichols. Perf. Al Pacino, Meryl Streep, Emma Thompson, Mary-Louise Parker, Jeffrey Wright, Patrick Wilson, and Justin Kerr. 2 episodes. HBO. 7 Dec. and 14 Dec. 2003.

Start with a title unless you are citing the work of a person or persons. The first example above lists (in quotation marks) an episode of a television program and then gives the writer's and director's names and the program title (underlined). The second example lists the writer first, then the title, the director, the main performers, and the number of episodes. Both entries end with the name of the network and the date(s).

58. A musical composition or work of art

Fauré, Gabriel. Sonata for Violin and Piano no. 1 in A Major, op. 15.

Don't underline musical compositions, such as the one above, that are identified only by form, number, and key. Do underline titled operas, ballets, and compositions (Carmen, Sleeping Beauty).

For a work of art, underline the title and include the name and location of the owner. For a work you see only in a photograph, provide the complete publication information, too, as in the following model. Omit such information only if you examined the actual work.

Sargent, John Singer. Venetian Doorway. Metropolitan Museum of Art, New York. Sargent Watercolors. By Donelson F. Hoopes. New York: Watson, 1976. 31.

59. A performance

The English Only Restaurant. By Silvio Martinez Palau. Dir. Susana Tubert. Puerto Rican Traveling Theater, New York. 27 July 2003.

Eddins, William, cond. Chicago Symphony Orch. Symphony Center, Chicago. 22 Jan. 2004.

As with films and television programs, place the title first unless you are citing the work of an individual (second example). Provide additional information about participants after the title, as well as the theater, city, and date. Note that the orchestra name in the second example is neither quoted nor underlined.

60. A letter

Buttolph, Mrs. Laura E. Letter to Rev. and Mrs. C. C. Jones. 20 June 1857. In The Children of Pride: A True Story of Georgia and the Civil War. Ed. Robert Manson Myers. New Haven: Yale UP, 1972. 334-35.

List a published letter under the writer's name. Specify that the source is a letter and to whom it was addressed, and give the date on which it was written. Treat the remaining information like that for a selection from an anthology (model 18, p. 486). (See also p. 490 for the format of a letter to the editor of a periodical.)

For a letter in the collection of a library or archive, specify the writer, recipient, and date, as in the previous example, and give the name and location of the archive as well:

James, Jonathan E. Letter to his sister. 16 Apr. 1970. Jonathan E. James Papers. South Dakota State Archive, Pierre.

For a letter you receive, give the name of the writer, note the fact that the letter was sent to you, and provide the date of the letter:

Packer, Ann E. Letter to the author. 15 June 2003.

Use the form above for personal e-mail as well, substituting "E-mail" for "Letter": E-mail to the author (see p. 500).

61. A lecture or address

Carlone, Dennis. "Architecture for the City of the Twenty-First Century." Symposium on the City. Urban Issues Group. Cambridge City Hall, Cambridge. 22 May 2003.

Give the speaker's name, the title (in quotation marks), the title of the meeting, the name of the sponsoring organization, the location of the lecture, and the date. If the lecture has no title, use Lecture, Address, or another description (not in quotation marks) instead.

Although the *MLA Handbook* does not provide a specific style for classroom lectures in your courses, you can adapt the preceding format for this purpose:

Ezzy, T. G. Class lecture on the realist novel. Dawson College. 20 Jan. 2004.

62. An interview

Graaf, Vera. Personal interview. 19 Dec. 2003.

Rumsfeld, Donald. Interview. <u>Frontline</u>. PBS. WGBH, Boston. 10 Oct. 2003.

Begin with the name of the person interviewed. For an interview you conducted, specify Personal interview or the medium (such as Telephone interview or E-mail interview)—without quotation marks or underlining—and then give the date. For an interview you read, heard, or saw, provide the title if any or Interview if there is no title, along with other bibliographic information and the date.

63. A map or other illustration

<u>Women in the Armed Forces</u>. Map. <u>Women in the World: An International Atlas</u>. By Joni Seager and Ann Olson. New York: Touchstone, 2003. 44-45.

List the illustration by its title (underlined). Provide a descriptive label (Map, Chart, Table), without underlining or quotation marks, and the publication information. If the creator of the illustration is credited in the source, put his or her name first in the entry, as with any author.

EXERCISE 56.1
Writing works-cited entries

Prepare works-cited entries from the following information. Follow the models of the *MLA Handbook* given in this chapter unless your instructor specifies a different style. For titles, use underlining (as here) unless your instructor requests italics. Arrange the finished entries in alphabetical order. (Do not number entries in a list of works cited.) Answers to the starred items appear at the end of the book.

*1. A journal article titled "Networking the Classroom" by Christopher Conte. The article appears in volume 5 of CQ Researcher, a journal that pages issues continuously throughout each annual volume. Volume 5 is dated 1999. The article runs from page 923 to page 943.

*2. A magazine article on CD-ROM that is also available in print. The author is Max Frankel. The title is "The Moon, This Time Around." The article appears in the May 5, 1996, issue of the New York Times Magazine, a weekly magazine, and starts on page 40. You consulted the article on the CD-ROM titled New York Times Ondisc, released by UMI-ProQuest in November 1996.

*3. A government document you consulted on March 12, 2004, over the Internet. The author is the National Center for Education Statistics, an agency within the United States Department of Education. The title of the document is Internet Access in Public Schools. It was published October 6, 2002, and can be accessed at http://www.ed.gov/nces/edstats.

*4. A book called Failure to Connect: How Computers Affect Our Children's Minds—For Better and Worse, written by Jane M. Healy and published in 2000 by Simon & Schuster in New York.

5. An article in the October 9, 2001, issue of the magazine The Nation titled "The Threat to the Net." The article is by Jeff Chester and appears on pages 6 to 7 of the magazine. You found it through Polk Library at Southeast State University on March 3, 2004, using the database Expanded Academic ASAP from the service InfoTrac. The home page address for the database is http://www.galegroup.com.

6. A pamphlet titled Equity on the Information Superhighway: Problems and Possibilities, with no named author. It was published in 2002 by the ALA in Chicago.

7. An article titled "Disparities along the Information Age Career Path" on a Web site titled Digital Divide Network at the address

http://www.digitaldividenetwork.org/content/index.cfm26. The Web site is sponsored by the Benton Foundation. The article is by Kade Twist and is dated 2002. You found it on March 3, 2004.

8. An e-mail interview you conducted with Mary McArthur on March 20, 2004.

56c Format the paper in MLA style.

The document format recommended by the *MLA Handbook* is fairly simple, with just a few elements. See also pages 75–85 for guidelines on type fonts, headings, lists, and other features that are not specified in MLA style.

The illustrations below show the formats for the first page and a later page of a paper. For the format of the list of works cited, see pages 479–80.

First page of paper

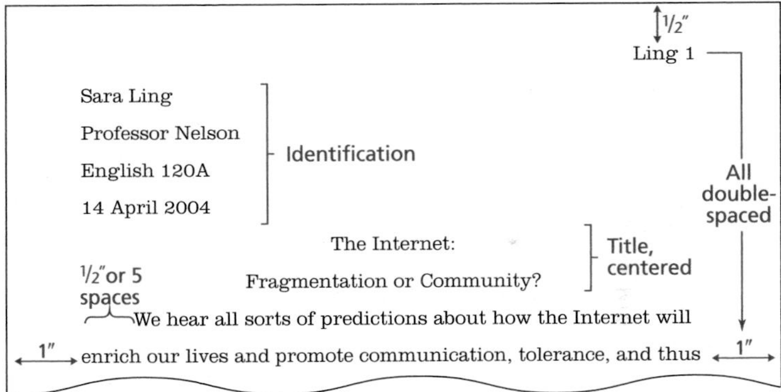

A later page of the paper

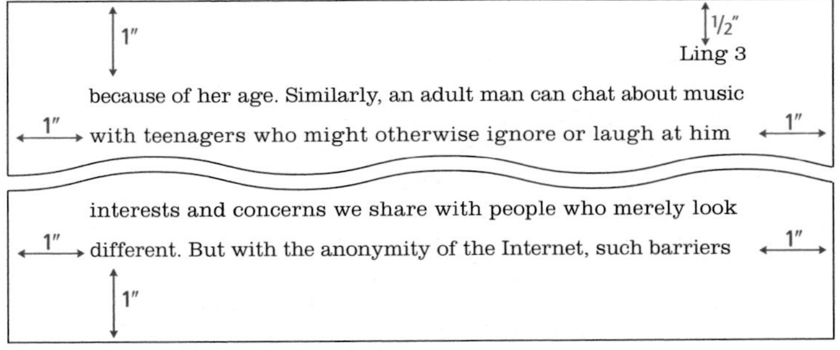

Margins

Use minimum one-inch margins on all sides of every page.

Spacing and indentions

Double-space throughout. Indent paragraphs one-half inch or five spaces. (See below for indention of set-off quotations.)

Paging

Begin numbering on the first page, and number consecutively through the end (including the list of works cited). Type Arabic numerals (1, 2, 3) in the upper right about one-half inch from the top. Place your last name before the page number in case the pages later become separated.

Identification and title

MLA style does not require a title page for a paper. Instead, give your name, your instructor's name, the course title, and the date on separate lines in the upper left of the first page—one inch from the top and the left of the paper. (See the sample on the previous page.) Double-space between all lines of this identification.

Double-space also around the title, and center it. If the title runs two lines, center both lines and double-space between them. Use capital and small letters for the title, capitalizing according to the guidelines on pages 393–94. Don't type the title in all-capital letters, underline it, or enclose it in quotation marks. (See the sample on the previous page.)

Poetry and long prose quotations

Treat a single line of poetry like any other quotation, running it into your text and enclosing it in quotation marks. You may run in two or three lines of poetry as well, separating the lines with a slash surrounded by space.

> An example of Robert Frost's incisiveness is in two lines from "Death of the Hired Man": "Home is the place where, when you have to go there / They have to take you in" (119-20).

Always set off quotations of more than three lines of poetry from your text. Use double spacing and a one-inch or ten-space indention. *Do not add quotation marks.*

> Emily Dickinson stripped ideas to their essence, as in this description of "A narrow Fellow in the Grass," a snake:
>
> I more than once at Noon
> Have passed, I thought, a Whip lash

> Unbraiding in the Sun
> When stopping to secure it
> It wrinkled, and was gone—(12-16)

Also set off prose quotations of five or more typed lines. *Do not add quotation marks.*

> In his 1967 study of the lives of unemployed black men, Elliot Liebow observes that "unskilled" construction work requires more experience and skill than is generally assumed:
>
> > A healthy, sturdy, active man of good intelligence requires from two to four weeks to break in on a construction job. . . . It frequently happens that his foreman or the craftsman he services is not willing to wait that long for him to get into condition or to learn at a glance the difference in size between a rough 2 x 8 and a finished 2 x 10. (62)

Do not use a paragraph indention for a quotation of a single complete paragraph or a part of a paragraph. Use paragraph indentions only for a quotation of two or more paragraphs.

56d A sample paper in MLA style

The sample paper beginning on page 511 follows the guidelines of the *MLA Handbook* for overall format, parenthetical citations, and the list of works cited. Marginal annotations highlight features of the paper.

Note Because the sample paper addresses a current Internet controversy, many of its sources come from the Internet and do not use page or other reference numbers. Thus, as noted in the annotations, the in-text citations of these sources do not give reference numbers. In a paper relying solely on printed journals, books, and other traditional sources, most if not all in-text citations would include page numbers.

A note on outlines

Some instructors ask students to submit a formal outline of the final paper. Advice on constructing such an outline appears on pages 25–26, along with an example written in phrases (a topic outline). The following outline of the sample paper is written in complete sentences. Note that the thesis statement precedes either a topic or a sentence outline.

Thesis statement

To improve equity between online and traditional stores and between consumers with and without Internet access, tax laws should be revised to allow collection of sales taxes on Internet purchases.

I. A Supreme Court ruling and congressional legislation presently govern Internet taxation.
   A. A 1992 Supreme Court decision frees vendors from collecting sales taxes from customers in states where the vendors have no physical presence.
   B. A 1998 law, extended in 2000, placed a moratorium on Internet taxes.

II. A tax-free Internet is unfair to traditional bricks-and-mortar stores.
   A. Sales taxes can make bricks-and-mortar purchases significantly more expensive than online purchases.
   B. Sales taxes exceed online merchants' shipping charges.

III. A tax-free Internet is unfair to consumers who lack Internet access.
   A. A government report shows a huge "digital divide" among US residents.
      1. The affluent are much more likely to have Internet access than the poor.
      2. Whites who are college educated are much more likely to have Internet access than nonwhites with elementary educations.
   B. The digital divide means the poor must pay sales taxes while the affluent can avoid the taxes by shopping online.

IV. The three main arguments against Internet taxation do not rebut the issue of fairness.
   A. Taxes on Internet commerce would not, as claimed, undermine the freedom of the Internet.
   B. Internet commerce does not, as claimed, deserve special protection and encouragement that is not given to traditional commerce.
   C. The very real complexities of Internet taxation do not, as claimed, justify a permanent ban on taxation.

Alder 1

Writer's name and page number.

Kisha Alder

Ms. Savarro

English 101

7 March 2004

Identification: writer's name, instructor's name, course title, date—all double-spaced.

Who Pays the Bill for
Internet Shopping?

Title centered.

Going to the mall may soon go out of style. These days more and more people are shopping from home over the Internet. In 2002 electronic commerce (e-commerce) took in approximately $40 billion from shoppers; by 2007 that amount is expected to be $105 billion or more ("Sales Tax"). These numbers are good news for the online stores and for online shoppers, who can anticipate increasing variety in e-commerce offerings. But because taxes are not collected on Internet sales as they are on purchases in almost all states, online stores compete unfairly with traditional "bricks-and-mortar" stores, and shoppers with Internet access have an unfair advantage over shoppers with no such access. To improve equity between online and traditional stores and between consumers with and without Internet access, tax laws should be revised to allow collection of sales taxes on Internet purchases.

Double-space throughout.

Introduction: gives background to establish the issue.

Citation form: shortened title for anonymous source; online source has no page number.

Thesis statement.

Internet commerce is regulated by the same tax laws that govern other commerce. However, in 1992 the Supreme Court ruled that vendors do not have to collect taxes on behalf of states where they do not have a physical presence, because such collection would place an unconstitutional burden on interstate commerce (<u>Quill Corp. v. North Dakota</u> 5-8). Buyers are supposed to send the correct taxes to their state governments voluntarily, but they rarely do and states currently have no way to collect (Zimmerman and Hoover 45). In a decision addressing mail-order sales but considered applicable to Internet sales, the Court's

Background on Internet taxation (next two paragraphs).

Citation form: law case; case title underlined in the text citation.

Citation form: source with two authors.

Alder 2

majority urged Congress to reexamine the tax laws governing interstate commerce:

> The underlying issue is not only one that Congress may be better qualified to resolve, but also one that Congress has the ultimate power to resolve. . . . Accordingly, Congress is now free to decide whether, when, and to what extent the States may burden interstate mail-order concerns with a duty to collect use taxes. (Quill Corp. v. North Dakota 18-19)

Quotation over four lines set off without quotation marks, indented one inch, and double-spaced.

Ellipsis mark signals omission from quotation.

Citation form: after displayed quotation, citation follows sentence period and one space.

Congress did take some action in 1998, when e-commerce was blossoming, by placing a temporary moratorium on new Internet taxes and by creating the Advisory Commission on Electronic Commerce to study the taxation issue and recommend solutions. A majority of the commission recommended extending the moratorium for another five years, through 2006, so that the taxation issue could be studied further and the state and local taxing authorities could simplify their complex and overlapping tax systems (US Advisory Commission). Congress agreed and voted to extend the moratorium (Bettelheim 27). Meanwhile, the debate over taxing e-commerce continues to heat up. On one side are state and local governments that have mounted a campaign for a uniform tax rate that would apply to Internet purchases. On the other side are those who would transform the moratorium on Internet sales taxes into a permanent ban ("E-Commerce").

Source: corporate author. Citation form: corporate author only, because online source has no page or other reference numbers.

Citation form: shortened title for anonymous source; no page number for one-page source.

As long as the moratorium is in effect, Internet shopping is essentially tax-free. Yet in almost all states, traditional shopping is subject to sales tax. Bricks-and-mortar stores that are required by law to charge and collect sales taxes are at a distinct disadvantage compared to the online stores with no such

Contrast between online and traditional commerce (next two paragraphs).

Alder 3

burden. The local bookstore, music store, and drugstore must charge sales tax; their competitors Amazon.com, CDNOW.com, and PlanetRx.com do not. And the difference can be significant: for instance, California and New York State charge residents at least 7 percent to shop in their own neighborhoods (Wiseman 60).

Selective use of data, with summary of source acknowledged.

Some online merchants claim that the shipping costs they charge offset the sales taxes they don't charge (Granfield 57). However, many online companies offer free shipping and handling as an incentive to online shoppers. And even without such promotions, state and local sales taxes far exceed most shipping costs. As one frequent online consumer said, "If I buy more than three CDs . . . , the shipping cost is less than the sales tax would have been" (James). On balance, the traditional purchase just costs more.

Paragraph integrates evidence from two sources.

Ellipsis mark indicates that omitted material fell before comma.

Primary source: e-mail interview. Citation form: source name only, because interview has no page or other reference numbers.

The Internet's tax-free shopping is also damaging to equality among groups of people. Governments, scholars, and businesspeople express concern about the "digital divide" between the affluent who have Internet access and the poor who do not. According to a US Department of Commerce study, Falling through the Net: Toward Digital Inclusion, "Households with incomes of $75,000 and higher are more than four times more likely to have access to the Internet than those at the lowest income levels [below $15,000]" (24; emphasis added). The same study shows that Internet access is three times more common among whites than among African Americans or Latinos (72) and twelve times more common among those with college educations than among those with elementary school educations (71).

Contrast between shoppers with and without Internet access (next two paragraphs).

Source named in the text, so not named in parenthetical citations that follow.

Brackets signal words added to clarify the quotation. Citation form: "emphasis added" indicates underlining was not in original quotation.

Paragraph draws together and acknowledges paraphrases of data from various places in the source.

The digital divide has implications for the relative abilities of people in different groups to function

Alder 4

effectively in an increasingly electronic world. But where sales taxes are concerned, it does further harm to the disadvantaged. For the most part, white, educated, and affluent consumers can shop tax-free because they can shop on the Internet, whereas nonwhite, uneducated, and poor consumers have no choice but to shop locally and pay the required taxes.

Writer's own conclusions from preceding data.

Equity thus requires sales taxes on e-commerce, but there are many who argue strongly against such taxes. The writing about Internet taxation (in articles and discussion groups and on Web sites) reveals three major arguments against it. (A fourth, against any new taxes of any kind, is not specifically relevant to Internet commerce.)

Statement and rebuttal of three opposing views (next five paragraphs).

The first argument holds that Internet freedom is sacred and should be protected. "To me," writes one discussion participant, "the Internet is . . . freedom of thought. We can't have the government meddling in the ability of its citizens to read, speak, and, yes, conduct free enterprise online" (Angeles). But Internet commerce is commerce, after all. Even if the network often serves as a site for free thought and communication, when it serves as a place of business it should be subject to the same rules as other businesses.

Signal phrase interrupts quotation and is set off by commas.

Citation form: author's name only, because online source has no page or other reference numbers.

Rebuttals are writer's own ideas and do not require source citations.

The second major argument against Internet taxes, related to the first, is expressed in this statement by a major opponent of the taxes, US Senator Ron Wyden: "State and local taxes could do irreparable harm to the Internet, killing the goose that could lay billions of dollars in golden eggs." But this argument, like the first one, assumes that Internet commerce deserves special protection and encouragement--even at the expense of bricks-and-mortar commerce. In fact, both kinds of commerce contribute to the health of the economy, and they should be protected, or taxed, equally.

Full-sentence introduction of a quotation is followed by a colon.

Citation form: no parenthetical citation because author is named in the text and online source has no page or other reference numbers.

Alder 5

Finally, the third major argument against Internet taxes holds that the issue is too complex to be resolved, a "logistical nightmare," in the words of a taxation opponent (Granfield 57). As outlined by more neutral observers--members of the respected accounting firm of Deloitte & Touche--the main complexities are very real: the existence of more than 3000 state and local taxing authorities in the United States, each with its own regulations and rates; the need to bring these jurisdictions into agreement on how to rationalize and simplify their systems; the concern that any federally imposed solution might violate states' rights; and finally the uncertainty about whether an online vendor conducts taxable business where its office, its server, its customer, or all three are located (67-72).

Citation form: author not named in the text.

Citation form (here and end of paragraph): corporate author named in the text.

Summary reduces six pages in the source to a list of four points.

Position of citation indicates that all preceding information comes from the Deloitte & Touche source.

The complexities do seem nightmarish, as tax opponents claim. But the sheer difficulty of creating an Internet tax structure is no justification for not doing what is fair. Both government and business members of the Advisory Commission on Electronic Commerce have expressed beliefs that the Internet should be taxed and optimism that the complexities can be resolved (Stamas). MCI's John Sidgmore says, "Massive changes are going to be required in the state and local tax frameworks, it is true. But there are ways to get through this to a system that is fair for everyone" (qtd. in Stamas).

Citation form: author's name only, because online source has no page or other reference numbers.

Citation form: indirect source (Sidgmore quoted by Stamas).

The Internet has introduced many improvements in our lives, including the ability to make purchases with the click of a mouse. But at the same time the tax-free status of Internet commerce allows it to compete unfairly with traditional businesses and gives an unfair financial advantage to those who most likely already have plenty of advantages. Congress and Internet businesses must recognize these inequities and must work with state and local taxing authorities to remedy them.

Conclusion: summary and a call for action.

Alder 6

New page for works cited.

Works Cited

Heading centered.

Angeles, Lemuel. "Internet Freedom." Online posting. 8 Oct. 2003. ZDNet Talkback. 8 Feb. 2004 <http://www.zdnet.com/tklbck/comment/22/0,7056.html>.

A posting to a Web forum.

Sources are alphabetized by authors' last names.

Second and subsequent lines of each source are indented one-half inch.

Bettelheim, Adrial. "Internet Tax Moratorium Extension Clears after Senate Rejects Plan for Multistate 'Compact.'" <u>CQ Weekly</u> 59.44 (2002): 27-45. <u>Academic Search Elite</u>. EBSCO. Southeast State U, Polk Lib. 15 Jan. 2004 <http://www.epnet.com>.

A journal article obtained through a library subscription service.

Deloitte & Touche. <u>Establishing a Framework to Evaluate E-Commerce Tax Policy Options</u>. Berkeley: U of California P, 1999.

A report by a corporate author.

"E-Commerce: Congress to Consider Extending Internet Tax Moratorium." <u>New York Times</u> 9 Jan. 2004, late ed.: C4. <u>LexisNexis Academic</u>. LexisNexis. Southeast State U, Polk Lib. 14 Jan. 2004 <http://www.lexisnexis.com>.

An anonymous newspaper article listed and alphabetized by title. Source obtained through a library subscription service.

Granfield, Anne. "Taxing the Internet." <u>Forbes</u> 17 Dec. 2002: 56-58.

An article in a magazine.

James, Nora. E-mail interview. 1 Feb. 2004.

An e-mail interview.

Quill Corp. v. North Dakota. 504 US 298. 1992.

A law case: title not underlined in list of works cited.

"Sales Tax on Internet Buys Could Help Fill Budget Gaps." <u>Associated Press State and Local Wire</u>. 26 Dec. 2002. <u>LexisNexis Academic</u>. LexisNexis. Southeast State U, Polk Lib. 13 Jan. 2004 <http://www.lexisnexis.com>.

An anonymous newswire article listed and alphabetized by title. Source obtained through a library subscription service.

Stamas, Vicky. "Tax-Free Web Goods May Disappear." <u>ZDNet News</u> 23 Jan. 2002. 13 Feb. 2004 <http://www.zdnet.com/zdnn/stories/news/0,4586.html>.

An article in an online magazine.

United States. Advisory Commission on Electronic Commerce. <u>Report to Congress</u>. Apr. 2000. 25 Jan. 2004 <http://www.ecommercecommission.org/report.htm>.

An online government publication with no named author, so government body given as author.

Alder 7

---. Dept. of Commerce. National Telecommunications and Information Admin. Falling through the Net: Toward Digital Inclusion. Oct. 2001. 2 Feb. 2004 <http://www.ntia.doc.gov/ntiahome/fttn00/contents00.html>.

Second source by author of two or more cited works: three hyphens replace author's name (*United States*).

Wiseman, Alan E. The Internet Economy: Access, Taxes, and Market Structure. Washington: Brookings, 2000.

A book.

Wyden, Ron. "Statement on the Internet Tax Non-Discrimination Act." Ron Wyden Online. 7 Jan. 2004. 13 Jan. 2004 <http://www.senate.gov/~wyden.docs.htm>.

A page on a Web site.

Zimmerman, Malai, and Kent Hoover. "Use of Third Parties to Collect State and Local Taxes on Internet Sales." Pacific Business Journal 26.2 (1999): 45-48.

An article from a journal that pages each issue separately. A source with two authors.

57 APA Documentation and Format

How do I cite sources and format papers in the social sciences?

The most widely used style guide in the social sciences is the *Publication Manual of the American Psychological Association* (5th ed., 2001). In APA documentation style, you acknowledge each of your sources twice:

- In your text, a brief parenthetical citation adjacent to the borrowed material directs readers to a complete list of all the works you refer to.
- At the end of your paper, the list of references includes complete bibliographical information for every source.

http://www.ablongman.com/littlebrown
➤ Research writing ➤ Exercises ➤ Exer. 11
➤ Documentation in the disciplines ➤ APA Style

Every entry in the list of references has at least one corresponding citation in the text, and every in-text citation has a corresponding entry in the list of references.

This chapter describes APA text citations (below) and references (p. 521), details APA document format (p. 535), and concludes with a sample APA paper (p. 538).

57a Use APA parenthetical citations in your text.

In the APA documentation style, parenthetical citations within the text refer the reader to a list of sources at the end of the text.

Note Models 1 and 2 show the direct relationship between what you include in your text and what you include in a parenthetical citation. The citation always includes a publication date (or "n.d." if the source has no date), and it may include a page or paragraph number. It also includes the author's last name if you do *not* name the author in your text (model 1). It does not include the author's name if you *do* name the author in your text (model 2).

1. Author not named in your text

One critic of Milgram's experiments said that the subjects "should have been fully informed of the possible effects on them" (Baumrind, 1968, p. 34).

When you do not name the author in your text, place in parentheses the author's last name and the date of the source. Separate the elements with commas. Position the reference so that it is clear what material is being documented *and* so that the reference fits as smoothly as possible into your sentence structure. (See pp. 476–78 for guidelines.) The next example would also be correct.

APA parenthetical text citations

> In the view of one critic of Milgram's experiments (Baumrind, 1968), the subjects "should have been fully informed of the possible effects on them" (p. 34).

Unless none is available, the APA requires a page or other identifying number for a direct quotation (as in the preceding examples) and recommends an identifying number for a paraphrase. Use an appropriate abbreviation or symbol before the number—for instance, "p." for *page* and "¶" for *paragraph* (or "para." if you do not have the symbol). The identifying number may fall with the author and date (as in the example on the facing page) or by itself in a separate pair of parentheses (as in the example above). See also model 11, page 521.

2. Author named in your text

> Baumrind (1968) said that the subjects in Milgram's study "should have been fully informed of the possible effects on them" (p. 34).

When you use the author's name in the text, do not repeat it in the reference. Place the source date in parentheses after the author's name. Place any page or paragraph reference either after the borrowed material (as in the example) or with the date: (1968, p. 34).

3. A work with two authors

> Pepinsky and DeStefano (1997) demonstrated that a teacher's language often reveals hidden biases.

> One study (Pepinsky & DeStefano, 1997) demonstrated hidden biases in teachers' language.

When given in the text, two authors' names are connected by "and." In a parenthetical citation, they are connected by an ampersand, "&."

4. A work with three to five authors

> Pepinsky, Dunn, Rentl, and Corson (1999) further demonstrated the biases evident in gestures.

In the first citation of a work with three to five authors, give all authors' last names, as in the example above. In the second and subsequent references to the work, generally give only the first author's name, followed by "et al." (Latin abbreviation for "and others"):

> In the work of Pepinsky et al. (1999), the loaded gestures included head shakes and eye contact.

However, two or more sources published in the same year could shorten to the same form—for instance, two references shortening to Pepinsky et al., 1999. In that case, cite the last names of as many authors as you need to distinguish the sources, and then give "et al.": for instance, Pepinsky, Dunn, et al., 1999 and Pepinsky, Bradley, et al., 1999.

5. A work with six or more authors

One study (Rutter et al., 1996) attempted to explain these geographical differences in adolescent experience.

For six or more authors, even in the first citation of the work, give only the first author's name, followed by "et al." If two or more sources published in the same year shorten to the same form, follow the instructions for model 4.

6. A work with a group author

An earlier prediction was even more somber (Lorenz Research, 2004).

For a work that lists an institution, agency, corporation, or other group as author, treat the name of the group as if it were an individual's name. If the name is long and has a familiar abbreviation, you may use the abbreviation in the second and subsequent citations. For example, you might abbreviate American Psychological Association as APA.

7. A work with no author or an anonymous work

One article ("Right to Die," 1996) noted that a death-row inmate may crave notoriety.

For a work with no named author, use the first two or three words of the title in place of an author's name, excluding an initial *The, A,* or *An.* Italicize book and journal titles. Place quotation marks around article titles, and capitalize the significant words in all titles cited in the text. (In the reference list, however, do not use quotation marks for article titles, and capitalize only the first word in all but periodical titles. See p. 523.)

For a work that lists "Anonymous" as the author, use this word in the citation: (Anonymous, 1999).

8. One of two or more works by the same author(s)

At about age seven, most children begin to use appropriate gestures to reinforce their stories (Gardner, 1973a).

If your reference list includes two or more works published by the same author(s) *in the same year,* the works should be lettered in the reference list (see p. 526). Then your parenthetical citation should include the appropriate letter, as in "1973a" in the example.

9. Two or more works by different authors

Two studies (Herskowitz, 1989; Marconi & Hamblen, 1999) found that periodic safety instruction can dramatically reduce employees' accidents.

List the sources in alphabetical order by the first authors' names. Insert a semicolon between sources.

10. An indirect source

Supporting data appeared in a study by Wong (cited in Marconi & Hamblen, 1999).

The phrase "cited in" indicates that the reference to Wong's study was found in Marconi and Hamblen. Only Marconi and Hamblen then appears in the list of references.

11. An electronic source

Ferguson and Hawkins (1998) did not anticipate the "evident hostility" of participants (¶ 6).

Electronic sources can be cited like printed sources, usually with the author's last name and the publication date. When quoting or paraphrasing electronic sources that number paragraphs instead of pages, provide the paragraph number preceded by the symbol "¶" if you have it, or by "para." Even if the source does not number its paragraphs, you can still direct readers to a specific location by listing the heading under which the quotation appears and then (counting paragraphs yourself) the number of the paragraph in which the quotation appears—for example, (Morrison & Lee, 2001, Method section, ¶ 4). When the source does not number pages or paragraphs or provide frequent headings, omit any reference number.

57b Prepare an APA reference list.

In APA style, the in-text parenthetical citations refer to the list of sources at the end of the text. This list, titled References, includes full publication information on every source cited in the paper. The list falls at the end of the paper, numbered in sequence with the preceding pages. The following sample shows the elements and their spacing.

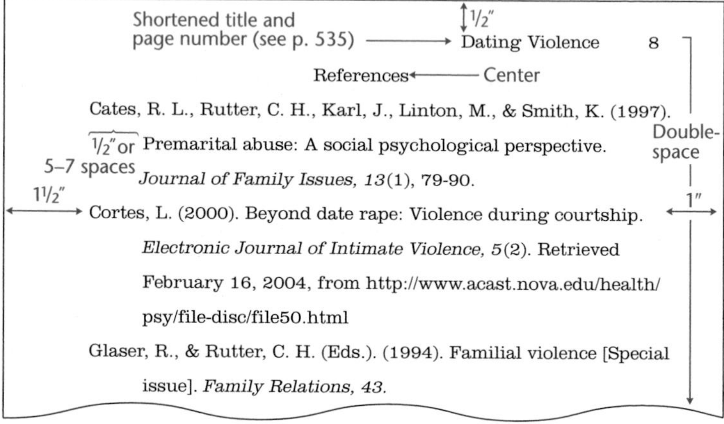

Arrangement

Arrange sources alphabetically by the author's last name or, if there is no author, by the first main word of the title. Do *not* group sources by type (books, journals, and so on).

Spacing

Double-space everything in the references, as shown in the sample, unless your instructor requests single-spacing. (If you do single-space the entries themselves, always double-space *between* them.)

Indention

As illustrated in the sample above, begin each entry at the left margin, and indent the second and subsequent lines five to seven spaces or one-half inch. Most word processors can produce this so-called hanging indent automatically.

Punctuation

Separate the parts of the reference (author, date, title, and publication information) with a period and one space. Do not use a final period in references to electronic sources, which conclude with an electronic address (see pp. 529–32).

Authors

For works with up to six authors, list all authors with last name first, separating names and parts of names with commas. Use initials for first and middle names. Use an ampersand (&) before the last author's name. See model 3 on page 525 for treatment of seven or more authors.

Publication date

Place the publication date in parentheses after the author's or authors' names, followed by a period. Generally, this date is the year only, though for some sources (such as magazine and newspaper articles) it includes month and sometimes day as well.

Titles

In titles of books and articles, capitalize only the first word of the title, the first word of the subtitle, and proper nouns; all other words begin with small letters. In titles of journals, capitalize all significant words (see p. 393). Italicize the titles of books and journals. Do not italicize or use quotation marks around the titles of articles.

City of publication

For print sources that are not periodicals (such as books or government publications), give the city of publication. The following US cities do not require state names as well: Baltimore, Boston, Chicago, Los Angeles, New York, Philadelphia, and San Francisco. Follow their names with a colon. For most other cities, add a comma after the city name, give the two-letter postal abbreviation of the state, and then add a colon. (You may omit the state if the publisher is a university whose name includes the state name, such as "University of Arizona.")

Publisher's name

For nonperiodical print sources, give the publisher's name after the place of publication and a colon. Use shortened names for many publishers (such as "Morrow" for William Morrow), and omit "Co.," "Inc.," and "Publishers." However, give full names for associations, corporations, and university presses (such as "Harvard University Press"), and do not omit "Books" or "Press" from a publisher's name.

Page numbers

Use the abbreviation "p." or "pp." before page numbers in books and in newspapers. Do *not* use the abbreviation for journals and magazines. For inclusive page numbers, include all figures: "667–668."

Note An index to the following models appears on the next two pages. Often, you will have to combine models to provide the necessary information on a source—for instance, combining "A book

APA references

with two to six authors" (2) and "An article in a journal" (12) for a journal article with two or more authors. If you don't see a model listed for the kind of source you used, try to find one that comes close, and provide ample information so that readers can trace the source.

1 • Books

1. A book with one author

Rodriguez, R. (1982). *A hunger of memory: The education of Richard Rodriguez.* Boston: Godine.

The initial "R" appears instead of the author's first name, even though the author's full first name appears on the source. In the title, only the first words of title and subtitle and the proper name *Richard Rodriguez* are capitalized.

2. A book with two to six authors

Nesselroade, J. R., & Baltes, P. B. (1999). *Longitudinal research in the study of behavioral development.* New York: Academic Press.

An ampersand (&) precedes the last author's name.

3. A book with seven or more authors

Wimple, P. B., Van Eijk, M., Potts, C. A., Hayes, J., Obergau, W. R., Zimmer, S., et al. (2001). *Case studies in moral decision making among adolescents.* San Francisco: Jossey-Bass.

Substitute "et al." (Latin abbreviation for "and others") for all authors' names after the first six.

4. A book with an editor

Dohrenwend, B. S., & Dohrenwend, B. P. (Eds.). (1999). *Stressful life events: Their nature and effects.* New York: Wiley.

List the editors' names as if they were authors, but follow the last name with "(Eds.)."—or "(Ed.)." with only one editor. Note the periods inside and outside the final parenthesis.

5. A book with a translator

Trajan, P. D. (1927). *Psychology of animals* (H. Simone, Trans.). Washington, DC: Halperin.

The name of the translator appears in parentheses after the title, followed by a comma, "Trans.," a closing parenthesis, and a final period. Note also the absence of periods in "DC."

6. A book with a group author

Lorenz Research (2004). *Research in social studies teaching.* Baltimore: Arrow Books.

For a work with a group author—such as a research group, government agency, institution, or corporation—begin the entry with the group name. In the references list, alphabetize the work as if the first main word (excluding *The, A,* and *An*) were an author's last name.

7. A book with no author or an anonymous book

Merriam-Webster's collegiate dictionary (11th ed.). (2003). Springfield, MA: Merriam-Webster.

When no author is named, list the work under its title, and alphabetize it by the first main word (excluding *The, A, An*).

For a work whose author is actually given as "Anonymous," use this word in place of the author's name and alphabetize it as if it were a name:

Anonymous. (1995). *Teaching research, researching teaching.* New York: Alpine Press.

8. Two or more works by the same author(s) published in the same year

Gardner, H. (1973a). *The arts and human development.* New York: Wiley.

Gardner, H. (1973b). *The quest for mind: Piaget, Lévi-Strauss, and the structuralist movement.* New York: Knopf.

When citing two or more works by exactly the same author(s), published in the same year—as in the examples above—arrange them alphabetically by the first main word of the title (here *arts*, then *quest*) and distinguish the sources by adding a letter to the date. Both the date *and* the letter are used in citing the source in the text (see p. 521).

When citing two or more works by exactly the same author(s) but *not* published in the same year, arrange the sources in order of their publication dates, earliest first.

9. A later edition

Bollinger, D. L. (1975). *Aspects of language* (2nd ed.). New York: Harcourt Brace Jovanovich.

The edition number in parentheses follows the title and is followed by a period.

10. A work in more than one volume

Lincoln, A. (1953). *The collected works of Abraham Lincoln* (R. P. Basler, Ed.). (Vol. 5). New Brunswick, NJ: Rutgers University Press.

Lincoln, A. (1953). *The collected works of Abraham Lincoln* (R. P. Basler, Ed.). (Vols. 1-8). New Brunswick, NJ: Rutgers University Press.

The first entry cites a single volume (5) in the eight-volume set. The second cites all eight volumes. Use the abbreviation "Vol." or "Vols." in parentheses, and follow the closing parenthesis with a period. In the absence of an editor's name, the description of volumes would follow the title directly: *The collected works of Abraham Lincoln* (Vol. 5).

11. An article or chapter in an edited book

Paykel, E. S. (1999). Life stress and psychiatric disorder: Applications of the clinical approach. In B. S. Dohrenwend & B. P. Dohrenwend (Eds.), *Stressful life events: Their nature and effects* (pp. 239-264). New York: Wiley.

Give the publication date of the collection (1999 above) as the publication date of the article or chapter. After the article or chapter title and a period, write "In" and then provide the editors' names (in normal order), "(Eds.)" and a comma, the title of the collection, and the page numbers of the article in parentheses.

2 • Periodicals: Journals, magazines, newspapers

12. An article in a journal with continuous pagination throughout the annual volume

Emery, R. E. (2001). Marital turmoil: Interpersonal conflict and the children of discord and divorce. *Psychological Bulletin, 92,* 310-330.

See page 425 for an explanation of journal pagination. Note that you do not place the article title in quotation marks and that you capitalize only the first words of the title and subtitle. In contrast, you italicize the journal title and capitalize all significant words. Separate the volume number from the title with a comma, and italicize the number. Do not add "pp." before the page numbers.

13. An article in a journal that pages issues separately

Dacey, J. (1998). Management participation in corporate buy-outs. *Management Perspectives, 7*(4), 20-31.

Consult page 425 for an explanation of journal pagination. In this case, place the issue number in parentheses after the volume number without intervening space. Do *not* italicize the issue number.

14. An abstract of a journal article

Emery, R. E. (2001). Marital turmoil: Interpersonal conflict and the children of discord and divorce. *Psychological Bulletin, 92,* 310-330. Abstract obtained from *Psychological Abstracts,* 2001, *69,* Item 1320.

When you cite the abstract of an article, rather than the article itself, give full publication information for the article, followed by Abstract obtained from and the information for the collection of abstracts, including title, date, volume number, and either page number or other reference number ("Item 1320" above).

15. An article in a magazine

William, N. (2002, October 24). Beethoven's late quartets. *The New York Review of Books,* 16-19.

If a magazine has volume and issue numbers, give them as in models 12 and 13. Also give the full date of the issue: year, followed by a comma, month, and day (if any). Give all page numbers even when the article does not appear on continuous pages, without "pp."

16. An article in a newspaper

Kolata, G. (2004, January 7). Kill all the bacteria! *The New York Times,* pp. B1, B3.

Give month *and* date along with year of publication. Use *The* in the newspaper name if the paper itself does. Precede the page number(s) with "p." or "pp.," and give all page numbers even when the article does not appear on continuous pages.

17. An unsigned article

APA 57b

The right to die. (1996, October 11). *Time, 121,* 101.

List and alphabetize the article under its title, as you would a book with no author (model 7, p. 526).

18. A review

Dinnage, R. (1987, November 29). Against the master and his men [Review of the book *A mind of her own: The life of Karen Horney*]. *The New York Times Book Review,* 10-11.

If the review is not titled, use the bracketed information as the title, keeping the brackets.

3 • Electronic sources

In general, the APA's electronic-source references begin as those for print references do: author(s), date, title. Then you add information on when and how you retrieved the source. For example, an online source might end Retrieved February 22, 2004, from http://www.isu.edu/finance-dl/46732 (in APA style, no period follows an electronic address at the end of the reference). Double-check Web addresses to be sure they are accurate and that they lead to the specific pages you consulted.

Using the following models for electronic sources, you may have to improvise to match your source to a model. Try to locate all the information required by a model, referring to pages 414–15 for help. However, if you search for and still cannot find some information, then give what you can find. If a source has no publication date, use "n.d." (for *no date*) in place of a publication date (see model 28, p. 531).

Note When you need to divide an electronic address from one line to the next, APA style calls for breaking *only* after a slash or before a period. Do not hyphenate an electronic address.

19. A journal article that is published online and in print

Palfrey, A. (1996). Choice of mates in identical twins [Electronic version]. *Modern Psychology, 4*(1), 26-40.

If you consulted the online version of a journal article that appears the same way both online and in print, insert [Electronic version] between the article title and the following period.

If you believe that the online version you consulted differs in some way from the print version, omit the bracketed insert and provide a retrieval statement with the date of your access and the complete electronic address for the article:

Grady, G. F. (2000). The here and now of hepatitis B immunization. *Today's Medicine, 13,* 145-151. Retrieved December 27, 2002, from http://www.fmrt.org/todaysmedicine/Grady050293.html

20. An article in an online journal

Wissink, J. A. (2000). Techniques of smoking cessation among teens and adults. *Adolescent Medicine, 2.* Retrieved August 16, 2003, from http://www.easu.edu/AdolescentMedicine/2-Wissink.html

If the article has an identifying number, give it after the volume number and a comma.

21. A journal article retrieved from an electronic database

Wilkins, J. M. (1999). The myths of the only child. *Psychology Update, 11*(1), 16-23. Retrieved December 20, 2003, from ProQuest Direct database.

Many reference works and periodicals are available full-text from electronic databases to which your library subscribes, such as ProQuest Direct or LexisNexis Academic. Your reference need not specify how you reached the database—for instance, through a Web site or on a CD-ROM. However, it should provide the appropriate information for the source itself—in the example above, for a journal article—and it should conclude with a retrieval statement giving the date of your access and the name of the database.

22. An abstract retrieved from an electronic database

Wilkins, J. M. (1999). The myths of the only child. *Psychology Update, 11*(1), 16-23. Abstract retrieved December 20, 2003, from ProQuest Direct database.

23. An article in an online newspaper

Pear, R. (2004, January 23). Gains reported for children of welfare to work families. *The New York Times on the Web.* Retrieved January 23, 2004, from http://www.nytimes.com/2004/01/23/national/23/WELF.html

24. An entire Web site (text citation)

The APA's Web site provides answers to frequently asked questions about style (http://www.apa.org).

Cite an entire Web site (rather than a specific page or document) by giving the electronic address in your text.

25. An independent document on the Web

Anderson, D. (2003, May 1). *Social constructionism and MOOs.* Retrieved August 6, 2003, from http://sites.unc.edu/~daniel/social_constructionism/

Treat the title of an independent Web document like the title of a book. If the document has no named author, begin with the title and place the publication date after the title.

26. A document from the Web site of a university or government agency

McConnell, L. M., Koenig, B. A., Greeley, H. T., & Raffin, T. A. (2003, August 17). *Genetic testing and Alzheimer disease: Has the time come?* Retrieved September 1, 2003, from Stanford University, Project in Genomics, Ethics, and Society Web site: http://scbe.stanford.edu/pges

Provide the name of the host organization and any sponsoring program as part of the retrieval statement.

27. An online government report

U.S. Department of Commerce. National Telecommunications and Information Administration. (2001, October). *Falling through the net: Toward digital inclusion.* Retrieved April 12, 2003, from http://www.ntia.doc.gov/ntiahome/fttnoo.html

28. A multipage online document

Elston, C. (n.d.). *Multiple intelligences.* Retrieved June 6, 2003, from http://education.com/teachspace/intelligences/

For an Internet document with multiple pages, each with its own electronic address, give the address of the document's home page. Note the use of "n.d." after the author's name to indicate that the document provides no publication date.

29. A part of an online document

Elston, C. (n.d.). Logical/math intelligence. In *Multiple intelligences.* Retrieved June 6, 2003, from http://education.com/teachspace/intelligences/logical.jsp

If the part of a document you site has a label (such as "chapter 6" or "section 4"), provide that in parentheses after the document title: *Multiple intelligences* (chap. 6).

30. A retrievable online posting

Tourville, M. (2004, January 6). European currency reform. Message posted to International Finance electronic mailing list, archived at http://www.isu.edu/finance-dl/46732

Include postings to discussion lists and newsgroups in your list of references *only* if they are retrievable by others. The source above is archived (as the reference makes plain) and thus retrievable at the address given.

31. Electronic mail or a nonretrievable online posting (text citation)

At least one member of the research team has expressed reservations about the design of the study (L. Kogod, personal communication, February 6, 2004).

Personal electronic mail and other online postings that are not retrievable by others should be cited only in your text, as in the example above.

32. Software

Project scheduler 9000 [Computer software]. (2004). Orlando, FL: Scitor.

No reference is needed for well-known software such as WordPerfect and Java. For a less familiar program, follow the model above, neither quoting nor italicizing the title. Provide an author's name if an individual has the rights to the program. If you obtain the software online, you can generally replace the producer's city and name with a retrieval statement that includes the electronic address.

4 • Other sources

33. A report

Gerald, K. (1998). *Medico-moral problems in obstetric care* (Report No. NP-71). St. Louis, MO: Catholic Hospital Association.

Treat a report like a book, but provide any report number in parentheses immediately after the title, with no punctuation between them.

For a report from the Educational Resources Information Center (ERIC), provide the ERIC document number in parentheses at the end of the entry:

Jolson, M. K. (1991). *Music education for preschoolers* (Report No. TC-622). New York: Teachers College, Columbia University. (ERIC Document Reproduction Service No. ED 264488)

34. A government publication

Hawaii. Department of Education. (2004). *Kauai district schools, profile 2002-03.* Honolulu, HI: Author.

Stiller, A. (1996). *Historic preservation and tax incentives.* Washington, DC: U.S. Department of the Interior.

U.S. House. Committee on Ways and Means. (2001). *Medicare payment for outpatient physical and occupational therapy services.* 107d Cong., 1st Sess. Washington, DC: U.S. Government Printing Office.

If no individual is given as the author, list the publication under the name of the sponsoring agency. When the agency is both the author and the publisher, use "Author" in place of the publisher's name.

35. A doctoral dissertation

A dissertation abstracted in DAI *and obtained from UMI:*

Steciw, S. K. (1986). Alterations to the Pessac project of Le Corbusier. *Dissertation Abstracts International, 46,* 565C. (UMI No. 6216202)

A dissertation abstracted in DAI *and obtained from the university:*

Chang, J. K. (2000). Therapeutic intervention in treatment of injuries to the hand and wrist (Doctoral dissertation, University of Michigan, 2000). *Dissertation Abstracts International, 50,* 162.

An unpublished dissertation:

Delaune, M. L. (2001). *Child care in single-mother and single-father families: Differences in time, activity, and stress.* Unpublished doctoral dissertation, University of California, Davis.

36. A published interview

Brisick, W. C. (1998, July 1). [Interview with Ishmael Reed]. *Publishers Weekly,* 41-42.

List a published interview under the interviewer's name. Provide the publication information appropriate for the kind of source the interview appears in (here, a magazine). Immediately after the date, in brackets, specify that the piece is an interview and give the subject's name if necessary. For an interview with a title, add the title (with an initial capital letter, no quotation marks, and no closing period) before the bracketed information.

An interview you conduct yourself should not be included in your list of references. Instead, use an in-text parenthetical citation, as shown in model 31 for a nonretrievable online posting.

37. A motion picture

Spielberg, S. (Director). (1993). *Schindler's list* [Motion picture]. United States: Viacom.

American Psychological Association (Producer). (2001). *Ethno-cultural psychotherapy* [Motion picture]. (Available from the American Psychological Association, 750 First Street, NE, Washington, DC 20002-4242, or online from http://www.apa.org/videos/4310240.html)

A motion picture may be a film or a video. Depending on whose work you are citing, begin with the name or names of the creator, director, producer, or primary contributor, followed by his or her function in parentheses. (The first model above would begin with the producer's name if you were citing the motion picture as a whole, not specifically the work of the director.) Add [Motion picture] after the title. For a motion picture in wide circulation (first example), give the country of origin and the name of the organization that released the picture. For a motion picture that is not widely circulated (second example), give the distributor's name and address in parentheses.

38. A musical recording

Springsteen, B. (2002). Empty sky. *The rising* [CD]. New York: Columbia.

Begin with the name of the writer or composer. (If you cite another artist's recording of the work, provide this information after the title of the work—for example, [Recorded by E. Davila].) Give the medium in brackets ([CD], [Cassette recording], and so on). Finish with the city and name of the recording label.

39. A television series or episode

Taylor, C., Cleveland, R., & Andries, L. (Producers). (2003). *Six feet under* [Television series]. New York: HBO.

Cleveland, R. (Writer), & Engler, M. (Director). (2003). Dillon Michael Cooper [Television series episode]. In C. Taylor, R. Cleveland, & L. Andries (Producers), *Six feet under*. New York: HBO.

For a television series, begin with the producers' names and identify their function in parentheses. Add [Television series] after the series title, and give the city and name of the network. For an episode, begin with the writer and then the director, identifying the function of each in parentheses, and add [Television series episode] after the episode title. Then provide the series information, beginning with "In" and the producers' names and function, giving the series title, and ending with the city and name of the network.

57c Format the paper in APA style.

The APA *Publication Manual* distinguishes between documents intended for publication (which will be set in type) and those submitted by students (which are the final copy). The following guidelines and the samples on the next two pages apply to most undergraduate papers. Check with your instructor for any changes in this format.

Note See pages 521–23 for the APA format of a reference list. And see pages 75–85 for guidelines on type spacing, type fonts, lists, and other elements of document design.

Margins

Use one-inch margins on the top, bottom, and right side. Add another half-inch on the left to accommodate a binder.

Spacing and indentions

Double-space your text and references. (See pp. 537–38 for spacing of displayed quotations.) Indent paragraphs and displayed quotations one-half inch or five to seven spaces.

Paging

Begin numbering on the title page, and number consecutively through the end (including the reference list). Type Arabic numerals (1, 2, 3) in the upper right, about one-half inch from the top.

Place a shortened version of your title five spaces to the left of the page number. (See the samples on the next page.)

Title page

Include the full title, your name, the course title, the instructor's name, and the date. Type the title on the top half of the page, followed by the identifying information, all centered horizontally and double-spaced. Include a shortened form of the title along with the page number at the top. (See the sample on the next page.)

Abstract

Summarize (in a maximum of 120 words) your subject, research method, findings, and conclusions. Put the abstract on a page by itself. (See the sample on the next page.)

Body

Begin with a restatement of the paper's title and then an introduction (not labeled). The introduction concisely presents the

Title page

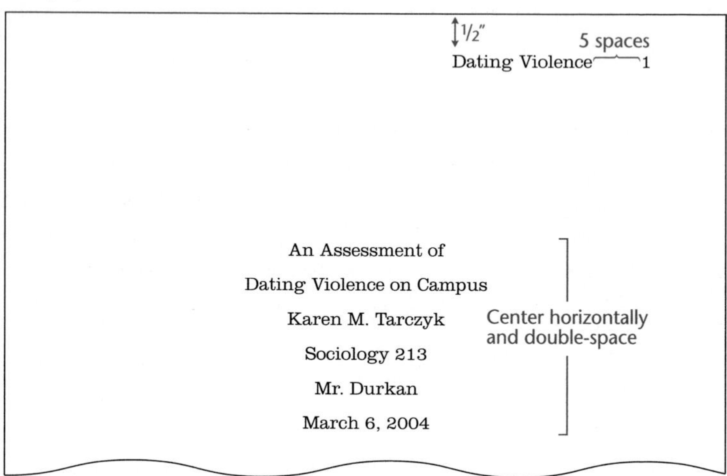

Abstract

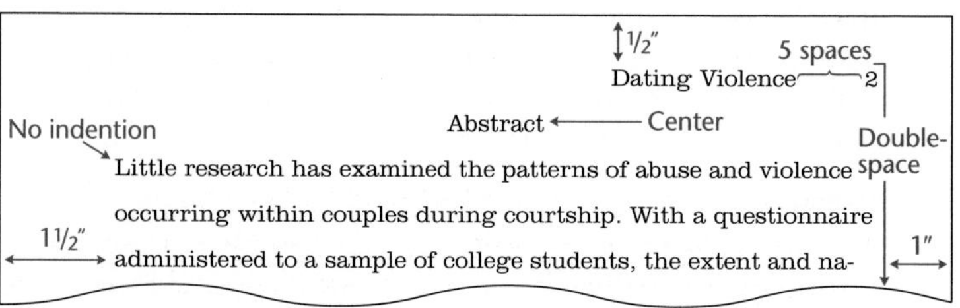

problem you researched, your research method, the relevant background (such as related studies), and the purpose of your research.

The next section, labeled "Method," provides a detailed discussion of how you conducted your research, including a description of the research subjects, any materials or tools you used (such as questionnaires or surveys), and the procedure you followed. In the bottom illustration on the facing page, the labels "Method" and "*Sample*" are first-level and second-level headings, respectively. When you need one, two, or three levels of headings, use the following formats, always double-spacing above and below:

First-Level Heading

Second-Level Heading

Third-level heading. Run this heading into the text paragraph.

First page of body

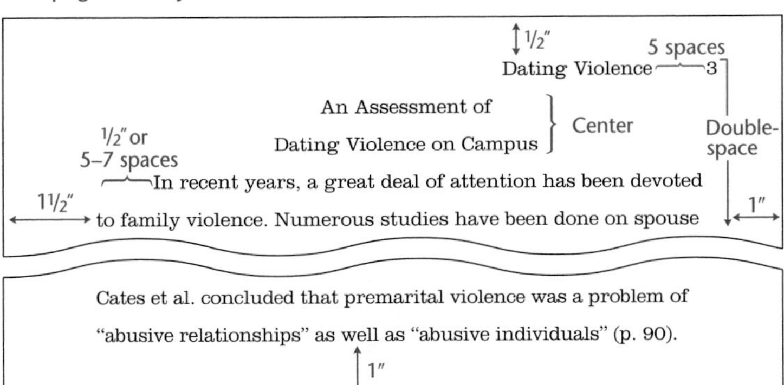
Dating Violence 3

An Assessment of

Dating Violence on Campus

In recent years, a great deal of attention has been devoted to family violence. Numerous studies have been done on spouse

Cates et al. concluded that premarital violence was a problem of “abusive relationships” as well as “abusive individuals” (p. 90).

Later page of body

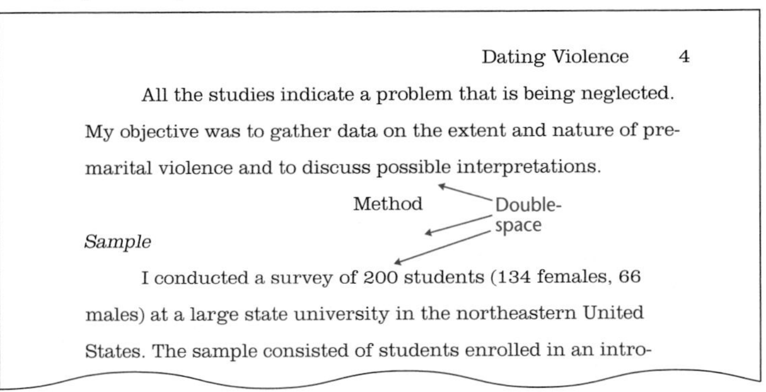
Dating Violence 4

All the studies indicate a problem that is being neglected. My objective was to gather data on the extent and nature of premarital violence and to discuss possible interpretations.

Method

Sample

I conducted a survey of 200 students (134 females, 66 males) at a large state university in the northeastern United States. The sample consisted of students enrolled in an intro-

The “Results” section (labeled with a first-level heading) summarizes the data you collected, explains how you analyzed them, and presents them in detail, often in tables, graphs, or charts.

The “Discussion” section (labeled with a first-level heading) interprets the data and presents your conclusions. (When the discussion is brief, you may combine it with the previous section under the heading “Results and Discussion.”)

The “References” section, beginning a new page, includes all your sources. See pages 521–23 for an explanation and sample.

Long quotations

Run into your text all quotations of forty words or less, and enclose them in quotation marks. For quotations of more than forty words, set them off from your text by indenting all lines one-half inch or five to seven spaces, double-spacing above and below. For student papers, the APA allows single-spacing of displayed quotations:

> Echoing the opinions of other Europeans at the time, Freud (1961) had a poor view of Americans:
>
> > The Americans are really too bad. . . . Competition is much more pungent with them, not succeeding means civil death to every one, and they have no private resources apart from their profession, no hobby, games, love or other interests of a cultured person. And success means money. (p. 86)

Do not use quotation marks around a quotation displayed in this way.

Illustrations

Present data in tables and figures (graphs or charts), as appropriate. (See p. 541 and pp. 82–83 for examples.) Begin each illustration on a separate page. Number each kind of illustration consecutively and separately from the other (Table 1, Table 2, etc., and Figure 1, Figure 2, etc.). Refer to all illustrations in your text—for instance, "(See Figure 3.)." Generally, place illustrations immediately after the text references to them.

57d A sample paper in APA style

The following excerpts from a sociology paper illustrate elements of a research paper using the APA style of documentation and format.

[Title page.]

Dating Violence 1 — Shortened title and page number.

APA 57d

An Assessment of
Dating Violence on Campus
Karen M. Tarczyk
Sociology 213
Mr. Durkan
March 6, 2004

Double-space all information: title, name, course title, instructor, date.

[New page.]

Dating Violence 2

Abstract

Little research has examined the patterns of abuse and violence occurring within couples during courtship. With a questionnaire administered to a sample of college students, the extent and nature of such abuse and violence were investigated. The results, interpretations, and implications for further research are discussed.

Abstract: summary of subject, research method, conclusions.

[New page.]

Dating Violence 3

Double-space throughout.

An Assessment of
Dating Violence on Campus

Title repeated on first text page.

In recent years, a great deal of attention has been devoted to spouse and child abuse. However, violent behavior occurs in dating relationships as well, yet the problem of dating violence has been relatively ignored by sociological research. It should be examined further since the premarital relationship is one context in which individuals learn and adopt behaviors that surface in marriage.

Introduction: presentation of the problem researched by the writer.

The sociologist James Makepeace (1989) contended that courtship violence is a "potential mediating link" between violence in one's family of orientation and violence in one's later family of procreation (p. 103). Studying dating behaviors at Bemidji State University in Minnesota, Makepeace reported that one-fifth of the respondents had had at least one encounter with dating violence. He then extended these percentages to students nationwide, suggesting the existence of a major hidden social problem.

Citation form: author named in the text.

Citation form: page number given for quotation.

More recent research supports Makepeace's. Cates, Rutter, Karl, Linton, and Smith (1997) found that 22.3% of respondents at Oregon State University had been either the victim or the perpetrator of pre-

Citation form: source with three to five authors, named in the text.

marital violence. Another study (Cortes, 2000) found that so-called date rape, while much more publicized, was reported by many fewer woman respondents (2%) than was other violence during courtship (21%). [The introduction continues.]

Citation form: author not named in the text.

All these studies indicate a problem that is being neglected. My objective was to gather data on the extent and nature of premarital violence and to discuss possible interpretations.

Method

First- and second-level headings.

Sample

"Method" section: discussion of how research was conducted.

I conducted a survey of 200 students (134 females, 66 males) at a large state university in the northeastern United States. The sample consisted of students enrolled in an introductory sociology course. [The explanation of method continues.]

The Questionnaire

A questionnaire exploring the personal dynamics of relationships was distributed during regularly scheduled class. Questions were answered anonymously in a 30-minute period. The survey consisted of three sections. [The explanation of method continues.]

Section 3 required participants to provide information about their current dating relationships: levels of stress and frustration, communication between partners, and patterns of decision making. These variables were expected to influence the amount of violence in a relationship. The next part of the survey, adapted from Murray Strauss's Conflict Tactics Scales (1982), contained 19 measures of conflict and the means of conflict resolution, including reasoning, verbal aggression, and actual violence. The final page of the questionnaire contained general questions on the couple's use of alcohol, sexual activity, and overall satisfaction with the relationship.

Results

The questionnaire revealed significant levels of verbal aggression and threatened and actual violence among dating couples. A high number of students, 50% (62 of 123 subjects), reported that they had been the victim of verbal abuse, either being insulted or sworn at. In addition, almost 14% (17 of 123) of respondents admitted being threatened with some type of violence, and more than 14% (18 of 123) reported being pushed, grabbed, or shoved. (See Table 1.)

"Results" section: summary and presentation of data.

Reference to table.

[The explanation of results continues.]

[Table on a page by itself.]

Table 1

Incidence of Courtship Violence

Table presents data in clear format. For student papers, the APA permits single-spacing within tables.

Type of violence	Number of students reporting	Percentage of sample
Insulted or swore	62	50.4
Threatened to hit or throw something	17	13.8
Threw something	8	6.5
Pushed, grabbed, or shoved	18	14.6
Slapped	8	6.5
Kicked, bit, or hit with fist	7	5.7
Hit or tried to hit with something	2	1.6
Threatened with a knife or gun	1	0.8
Used a knife or gun	1	0.8

Discussion

Violence within premarital relationships has been relatively ignored. The results of the present study indicate that abuse and force do occur in dating relationships. Although the percentages are small, so

"Discussion" section: interpretation of data and presentation of conclusions.

Dating Violence 6

was the sample. Extending them to the entire campus population of 5,000 would mean significant numbers. For example, if the nearly 6% incidence of being kicked, bitten, or hit with a fist is typical, then 300 students might have experienced this type of violence. [The discussion continues.]

If the courtship period is characterized by abuse and violence, what accounts for it? The other sections of the survey examined some variables that appear to influence the relationship, particularly level of stress and frustration and level of communication between partners. [The discussion continues.]

The method of analyzing the data in this study provided a clear overview. However, more tests of significance and correlation and a closer look at the variables affecting the relationship are warranted. The courtship period may set the stage for patterns of married life. It merits more attention.

[New page.]

New page for reference list.

Dating Violence 7

References

Heading centered.

Cates, R. L., Rutter, C. H., Karl, J., Linton, M., & Smith, K. (1997). Premarital abuse: A social psychological perspective. *Journal of Family Issues, 13*(1), 79-90.

Cortes, L. (2000). Beyond date rape: Violence during courtship. *Electronic Journal of Intimate Violence, 5*(2). Retrieved February 16, 2004, from http://acast.nova.edu/health/psy/file-disc/file50.html

Glaser, R., & Rutter, C. H. (Eds.). (1994). Familial violence [Special issue]. *Family Relations, 43.*

Makepeace, J. M. (1989). Courtship violence among college students. *Family Relations, 28,* 97-103.

Strauss, M. L. (1982). *Conflict Tactics Scales.* New York: Sociological Tests.

An article in a print journal.

Double-space throughout.

An article in an online journal.

Sources are alphabetized by first authors' last names.

Second and subsequent lines of each source are indented ½" or 5–7 spaces.

A book. ("Tactics Scales" is part of a name and so is capitalized.)

Glossary of Usage

This glossary provides notes on words or phrases that often cause problems for writers. The recommendations for standard American English are based on current dictionaries and usage guides. Items labeled **nonstandard** should be avoided in speech and especially in writing. Those labeled **colloquial** and **slang** occur in speech and in some informal writing but are best avoided in the more formal writing usually expected in college and business. (Words and phrases labeled *colloquial* include those labeled by many dictionaries with the equivalent term *informal.*)

Note Two lists in the text supplement this glossary: idioms with prepositions, such as *part from* and *part with* (p. 196); and words that are pronounced the same or similarly but spelled differently, such as *heard* and *herd* (pp. 383–84).

a, an Use *a* before words beginning with consonant sounds, including those spelled with an initial pronounced *h* and those spelled with vowels that are sounded as consonants: *a historian, a one-o'clock class, a university.* Use *an* before words that begin with vowel sounds, including those spelled with an initial silent *h: an orgy, an L, an honor.*

The article before an abbreviation depends on how the abbreviation is to be read: *She was once an AEC undersecretary* (*AEC* is to be read as three separate letters). *Many Americans opposed a SALT treaty* (*SALT* is to be read as one word, *salt*).

See also pp. 302–04 on the uses of *a/an* versus *the.*

accept, except *Accept* is a verb meaning "receive." *Except* is usually a preposition or conjunction meaning "but for" or "other than"; when it is used as a verb, it means "leave out." *I can accept all your suggestions except the last one. I'm sorry you excepted my last suggestion from your list.*

advice, advise *Advice* is a noun, and *advise* is a verb: *Take my advice; do as I advise you.*

affect, effect Usually *affect* is a verb, meaning "to influence," and *effect* is a noun, meaning "result": *The drug did not affect his driving; in fact, it seemed to have no effect at all.* But *effect* occasionally is used as a verb meaning "to bring about": *Her efforts effected a change.* And *affect* is used in psychology as a noun meaning "feeling or emotion": *One can infer much about affect from behavior.*

agree to, agree with *Agree to* means "consent to," and *agree with* means "be in accord with": *How can they agree to a treaty when they don't agree with each other about the terms?*

all ready, already *All ready* means "completely prepared," and *already* means "by now" or "before now": *We were all ready to go to the movie, but it had already started.*

all right *All right* is always two words. *Alright* is a common misspelling.

all together, altogether *All together* means "in unison" or "gathered in one place." *Altogether* means "entirely." *It's not altogether true that our family never spends vacations all together.*

allusion, illusion An *allusion* is an indirect reference, and an *illusion* is a deceptive appearance: *Paul's constant allusions to Shakespeare created the illusion that he was an intellectual.*

almost, most *Almost* means "nearly"; *most* means "the greater number (or part) of." In formal writing, *most* should not be used as a substitute for *almost: We see each other almost* [not *most*] *every day.*

a lot *A lot* is always two words, used informally to mean "many." *Alot* is a common misspelling.

among, between In general, use *among* for relationships involving more than two people or for comparing one thing to a group to which it belongs. *The four of them agreed among themselves that the choice was between New York and Los Angeles.*

amount, number Use *amount* with a singular noun that names something not countable (a noncount noun): *The amount of food varies.* Use *number* with a plural noun that names more than one of something countable (a plural count noun): *The number of calories must stay the same.*

and/or *And/or* indicates three options: one or the other or both (*The decision is made by the mayor and/or the council*). If you mean all three options, *and/or* is appropriate. Otherwise, use *and* if you mean both, *or* if you mean either.

ante-, anti- The prefix *ante-* means "before" (*antedate, antebellum*); *anti-* means "against" (*antiwar, antinuclear*). Before a capital letter or *i*, *anti-* takes a hyphen: *anti-Freudian, anti-isolationist.*

anxious, eager *Anxious* means "nervous" or "worried" and is usually followed by *about. Eager* means "looking forward" and is usually followed by *to. I've been anxious about getting blisters. I'm eager* [not *anxious*] *to get new running shoes.*

anybody, any body; anyone, any one *Anybody* and *anyone* are indefinite pronouns; *any body* is a noun modified by *any; any one* is a pronoun or adjective modified by *any. How can anybody communicate with any body of government? Can anyone help Amy? She has more work than any one person can handle.*

any more, anymore *Any more* means "no more"; *anymore* means "now." Both are used in negative constructions. *He doesn't want any more. She doesn't live here anymore.*

are, is Use *are* with a plural subject (*books are*), *is* with a singular subject (*book is*).

as Substituting for *because, since,* or *while, as* may be vague or ambiguous: *As the researchers asked more questions, their money ran out.* (Does *as* mean "while" or "because"?) *As* should never be used as a substitute for *whether* or *who. I'm not sure whether* [not *as*] *we can make it. That's the man who* [not *as*] *gave me directions.*

as, like In formal speech and writing, *like* should not introduce a full clause (with a subject and a verb) because it is a preposition. The preferred choice is *as* or *as if: The plan succeeded as* [not *like*] *we hoped. It seemed as if* [not *like*] *it might fail. Other plans like it have failed.*

assure, ensure, insure *Assure* means "to promise": *He assured us that we would miss the traffic. Ensure* and *insure* often are used interchangeably to mean "make certain," but some reserve *insure* for matters of legal and financial protection and use *ensure* for more general meanings: *We left early to ensure that we would miss the traffic. It's expensive to insure yourself against floods.*

awful, awfully Strictly speaking, *awful* means "awe-inspiring." As intensifiers meaning "very" or "extremely" (*He tried awfully hard*), *awful* and *awfully* should be avoided in formal speech or writing.

a while, awhile *Awhile* is an adverb; *a while* is an article and a noun. *I will be gone awhile* [not *a while*]. *I will be gone for a while* [not *awhile*].

bad, badly In formal speech and writing, *bad* should be used only as an adjective; the adverb is *badly. He felt bad because his tooth ached badly.* In *He felt bad,* the verb *felt* is a linking verb and the adjective *bad* describes the subject. See also p. 295.

being as, being that Colloquial for *because,* the preferable word in formal speech or writing: *Because* [not *Being as*] *the world is round, Columbus never did fall off the edge.*

beside, besides *Beside* is a preposition meaning "next to." *Besides* is a preposition meaning "except" or "in addition to" as well as an adverb meaning "in addition." *Besides, several other people besides you want to sit beside Dr. Christensen.*

better, had better *Had better* (meaning "ought to") is a verb modified by an adverb. The verb is necessary and should not be omitted: *You had better* [not just *better*] *go.*

between, among See *among, between.*

bring, take Use *bring* only for movement from a farther place to a nearer one and *take* for any other movement. *First take these books to the library for renewal; then take them to Mr. Daniels. Bring them back to me when he's finished.*

but, hardly, scarcely These words are negative in their own right; using *not* with any of them produces a double negative (see pp. 299–300). *We have but* [not *haven't got but*] *an hour before our plane leaves. I could hardly* [not *couldn't hardly*] *make out her face.*

but, however, yet Each of these words is adequate to express contrast. Don't combine them. *He said he had finished, yet* [not *but yet*] *he continued.*

can, may Strictly, *can* indicates capacity or ability, and *may* indicates permission or possibility: *If I may talk with you a moment, I believe I can solve your problem.*

censor, censure To *censor* is to edit or remove from public view on moral or other grounds; to *censure* is to give a formal scolding. *The* *lieutenant was censured by Major Taylor for censoring the letters her soldiers wrote home from boot camp.*

cite, sight, site *Cite* is a verb usually meaning "quote," "commend," or "acknowledge": *You must cite your sources. Sight* is both a noun meaning "the ability to see" or "a view" and a verb meaning "perceive" or "observe": *What a sight you see when you sight Venus through a strong telescope. Site* is a noun meaning "place" or "location" or a verb meaning "situate": *The builder sited the house on an unlikely site.*

climatic, climactic *Climatic* comes from *climate* and refers to the weather: *Last winter's temperatures may indicate a climatic change. Climactic* comes from *climax* and refers to a dramatic high point: *During the climactic duel between Hamlet and Laertes, Gertrude drinks poisoned wine.*

complement, compliment To *complement* something is to add to, complete, or reinforce it: *Her yellow blouse complemented her black hair.* To *compliment* something is to make a flattering remark about it: *He complimented her on her hair. Complimentary* can also mean "free": *complimentary tickets.*

conscience, conscious *Conscience* is a noun meaning "a sense of right and wrong"; *conscious* is an adjective meaning "aware" or "awake." *Though I was barely conscious, my conscience nagged me.*

continual, continuous *Continual* means "constantly recurring": *Most movies on television are continually interrupted by commercials. Continuous* means "unceasing": *Some cable channels present movies continuously without commercials.*

could of See *have, of.*

credible, creditable, credulous *Credible* means "believable": *It's a strange story, but it seems credible to me. Creditable* means "deserving of credit" or "worthy": *Steve gave a creditable performance. Credulous* means "gullible": *The credulous Claire believed Tim's lies.* See also *incredible, incredulous.*

criteria The plural of *criterion* (meaning "standard for judgment"): *Our criteria are strict. The most important criterion is a sense of humor.*

data The plural of *datum* (meaning "fact"). Though *data* is often used as a singular noun, many careful writers still treat it as plural: *The data fail* [not *fails*] *to support the hypothesis.*

device, devise *Device* is the noun, and *devise* is the verb: *Can you devise some device for getting his attention?*

different from, different than *Different from* is preferred: *His purpose is different from mine.* But *different than* is widely accepted when a construction using *from* would be wordy: *I'm a different person now than I used to be* is preferable to *I'm a different person now from the person I used to be.*

Usage

differ from, differ with To *differ from* is to be unlike: *The twins differ from each other only in their hairstyles.* To *differ with* is to disagree with: *I have to differ with you on that point.*

discreet, discrete *Discreet* (noun form *discretion*) means "tactful": *What's a discreet way of telling Maud to be quiet? Discrete* (noun form *discreteness*) means "separate and distinct": *Within a computer's memory are millions of discrete bits of information.*

disinterested, uninterested *Disinterested* means "impartial": *We chose Pete, as a disinterested third party, to decide who was right. Uninterested* means "bored" or "lacking interest": *Unfortunately, Pete was completely uninterested in the question.*

don't *Don't* is the contraction for *do not,* not for *does not: I don't care, you don't care,* and *he doesn't* [not *don't*] *care.*

due to the fact that Wordy for *because.*

eager, anxious See *anxious, eager.*

effect See *affect, effect.*

elicit, illicit *Elicit* is a verb meaning "bring out" or "call forth." *Illicit* is an adjective meaning "unlawful." *The crime elicited an outcry against illicit drugs.*

emigrate, immigrate *Emigrate* means "to leave one place and move to another": *The Chus emigrated from Korea. Immigrate* means "to move into a place where one was not born": *They immigrated to the United States.*

ensure See *assure, ensure, insure.*

enthused Used colloquially as an adjective meaning "showing enthusiasm." The preferred adjective is *enthusiastic: The coach was enthusiastic* [not *enthused*] *about the team's victory.*

et al., etc. Use *et al.,* the Latin abbreviation for "and other people," only in source citations: *Jones et al.* Avoid *etc.,* the Latin abbreviation for "and other things," in formal writing, and do not use it to refer to people or to substitute for precision, as in *The government provides health care, etc.*

everybody, every body; everyone, every one *Everybody* and *everyone* are indefinite pronouns: *Everybody* [*everyone*] *knows Tom steals. Every one* is a pronoun modified by *every,* and *every body* a noun modified by *every.* Both refer to each thing or person of a specific group and are typically followed by *of: The game commissioner has stocked every body of fresh water in the state with fish, and now every one of our rivers is a potential trout stream.*

everyday, every day *Everyday* is an adjective meaning "used daily" or "common"; *every day* is a noun modified by *every: Everyday problems tend to arise every day.*

everywheres Nonstandard for *everywhere.*

except See *accept, except.*

except for the fact that Wordy for *except that.*

explicit, implicit *Explicit* means "stated outright": *I left explicit instructions. Implicit* means "implied, unstated": *We had an implicit understanding.*

farther, further *Farther* refers to additional distance (*How much farther is it to the beach?*), and *further* refers to additional time, amount, or other abstract matters (*I don't want to discuss this any further*).

fewer, less *Fewer* refers to individual countable items (a plural count noun), *less* to general amounts (a noncount noun, always singular). *Skim milk has fewer calories than whole milk. We have less milk left than I thought.*

flaunt, flout *Flaunt* means "show off": *If you have style, flaunt it. Flout* means "scorn" or "defy": *Hester Prynne flouted convention and paid the price.*

flunk A colloquial substitute for *fail.*

fun As an adjective, *fun* is colloquial and should be avoided in most writing: *It was a pleasurable* [not *fun*] *evening.*

further See *farther, further.*

get This common verb is used in many slang and colloquial expressions: *get lost, that really gets me, getting on. Get* is easy to overuse: watch out for it in expressions such as *it's getting better* (substitute *improving*) and *we got done* (substitute *finished*).

good, well *Good* is an adjective, and *well* is nearly always an adverb: *Larry's a good dancer. He and Linda dance well together. Well* is properly used as an adjective only to refer to health: *You look well.* (*You look good,* in contrast, means "Your appearance is pleasing.")

good and Colloquial for "very": *I was very* [not *good and*] *tired.*

had better See *better, had better.*

had ought The *had* is unnecessary and should be omitted: *He ought* [not *had ought*] *to listen to his mother.*

hanged, hung Though both are past-tense forms of *hang, hanged* is used to refer to executions and *hung* is used for all other meanings: *Tom Dooley was hanged* [not *hung*] *from a white oak tree. I hung* [not *hanged*] *the picture you gave me.*

hardly See *but, hardly, scarcely.*

have, of Use *have,* not *of,* after helping verbs such as *could, should, would, may,* and *might: You should have* [not *should of*] *told me.*

he, she; he/she Convention has allowed the use of *he* to mean "he or she": *After the infant learns to creep, he progresses to crawling.* However, many writers today consider this usage inaccurate and unfair because it seems to exclude females. The construction *he/she,* one substitute for *he,* is awkward and objectionable to most readers. The better choice is to make the pronoun plural, to rephrase, or, sparingly, to use *he or she.* For instance: *After infants learn to creep, they progress to crawling. After learning to creep, the infant progresses to crawling. After the infant learns to creep, he or she progresses to crawling.* See also pp. 188 and 287–88.

herself, himself See *myself, herself, himself, yourself.*

hisself Nonstandard for *himself.*

hopefully *Hopefully* means "with hope": *Freddy waited hopefully for a glimpse of Eliza.* The use of *hopefully* to mean "it is to be hoped," "I hope," or "let's hope" is now very common; but since many readers continue to object strongly to the usage, try to avoid it. *I hope* [not *Hopefully*] *the law will pass.*

idea, ideal An *idea* is a thought or conception. An *ideal* (noun) is a model of perfection or a goal. *Ideal* should not be used in place of *idea: The idea* [not *ideal*] *of the play is that our ideals often sustain us.*

if, whether For clarity, use *whether* rather than *if* when you are expressing an alternative: *If I laugh hard, people can't tell whether I'm crying.*

illicit See *elicit, illicit.*

illusion See *allusion, illusion.*

immigrate, emigrate See *emigrate, immigrate.*

implicit See *explicit, implicit.*

imply, infer Writers or speakers *imply,* meaning "suggest": *Jim's letter implies he's having a good time.* Readers or listeners *infer,* meaning "conclude": *From Jim's letter I infer he's having a good time.*

incredible, incredulous *Incredible* means "unbelievable"; *incredulous* means "unbelieving": *When Nancy heard Dennis's incredible story, she was frankly incredulous.* See also *credible, creditable, credulous.*

individual, person, party *Individual* should refer to a single human being in contrast to a group or should stress uniqueness: *The US Constitution places strong emphasis on the rights of the individual.* For other meanings *person* is preferable: *What person* [not *individual*] *wouldn't want the security promised in that advertisement? Party* means "group" (*Can you seat a party of four for dinner?*) and should not be used to refer to an individual except in legal documents. See also *people, persons.*

infer See *imply, infer.*

in regards to Nonstandard for *in regard to, as regards,* or *regarding.*

insure See *assure, ensure, insure.*

irregardless Nonstandard for *regardless.*

is, are See *are, is.*

is because See *reason is because.*

is when, is where These are faulty constructions in sentences that define: *Adolescence is a stage* [not *is when a person is*] *between childhood and adulthood. Socialism is a system in which* [not *is where*] *government owns the means of production.* See also p. 330.

its, it's *Its* is the pronoun *it* in the possessive case: *That plant is losing its leaves. It's* is a contraction for *it is* or *it has: It's* [*It is*] *likely to die. It's* [*It has*] *got a fungus.* Many people confuse *it's* and *its* because possessives are most often formed with *-'s;* but the possessive *its,* like *his* and *hers,* never takes an apostrophe.

kind of, sort of, type of In formal speech and writing, avoid using *kind of* or *sort of* to mean "somewhat": *He was rather* [not *kind of*] *tall.*

Kind, sort, and *type* are singular and take singular modifiers and verbs: *This kind of dog is easily trained.* Agreement errors often occur when these singular nouns are combined with the plural adjectives *these* and *those: These kinds* [not *kind*] *of dogs are easily trained. Kind, sort,* and *type* should be followed by *of* but not by *a: I don't know what type of* [not *type* or *type of a*] *dog that is.*

Use *kind of, sort of,* or *type of* only when the word *kind, sort,* or *type* is important: *That was a strange* [not *strange sort of*] *statement.*

lay, lie *Lay* means "put" or "place" and takes a direct object: *We could lay the tablecloth in the sun.* Its main forms are *lay, laid, laid. Lie* means "recline" or "be situated" and does not take an object: *I lie awake at night. The town lies east of the river.* Its main forms are *lie, lay, lain.* (See also p. 240.)

leave, let *Leave* and *let* are interchangeable only when followed by *alone; leave me alone* is the same as *let me alone.* Otherwise, *leave* means "depart" and *let* means "allow": *Jill would not let Sue leave.*

less See *fewer, less.*

lie, lay See *lay, lie.*

like, as See *as, like.*

like, such as Strictly, *such as* precedes an example that represents a larger subject, whereas *like* indicates that two subjects are comparable. *Steve has recordings of many great saxophonists such as Ben Webster and Lee Konitz. Steve wants to be a great jazz saxophonist like Ben Webster and Lee Konitz.*

literally This word means "actually" or "just as the words say," and it should not be used to qualify or intensify expressions whose words are not to be taken at face value. The sentence *He was literally climbing the walls* describes a person behaving like an insect, not a person who is restless or anxious. For the latter meaning, *literally* should be omitted.

lose, loose *Lose* means "mislay": *Did you lose a brown glove? Loose* means "unrestrained" or "not tight": *Ann's canary got loose. Loose* also can function as a verb meaning "let loose": *They loose the dogs as soon as they spot the bear.*

lots, lots of Colloquial substitutes for *very many, a great many,* or *much.* Avoid *lots* and *lots of* in college or business writing.

may, can See *can, may.*

may be, maybe *May be* is a verb, and *maybe* is an adverb meaning "perhaps": *Tuesday may be a legal holiday. Maybe we won't have classes.*

may of See *have, of.*

media *Media* is the plural of *medium* and takes a plural verb: *All the news media are increasingly visual.* The singular verb is common, even in the media, but most careful writers still use the plural verb.

might of See *have, of.*

moral, morale As a noun, *moral* means "ethical conclusion" or "lesson": *The moral of the story escapes me. Morale* means "spirit" or "state of mind": *Victory improved the team's morale.*

most, almost See *almost, most.*

must of See *have, of.*

myself, herself, himself, yourself The *-self* pronouns refer to or intensify another word or words: *Paul helped himself; Jill herself said so.* The *-self* pronouns are often used colloquially in place of personal pronouns, but that use should be avoided in formal speech and writing: *No one except me* [not *myself*] *saw the accident. Our delegates will be Susan and you* [not *yourself*]. See also p. 278 on the unchanging forms of the *-self* pronouns in standard American English.

nowheres Nonstandard for *nowhere.*

number See *amount, number.*

of, have See *have, of.*

off of *Of* is unnecessary. Use *off* or *from* rather than *off of: He jumped off* [or *from,* not *off of*] *the roof.*

OK, O.K., okay All three spellings are acceptable, but avoid this colloquial term in formal speech and writing.

on the other hand This transitional expression of contrast should be preceded by its mate, *on the one hand: On the one hand, we hoped for snow. On the other hand, we feared that it would harm the animals.* However, the two combined can be unwieldy, and a simple *but, however, yet,* or *in contrast* often suffices: *We hoped for snow. Yet we feared that it would harm the animals.*

owing to the fact that Wordy for *because.*

party See *individual, person, party.*

people, persons In formal usage, *people* refers to a general group: *We the people of the United States. . . . Persons* refers to a collection of individuals: *Will the person or persons who saw the accident please notify. . . .* Except when emphasizing individuals, prefer *people* to *persons.* See also *individual, person, party.*

per Except in technical writing, an English equivalent is usually preferable to the Latin *per: $10 an* [not *per*] *hour; sent by* [not *per*] *parcel post; requested in* [not *per* or *as per*] *your letter.*

percent (per cent), percentage Both these terms refer to fractions of one hundred. *Percent* always follows a numeral (*40 percent of the voters*), and the word should be used instead of the symbol (%) in general writing. *Percentage* stands alone (*the percentage of voters*) or follows an adjective (*a high percentage*).

person See *individual, person, party.*

persons See *people, persons.*

phenomena The plural of *phenomenon* (meaning "perceivable fact" or "unusual occurrence"): *Many phenomena are not recorded. One phenomenon is attracting attention.*

plenty A colloquial substitute for *very: The reaction occurred very* [not *plenty*] *fast.*

plus *Plus* is standard as a preposition meaning "in addition to": *His income plus mine is sufficient.* But *plus* is colloquial as a conjunctive adverb: *Our organization is larger than theirs; moreover* [not *plus*], *we have more money.*

precede, proceed The verb *precede* means "come before": *My name precedes yours in the alphabet.* The verb *proceed* means "move on": *We were told to proceed to the waiting room.*

prejudice, prejudiced *Prejudice* is a noun; *prejudiced* is an adjective. Do not drop the *-d* from *prejudiced: I knew that my parents were prejudiced* [not *prejudice*].

pretty Overworked as an adverb meaning "rather" or "somewhat": *He was somewhat* [not *pretty*] *irked at the suggestion.*

principal, principle *Principal* is an adjective meaning "foremost" or "major," a noun meaning "chief official," or, in finance, a noun meaning "capital sum." *Principle* is a noun only, meaning "rule" or "axiom." *Her principal reasons for confessing were her principles of right and wrong.*

proceed, precede See *precede, proceed.*

question of whether, question as to whether Wordy substitutes for *whether.*

raise, rise *Raise* means "lift" or "bring up" and takes a direct object: *The Kirks raise cattle.* Its main forms are *raise, raised, raised. Rise* means "get up" and does not take an object: *They must rise at dawn.* Its main forms are *rise, rose, risen.* (See also p. 240.)

real, really In formal speech and writing, *real* should not be used as an adverb; *really* is the adverb and *real* an adjective. *Popular reaction to the announcement was really* [not *real*] *enthusiastic.*

reason is because Although colloquially common, this expression should be avoided in formal speech and writing. Use a *that* clause after *reason is: The reason he is absent is that* [not *is because*] *he is sick.* Or: *He is absent because he is sick.* (See also p. 330.)

respectful, respective *Respectful* means "full of (or showing) respect": *Be respectful of other people. Respective* means "separate": *The French and the Germans occupied their respective trenches.*

rise, raise See *raise, rise.*

scarcely See *but, hardly, scarcely.*

sensual, sensuous *Sensual* suggests sexuality; *sensuous* means "pleasing to the senses." *Stirred by the sensuous scent of meadow grass and flowers, Cheryl and Paul found their thoughts growing increasingly sensual.*

set, sit *Set* means "put" or "place" and takes a direct object: *He sets the pitcher down.* Its main forms are *set, set, set. Sit* means "be seated" and does not take an object: *She sits on the sofa.* Its main forms are *sit, sat, sat.* (See also p. 240.)

shall, will *Will* is the future-tense helping verb for all persons: *I will go, you will go, they will go.* The main use of *shall* is for first-person questions requesting an opinion or consent: *Shall I order a pizza? Shall we dance? Shall* can also be used for the first person when a formal effect is desired (I *shall expect you around three*), and it is occasionally used with the second or third person to express the speaker's determination (*You shall do as I say*).

should of See *have, of.*

sight, site, cite See *cite, sight, site.*

since *Since* mainly relates to time: *I've been waiting since noon.* But *since* is also often used to mean "because": *Since you ask, I'll tell you.* Revise sentences in which the word could have either meaning, such as *Since you asked, I've researched the question.*

sit, set See *set, sit.*

site, cite, sight See *cite, sight, site.*

so Avoid using *so* alone or as a vague intensifier: *He was so late. So* needs to be followed by *that* and a clause that states a result: *He was so late that I left without him.*

somebody, some body; someone, some one *Somebody* and *someone* are indefinite pronouns; *some body* is a noun modified by *some;* and *some one* is a pronoun or an adjective modified by *some. Somebody ought to invent a shampoo that will give hair some body. Someone told Janine she should choose some one plan and stick with it.*

sometime, sometimes, some time *Sometime* means "at an indefinite time in the future": *Why don't you come up and see me sometime? Sometimes* means "now and then": *I still see my old friend Joe sometimes. Some time* means "a span of time": *I need some time to make the payments.*

somewheres Nonstandard for *somewhere.*

sort of, sort of a See *kind of, sort of, type of.*

such Avoid using *such* as a vague intensifier: *It was such a cold winter. Such* should be followed by *that* and a clause that states a result: *It was such a cold winter that Napoleon's troops had to turn back.*

such as See *like, such as.*

supposed to, used to In both these expressions, the *-d* is essential: *I used to* [not *use to*] *think so. He's supposed to* [not *suppose to*] *meet us.*

sure Colloquial when used as an adverb meaning *surely: James Madison sure was right about the need for the Bill of Rights.* If you merely want to be emphatic, use *certainly: Madison certainly was right.* If your goal is to convince a possibly reluctant reader, use *surely: Madison surely was right.*

sure and, sure to; try and, try to *Sure to* and *try to* are the correct forms: *Be sure to* [not *sure and*] *buy milk. Try to* [not *Try and*] *find some decent tomatoes.*

take, bring See *bring, take.*

than, then *Than* is a conjunction used in comparisons, *then* an adverb indicating time: *Holmes knew then that Moriarty was wilier than he had thought.*

that, which *That* introduces an essential clause: *We should use the lettuce that Susan bought* (*that Susan bought* limits the lettuce to a particular lettuce). *Which* can introduce both essential and nonessential clauses, but many writers reserve *which* only for nonessential clauses: *The leftover lettuce, which is in the refrigerator, would make a good salad* (*which is in the refrigerator* simply provides more information about the lettuce we already know of). Essential clauses (with *that* or *which*) are not set off by commas; nonessential clauses (with *which*) are. See also pp. 344–46.

that, which, who Use *that* for animals, things, and sometimes collective or anonymous people: *The rocket that failed cost millions. Infants that walk need constant tending.* Use *which* only for animals and things: *The river, which flows south, divides two countries.* Use *who* only for people and for animals with names: *Dorothy is the girl who visits Oz. Her dog, Toto, who accompanies her, gives her courage.*

their, there, they're *Their* is the possessive form of *they: Give them their money. There* indicates place (*I saw her standing there*) or functions as an expletive (*There is a hole behind you*). *They're* is a contraction for *they are: They're going fast.*

theirselves Nonstandard for *themselves.*

them In standard American English, *them* does not serve as an adjective: *Those* [not *them*] *people want to know.*

then, than See *than, then.*

these kind, these sort, these type, those kind See *kind of, sort of, type of.*

this, these *This* is singular: *this car* or *This is the reason I left. These* is plural: *these cars* or *These are not valid reasons.*

thru A colloquial spelling of *through* that should be avoided in all academic and business writing.

to, too, two *To* is a preposition; *too* is an adverb meaning "also" or "excessively"; and *two* is a number. *I too have been to Europe two times.*

too Avoid using *too* as a vague intensifier: *Monkeys are too mean.* When you do use *too,* explain the consequences of the excessive quality: *Monkeys are too mean to make good pets.*

toward, towards Both are acceptable, though *toward* is preferred. Use one or the other consistently.

try and, try to See *sure and, sure to; try and, try to.*

type of See *kind of, sort of, type of.* Don't use *type* without *of*: *It was a family type of* [not *type*] *restaurant.* Or better: *It was a family restaurant.*

uninterested See *disinterested, uninterested.*

unique *Unique* means "the only one of its kind" and so cannot sensibly be modified with words such as *very* or *most*: *That was a unique* [not *a very unique* or *the most unique*] *movie.*

usage, use *Usage* refers to conventions, most often those of a language: *Is "hadn't ought" proper usage? Usage* is often misused in place of the noun *use*: *Wise use* [not *usage*] *of insulation can save fuel.*

use, utilize *Utilize* can be used to mean "make good use of": *Many teachers utilize computers for instruction.* But for all other senses of "place in service" or "employ," prefer *use.*

used to See *supposed to, used to.*

wait for, wait on In formal speech and writing, *wait for* means "await" (*I'm waiting for Paul*) and *wait on* means "serve" (*The owner of the store herself waited on us*).

ways Colloquial as a substitute for *way*: *We have only a little way* [not *ways*] *to go.*

well See *good, well.*

whether, if See *if, whether.*

which, that See *that, which.*

which, who, that See *that, which, who.*

who's, whose *Who's* is the contraction of *who is* or *who has*: *Who's* [*Who is*] *at the door? Jim is the only one who's* [*who has*] *passed. Whose* is the possessive form of *who*: *Whose book is that?*

will, shall See *shall, will.*

would have Avoid this construction in place of *had* in clauses that begin *if* and state a condition contrary to fact: *If the tree had* [not *would have*] *withstood the fire, it would have been the oldest in town.* See also p. 264.

would of See *have, of.*

you In all but very formal writing, *you* is generally appropriate as long as it means "you, the reader." In all writing, avoid indefinite uses of *you*, such as *In one ancient tribe your first loyalty was to your parents.* See also pp. 292–93.

your, you're *Your* is the possessive form of *you*: *Your dinner is ready. You're* is the contraction of *you are*: *You're bound to be late.*

yourself See *myself, herself, himself, yourself.*

(continued from p. iv)

Drucker, Peter F. "How Best to Protect the Environment," *Harper's* Magazine, January 1972.

Dyson, Freeman. Excerpt reprinted with permission of Perseus Books, LLC, from *Disturbing the Universe* by Freeman Dyson. Copyright © 1979 by Freeman J. Dyson. Permission conveyed through Copyright Clearance Center, Inc.

EBSCO Publishing. Screen shots of initial keyword search, partial search results, and full record with abstract from EBSCOhost database used with permission from EBSCO Publishing.

Eisinger, Peter K. et al. *American Politics: The People and the Polity*. Boston: Little, Brown, 1978, p. 44.

Farb, Peter K. *Word Play: What Happens When People Talk*. New York: Knopf, 1973, p. 107.

Gaylin, Willard. "Feeling Anxious." Excerpt from *Feelings: Our Vital Signs*. New York: Harper & Row, 1979, p. 23.

Google. Screen shots used with permission from *Google.* GOOGLE is a trademark of Google Inc.

Goreau, Angeline. Excerpt from "Worthy Women Revisited," *The New York Times*, December 11, 1986, p. C2. Copyright © 1986 by the New York Times Co. Reprinted with permission.

Hartmann, Thomas. "How Dangerous Is Your Computer?" (*http://www.atariarchives.org/deli/how_dangerous.php*).

Ik, Kim Yong. "A Book-Writing Venture," *The Writer*, October 1965.

King, Martin Luther, Jr. Excerpt from "I Have a Dream." Reprinted by arrangement with the Estate of Martin Luther King Jr., c/o Writer's House as agent for the proprietor, New York, NY. Copyright 1963 Martin Luther King, Jr., copyright renewed 1991 Coretta Scott King.

Kuralt, Charles. *Dateline America*. New York: Harcourt, 1979.

Mayer, Lawrence A. "The Confounding Enemy of Sleep," *Fortune*, June 1974.

Merriam-Webster. Definition of "reckon." By permission. From *Merriam-Webster's Collegiate® Dictionary*, Eleventh Edition, © 2003 by Merriam-Webster, Incorporated (*www.Merriam-Webster.com*).

Microsoft Corporation. Screen shots reprinted by permission from Microsoft Corporation.

Miller, Arthur. *Death of a Salesman*. New York: Penguin, 1949.

Nadelmann, Ethan A. "Shooting Up," *The New Republic*, June 1988.

Otten, Charlotte F. *English Women's Voices, 1540-1700*. Miami: Florida International University Press, 1992.

Ouchi, William. *Theory Z: How American Business Can Meet the Japanese Challenge*. Reading, MA: Addison-Wesley, 1981.

Posey, Michael W. "I Did Drugs Until They Wore Me Out. Then I Stopped," *The New York Times*, December 15, 1989.

Reston, James, Jr. Adapted from "You Cannot Refine It," *The New Yorker*, 1985.

Rosen, Ruth. "Search for Yesterday," in Todd Gitlin, ed., *Watching Television*. New York: Pantheon, 1986.

Sowell, Thomas. "Students Loans" from *Is Reality Optional?* by Thomas Sowell. Copyright © 1993 by Thomas Sowell. Reprinted by permission of the author.

Tuchman, Barbara. Excerpt from "The Decline of Quality," *The New York Times*, November 2, 1980. Reprinted by the permission of Russell & Volkening as agents for the author. Copyright © 1980 by Barbara Tuchman.

Vaillant, George E. *Adaptation to Life*. Boston: Little, Brown, 1977, p. 361.

Woolf, Virginia. *The Waves*. New York: Harcourt, 1931.

Answers to Selected Exercises

These pages provide answers to all exercise items and sentences that are labeled with a star (∗) in the book.

Exercise 10.5, p. 119

Possible answers

1. Sweeping generalization and begged question.
   A revision: A successful marriage demands a degree of maturity.
2. Hasty generalization and non sequitur.
   A revision: Students' persistent complaints about the unfairness of the grading system should be investigated.
3. Reductive fallacy.
   A revision: The United States got involved in World War II for many complex reasons. The bombing of Pearl Harbor was a triggering incident.
4. Either/or fallacy and hasty generalization.
   A revision: People watch television for many reasons, but some watch because they are too lazy to talk or read or because they want mindless escape from their lives.
5. Reductive fallacy and begged question.
   A revision: Racial tension may occur when people with different backgrounds live side by side.

Exercise 15.1, p. 164

Possible answers

1. Many heroes helped to emancipate the slaves.
2. Harriet Tubman, an escaped slave herself, guided hundreds of other slaves to freedom on the Underground Railroad.

Exercise 15.2, p. 167

Possible answers

1. Pat Taylor strode into the packed room, greeting students called "Taylor's Kids" and nodding to their parents and teachers.
2. This wealthy Louisiana oilman had promised his "Kids" free college educations because he was determined to make higher education available to all qualified but disadvantaged students.

Exercise 15.3, p. 170

Possible answers

1. Because soldiers admired their commanding officers, they often gave them nicknames containing the word *old,* even though not all of the commanders were old.
2. General Thomas "Stonewall" Jackson was also called "Old Jack," although he was not yet forty years old.

Exercise 15.4, p. 172

Possible answers

1. Because Genaro González is a talented writer, his stories and novels have been published to critical acclaim.
2. Although he loves to write, he has also earned a doctorate in psychology.

Exercise 15.5, p. 173

Possible revision

Sir Walter Raleigh personified the Elizabethan Age, the period of Elizabeth I's rule of England, in the last half of the sixteenth century. Raleigh was a courtier, a poet, an

Ans

explorer, and an entrepreneur. Supposedly, he gained Queen Elizabeth's favor by throwing his cloak beneath her feet at the right moment, just as she was about to step over a puddle.

Exercise 16.1, p. 176

Possible answers

1. The ancient Greeks celebrated four athletic contests: the Olympic Games at Olympia, the Isthmian Games near Corinth, the Pythian Games at Delphi, and the Nemean Games at Cleonae.
2. Each day of the games consisted of either athletic events or ceremonies and sacrifices to the gods.
3. In the years between the games, competitors were taught wrestling, javelin throwing, and boxing.
4. Competitors ran sprints, participated in spectacular chariot and horse races, and ran long distances while wearing full armor.
5. The purpose of such events was developing physical strength, demonstrating skill and endurance, and sharpening the skills needed for war.

Exercise 16.2, p. 177

Possible answers

1. People can develop post-traumatic stress disorder (PTSD) after experiencing a dangerous situation and fearing for their survival.
2. The disorder can be triggered by a wide variety of events, such as combat, a natural disaster, or a hostage situation.

Exercise 17.1, p. 182

Possible revision

After being dormant for many years, the Italian volcano Vesuvius exploded on August 24 in the year AD 79. The ash, pumice, and mud from the volcano buried two towns—Herculaneum and the more famous Pompeii—which lay undiscovered until 1709 and 1748, respectively.

Exercise 18.1, p. 188

Possible answers

1. Acquired immune deficiency syndrome (AIDS) is a serious threat all over the world.
2. The disease is transmitted primarily by sexual intercourse, exchange of bodily fluids, shared needles, and blood transfusions.
3. Those who think the disease is limited to homosexuals and drug users are quite mistaken.
4. Statistics suggest that in the United States one in every five hundred college students carries the virus.
5. People with AIDS do not deserve others' exclusion or callousness. Instead, they need all the compassion, medical care, and financial assistance due the seriously ill.

Exercise 18.2, p. 189

Possible answers

1. When people apply for a job, they should represent themselves with the best possible résumé.
2. A person applying for a job as a mail carrier should appear to be honest and responsible.
3. Applicants for a position as an in-home nurse should also represent themselves as honest and responsible.
4. Of course, the applicant should also have a background of capable nursing.
5. The business executive who is scanning a stack of résumés will, of necessity, read them all quickly.

Exercise 18.4, p. 193

1. Maxine Hong Kingston was awarded many prizes for her first two books, *The Woman Warrior* and *China Men.*
2. Kingston cites her mother's tales about ancestors and ancient Chinese customs as the sources of these memoirs.
3. Two of Kingston's progenitors, her great-grandfathers, are focal points of *China Men.*
4. Both men led rebellions against oppressive employers: a sugarcane farmer and a railroad-construction engineer.
5. In her childhood Kingston was greatly affected by her mother's tale about a pregnant aunt who was ostracized by villagers. [*Ostracized* is correct.]

Exercise 18.5, p. 194

1. AIDS is a serious health problem.
2. Once the virus has entered the blood system, it destroys T-cells.

Exercise 18.7, p. 197

1. The friend who introduced Mark and Lana was proud of his matchmaking.
2. They had fallen in love on their first date.
3. Mark and Lana had become so dependent upon [*or* on] each other that they talked on the phone several times every day.
4. Certain of their love, Mark and Lana decided to get married.
5. Now, as Mark and Lana waited for the justice of the peace, they seemed oblivious to [*or* of] the other people in the lobby.

Exercise 18.8, p. 197

1. The Eighteenth Amendment to the Constitution of the United States was ratified in 1919.
2. It prohibited the "manufacture, sale, or transportation of intoxicating liquors."

Exercise 18.10, p. 200

Possible answers

1. The disasters of the war have shaken the small nation severely.
2. Prices for food have risen markedly, and citizens suspect that others are profiting on the black market.
3. Medical supplies are so scarce that even very sick civilians cannot get treatment.
4. With most men fighting or injured or killed, women have had to take men's places in farming and manufacturing.
5. Finally, the war's high cost has destroyed the nation's economy.

Exercise 19.1, p. 202

1. The first ice cream, eaten in China in about 2000 BC, was lumpier than modern ice cream.
2. The Chinese made their ice cream of milk, spices, and overcooked rice and packed it in snow to solidify.

Exercise 20.1, p. 207

Possible answers

1. If sore muscles after exercising are a problem for you, there are some things you can do to ease the discomfort.
2. First, apply cold immediately to reduce inflammation.
3. Cold constricts blood vessels and keeps blood away from the injured muscles.
4. Avoid heat for the first day.
5. Applying heat within the first twenty-four hours can increase muscle soreness and stiffness.

Ans

Exercise 20.2, p. 208

Possible answers

After much thought, he concluded that carcinogens could be treated like automobiles. Instead of giving in to a fear of cancer, we should balance the benefits we receive from potential carcinogens (such as plastic and pesticides) against the damage they do.

Exercise 21.1, p. 214

1. Ancestors (N) of the ginkgo tree (N), a relic (N) from the age (N) of the dinosaurs (N), lived (V) 175 to 200 million years (N) ago.
2. The tree (N) sometimes grows (V) to over a hundred feet (N) in height (N).
3. It (P) has (V) fan-shaped leaves (N) about three inches wide.
4. A deciduous tree (N), the ginkgo (N) loses (V) its (P) leaves (N) in the fall (N) after they (P) turn (V) bright yellow.
5. The ginkgo tree (N) is (V) esteemed in the United States (N) and Europe (N) as an ornamental tree (N).

Exercise 21.2, p. 215

1. You can reduce stress by making a (ADJ) few (ADJ) simple (ADJ) changes.
2. Get up (ADV) fifteen (ADJ) minutes earlier (ADV) than you ordinarily (ADV) do.
3. Eat a (ADJ) healthy (ADJ) breakfast, and eat it slowly (ADV) so that you enjoy it.
4. Do your unpleasant (ADJ) tasks early (ADV) in the (ADJ) day.
5. Every (ADJ) day, do at least one (ADJ) thing you really (ADV) enjoy.

Exercise 21.3, p. 217

1. Just about everyone has heard the story of the Trojan Horse.
2. This incident happened at the city of Troy and was planned by the Greeks.
3. The Greeks built a huge wooden horse; inside it was a hollow space big enough to hold many men.
4. At night, they rolled the horse to the gate of Troy and left it there before sailing their ships out to sea.
5. In the morning, the Trojans were astonished to see the enormous horse.

Exercise 22.1, p. 220

1. The horse | has a long history of serving humanity but today is mainly a show and sport animal.
2. A member of the genus *Equus,* the domestic horse | is related to the wild Przewalski's horse, the ass, and the zebra.
3. The domestic horse and its relatives | are all plains-dwelling herd animals.
4. An average-sized adult horse | may require twenty-six pounds or more of pasture feed or hay per day.
5. Racehorses | require grain for part of their forage.

Exercise 22.2, p. 223

1. The number (S) of serious crimes in the United States decreased (V).
2. A decline (S) in serious crimes occurred (V) each year.
3. The Crime Index (S) measures (V) serious crime (DO).
4. The FBI (S) invented (V) the index (DO).
5. The four serious violent crimes (S) are (V) murder (SC), robbery (SC), forcible rape (SC), and aggravated assault (SC).

Exercise 22.3, p. 226

1. Ron Kovic cowrote the screenplay for *Born on the Fourth of July.*
2. Oliver Stone directed the film.

Exercise 23.1, p. 230

prepositional phrase / appositive phrase / prepositional phrase / infinitive phrase

1. Because of its many synonyms, or words with similar meanings, English can make it difficult to choose the exact word.

participial phrase / prepositional phrase / appositive phrase / prepositional phrase

2. Borrowing words from other languages such as French and Latin, English acquired an unusual number of synonyms.

participial phrase / prepositional phrase / prepositional phrase

3. Having so many choices, how does a writer decide between *motherly* and *maternal* or among *womanly, feminine,* and *female?*

infinitive phrase / prepositional phrase

4. Some people prefer longer and more ornate words to avoid the flatness of shortened words.

prepositional phrase / prepositional phrase / participial phrase / participial phrase

5. During the Renaissance a heated debate occurred between the Latinists, favoring Latin words, and the Saxonists, preferring native Anglo-Saxon words.

Exercise 23.2, p. 232

1. The Prophet Muhammad, who was born about AD 570 in the city of Mecca, was the founder of Islam. [ADJ]
2. He grew up in the care of his grandfather and an uncle because both of his parents had died. [ADV]
3. His family was part of a powerful Arab tribe that lived in western Arabia. [ADJ]
4. When he was about forty years old, he had a vision in a cave outside Mecca. [ADV]
5. He believed that God had selected him to be the prophet of a true religion for the Arabs. [N]

Exercise 24.1, p. 234

1. Our world has many sounds, but they all have one thing in common. [Compound.] (main clause / main clause)
2. The one thing that all sounds share is that they are produced by vibrations. [Complex.] (main clause; subordinate clause / subordinate clause)
3. The vibrations make the air move in waves, and these sound waves travel to the ear. [Compound.] (main clause / main clause)
4. When sound waves enter the ear, the brain has to interpret them. [Complex.] (subordinate clause / main clause)
5. Sound waves can also travel through other material, such as water and even the solid earth. [Simple.] (main clause)

Exercise 25.1, p. 239

1. The world population has grown by two-thirds of a billion people in less than a decade. [Past participle.]

2. Recently it broke the 6 billion mark. [Past tense.]
3. Experts have drawn pictures of a crowded future. [Past participle.]
4. They predict that the world population may have slid up to as much as 10 billion by the year 2050. [Past participle.]
5. Though the food supply rose in the last decade, the share to each person fell. [Both past tense.]

Exercise 25.2, p. 240

1. Yesterday afternoon the child lay down for a nap.
2. The child has been raised by her grandparents.

Exercise 25.3, p. 242

1. A teacher sometimes asks too much of a student.
2. In high school I was once punished for being sick.
3. I had missed a week of school because of a serious case of the flu.
4. I realized that I would fail a test unless I had a chance to make up the class work.
5. I discussed the problem with the teacher.

Exercise 25.4, p. 248

1. Each year thousands of new readers have been discovering Agatha Christie's mysteries.
2. The books were written by a prim woman who had worked as a nurse during World War I.

Exercise 25.5, p. 248

1. A report from the Bureau of the Census has confirmed a widening gap between rich and poor.
2. As suspected, the percentage of people below the poverty level did increase over the last decade.

Exercise 25.6, p. 251

1. A program called HELP Wanted tries to encourage citizens to take action on behalf of American competitiveness.
2. Officials working on this program hope to improve education for work.

Exercise 25.7, p. 253

1. American movies treat everything from going out with [correct] someone to making up [correct] an ethnic identity, but few people look into their significance.
2. While some viewers stay away from [correct] topical films, others turn up at the theater simply because a movie has sparked debate.

Exercise 26.1, p. 261

1. Diaries that Adolf Hitler was supposed to have written had surfaced in Germany.
2. Many people believed that the diaries were authentic because a well-known historian had declared them so.

Exercise 26.2, p. 261

1. When an athlete turns professional, he or she commits to a grueling regimen of mental and physical training.
2. If athletes were less committed, they would disappoint teammates, fans, and themselves.
3. If professional athletes are very lucky, they may play until age forty.
4. Unless an athlete achieves celebrity status, he or she will have few employment choices after retirement.
5. If professional sports were less risky, athletes would have longer careers and more choices after retirement.

Exercise 26.3, p. 262

1. In his speech accepting the Nobel Prize, William Faulkner said that he believed that man would not merely endure: he would prevail.
2. Cornelia Otis Skinner commented cynically that woman's virtue is man's greatest invention.

Exercise 27.1, p. 264

1. If John Hawkins had known of all the dangerous side effects of smoking tobacco, would he have introduced the dried plant to England in 1565?
2. Hawkins noted that if a Florida Indian man were to travel for several days, he would smoke tobacco to satisfy his hunger and thirst.

Exercise 28.1, p. 267

Possible answers

1. Many factors determine water quality.
2. All natural waters contain suspended and dissolved substances.
3. The environment controls the amounts of the substances.
4. Pesticides produce some dissolved substances.
5. Fields, livestock feedlots, and other sources deposit sediment in water.

Exercise 28.2, p. 268

Possible answers

1. When engineers built the Eiffel Tower in 1889, the French thought it to be ugly.
2. At that time, industrial technology was still resisted by many people.

Exercise 29.1, p. 275

1. Weinstein & Associates is a consulting firm that tries to make businesspeople laugh.
2. Statistics from recent research suggest that humor relieves stress.
3. Reduced stress in businesses in turn reduces illness and absenteeism.
4. Reduced stress can also reduce friction within an employee group, which then works together more productively.
5. In special conferences held by one consultant, each of the participants practices making others laugh.

Exercise 29.2, p. 276

The Siberian tiger is the largest living cat in the world, much bigger than its relative the Bengal tiger. It grows to a length of nine to twelve feet, including its tail, and to a height of about three and a half feet. It can weigh over six hundred pounds. This carnivorous hunter lives in northern China and Korea as well as in Siberia. During the long winter of this Arctic climate, the yellowish striped coat gets a little lighter in order to blend with the snow-covered landscape. The coat also grows quite thick, since the tiger has to withstand temperatures as low as –50°F.

Exercise 30.1, p. 280

1. Jody and I had been hunting for jobs.
2. The best employees at our old company were she and I, so we expected to find jobs quickly.

Exercise 30.2, p. 282

1. The school administrators suspended Jurgen, whom they suspected of setting the fire.
2. Jurgen had been complaining to other custodians, who reported him.
3. He constantly complained of unfair treatment from whoever happened to be passing in the halls, including pupils.
4. "Who here has heard Mr. Jurgen's complaints?" the police asked.
5. "Whom did he complain most about?"

Exercise 30.3, p. 284

1. Sentence correct.
2. Sentence correct.
3. Immediately, he and Gilgamesh wrestled to see who was more powerful.
4. Sentence correct.
5. The friendship of the two strong men was sealed by their fighting.

Exercise 31.1, p. 288

Possible answers

1. Each girl raised in a Mexican American family in the Rio Grande valley of Texas hopes that one day she will be given a *quinceañera* party for her fifteenth birthday.
2. Such a celebration is very expensive because it entails a religious service followed by a huge party. [*Or:* Such celebrations are very expensive because they entail a religious service followed by a huge party.]
3. A girl's immediate family, unless it is wealthy, cannot afford the party by itself.
4. Her parents will ask each close friend or relative if he or she can help with the preparations. [*Or:* Her parents will ask close friends or relatives if they can help with the preparations.]
5. Sentence correct.

Exercise 32.1, p. 293

Possible answers

1. "Life begins at forty" is a cliché many people live by, and this saying may or may not be true.
2. Living successfully or not depends on one's definition of success.
3. When Pearl Buck was forty, her novel *The Good Earth* won the Pulitzer Prize.
4. Buck was raised in a missionary family in China, which [*or* whom] she wrote about in her novels.
5. In *The Good Earth* the characters have to struggle, but fortitude is rewarded.

Exercise 33.1, p. 296

1. The eighteenth-century essayist Samuel Johnson suffered badly in his early life.
2. Sentence correct.
3. After failing as a schoolmaster, Johnson moved to London, where he did well.
4. Johnson was taken seriously as a critic and dictionary maker.
5. Johnson was really surprised when he received a pension from King George III.

Exercise 33.2, p. 300

1. Several critics found Alice Walker's *The Color Purple* to be a fascinating book.
2. Sentence correct.
3. Another critic argued that although the book contained many depressing episodes, the overall effect was exciting.
4. Since other readers found the book annoying, this critic pointed out its many surprising [correct] qualities.
5. In the end most critics agreed that the book was a satisfying novel about the struggles of an African American woman.

Exercise 33.3, p. 305

From the native American Indians who migrated from Asia 20,000 years ago to the new arrivals who now come by planes, the United States is a nation of foreigners. It is a country of immigrants who are all living under a single flag.

Back in the seventeenth and eighteenth centuries, at least 75 percent of the population came from England. However, between 1820 and 1975 more than 38 million immigrants came to this country from elsewhere in Europe.

Exercise 33.4, p. 306

1. Americans often argue about which professional sport is best: basketball, football, or baseball.
2. Basketball fans contend that their sport offers more action because the players are constantly running and shooting.
3. Because it is played indoors in relatively small arenas, basketball allows fans to be closer to the action than the other sports do.
4. Football fanatics say they hardly stop yelling once the game begins.
5. They cheer when their team executes a really complicated play well.

Exercise 34.1, p. 311

1. People who are right-handed dominate in our society.
2. Hand tools, machines, and even doors are designed for right-handed people.
3. However, nearly 15 percent of the population may be left-handed.
4. When they begin school, children often prefer one hand or the other.
5. Parents and teachers should not try deliberately to change a child's preference for the left hand.

Exercise 34.2, p. 312

1. A young Chinese computer specialist developed image controls.
2. A skeptical American engineer assisted the specialist.
3. Several university researchers are carrying out further study.
4. The controls depend on a hand-sized, T-shaped object connected by wires to the computer.
5. The image allows a biochemist to walk into a gigantic holographic display of a molecule.

Exercise 34.3, p. 314

Possible answers

1. After Andrew Jackson had accomplished many deeds of valor, his fame led to his election to the presidency in 1828 and 1832.
2. While Jackson was still very young, both of his parents had died.
3. To aid the American Revolution, Jackson chose service as a mounted courier.
4. Sentence correct.
5. Though not well educated, Jackson proved his ability in a successful career as a lawyer and judge.

Exercise 35.1, p. 319

Possible answers

1. Human beings who perfume themselves are not much different from other animals.
2. Animals as varied as insects and dogs release pheromones, chemicals that signal other animals.
3. Human beings have a diminished sense of smell and do not consciously detect most of their own species' pheromones.
4. No sentence fragment.
5. Some sources say that people began using perfume to cover up the smell of burning flesh during sacrifices to the gods.

Exercise 35.2, p. 320

Possible answers

People generally avoid eating mushrooms except those they buy in stores. But in fact many varieties of mushrooms are edible. Mushrooms are members of a large group of vegetation called nonflowering plants, including algae, mosses, ferns, and coniferous trees, even the giant redwoods of California. Most of the nonflowering plants prefer moist environments such as forest floors, fallen timber, and still water. Mushrooms, for example, prefer moist, shady soil. Algae grow in water.

Exercise 36.1, p. 326

Possible answers

1. Some people think that dinosaurs were the first living vertebrates, but fossils of turtles go back 40 million years or further.
2. Although most other reptiles exist mainly in tropical regions, turtles inhabit a variety of environments worldwide.
3. Turtles do not have teeth; their jaws are covered with a sharp, horny sheath.
4. Turtles cannot expand their lungs to breathe air; as a result, they make adjustments in how space is used within the shell.
5. Some turtles can get oxygen from water; therefore, they don't need to breathe air.

Exercise 36.2, p. 327

Possible answers

1. Money has a long history. It goes back at least as far as the earliest records.
   Money has a long history; it goes back at least as far as the earliest records.
2. Many of the earliest records concern financial transactions. Indeed, early history must often be inferred from commercial activity.
   Many of the earliest records concern financial transactions; indeed, early history must often be inferred from commercial activity.
3. Sentence correct.
4. Sometimes the objects have had real value; however, in modern times their value has been more abstract.
   Although sometimes the objects have had real value, in modern times their value has been more abstract.
5. Cattle, fermented beverages, and rare shells have served as money, and each one had actual value for the society.
   Cattle, fermented beverages, and rare shells have served as money. Each one had actual value for the society.

Exercise 36.3, p. 328

Possible answers

What many call the first genocide of modern times occurred during World War I, when the Armenians were deported from their homes in Anatolia, Turkey. The Turkish government assumed that the Armenians were sympathetic to Russia, with whom the Turks were at war. Many Armenians died because of the hardships of the journey, and many were massacred. The death toll was estimated at between 600,000 and 1 million.

Exercise 37.1, p. 331

Possible answers

1. A hurricane occurs when the winds in a tropical depression rotate counterclockwise at more than seventy-four miles per hour.
2. Because hurricanes can destroy so many lives and so much property, people fear them.
3. Through high winds, storm surge, floods, and tornadoes, hurricanes have killed thousands of people.
4. Storm surge occurs when the hurricane's winds whip up a tide that spills over seawalls and deluges coastal islands.
5. Hurricanes have become less deadly since 1950.

Exercise 37.2, p. 333

1. Archaeologists and other scientists can often determine the age of their discoveries by means of radiocarbon dating.
2. This technique can be used on any material that once was living.

3. This technique is based on the fact that all living organisms contain carbon.
4. The most common isotope is carbon 12, which contains six protons and six neutrons.
5. A few carbon atoms are classified as the isotope carbon 14, where the nucleus consists of six protons and eight neutrons.

Exercise 38.1, p. 338

When visitors first arrive in Hawaii, they often encounter an unexpected language barrier. Standard English is the language of business and government, but many of the people speak Pidgin English. Instead of an excited "Aloha!" the visitors may be greeted with an excited Pidgin "Howzit!" or asked if they know "how fo' find one good hotel."

Exercise 39.1, p. 341

1. Parents once automatically gave their children the father's last name, but some no longer do.
2. Parents were once legally required to give their children the father's last name, but these laws have been contested in court.
3. Parents may now give their children any last name they choose, and the arguments for choosing the mother's last name are often strong and convincing.
4. Sentence correct.
5. The child's last name may be just the mother's, or it may link the mother's and the father's with a hyphen.

Exercise 39.2, p. 343

1. Veering sharply to the right, a large flock of birds neatly avoids a high wall.
2. Sentence correct.
3. With the help of complex computer simulations, zoologists are learning more about this movement.
4. Because it is sudden and apparently well coordinated, the movement of flocks and schools has seemed to be directed by a leader.
5. Almost incredibly, the group could behave with more intelligence than any individual seemed to possess.

Exercise 39.3, p. 348

1. Italians insist that Marco Polo, the thirteenth-century explorer, did not import pasta from China.
2. Pasta, which consists of flour and water and often egg, existed in Italy long before Marco Polo left for his travels.
3. Sentence correct.
4. Most Italians dispute this account, although their evidence is shaky.
5. Wherever it originated, the Italians are now the undisputed masters in making and cooking pasta.

Exercise 39.4, p. 350

1. Shoes with high heels were originally designed to protect feet from mud, garbage, and animal waste in the streets.
2. Sentence correct.
3. The heels were worn by men and made of colorful silk fabrics, soft suedes, or smooth leathers.
4. High-heeled shoes became popular when the short, powerful King Louis XIV of France began wearing them.
5. Louis's influence was so strong that men and women of the court, priests and cardinals, and even household servants wore high heels.

Exercise 39.5, p. 354

1. An important source of water is underground aquifers.

2. Underground aquifers are deep and sometimes broad layers of water that are trapped between layers of rock.
3. Porous rock or sediment holds the water.
4. Deep wells drilled through the top layers of solid rock produce a flow of water.
5. Such wells are sometimes called artesian wells.

Exercise 39.6, p. 355

Ellis Island, New York, reopened for business in 1990, but now the customers are tourists, not immigrants. This spot, which lies in New York Harbor, was the first American soil seen or touched by many of the nation's immigrants. Though other places also served as ports of entry for foreigners, none has the symbolic power of Ellis Island. Between its opening in 1892 and its closing in 1954, over 20 million people, about two-thirds of all immigrants, were detained there before taking up their new lives in the United States. Ellis Island processed over 2000 [*or* 2,000] newcomers a day when immigration was at its peak between 1900 and 1920.

Exercise 40.1, p. 358

Possible answers

1. Electronic instruments are prevalent in jazz and rock music; however, they are less common in classical music.
2. Jazz and rock change rapidly; they nourish experimentation and improvisation.
3. The notes and instrumentation of traditional classical music were established by a composer writing decades or centuries ago; therefore, such music does not change.
4. Contemporary classical music not only can draw on tradition; it can also respond to innovations such as jazz rhythms and electronic sounds.
5. Much contemporary electronic music is more than just jazz, rock, or classical; it is a fusion of all three.

Exercise 40.2, p. 360

The set, sounds, and actors in the movie captured the essence of horror films. The set was ideal: dark, deserted streets; trees dipping their branches over the sidewalks; mist hugging the ground and creeping up to meet the trees; looming shadows of unlighted, turreted houses. The sounds, too, were appropriate; especially terrifying was the hard, hollow sound of footsteps echoing throughout the film.

Exercise 41.1, p. 362

1. Sunlight is made up of three kinds of radiation: visible rays; infrared rays, which we cannot see; and ultraviolet rays, which are also invisible.
2. Especially in the ultraviolet range, sunlight is harmful to the eyes.
3. Ultraviolet rays can damage the retina; furthermore, they can cause cataracts on the lens.
4. Infrared rays are the longest, measuring 700 nanometers and longer, while ultraviolet rays are the shortest, measuring 400 nanometers and shorter.
5. The lens protects the eye by absorbing much of the ultraviolet radiation and thus protecting the retina.

Exercise 42.1, p. 366

1. In the myths of the ancient Greeks, the goddesses' roles vary widely.
2. Demeter's responsibility is the fruitfulness of the earth.
3. Athena's role is to guard the city of Athens.
4. Artemis's function is to care for wild animals and small children.
5. Athena and Artemis's father, Zeus, is the king of the gods

Exercise 42.2, p. 368

Landlocked Chad is among the world's most troubled countries. The peoples of Chad are poor: their average per capita income equals $1000 per year. Just over 30 percent of Chad's population is literate, and every five hundred people must share only two teachers.

Exercise 43.1, p. 373

In one class we talked about a passage from "I Have a Dream," the speech delivered by Martin Luther King, Jr., on the steps of the Lincoln Memorial on August 28, 1963:

> When the architects of our republic wrote the magnificent words of the Constitution and the Declaration of Independence, they were signing a promissory note to which every American was to feel heir. This note was a promise that all men would be guaranteed the unalienable rights of life, liberty, and the pursuit of happiness.

"What did Dr. King mean by this statement?" the teacher asked. "Perhaps we should define 'promissory note' first."

Exercise 44.1, p. 379

1. "To be able to read the Bible in the vernacular was a liberating experience . . . ."

Exercise 44.2, p. 380

"Let all the learned say what they can, / 'Tis ready money makes the man." These two lines of poetry by the Englishman William Somerville (1645–1742) may apply to a current American economic problem. Non-American investors with "ready money" pour some of it—as much as $1.3 trillion in recent years—into the United States. Stocks and bonds, savings deposits, service companies, factories, artworks, political campaigns—the investments of foreigners are varied and grow more numerous every day.

Exercise 45.1, p. 386

1. Science affects many important aspects of our lives.
2. Many people have a poor understanding of the role of scientific breakthroughs in their health.
3. Many people believe that doctors, more than science, are responsible for improvements in health care.
4. But scientists in the laboratory have made crucial steps in the search for knowledge about health and medicine.
5. For example, one scientist whose discoveries have affected many people is Ulf Von Euler.

Exercise 45.2, p. 387

I have a spelling checker,
It came with my PC;
It plainly marks for my review
Mistakes I cannot see.

Exercise 46.1, p. 389

1. Sentence correct.
2. Sentence correct.
3. The non-African elephants of south-central Asia are somewhat smaller.
4. A fourteen- or fifteen-year-old elephant has reached sexual maturity.
5. The elephant life span is about sixty-five or seventy years.

Exercise 47.1, p. 394

1. San Antonio, Texas, is a thriving city in the Southwest.
2. The city has always offered much to tourists interested in the roots of Spanish settlement of the New World.
3. The Alamo is one of five Catholic missions built by priests to convert Native Americans and to maintain Spain's claims in the area.

4. But the Alamo is more famous for being the site of an 1836 battle that helped to create the Republic of Texas.
5. Many of the nearby streets, such as Crockett Street, are named for men who died in that battle.

Exercise 48.1, p. 398

1. Of the many Vietnam veterans who are writers, Oliver Stone is perhaps the most famous for writing and directing the films Platoon and Born on the Fourth of July.
2. Tim O'Brien has written short stories for Esquire, GQ, and Massachusetts Review.
3. Going After Cacciato is O'Brien's dreamlike novel about the horrors of combat.
4. The word Vietnam is technically two words (Viet and Nam), but most American writers spell it as one word. [*Viet* and *Nam* were correctly highlighted. Highlighting removed from *one.*]
5. American writers use words or phrases borrowed from Vietnamese, such as di di mau ("go quickly") or dinky dau ("crazy").

Exercise 49.1, p. 401

1. Sentence correct.
2. About 65 million years ago, a comet or asteroid crashed into the earth.
3. The result was a huge crater about 10 kilometers (6.2 miles) deep in the Gulf of Mexico.
4. Sharpton's new measurements suggest that the crater is 50 percent larger than scientists had previously believed.
5. Indeed, 20-year-old drilling cores reveal that the crater is about 186 miles wide, roughly the size of Connecticut.

Exercise 50.1, p. 404

1. The planet Saturn is 900 million miles, or nearly 1.5 billion kilometers, from the sun.
2. Sentence correct.
3. Thus, Saturn orbits the sun only 2.4 times during the average human life span.
4. It travels in its orbit at about 21,600 miles per hour.
5. Fifteen to twenty times denser than Earth's core, Saturn's core measures seventeen thousand miles across.

Exercise 56.1, p. 506

The entries below follow the order of the exercise and so are not alphabetized.

Conte, Christopher. "Networking the Classroom." CQ Researcher 5 (1999): 923–43.

Frankel, Max. "The Moon, This Time Around." New York Times Magazine 5 May 1996: 40+. New York Times Ondisc. CD-ROM. UMI-ProQuest. Nov. 1996.

United States. Dept. of Education. National Center for Education Statistics. Internet Access in Public Schools. 6 Oct. 2002. 12 Mar. 2004 <http://www.ed.gov/nces/edstats>.

Healy, Jane M. Failure to Connect: How Computers Affect Our Children's Minds—For Better and Worse. New York: Simon, 2000.

Index

E

Index

G

Index

H

Index

Index

M

N

Q

R

S

Index

Index

U

V

Guide to CULTURE LANGUAGE Topics

Throughout the handbook, the symbol CULTURE LANGUAGE signals topics for writers who are using standard American English as a second language or a second dialect. This guide indexes these topics, with * marking exercises.

Editing Symbols

Boldface numbers and letters refer to chapters and sections of the handbook.

ab	Faulty abbreviation, **49**
ad	Misused adjective or adverb, **33**
agr	Error in agreement, **29**, **31**
ap	Apostrophe needed or misused, **42**
appr	Inappropriate word, **18a**
arg	Faulty argument, **10b–d**
awk	Awkward construction
cap	Use capital letter, **47**
case	Error in case form, **30**
cit	Missing source citation or error in form of citation, **54e**
coh	Coherence lacking, **3b-3**, **6b**
con	Be more concise, **20**
coord	Coordination needed, **15c**
crit	Think or read more critically, **9a–b**
cs	Comma splice, **36**
d	Ineffective diction (word choice), **18**
des	Ineffective or incorrect document design, **7**
det	Error in use of determiner, **33f**
dm	Dangling modifier, **34b**
emph	Emphasis lacking or faulty, **15**
exact	Inexact word, **18b**
frag	Sentence fragment, **35**
fs	Fused sentence, **36**
gram	Error in grammar, **21–24**
hyph	Error in use of hyphen, **46**
inc	Incomplete construction, **19**
ital	Italicize or underline, **48**
k	Awkward construction
lc	Use lowercase letter, **47**
mixed	Mixed construction, **37**
mm	Misplaced modifier, **34a**
mng	Meaning unclear
no cap	Unnecessary capital letter, **47**
no ^,	Comma not needed, **39h**
no ¶	No new paragraph needed, **6**
num	Error in use of numbers, **50**
p	Error in punctuation, **38–44**
. ? !	Period, question mark, exclamation point, **38**

^,	Comma, **39**
;	Semicolon, **40**
:	Colon, **41**
’∨	Apostrophe, **39**
“ ”	Quotation marks, **40**
— () … [] /	Dash, parentheses, ellipsis mark, brackets, slash, **44**
par, ¶	Start new paragraph, **6**
¶ coh	Paragraph not coherent, **6b**
¶ dev	Paragraph not developed, **6c**
¶ un	Paragraph not unified, **6a**
pass	Ineffective passive voice, **28a**
pn agr	Error in pronoun-antecedent agreement, **31**
ref	Error in pronoun reference, **32**
rep	Unnecessary repetition, **20c**
rev	Revise or proofread, **5**
run-on	Run-on (fused) sentence, **36**
shift	Inconsistency, **26d**, **27b**, **28b**, **32f**
sp	Misspelled word, **45**
spec	Be more specific, **6c**, **18b-2**
sub	Subordination needed or faulty, **15d**
t	Error in verb tense, **26**
t seq	Error in tense sequence, **26e**
trans	Transition needed, **6b-6**
und	Underline or italicize, **48**
usage	See Glossary of Usage, p. 543
var	Vary sentence structure, **17b**
vb	Error in verb form, **25**
vb agr	Error in subject-verb agreement, **29**
w	Wordy, **20**
ww	Wrong word, **18b-1**
//	Faulty parallelism, **16**
#	Separate with a space
⁀	Close up the space
∂	Delete
the	Capitalize, **47**
The	Use a small letter, **47**
teh	Transpose letters or words
x	Obvious error
^	Something missing, **19**
??	Document illegible or meaning unclear

Contents

← "Editing Symbols" and "Guide to CULTURE LANGUAGE Topics"